A TEXTBOOK OF ECONOMICS

To Grace, Shauna, Karen,
Susan and St John
with love

A TEXTBOOK OF ECONOMICS
Third edition

by Frank Livesey

formerly Professor and Head of the
School of Economics,
Lancashire Polytechnic

Longman
London and New York

Longman Group UK Limited,
Longman House, Burnt Mill, Harlow,
Essex CM20 2JE, England
and Associated Companies throughout the world.

Published in the United States of America
by Longman Inc., New York

First published 1978
Second edition 1982
Third edition 1989

**British Library Cataloguing in Publication
Data**
Livesey, Frank
  A textbook of economics. – 3rd ed.
  1. Economics
  I. Title
  330
  ISBN 0-582-44711-9

**Library of Congress Cataloging in Publication
Data**
Livesey, Frank.
  A textbook of economics/by Frank Livesey.
  – 3rd ed.
    p.   cm.
  Includes index.
  ISBN 0-582-44711-9
  1. Economics.   I. Title.
HB171.5.L7338 1989
330 – dc 19

Set in Linotron 202 9/11 pt Palatino Roman
Produced by Longman Singapore Publishers
(Pte) Ltd.
Printed in Singapore

Contents

Preface to the First Edition

This book is written primarily for students taking economics at 'A' level or in the first year of a degree course. Although there is a substantial list of books available to such students, the author believes that the present book can be justified by several recent developments.

First, there is the increasing emphasis on the incorporation into economics teaching of quantitative data. The desirability of this development was highlighted in 1973 in *The Teaching of Economics in Schools*, a report of a Joint Committee of the Royal Economic Society, the Association of University Teachers of Economics and the Economics Association. Impetus was subsequently given to this development by the introduction by a number of 'A' level Examination Boards of complete or part-papers comprising questions containing quantitative data.

Several people, including the present author, have written books of specimen questions and it is to be hoped that teachers and students have found these books useful in preparing for examinations. Moreover various commentaries utilizing quantitative data, such as *The Economist*'s 'Schools Briefs', have been published and again these have no doubt proved helpful. However, there would appear to be advantages in having a textbook in which such data are integrated with the theoretical arguments, and this integration has been one of my primary objectives. The main body of the text contains a great deal of material relating to actual economic events and processes, while further material is contained in the exercises which are to be found at the end of each chapter.

Incidentally the use of quantitative data should not be confused with a move towards 'mathematical economics'. There is nothing in this present volume that requires mathematics beyond that taught at 'O' level.

The second development has been the emergence of a certain degree of disenchantment with 'positive economics'. Conversations with teachers of economics at all levels have indicated a frequent (although not universal) desire to reintroduce certain elements of 'political economy', and to recognize the fact that the economic actions of individuals, firms and governments may be influenced by a wide range of motives and objectives. I have taken these diverse motives and objectives into account in the discussion of incomes policies, pricing decisions, alternative economic systems, and indeed wherever it seemed appropriate to do so within the confines of an economics textbook.

Third, there has recently been a revival of 'monetarism' which has led to a challenging of the 'Keynesian conventional wisdom' and to a widespread debate concerning the respective roles of fiscal and monetary policy. One of the most useful outcomes of this debate has been a recognition of the fact that fiscal policy may have very important monetary implications, and I discuss this point at length in Chapter 13.

Finally, there has been a tendency in recent years to move away from the rigid distinction between macro- and micro-economics, and this tendency is reflected to some extent in the present volume. For example, although Chapter 6 is mainly concerned with the macro-economic implications of investment expenditure, it also explores the factors which may influence the investment programmes of individual firms. Again macro and micro elements appear in most of the chapters on government policy, and especially in the chapters on regional and manpower policy.

I have, however, retained a broad division between the two areas, the major macro aspects being discussed in the first part of the book, and the major micro aspects in the second. As pointed out in Chapter 1, it is hoped that this reversal of the usual order of presentation will enable the student to 'get at' topics of current interest as quickly as possible.

As noted above, the exercises are intended to be an integral part of the book, and to reinforce the parts of the text to which they relate. Some of the exercises have appeared in two of the author's previous publications. *Economics and Data Response Questions in Economics*. However, the majority are new.

Mrs Muriel Shingler, together with Miss Mary O'Mohony, my daughter Shauna and my wife Grace, transformed a chaotic manuscript into a typescript fit for presentation to the printer. My thanks are due to the entire team.

The complete manuscript was read by John Oliver and Alan Turner. Both agreed to take on this task despite having work to do on manuscripts of their own, and I am extremely grateful for the numerous improvements which each suggested.

I acknowledge with thanks the material from HMSO publications which is reproduced with the permission of the Controller of Her Majesty's Stationery Office.

Preface to the Second Edition

In the preface to the first edition the author suggested that the publication of another textbook could be justified by recent developments in the teaching and examining of economics and by changes in emphasis in economic policy. Since this belief has been confirmed by the market, the second edition retains the original approach. Indeed certain elements of this approach have been strengthened. The first edition, while acknowledging the need to give distinct accounts of fiscal and monetary policy, included a chapter (13) on 'The interaction between fiscal and monetary policy'. Since then the importance of this interaction has become common ground among economists, and this has allowed attention to be focused on the effectiveness, or lack of effectiveness, of demand management policies in general. This change in focus is reflected in the discussion in Chapter 13, now retitled 'An evaluation of demand management policies'.

The election of a new government in 1979 led to a more substantial shift in policy than normally follows changes in government in the UK. This has required extensive revision of the discussion of government policy, most notably in Chapters 12 (Monetary policy), 16 (Regional policy), 17 (Manpower policy) and 19 (The nationalized industries). The discussion encompasses changes in policy up to May.

There have also been important changes in the UK economy since the preparation of the first edition. Most notable have been the improvement of the balance of payments following the development of North Sea oil, the consequent improvement in the sterling exchange rate (subsequently partially reversed), and the rising level of unemployment. The statistical material and accompanying commentary have been updated to take account of these changes.

The text has also been revised to take account of recent changes in examination syllabuses, e.g. the extensive revision undertaken by the Associated Examining Board (AEB), and to incorporate additional topics, such as oligopoly and monopolistic competition. These market structures were not discussed in the first edition because of the author's reservations about their usefulness as usually presented at this level. They are now included to extend the book's coverage of examination syllabuses. However, the author's reservations are expressed at the relevant points in the text.

Teachers are divided on the question of whether it is better to begin by teaching macro- or micro-economics. Although this book puts macro first, for the reasons given in the preface to the first edition, it can easily be adapted to the alternative approach. After the introductory first chapter, teachers who wish to begin with micro-economics should move to Chapters 22–28. They could then deal with micro-economic policy (Chapters 16–20) and finally with macro theory and policy (Chapters 2–15). An alternative approach would be to teach micro theory (Chapters 22–28), followed by macro theory (2–9) and economic policy (10–21).

In reading all the new material prepared for the second edition my wife Grace has performed her usual role of 'informed layman' (a term which meets with her approval!) I am very grateful for her assistance and also for that of Mrs Rita Dickinson and Miss Alison Ormsby who, as always, performed their secretarial duties efficiently and cheerfully.

Preface to the Third Edition

This edition retains many of the features of previous editions, including a blend of theory and application and a range of different types of questions to test the reader's understanding. However, the text has been extensively rewritten, reflecting changes that have occurred in the world of economics and in the teaching of the subject.

During extensive discussions with teachers I have sensed an increasing dissatisfaction with the content of introductory economics courses. (This dissatisfaction surfaces regularly in *Economics*, the journal of the Economics Association.) I believe that a textbook should report at least some of these controversies if the student is to be given an accurate picture of the subject.

Consequently, in Chapter 1 the traditional view of economic man is contrasted with an alternative, more realistic view. In subsequent chapters there is an examination of alternative approaches to the theory of the firm, in which the advantages and disadvantages of each approach are discussed. Given the strong passions aroused by this area of the syllabus, the discussion is detailed (marginal analysis having a chapter to itself!). In other instances it has been necessary to confine the examination of an alternative approach to a short appendix to the relevant chapter. The state of macro-economic theory has also been a cause of dissatisfaction, and not only to teachers. In Chapter 19 the images of the macroeconomic system held by different 'schools' of economists are examined, and the implications of these different images for government policy are outlined.

Reference was made in the preface to the previous edition to changes in policy made by the recently elected government. As these policies have matured a fuller evaluation can now be attempted. Much of the completely rewritten Chapter 22 is in effect a large case-study of recent UK economic performance. In preparing this case-study the author had two questions in mind: (a) What is the relative effectiveness of fiscal and monetary policies? (b) How effective are demand-management policies as a whole? The reader is warned in advance that the case-study allows alternative answers to be given to these two questions. This may come as a disappointment to anyone who was hoping to find unequivocal answers. But the author makes no apologies for presenting economic life as it is, shot through with uncertainty and ambiguity.

Policies designed to influence the supply side of the economy have received increased emphasis under recent governments. These policies are discussed in several chapters and especially in Chapter 24, which builds on the theoretical discussion in Chapter 19.

Revisions have also been made to incorporate policy changes in other areas, for example regional and urban policy, nationalization and privatization.

The preface to the first edition presented the case for teaching macro- before micro-economics. Recent developments in the theory relating to supply-side economics have weakened this case, and the chapters have been reordered accordingly. Taken together, Chapters 1–3 constitute on overview of the subject as a whole. Micro-economic theory (together with relevant applications) is dealt with in Chapters 4–8. Chapter 9 examines the theoretical justification for government intervention at the micro level, and different aspects of intervention are discussed in this and the following three chapters.

The treatment of macro-economics is broadly similar to that adopted in previous editions. It begins in Chapter 13 with an examination of the national accounts. However, an additional section on value added has been included in this chapter in order to help the student to understand the basis on which the national accounts are constructed.

The major expenditure flows identified in the national accounts are discussed in detail in Chapters 14 to 17 and these are then brought together again, but this time in the form of a simple economic model, in Chapter 18.

In Chapter 19 this model is used to explain the different images, referred to above, and to provide a framework for the discussion of macro-economic policies in the remaining chapters.

Readers of previous editions have commented favourably on the inclusion of different types of question, as noted above. Additional data-response questions will be found in the third edition of the author's *Data Response Questions in Economics*. There has previously been some overlap between the material in the two books, but this has now been eliminated. A *Teacher's Manual*, giving answers to the exercises in both books, is available.

List of Abbreviations

AEB	Associated Examining Board	IED	income elasticity of demand
AFC	average fixed cost	IFC	International Finance Corporation
AMD	aggregate monetary demand	IMF	International Monetary Fund
APC	average propensity to consume	LAs	local authorities
APS	average propensity to save	LAPFs	life assurance and pension funds
ATC	average total cost	LBC	London Brick Company
AVC	average variable cost	LDCs	less developed countries
BAT	British American Tobacco	LGS	Loan Guarantee Scheme
BES	Business Expansion Scheme	MES	minimum efficient scale
BMA	British Medical Association	MFA	Multifibre Arrangement
BMC	British Mountaineering Council	MMC	Monopolies and Mergers Commission
BT	British Telecom	MNE	multinational enterprise
CAP	Common Agricultural Policy	MPC	marginal propensity to consume
CBI	Confederation of British Industry	MPE	marginal propensity to spend
CCA	current cost accounting	MPP	marginal physical product
CEGB	Central Electricity Generating Board	MPS	marginal propensity to save
CO	cash outflow	MPW	marginal propensity to withdraw
CPI	consumer price index	MRP	marginal revenue product
CSO	Central Selling Organization	MSC	Manpower Services Commission
DCF	discounted cash flow	NCIs	net cash inflows
DFI	direct foreign investment	NICs	newly industrialized countries
DHSS	Department of Health and Social Security	NSM	new smoking materials
EC	European Community	ODA	Official Development Assistance
ECSC	European Coal and Steel Community	OECD	Organization for Economic Co-operation and Development
EEA	Exchange Equalization Account		
EEC	European Economic Community	OFT	Office of Fair Trading
EFL	external financing limit	OFTEL	Office of Telecommunications
EIB	European Investment Bank	OPEC	Organization of Petroleum Exporting Countries
EL	eligible liabilities	PED	price elasticity of demand
EMF	European Monetary Fund	PLC, plc	public limited company
EMS	European Monetary System	PSBR	public sector borrowing requirement
ERDF	European Regional Development Fund	R & D	research and development
Euratom	European Atomic Energy Community	RDG	Regional Development Grant
GATT	General Agreement on Tariffs and Trade	RPI	retail price index
GDP	gross domestic product	RPM	resale price maintenance
GNP	gross national product	RRR	required rate of return
IBRD	International Bank for Reconstruction and Development	SDRs	Special Drawing Rights
		TDR	test discount rate
ICFC	Industrial and Commercial Finance Corporation	TVEI	Technical and Vocational Education Initiative

UNCTAD	United Nations Conference on Trade and Development
USM	Unlisted Securities Market
VAT	Value added tax
VERs	voluntary export restraints
YWS	Young Workers Scheme

Acknowledgements

We are grateful to the following for permission to reproduce copyright material:

Philip Allan Publishers Ltd. for tables 22.3 & 22.4 from *The Economic Review* (May 1986, September 1984); Bank of England for figs. 2.3, 10.2 and tables 17.8, 21.1 from *Quarterly Bulletin* (June 1986, August 1987, November 1987); Barclays Bank Plc for figs. 21.5, 22.5, 22.6, 22.7, 22.9 & 22.11 from *Barclays Review* © Nov. 1981, Aug. 1985, Feb. 1986; Basil Blackwell Ltd. for table 4.4 by J. Muellbauer from *The Economic Journal* 1977 © Royal Economic Society; Cambridge University Press for tables 5.1 & 5.2 by C. F. Pratten from *Economies of Scale in Manufacturing Industry* 1971; Financial Times for fig. 8.11 and tables 11.2, 21.6 from *Financial Times* (20.12.83, 11.8.86, 10.5.86); the Controller of Her Majesty's Stationery Office for various data, figures and tables; International Monetary Fund for table 25.2 from *World Economic Outlook* (1984, 1985); Lloyds Bank Plc for figs. 20.10, 20.12 and table 22.6 from *Economic Bulletin* (1986, 1987); Midland Bank Plc for figs. 8.12, 17.11, 22.12 and table 22.5 from *Midland Bank Review* (Spring 1985, Summer 1985, Winter 1985); The Times Newspaper for fig. 5.9 from *The Times* (3.11.83); University of Chicago Press for table 5.3 from *Journal of Law and Economics* 1973 © University of Chicago Press; The World Bank for table 25.1 from *World Development Report 1984*.

Whilst every effort has been made to trace the owners of copyright material, in some cases this has proved impossible and we take this opportunity to offer our apologies to any copyright holders whose rights we may have unwittingly infringed.

Objective Test Questions

Three types of objective test questions are included in the book: *Simple completion*, where the student chooses one of the five options, A to E. *Multiple completion*, where,

A   indicates that all three options are correct,
B   indicates that options 1 and 2 are correct,
C   indicates that options 2 and 3 are correct,
D   indicates that option 1 only is correct,
E   indicates that option 3 only is correct.

Double statement, where,

A   indicates that both statements are true, and that the second statement is an explanation of the first,
B   indicates that both statements are true, but that the second statement is not an explanation of the first,
C   indicates that the first statement is true and the second statement is false,
D   indicates that the first statement is false and the second statement is true,
E   indicates that both statements are false.

CHAPTER ONE
Economic Man

Introduction

A quick survey of economics textbooks reveals alternative definitions of economics. For example economics has been defined as the study of:

(a) mankind in the ordinary business of life;

(b) that part of human behaviour which relates to the production, exchange and use of goods and services;

(c) how people and society choose to employ scarce resources that could have alternative uses;

(d) how people allocate their scarce resources to provide for their wants.

Despite differences in emphasis, there is general agreement among economists that at the heart of the subject is the study of how people behave given the assumption that they have limited resources, i.e. the study of economic man.

The nature of economic man

In a recent article in *Economics* Dr Lee argued that the picture of economic man usually presented is 'very *narrow* (for example, in terms of the range of motives assumed to condition human behaviour) and very *simplistic* (for example in terms of the knowledge and rationality which human beings are assumed to possess)'.[1]

Lee suggested that a broader and deeper concept of economic man should be presented, and he gave (in question form) two lists of characteristics, which form the basis of Table 1.1. The left-hand list refers to the picture of economic man as presented in most (general) economics textbooks, and the right-hand list to the picture advocated by Lee.

These questions provide a useful starting-point for our discussion of econ-

Table 1.1
The nature of economic man

Does he act as an individual decision-maker (e.g. individual consumer, producer, citizen etc.)?	or	Does he act as part of a group (e.g. household, business organization, trade union, political pressure group)?
Is his behaviour always rational?	or	Does he engage in some forms of non-maximizing behaviour?
Is he entirely selfish?	or	Does concern for the well-being of others also influence his decisions?
Are his objectives solely materialistic in nature?	or	Does he also have significant non-materialistic objectives?
Is he unconstrained in the pursuit of his own goals?	or	Is his personal behaviour constrained by adherence to laws, codes of professional conduct, etc.?
Is he perfectly well informed?	or	Does he possess incomplete information for decision-making?
Are his tastes self-determined?	or	Are his tastes, in part, socially determined (e.g. through advertising)?

omic man, and we further explore some of the questions in the following sections.

Individual or group decision-making

All economics textbooks discuss men (and women, of course) both as individuals and as members of groups such as firms and trade unions. But they say little or nothing about how decisions are reached by these groups. The assumption is usually made that the group has a single, clearly defined objective. In practice group decisions are often subject to negotiation and bargaining, whose outcome is by no means certain.

For example, firms frequently have to decide how much money to spend on research and development (R & D). Heavy spending on R & D may offer the prospect of growth in future years. On the other hand *current* profits are likely to be higher if nothing is spent this year on R & D. The first alternative may be chosen by a firm controlled by people who attach great importance to growth and are willing to take the necessary risks. The second alternative may be chosen by a firm controlled by more cautious people for whom maintaining current profitability is of paramount importance. A third alternative would be to give some weight to both objectives, and to steer a path between the two extremes, i.e. to spend a modest amount on R & D. Incidentally, spending on R & D (or on any item) may change over time, as the influence exercised by different people within the firm changes.

Taking a second example, consider the decisions taken by a household. There are many competing demands on a household's budget. Mum might wish to buy a new washing-machine because the existing one keeps breaking down, Dad might feel that the house should be repainted, the children might like a holiday abroad. The eventual decision might be to buy the washing-machine now, but on the understanding that the desires of Dad and the children will have preference next time round. Once more we see that group decision-making may be characterized by

compromise and an attempt to achieve more than one objective.

However, as noted above, these are features which are ignored in many textbooks. It is often assumed that a group has a single well-defined, unchanging objective, and that the decisions of groups and individuals can be analysed in precisely the same way.

Rational or non-maximizing behaviour

By posing the question in this way, Lee draws attention to the fact that economists often equate rational behaviour with maximization. Consumers are assumed to maximize the satisfaction derived from the goods and services that they buy. Firms are assumed to maximize their profits. There is obviously a link here with two of the other questions given in Table 1.1: whether man is entirely selfish, having solely materialistic objectives, or whether he is influenced by concern for others and has significant non-materialistic objectives.

Although it would be difficult to argue that people take decisions intended to *reduce* their level of satisfaction, this does not mean that they pursue purely materialistic aims. To assume that they do is to ignore motivations which can be very important in practice. Many consumers give to charity money that they might have spent on themselves; firms often provide facilities for their employees because of their desire to be good employers, not because it is in the best interest of the firm or because they are forced to do so.

Unconstrained or constrained behaviour

As we have just shown, man's decisions are frequently influenced by other motivations in addition to a desire to improve his material well-being. In some instances these motivations may arise from a wish to observe codes of professional conduct, for example with respect to the content of advertising. In other instances behaviour is constrained by the law, for example mergers and take-overs are subject to various pieces of legislation, as shown in Chapter 10. Of these various influences on behaviour, textbooks are usually interested only in legal constraints.

Perfect or incomplete information

Textbooks usually proceed on the basis of perfect information. Consumers are assumed to be aware of all the goods and services that they could buy, of their prices and of the satisfaction that they would yield. Firms are assumed to know what quantity of each product they would sell at any price, and exactly how much it would cost to produce a given quantity. Trade unions are assumed to know how many people would be employed at any wage rate that they might negotiate.

In practice, however, information is far from perfect. Consumers are often unaware of some of the products that they could buy, and cannot be certain how much satisfaction they will derive from the products of which they are aware. It follows that the information possessed by consumers is likely to change over time, and this may well cause them to modify their spending patterns.

The last question listed in Table 1.1 is also relevant here. Textbooks usually mention that consumers can be influenced by advertising, i.e. tastes are partially socially determined. However, the role of advertising in providing information to consumers is seldom discussed.

The information available to firms and trade unions is also less than is usually assumed in textbooks. This means that these groups may in practice make different decisions than they are assumed to make on the basis of perfect information.

It can be seen that economic man as presented in textbooks is different in many important respects from the people whose behaviour economists are reputed to study. In order to explain why this is so it is necessary briefly to discuss the nature and role of economic models.

Economic models

Economic models provide 'pictures' of the behaviour of individuals and of groups, and of the relationships between these individuals and groups. However, most models do not describe in detail the situation facing any particular individual or group. Many aspects are deliberately ignored in order to simplify the analysis. It is believed that by concentrating on a few major aspects, our ability to *predict* behaviour is improved. For example a model constructed by Lord Keynes leads to the prediction that when incomes increase, consumers' expenditure will also increase, but by less than the increase in income. We are able to make this prediction because we ignore the many factors which might cause some individual consumers to behave in other ways. (The strengths and weaknesses of this model are discussed in Ch. 14.) (It follows that the term 'economic law', sometimes used to describe the conclusions drawn from an economic model, indicates a general tendency to behave in a certain way, rather than a pattern of behaviour that occurs in every instance.)

All economists agree that simplification is a necessary part of model-building. However, there is some disagreement about what the process of simplification should involve, i.e. about economic methodology.

Economic methodology

Economic models incorporate *assumptions* about motivations. For example, as noted above, consumers are assumed to wish to maximize their utility or satisfaction. Firms are assumed to wish to maximize their short-run profits. Given these assumptions it is then possible to *deduce* how individuals and firms will behave in order to achieve their objectives.

The deductive method is a very powerful analytical tool. However, since the predictions derived from a model depend upon the assumptions built in, the nature of these assumptions becomes critical. If the assumptions are incorrect or inadequate, the model might yield incorrect or inadequate predictions. For example, the assumption of short-run profit maximization yields predictions about the behaviour of firms which conflict with the behaviour that we observe.

This, of course, brings us back to Lee's suggestion that in building our models we should take more account of what we know in practice about people's motivations and about the information they possess.[2] By doing this, our ability to predict behaviour will be improved.

One reason for trying to improve our predictive ability is to provide sound guidelines for government policy. As we demonstrate in later chapters, different models, incorporating different assumptions, have led to conflicting guidelines concerning government policy towards unemployment, inflation, mergers, etc.

The approach adopted in this book

This is not the place to give a detailed account of the assumptions made in this book. However, it is appropriate to indicate some of the ways in which we depart from the assumptions that are usually made.

Although we do not explore the processes of negotiation and bargaining that are often involved in making business decisions, we recognize that firms may have a number of objectives, that these may sometimes conflict and that they may change over time.

We examine the possibility that trade unions act to benefit some of their members, even though this may be at the expense of other members and of other workers in general.

In many places, in particular when we discuss the decisions taken by firms, we emphasize the existence of uncertainty and the incompleteness of information. Incomplete information is one reason why

firms adopt cost-based pricing (Ch. 5), relying on procedures that have proved satisfactory in the past. Moreover, the crucial difference between marginal models and the models of open markets (Chs 6 and 7) is the assumption in the latter of imperfect information.

We referred above to models which gave rise to different guidelines for government policy. We show that one of the reasons for this is that the models make different assumptions about the availability of information and about people's reactions to information.

We do not define rationality purely in terms of maximizing behaviour. We assume that it may be entirely rational for people to adopt objectives other than maximization, being influenced by customs and by non-selfish motives.

Positive and normative statements

Examiners are fond of setting questions about the difference between positive and normative statements. A positive statement refers to what *is*, a normative statement to what *should* or *ought to be*. For example, 'The richest 5 per cent of the population owns 50 per cent of the nation's wealth' is a positive statement. 'Inequalities of wealth are undesirable and the government should tax rich people more heavily' is a normative statement.

It is often said that in their professional capacity, economists should be concerned only with positive statements. They should confine themselves to an analysis of the current situation, and to predicting how that situation might change. For example, if a government proposed to tax wealth more heavily, economists would be expected to give advice (i.e. to make positive statements) about the effects on consumption, on people's desire to work, etc. However, as we showed above, there may be considerable disagreement about the likely effects. In other words, some 'positive' statements may be erroneous.

Summary

1. The study of human behaviour and the allocation of resources form the core of economics.
2. Individuals and groups have a wider range of motives than is often assumed by economists.
3. Behaviour is influenced by conventions and by laws as well as by self-interest.
4. Individuals and groups have less complete information than is often assumed by economists.
5. Economic models give a highly simplified picture of behaviour.
6. Economic models are used to help us to predict behaviour.
7. Given the assumptions built into a model, a process of deduction enables us to predict how individuals and groups will behave.
8. Models based on different assumptions may give rise to conflicting predictions.
9. An economic law states a general tendency, not a universal rule.
10. A positive statement refers to what is, although some positive statements may be factually incorrect.
11. A normative statement refers to what ought to be.

Key terms

Economic man

Allocation of resources

Decision-making

Motivations

Objectives

Information

Rational behaviour

Maximization

Constraints

Economic model

Economic law

Assumptions

Prediction

Deductive method

Positive statements

Normative statements

Notes

1. Lee N, Putting the heart back into Economic Man, *Economics*, Autumn 1986.
2. This *inductive* approach is used, but not as frequently as some economists would wish.

Essay questions

1. In what respects does economic man (as portrayed by economists) differ from the man in the street?
2. Write notes on the following terms: (a) rational behaviour; (b) perfect information; (c) prediction; (d) economic law.
3. What are the main purposes and features of economic models?
4. Explain, giving examples, why it is helpful to distinguish between positive and normative statements.

Exercises

1.1 (a) A farmer has to decide the use to which he should put a plot of land. Explain how his decision might be influenced by the amount of information that he possesses. (b) The previous year the farmer bought a new piece of equipment, but he now discovers that he could have bought, for the same price, a much more efficient machine. Say whether his purchase represented rational behaviour, giving reasons for your answer.

1.2 Which column of Table 1.1 gives the more accurate picture of the people that you know?

CHAPTER TWO
Economic Resources

Introduction

We noted in Chapter 1 that the allocation of resources is a core area of economics. In this chapter we describe the nature of economic resources, and in Chapter 3 we examine how these resources are allocated.

The stock of economic resources can be divided into two broad categories – human and non-human resources – and we consider each category in turn.

Human resources

The stock of human resources in an economy (in less technical language the size of a country's population) depends upon the birth- and death-rates and upon international migration flows. In many countries economic development has led to periods of rapid population growth, as improved medical facilities reduced the death-rate, followed by periods of less rapid growth as the birth-rate declined.

At present there is a tendency for the birth-rate, and hence the rate of population growth, to be higher in developing countries than in countries with more fully developed, highly industrialized economies. This is due to several factors, non-economic as well as economic. For example it has been claimed that programmes designed to encourage the use of various contraceptive techniques in underdeveloped countries would have had a greater measure of success if greater attention had been given to the social structures of the communities and to the role of certain key members in influencing attitudes and behaviour.

While such social factors are no doubt important, economic considerations also help to explain why such programmes have sometimes been less successful than anticipated. The survival of many peasant families depends upon there being sufficient labour to tend the family farm or smallholding. When sickness and disease are common, the birth of additional children may be seen as a form of insurance against the possible future loss of active members of the family. (In more advanced societies families are cushioned to some extent by social security provisions against the loss of income following the death of a breadwinner.)

Economic factors are also an important determinant of migration patterns. People tend to emigrate from less to more developed economies, attracted by the prospect of better employment opportunities and living standards. Sometimes emigration is temporary, the emigrant's motive being to obtain education and training which he can then utilize in his own country. But often it is permanent.

The flow of labour inputs

The flow of labour inputs has two major aspects, quantity and quality. The quantity of labour derived from a given stock or population depends upon several factors. The age and sex structure of the population determine the proportion of the inhabitants who are physically capable of working. Of these people a substantial proportion will not in practice be available for work because of legislation or social conventions.

Legislation reduces the size of the potential work-force by specifying a minimum school-leaving age. At the other end of the age-scale, although compulsory withdrawal from the labour force is unusual, the provision of state retirement pensions obviously reduces the need for older people to work.

In many countries social convention has decreed that married women, and especially the mothers of young children, should not work. Although attitudes and practice have changed considerably in recent years, 'participation rates' for females remain well below those for males.

The increase that has occurred in the proportion of married women who work is again due to a mixture of economic and non-economic motives. The idea that a woman should be content to act only as wife and mother has been challenged ever more strongly, the most extreme form of this challenge being represented by the 'women's liberation' movement. At the same time economic changes have led to an increase in the opportunities for women to find paid employment. On the one hand there has sometimes been insufficient male workers to fully meet the increasing demand for labour. On the other hand an increase in the availability of domestic labour-saving devices has left women with more time to spend outside the home.

Together these factors can lead to substantial differences in the flow of labour inputs between one country and another. In a survey undertaken in the early 1980s the Organization for Economic Co-operation and Development (OECD) found that the labour force as a percentage of the total population ranged from over 70 per cent in the UK, the USA and Japan, through 60 to 70 per cent in France, West Germany and Italy, to less than 60 per cent in the Netherlands and Spain. When an allowance was made for unemployment, the percentage of the population in employment ranged from 71 per cent in Japan to 47 per cent in Spain.

The final important influence on the quantity of labour inputs is the average number of hours worked. This is determined by the average length of the working week and by the number of weeks worked per year, both of which have tended to decline in many countries in recent years. The average hours worked is influenced by legislation, by custom – in some less developed countries it is usual to work only during daylight hours

– and by negotiations between representatives of employers and workers.

Optimum population

The optimum population is the size of population at which, given the volume of other resources, the output of goods and services per head of population would be maximized. Since the volume of other resources is constantly changing, it follows that the optimum population will also constantly change. As the volume of other resources, and especially of capital, increases, the size of the optimum population will tend to increase. However, increasing concern has been expressed about the continued growth in world population.

There are several reasons for this concern. In some countries the rate of growth of population may outstrip the increase in the availability of certain vital commodities, e.g. staple foodstuffs in India and certain African countries. In many of these countries the population is increasing by 2 or 3 per cent a year, implying a doubling of the population in thirty years or less. Elsewhere the growth of population may lead to a deterioration in living conditions, as has occurred in some parts of large cities such as Tokyo, New York and London. (The population per square kilometre is over 4,300 in Greater London, as compared to 230 for the UK as a whole and only 2 in Australia and Canada.) Furthermore, rapid population growth may contribute to the early exhaustion of vital resources such as oil, which could cause future living standards to decline. This suggests that our initial definition of optimum population might in some circumstances be inadequate. Rather than confining our attention to the situation at a given point in time, it might be more appropriate to consider the implications of a change in population for both the current and future generations.

A country wishing to limit its population may discourage immigration and encourage emigration. In addition it may encourage birth control by providing information and financial incentives, for example the Indian government offered transistor radios to men having a vasectomy.

The growth of population has not been a problem in all countries. Indeed some governments have adopted policies intended to increase the population. If a government wishes to see an increase in population it may encourage immigration, and discourage emigration. It may also provide assistance, via tax reliefs or grants, to large families, as has happened in France. Some countries, such as Australia, have been particularly concerned to increase the supply of skilled labour; they have made visas freely available and have sometimes provided financial assistance to the immigrants possessing the required skills. (In such instances, optimum population is seen in terms of its composition as well as the total number.)

The age structure

Most Western countries have experienced a sharp slowing in the rate of population growth in recent years. In the UK the increase in population over the last decade has been very small, and in some years the population fell. This fall in the rate of population growth can be seen as part of a long-term trend in operation since the early years of this century. This reflects an underlying tendency for the birth-rate to decline.

Another feature of the UK population (reflecting the long-term decline in the birth-rate) is the progressive ageing of the population. Figure 2.1 shows how the proportion of the population in the older age-groups increased from 1901 to 1981 and is projected to further increase by the twenty-first century.

The dependent population

The dependent population is usually taken to refer to those people of an age at which it is uncommon to have paid

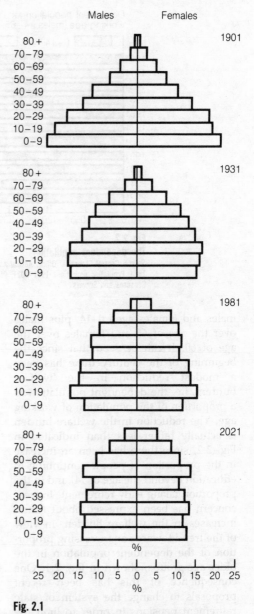

Fig. 2.1
UK population: age and sex distribution
Source: Central Statistical Office, *Annual Abstract of Statistics*, 1984; Population projections 1981–2021, Office of Population Censuses and Surveys

employment. We have shown that this age may change over time due to changes in legislation and custom. Such changes are ignored in Fig. 2.2 where for each year the dependent population is defined as

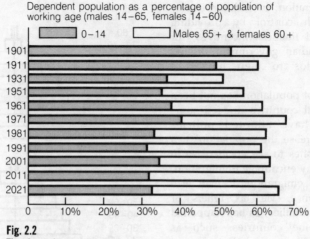

Dependent population as a percentage of population of working age (males 14–65, females 14–60)

☐ 0–14   ☐ Males 65+ & females 60+

Fig. 2.2
The dependent population
Source: Central Statistical Office, *Annual Abstract of Statistics*,
1984; Population projections 1981–2021, Office of Population
Censuses and Surveys

males and females aged 0–14, plus males over the age of 65 and females over the age of 60. It can be seen that since the beginning of the century there has been a modest reduction in the 'welfare burden', i.e. the dependent population as a proportion of the population of working age. The reduction in the welfare burden is actually rather less than indicated in Fig. 2.2, since there has been an increase in the proportion of people continuing in education beyond the age of 14, and in the proportion taking early retirement. Indeed, concern has been expressed about future increases in the welfare burden, in view of the trend towards an increasing proportion of the dependent population in the older age-groups, shown in Fig. 2.1. One consequence of this has been recent proposals to change the system of state retirement pensions in order to limit the state's liability.

The quality of labour

In principle, if not always in practice, one can distinguish between workers in terms of inherent (natural) and acquired characteristics. On the one hand, some people are naturally more intelligent, energetic, diligent or stronger than others. On the other hand, some people have received more education and/or training than others. It follows that the quality of a nation's labour force can be influenced at least to some extent by the education and training facilities provided by the state, employers, etc. and by the willingness and ability of citizens to make use of these facilities. The increase in spending on education, and especially on higher and further education, in the post-war period was *partly* due to the belief that this would result in an improvement in the quality of the labour force and thus to an increase in productivity (the ratio of outputs to inputs), and in the rate of economic growth.

The facilities are frequently supplied without charge, especially when provided by the state. There is, however, a very substantial opportunity cost[1] involved in their provision; if the state spent less on schools, technical colleges and universities, it would be able to spend more on hospitals, roads and prisons.

The concept of opportunity cost is also involved in a person's decision as to whether or not he or she should undertake further education or training. The opportunity cost of a period of training is the additional income (wages or salary minus any grant received while training) that would have been obtained by working. The loss of this income must be balanced against the potentially higher earnings in future years. (Other non-monetary factors such as the greater freedom enjoyed by students would also be taken into account, i.e. education is both an investment and a consumption good, to use the classification adopted in later chapters.)

As we show in Chapter 15 British governments have also attempted, by means of legislation and other methods, to increase the resources devoted to training. Here again it was believed that the improvement in the quality of the labour force would result in higher productivity and faster economic growth.

If increased training and education are to lead to higher productivity and faster economic growth, the skills and abilities acquired and developed must be those that are demanded by employers. Technological change means that the most appropriate mix of skills is constantly changing. This implies that part of the training effort should be devoted to the retraining of workers whose skills have become obsolete or less useful, in order to increase their occupational mobility.

Non-human resources

We follow the usual convention of distinguishing between two non-human resources, land and capital, although in practice these two resources are normally combined in use.[2]

Land

If land is defined as the total surface area of the planet, including oceans, lakes and rivers, then its total quantity is fixed. If the definition is restricted to dry land, some increase in quantity may occur as a result of drainage schemes, etc., but such increases will clearly be very small in relation to the existing stock.

If we extend our definition of land to include the 'free gifts of nature' – mineral wealth, soil fertility, etc. – it is clear that considerable changes may occur in the quality of land and therefore in the flow of inputs derived from a given quantity or stock. This flow may either increase or decrease over time. In agriculture selective breeding can lead to higher yields. On the other hand, over-intensive cultivation can lead to a reduction in the quality of the land and in crop yields, as shown by the creation of huge 'dust-bowls' in the USA in the inter-war period, and in Africa more recently.

An increase in the flow of inputs from the land often requires the application of capital, sometimes in vast quantities, as illustrated by the development of North Sea oil. In addition labour is also required, of course. In such instances it is clearly impossible to determine the relative contributions to output of the different resources, the different *factors of production*.

Capital

Capital is any resource – other than what is defined as land and labour – that is used in the production and distribution of goods and services. Two types of capital are normally distinguished: fixed capital consisting of buildings, plant and machinery, and circulating capital (termed working capital by some writers) consisting of stocks of components, raw materials, etc. The main basis of this distinction is that fixed capital may provide a flow of inputs over a long period – typically ten or so years for machinery and much longer for buildings – whereas circulating capital is used up much more quickly and needs to be constantly replaced. Another difference between the two is that circulating capital is much the more mobile geographically.

We have not made a distinction between capital used in the production of those outputs (goods or services) which are marketed and those which are provided free. Thus we would include within capital not only industrial buildings and equipment but also schools, hospitals, roads, etc. Some writers do seek to make a distinction, but the outcome is seldom satisfactory. To take but one example, it would seem to be illogical to include railways within capital because their output is marketed, but to exclude roads because people are not charged directly for their use.

Moreover, all capital assets, whether used in the production of marketed or non-marketed outputs, have the important common characteristic that they are physical or 'real' (as opposed to monetary) assets. Furthermore, an increase in the output of capital goods is likely to mean that the current consumption of goods and services is less than it might have been. (The only situation in which this would not be so is if the additional capital goods could be produced by resources which would otherwise have remained idle.) The reduction in the current output of consumption goods constitutes the opportunity cost of producing additional capital goods. This cost must be balanced against the benefit that an increased stock of capital goods would enable a greater quantity of consumption goods to be produced in future periods.

If the size of the labour force increases, an increase in the capital stock is required in order to maintain the existing capital–labour ratio. This process is known as capital widening. In practice most industrialized economies have been characterized by a faster rate of growth in the capital than in the labour stock, i.e. the capital–labour ratio has increased, a process known as capital deepening.

Additional capital may be either labour-saving or capital-saving or both. Recent developments in micro-processors have reduced the amount of labour and capital required to produce a given volume of output. Looking at the situation from another point of view we can say that technological progress has made it possible to increase the output of consumption goods without any increase in the stock of capital. We could define this process as

one involving an increase in the *quality* of capital.

A different aspect of the quality of capital has received considerable attention in the less developed countries. In such countries it is often possible to achieve spectacular increases in labour productivity in particular industries by introducing production methods incorporating the latest technical innovations. However, since such countries are often characterized by a labour surplus, many of the workers displaced by the new equipment may remain unemployed. If this occurs labour productivity in the country as a whole may be virtually unchanged, while social distress may result from the higher unemployment.

This result is especially likely if the production process 'imported' from more developed countries requires supplies of components, etc. and maintenance facilities which must also be provided by these countries. Experience of such situations has led to proposals that more of the capital assets of less developed countries should incorporate an 'intermediate technology', less capital intensive than that used in more developed countries. These proposals are discussed further in Chapter 25.

Capital and economic growth

An increase in the capital–labour ratio normally increases labour productivity (output per worker), and in many industrialized economies whose labour force is static or growing only very slowly, an increase in the capital–labour ratio is seen as the mainspring of economic growth. However, while there appears to be a link between changes in the capital stock and the rate of economic growth, the connection is by no means straightforward.

Figure 2.3 shows that Japan has achieved the highest rate of investment and economic growth. On the other hand the UK's growth rate has been below that of the USA and Italy despite very similar investment rates.

Investment as a proportion
of GNP (%) 1960–85

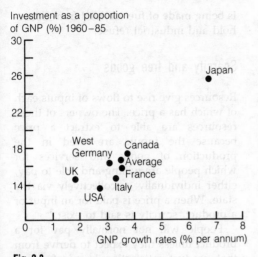

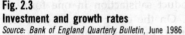

Fig. 2.3
Investment and growth rates
Source: Bank of England Quarterly Bulletin, June 1986

This suggests that although the UK's relatively slow rate of growth might be partly due to a low investment rate, other factors also contributed to the UK's poor performance. Stafford found that too much investment had been made in the wrong type and quality of plant and machinery.[3] There is also reason to believe that even machinery of a given type and quality has tended to be used less effectively in the UK. This might be due to poor maintenance, inadequate production planning, overmanning or other restrictive labour practices. A number of studies have shown that in industries as diverse as newspapers, railways, steel and shipbuilding, new equipment is manned by more workers in the UK than in many other countries. (We show in Ch. 22 that in the 1980s, in contrast to earlier experience, productivity increased more rapidly in the UK than in many other countries.)

It is sometimes argued that a low level of demand has resulted in plant and machinery being operated less intensively in the UK than elsewhere. Although this factor might have affected some industries at certain times there is little evidence that it is of general importance. The post-war period has seen a decline in the UK's share of world exports of many products, suggesting that the UK has been less successful than other countries in satisfying the *increase* in demand that has occurred.

The direction of investment may also be important. There is an inverse relationship between the proportion of a country's resources devoted to military research and development and international competitiveness in manufacturing (which in turn aids economic growth). For much of the post-war period the UK has been near the top of the table for military R & D, and near the bottom of the table for growth.[4]

The entrepreneur

Some writers have identified a further factor of production 'enterprise' one of whose functions is to co-ordinate the other factors. This is now considered to be an unsatisfactory distinction since the process of co-ordination is undertaken by one of those other factors, labour. However, the importance of this co-ordination process is accepted; indeed it has received increasing attention of late, as part of the discussion of the role of the entrepreneur.

Although co-ordination may involve some routine procedures, the entrepreneur plays a more active, dynamic role. He is constantly searching for more profitable ways of using resources, by finding more efficient ways of producing existing goods and services and by introducing new goods and services.

Producers operate in a climate of uncertainty, and this applies particularly to the activities of the entrepreneur. Since he is seeking to effect change, to do things differently from the way they have been done in the past, he cannot be certain what the result of his efforts will be.

In those businesses which are managed by their owners, for example one-man businesses, the owner-manager is obviously the entrepreneur. It is not, however, so easy to identify the entrepreneur in large companies where there is a divorce between ownership and control, where most directors have only small shareholdings, and where most shareholders take little or no part in the running of the business. In these companies the allocation and co-ordination of resources, the searching for new opportunities, is undertaken by the directors and senior managers. Although these directors and managers may also be shareholders, most of the financial risks, which are basically due to the existence of uncertainty, are borne by the many other shareholders.

Renewable and non-renewable resources

Non-human resources may be renewable or non-renewable. Timber is renewed when new trees are planted to replace those that are felled. On the other hand coal, formed from trees that died millions of years ago, is not renewable within the time period for which plans can be made. This is also true of other major sources of energy: oil and gas. Concern has been expressed about the possible exhaustion of these latter fuels in the foreseeable future, and greater attention has been given to the possible development of alternative renewable sources including solar energy, wind and water power, e.g. the proposed Severn barrage, and 'fast breeder' reactors involving nuclear fusion.

One might think of all metals and minerals as non-renewable in that the existing supplies were formed many years ago, as with coal. However, it is often possible to salvage and reuse such materials, and the use of recycled materials has increased considerably in recent years. Furthermore, scientists have discovered alternative, and potentially very valuable uses for materials that were previously considered as waste products. For example a method of turning plastic waste into high-quality protein has been developed at Manchester University, increasing use

is being made of fuel derived from household and industrial refuse.

Scarcity and free goods

Resources give rise to flows of inputs each of which has a price. The owners of these resources are able to extract a price because the inputs are used in the production of goods and services for which people are willing and able to pay, either individually or collectively via the state. When a price is paid for an input or a product, scarcity is said to exist.[5]

People will not normally pay for a product unless they expect to derive from that product satisfaction in one form or another. On the other hand, it does not follow that they must always pay for something from which they derive satisfaction. Consider, for example, the person walking in the country who derives deep satisfaction from breathing fresh air and, when thirsty, from drinking from a mountain stream – both obtained at a zero price.

Why is it that these benefits are available free? Part of the explanation is that the 'products' in question are abundant. Indeed this is sometimes given as the sole explanation.[6] However, there is a more fundamental reason, namely that property or ownership rights in the use of the product or resource have not been established or, if established, have not been exercised. Had the owner of the stream been able to control access he would have been able to make a charge for its use.

Property rights

The importance of property rights – or the lack of them – can be further demonstrated by means of three more examples. First, the 1970s and 1980s saw the extension of the area of the oceans in which individual countries claimed exclusive fishing rights. This meant that whereas previously ships from any country had been able to fish in these waters at no cost (apart, of course, from the cost of operating the ships), henceforth foreign ships incurred a cost in terms of the danger of arrest followed by a fine, impounding of their catch, etc.

Second, where no property rights in lakes and inland waterways have been established, or where the owners have chosen not to exercise these rights, anyone has been able to use such waterways without charge for the discharge of effluent. On the other hand where property rights are established and exercised, as by the regional water authorities in the UK, this free use is often no longer possible. The authorities may forbid the discharge of effluent, in which case the cost to a discharger becomes the risk of punishment if detected. Alternatively, the authorities may allow discharge only after appropriate treatment, in which case the cost comprises the installation and operation of the treatment plant. A third possibility, not common in the UK, is charging a price related to the volume and type of effluent discharged.

The final example, closely comparable to the previous one, is the discharge of smoke and other substances into the air. Parliament has vested property rights in residents if local authorities introduce clean air regulations preventing discharge. The resultant cost to users arises from the need to treat the discharge or change to substitute fuels.

It is often difficult to establish property rights when more than one country is involved, as illustrated by the controversy over acid rain. This is the term given to the pollution which results when emissions of sulphur dioxide, nitrogen oxides and ozone undergo chemical changes in the atmosphere. The pollution can be carried thousands of kilometres and so cause damage in countries other than the country of origin. It is believed, for example, that much of the 4 million tonnes of sulphur dioxide that is found each year in the atmosphere above the UK is deposited in other parts of Europe and in Scandinavia.

The damage alleged to be caused by acid rain includes the destruction of trees

(at least 30 per cent of West Germany's forests are estimated to have been damaged), the pollution of lakes (in Sweden more than 10,000 lakes are said to be under threat, with the fish being unable to reproduce as a direct result of acid in the water), and damage to plant life. To mitigate the damage caused by such 'transboundary pollutants' international co-operation is required on a scale that is not easy to achieve, partly because of a lack of agreement about the precise cause and extent of the damage.

In 1987 the Central Electricity Generating Board announced a programme to install equipment that would remove almost 1 million tonnes of sulphur dioxide – the chemical responsible for acid rain – from the atmosphere by the year 2000 at a cost of more than £1 bn. But the programme was described as inadequate by Friends of the Earth who pointed out that West Germany planned to spend £2.5 bn. by 1989. (Throughout the book billion (bn.) means a thousand million (m.))

Opportunity cost

The opportunity cost of utilizing a free good is zero; the water that the thirsty man drinks from the mountain stream would otherwise have run to waste. On the other hand, there *is* an opportunity cost in utilizing a river for effluent disposal, namely the loss of amenity, e.g. for swimming or fishing, suffered by other potential users; consequently the river can no longer be treated as a free good. (However, as we noted above, a charge will be levied only if property rights are established.)

Moreover a product would be free only if *all* the resources required for its supply were free. In practice, as we noted above, even the free gifts of nature can normally be utilized only through the application of additional, scarce resources; to bring mountain water into our homes requires costly capital equipment and considerable manpower. It follows that as a rule the term 'free good' is applied to resources and not to products.[7]

Summary

1. Resources can be divided into two broad categories: human and non-human.
2. The stock of human resources in an economy depends upon the birth- and death-rates and upon international migration flows.
3. The quantity of labour derived from a given population depends upon the age and sex structure, legislation and social conventions. These factors also affect the size of the dependent population.
4. The quality of labour depends upon workers' inherent and acquired characteristics.
5. Land may be defined as the surface area or, more widely, to include mineral wealth and soil fertility. Any changes in quantity are very small in relation to the existing stock.
6. Capital is any resource, other than land and labour, that is used in the production and distribution of goods and services.
7. An increase in the capital–labour ratio normally leads to an increase in labour productivity. Labour productivity has tended to grow more slowly in the UK than in many other countries.
8. Entrepreneurs constantly search for more profitable ways of using resources.
9. Financial risks arise basically because of uncertainty.
10. Resources may be renewable or non-renewable. Resources can be 'renewed' by recycling. The use of recycled materials has increased considerably in recent years.
11. When a price is paid for a product, scarcity is said to exist. When property rights in a product are not established the product will be available at a zero price.

Key terms

Labour	Productivity
Structure of population	Entrepreneurial activity
Optimum population	Uncertainty
Dependent population	Risk
Land	Opportunity cost
Capital	Property rights
Capital widening	Free good
Capital deepening	
Factor mobility	

Notes

1. The opportunity cost of using resources in one way is the maximum benefit that could have been obtained from using them in another way. Opportunity cost is one of the most important concepts in economics.
2. We also continue to speak of the flow of *inputs* derived from a resource, although in another context some of these inputs, e.g. agricultural products and minerals derived from the land, might be termed outputs.
3. Stafford B, *The End of Economic Growth? Growth and Decline in the UK Since 1945.* Martin Robertson, 1981.
4. Koldor M, Sharp M and Walker W, Industrial competitiveness and Britain's defence, *Lloyds Bank Review*, Oct. 1986.
5. It is clear that this use of the term 'scarcity' differs from the everyday use.
6. 'Free goods are goods which are not relatively scarce, and therefore which do not

have a price' (Bannock G, Baxter R E and Rees R, *The Penguin Dictionary of Economics*. Penguin, 1972). We show below that the term 'free good' can be properly applied only to resources.

7. The walker breathing fresh air and drinking water from a stream is a very special case in that the air and the water are resources that could also be seen as products.

Essay questions

1. What are the major determinants of a country's stock of (a) human, and (b) non-human resources?
2. Explain the significance of the statement that optimum population is a dynamic and not a static concept.
3. 'Opportunity cost is a key economic concept.' Discuss.
4. Discuss the relationship between investment and economic growth.
5. Explain what is meant by a 'free good'. What is the fundamental reason for the existence of free goods?
6. 'There is no such thing as a free lunch.' Comment.
7. Explain what is meant by the statement that the stock of resources is determined by both economic and non-economic factors.
8. Explain what you understand by the term 'scarcity'.
9. Why is it difficult to predict the rewards to entrepreneurial activity?

Exercises

2.1 When a large estate in Cheshire was auctioned, a plot of 1,134 acres was bought by two farmers, Messrs Edgecox and Sykes, for £60,000 (£53 an acre), £10,000 more than the Peak National Park's bid, which was limited by the district valuer's estimate.

The new owners introduced sheep on to the former grouse moors. This required wire fencing, at a cost of £20,000, and restricted the activities of the walkers and climbers who hitherto had generally been allowed free access to the area. The previous owner, a keen climber, had charged police and service units 15p a head to train there. This charge had been raised to 25p and, said Mr Edgecox, 'if the services are offering to pay for essential training, surely the average climber ought to pay for his pleasure' (*The Guardian*, 11 July 1979). He also claimed that payment was required to compensate for damage caused by walkers and climbers: 'While 90 per cent of the visitors keep to the public paths, the rest spoil it all with abuse, insults and litter. There is a risk of loss of grazing land through erosion when people approach from all directions. With £80,000 of sheep we now have about £200,000 tied up in this venture and we have to protect our investment and property rights.'

Concerned about the loss of access the Peak Park Planning Board attempted to buy part of the plot from the new owners. The price asked was £200 an acre for a plot of 200 acres (or £300 an acre for 140 acres), whereas the Board offered £110 an acre for 200 acres.

Faced with the failure of these negotiations the Board considered two other alternatives. The first was a compulsory purchase order, but this would be the first in the twenty-eight years' history of the Park. The second was an access order. This was favoured by the Board, but was opposed by the British Mountaineering Council (BMC) which had offered £1,000 to the Board for the purchase of the crags. The secretary to the BMC pointed out that to pay a fee for access to land within a national park that had been climbed for a long time was against the Council's policy. 'It would be the thin edge of the wedge. Some future government could then well charge for access to the Kinder (an area much used by climbers). Our policy is for free access with proper protection for the farming interests, which we respect.'

(i)   Does the fact that climbers had previously been able to use the area without payment indicate that there was no scarcity of rocks suitable for climbing?

(ii)   Why do you think the previous owner had made a charge to the services but not to individual climbers?

(iii)   If the new owners were to make a charge to individual climbers what would be an appropriate basis for the charge?

(iv)   How would you explain the fact that the new owners were willing to pay a price in excess of the district valuer's estimate?

(v)   If the Planning Board was unable to buy part of the plot, either by negotiation or at auction, do you think that it should:
    (a)   enforce a compulsory purchase order;
    (b)   enforce an access order?

2.2   Discuss the possible implications of the changes in population *projected* in Fig. 2.1 and 2.2.

2.3

Table 2.1
Employment and labour productivity (1980 = 100)

	Total employed labour force	Output per person employed
1976	99	94
1977	100	96
1978	100	99
1979	102	101
1980	100	100
1981	96	102
1982	94	106
1983	94	110
1984	96	112
1985	97	114
1986	98	117

Source: Economic Trends

(i)   With reference to the data in Table 2.1 estimate the change in output between 1976 and 1986.

(ii)   What factors might account for the change in productivity that occurred in (a) 1979–80, (b) 1985–86?

(iii)   Write a brief account of the benefits and costs of increases in productivity.

(iv)   What conclusions do you draw from Table 2.1 about changes in economic capacity?

CHAPTER THREE
Economic Systems

Introduction

In Chapter 2 we discussed the main types of economic resources and the inputs derived from these resources. We now examine the mechanisms by which resources are allocated among competing users. We show that the mechanisms differ from one type of economic system to another. But first we present a model that could in principle apply to any type of economic system.

A model of an economic system

Figure 3.1 is a highly simplified representation of a national economy. It shows that the owners of resources supply inputs to producers (flow A) in return for rewards of various kinds – wages and salaries, rent, interest and dividends (flow B). The producers utilize these inputs in the creation of a flow of outputs – goods and services of various kinds (flow C). These goods and services are bought by the owners of resources – now acting as consumers – the expenditure (flow D) being financed out of the rewards (income) received from the producers.

The economy represented in Fig. 3.1 is a closed economy, i.e it engages in no international economic transactions. In practice all modern economies are open – to a greater or lesser extent – and the international economic system could be represented by a diagram showing a series of national economies linked by international economic flows. Almost all countries obtain some inputs from abroad and sell goods and services abroad.

No government sector was separately identified in Fig. 3.1 since we wished to concentrate on the relationships that are common to all economic systems – free market, planned and mixed economies.

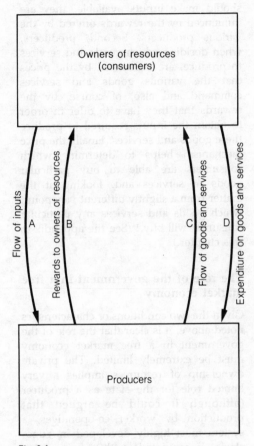

Fig. 3.1
A simple national economy

The role of the government, or the state, in these different systems is explored briefly in the following sections.

Alternative economic systems

The free market economy

The two most important characteristics of a free market economy are first that resources are owned by the private sector and not by the government or the state, and second that these resources are allocated via the price mechanism. Allocation of resources via the price mechanism has several aspects. First, when the owners of resources decide to which producers they should make inputs available, they are influenced by the rewards offered by the various producers. Second, producers, when deciding which goods and services to produce, are influenced by the prices that the various goods and services command and also, of course, by the rewards that they have to offer in order to obtain the inputs required to produce these goods and services. Finally the price mechanism helps to determine which consumers are able to buy particular goods or services and, looking at the matter from a slightly different viewpoint, which goods and services any particular consumer will buy.[1] (See the appendix to this chapter.)

The role of the government in a free market economy

Given the two conditions or characteristics noted above, it is clear that the role of the government in a free market economy must be extremely limited. The private ownership of resources implies a very limited role for the state as a producer (although it could be argued that production by worker co-operatives, a system most highly developed in Yugoslavia, is compatible with a free market economy). The state could, however, act as a consumer. It could obtain revenue by taxing the rewards accruing to owners of resources, and use this revenue to buy goods and services. An important form of expenditure would probably be on collective consumption goods such as defence, which it is not usually feasible for consumers to purchase individually. In addition the state might buy products for resale at a price below the free market price. Such products are known as merit goods – medical and educational facilities being common examples.

An alternative method of influencing the price and availability of merit goods is to subsidize their production (the cost of the subsidies again being met out of taxation). Whether the government chooses this method or whether it enters the market as a consumer, there is some interference with the operation of the price mechanism. It is a matter for debate as to what degree of interference can be said to be compatible with the existence of a free market economy.

The government might also intervene in response to the existence of *externalities*. (Again what degree of intervention is compatible with the existence of a free market economy is debatable.) An externality arises whenever a production or consumption decision of an individual or group of individuals (such as a firm) affects the production or consumption of others, except through market transactions. Externalities can be either negative (yielding costs or disbenefits) or positive (yielding benefits).

If a factory making detergents discharged wastes into a nearby river, the resulting pollution might prevent anglers and swimmers from enjoying the amenities of the river, and might prevent other factories lying downstream from using the water in their production processes. This would be an example of a negative externality. In order to minimize the externality the government might require the detergent manufacturer to install equipment which would reduce the quantity of pollution. (Government policy relating to externalities is discussed at greater length in Ch. 9.)

Finally, the government might intervene in order to 'oil the wheels' of the free market economy. The price mechanism involves decisions made by a large number of producers and consumers. If the mechanism is to work freely, producers and consumers should be well informed about the costs and benefits of the alternative courses of action that they might follow.

It would not be feasible to attempt to provide perfect information. But it may be possible and useful to reduce the degree of ignorance in a number of respects. Useful information might relate to the dangers inherent in the consumption of certain goods, for example cigarettes, the names and locations of suppliers of products, the existence of job vacancies, the availability of unemployed workers having skills required by employers, etc. In some instances this information will be provided through market mechanisms. In other instances the government may feel that it should supplement the amount of information provided privately. (In these instances information is seen as a merit good.)

The planned economy

In a fully planned economy, sometimes known as a command economy, resources are allocated by a centralized administrative process. Decisions as to which goods and services should be produced may be influenced by the planning authority's perception of consumers' desires, perhaps as indicated by 'queues' for some products and unwanted stocks of others, indicators which are also important in the free market economy. But the decisions are likely to be heavily influenced by the planners' views of what would be beneficial for the community and the state as a whole. This may involve expanding the output of individual merit goods, and reducing the output of goods deemed to be undesirable. It may also involve the expansion of whole industries or sectors of the economy, for example the output of capital goods, of the defence industry, of the agricultural sector.

In a fully planned economy decisions about the desired output of final goods and services are only the start of the planning process. In order to meet this ultimate objective the planners must ensure that the required inputs are available. Thus a series of quotas is established for producers of both final and intermediate goods – components, raw materials, etc. This in turn implies that control must be imposed over the flow of inputs and thus over the allocation of resources.

It is clear that the implementation of the plans will be very much easier if resources are owned by the state. Consequently, planned economies are normally characterized by extensive public ownership, as well as by the very limited role accorded to the price mechanism. Indeed, in the pure form of the command economy all resources would be publicly owned and the price mechanism would not operate.

In practice, even in countries such as the USSR and China where central planning is highly developed, some resources are privately owned and the price mechanism operates, albeit on a limited scale. This sometimes involves illegal economic activities, but in the USSR there has recently been a move to extend the range of private activities permitted by law. Legislation which came into effect in 1987 provided for the establishment of private businesses in a range of trades including tailoring, building repairs, tutoring and taxi services. These businesses can employ only members of the owner's family and workers are expected to work on a part-time basis, continuing in full-time jobs in state-owned organizations. Consequently the private businesses will remain small. But in total their share of economic activity was expected to be around 4 per cent by the early 1990s.

The legislation also provided for producer co-operatives to be established by workers (as opposed to state-sponsored co-operatives). When this development was announced, Mr Gorbachev, the Soviet leader, said that he expected it to have an even bigger impact than the legalization of family businesses. One Soviet economist estimated that in ten years' time they might account for 10–12 per cent of total output.

An enhanced role for the price mechanism was also announced. Food subsidies were to be phased out, and prices adjusted to cover costs of production (enterprises that could not cover their costs at the higher prices would be allowed to go bankrupt). Moreover, enterprises which produced better-quality goods were to be allowed to charge higher prices than the producers of poorer-quality goods.

Although in planned economies many wage rates are set centrally, wage differentials do exist. (Indeed some observers have claimed that when account is taken of fringe benefits and the tax structure, differentials in real incomes may be greater in the USSR than in many Western countries.) One function of wage differentials may be to influence people's decisions as to which occupation they should try to enter, i.e. to influence the allocation of human resources.

The existence in planned economies of these elements of the free market system is largely due to three factors. First, the process of planning itself requires resources, and the more detailed the planning procedures the more resources are required. Costs are likely to be especially high when attempts are made to plan the activities of industries in which there are a large number of small producers, widely scattered geographically, as in agriculture and, to a lesser extent, retailing.

Second, although this might in fact be denied by the advocates of planning, experience has shown that complete state control of an industry sometimes leads to a dramatic fall in productivity. The poor performance of the collective farms in the USSR in the early years of centralization appears to have been an important factor in the decision to maintain some private ownership of land and indeed to return some land to private owners. A similar reversal of policy occurred in China.

Finally, 'ownership' of labour in the sense that labour can be directed into particular occupations and areas, is likely to be highly unpopular politically. (The direction of labour on a temporary basis, as practised in China, was probably due to ideological rather than economic motives, and as the dominant ideology changed the practice was accepted less

readily.) The less the ability to direct labour centrally, the greater the scope for the operation of the price mechanism.

The mixed economy

All contemporary economies are mixed. Resources are owned part privately and part publicly, and are allocated partly by means of the price mechanism (modified by government intervention) and partly in accordance with a centralized planning mechanism. But although every economy has both free market and planned elements, these elements are found in very different proportions in different economies. Taking the following sample of eight countries, as we move from the command (or planned) end of the spectrum to the free market end we would first encounter Albania, followed by the Soviet Union, Yugoslavia, Hungary, France, UK, the USA and finally Hong Kong.

A comparison of alternative systems

There has been a great deal of discussion about the relative efficiency of free market and planned economies, and of mixed economies that approximate more closely to one or the other of these extremes. The major *potential* strengths and benefits claimed for each type of economy are as follows.

The free market economy is said to be more flexible; the reallocation of resources in response to changes in the demands of consumers occurs more quickly via the price mechanism than through a centralized planning procedure. Moreover the private ownership of resources provides an incentive to utilize these resources in order to meet the requirements of consumers as expressed in their desire to purchase goods and services. (It is pointed out that the legalization of private businesses in the Soviet Union, discussed above, occurred because of persistent shortages of the products that these businesses are allowed to supply.)

It is claimed that in a planned economy resources can be allocated in accordance with consumers' needs, rather than their ability to pay. Morever, by giving priority to the capital goods industries, the planners can ensure a rapid rate of economic growth. It is also claimed that planning can ensure that work is available for all those who wish to work (although it was admitted in 1987 that 3 million workers had recently been 'released' from manufacturing industries in the Soviet Union) and that rewards can be matched to effort.

Appendix: The price mechanism

The operation of the price mechanism is discussed in detail in later chapters, but since the price mechanism plays an important role in all mixed economies it will be helpful to give a brief explanation here. Figure 3.2 refers to the market for a given product, say sugar or bicycles. Line D, the demand curve, indicates the quantities of the product that consumers would offer to buy at various prices. Line S, the supply curve, indicates the quantities that producers would offer to supply at various prices. (The reasons why demand and supply curves may have the shapes shown in Fig. 3.2 are given in Chs 4 and 5.)

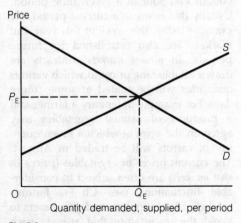

Price

Fig. 3.2
Equilibrium price and output

It can be seen that there is only one price at which the suppliers' offer matches that of the purchasers. This price is known as the *equilibrium price* and is designated P_E. The quantity traded (bought and sold) at this price is known as the *equilibrium output* and is designated Q_E.

Let us now consider what happens when the demand for the product changes. In Fig. 3.3 the initial demand curve is D_1. D_2 represents an increase in demand; for example the demand for bicycles might increase because of an increase in the number of children in the population. This increase in demand causes the price to rise from P_1 to P_2. At this higher price producers are willing to supply more, and the amount traded rises from Q_1 to Q_2.

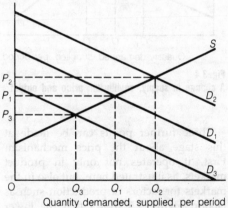

Price

Fig. 3.3
A change in demand, equilibrium price and output

A fall in demand is represented by a shift of the demand curve from D_1 to D_3; for example the demand for sugar might fall because people believe that a reduction in their consumption of sugar will lead to an improvement in their health. It can be seen that the fall in demand causes a fall in the equilibrium price to P_3 and in the equilibrium output to Q_3.

A change in equilibrium price and output also occurs following a change in supply. In Fig. 3.4 the initial supply curve is S_1. An increase in supply to S_2 which might occur following a reduction to suppliers' costs, causes prices to fall to P_2 and the quantity traded to rise to Q_2. Conversely a fall in supply to S_3, following an increase in suppliers' costs, causes prices to rise to P_3 and the quantity traded to fall to Q_3.

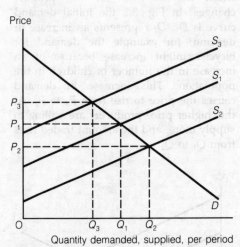

Price

Quantity demanded, supplied, per period

Fig. 3.4
A change in supply, equilibrium price and output

Three further points can be made at this stage about the price mechanism. First, it operates not only in product markets, as illustrated here, but also in the markets for factors of production such as labour. Figure 3.5 shows that the lower the real wage the more labour is demanded and the less labour is supplied. The *equilibrium wage* is W_E and Q_E is the *equilibrium employment*. (Factor markets are discussed in greater detail in Ch. 8.)

Second, the changes that occur in one market have an impact on other markets. For example, it is likely that at least some of the additional resources required to increase the quantity of bicycles supplied (Fig. 3.3) would have to be transferred from other product markets. If we take labour as an example, the producers of bicycles might offer higher wages in order

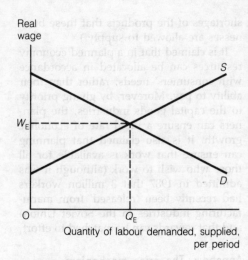

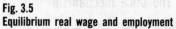

Quantity of labour demanded, supplied, per period

Fig. 3.5
Equilibrium real wage and employment

to attract workers currently employed in the production of toys. If the toy producers responded by raising wages in order to try to retain their workers, their supply curve would shift to the left (to S_3 in Fig. 3.4). As we have seen, this causes a change in the equilibrium price and output in the product market. (It also follows, of course, that changes occur in the market for labour.)

The final point relates to the time period to which the market refers. Figures 3.2–3.4 indicate the output that would be bought and sold in a given time period. Usually this refers to a current period, for example today, this week or this year. But markets are also established for future periods. In *futures markets* contracts are drawn establishing prices at which various quantities will be traded at some future date. For example in January a farmer and a producer of canned vegetables may agree on the price at which a given quantity of carrots will be traded in August. The current prices of vegetables (prices in *spot markets*) are often subject to considerable fluctuations (see Ch. 7). Futures markets allow suppliers and purchasers to avoid the uncertainty that attends such fluctuations.

Summary

1. An economy comprises a set of flows: of inputs (derived from resources), of rewards to owners of resources, of goods and services, and of expenditure on goods and services.
2. In a free market economy resources are owned by the state and allocated via the price mechanism. The price mechanism helps to determine what should be produced, how it should be produced, and for whom it should be produced.
3. An externality arises whenever a production or consumption decision of an individual or group affects the production or consumption of others, except through market prices. Governments may intervene to reduce the incidence of negative externalities arising from the operation of the price mechanism.
4. Governments may also intervene in order to make the price mechanism work more freely, e.g. by providing information to consumers and producers.
5. In a planned or command economy there is extensive public ownership, and resources are allocated by a centralized administrative process.
6. All modern economies are mixed. Resources are owned part privately and part publicly, and are allocated partly by means of the price mechanism (modified by government intervention) and partly in accordance with a centralized planning mechanism.
7. The equilibrium price is that at which the suppliers' offer matches that of the purchasers. The equilibrium output is the quantity traded at the equilibrium price. A change in either demand or supply may cause the equilibrium price and output to change.
8. The equilibrium wage is that at which the quantity of labour supplied equals the quantity demanded. The equilibrium employment is the amount of labour employed at that wage. A change in either supply or demand may cause the equilibrium wage and employment to change.

Key terms

Economic system	Equilibrium price
Free market economy	Equilibrium output
Planned (command) economy	Equilibrium wage
Mixed economy	Equilibrium employment
Price mechanism	Externalities
Allocation of resources	

Notes

1. The functions of the price mechanism are sometimes summarized as follows: it helps to determine what should be produced, how it should be produced and for whom it should be produced.

Essay questions

1. What are the major characteristics of free market, planned and mixed economies?
2. To what extent do you agree with the view that the needs of consumers are more likely to be satisfied in a planned than in a market economy?

3. How would you explain the increasing importance of mixed economies?
4. Why is it often difficult to obtain agreement about which type of economy is preferable?
5. Explain how an increased demand for a product is likely to affect (a) the price of that product, (b) the quantity produced, (c) the price of other products.

Exercises

3.1 The passage below, adapted from an article in the *Financial Times*, 1 May 1987, refers to changes in the Soviet economy. What light does the passage throw on: (a) efficiency/inefficiency in a planned economy; (b) the problems that can arise in introducing aspects of a market economy; (c) the likely effects of the proposed changes on the distribution of income?

By the end of this year about 1,500 service co-operatives are expected to be in existence – and this excludes other forms of co-operative. Their popularity reflects a desire on the part of ordinary Soviets to earn extra money through a second job: a recent poll carried out by the Institute of Sociological Research in Moscow showed that 27 per cent of those questioned wanted to earn more in this way.

The new law makes it legal for individuals to engage in 29 different activities, including flat repair, tailoring, photographic services, tutoring, taxis and mending fishing rods.

In many cases it will simply allow people to do legally what they have previously done on the side. Soviet surveys show that between 17 m and 20 m people out of a total labour force of 155 m make money through second jobs.

The incomes of Soviet wage-earners have increased faster than the supply of consumer goods and services over the past 30 years. The result is that private handymen working on their own account supply 50 per cent of all shoe repairs, 45 per cent of apartment repairs, 40 per cent of car repairs and 30 per cent of repairs to household appliances. In the countryside the figure rises to 80 per cent.

In the republic of Russia, the Transport Ministry says it meets only 42 per cent of the public needs for taxis, the rest being met, if at all, by drivers of the 12 m privately owned cars.

Failure to meet demand, surveys show, means that the average Soviet citizen spends 10 per cent of income on services, but would like to spend twice as much. Instead bank savings have risen steeply, so even high-priced goods such as new cars or expensive furniture find immediate buyers.

Co-operatives already exist in the co-operative farms (kolkhoz) set up after the collectivization of agriculture in 1929. But the peasants were coerced into joining kolkhoz and the appointment of chairmen is always from above.

The new co-operatives are different. In theory individuals can set them up by registering with local financial authorities and paying a small fee. There is plenty of demand for jobs. When a co-operative providing some 30 different services in Ulyanovsk advertised for up to 50 people wanting a second job, it had 800 applicants.

However, the co-operatives face three serious difficulties. These are supplies of raw materials and machinery, provision of full-time skilled labour and relations with local government and ministries.

The greatest difficulty is supplies. The wholesale customer in the Soviet Union cannot just arrive at the appropriate state organization with a cheque and sign an order for raw materials or equipment. Allocation of resources is decided centrally by the State Supplies Committee (Gosnab) which is not geared to supplying the new co-operatives with small batches of material or a few machines.

The supply of labour for second jobs is no problem and the co-operatives will also use pensioners (Soviet women retire at 55, men at 60), housewives and students. A difficulty is that the co-operatives will also need full-time skilled workers and technicians whom state enterprises want to keep. In some cases, part-time workers, such as would-be taxi drivers in Tallin, Estonia, have been unable to get documents from their main place of work to allow them to take on secondary employment.

It is vital that the Government should not try to control the new co-operative or individual ventures to the point where they are stifled. For instance the Transport Ministry wanted to decide the prices charged by private taxis and exactly when and how they should operate. Other ministries have tried to keep a grip on costs, salaries and management because this is their traditional behaviour and because they want to prevent competition with state services.

Tax rates demonstrate the Government's determination to stop entrepreneurs becoming millionaires. It has introduced for the first time a progressive tax. On an individual's net profit up to 3,000 roubles per annum tax is levied on only 11 per cent of income but then jumps to 60 per cent on profits between 3,000 and 5,000 roubles. Co-operatives pay 5 per cent for three or four years and then 10 per cent.

3.2 Exercise 3.2 is based on the operation of the Stock Exchange. The shares of most companies which are quoted on the Stock Exchange are distributed among a large number, often thousands, of investors. These investors will have different views about the future prospects of any particular company in which they hold shares, and therefore about the price for which they would be willing to sell these shares. Let us take as a hypothetical example the shares of the Vestas Pottery Co. Sixty thousand Vestas shares have been issued, and the holders of these shares would be willing to sell at the following prices:

Supply schedule for Vestas Pottery Co. shares

Price (£)	No. of shares offered for sale
1.60	60,000
1.50	40,000
1.40	25,000
1.30	15,000
1.20	7,000
1.10	2,000

At a price of £1.60 all of the existing holders would be willing to sell their shares. At a price of £1.10, only 2,000 shares would be offered for sale, and below this price no shares would be offered.

There are also many potential buyers of Vestas shares, again with different views about the company's prospects. The view of these investors can be summarized as follows:

Demand schedule for Vestas Pottery Co. shares

Price (£)	No. of shares demanded
1.50	2,000
1.40	7,000
1.30	15,000
1.20	25,000
1.10	40,000
1.00	60,000

Investors buy and sell shares through stockbrokers who transmit the instructions of their clients to jobbers who undertake the actual trading.

(i)   Draw the demand and supply curves corresponding to the above schedules.

(ii)   Given that on any one day stockbrokers receive buying and selling instructions as indicated by the above demand and supply schedules, how many shares will change hands?

(iii) At what price will these shares be traded?

(iv) Show by means of diagrams how the shares traded would differ from that indicated above if the following changes were to take place:

    (a)   The existing shareholders receive a statement from the company's chairman, which has not yet been released to members of the general public, indicating that profits are likely to be considerably greater than he had forecast at the last annual general meeting.

    (b)   A financial journalist with a very large following amongst investors writes an article about Vestas in which he forecasts a doubling of profits in the current year.

    (c)   Several very large potential buyers of Vestas shares are advised by a reliable contact within the company that the company's sales are well below target.

    (d)   An extensive fire destroys the company's main factory, which is discovered to be considerably under-insured.

CHAPTER FOUR
Demand

Introduction

In this chapter we discuss the various factors which influence demand, developing the analysis presented in the previous chapter. In that chapter we showed that a demand curve, which indicates the various quantities of a product (or input) that would be demanded at various prices in a given time period, has two important aspects. The *shape* of the curve indicates how the quantity demanded would change in response to a change in price. The *position* of the curve indicates the quantity that would be demanded at any given price. (When we draw a demand curve we assume, of course, that we know both its shape and its position.)

In the first part of the chapter we examine the determinants of the shape of the demand curve, and in the second part the determinants of its position.

The determinants of the shape of the demand curve

Several alternative theories have been advanced which purport to explain the shape of the demand curve. We consider two of these alternatives, beginning with the marginal utility theory.

The marginal utility theory

This theory is based on the proposition that products are bought because of the satisfaction or utility they yield to the purchaser. Marginal utility is the satisfaction obtained from the consumption of one additional unit of a product. The *law of diminishing marginal utility* states that, within any given period, the marginal utility of any product declines as the quantity consumed increases, the consumption of other products remaining constant.

Consider a housewife deciding how many potatoes she should buy each week for the family. She might decide that if she were to buy 2 kg the family would obtain more satisfaction than if she bought only 1 kg, but that their satisfaction would not be doubled. Again, if she were to buy 3 kg there would be a further increase in satisfaction, but the additional satisfaction would be less than would be yielded by the second kilogram. Finally, if she were to buy 4 kg total satisfaction would decline as the members of the family would have to eat more potatoes than they would wish, i.e. the marginal utility of the fourth kilogram would be negative. This relationship between utility and the quantity consumed is shown in Fig. 4.1. It will be noticed that total utility is maximized at the point at which marginal utility is zero, i.e. at a weekly consumption of between 3 and 4 kg.

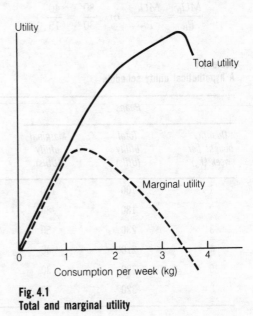

Fig. 4.1
Total and marginal utility

In order to explain the overall equilibrium position of the consumer or household we have to take into account the relative prices of all the products that might be bought. If the consumer is to maximize his (or her) utility, his pattern of consumption must be such that he equalizes the ratios of the marginal utilities of each product to their prices. Using symbols this condition can be expressed as follows:

$$\frac{MU_a}{P_a} \ldots = \ldots \frac{MU_n}{P_n}$$

where $a \ldots n$ represents the range of products purchased.

To illustrate this point let us assume that the consumer derives utility from a pair of products, carrots and beans, as shown in Table 4.1. If we assume that beans are twice as expensive as carrots, e.g. 30p and 15p a kilogram, we know that for the consumer to be in equilibrium the ratio of the marginal utilities must also be 2 : 1. There are, in fact, two alternative combinations that would fulfil this condition. If the consumer purchased 2 kg of beans and 2 kg of carrots a week we would have:

$$\frac{MU_B}{P_B} = \frac{MU_C}{P_C} \quad \text{or} \quad \frac{80}{30} = \frac{40}{15}$$

Alternatively, if he purchased 4 kg of beans and 4 kg of carrots we would have:

$$\frac{MU_B}{P_B} = \frac{MU_C}{P_C} \quad \text{or} \quad \frac{40}{30} = \frac{20}{15}$$

Note that we have described the relationship between the relative prices of various products and the relative quantities purchased. We have not explained how much of a given product would be bought. Indeed we have shown that at 30p a kilogram the consumer might buy either 2 kg or 4 kg of beans a week. In order to determine the actual quantities bought we would need to know not only the prices of each product but also the consumer's income. In other words the marginal utility theory does not enable us to determine the *position* of the consumer's demand curve.

The theory does, however, enable us to predict the way in which the consumption of a product will change as its price changes. To illustrate this let us assume that the price of beans falls to 15p a kilogram, i.e. the ratio of the prices of beans to carrots becomes 1 : 1. At the previous pattern of consumption the condition for the consumer's equilibrium would no longer be fulfilled. In order to restore equilibrium the consumer must increase

Table 4.1
A hypothetical utility schedule

	Beans			Carrots	
Quantity bought per week (kg)	Total utility (Utils)	Marginal utility (Utils)	Quantity bought per week (kg)	Total utility (Utils)	Marginal utility (Utils)
1	100	100	1	60	60
2	180	80	2	100	40
3	230	50	3	130	30
4	270	40	4	150	20
5	300	30	5	155	5
6	320	20	6	155	0

his consumption of beans relative to that of carrots. For example if he previously purchased 2 kg of beans a week (and 2 kg of carrots) he may now purchase 4 kg of beans (and 2 kg of carrots), i.e.:

$$\frac{MU_B}{P_B} = \frac{MU_C}{P_C} \quad \text{or} \quad \frac{40}{15} = \frac{40}{15}$$

Alternatively, if he previously purchased 4 kg of beans (and 4 kg of carrots) he may now purchase 6 kg of beans (and 4 kg of carrots), i.e.:

$$\frac{MU_B}{P_B} = \frac{MU_C}{P_C} \quad \text{or} \quad \frac{20}{15} = \frac{20}{15}$$

Whichever of these combinations of purchases we start from, a fall in the price of beans leads to an increase in the quantity bought, i.e. the demand curve slopes downwards from left to right.

Price elasticity of demand

The price elasticity of demand[1] is defined as:

$$\frac{\Delta Q}{Q} \div \frac{\Delta P}{P}$$

where Q is the initial quantity demanded,
P is the initial price, and
Δ denotes a small change in the variable.

As shown below, price elasticity of demand is an extremely important concept, and it is sometimes claimed that the marginal utility theory can help to predict its value. This claim is usually justified by reference to a situation such as that portrayed in Fig. 4.2, where two alternative marginal utility curves for a given product are shown.

We start from a situation where the consumer is in equilibrium with a marginal utility of U_1 derived from this product. This implies a consumption of Q_1 with marginal utility curve M_1, and of R_1 with curve M_2. Let us assume that, the prices of all other products remaining

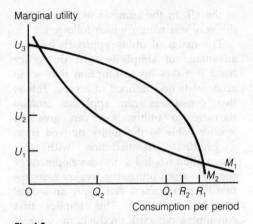

Fig. 4.2
Marginal utility and changes in consumption

equal, the price of this product now doubles. In order to restore equilibrium, consumption is reduced to the point where marginal utility is doubled, from U_1 to U_2. With curve M_1 this implies a fall in consumption from Q_1 to Q_2, i.e. a reduction of about one-half. With M_2 it implies a fall in consumption from R_1 to R_2, or about one-tenth.

It seems then that demand is far more elastic with marginal utility curve M_1 than M_2. However, we must remember that this conclusion refers only to the particular ranges of consumption considered here. It need not apply when other ranges are considered. Indeed we would reach a different conclusion if we started from, say, the level of marginal utility U_3. This is an extremely important qualification since, as we have already shown, we cannot predict what levels of consumption will be associated with given prices.

The concept of marginal utility does help us to understand why a given product can command very different prices in different circumstances. A very dramatic, if somewhat unreal, example is the different prices that might be offered for a glass of water by a man dying of thirst and another who was in danger of drowning. More realistic is the difference in the relative value of an additional litre of water during the drought experienced in the UK in the summer of 1976 and in the very wet winter which followed.

The marginal utility approach has the advantage of simplicity. On the other hand it makes an assumption that some economists find difficult to accept. This is that consumers can apply a *cardinal* measure to utility, i.e. can give an *absolute* value to the utility derived from a product. Dissatisfaction with this assumption has led to the development of theories which utilize the weaker assumption that consumers can apply an *ordinal* measure to utility. This implies that consumers can rank products in order of preference, although they may not be able to say by how much they prefer one product (or one combination of products) to another. This assumption is utilized in indifference analysis.

Indifference analysis

In Fig. 4.3 the indifference curve *I* indicates the various combinations of two products, beans and carrots, that would give the consumer an identical amount of satisfaction. (The consumer would be indifferent as between any of the combinations represented by the curve.)

Although it is sometimes claimed that in principle it would be possible to derive a consumer's indifference curve by experimentation, in practice the shape of the curve in Fig. 4.3 is based upon the assumption that the less a consumer has of one product the less of that product he would be willing to give up in exchange for one additional unit of another product. If he were at E he would be willing to give up 2 kg of carrots (EF) in exchange for 1 kg of beans (FD), whereas if he were at B he would be willing to exchange only 1 kg of carrots (BC) for 1 kg of beans (CA). This concept of a *declining* (*or diminishing*) *marginal rate of substitution* is clearly analogous to the proposition that marginal utility changes with the amount consumed per period, or the rate of consumption.

In order to determine the quantity demanded we introduce the consumer's budget constraint, which takes account of the relative prices of products and the consumer's income. In Fig. 4.4 we show a 'family' of indifference curves, representing different levels of satisfaction. The highest level of satisfaction is represented by curve I_1. However, the consumer cannot reach this level. His income is only sufficient to allow him to buy the various combinations represented by the budget line AB. The highest level of satisfaction that he can attain is indicated by point X, where the budget line

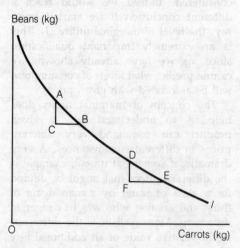

Beans (kg)

Carrots (kg)

Fig. 4.3
An indifference curve

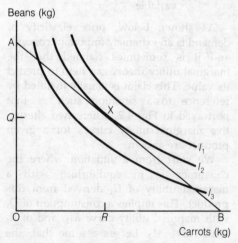

Beans (kg)

Carrots (kg)

Fig. 4.4
The equilibrium of the consumer

is tangential to I_2. This shows that he is in equilibrium when he purchases Q kilos of beans and R kilos of carrots per week.

The equilibrium will be disturbed by any change in the consumer's budget line. Let us consider first a change in income, the prices of all products remaining unchanged. An increase in income would be represented by an outward shift of the budget line, from AB to A'B' in Fig. 4.5. (The two lines are parallel because the relative prices of beans and carrots are unchanged.) A fall in income would be represented by an inward shift of the budget line, from AB to A"B".

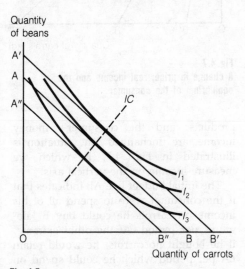

Fig. 4.5

A change in income and in the equilibrium of the consumer

As income changes, a change occurs in the combinations of products available to the consumer, and he moves to a new equilibrium position. In each instance the equilibrium position is given by the point of tangency of the budget line to an indifference curve.[2] These points of tangency, these equilibrium positions, may be joined to form an income–consumption line, designated IC in Fig. 4.5. The path traced by IC indicates that an increase in income leads to an increase in the consumption of both beans and carrots, i.e. both are *normal goods* (see below).

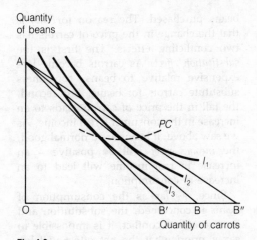

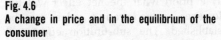

Fig. 4.6

A change in price and in the equilibrium of the consumer

The other factor which will cause a change in the consumer's equilibrium position is a change in the relative prices of products. In Fig. 4.6 we illustrate the effect of a change in the price of carrots, the price of beans being unchanged.

The initial budget line AB corresponds to that shown in Fig. 4.4. Since both the consumer's money income and the price of beans remain unchanged, the consumer could, if he wished, continue to buy A kilograms of beans. However, the change in the price of carrots changes the quantity of carrots that he could buy. As carrots become dearer, the budget line pivots to AB'. Conversely, as carrots become cheaper the budget line pivots to AB".

Equilibrium is again determined by the points of tangency of the budget line to the indifference curves. In this instance the equilibrium points may be joined to form a price–consumption curve, designated PC in Fig. 4.6. The path traced by PC indicates that as the price of carrots falls the quantity purchased increases. This has clear implications for the shape of the demand curve for carrots, and we return to this point below. But first we consider the consumption of beans.

The path of PC indicates that a fall in the price of carrots may lead to either an increase or a decrease in the quantity of beans purchased. The reason for this is that the change in the price of carrots has two conflicting effects. The first is the *substitution effect*. As carrots become less expensive relative to beans, consumers substitute carrots for beans. But second, the fall in the price of carrots leads to an increase in the consumer's real income. As we saw above, if beans are a normal good, the *income effect* will be positive – an increase in real income will lead to an increase in consumption.

Since, as far as the consumption of beans is concerned, the substitution and income effects conflict, it is impossible to say a priori what the net effect will be. However, some ground rules can be established. The substitution effect will obviously be greater the more likely it is that consumers will substitute one product for another. We would expect a change in the price of carrots to have a greater effect on the consumption of beans than on the consumption of a less close substitute, such as oranges.

The magnitude of the income effect depends upon two factors. The first is the extent of the change in the consumer's real income. This in turn depends upon both the proportion of the consumer's income spent on the product whose price changes and the magnitude of the price change. The second factor is the value of the income elasticity of demand for the product in question (see below).

Let us now consider further the consumption of the product whose price changes – in this instance carrots. Here the substitution and income effects normally work in the same direction. A fall in the price of carrots will cause consumers to substitute carrots for beans, while the increase in real income will also encourage an increase in the consumption of carrots.

As we said above, this analysis has clear implications for the shape of the demand curve. However, we must extend the analysis a little further. A demand curve is drawn on the assumption that only the price of the product in question changes, i.e. that the prices of *all* other

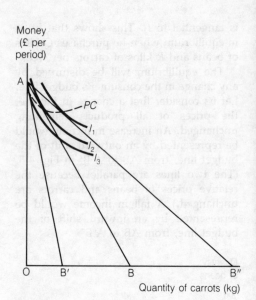

Fig. 4.7
A change in price, real income and the equilibrium of the consumer

products, and the consumer's money income, are unchanged. The situation is illustrated in Fig. 4.7, in which we measure income on the vertical axis.

The initial budget line AB indicates that if the consumer were to spend all of his income on carrots he could buy B kilograms per period. At the other extreme, if he bought no carrots, he would retain £A per period which he could spend on other goods. His equilibrium position is denoted by the point of tangency of AB to I_2.

As before, a change in the price of carrots causes the budget line to pivot – to AB' as carrots become dearer, or AB" as they become cheaper. Also as before, the points of equilibrium may be joined to form a price consumption curve PC. The path of PC indicates that the quantity of carrots increases as the price falls, i.e. that the demand curve slopes down from left to right. This again can be explained in terms of a combination of substitution and income effects, although now the substitution effect refers to the substitution of carrots for all other products.

Indifference analysis suggests that the substitution effect always operates so as to increase the quantity bought when price is reduced. It follows from this assumption that if a reduction in price results in a fall in consumption, this must be due to a negative income effect outweighing the substitution effect.

This is illustrated in Fig. 4.8. The initial budget line AB is tangential to I_1 at point X. A fall in the price of bread causes the budget line to pivot to AB″ and leads to a new equilibrium position Z, where AB″ is tangential to I_2. (By drawing a hypothetical budget line A′ B′ tangential to I_1, we cancel out the income effect; the move from X to Y denotes the substitution effect).

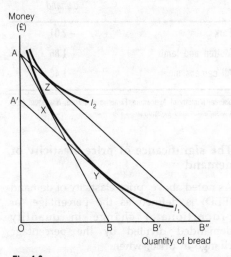

Fig. 4.8
A fall in price and in consumption

Products for which the income effect is negative, i.e. products with a negative income elasticity of demand, are known as *inferior goods*. When the negative income effect is sufficient to outweigh the substitution effect, as here, the product is known as a *Giffen good*. Giffen goods are named after Sir Robert Giffen who was said to have observed in the 19th century that when the price of a product rose, its consumption by certain groups in society also rose. The product is said by some writers to have been bread, and by others potatoes. In fact it seems unlikely that the alleged observation actually occurred.

A Giffen good is one of the types of product whose demand curves slope upwards from left to right (or at least have an upward-sloping portion). The other types of product which may have a similar shape of demand curve are those whose price is taken by consumers as an indicator of quality, and those which are bought for the purpose of conspicuous consumption. In these instances the shape of the demand curve can be explained by a substitution effect different from usual. As a result of the lower price, consumers will be disposed to buy less of that product and more of substitute products. If this substitution effect is sufficiently strong to outweigh any positive income effect, consumption of that product will fall as its price is reduced. (The reactions of consumers to changes in the price of such a product might be interpreted as indicating a change in tastes. It would not, however, be possible to use a single demand curve to demonstrate this effect, since a demand curve is drawn on the assumption that the conditions of demand, including consumers' tastes, are unchanged.)

A comparison of utility and indifference analysis

The purpose of this section is not to suggest a 'best buy' from among the competing approaches – indeed experience suggests that some students are likely to be happier with one approach and other students with another – but to review the criteria against which the different approaches might be evaluated.

As we noted when discussing the controversies between Keynesians and monetarists, economists of a 'positivist' persuasion take the view that the predictive value of a theory is the most important (and perhaps the only valid) criterion. Unfortunately this does not get us very far in this instance since the same prediction emerges from both approaches, namely that a fall in the price of a product will normally lead to an increase in the quantity demanded. The only distinction that we could make on this score is that the marginal utility approach has not provided an explanation as to why for some products (Giffen goods) price and quantity are positively related.

Again, although each approach leads to the conclusion that the demand curve slopes down from left to right, neither enables us to draw conclusions about the precise shape of the curve, i.e. about its elasticity. We showed that certain tentative conclusions could be drawn about elasticity on the basis of alternative marginal utility schedules or curves. The price–consumption curves derived from indifference analysis are also an indicator of demand elasticities. However, the utility schedules and the indifference curves that we presented were hypothetical; indeed no empirical evidence relating to either concept has ever been presented. This is, in fact, simply one example of the deductive nature of both approaches. Each approach starts from certain assumptions about consumers' motivations and preferences, and derives conclusions about behaviour from these assumptions.

Although the deductive method is well established in economics, the assumptions made in some models have been criticized. For example, the assumption of a constant scale of preferences, which underlies indifference analysis, is dubious in the extreme, if only because it implies that consumers do not learn anything from their past experience. (The same point applies to the assumption of consistent behaviour which is central to the revealed preference theory.)

A final criterion by which we might evaluate alternative theories is the extent to which they aid one's understanding of economic processes. Indifference analysis enables both the income and substitution effects of a price change to be explored in detail. Many people would consider this to be an advantage, although others might consider this advantage to be outweighed by the greater simplicity of alternative approaches.

The measurement of elasticity

Table 4.2 gives estimates of demand elasticities derived from observation (using statistical analysis) of actual expenditure patterns. It will be noticed that the elasticity is highest for the narrow groups (pork and mutton and lamb) and lowest for the wide group (all carcass meat). The reason for this is that there are more close substitutes for pork and for mutton and lamb than for all carcass meat.

Table 4.2
Estimated price elasticities of demand

Product	Price elasticity of demand
Pork	−2.01
Mutton and lamb	−1.86
All carcass meat	−1.46

Source: Ministry of Agriculture, Fisheries and Food, *Household Food Consumption and Expenditure*, 1986

The significance of price elasticity of demand

As noted above, price elasticity of demand (PED) is defined as the percentage (or proportionate) change in quantity demanded divided by the percentage change in price, when:

PED > (−)1, as in Table 4.2, demand is said to be (price) elastic

PED < (−)1, e.g. −0.89, demand is said to be (price) inelastic

PED = (−)1, demand is said to be of unitary (price) elasticity

The change in revenue that results from a given change in price is determined by the value of PED. In Figure 4.9 a reduction in price, from A to B, causes a much bigger *percentage* increase in the quantity demanded from M to N. (Remember that A, M, etc. is shorthand for OA, OM, etc.) In other words demand is elastic in the price range AB. It can be seen that

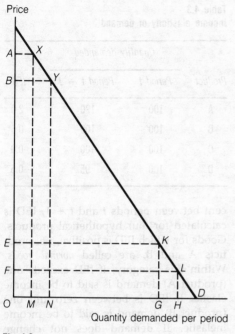

**Fig. 4.9
Elastic and inelastic demand**

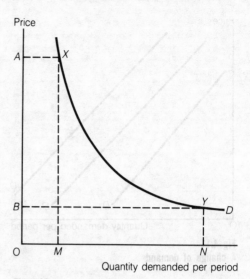

**Fig. 4.10
Demand of unitary elasticity**

following this price change, revenue increases: *OBYN > OAXM*. Conversely, since demand is elastic, an increase in price from *B* to *A* would, of course, cause a fall in revenue.

On the other hand a reduction in price from *E* to *F* causes a smaller *percentage* increase in quantity demanded, i.e. demand is inelastic. In this situation a fall in price causes revenue to fall (*OFLH < OEKG*). Conversely, an increase in price causes revenue to increase.

Finally the demand curve in Fig. 4.10, a rectangular hyperbola, is of unitary elasticity throughout its length. A change in price causes an identical percentage change in output, and revenue is the same whatever the price (*OAXM = OBYN*).

The relationships that we have identified are summarized below:

Demand	Change in price	Change in revenue
Elastic	Decrease	Increase
	Increase	Decrease

Demand	Change in price	Change in revenue
Inelastic	Decrease	Decrease
	Increase	Increase
Unitary	Decrease	None
	Increase	None

Time and elasticity

The response of quantity demanded to a change in price is likely to become greater over time. Time gives customers more opportunity to search for alternative products and brands, and to make contact with alternative suppliers. Technological constraints, which may present a change in purchasing patterns in the short term, can be removed in the longer term. For example a change in the relative prices of different fuels may have little effect until customers have the opportunity to change their appliances to run on the alternative fuel.

The position of the demand curve

We now move to the second major topic covered in this chapter, namely the factors which influence the position of the demand curve. Referring to Fig. 4.11, we

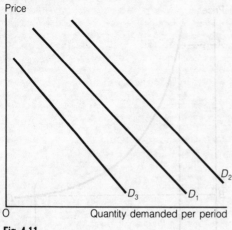

Price

D_2

D_3 D_1

O   Quantity demanded per period

Fig. 4.11
A change of demand

Table 4.3
Income elasticity of demand

Product	*Quantity demanded*		IED
	Period t	*Period t + 1*	
A	100	120	2.0
B	100	105	0.5
C	100	100	0.0
D	100	95	−0.5

are concerned with factors which result in either an increase in demand (a shift from D_1 to D_2), or a decrease in demand (a shift from D_1 to D_3).

The conditions of demand

A shift of the demand curve – in either direction – indicates a change in the conditions of demand. It would be impossible to discuss all the factors which might influence demand, i.e. all the conditions of demand. However, we examine the most important, beginning with income.

Income
A change in real national income is likely to affect the demand for almost every product. However, the response of demand to a change in income varies from product to product. A precise measure of this response is the income elasticity of demand (IED), defined as:

$$\frac{\Delta Q}{Q} \div \frac{\Delta Y}{Y}$$

where Q is the quantity demanded per period,
Y is national income, and
Δ denotes a small change in the variable.

In Table 4.3 where it is assumed that national income (Y) increases by 10 per

cent between periods t and $t + 1$, IED is calculated for four hypothetical products. Goods for which IED is positive, i.e. products A and B, are called *normal goods*. Within this category, if IED exceeds one (product A) demand is said to be income elastic. If IED is between zero and one (product B) demand is said to be income inelastic. If demand does not change following a change in income (product C) IED is zero. Finally, goods whose IED is negative (product D) are called *inferior goods*.

As national income increases, the volume of sales of most products increases, suggesting that normal goods are more common than inferior goods. This implies that in Fig. 4.11 an increase in income is most likely to cause the demand curve to shift from D_1 to D_2.

Demand is influenced by many factors in addition to income, as we show below. In order to estimate IED allowances have to be made, as far as possible, for changes in these other influencing factors, and this may require the use of elaborate statistical or econometric techniques. Table 4.4 gives estimates of IED derived in this manner.

It should be emphasized that these values of IED relate only to the periods studied (1968–73). Other periods would yield different values. The IED for particular consumer durables is often high in the early years but falls when most households have acquired the product, the main demand then being for replacement purposes. Moreover, one can find examples of products whose IED becomes

Table 4.4
Estimated income elasticities of demand

Product group	IED
Fuel and light	0.41
Food	0.24
Alcoholic drinks	0.61
Tobacco	0.16
Clothing	0.53
Durable goods	0.58
Private transport	0.49
Public transport	0.47
Services	0.52

Source: Muellbauer J, Testing the Barteen model of household composition effects and the cost of children, *Economic Journal*, 1977

negative after a certain point, i.e. the good changes from being a normal to an inferior good. This is especially likely to happen when a more expensive substitute exists which more people are able to afford as income increases. In the UK the demand for bicycles increased for some time with increasing income, but then fell as many people switched to motor cycles and cars.

Figure 4.12 gives details of changes in the relative importance of various items of expenditure. It can be seen that as incomes have risen the proportion spent on housing, transport and vehicles, and services has increased, while the proportion spent on food, clothing and footwear has declined. This suggests that IED is higher for the former than the latter group of commodities.

We have been concerned in this section with the effect of changes in aggregate national income. But a given change in national income might, of course, take many different forms. The implications of this are discussed in the following section.

The distribution of income
The distribution of income may change as national income changes or while national

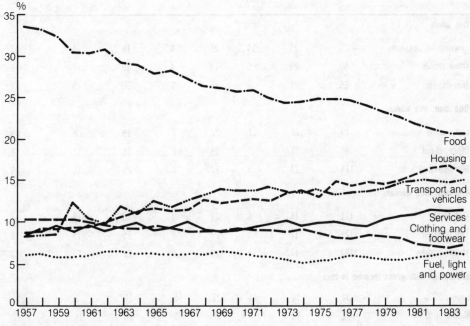

Fig. 4.12
Changes in the pattern of expenditure. *Note*: **Percentages are expenditure on commodity or service group as a percentage of total household expenditure**
Source: Family Expenditure Survey reports, 1957–84

income remains constant. The relative incomes of different sectors may alter, for example the share of the national income going to wage- and salary-earners may rise while that going to companies falls. This is likely to alter the demand for both consumer and investment goods. Or the change may occur within a sector, e.g. the share of the wage and salary bill going to the lowest paid may rise while that going to the highest paid falls. Different household types and income groups have different consumption patterns, as shown in Table 4.5. Consequently a change in income distribution will cause a change in the overall pattern of consumption.

Changes in population

A change in total population usually leads to a change in national income, with the consequences discussed above. Even if total population is constant, changes may occur in its structure, with important implications for the pattern of demand. For example an increase in the proportion of children leads to an increase in the demand for baby food and clothes and subsequently for pop records, cosmetics, etc. Conversely, an increase in the proportion of elderly citizens may lead to an increase in the demand for false teeth, hearing aids, bungalows, etc.

Table 4.5
Patterns of household expenditure, by household composition and income level

Household composition	Index of expenditure (all households = 100)	Percentage of expenditure allocated to:						
		Housing	Fuel, light and power	Food	Alcohol, tobacco	Durable goods	Transport vehicles	Services, miscellaneous
One adult:								
Low-income pensioner	28	21	14	26	4	18	4	13
Other retired	50	29	9	17	4	19	7	16
Non-retired	65	21	6	16	9	20	19	14
One man, one woman:								
Low-income pensioner	49	20	11	27	7	19	8	9
Other retired	86	22	7	19	6	18	11	18
Non-retired	114	17	5	17	7	25	15	16
One man, one woman:								
One child	111	16	6	20	7	23	16	13
Two children	128	17	5	20	6	25	15	13
Three children	137	17	5	20	6	27	13	12
Households with gross income in the:								
Lowest 20%	34	16	13	27	8	20	7	11
Middle 60%	92	18	6	20	7	23	14	12
Highest 20%	190	14	4	17	6	25	18	16

Source: Family Expenditure Survey 1986, published in Employment Gazette, Dec. 1987

The introduction of new products

Increases in demand for consumer durables are partly due to the fact that manufacturers have introduced a large number of new and improved products e.g. fridge-freezers, video-recorders, personal stereos. Other illustrations can be drawn from other product fields. For example the growth in the sales of frozen foodstuffs has been influenced by extensions in the range supplied by manufacturers. Many manufacturers started with such basic products as peas and fish fingers and subsequently introduced complete dinners, dishes of foreign origin, etc. (Incidentally increased sales of frozen foods have gone hand in hand with an increase in the ownership of home freezers, from 26 per cent of households in 1975 to 74 per cent in 1986.)

The introduction of new products and improved versions of existing products means that one has to be very careful in applying demand analysis. In principle, a series of demand curves for different periods should relate to a given product with unchanged characteristics; in practice this requirement may be difficult to fulfil.

The price and availability of substitutes

As noted earlier, the demand for a product is influenced by the availability of substitutes. The more close substitutes are available the more elastic demand is likely to be. In other words the availability of substitutes affects the shape of the demand curve.

The availability and price of substitutes also affect the position of the curve. The effect of a change in the price of one product on the quantity demanded of another product is measured by the cross-elasticity of demand.

$$\text{Cross elasticity of demand} = \frac{\Delta Q_A}{Q_A} \div \frac{\Delta P_B}{P_B}$$

where A and B are two products,
 Q and P denote the initial quantity demanded and price,
 Δ denotes a small change in the variable.

The bigger the value of cross-elasticity of demand the closer substitutes the two products are considered to be.

The availability of substitutes is especially important in relation to the introduction of new products. For example the introduction of colour television sets led to a fall in the demand for monochrome sets. (Incidentally it is interesting to note that some manufacturers responded by introducing an improved range of smaller, portable televisions, with the result that the total demand for all monochrome sets actually increased for some time.) Taking an example from a different market, the decline of the traditional fish and chip shop has been hastened by the growth of alternative quick-food outlets serving hamburgers, chicken, Chinese food, etc.

The price and availability of complements

Here the reverse process applies. Complementarity is said to exist when an increase in the quantity of one product sold leads to an increase in the demand for another product. The effect of a change in price can again be measured by the cross-elasticity of demand, although a fall in the price of A (and hence an increase in the quantity bought) now leads to an increase in the quantity of B demanded.

The greater the degree of complementarity, the higher the (negative) value of the cross-elasticity of demand. Examples of pairs of complementary products are bread and butter, cricket bats and balls, shoes and shoe laces, cars and petrol. (Some writers use the term 'joint demand' as being synonymous with complementary demand, while others reserve the former term for products, or factors, which must be used together.)

The promotional activities of suppliers

A wide variety of activities can be included under this heading, including advertising, personal visits by salesmen and, possibly, some forms of packaging. The promotional activities whose success in stimulating demand come most readily to mind are, perhaps, the long-running advertising campaigns such as 'Drinka-Pinta-Milka-Day' and 'The Genius of Guinness'. But other activities less visible to the general public may be just as effective. Much of the promotional activity devoted to ethical pharmaceutical products comprises expenditure on communication to doctors, including visits by professionally qualified representatives.

The tastes of consumers

Considerable fluctuations in the demand for some products result from changes in consumers' tastes. When mini-skirts were in fashion the demand for cloth decreased but the demand for nylon tights increased. Subsequently, as hem-lines dropped, the demand for cloth increased and the demand for tights decreased. (There was clearly a substitution effect here.) There has been a long-standing controversy as to whether or not the tastes of consumers can be changed by the promotional activities of suppliers, and especially by advertising. Fortunately, we need not enter into this controversy since we have included both factors in our list of determinants of demand.

The demand for investment goods

Many of the factors listed above can affect the demand for investment or capital goods. However, a change in demand for investment goods often originates in a change in demand for consumption goods (see Ch. 16).

Summary

1. The law of diminishing marginal utility states that within any given period the marginal utility of any product declines as the quantity consumed increases, the consumption of other products remaining constant. If the consumer is to maximize his (or her) utility, his pattern of consumption should be such that he equalizes the ratios of the marginal utilities of each product to their prices.
2. The shape of a consumer's indifference curve is determined by the concept of a declining or diminishing marginal rate of substitution. A consumer's equilibrium pattern of consumption is that at which his budget line is tangential to the highest indifference curve.
3. The law of diminishing marginal utility and indifference analysis both lead to the conclusion that demand is usually inversely related to price, i.e. demand curves normally slope down from left to right. But neither allows conclusions to be drawn about the precise shape of the curve, i.e. about its elasticity.
4. Price elasticity of demand is the percentage (or proportional) change in quantity demanded divided by the percentage change in price. Estimates of elasticity can be obtained from observation and statistical analysis. Elasticity is affected by the availability and price of substitutes. If elasticity exceeds one, a price reduction leads to an increase in revenue; if elasticity is less than one, a price reduction leads to a fall in revenue.
5. Income elasticity of demand is the percentage change in quantity demanded divided by the percentage change in income. An increase in real national income causes the demand for most ('normal') goods to increase. Goods for which demand falls following an increase in income are known as inferior goods.
6. Demand is also affected by changes in the distribution of income, changes in population, by the introduction of new products, by the promotional activities of suppliers, and by changes in consumer tastes.

Key terms

Total and marginal utility
Law of diminishing marginal utility
Indifference curve
Declining (diminishing) marginal rate of substitution
Budget line
Substitution effect
Income effect
Giffen good
Equilibrium of the consumer
Price elasticity of demand
Normal good
Inferior good
Conditions of demand
Income elasticity of demand

Notes

1. This is a definition of the point elasticity of demand.
2. At any point of tangency

$$\frac{P_{beans}}{P_{carrots}} = \frac{MU_{beans}}{MU_{carrots}}$$

Essay questions

1. State the law of diminishing marginal utility and show how it can help to explain the shape of demand curves.
2. Using indifference analysis explain the effect on the quantity of a product demanded of a change in (a) income, (b) the price of the product, (c) the price of a substitute.
3. Discuss the relative advantages and disadvantages of any two theories which attempt to explain the shape of demand curves.
4. Define price elasticity of demand and illustrate its relevance to decisions taken by (a) producers, (b) the government.
5. What types of decision might be improved by information concerning the value of each of the following: price, income and cross-elasticity of demand?
6. What factors might you expect to cause a reduction in the demand for the following products: bread, ice-cream, gas, petrol, public transport?
7. 'The most important influence on the current pattern of demand is the activity of producers, past and present.' Discuss.
8. 'The test of a theory's validity is its usefulness in illuminating observed reality.' Discuss this statement with reference to theories of demand.

Exercises

4.1 A hypothetical utility schedule.

	Apples		Pears	
	Quantity bought per week (kilos)	Total utility (utils)	Quantity bought per week (kilos)	Total utility (utils)
	1	100	1	100
	2	175	2	175
	3	225	3	225
	4	265	4	265
	5	300	5	300
	6	325	6	325
	7	320	7	320

(i) Which combinations of apples and pears would be consistent with the maximization of the consumer's utility when (a) 1 kg of apples cost the same as 1 kg of pears, (b) 1 kg of apples cost twice as much as 1 kg of pears?

(ii) Explain, by means of an arithmetic example, why other combinations would not be consistent with the maximization of the consumer's utility.

(iii) How many apples and pears would be consumed if they were free?

(iv) Explain carefully what, if anything, can be deduced from the answers to question (i) about (a) the shape, and (b) the position, of the individual's demand curves for apples and pears.

4.2 The following data relate to the quantity sold of a number of products in each of two years. Given that national income rose by 10 per cent between years 1 and 2, calculate IED for each product and say whether IED is elastic, unity, inelastic, zero or negative.

				Sales of product			
Year	A	B	C	D	E	F	G
1	18,000	900	650	9,000	750	910	500
2	19,000	1,000	730	9,000	825	900	525

4.3 What factors might explain the patterns of expenditure shown in Table 4.5?

4.4 (i) Discuss, with reference to Table 4.6, 'the conditions of demand for foodstuffs'.

(ii) What changes in trends in food consumption might you expect to occur over the subsequent decade?

4.5 Calculate price elasticity of demand for the following products and say for which products demand is (a) price elastic, (b) price inelastic.

	Product A		Product B		Product C		Product D	
	Price	Demand	Price	Demand	Price	Demand	Price	Demand
Period 1	£20	100	£70	110	£0.05	70	£1.10	700
Period 2	£40	70	£63	123	£0.06	70	£0.99	800

Table 4.6
Consumption in the home of selected foods
(indices of average quantities per person per
week in 1984; 1974 = 100)

Bread	91
Cakes and pastries	74
Sugar	70
Tea	80
Instant coffee	106
Fresh potatoes	87
Fresh green vegetables	85
Other fresh and frozen vegetables	130
Butter	51
Magarine	157
Other fats	83
Beef and veal	85
Mutton and lamb	81
Pork	103
Poultry and cooked chicken	140

Source: National Food Survey

4.6   Mr Greave is managing director of a prominent engineering firm which makes
vast quantities of three basic products – springs, clips and bolts. Worried by
increases in his costs of production he wished to increase his prices, and favoured
an across-the-board price increase of about 5 per cent on all three products.
However, the company chief economist, John Slater, to whom Greave turned for
advice, was rather unhappy about this proposal. An examination of the firm's
sales records suggested that the sales of some products were far more sensitive
than others to changes in price. He estimated price elasticities to be as follows:
springs 0.2, clips 1.0, bolts 1.5. What modification would you suggest to Mr
Greave's proposal?

Objective test questions: set 1

1.   A demand curve indicates:
   A   the quantities that were demanded in past periods;
   B   the quantities that were demanded at various prices in past periods;
   C   the quantities that would be demanded at various prices;
   D   the quantities that would be demanded at various prices in a given period;
   E   the quantities that would be demanded at various prices in different periods.

2. If the demand curve slopes down and the supply curve slopes up to the right, a fall in demand causes:
   A an increase in both price and quantity traded;
   B an increase in price and a fall in quantity traded;
   C a fall in price and an increase in quantity traded;
   D a fall in both price and quantity traded;
   E a fall in quantity traded, price being unchanged.

3. In order to maximize his satisfaction from a given level of income a consumer should spend his income in such a way that:
   A total utility derived from each product is equalized;
   B marginal utility derived from each product is maximized;
   C marginal utility derived from each product is equalized;
   D marginal utility derived from each product is zero;
   E ratios of the marginal utilities to the prices of each product are equalized.

4. In drawing a demand curve we make all of the following assumptions except that:
   A prices of all substitutes remain unchanged;
   B prices of all complements remain unchanged;
   C availability of both complements and substitutes remains unchanged;
   D consumers' real income remains unchanged;
   E consumers' money income remains unchanged.

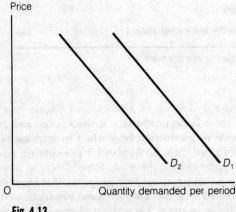

Fig. 4.13

5. The shift in the demand curve from D_1 to D_2 in Fig. 4.13 is *least* likely to have been caused by:
   A a fall in national income;
   B a fall in the price of substitutes;
   C an increase in the price of complements;
   D an increase in population;
   E a redistribution of income from low- to high-income groups.

6. In Fig. 4.14 the demand curve for peas is *least* likely to have shifted from D_1 to D_2 because of:
   A an increase in the price of beans;
   B a fall in the price of peas;

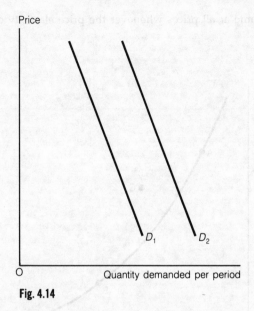

Fig. 4.14

C   an increase in population;
D   an increase in national income;
E   an increase in advertising by firms selling canned peas.

7.   Some resources are allocated by means of the price mechanism in:
1   a fully planned economy;
2   a mixed economy;
3   a market economy.

8.   A demand curve might slope from right to left if:
1   consumers see the price of the product as an indicator of its quality;
2   the purchase of the product represents conspicuous consumption;
3   the product is a Giffen good.

9.   The consumption of a product whose price is zero will be such that:
1   marginal utility derived from the product is zero;
2   total utility derived from the product is at a maximum;
3   marginal utility derived from the product equals the marginal utility derived from all other products.

10.

Product X		Product Y	
Consumption (units)	*Marginal utility* (utils)	*Consumption* (units)	*Marginal utility* (utils)
1	100	1	60
2	60	2	50
3	30	3	30

If product X cost twice as much per unit as product Y, which of the following combinations of purchases would be consistent with the maximization of the consumer's utility?
1   3 units of X plus 3 units of Y;
2   2 units of X plus 2 units of Y;
3   1 unit of X plus 2 units of Y.

11. Revenue is the same at all prices whenever the price elasticity of demand is:
    1 unity;
    2 constant;
    3 infinite.

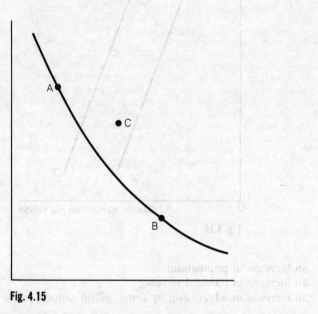

Fig. 4.15

12. From the indifference curve shown in Fig. 4.15 we can conclude that the:
    1 combinations of products represented by points A and B yield equal satisfaction;
    2 marginal rate of substitution is equal at points A and B;
    3 combination of products represented by A yields more satisfaction than the combination represented by C.

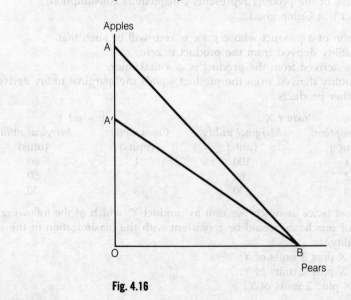

Fig. 4.16

13. In Fig. 4.16 the movement of the budget line from AB to A'B could have been caused by:
    1 an increase in the consumer's money income;
    2 a decrease in the price of pears;
    3 an increase in the price of apples.

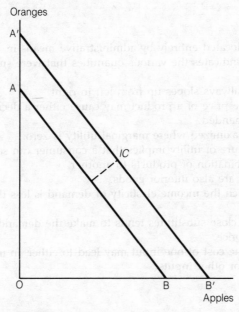

Fig. 4.17

14. In Fig. 4.17 AB and A'B' represent a consumer's budget line in two periods and IC represents his income consumption curve. From the diagram we can deduce that:
    1 oranges are a normal good;
    2 apples are a normal good;
    3 the price of oranges relative to the price of apples remained constant from one period to the next.

15. The price elasticity of demand for a product is likely to be higher:
    1 the less is spent on the product;
    2 the more close substitutes for the product exist;
    3 the longer the time that elapses since a change in the product's price.

16. In fully planned economies barter is an important form of exchange.
    In fully planned economies resources are not allocated by means of the price mechanism.

17. An increase in demand may cause either an increase or a decrease in the quantity traded.
    The effect of a change in demand on the quantity traded depends upon the shape of the supply curve.

18. An increase in demand may cause either an increase or a decrease in price.
    The effect of a change in demand on price depends upon the shape of the supply curve.

19. Indifference analysis shows that a fall in the price of a product always leads to an increase in its consumption.
    A fall in the price of a product has both an income and a substitution effect.
20. A fall in the price of an inferior good will lead to a fall in the quantity demanded.
    The income elasticity of demand of an inferior good is negative.

True/false

1. Resources are allocated entirely by administrative means in a mixed economy.
2. A supply curve indicates the various quantities that were supplied at different prices.
3. A supply curve always slopes up from left to right.
4. A decrease in the price of a product may cause either a decrease or an increase in the quantity demanded.
5. Total utility is maximized where marginal utility is zero.
6. An ordinal measure of utility implies that a consumer can say by how much he prefers one combination of products to another.
7. All Giffen goods are also inferior goods.
8. Products for which the income elasticity of demand is less than one are known as inferior goods.
9. The existence of close substitutes tends to make the demand for a product elastic with respect to price.
10. An increase in the cost of one input may lead to either an increase or a decrease in the demand for other inputs.

CHAPTER FIVE
Supply

Introduction

We showed in Chapter 3 that the price of a product or input is determined by the interaction of demand and supply. Having examined demand in Chapter 4 we now consider the factors influencing supply.

This chapter follows the pattern of the previous one in that we first discuss the factors which influence the *shape* of the supply curve, and subsequently examine the determinants of the *position* of the curve.

A supply curve indicates the quantity of a product (or input) that would be supplied at various prices in a given time period. There are several alternative ways of explaining the shape of supply curves. The approach adopted in this chapter starts with the costs incurred by the firm. So, to preview our conclusions, the supply curve S_1 in Fig. 5.1 implies that the cost per unit of output is roughly constant, S_2 implies that the cost per unit rises as output increases, and S_3 implies

that the cost per unit falls as output increases. An explanation of why cost might behave in these ways occupies much of the chapter. We consider first the behaviour of costs when the scale of organization is given.

The relationship between output and cost at a given scale of organization

The scale of organization refers to the maximum rate of output that the firm could achieve. The larger the scale, the greater the volume of output the firm could produce in a given period – say a week or month. Whatever the scale of organization an ultimate limit to output is set by the fact that there is at least one input, one factor of production, whose quantity is limited. The longer the time period considered, the greater the opportunity for increasing the quantity of the limiting input, i.e. for increasing the scale of organization.

Some writers make a distinction between the short run, in which at least one factor is fixed, and the long run in which all factors are variable in quantity. This distinction corresponds to our distinction between a given and a changing scale of organization. We have not used the more traditional terminology because the phrases short and long run (or short and long period) may be interpreted as referring to fixed periods of time. As we shall see, such an interpretation would not be justified. A change in the scale of organization may be accomplished far more quickly in some instances than in others.

The limit to output is most likely to be determined by the quantity of capital inputs – land, factories, plant and equipment. However, other limiting factors may exist. A firm may have spare capacity in plant and machinery, but may be

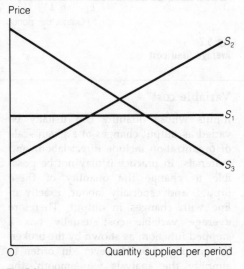

Price

S_2

S_1

S_3

O   Quantity supplied per period

Fig. 5.1
Alternative supply curves

prevented from increasing its output because it is unable to recruit additional labour.

When planning its scale of organization a firm will normally take into account its expected volume of output and sales. Since these cannot be predicted precisely, firms often install capacity in excess of their best estimate of output. In this way they reduce the possibility that, should demand turn out to be higher than expected, they may have to turn away regular customers, with a consequent loss of goodwill. Similarly, they will be in a better position to gain customers from rival suppliers should the capacity of those rivals be insufficient to meet their peak demand.

Each firm has to balance these potential benefits against the costs incurred in installing the additional capacity. The balance is most likely to swing towards installing additional capacity under the following circumstances:

(a) There are no important physical differences between the products of rival suppliers, so that ability to supply becomes very important.

(b) Demand in the market is increasing, so that even if the excess capacity is not utilized in the near future, it is likely to be required eventually.

(c) There are indivisibilities in inputs; the alternative to installing capacity in excess of expected quantity demanded may be to install capacity less than expected quantity demanded.

Having explored the possible relationship between capacity and *expected* output, we now examine the behaviour of costs as actual output changes. An important distinction is between the costs of those inputs whose quantity is fixed during the relevant time period and the costs of those inputs whose quantity can be varied. We deal with each of these in turn.

Fixed cost

As we indicated above, the inputs whose quantity (and hence cost) is most likely to

be fixed are land, buildings, plant and equipment. Since the total cost of these inputs is fixed, the average cost, the cost per unit produced, falls as output increases. In Fig. 5.2 the average fixed cost declines steadily, beyond E, the expected output, up to L, the ultimate limit. The broken line indicates that to increase output beyond L would require an increase in the scale of organization. (As additional plant, equipment, etc. was installed, average fixed cost would rise but then decline once more as output increased.)

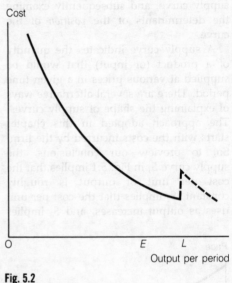

Fig. 5.2
Average fixed cost

Variable cost

Inputs whose quantity can usually be varied as output changes at a given scale of organization include direct labour and materials. In practice it may not be possible to change the quantity of these inputs, and especially labour, exactly in line with changes in output. Therefore average variable cost usually has a stepped function, as shown by the broken line in Fig. 5.3. However, in order to simplify the analysis we 'smooth' the curve, as shown by the unbroken line in that diagram.

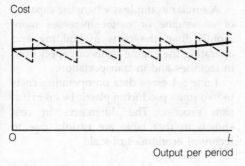

Fig. 5.3
Average variable cost

It will be noticed that average variable cost is constant over a wide range of output, but that it rises slightly as output approaches the ultimate limit. This may occur for several reasons. A rise in labour costs per unit of output may occur as additional, less efficient, workers are recruited in order to increase output beyond the expected level, or because of an increase in overtime working at higher wage rates. An increase in material costs may occur because of higher scrap rates resulting from increased machine speeds.

Semi-variable costs

There are many inputs whose quantity can be varied, but not precisely in line with changes in output, and whose costs can therefore be classified as semi-variable. Examples are the cost of fuel and power, and of indirect materials and labour. (We have seen that even direct labour costs, normally given as an example of a variable cost, may in practice be semi-variable.)

In order to simplify the analysis we assume that semi-variable costs can be split into a fixed and variable component. In this way we can continue to operate with two categories of cost.

Total cost

Since we have defined costs as either fixed or variable it follows that average total cost (ATC) at any level of output, is obtaining by adding together average

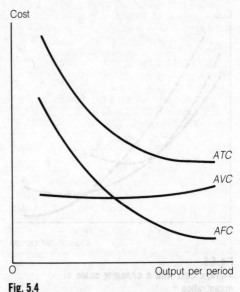

Fig. 5.4
Average fixed, variable, total cost

fixed cost (AFC) and average variable cost (AVC). Figure 5.4 shows that at first ATC falls as output increases. Eventually a point is reached (perhaps round about the expected level of output) beyond which ATC becomes more or less constant. This occurs because over this range of output a fall in AFC is roughly balanced by a rise in AVC.

The relationship between output and cost as the scale of organization changes

In Fig. 5.4 ATC indicates how cost is likely to vary with output at a given scale of organization. In Fig. 5.5 three average (total) cost curves are shown, each relating to a particular scale of organization. At any output up to M, the lowest average cost is attained with the smallest scale of organization (giving rise to AC_1). Beyond M average cost would be lower if a larger scale of organization (giving rise to AC_2) were adopted. Finally, beyond N average cost can be reduced by adopting an even larger scale of organization (giving rise to AC_3).

Cost

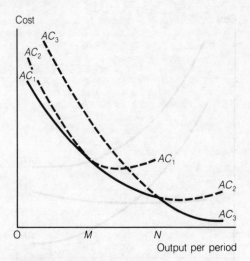

Output per period

Fig. 5.5
Average cost with a changing scale of organization

The lowest cost that could be attained at each output, given that the firm was always able to adopt the most appropriate scale of organization, is indicated by the unbroken line. Up to output *M* this curve slopes down because fixed factors are being utilized more fully, as discussed in the previous section. Beyond *M* the fall in average cost also reflects the fact that at a bigger scale of organization economies of scale arise. (These internal economies of scale are to be distinguished from external economies which are discussed later in the chapter.)

Internal economies of scale

These economies can be grouped into several categories.

Technical economies
Technical economies mainly relate to the scale of the production unit. Cost savings may arise because of changes in physical dimensions. One example is where cost depends upon area, and capacity or output upon volume, for example gas storage, oil tankers. In these instances an increase in capacity is accompanied by a less than proportionate increase in the cost of construction.

A similar example is where the capacity of an engine or motor increases more rapidly than the costs of building and operating the engine – this can apply both in factories and in transportation.

Table 5.1 gives data on operating costs in two units producing plastic by an extrusion process. The differences in cost shown in that table are mainly due to technical economies of scale.

Table 5.1
Operating costs for plastic extruders

Extruder capacity (lbs per hour)	135	1230
Cost per lb (p):		
Depreciation of machines and tools	0.59	0.13
Direct labour	0.42	0.22
Other works costs	0.96	0.57
Total operating costs	1.96	0.92

Source: Pratten C F, *Economies of Scale in Manufacturing Industry.* Cambridge Univ. Press, 1971

Technical economies may be enhanced by the introduction of a different technology such as the continuous strip mill in steel and plate-glass manufacture. The automatic control of production processes has become increasingly common in recent years. The cost of electronic control equipment is often high, and considerable economies can be achieved by spreading this cost over a higher output. Automatic data-processing equipment, and especially the computer, has also become more widely used and again substantial reductions in the average cost of equipment can be obtained by increases in scale. In this instance, the scale of the entire organization, i.e. the company, may be more important than the scale of individual production units.

The change-over from electro-mechanical to computerized digital technology increased the initial costs of developing telephone exchanges for public networks to between $500m. and $1bn. It is estimated that to justify such an expenditure a manufacturer must sell $1\frac{1}{2}$–2 million exchange lines a year. Moreover, the threshold is rising as prices fall by about 20 per cent a year.[1] Very few of the world's suppliers can achieve such sales in their domestic markets, and there is intense competition for export order among manufacturers such as AT & T (USA), Siemens (West Germany) and Ericson (Sweden).

However, technological change does not always lead to greater economies of scale. Indeed it appears that some recent changes in technology have reduced the advantages previously enjoyed by large firms. Micro-computers can put more sophisticated production techniques within the reach of smaller firms so that they are at less of a disadvantage *vis-à-vis* large firms. Several other illustrations are given by Bollard. For example in the printing industry traditional methods of composition require heavy machines which use substantial quantities of metal type that are expensive and bulky to store. But photocomposition is replacing metal type by a keyboard that records the text, a visual display unit, tapes or discs to store it and a photo-unit to produce film or paper for plate-making. A typical unit would cost £20,000 or less.[2]

In 1987 the Central Electricity Generating Board (CEGB) estimated that splitting the Board into five separately owned units would cause operating costs to rise by £700m. a year, because of a loss of economies of scale. The proportion of reserve capacity would have to rise from 22 per cent to 38 per cent over maximum demand at an extra cost of £150m. The loss of the integrated structure, whereby power stations could be employed according to a 'merit order' of efficiency, would cost £250m. The loss of the ability to co-ordinate repair and maintenance of the power generation and supply infrastructure would cost an extra £100m. About a quarter of the total electricity produced would end up being traded between different generators at a cost of £200m.

The increase in cost would be equivalent to an increase in the price of electricity of 7 per cent, a substantial burden for the consumer. (However, it must be remembered that these estimates were published as part of a campaign waged by the CEGB in order to try to persuade the government not to split it.)

Where technical economies involve the installation of more equipment, the *division of labour* – the specialization by each worker on a narrow range of tasks – is likely to be enhanced. However, the growth of a firm could lead to an increase in the division of labour quite apart from any change in technical economies. The bigger the firm the greater the opportunity for each worker to specialize in those tasks for which he is best fitted. Moreover, as workers specialize, their efficiency is increased by experience in a particular job (unless boredom sets in).

Marketing economies

Economies may arise in selling costs, including the distribution of products from factory to customer – wholesaler, retailer or consumer. Selling in bulk may enable savings to be made in invoicing and other costs. Distribution on a larger scale may enable the firm fully to utilize larger warehouses, delivery vehicles, etc. Furthermore, once the volume of goods to be distributed reaches a certain point, the firm may be able to reduce its costs by establishing its own distribution fleet instead of hiring transport services.

Large firms may also enjoy economies in advertising. This is especially important for firms which serve a national market, since the total cost of advertising on a nation-wide basis may be very expensive. An official from Pickfords, a prominent chain of travel agents, was quoted as saying that: 'If you want to optimize television advertising, for example, you need around 400 outlets.'[3]

Buying economies

Some savings may be made by setting up a more efficient form of buying organization. The larger firm is more likely to be able to employ buyers who are experienced in buying particular products, whereas in a small firm the buyer may have to deal with a wider range of products. (In other words the large firm can take more advantage of the division of labour.)

Another, probably more important, advantage enjoyed by large firms is the ability to buy supplies at lower prices. In addition to being able to take advantage of the terms embodied in the quantity discount schedules operated by many suppliers, the largest buyers may be able to negotiate special terms.

The Monopolies and Mergers Commission's *Report on Metal Containers* showed that Metal Box, the dominant supplier, granted a discount of up to 6 per cent on annual purchases of 200 million cans, together with additional rebates relating to the quantity of any one kind of can bought in one year. Of Metal Box's 624 customers all but 45 bought at the terms specified in the published quantity discount schedules. These 45 were able to gain additional cost-savings by special negotiations. The importance of these special negotiations can be judged from the fact that these 45 customers accounted for 88 per cent of the company's sales.

Buying economies are especially important in retailing since the cost of goods sold is by far the most important single cost. The discounts granted by manufacturers to retailers are well-kept secrets. However, the larger discounts obtained by multiple retailers have undoubtedly been one of the major factors enabling these retailers to undercut their small rivals and thus obtain a substantial increase in market share. (In some instances retailers take at least part of the benefit of buying economies in the form of higher profit margins.) In its report *Discounts to Retailers*, issued in 1981, the Monopolies and Mergers Commission showed that the additional discounts obtained by the three largest and most rapidly expanding multiple grocery chains from fifteen major manufacturers averaged almost 8 per cent.

Financial economies

Large firms can often obtain finance more cheaply and/or more easily than smaller firms. For reasons that are discussed in Chapter 16, small firms may have to offer a higher return to investors. In addition, the costs of issuing capital do not increase as quickly as the size of the issue. A study published by the Bank of England in 1986 showed that the average issue costs on offers raising up to £3m. accounted for nearly 18 per cent of the sum raised, but fell to less than 5 per cent on offers raising over £10m. (We show in Chapter 16 that the Unlisted Securities Market (USM) has lessened the disadvantages faced by small firms.)

Risk-bearing economies

A number of different advantages can be considered under this heading, but the underlying factor enabling the large firm to enjoy these advantages is that its activities are usually more diverse than those of the small firm. This means that a failure or loss in any one line of activity is less likely to endanger the viability of the whole enterprise.

Research and development is an activity whose rewards are, as matter of definition, uncertain. Substantial costs may have to be incurred before revenue, if any, begins to flow in, and large firms can best afford to take the risks inherent in this situation. A good example of the need to incur costs in advance of revenue is the conversion of oil to make protein for use as an animal food. Although the first experiments which opened up this possibility were conducted in the 1950s, the first commercial plants were not established until the 1970s by BP and later by ICI. Shell, which began conducting its own experiments in 1965, announced ten years later that although it had successfully manufactured a high-protein product in trials, it was to delay the construction of a full-scale experimental plant until it had re-examined the economics of the operation. One of the events that had occurred since trials began was, of course, a steep rise in the price of oil, the primary raw material. This illustrates the risks that are inherent in developments that have a very long gestation period.

Another example is the market for new smoking materials (NSM). The link between cigarette smoking and ill health led a number of companies to begin research in the 1950s and 1960s into possible substitutes for tobacco. The two major areas of uncertainty facing these companies were first the attitude of the health authorities towards such substitutes, and second the reactions of consumers towards any substitutes that might be approved by the authorities. This uncertainty no doubt limited the number of companies initially undertaking research, and subsequently caused some of these pioneers to rethink this strategy.

The failure in West Germany of two cigarette brands containing a tobacco substitute led at least two companies – Bayer in West Germany and Polystrep in Switzerland – to reduce their R & D expenditure. In the UK expenditure was halted by Courtaulds and the Scottish Co-operative Wholesale Society when the Hunter Committee published its guidelines outlining the programme of testing required of manufacturers before being able to market their products. Courtaulds, which had already spent about £1m. on R & D over the previous ten years, estimated that it would cost a further £2–3m. to fulfil these requirements. In addition a further investment of £10–20m. would be required before production could begin – all of this without any guarantee of acceptance of the new product by the consumer.

In view of the uncertainty surrounding the new product it was, perhaps, not surprising that only two companies – the Celanese Corporation of the USA and a company formed jointly by two UK giants – ICI and Imperial Tobacco – entered the UK market. Even then demand was over-estimated, production had to be cut back and a large number of cigarettes scrapped.

Many manufacturers of semiconductors (silicon chips) spend between 25 and 40 per cent of their sales revenue on R & D and capital equipment for the manufacture of products with a short 'life cycle'. In the 1960s a chip took two to three years to develop and had a life-span of five to ten years. By the mid 1980s the development time had fallen to twelve to eighteen months, and the life-span to two to four years.[4] The cost of launching a new pharmaceutical product is now £100m. and is expected to increase to £500m. by the late 1990s.[5] Clearly, only the largest firms are able to take the risks inherent in expenditure on this scale.

Finally, a large firm may need to keep proportionately less spare machinery and parts in case of breakdown, and to stockpile proportionately less raw materials in case of interruptions of supply. This saving is due to the operation of the 'law of large numbers' or the 'principle of massed reserves' and is not dependent upon the firm having a diverse range of activities. It could, in fact, be seen either as a risk-bearing or a technical economy.

Managerial economies

This term is given to a miscellaneous group of economies pertaining to the administration of the enterprise. It includes the ability to offer the high rewards needed to attract highly talented staff in various fields – personnel, purchasing, marketing, etc. It also includes the ability to utilize more efficient administrative procedures. Figure 5.6 shows the lower management costs enjoyed by the larger building societies.

Joint ventures

In some industries the costs and risks associated with new developments are so great that even the largest firms may be unwilling to shoulder the entire burden. Instead two or more firms may undertake a joint venture, sharing the cost (each contributing equipment and expertise) and, it is hoped, the rewards.

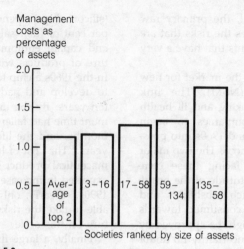

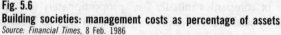

Fig. 5.6
Building societies: management costs as percentage of assets
Source: Financial Times, 8 Feb. 1986

Joint ventures are especially common in the vehicle industries. For example Honda and Rover have co-operated in the design of new models; Alfa-Romeo and Fiat in the development of components such as chassis and gear-boxes; Renault and Volvo (15 per cent owned by Renault) in the development of new vehicles and components; six European producers, including Rover, have entered into a long-term agreement on basis research. In aircraft production several European manufacturers, including British Aerospace, have co-operated in aircraft production in order to try to match the scale economies enjoyed by US aircraft manufacturers. In computers, where the cost of development is often very high, ICL markets the very large data-processing centres manufactured by the Japanese Fujitsu Company. In exchange ICL has gained access to Fujitsu's technology in very large scale integrated circuit chips. ICL has also made a technological exchange agreement with CDC, the US computer manufacturer.

Other aspects of economies of scale

Having analysed the various types of scale economy, we make three final points in order to link the analysis to the previous discussion of the behaviour of costs – in particular as shown in Fig. 5.5.

In order to make the first point we assume that the reduction in average cost which that diagram shows to be possible at an output greater than *M* would involve the installation of more expensive machinery embodying a superior technology. In other words we assume that technical economies of scale can be attained. If, this new equipment having been installed, output subsequently fell below *M*, average cost would be higher at the new, larger, scale of organization than it would have been if the smaller scale had been retained. It might be possible for the organization eventually to revert to the smaller scale, but only after a considerable time-lag.

In this respect technical economies are rather different from other types. In these other instances an increase in the scale of organization is less likely to involve changes which are difficult to reverse. Consequently there is less likelihood that, if output turns out to be lower than expected, average cost will continue to be higher than it would have been at a smaller scale of organization.

Second, some advantages of large-scale operation are not fully encompassed in the behaviour of costs, and therefore cannot be satisfactorily represented in Fig. 5.5. As noted above, advertising and other marketing activities may lead to an increase in the volume of sales. In addition, or alternatively, they may make it easier for the firm to increase its prices.

Finally, although Fig. 5.5 does not show any tendency for average cost to rise at the largest scale of organization, it may do so in practice, i.e. diseconomies of scale may exist.

Diseconomies of scale

Engineering studies have shown that technical diseconomies can arise in principle. For example in petrochemicals the largest ethylene cracker in production in the late 1970s had an annual capacity of 500,000 tonnes of ethylene. Up to that size substantial economies were achieved; it was estimated that the cost per unit of output of this cracker, when working at full capacity, was only 30 per cent of the cost of the smallest cracker then in operation. However, given the current state of technology, the construction of plants with a greater capacity would have resulted in diseconomies for several reasons including the need for on-site fabrication of towers and vessels, and the fact that the technical limit to compressor size had been reached. Moreover, more capital would have been tied up, making any delays in commissioning very expensive.

Since it is possible to identify potential technical diseconomies in advance, the firm should be able to avoid them by not building the bigger plant. Prior identification is also likely for other potential diseconomies, e.g. buying terms for small and big orders are known or can be estimated, as can the cost of raising various amounts of capital.

It is more difficult to predict how administrative and management expenses will change as the organization grows. However, theoretical considerations suggest two possible sources of managerial diseconomies.

First, large firms, and especially those operating large plants, may become very impersonal and bureaucratic with a consequent loss of job satisfaction. This can be reflected in high labour turnover, absenteeism, poor timekeeping and a high incidence of strikes. Figures published by the Department of Employment in 1978 showed that in a typical year 99.3 per cent of small establishments (11–99 employees) were strike-free, as compared to only 51 per cent of very large establishments (1,000 + employees).

Second, large firms with potentially lower costs than their smaller competitors may dissipate their advantage by inadequate controls which allow costs to rise, or even by distributing the benefits within the firm, for example by providing staff with extra 'perks' (perquisites) of various kinds.

In fact much of the evidence relating to diseconomies of scale is circumstantial; despite clear evidence of economies of scale, large firms frequently fail to earn above-average profits, and this might be explained by the existence of compensating diseconomies.

The significance of economies of scale

Two factors determine the significance of economies of scale in a given industry. This can be illustrated by the cost curves in Fig. 5.7. In both industries A and B the size of the market (current volume of sales) is denoted by the index number 100. The minimum efficient scale (MES) is the level of output at which average cost becomes constant, scale economies being exhausted. In industry A an output of 70 per cent of the market is required in order to attain the MES. Moreover, there is a substantial penalty for not attaining the MES; for example average cost at half MES (sales = 35) is 20 per cent greater than at MES (24 as compared to 20).

By contrast in industry B MES is attained by a firm having only 10 per cent of the market. Moreover, the penalty for not attaining this output is much smaller than in industry A. Average cost at half

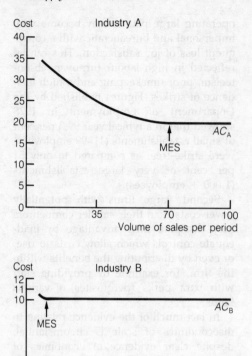

Volume of sales per period

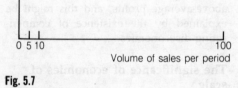

Volume of sales per period

Fig. 5.7
Minimum efficient scale

Table 5.2
Minimum economic scale in various industries

Industry	MES as % of UK market	% increase in cost at 50% of MES
Dyes	>100	22
Aircraft: one type	>100	20
Electric motors	60	15
Footwear	0.2	2
Diesel engines: models	10	4
Bricks	0.5	25
Sulphuric acid	30	1

Source: Pratten C F, *Economies of Scale in Manufacturing Industry*. Cambridge Univ. Press, 1971

MES (sales = 5) is 5 per cent higher than at MES (10.5 as compared to 10).

Economies of scale are far more significant in industry A. There is only room for one optimum-scale plant (and firm). Moreover, the remaining firm or firms, operating at smaller scales, will suffer a very severe cost disadvantage. Competition to win customers is likely to be intense. In industry B there is room for more optimum-scale plants (and therefore for more firms provided that each firm operates only one plant). Moreover, any firm operating at a lower scale will suffer less of a disadvantage than in industry A.

Table 5.2 presents estimates of these relationships for a number of industries. These estimates suggest that economies of scale are likely to be more significant in dyes, aircraft and electric motors than in diesel engines and footwear. (Bricks and sulphuric acid have been included as less straightforward examples.)

The experience effect
We showed that in industry A (Fig. 5.7) a firm operating at the MES would have a considerable cost advantage over other firms. This advantage is likely to become more pronounced over time because of the experience or learning effect. This

effect relates to the fact that average cost depends upon not only the current rate of output but also the cumulative output to date.

The experience effect can be illustrated by reference to Fig. 5.8 in which AC_1 indicates the average cost during the current time period. Average cost is lower with an output of OM than ON because of economies of scale and/or a higher rate of capacity utilization.

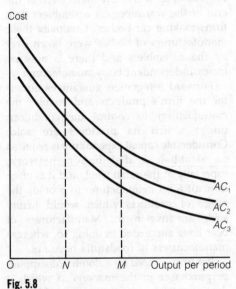

Fig. 5.8
The experience effect

If we were to measure cost in a subsequent period we would expect to find that real cost (i.e. after allowing for changes in input prices) had fallen because of the experience in production gained by the firm. Moreover, the greater the output in previous periods the greater the firm's experience, and hence the greater the fall in cost. So if the firm had produced ON its cost curve might be predicted to fall to AC_2, whereas if it had produced OM it would fall further to AC_3.

The first systematic observations of the experience effect were made in the production of aircraft in the 1930s. In the Second World War the production of the famous Liberty ships showed similar

effects, the first taking many months to build and the last only three days. Subsequently, after examining a wide range of manufacturing and non-manufacturing industries, the Boston Consulting Group concluded that the decline in unit cost 'is consistently 20 to 30 per cent each time accumulated production is doubled'.[6]

Industries in which the experience effect is important are characterized by bursts of intense price competition, especially in periods when supply expands more rapidly than demand. So, for example, in 1985 the price of a certain type of semiconductor, the 64K D-Ram (dynamic random access memory) chip fell in five months from around $3 to 50 cents. Over a period of eight months, the price of the more complex 256K D-Ram fell from $18 to $2.50.

External economies

Internal economies of scale arise out of the expansion of an individual firm. They are to be distinguished from external economies, which arise for two basic reasons. First, some operations previously undertaken by individual firms are taken over and performed more efficiently by a central organization, e.g. a central training unit is established. Second, the expansion of an industry leads to improvements in efficiency. This improvement may occur because the expansion of the industry makes it worth while establishing a central facility, because a large and more flexible labour market is created, or because new suppliers of components, services, etc. are established to meet the increased demand.

When discussing internal economies we noted that new technology may operate to increase economies of scale because the new equipment is so expensive to purchase and operate that it requires a large output to justify its installation. The disadvantages faced by small firms will be reduced if they are given access to centrally owned equipment. In a number of industries central research facilities have been established, which can be used by small as well as large firms.

Whatever its source, an external economy can be distinguished from an internal economy because it leads to a fall in the costs of the individual firm *even if the scale of that firm is unchanged.* (If the scale of all existing firms is unchanged, an expansion of the industry will, of course, require the entry of new firms.)

The direction of growth, economies of scale and other advantages

A firm may grow in several alternative directions, each direction having different implications and consequences.

Horizontal growth

This involves an expansion of the firm's existing activities. An example would be a car assembler which started to assemble more cars (internal expansion) or which merged with another car assembler. Horizontal growth is likely to give rise to most of the economies that we considered above, although not to those risk-bearing economies which depend upon a diversified range of activities. In addition, if horizontal growth leads to an increase in market share, the firm may be able to exert more control over prices, as shown below. This is most likely when growth is achieved by merging with, or taking over, competitors. This helps to explain why, as shown in Chapter 10, legislation has been passed to control mergers but not internal growth.

Vertical growth

This involves an extension of the firm's activities into another stage of the production and distribution process. If the extension is towards the beginning of the process, it is known as backward integration, e.g. a car assembler might begin the manufacture (or might take over a manufacturer) of components which it had previously bought. If the extension is towards the end of the process it is known as forward integration, e.g. a car assembler might establish (or take over) a distri-

bution network in order to sell the cars that it produces.

Vertical growth may give rise to some of the economies of scale associated with the size of the firm, e.g. the full utilization of elaborate data-processing facilities. But in general a more important motive for vertical growth is additional security. Backward integration gives security of supplies, and is most likely to occur when specialist sources of supply are limited. For example in the UK there were at the end of the war more car assemblers than firms making car bodies. Gradually these manufacturers of bodies were taken over by the assemblers and there is now no major independent body manufacturer.

Forward integration guarantees outlets for the firm's products and enables the manufacturer to control the conditions under which its products are sold. Considerable capital expenditure is required to establish a distribution network, especially at the retail level, and it is often difficult for a manufacturer to provide the range of products which would justify such an investment. Manufacturers of beer have succeeded in doing so, whereas manufacturers of foodstuffs have not.

If a firm is faced by a dominant supplier or purchaser in the markets in which it deals, vertical expansion may enable it to obtain inputs at a lower cost and sell its output at a higher price. (However, any firm which has the financial resources to expand vertically is usually able to obtain reasonable terms from suppliers or purchasers. This helps to explain why a large retailer such as Marks and Spencer has not felt it necessary to develop its own manufacturing facilities.)

Diversified growth

This involves an extension of the range of products handled by the firm. For example a car assembler might begin to assemble lorries or motor cycles. Most of the scale economies discussed above are likely to arise, although to a lesser degree in some instances. For example, quantity discounts may be less than they would be if a narrower range and bigger quantities of materials and components were bought. On the other hand, diversified growth is more likely to give rise to risk-bearing economies. Indeed risk-bearing economies may be the only important type when growth involves the production of dissimilar products.

The classic background to a policy of diversification is an industry in which current profits (and especially cash flow) are high but future growth prospects are poor. It is therefore not surprising that most tobacco manufacturers have adopted an energetic diversification programme. Fairly typical in this respect is BAT Industries (formerly British American Tobacco), the world's largest private sector tobacco manufacturer, whose 1983 profile is presented in Fig. 5.9.

It can be seen that although by 1983 tobacco accounted for less than half of the group's assets, it still provided almost three-quarters of its profits, an indication that diversification is not without its problems. Since 1983 BAT's profile has shifted considerably. The acquisition at a cost of £969m. of the Eagle Star insurance company took the group into the booming financial services sector. This was followed by the purchase in 1984 of Hambro Life Assurance (later renamed Allied Dunbar) for £664m. In 1988 BAT paid £3.1bn. for Farmers Group, a US insurance company. It estimated that the acquisition of Farmers would, for the first time, reduce the proportion of profits derived from tobacco to less than 50 per cent. On the other hand, it has sold some of its retailing interests, including International Stores, a British supermarket chain sold to Dee Corporation for £180m., and several US retailing companies.

Costs and the supply curve

Having examined the relationships between output and costs, we now show how the behaviour of cost may be reflected in the supply curve. For this purpose it is convenient to make a distinction between two types of market. In the markets for many manufactured goods and services, cost-based pricing is practised. These markets are discussed in the remainder of this chapter and in Chapter 7. Raw materials and agricultural products are usually sold in open markets, where the influence of cost on supply is much less pronounced. Price determination in open markets is discussed in Chapter 7.

Cost-based pricing

Since considerable trouble and expense may be involved in changing prices, firms prefer to set and maintain a price for a given period. The length of this period varies. At one time there was in many

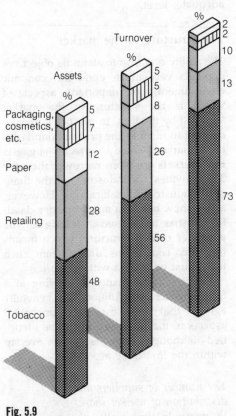

Fig. 5.9
BAT Industries
Source: The Times, 3 Nov. 1983

markets an annual pricing cycle or season. During periods of more rapid inflation prices are revised more frequently, perhaps every six months.

Whatever the length of the season, a price is set which relates to the average cost at the expected level of output during that period. In Fig. 5.10 the firm expects to produce quantity E at an average cost of EF. It adds the profit margin FG and sets price P ($OP = EG$). (The firm's estimate of output takes account of the price. What we have described as a process with two distinct stages is in practice a single process in which several alternative combinations of price and output are usually considered.)

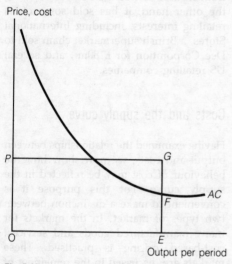

Fig. 5.10
Cost-based pricing

The size of the profit margin added by the firm is influenced by three factors: the firm's objectives; the structure of the market; and the firm's assessment of the overall level of market demand. We consider these in turn.

The objectives of firms

The following conclusions should be seen as a summary of what is an extremely complicated issue. First, profitability is normally the primary objective of private sector producers, since unless the firm

earns adequate profits it will not survive – it may be taken over by another firm or may go out of business. Second, although profitability is important it may mean different things to different firms. Some firms aim to maximize profitability, some to earn an 'adequate' profit, and some, between the two, to earn not less than and preferably more than in previous years. Third, other objectives may be very important – in particular an increase in the volume of sales or in market share. (This may in turn contribute to further objectives such as an increase in the assets of the firm and in the number of employees.) An increase in the volume of sales often implies an increase in profitability, but this is not always so, and firms sometimes compromise, aiming to increase the volume of sales provided this does not cause profitability to fall below a minimum, adequate, level.

The structure of the market

The ability of a firm to attain its objectives depends very much upon its economic environment, an important aspect of which is the structure of the market supplied by the firm. In practice it may be difficult to identify the precise boundaries of a market. Creedy correctly suggests that markets are often narrower than the 334 'activities' (or industries) of the Standard Industrial Classification.[7] However, as we show below, a much broader classification has to be used in testing for the effects of market structure, which means that any conclusions drawn from such tests must be treated with caution.

Despite the difficulty in arriving at a fully satisfactory definition, it is generally agreed that four especially important aspects of market structure can be identified (although there is some overlap within the first three aspects).

The number of suppliers and the distribution of market shares

In principle the smaller the number of suppliers the more control they can exercise over prices. Moreover, given the number of suppliers, the control of prices tends to be greatest, again in principle, when a large share of the market is in the hands of a few firms. (The control is, of course, mainly exercised by the large firms; the small firms may have little or no influence.)

The degree of product differentiation

A producer may seek to differentiate its product from those of its competitors in a number of ways: by offering improved performance, better styling, better after-sales service, advertising, etc. If these attempts are successful, a market may in effect be split into a number of separate submarkets, each having very few suppliers, i.e. having a high level of concentration.

Barriers to entry

The third aspect of market structure is the existence or absence of barriers which make it difficult for new firms to enter the market (or submarket).

Among the most important barriers to entry are:

(a) the capital cost of establishing production and distribution facilities – this barrier is especially important if substantial economies of scale are enjoyed by existing firms;

(b) absolute cost advantages arising from control over some vital input such as a raw material or skilled labour;

(c) scientific or technological know-how arising from a sustained research and development programme and perhaps protected by patents;

(d) marketing activities leading to a high degree of consumer loyalty, a well-regarded brand-name, etc.

It is important to recognize that some of these factors can also operate so as to break down or overcome entry barriers. For example a firm that has benefited from entry barriers and has been very successful in one market, may use its profits to finance the advertising that enables it to enter another market. Technological change may facilitate new entry; the introduction of electronic, quartz watches enabled Japanese companies to break down the domination of the Swiss watchmakers.

The concentration of buying power

The above aspects of market structure relate to the supply side of the market. The final aspect relates to the demand side; the larger the share of output bought by a few firms, i.e. the more concentrated is buying power, the less control will suppliers have over prices.

Concentration, entry barriers and profitability

Studies by Bain[8] and Mann[9] in the USA seemed to suggest that once concentration reached a certain point, higher profits resulted. Mann examined the profitability of thirty industries over the period 1950–60. He found that the average rate of return in the more concentrated industries (where the leading eight firms accounted for more than 70 per cent of sales) was 13.3 per cent as compared to 9 per cent in the less concentrated industries, i.e. average profitability was around 50 per cent higher in the more concentrated industries.

However, the link between concentration was by no means automatic. Profitability in some less concentrated industries (e.g. petroleum refining 12.2 per cent) exceeded that in some concentrated industries (e.g. rayon 8.5 per cent). Moreover, industry averages sometimes concealed wide variations among individual firms; for example the rate of return of 15.5 per cent in automobiles was an average of the 21.5 per cent earned by General Motors, 14.5 per cent by Ford and 10.5 per cent by Chrysler. Even more important, as we show below, the link between concentration and profitability does not appear to persist over time.

As we noted above, barriers to entry may be one cause of a high level of concentration. However, Bain and Mann suggested that high entry barriers may be an independent source of high profits. Mann found that within the group of concentrated industries the rate of return in industries with very high entry barriers was 16.1 per cent as compared to 12.7 per cent in industries with moderate to low barriers. (However, industries with substantial barriers had even lower profits (11.3 per cent), suggesting that the link between entry barriers and profitability is loose.)

Changes in profitability over time
When Brozen[10] carried out a later investigation of the industries studied by Bain and Mann he found that differences in profitability diminished over time. The differential between those industries classified by Bain as concentrated and those classified as less concentrated had fallen from 57 per cent in 1936–40 to 10 per cent in 1953–57. This suggests that differences in profitability may be due to other factors in addition to the level of concentration. An alternative view of markets emphasizes ignorance, error and the (partial) correction of error over time: 'The over-ambitious plans of one period will be replaced by more realistic ones; market opportunities overlooked in one period will be exploited in the next.'[11]

This view implies, of course, that firms and markets are not usually in equilibrium. Moreover, it also implies that industries with above-average profit rates will attract new entry, and that the changing balance between supply and demand will

cause profits to decline. (Alternatively, the threat of new entry might be sufficient to persuade existing firms to accept lower profits.) Conversely, in industries with below-average profits, there tends to be a contraction of supply, causing profit rates to rise. This is precisely what Brozen found had happened.

Demsetz has also cast doubt on the importance of concentration as a determinant of profitability. He pointed out that if it were true that firms in highly concentrated industries could collude in order to earn above-average profits, this should benefit all firms in that industry including small firms who are not party to the collusion but are able to set high prices, sheltering under the 'umbrella' put up by the leading firms. Demsetz found no evidence that small firms were more profitable in concentrated than in less concentrated industries. Any association between concentration was entirely explained by differences in profitability within large firms, as shown in Table 5.3. This suggests that high profit rates were a return to the superior efficiency of the large firms, rather than the result of collusion.

The level of market demand

The final factor influencing the size of the profit margin is the producers' assessment

Table 5.3
Rates of return by asset size and concentration ratios, 1963

Four-firm concentration ratio (%)	Number of industries	Rate of return (%), asset size (m.)				
		0.5	0.5–5.5	5.5–50	Over 50	Average
10–20	14	7.3	9.9	10.6	8.0	8.8
20–30	22	4.4	8.6	9.9	10.6	8.4
30–40	24	5.1	9.0	9.4	11.7	8.8
40–50	21	4.8	9.5	11.2	9.4	8.7
50–60	11	0.9	9.6	10.8	12.2	8.4
Over 60	3	5.0	8.6	10.3	21.6	11.3

Source: Demsetz H, Industry structure, market rivalry and public policy, *Journal of Law and Economics*, 1973

of the overall level of market demand. If they perceive demand as high or rising, for example because the government has taken steps to boost the economy, they may take the opportunity to widen their profit margins. (This is especially likely if previous profit margins were unsatisfactory.) Conversely, in a recession producers are more likely to reduce, or at best maintain, their existing profit margins.

The determinants of the profit margin: summary

The influence of the three factors considered above can be illustrated by reference to Fig. 5.11. (This figure relates to different markets, and we assume for the sake of convenience that the two producers have identical cost curves. Producer A wishes to achieve a high profit margin and faces a favourable market situation; it is a dominant firm in a highly concentrated market supplying a product for which demand is expanding. It sets price P_A at which it expects to sell Q, giving a margin EG. On the other hand producer B is satisfied with a more modest profit margin, which is just as well because it is one of a large number of suppliers of a product for which demand has been declining, and it is faced by a

single large purchaser. It sets price P_B at which it expects to sell Q, giving a margin EF. Here G is a point on A's supply curve, and F a point on B's supply curve.

The supply curve with a given scale of organization

Producers' expectations may or may not be fulfilled. If demand is as expected, as denoted by D_E in Fig. 5.12, the firm sells Q_E at price P_E. (If this firm is representative of the n firms in the industry, market supply at P_E will be $Q_E \times n$.)

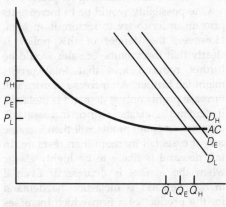

Fig. 5.12
Changes in demand, price and output

If demand is higher than expected, D_H, the firm may choose to sell Q_E at a higher price P_H, Q_H at price P_E, or an output between Q_E and Q_H at a price between P_E and P_H.

There are several reasons for believing that of these alternatives the firm is most likely to choose to maintain price P_E during the current pricing season and increase sales to Q_H. First, as we have seen, an increase in the volume of sales is often an important objective. Second, firms incur certain additional costs whenever they change price. Third, the lower the price the less likely it is that new firms will attempt to enter the market. These considerations would have less weight if profits were reduced following the increase

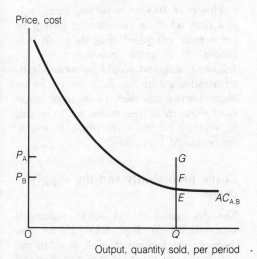

Price, cost

Output, quantity sold, per period

Fig. 5.11
Alternative profit margins and prices

in output – as might happen if a steep rise were to occur in average cost. However, it can be seen that average cost does not rise and that profit margins are maintained. Consequently total profits, and profit expressed as a rate of return on capital employed, will increase.

Let us now consider the situation where demand turns out to be less than expected, at D_L. If the firm maintains its price at P_E it will sell only Q_L, and its profitability will therefore be less than expected. (Profit would be reduced further if the fall in demand was so great as to cause an increase in average cost.) Faced with this unsatisfactory profit position the firm will consider changing its price.

One possibility would be to increase its price in order to try to restore its profits. However, the danger of this policy is clearly that the volume of sales would be further reduced and that total profits might fall further. An increase in price will increase profits only if demand is inelastic. If demand is elastic a price increase will decrease revenue; profits will then increase only if costs fall by more than revenue. In fact demand is likely to be highly elastic when the market is depressed. Even if market demand is inelastic, the demand for the product of a firm which increases its price is likely to be highly elastic. The reason for this is that rival suppliers, rather than following the price increase, are likely to maintain their prices in the hope of attracting customers from the higher-price firm. (The demand curves in Fig. 5.12 are drawn on the assumption that all firms charge the same price. If only one firm raised its price, its demand curve would be far more elastic than shown there, unless its product is highly differentiated from competing products.)

An alternative response to the fall in demand is to reduce price to P_L in an attempt to maintain sales at the expected level. Again the elasticity of market demand must be taken into account – the more elastic the demand the more likely it is that profits will increase following a reduction in price. If only one firm were to reduce its price, demand might be very

elastic. However, the reduction is likely to be matched by other firms. Again, therefore, there are strong pressures discouraging a change in price following a failure of demand to reach the expected level. (Price reductions are most likely to occur if they can be concealed from competitors, e.g. by transacting business via negotiations with individual customers, rather than by selling to all customers at the list price.) If price is maintained at P_E, the quantity sold will be Q_L.

We can conclude then that where firms initially set a price which includes an adequate profit margin, price is likely to be held stable during the pricing season over quite a wide range of output, both greater and less than expected. In other words the supply curve will be horizontal over that range of output.

If the original profit margin was not considered to be adequate and demand is less than expected, the response is likely to be as before. But when demand turns out to be greater than expected (D_H in Fig. 5.12), suppliers are likely to take the opportunity to improve their profit margins. Since they may also wish to increase their sales volume, the most likely response is to set a price between P_E and P_H, at which price their output will be between Q_E and Q_H.

However, this response will occur only if a firm which is considering raising its price feels confident that its rivals will follow. If a price increase were not followed, demand would be more elastic than indicated in Fig. 5.12. As we noted above, firms are likely to be most confident about rivals' responses, i.e. to be able to exercise control over price, in highly concentrated industries.

Costs, profitability and the supply curve

The discussion in the above section is summarized in Fig. 5.13. If for the moment we assume that all firms in the industry have identical cost and demand curves, S_1 represents the market supply curve when the original price was

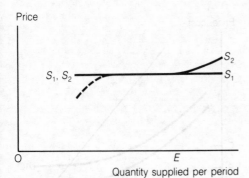
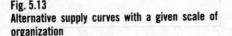

Price

S_2

S_1, S_2 ———————— S_1

O   E

Quantity supplied per period

Fig. 5.13
Alternative supply curves with a given scale of organization

considered satisfactory; S_2 refers to the situation where the firms felt obliged to set an original price that they considered to be too low, and which they subsequently raised when demand turned out to be higher than expected.

We showed that initially price is unlikely to fall in response to a fall in demand. However, if the fall in demand is prolonged and substantial, prices will eventually weaken. Once one firm breaks out of line, others will follow and a cumulative series of price reductions may ensue. This process is represented in Fig. 5.13 by the dotted portion of the supply curves, which might apply to both S_1 and S_2. The ultimate floor to the price reductions is set by average variable cost, or by opportunity cost should this be greater.

The supply curve with a changing scale of organization

When the analysis is extended to encompass changes in scale, the supply curve may assume shapes other than those discussed above. If economies of scale arise, producers may wish to pass on the reduction in costs in the form of price reductions – this is most likely if demand is highly elastic and if an increase in sales is an important objective. Moreover, even if producers would prefer not to reduce their prices they may feel obliged to do so.

Very large buyers may be able to insist on being given at least a share of the cost savings. If prices are reduced as economies of scale arise, the supply curve will be downward sloping as shown by S_1 in Fig. 5.14.

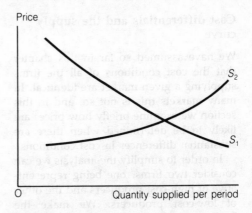
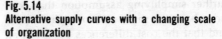

Price

S_2

S_1

O   Quantity supplied per period

Fig. 5.14
Alternative supply curves with a changing scale of organization

Alternatively the supply curve may slope upwards, as shown by S_2. This may reflect diseconomies of scale. But the main cause of an upward-sloping supply curve (with a changing scale of organization) is that as output increases the additional demand for factor inputs – labour, raw materials, etc. – causes an increase in their price. (As we shall see in later chapters, the prices of such inputs are much more sensitive to changes in demand than are the prices of types of products considered in this chapter.) In order to compensate for the increase in their costs, producers increase their prices.

This effect of an increase in output is likely to be most pronounced when the economy as a whole is operating near full capacity, so that producers have to offer higher prices in order to try to attract resources away from other uses. Even if resources are not fully employed, the costs of a particular industry may rise as output increases if that industry is a major purchaser of a particular input. Incidentally an increase in output may lead to an increase in factor prices, and hence in product prices, even when the scale of organization is unchanged. But the effect is clearly likely to be greater over a longer period when the scale of organization can change, since there is then scope for a bigger increase in output.

Cost differentials and the supply curve

We have assumed so far in this chapter that the cost conditions of all the firms supplying a given market are identical. In many markets this is not so, and in this section we examine briefly how prices are likely to be determined when there are substantial differences in cost conditions.

In order to simplify the analysis we can consider two firms, one being representative of high-cost producers and the other of low-cost producers. We make the further simplifying assumption that both firms have the same scale of organization, and that the cost differences persist at all levels of output. Such cost differences could be due to differences in labour productivity, to different prices paid for inputs, etc. Finally, we assume that both firms have identical demand curves whose elasticity is the same as the market demand curve. This may occur because the products are identical (homogeneous). Alternatively it may occur because, although the products are differentiated with some consumers preferring one 'brand' and other consumers another, the preferences of consumers as a whole are divided equally among all the brands.

This situation is illustrated in Fig. 5.15. It is extremely likely that the lead in setting prices will be taken by B, the lower-cost firm. Firm B has basically two choices. It can set a price P_1 which yields adequate profits to firm A (and also, of course, firm B). Alternatively it can set a lower price P_2, designed to drive A out of the market. Although B's profits during this period would be lower with price P_2 than P_1, this might be compensated by higher profits in future periods, if and when A had left the market. (If A left the market, B's demand curve would shift to

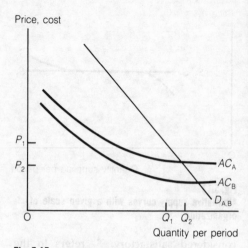

Fig. 5.15
Alternative prices of the dominant firm

the right.) Firm B would be most likely to earn higher profits if, as it expanded its output to meet the additional demand from A's former customers, it gained economies of scale. Moreover, if B forced some competitors out of the market, it might subsequently be able to raise its price above P_2.

If B chooses the first alternative we can apply the analysis of the earlier sections in explaining the shape of the supply curve. At price P_1 the quantity supplied is $Q_1 \times n$, where n is the number of suppliers. This gives us one point on the supply curve. The location of the other points on the curve will be influenced by all the factors considered above. If, on the other hand, B sets price P_2 it becomes impossible to derive a supply curve, because we do not know how quickly high-cost firms will leave the market. Nor do we know what price B would set once these firms have left the market.

A similar choice faces the firms in an industry in which there are substantial entry barriers. In Fig. 5.16 AC_B represents the cost curve of an existing firm, and AC_A refers to a potential entrant. The difference in costs between the two firms constitutes a barrier to entry.

If B set price P_1 it would earn much higher current profits than if it set price P_2. However, P_1 may encourage new firms

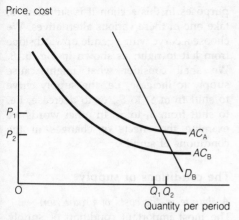

Fig. 5.16
Barriers to entry and alternative prices

to enter the industry whereas P_2 will deter entry. If new entry occurs, prices in future periods may be forced down below P_2. Consequently B must weigh up the benefit of higher current profits against the possibility of lower profits in the future.

The demand curves in Fig. 5.15 are drawn on the assumption that all firms set the same price. If this condition does not hold the demand curves will have quite a different shape. In order to simplify the analysis we confine our attention to the situation facing the high-cost firm A. We have suggested that if B were to set price P_1, A would be happy to follow this price since it yields adequate profits. However, let us now consider the situation where B sets a lower price, P, in Fig. 5.16. Although, if A were to sell Q at this price it would earn a profit, it would not feel this profit to be adequate. A might, therefore, consider setting other prices.

If, in order to increase its profit margin, A were to set a higher price, it would probably find that demand was highly elastic, as consumers switched to the cheaper alternatives offered by B. On the other hand, if A were to reduce its price in the hope of increasing its profits via a large increase in the volume of sales, it would probably be frustrated, finding demand inelastic. The reason for this is that B would match A's price cut in order

to avoid losing sales. As the lower-cost firm, B is likely to be in a better position than A to withstand a price war. Consequently A is most unlikely to initiate price competition. It is more likely to accept the price set by B. We can therefore say that B acts as a *price leader* and A as a *price follower*. Alternatively we can say that B acts as *price maker* and A as a *price taker*.

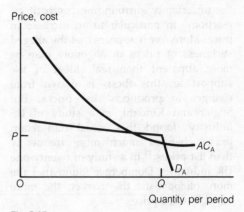

Fig. 5.17
The demand curve of a price follower

There are many recorded examples of firms which, unable to increase profits via higher prices, have successfully sought to reduce their cost of production, and have thus achieved more satisfactory profits. This process has been termed 'price-minus costing' by some commentators.

Oligopoly and the kinked demand curve

An oligopolistic market is one in which a few producers account for a substantial proportion of sales. Each producer knows that, because of its importance in the market, its actions will impinge on other producers, who will react in turn. Specifically it is assumed that a price reduction by one producer would be matched by other producers, causing demand to be inelastic (unless market demand is elastic). On the other hand a price increase would not be matched by other producers, causing demand to be elastic. The resulting kinked demand curve has the shape shown in Fig. 5.17.

The analysis presented earlier in the chapter implies that a reluctance to change price, because of the reactions (or lack of reaction) of competitors, is by no means confined to oligopolistic markets. Indeed it was suggested that the smaller the number of suppliers the easier it may be to reach an understanding that will reduce the uncertainty surrounding competitors' reactions, in particular to an increase in price. Moreover it appears that the alleged stickiness of prices in oligopoly may be more apparent than real. Most of the support for this thesis is drawn from changes in producers' list prices. But Stigler and Kindahl, in a study of US industry, found that actual transaction prices changed much more frequently than list prices.[12] In a study of twenty-one UK industries Domberger found that the more oligopolistic the market, the more variable were prices.[13]

The position of the supply curve

So far in this chapter we have been concerned with the shape of the market or industry supply curve. We now turn our attention to the factors which influence the position of the curve. We have seen that supply curves may have numerous alternative shapes. For our purposes in this section it is sufficient to take one of these various alternatives. We choose a curve with a gentle upward slope from left to right, as shown in Fig. 5.18. We shall consider what might cause supply to increase, i.e. the supply curve to shift from S_1 to S_2, or to decrease, i.e. to shift from S_1 to S_3. In other words we examine the effects of changes in the conditions of supply.

The conditions of supply

A change in the costs of production
The most important condition of supply is the cost of production and distribution. An increase in average cost causes a decrease in supply. In order to supply a given quantity of output, producers will require a higher price than previously, i.e. the supply curve will shift upwards (to the left).

Conversely, a fall in average cost will cause an increase in supply. Producers will be willing to supply a given quantity at a lower price than previously. (Some producers might wish to maintain the price and thus increase their profit margins but, in the absence of collusion, competition will cause the cost reduction to be passed on in the form of a lower price.) The supply curve will shift downwards (to the right).

Note that average cost is affected both by the prices of inputs and by their productivity. So, for example, average cost would rise either if wage rates increased or labour productivity fell. (It is, of course, possible that compensating changes could occur. For example an increase in wage rates could be balanced by an increase in labour productivity, leaving labour costs unchanged.)

It is important to distinguish between *autonomous* changes in input costs, and changes which occur because of change in output (discussed above). Autonomous changes in cost cause a shift in the position of the supply curve. Output-induced changes in cost are encompassed in the shape of the curve.

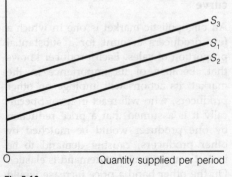

Price

S_3

S_1

S_2

O   Quantity supplied per period

Fig. 5.18
A shift in the supply curve

Supply conditions may also be affected by technological change. Technological change normally reduces average cost, i.e. causes the supply curve to shift downward. The same effect follows from an increase in the efficiency with which production is organized.

A change in profit margins

If suppliers set their prices so as to achieve a constant profit per unit under all circumstances, a change in average cost is directly reflected in a shift of the supply curve. In Fig. 5.19 a reduction in average cost of MN causes the supply curve to shift from S_1 to S_2. If, on the other hand, suppliers decide not to pass on all of the cost reduction, the curve will shift less. For example, if they increase their profit margin by NP, the supply curve will shift to S_3.

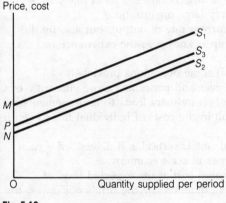

Price, cost

S_1
S_3
S_2

M
P
N

O   Quantity supplied per period

Fig. 5.19
Alternative shifts in the supply curve

A change in opportunity cost

A firm's desired profit margin on one product may be influenced by the (maximum) profits that it could earn by producing other products, i.e. by the opportunity cost of the present use of its resources. If prospective profitability in other markets rose, i.e. if opportunity cost increased, the firm might require higher profits from its existing markets. This

higher target profit would cause the supply curve to shift upward.

A change in the number of producers

An increase in the number of producers will cause an increase in supply, a fall in the number of producers a decrease in supply. The precise nature of the change in supply will depend upon the change that occurs in the overall cost conditions of producers.

The number of producers may change for various reasons. But especially important is a change in profitability in this market as compared to prospective profitability in other markets. (Such a change may itself be due to a wide variety of factors.) A change in entry barriers – both in this and other markets – may also be important.

Indirect taxation

As far as the producer is concerned, the imposition of an indirect tax on a product is equivalent to an increase in that product's cost of production. It is a further expense which must be covered by the product's price. In Fig. 5.20 we illustrate the effect of two different types of indirect or expenditure tax. (We assume that in each case the imposition of the tax is fully reflected by the shift in the supply curve.)

The original supply curve is S_1. After the imposition of a *specific tax*, i.e. a tax of

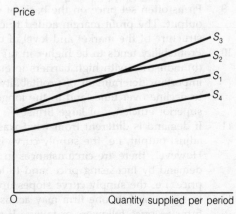

Price

S_3
S_2
S_1
S_4

O   Quantity supplied per period

Fig. 5.20
Indirect taxes and the supply curve

a fixed amount per unit, the supply curve shifts to S_2. After the imposition of an *ad valorem tax*, i.e. a tax whose rate varies in accordance with the price of the product, the supply curve shifts to S_3. Finally note that a (specific) subsidy causes the supply curve to shift downward to S_4. A subsidy is, in effect, a negative tax.

Summary

1. When planning its scale of organization a firm takes into account its expected volume of output and sales. Since these cannot be predicted precisely, firms often install capacity in excess of their best estimate of output.

2. A distinction can be made between the costs of those inputs whose quantity is fixed, given the existing scale of organization (fixed costs), and of those inputs whose quantity can be varied (variable costs).

3. As output increases at a given scale of organization, average fixed cost falls. Average variable cost is constant over a wide range of output, but rises slightly as output approaches the ultimate limit. As output increases average total cost falls at first, and then becomes roughly constant.

4. As the scale of organization increases, firms have more opportunity to take advantage of economies of scale. These can be classified as technical, marketing, buying, financial, risk-bearing and managerial economies. Economies of scale lead to reductions in average cost as output increases.

5. Beyond a certain point, diseconomies of scale may arise, causing average cost to rise as output increases. The main source of diseconomies is most likely to be difficulties in managing and controlling very large organizations.

6. Average cost is affected not only by the current rate of output, but also by the cumulative output to date. This relationship is known as the experience or learning effect.

7. External economies of scale arise when: (a) some operations previously undertaken by individual firms are taken over and performed more efficiently by a central organization; (b) the expansion of an industry leads to improvements in efficiency. External economies lead to a fall in the costs of individual firms even if the scale of those firms is unchanged.

8. There are different forms of growth – horizontal, vertical and diversified – each providing the opportunity for different types of scale economy.

9. Firms often set price on the basis of estimated cost at the expected level of output. The profit margin added to cost is influenced by the firm's objectives, the structure of the market and level of demand.

10. Profitability tends to be higher in (a) highly concentrated industries, (b) industries with high barriers to entry, suggesting that market structure is an important determinant of profitability. However, differentials in profitability tend to decline over time, and in the longer term higher profits might reflect the superior efficiency of large firms.

11. If demand is different from what was expected, firms often maintain price and adjust output, i.e. the supply curve is horizontal over that range of output. However, there are circumstances in which firms respond to higher than expected demand by increasing price, and to lower than expected demand by lowering price, i.e. the supply curve slopes up from left to right.

12. In some markets one firm may act as a price leader or maker, and the remaining firms as price followers or takers. If the existing price yields unsatisfactory profits, firms may attempt to reduce their costs of production.

13. The supply curve will shift with a change in any of the conditions of supply: costs of production, profit margins, opportunity cost, the number of producers and indirect taxation.

Key terms

Supply curve	Cost-based pricing
Scale of organization	Market structure
Fixed cost	Concentration
Variable cost	Barriers to entry
Total cost	Cost differentials
Economies of scale	Price leader (maker)
Diseconomies of scale	Price follower (taker)
Experience effect	Kinked demand curve
External economies	Conditions of supply
Growth of the firm	Price-minus costing

Notes

1. De Jonquieres G, The mountain starts to move but may still meet resistance, *Financial Times*, 4 Dec. 1985. This article was concerned primarily with GEC's bid for Plessey, firms which were eleventh and fourteenth respectively in world sales of telecommunications equipment, their combined sales being one-quarter of the sales of AT & T.
2. Bollard A, Technology, economic change, and small firms, *Lloyds Bank Review*, 1983.
3. Sandles A, Independent travel agents under siege, *Financial Times*, 7 April 1984.
4. Dodsworth T, Shooting for the magic billion, *Financial Times*, 1 April 1987.
5. Sir John Harvey-Jones, then chairman of ICI, in speech given at the Royal Institute of International Affairs, 19 Sept. 1986.
6. Boston Consulting Group, *Perspectives on Experience*, 1970. See also Department of Trade, *A Review of Monopolies and Mergers Policy*. HMSO, 1978.
7. Creedy J et al., *Economics: An Integrated Approach*. Prentice-Hall, 1984.
8. Bain J S, Relation of profit rate to industry concentration: American manufacturing 1936–40, *Quarterly Journal of Economics*, 1951.
9. Mann H M, Seller concentration, barriers to entry, and rates of return in thirty industries, 1950–60, *Review of Economics and Statistics*, 1966.
10. Brozen Y, The antitrust task force deconcentration recommendation, *Journal of Law and Economics*, 1970.
11. Kirzner I M, *Competition and Entrepreneurship*. Chicago Univ. Press, 1973.
12. Stigler G J and Kindahl J K, *The Behaviour of Industrial Prices*. National Bureau of Economic Research, 1970.
13. . Domberger S, Mergers, market structure and the rate of price adjustment. In Cowling K et al., *Mergers and Economic Performance*. Cambridge Univ. Press, 1980.

Essay questions

1. How would you explain the fact that, despite the widespread existence of economies of scale, many small firms survive?

2. Explain the reasons for believing that average total cost is often constant over quite a wide range of output, and discuss the significance of this fact.
3. Outline the various possible forms of internal growth and discuss the types of scale economy most likely to be associated with each form.
4. Discuss the advantages and disadvantages of internal growth as compared to growth by merger.
5. Why do so many firms adopt a policy of cost-based pricing?
6. 'Cost-based pricing ensures that adequate profits are earned.' 'Cost-based pricing is a certain road to bankruptcy.' Comment.
7. Examine the factors which might determine the margin added to cost in arriving at a firm's target price.
8. 'The response of price to a change in demand is likely to depend upon the time period under consideration.' Discuss.
9. 'The greatest problems facing a firm which is considering changing its price arise from uncertainty concerning the reactions of its rivals.' Explain this statement and show how a firm may try to reduce the degree of uncertainty.
10. Examine the alternative policies open to a price leader and discuss the relative merits of each policy.
11. Explain the circumstances in which a policy of 'price-minus costing' is most likely to be adopted.
12. What factors will a firm take into account in deciding whether or not to change its prices following (a) an increase, (b) a decrease in average cost?

Exercises

5.1 The Fishburn Machine Co. was about to begin the manufacture of a new type of metal fastener which they had not made before. Two machines suitable for making this fastener were on the market. Machine A, the cheaper of the two, had a rated capacity equivalent to an output of 400 units a day. It was in fact possible to increase output beyond this point by running the machines more quickly. However, this required additional labour, since each worker could look after fewer machines. Moreover, it had been found that there was an appreciable increase in the scrap rate, and hence in material costs.

Machine B had a greater capacity and, being fitted with more automatic devices, required fewer workers to operate it. Unfortunately, it was more expensive than machine A.

Using its usual method of depreciation, the company estimated its fixed costs would be £50 a day with machine A, and £100 a day with machine B. It estimated its variable costs to be as follows:

Daily output	Material costs (£ per unit)		Labour costs (£ per unit)	
(units)	Machine A	Machine B	Machine A	Machine B
100	0.25	0.25	0.40	0.30
200	0.25	0.25	0.40	0.30
300	0.25	0.25	0.40	0.30
400	0.25	0.25	0.40	0.30
500	0.30	0.25	0.50	0.30
600	0.35	0.25	0.60	0.30

(i) Draw the average total cost curves for both types of machine and indicate the single curve that would apply if the company could always choose the scale of organization appropriate to each level of output.

(ii) While the firm expects to sell 400 units a day, it realizes that sales could either exceed or fall short of this level. Examine the arguments in favour of installing each type of machine.

5.2 Each of ten manufacturers of a certain product has the following cost schedule:

Output (000s)	Average cost (p)	Average variable cost (p)
1	80	30
2	55	30
3	47	30
4	43	30
5	40	30

Each firm expects to produce 5,000 units, and sets a price of 60p in order to achieve a target profit of £1,000.

Below are three alternative market demand schedules for this product.

	Demand (000 units)		
Price (p)	I	II	III
30	65	55	50
40	60	50	40
50	55	45	25
60	50	30	10

(i) Calculate each firm's total profit with demand schedule I.
(ii) With demand schedule II calculate each firm's total profit if they:
   (a) maintain price at 60p;
   (b) reduce price to the level of average cost at the output initially expected.
(iii) With demand schedule III calculate each firm's total profit if they:
   (a) maintain price at 60p;
   (b) reduce price to the level of average cost at the output initially expected.
(iv) Calculate each firm's total contribution in situations (iii) (a) and (b).
   (Contribution = sales revenue minus variable cost.)

5.3 Figure 5.21, which appeared in *Economic Progress Report*, Oct. 1983, shows how the

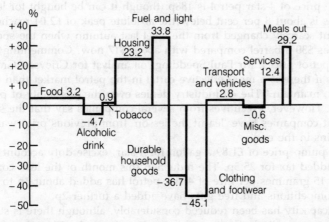

Fig. 5.21
Changes in relative prices, 1963–83. *Note*: width of bars indicated 1983 weights in RPI
Source: Department of Employment

prices of various product groups changed in comparison with the change in the retail price index.

(i) What factors might have accounted for the change in relative prices?

(ii) Outline the probable consequences of these changes.

5.4 The passage below is from G. and P. Polyani, *Parallel Pricing: a Harmful Practice*. Moorgate and Wall Street, Spring 1974, p. 59.

It is clear in one sense price leadership must restrict 'competition'. For if this is defined as fully independent action, then price leadership must restrain it. But if by competition is meant the bringing into existence of prices and costs that correspond with the requirements of efficient supply (i.e. the same as would emerge in a market with many sellers competing independently) then barometric price leadership is a device for creating these conditions, and therefore a means of making price competition effective where it would otherwise be hampered. For if there were fully independent pricing there would either be a tendency towards price rigidity or a 'price war' which might reach the point of price cutting aimed at mutual elimination. The first is clearly inefficient because it paralyses the price mechanism which is the means of attracting scarce resources into the uses where they can best satisfy customers' wants. And the second is also undesirable because in cut-throat 'price wars' prices may no longer correspond with costs but fall below them, and the end-result may be the survival not of the most efficient supplier but of the firm with the strongest financial resources. Even if the process stops short of this stage, resource allocation will still be distorted because prices and profits will fall below the level which correctly reflects the requirement of resources to meet customers' wants (i.e. the effect of interdependence in oligopoly will have been to force prices below the level that would emerge in independent competition between many small suppliers).

(i) What is the justification for the statement that 'if there were fully independent pricing there would either be a tendency towards price rigidity or a price war'? Do you agree with this statement?

(ii) Comment upon the authors' conclusion that interdependence in oligopoly is undesirable if its effect is to force prices below the level that would emerge in independent competition between many small suppliers.

5.5 The following passage was adapted from the *Financial Times*, 4 Feb. 1986.

The average price of 4-star petrol is 188p (though it can be bought for less in some places). This is about 8 per cent below the absolute peak of £2.04 reached in April last year, but scarcely changed from the level last autumn when the spot price of crude oil was $30 a barrel compared with about $17 now. Commenting on the stability of petrol prices, Mr Paul Spedding, oil analyst for Grievson Grant, said: 'It seems as if there is a more effective cartel in the petrol market than Opec has been able to maintain.' The oil industry denies even the possibility of pricing agreements. However, executives from several companies say that the smaller independent companies have 'learnt the lesson' from previous price wars that 'nobody gains in the end'.

Out of a pump price of £1.89 a gallon for 4-star, excise duty accounts for 81.4p and value added tax for 25.5p. The reduction this month of the lead content from 4 to 0.15 grammes per litre of 4-star petrol has added about 3p to the cost of a gallon. Competitions and free gifts have added a further 2p.

Refinery capacity has been reduced considerably, although there is still 20 to 30 per cent excess capacity in Europe. The number of petrol stations has fallen in the last 10 years from about 40,000 to about 22,000, most of the closures being small outlets. Many of the remaining stations have been refurbished, the average cost of refurbishing a large station being around £500,000. The result has been larger, brighter, stations, usually incorporating a self-service shop.

(i) Why do you think petrol could be bought more cheaply in some places than others?

(ii) Explain Mr Spedding's statement.

(iii) Is it true that 'nobody gains in the end' from price wars?

(iv) Explain, using a numerical example, why high indirect taxes may inhibit price competition.

(v) List the factors discussed in the passage which might (a) encourage, (b) discourage, price competition.

(vi) Discuss the impact on the welfare of consumers of the various factors listed in the passage.

CHAPTER SIX
The Marginal Analysis

Introduction

The models of price determination presented in Chapter 5 approximate closely to actual business behaviour. In this chapter we present an alternative series of models based on the marginal analysis. These models assume that the firm aims to maximize its short-run profits, and show that in order to attain this objective it should produce the output at which marginal cost equals marginal revenue. (More precisely it should produce the output at which the marginal cost curve cuts the marginal revenue curve from below.)

Total, average and marginal cost

Marginal cost is the change in total cost that occurs as a result of a change in output of one unit. The relationship between total, average and marginal cost is shown in Table 6.1, and the corresponding Fig. 6.1.

It can be seen that as output increases, average variable cost (and hence average total cost) and marginal cost fall at first and subsequently rise. This is due to the

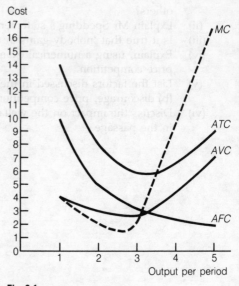

Fig. 6.1
Average and marginal cost

operation of the law or principle of *diminishing marginal productivity*. This law applies when (at least) one factor of production is fixed, and is used in conjunction with increasing quantities of other factors. It can easily be demonstrated that in this situation the return to

Table 6.1
Total, average and marginal cost

Output (units)	Fixed cost (£)	Average fixed cost (£)	Variable cost (£)	Average variable cost (£)	Total cost (£)	Average total cost (£)	Marginal cost (£)
1	10	10	4	4	14	14	4
2	10	5	6	3	16	8	2
3	10	3.3	8	2.7	18	6	2
4	10	2.5	18	4.5	28	7	10
5	10	2	35	7	45	9	17

the variable factor(s) will eventually decline.

As an example consider the farmer with a fixed amount of land on which he can employ different numbers of workers. It is likely that employing a second worker would lead to a more than proportionate increase in output, since there may be some tasks which are extremely difficult, even impossible, for a single worker to perform. Since output increases more than proportionately, we say that the returns to the variable factor (labour) increase. However, as more workers are employed output is likely to increase less than proportionately (i.e. returns begin to diminish or decrease), since the most important jobs will have already been completed. We might, for example, envisage the first workers employed undertaking the tasks of planting, weeding and harvesting, and later workers as sweeping the farmyard. This process is illustrated in Fig. 6.2. The marginal physical productivity of labour declines when more than X workers are employed; the average physical productivity declines beyond Y.

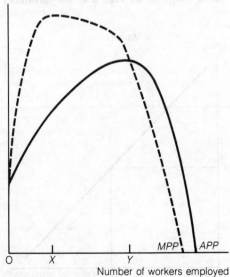

Fig. 6.2
Average (AAP) and marginal (MPP) physical productivity

Let us assume that each worker is paid the same wage. The consequence of these changes in productivity is that marginal and average variable cost falls at first and then rises. This is, of course, the situation illustrated in Fig. 6.1, which can be seen as the mirror image of Fig. 6.2.

Total, average and marginal revenue

Marginal revenue is the change in revenue that occurs as a result of a change in output (or sale) of one unit. The relationship between total, average and marginal revenue depends upon the type of market in which the product is sold. A broad distinction can be made between perfectly and imperfectly competitive markets.

A perfectly competitive market

A perfectly competitive market comprises a large number of producers (and consumers) of a homogeneous (undifferentiated) product. There are no barriers preventing entry to, or exit from, the market. Since consumers have no reason to prefer one supplier's product to another, any supplier that raised his price above that of rival suppliers would sell nothing. Consequently each supplier accepts the market price (i.e. acts as a price taker), and sells the amount he wishes at that price. This situation is illustrated in Table 6.2.

Table 6.2
Revenue in a perfectly competitive market

Output (units)	Price (= average revenue) (£)	Total revenue (£)	Marginal revenue (£)
1	7	7	7
2	7	14	7
3	7	21	7
4	7	28	7
5	7	35	7

Profit maximization in perfect competition

The operation of the profit-maximizing rule is illustrated in Fig. 6.3. Since the producer can sell any quantity that he is capable of producing at price P, his demand or average revenue curve is horizontal. Consequently his average and marginal revenue curves coincide. In order to maximize his profits he produces to the point at which the marginal cost curve cuts the marginal revenue curve from below. This occurs at output Q. His average cost curve is assumed to include an allowance for 'normal' profit. Since average cost equals average revenue at output Q, normal profit is earned.

In order to show why profits are maximized at this output, consider two other levels of output. If he produced less than Q, say R, he would forgo profits indicated by the shaded area lying beneath the marginal revenue curve and above the marginal cost curve. Conversely, if he produced more than Q, say T, his profits would be reduced by the shaded area lying above the marginal revenue and below the marginal cost curve.

The supply curve in a perfectly competitive market

As noted above, the supply curve indicates the amount of a product that a producer is willing to supply in a given time period at various prices. In the left-hand diagram in Fig. 6.4, the producer

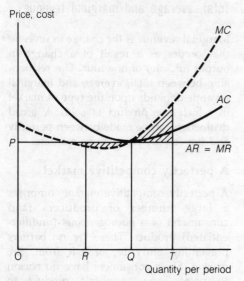

Fig. 6.3
Equilibrium in a perfectly competitive market

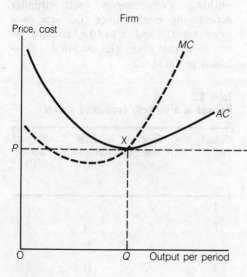

Fig. 6.4
Firm and market equilibrium

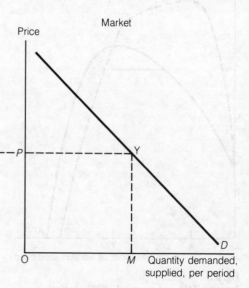

would supply Q units at price P, implying that X is a point on that producer's supply curve. The right-hand diagram refers to the market. Given demand D, M units are sold at price P. (If there are n firms each producing Q units, M = nQ.) Here Y is a point on the market supply curve.

To identify other points on the supply curve we must consider output at other prices. In Fig. 6.5 demand increases from D to D'. It will pay each producer to increase output provided the marginal (additional) revenue covers the marginal (additional) cost. The marginal cost curve indicates the expansion path of output; at price P', output is Q'. In other words XT is a segment of the firm's supply curve. Market output is M' (= nQ'), and YZ is a segment of the market supply curve.

A similar process applies, but in reverse, following a fall in demand. The firm's output falls along the path of the marginal cost curve, and there is a corresponding fall in market supply. Even though price is below average total cost producers continue to supply, since they are still covering the variable costs incurred in producing the current output. The process will end, however, if price falls below average variable cost, since revenue would no longer cover costs currently incurred.

We can therefore define the supply curve of the firm in perfect competition as that segment of the marginal cost curve that lies on and above the average variable cost curve. The market supply curve is, of course, the summation of the individual producers' supply curves.

Time and the supply curve

In the above section we assumed that when demand increased there was sufficient time to enable existing producers to increase output, but not to allow the entry of new firms. If the time period under consideration is shorter than that assumed above, output may increase less, i.e. supply may be less elastic. Indeed in some instances it may be impossible to increase output at all, as when only a fixed amount of fresh foods are supplied to a certain market on a given day. In such a situation the supply curve is vertical, and supply is said to be absolutely or infinitely inelastic.

On the other hand the time period may be longer than assumed above, allowing other producers to enter the market.

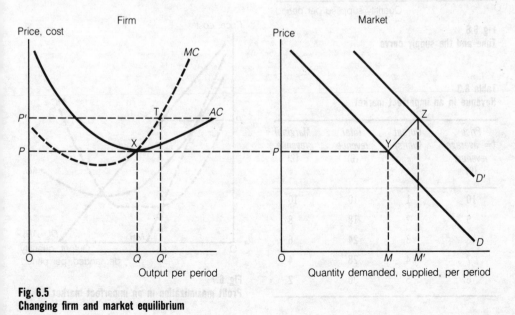

Fig. 6.5
Changing firm and market equilibrium

Output will therefore increase more than assumed above, i.e. supply will be more elastic. Indeed if the new entrants are as efficient as existing producers, the additional output required to meet the higher demand will be supplied at the initial price; i.e. the supply curve will be horizontal, and supply is said to be infinitely elastic.

These three situations are illustrated in Fig. 6.6, where S_{vs} denotes supply in the very short period, S_s supply in the short period and S_L supply in the long period.

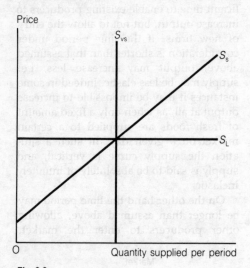

Fig. 6.6
Time and the supply curve

Table 6.3
Revenue in an imperfect market

Price (= average revenue) (£)	Output (units)	Total revenue (£)	Marginal revenue (£)
10	1	10	10
9	2	18	8
8	3	24	6
7	4	28	4
6	5	30	2

An imperfectly competitive market

There are several types of imperfect market. (As shown below, a distinction can be made between monopoly, monopolistic competition and oligopoly.) But in the present context the important feature of an imperfect market is that the firm has to reduce its price in order to increase the quantity that it sells. The relationship between total, average marginal revenue in an imperfect market is shown in Table 6.3.

Profit maximization in an imperfect market

The application of the profit-maximizing rule in an imperfect market is illustrated in Fig. 6.7. The equilibrium output Q is, as before, given by the point of intersection of the marginal cost and marginal revenue curves. This output is sold at price P.

In view of the preceding analysis, since Q is sold at price P, it might be thought that X is a point on the firm's supply curve. Unfortunately this is not so. In fact

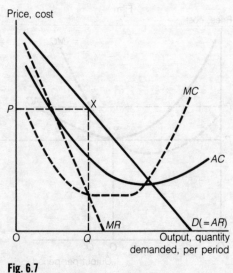

Fig. 6.7
Profit maximization in an imperfect market

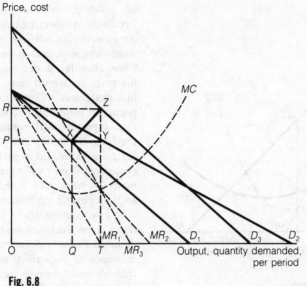

Fig. 6.8
Alternative supply curves

a supply curve for an imperfect market cannot be derived from a model based on marginal analysis.

To see why this is so consider Fig. 6.8 (the average cost curve has been omitted to simplify the diagram). With demand D_1 and marginal revenue MR_1, Q units would be sold at price P. If the demand curve shifted from D_1 to D_2, T units would be sold at price P, implying a horizontal supply curve (XY). On the other hand, if demand shifted from D_1 to D_3, T units would be sold at price R, implying an upward-sloping supply curve (XZ).

We arrive, therefore, at the conclusion that the shape of the supply curve is influenced by the shape of the demand curve. But this conclusion is incompatible with the assumption underlying models incorporating marginal analysis, that supply and demand are determined independently.

A fuller evaluation of marginal models is reserved until later. But the fact that a supply curve can be derived only for one type of market, perfect competition, must be considered as a deficiency of these models. Markets that even approximate to the model of perfect competition are very

much the exception. Consequently there is no link between producers' decisions on the one hand, and much of the analysis of markets on the other.

Types of imperfect market

As noted above, a distinction can be made between three types of imperfect market: monopoly, monopolistic competition and oligopoly. We discuss each type in turn, beginning with monopoly.

Monopoly
In a monopoly market the entire output is supplied by a single producer (we shall see in Ch. 10 that monopoly is defined differently for the purpose of competition policy). Consequently Fig. 6.9 refers both to the firm and the market (or industry). Equilibrium output is again given by the point of intersection of the marginal revenue and marginal cost curves. This output, Q, is sold at price P.

Models incorporating marginal analysis assume that cost includes normal profit, defined as the profit required if the firm is to remain in this market. Since revenue exceeds cost (including normal profit), the

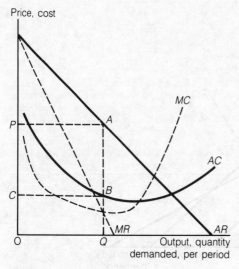

Fig. 6.9
Equilibrium in monopoly

monopolist represented in Fig. 6.9 is earning supernormal profit. The supernormal or monopoly profit per unit of output is *AB* (average revenue minus average cost) and the total amount of monopoly profit is the area *ABCP*.

The existence of supernormal profit will cause potential competitors to seek to enter the market. However, barriers prevent the entry of potential competitors (barriers to entry were discussed in Ch. 5). Consequently supernormal profits can persist in the long term.

Monopolistic competition
In monopolistic competition there are a large number of suppliers. However, each supplier offers consumers something that is not offered by other suppliers. In some instances a supplier's *product* may be differentiated from competitive products in one way or another: by quality, styling, advertising, etc. In other instances there may be differences in other aspects of the supplier's offer, for example better after-sales service, a more convenient location, longer opening hours.

The term 'product differentiation' is applied to all these differences (whether

in product or non-product aspects). Product differentiation means that consumers do not see the products of competing suppliers as perfect substitutes. Consequently, if one supplier increased his price he would not expect to lose all his customers. Consumers who attach particular importance to what is offered by this supplier, will continue to buy his product. Similarly, if a supplier reduced his price he would expect to attract some customers from rival suppliers, but not as many as he would if the products were seen as perfect substitutes.

We can summarize by saying that when there is product differentiation the firm's demand curve is downward sloping. The existence of (imperfect) substitutes means that demand curves tend to be more elastic in monopolistic competition than in monopoly. Nevertheless, supernormal profits can be earned in monopolistic competition, as previously illustrated in Fig. 6.9.

The existence of supernormal profits will again attract potential competitors. Whereas barriers prevent the entry of potential competitors into a monopoly

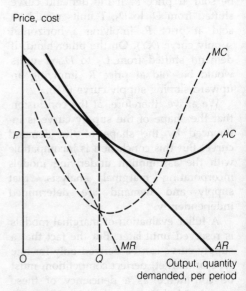
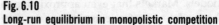

Fig. 6.10
Long-run equilibrium in monopolistic competition

market, in monopolistic competition competitors can enter, supplying products that attract some customers away from existing suppliers. This causes the demand curves of existing suppliers to shift to the left, a process that continues until supernormal profits have been competed away. This is illustrated in Fig. 6.10. The firm sells Q at price P, and normal profit is earned.

Oligopoly
Oligopoly denotes that the whole, or at least a large part, of the market is supplied by a few firms. As we saw in Chapter 5, firms in an oligopolistic market are *assumed* to face a demand curve that is kinked at the going market price.

Marginal analysis cannot explain the determination of the going price. But it does seek to explain why prices may be 'sticky', failing to change in response to factors that would cause prices to change in other types of market. In Fig. 6.11, with demand D the marginal revenue curve has a vertical segment. Marginal analysis suggests that Q will continue to be supplied at price P even if costs change, provided that the marginal cost curve continues to intersect the vertical portion of the marginal revenue curve.[1]

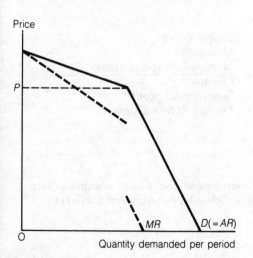

Fig. 6.11
Kinked demand curve

A critique of the marginal analysis

We have shown that marginal analysis is unable to explain the derivation of supply curves except in perfect competition. We have also shown that it cannot be used to explain price determination in oligopoly, a common type of market.

In other types of market, perfect competition, monopoly and monopolistic competition, models incorporating marginal analysis are able to present an apparently simple rule for profit maximization. This advantage should not be dismissed lightly. However, simplicity is attained only by making the very dubious assumption that firms wish to maximize their *short-run* profits. In practice most suppliers have a longer time horizon. They are interested in building up a market position which will guarantee their profitability, and hence their survival, in future years. This is a very important distinction since, as we saw during the discussion of new entry in Chapter 5, higher profits today may mean lower profits tomorrow.

Moreover, even if the analysis is confined to the short run, the models assume a much greater degree of certainty about demand conditions than usually exists in practice. One could take the view that the demand curves shown in the diagrams represent the firm's best estimate of market conditions, and that firms take price and output decisions in the light of these estimates. However, this is an unsatisfactory assumption. Many firms are so uncertain about the reactions of their rivals that it would not be meaningful to think of a demand curve on the basis of which marginal adjustments to price and output could be made. Instead firms usually prefer to set a price for a season, and to adjust output rather than price if demand conditions are not as expected.

This does not mean that marginal principles are of no account. Indeed, as we show in Chapter 7, firms may face many decisions in which incremental analysis – which embodies marginal principles – can be applied. However, these decisions often cannot be satisfactorily analysed in terms of models which assume the existence of distinct markets (or submarkets) each having clearly defined demand and cost schedules or curves.

Summary

1. Models based on the marginal analysis assume that the firm aims to maximize its short-run profits. In order to achieve this objective the firm produces the output at which marginal cost equals marginal revenue. (Marginal cost and revenue are the change in cost and revenue that occur as a result of a change in output of one unit.)
2. As output increases, average variable cost, average total cost and marginal cost fall at first and subsequently rise. This happens because of the operation of the law of diminishing marginal productivity.
3. In a perfectly competitive market an individual supplier can sell any quantity at the market price, i.e. price, average revenue and marginal revenue are equal and constant.
4. Changes in demand lead to a change in price and in the output of each producer. The short-run supply curve of a producer is the segment of the marginal cost curve that lies on and above the average variable cost curve. The market supply curve is the summation of the individual producers' supply curves. The supply curve is normally more elastic in the long than the short run.
5. In an imperfect market the individual supplier faces a downward-sloping demand curve, and a marginal revenue curve that lies below the demand (average revenue) curve. The application of the profit-maximizing rule often leads to supernormal profits being earned in the short run. In monopolistic competition excess profits are usually competed away in the long run, and only normal profits are earned. In monopoly barriers prevent the entry of new firms, and supernormal (monopoly) profits can be earned in both the short and the long run.

Key terms

Profit maximization
Marginal cost
Law of diminishing marginal productivity
Marginal revenue
Perfect competition
Normal profit

Supply curve
Monopoly
Monopolistic competition
Oligopoly
Supernormal profit
Product differentiation

Note

1. We showed in Chapter 5 that there is considerable doubt as to whether in fact prices are more sticky in oligopoly than in other types of imperfect market.

Essay questions

1. Explain the relationships between total, variable and marginal costs.
2. Show how the law of diminishing marginal productivity may affect (a) average variable cost, (b) average fixed cost.

3. Explain the statement that the relationship between total, average and marginal revenue depends upon the type of market in which the product is sold.
4. 'In perfect competition producers make decisions on output, not on price.' Discuss.
5. Show how a supply curve can be derived for (a) a firm, (b) a market or industry.
6. Explain why a supply curve cannot be derived from models of imperfect markets which are based on marginal analysis.
7. Discuss, with illustrations, how elasticity of supply may change over time.
8. Using marginal analysis, show why barriers to entry may affect profitability.
9. Define and explain the significance of product differentiation.
10. Discuss the cause and significance of the kinked demand curve.

Objective test questions: set 2

1. The best definition of a supply curve is that it shows:
    A   the relationship between average cost and price;
    B   the relationship between price and the quantity supplied;
    C   the quantity supplied at various prices;
    D   the quantity that would be supplied at various prices;
    E   the quantity that would be supplied at various prices in a given period.
    Questions 2–7 are based on Fig. 6.12 which relates to the market for bauxite (aluminium ore). The unbroken lines are the initial demand and supply curves and the broken lines are the demand and supply curves which might arise as a result of the various changes listed below. Starting each time from the original equilibrium position X, indicate the new equilibrium position A, B, C, D or E. Each letter may be used once, more than once, or not at all.

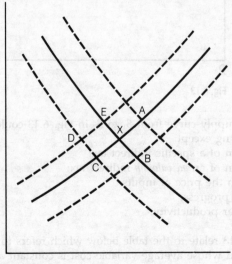

Fig. 6.12

2. The price of copper, a substitute for aluminium, falls.
3. The cost of transporting bauxite increases.
4. An increase occurs in the price of electricity, used in the process of transforming bauxite into aluminium.

5. New low-cost deposits of bauxite are discovered.
6. The demand for aluminium goods falls; a strike by bauxite miners reduces supplies from low-cost mines.
7. The government places a tax on copper goods; an increase occurs in real national income.

8. Which of the following could *not* explain why a firm's average total cost decreased as its output increased at a given scale of organization? (AFC = average fixed cost; AVC = average variable cost.)
   A Both AFC and AVC decreased.
   B AVC decreased while AFC remained constant.
   C AFC decreased while AVC remained constant.
   D The decrease in AFC outweighed the increase in AVC.
   E AVC decreased more rapidly than AFC.

9. If a grocery wholesaler took over a retail grocery chain this would be an example of:
   A horizontal growth;
   B backward integration;
   C backward growth by internal expansion;
   D forward integration;
   E forward growth by internal expansion.

Fig. 6.13

10. The shift of the supply curve from S_1 to S_2 in Fig. 6.13 could have been caused by any of the following except:
    A the imposition of a specific indirect tax;
    B the imposition of an *ad valorem* indirect tax;
    C an increase in the price of inputs;
    D technological progress;
    E a fall in labour productivity.

Questions 11–13 relate to the table below which refers to a product whose fixed cost is £1,000, and whose average variable cost is constant at all levels of output.

Output	Average cost (£)
2	520
3	353.3
4	—
5	220

11. The average total cost at an output of 4 units would be (£):
    A 300;
    B 286.7;
    C 280;
    D 270;
    E 250.

12. The incremental cost incurred in increasing output from 2 to 5 units would be (£):
    A 300;
    B 100;
    C 80;
    D 60;
    E 20.

13. The marginal cost at all levels of output is (£):
    A 300;
    B 100;
    C 80;
    D 60;
    E 20.

14. Assuming a given scale of organization, a producer will cease production if there is no output at which revenue equals or exceeds:
    A total cost;
    B fixed cost;
    C variable cost;
    D sunk cost;
    E escapable cost.

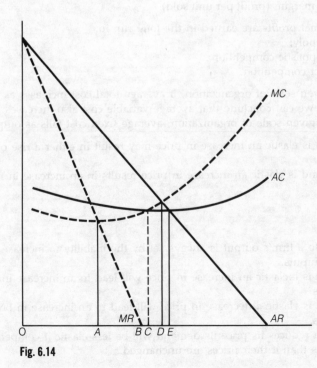

Fig. 6.14

15. If a firm were certain that its cost and revenue conditions were as shown in Fig. 6.14, and if it wished to maximize its short-run profits, what output would it produce – A, B, C, D or E?

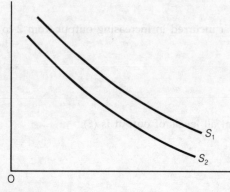

Fig. 6.15

16. The shift in the supply curve from S_1 to S_2 in Fig. 6.15 could have been due to:
    1. economies of scale being attained as output increased;
    2. a fall in the cost of production at all levels of output;
    3. the granting of subsidies to producers.

17. If demand is inelastic an increase in price must result in an increase in:
    1. total revenue;
    2. total profits;
    3. profit margins (profit per unit sold).

18. Supernormal profits are earned in the long run in:
    1. monopoly;
    2. monopolistic competition;
    3. perfect competition.

19. With a given scale of organization, if average total cost increases as output increases, we can conclude that average variable cost also increases.
    With a given scale of organization, average fixed cost falls as output increases.

20. If demand is elastic an increase in price may result in either a rise or a fall in total profits.
    If demand is elastic an increase in price results in an increase in revenue.

True/false

1. The limit to a firm's output is always set by the inability to increase the quantity of capital inputs.
2. If demand is inelastic an increase in price will lead to an increase in both revenue and profits.
3. If demand is elastic a decrease in price will lead to an increase in both revenue and profits.
4. If one firm reduces its price its demand will be less elastic if competitors reduce their prices than if their prices are unchanged.

5. When the supplier of a given product sets different prices that do not reflect cost differences he is said to practise price discrimination.
6. A firm which obtained greater economies of scale than other firms would have lower average costs than these other firms at all levels of output.
7. Technical economies of scale are more likely to result from a process of horizontal than diversified growth.
8. The marginal cost curve always cuts the average cost curve at the latter's minimum point.
9. The marginal cost curve always cuts the average fixed cost curve at the latter's minimum point.
10. Average revenue equals marginal revenue in both monopoly and perfect competition.

CHAPTER SEVEN
Additional Issues in Pricing

Introduction

In Chapters 5 and 6 we have presented alternative theoretical models of price and output determination. The first set of models was based on the assumption that firms base their price on the average cost at the expected level of output. The profit margin that is added to this cost is influenced by the motivations of producers, the structure of the market and the producers' assessment of the level of market demand. (We showed that in some markets price followers accept the price set by the price leaders.) The second set of models was based on the assumption that firms maximize their short-run profits by producing the output at which marginal cost equals marginal revenue.

In this chapter we build on these models as we consider additional aspects of price determination. First, we relax the assumption that a supplier charges the same price to all customers, and discuss the circumstances in which different prices may be charged. (This discussion involves cost concepts not considered so far.) We then discuss at length those situations in which price is determined by the interaction of market demand and supply, and all suppliers act as price takers.

Price discrimination

Price discrimination denotes that different prices are set for different customers even though the cost of supplying these customers is identical. The term 'discriminating monopoly' is sometimes used to describe this situation, but price discrimination is not confined to monopoly.

When a producer sells a given product in two (or more) distinct markets he will obtain greater profits by setting different prices in the different markets than he

would by setting the same price, providing the following conditions apply:
1. The different markets have different price elasticities of demand.
2. There is no 'leakage' between the markets. This implies that:
   (a) customers are unable to benefit by buying in one market and reselling in another;
   (b) customers are unable to transfer from one market to another (this condition assumes particular importance in markets for services).

We can demonstrate that price discrimination increases profits where demand elasticities differ by reference to Fig. 7.1. We start from a position where the firm sets the same price, P, in both markets and in order to simplify the analysis we assume that quantity Q is sold in both markets, i.e. the two demand curves coincide at point X.

The firm now increases its price in the less elastic market B, and reduces its price

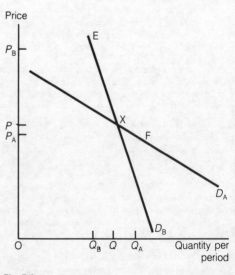

Fig. 7.1
Price discrimination

in the more elastic market A. In order further to simplify the analysis we assume that the price adjustments are such as to leave total output unchanged. Since we have assumed that the average cost of supplying both markets is the same, total cost will also be unchanged. However, it can be seen that total revenue, and therefore total profit, has increased:

$$[OP_BEQ_B + OP_AFQ_A] > [2(OPXQ)]$$

The subdivision of markets

We now consider the various ways in which a market might be differentiated, i.e. divided into submarkets. The most obvious basis is probably geographical (differentiation by space). In large countries, such as the USA, differentiation between regional markets may be practical. Producers in smaller countries may be restricted to differentiation between home and export markets.

A second basis is differentiation by time. Consumers may put different values on a product which is made available at different times. If, as a result, demand elasticities differ at different times, profits will be increased by price discrimination. So we find that telephone calls are cheaper in the evening, early morning and at weekends; railway travel is cheaper at off-peak times; cinema and theatre tickets are sometimes cheaper for matinee performances. Also, many products are offered at lower prices in end-of-season sales.

The final basis for differentiation that we consider is the type of customer. In some instances this is tied up with another form of differentiation. For example *some* price concessions to retirement pensioners, females or children are available only for off-peak purchases. Again a price discount offered by a manufacturer to a wholesaler might be partly due to the fact that, as a wholesaler, the purchaser undertakes certain functions that are helpful to the manufacturer and that are not undertaken by other types of customer. But the discount may also take into account the quantity of the

product bought by the purchaser. In other instances price differentials may be made purely on the basis of the type of customer – whether he is a child or an adult, a manufacturer, wholesaler or retailer, etc.

Price and cost differentials

In the introduction we defined price discrimination as the charging of different prices to different customers when the cost of supplying those customers is identical. It follows that if differences in price reflect differences in cost, this does not constitute price discrimination in an economic sense (although customers who are charged the higher price may feel that they are being discriminated against).

It is not difficult to think of reasons why costs may differ. The cost of supplying two different geographical markets may differ because of differences in transport costs or because the two markets are supplied from two factories which have different levels of efficiency. The cost per unit of a large order may be less than of a small order because of the economies of a large production run. The cost of supplying services at different times may differ because of the need to pay workers premium rates for 'unsocial' hours of work.

In some of these cases the analysis is straightforward. Two different average cost curves and therefore two different supply curves exist for the two markets. The analysis becomes more complicated when it is not possible to make a clear distinction between the costs that are incurred in supplying one market (or submarket) and those incurred in supplying another. In order to analyse this situation we must refer to certain cost concepts that have not so far been required.

Additional cost concepts

Incremental cost
Incremental cost is the additional cost that results from an increase in output. A small increase in output may require an increase

only in the quantity of direct materials used, since spare capacity may exist in other inputs. Larger increases in output are likely to require an increase in more inputs and even, perhaps, an increase in the scale of organization.

As we saw in Chapter 6, marginal cost is a similar concept to incremental cost, but it refers to a change in output of one unit. Although in principle such a change *could* require an increase in the scale of organization it is most unlikely to do so in practice. Consequently, marginal cost normally relates to a change in the cost of variable inputs such as direct labour and materials.

Escapable cost
Escapable cost is the opposite of incremental cost. It is the reduction in cost that occurs when output falls. The reduction may apply to any input, e.g. less labour may be employed, fewer raw materials may be bought, machines may be scrapped. If the reduction in output refers to a single unit, the term 'marginal cost' can be applied to the reduction in cost.

Sunk cost
A sunk cost is a cost that has already been incurred, and is therefore not affected by a change in output. If a machine has already been purchased the purchase price represents a sunk cost – only the operating costs would be saved by scrapping the machine. This is an extremely important point, since many of the fixed costs that we considered in Chapter 6 are in fact sunk costs. In order to explain the connection between these two cost concepts we need to explore briefly the meaning and purpose of depreciation.

Depreciation
When capital equipment is purchased the firm usually tries to recover its cost, not in the year of its purchase, but over a number of years – perhaps five or ten for machinery, longer for a factory. For example, if a firm purchased for £100,000

a machine which it expected to use for ten years its annual cost would be considered to be £10,000. (If the firm used a replacement cost rather than a historical cost basis of depreciation, and it expected a new machine to cost £120,000 in ten years' time, its annual cost would be £12,000.) The spreading of the initial, fixed, cost over a number of years is known as depreciation. (The number of years over which equipment and other assets are depreciated or written off may, of course, differ from that assumed here.)

The firm would hope and expect to charge a price that would cover this annual cost (together with the cost of all other inputs). However, it might not always be able to do so. It might find that its customers would accept a price above variable cost but below total cost. As we said above, many fixed costs are sunk costs. If we make the simplifying assumption that all fixed costs are sunk we reach the conclusion that the firm would be better off, i.e. its *cash flow* would be greater, if it sold its output at a price above variable cost than if it did not produce at all.

Alternative cost concepts and pricing decisions

In order to link these concepts with the analysis presented in the previous chapter consider Fig. 7.2. Since average variable cost (AVC) is constant up to output Q, marginal cost (MC) equals AVC up to that point. Then as AVC begins to increase, MC rises above AVC. As we noted above, marginal cost refers to a change in output of one unit. So the marginal cost of increasing output by one unit to Q is QA. Similarly the marginal cost of increasing output by one unit to R is RB. It follows that the incremental cost of increasing output from Q minus one unit ($Q - 1$) to R is the area under the relevant part of the marginal cost curve, i.e. $QABR$.

Price, cost

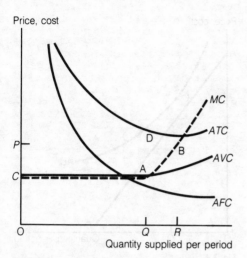

Fig. 7.2
Average total, fixed, variable and marginal cost

Escapable cost is found by moving down the marginal cost curve. The reduction in marginal cost resulting from a reduction in output by one unit to R is RB, and by one unit Q is QA. If the firm were producing output Q the escapable cost if were to cease production would be the area $QACO$.

If the firm sold quantity Q at price P it would fail to cover its total cost. Nevertheless, it would be better to sell at this price than to cease production. If it ceased production its revenue would fall by $QDPO$ whereas, as we have seen, its cost would fall by only $QACO$. In this decision the firm ignores sunk, or fixed, cost.[1]

The above conclusion depends, of course, upon the assumption that the firm could not use its assets in a more profitable way. If it believes that the maximum revenue that it could obtain in a given time period is $OQDP$, and if it could sell up, withdraw its resources from this market and invest them in an alternative use that would yield more than $OQDP$ per period, it would pay it to redeploy its resources. We say that the opportunity cost of resources is greater than $OQDP$.

We can summarize by saying that the ultimate 'floor price' is equal to average variable cost (or opportunity cost if this is

greater). However, it is important to remember that when the time period is sufficiently long to enable the scale of organization to be changed, all inputs and costs become variable. As the existing machinery wears out new machinery must be bought (unless the firm is willing to move to a smaller scale). Consequently it is not possible for firms to permanently maintain price below average total cost. If the firm is unable to cover total cost and to earn a satisfactory profit at any scale of organization, it will eventually leave the market.

Price differentials

In the shorter period, if the firm is unable to sell its output at its target price, it may still be able to sell part at this price and part at lower prices. (Alternatively, if it is unable to sell any at the target price, it may offer smaller reductions to some customers than others.)

It might appear that such a policy would represent price discrimination. But further exploration of the meaning of 'cost' may lead to a different conclusion. In order to simplify the analysis we assume in Fig. 7.3 that average variable cost is constant over the relevant range of output, and so is equal to marginal cost. We omit the average fixed cost curve from

Price, cost

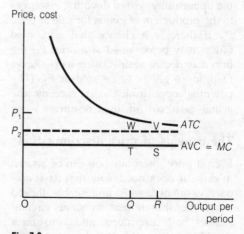

Fig. 7.3
Differential pricing

the diagram, since this is not relevant to the decision considered here.

The current pattern of orders might suggest that during the present 'season' the firm will be able to sell output Q at price P_1. This price is lower than the firm hoped to obtain, and does not yield a satisfactory profit. The firm then has the opportunity to sell an additional amount QR at a price P_2. The revenue from this order would be $QWVR$. The cost would be $QTSR$. Consequently the additional profit from the order, i.e. the incremental profit, would be $TWVS$.

It will probably now be clear why it is not easy to decide whether taking this order would represent price discrimination. Although the price is below that charged to other customers, it yields a profit over the costs incurred in meeting the order.

In deciding whether to accept the order the firm must take into account the factors outlined above. It must ensure that there is no leakage between the markets, i.e. that the purchaser will not resell the output QR to customers who would otherwise have purchased from the producer at price P_1. It must also ensure that these other customers do not realize that sales have been made at P_2 and demand a similar reduction in price on their purchases. Finally it must consider the opportunity cost of devoting resources to the production of goods for sale at price P_2. If there is a chance that additional orders may be obtained at a price P_1, the firm may decide against using its resources to produce goods to be sold at P_2. (The potential opportunity cost exceeds the actual 'cash' cost of these resources.)

The benefits of price discrimination

Even if price discrimination can be shown to exist, it does not follow that its consequences are necessarily undesirable. Indeed it can be shown that in some circumstances both producers and consumers would be worse off in the absence of price discrimination. In Fig. 7.4 the producer

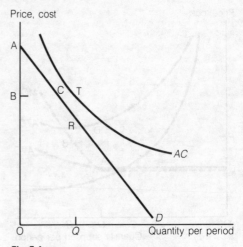

Fig. 7.4
Cost and revenue under perfect price discrimination

would be unable to cover his costs at any price that was uniformly applied. He would therefore eventually leave the market. On the other hand, if he was able to practise perfect price discrimination, to charge each consumer what he or she was prepared to pay, he could make a profit and stay in business. At output Q total revenue would be $OQRA$, which exceeds total cost $OQTB$. (This can be clearly seen since the area of the triangle ABC exceeds that of CTR.)

Marginal analysis and price discrimination

The marginal analysis can also be used to explain profit maximization when price discrimination is practised. In Fig. 7.5 the firm supplies two markets with different elasticities, as shown by the demand curves D_A and D_B. If it follows the profit-maximizing rule, the firm will equate marginal cost and marginal revenue in each market. In the less elastic market A, Q_A is sold at price P_A. In the more elastic market B, Q_B is sold at the lower price P_B. (Note that at any price, total demand equals the sum of the demand in the two markets, i.e. $D = D_A + D_B$. Similarly MR

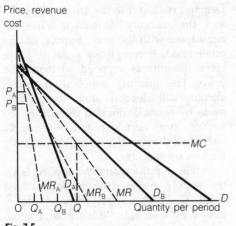

Fig. 7.5
Marginal analysis and price discrimination

$= MR_A + MR_B$. The equilibrium output Q $(= Q_A + Q_B)$ occurs at the intersection of MC and MR.)

The pricing of services

The principles discussed in the above sections may be applied to markets for both goods and services. But services have certain characteristics which often make price differentials especially appropriate. The most important of the characteristics is that services cannot be 'stored'. If a person wishes to travel by public transport at 8.00 a.m. or to attend the theatre at 8.00 p.m., the facilities must be made available at those times.

This has a very important implication if demand has an uneven pattern over time, as often occurs in service markets. If sufficient facilities are provided to meet the peak demand, excess capacity will occur at other times. Consequently marginal or incremental cost in off-peak periods is likely to be relatively low. For example whereas an increase in the peak demand for rail travel might require an increase in capacity, e.g. the purchase of more rolling-stock, an increase in off-peak demand may simply mean that seats previously unoccupied are now occupied. One of the purposes of price concessions

at off-peak times is to encourage the utilization of excess capacity.

The elasticity of demand is, of course, also relevant to the pricing of services. In many service markets demand is likely to be far less elastic at peak than at off-peak times. This again would suggest that a system of differential pricing would be likely to increase total revenue.

Moreover, even if some transfer of custom occurs from the high to the low price market, leading to a reduction in total revenue, price differentials may still increase profitability because of the favourable compensating effect on cost. If the peak demand falls the producer needs less capacity, and this reduction in 'capacity costs' may outweigh the loss of revenue. This is an especially important consideration in markets in which demand is growing overall, where the need to increase capacity, and hence incur additional capacity costs, would be reduced.

Price takers

So far in this chapter we have been concerned with situations in which individual firms set prices. We now examine situations in which price is determined by the interaction of aggregate (market) demand and aggregate (market) supply. No individual supplier can influence price; all suppliers are price takers. (It follows that cost is a much less important influence on price than in the markets discussed earlier in the chapter. However, we shall see that the influence of cost is not completely absent.)

We saw in Chapter 6 that in perfect competition all suppliers are price takers and we refer to perfectly competitive markets below. However, one of the assumptions of the model of perfect competition – that price is known when output decisions are made – reduces the usefulness of that model for our present purposes. Consequently we begin with an alternative model, that of the open market.

Open markets

The term 'open market' denotes that there are few or no restrictions on the interplay of market forces.[2] Open markets are characterized by: (a) a high level of uncertainty, at the time that production decisions are made, about future price levels; (b) the impossibility, or at least extreme difficulty, of co-ordinating the activities of producers.

Many open markets also have a large number of producers, very little or no product differentiation, and easy entry to and exit from the market. But these features are important mainly in so far as they affect the two characteristics noted previously.

A basic model of an open market

Probably the best example of an open market is the sale by auction of a perishable product such as fish or tomatoes. In such instances the pricing season is extremely short, lasting only as long as the auction – normally less than one day. Price is determined by the interaction between demand and supply on that day.

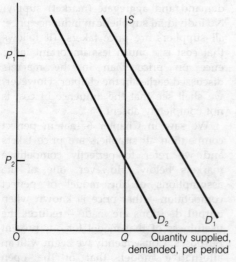

Fig. 7.6
Equilibrium price in an open market

Demand is subject to the usual influences, and the quantity demanded varies in accordance with the price. Supply, on the other hand, is completely inelastic, i.e. a given quantity is supplied whatever the price. The quantity supplied at a fish auction will depend upon the catches made by boats landing on the day of the auction; at an auction of tomatoes supply will depend upon the deliveries made by farmers on that day.

In Fig. 7.6 the quantity supplied is Q, the supply curve being vertical at that point. Given this supply, price is determined by demand. With demand at D_1 price is P_1; with demand at D_2, price is P_2. At both prices quantity traded is, of course, Q.

The influence of cost

Although prices in open markets are often said to be 'demand determined', cost may still influence price in several ways. First, continuing our previous example, let us assume that fishermen wish to insure themselves against the fluctuations in price, and hence in revenue, which characterize auction markets. Rather than allow all their fish always to be sold by auction for human consumption, they might seek an alternative market to which supplies could be diverted if the price at auction was unsatisfactory. The manufacturers of pet food might provide such an alternative market. (The revenue obtainable from the pet-food manufacturers would constitute the opportunity cost of supplying fish to the auction market.)

Since the manufacturers guarantee to pay a given price, and thus give suppliers the additional security they require, this price will obviously be below the average price expected in the auction market over a long period. In Fig. 7.7 the average expected price is designated as P_E, and the guaranteed, floor, price as P_F. With demand at D_E the entire supply would be sold at auction at price P_E. On the other hand if demand on a given day were to fall to D_A, the agreement with the manufacturers would be activated. Quantity OR

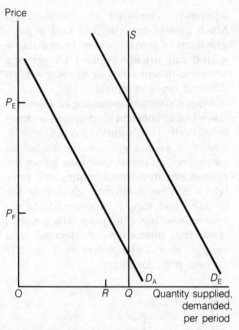

Fig. 7.7
A floor price in an open market

would be sold at auction, and RQ to the manufacturers – the price being P_F in both instances.

The floor price might also be reached because the quantity supplied is very large on a particular day. In Fig. 7.8 S_E is the expected supply and P_E the expected price. When supply is S_A, quantity OQ is sold at auction and QR to the manufacturers at price P_F.

Similar agreements might be made by the suppliers of other perishable products such as fruit and vegetables. In addition the amount of produce that farmers bring to the market on any given day may be influenced by the price that they obtained on previous days. This influence will be particularly strong where prices fall to a level at which the variable cost of 'harvesting' and bringing the crop to market is not covered. If farmers expect these demand conditions to continue they will temporarily withdraw from the market. The effect of this withdrawal is shown in Fig. 7.9.

On day 1 quantity Q_1 is sold at price P_1, which is below the average variable cost.

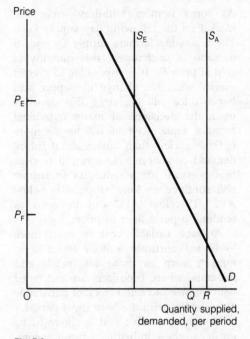

Fig. 7.8
A floor price when supply exceeds the expected level

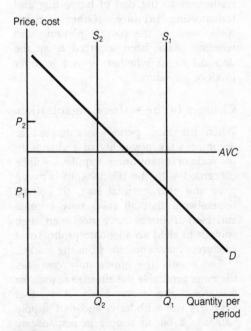

Fig. 7.9
Changes in daily supply and price in an open market

As some farmers withdraw from the market on the following day supply falls. The remaining farmers supply Q_2 and, if demand is unchanged, this quantity is sold at price P_2. It is impossible to predict exactly what the change in supply and hence price will be, since this depends upon the decisions of many individual farmers, some of whom will have a more optimistic view than others about future demand conditions. However, it is clear that pressure for a reduction in supply will continue as long as price is below *AVC*. Therefore *AVC* can be seen as tending to put a floor to price.

Average variable cost is even more likely to constitute a floor to price in markets such as those for metals and minerals, where producers are not faced with the need to sell a stock of perishable commodities within a very short period.

Moreover variable cost is likely to be greater in these industries since it encompasses a greater part of the total production process than in agriculture or horticulture where, as we saw, it may relate only to the cost of harvesting and transporting produce. (Other variable costs, such as the cost of planting and weeding, have been incurred *before* the decision as to whether or not to offer produce for sale.)

Changes in the scale of organization

When the time period is extended to encompass the possibility of a change in the scale of organization, suppliers will be concerned with the relationship between price and average total cost. (It will be remembered that all costs now become variable.) If prices have not been high enough to yield an adequate profit, some producers may withdraw from the market.

The greater the opportunity cost, i.e. the more profitable the alternative uses for resources, the more likely it is that suppliers will withdraw, and that supply will fall. A fall in supply in response to inadequate profits will be relatively slow in fishing, since it is difficult to find alternative uses for most of the capital

equipment employed in the industry. Much greater opportunities for the redeployment of resources exist in agriculture – land can usually be used for growing several different crops or keeping several different types of animal.

Where constant switching of resources takes place, constant fluctuations in price may result. This is illustrated in Fig. 7.10, which we assume refers to the market for cucumbers. In this diagram we ignore the fluctuations in demand, supply and price which may occur during a given year; the demand and supply curves relate to the year as a whole. (The price which results from the interaction of demand and supply should be interpreted as the average price for the year.)

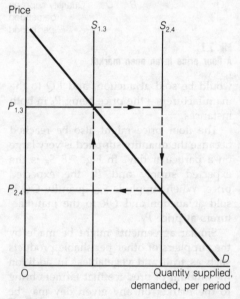

Fig. 7.10
The cobweb: price fluctuations in an open market

In year 1, with supply S_1, price is P_1 which we assume yields a higher rate of return than was obtained from the growing of other crops such as lettuces. Consequently in year 2 some land is taken out of lettuce production and used for growing cucumbers. This results in an increase in supply (S_2). With an unchanged demand, price falls to P_2 at which the returns are less than those obtained from other crops. Consequently in year 3 supply decreases (S_3) with the result that price rises (P_3). In year 4, with supply S_4, price is P_4.

The path traced by price, via the changing supply curves, is shown by the dotted line in Fig. 7.10. Because of the configuration of this path this process has been called the cobweb. There is no reason why price fluctuations should not continue indefinitely, since the actions of suppliers are uncoordinated. Each supplier who considers entering the market may recognize that if sufficient suppliers enter, the price may fall to an unacceptable level. But he cannot tell, until after his own decision is made, what other suppliers have decided to do.

Figure 7.10 shows that price fluctuates between two points. This follows, of course, from the assumption that supply fluctuates between two levels. But in practice supply, and therefore price, may behave in other ways. If fluctuations in supply increased over time, i.e. if S_3 lay to the left of S_1 and S_4 to the right of S_2, price fluctuations would become greater. (This is known as a divergent cobweb.) Conversely if fluctuations in supply decreased (if S_3 lay to the right of S_1 and S_4 to the left of S_2) price fluctuations would decrease and eventually disappear (a convergent cobweb).

The basic model: summary

Even in open markets cost influences price, since unless firms earn adequate profits, i.e. unless the relationship between revenue and cost is satisfactory, resources will be withdrawn from the market, either temporarily or permanently. Nevertheless, during a pricing season suppliers act as price takers, except in extremely adverse circumstances when a price floor – related in some way to cost – may operate.

Price may fluctuate primarily either because of changes in demand (Figs 7.6,

7.7) or in supply (Figs 7.8–7.10). We show below that the relative importance of these two factors depends upon the nature of the product and the time period being considered.

Inelastic supply

In the basic model supply was presented as fixed or perfectly inelastic (above any floor price). In many instances this assumption is highly realistic. This is most obvious when the time period is very short (in these instances the vertical supply curve corresponds to the very short run supply curve in the perfect competition model). But even when a period as long as a year is considered it is reasonable to consider supply as being fixed, i.e. not responsive to changes in current prices, in many agricultural markets, since the quantity supplied depends on prior production decisions (e.g. the amount of land planted) which are influenced by expectations about *future* prices. The quantity supplied is also affected, of course, by climatic conditions, but this does not detract from the proposition that a given amount will be supplied regardless of the current price.

There may be some circumstances in which supply is not perfectly inelastic within a pricing season and these circumstances are explored briefly in the following section. However, there is no doubt that overall open markets are characterized by a highly inelastic supply, so that changes in demand give rise to substantial fluctuations in price.

Changes in the quantity supplied

In some agricultural markets a higher price will call forth an increase in the quantity supplied. For example additional supplies of raw cotton and tea can be obtained by reworking bushes that have already been picked. The yield of minerals can sometimes be increased by more intensive exploitation of deposits, even extending to the reworking of spoil tips.

Supply is most likely to change in response to a change in demand when a

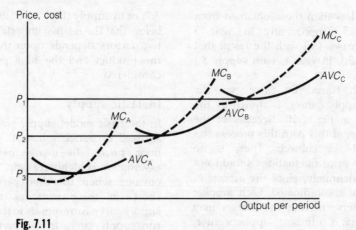

Fig. 7.11
A fall in price and a closure of production units

producer owns several production units of differing efficiency. Figure 7.11 illustrates the situation that might face a company operating three mines. We assume that demand is so depressed that the company has decided to keep the mines open as long as revenue covers variable cost. At price P_1 all three mines operate. If price fell to P_2 only mines A and B would remain open, and a further fall to P_3 would result in the closure of mine B.

If the producer closes a mine whose output accounts for a significant share of the market this might, for course, halt and even reverse the fall in price. In such a situation it is debatable whether that producer is acting as a price follower. In practice even large producers of minerals and metals have found it extremely difficult to prevent prices falling in the face of a steep fall in demand. If they cut back production in order to try to stabilize price, they invariably find that other producers are only too happy to take their place.

Fluctuations in demand

The demand for some foodstuffs can vary considerably from day to day because of changes in the weather. But if we ignore such short-term fluctuations we can say that in general demand tends to fluctuate most for raw materials used in the

manufacture of capital goods, for example many metals, and least for foodstuffs. The intermediate case is the demand for raw materials used in the manufacture of consumer goods, e.g. wool and cotton.

Speculation and demand

Although the basic factor underlying demand is that the commodity is required for use, some products also attract a speculative demand. Indeed one informed observer of commodity markets expressed the view that in the metal markets 'prices appear to be mainly moved by the reaction of speculators to a wide variety of influences. Very often fundamental supply–demand developments are swamped by speculators reacting to non-trade influences, particularly changes in exchange and interest rates, economic forecasts and political considerations.'[3] Even though it can be argued that any price movements resulting from speculation will eventually be corrected, speculation can certainly lead to more extreme fluctuations in the shorter term.

Commodity prices in practice

Figure 7.12 shows the changes that have occurred in real commodity prices, i.e.

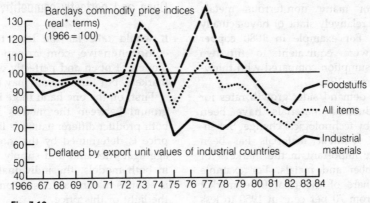

Fig. 7.12
Commodity price indices
Source: Barclays Review, Feb. 1985

commodity prices deflated by an index of export unit values of industrial countries. Several factors are of special importance in an explanation of these price changes.[4]

It can be seen that prices rose rapidly in 1973. This followed a period in which expansionary monetary policies throughout the industrialized world encouraged rapid economic growth which subsequently led to a build-up of inflationary pressures. There was also in this period a widespread move from fixed to floating exchange rates. These factors combined to produce strong speculative activity in commodities on top of the increased demand due to rising output and incomes in the industrialized countries.

On the supply side, stocks of many commodities had previously been run down to very low levels as a result of government policies, economic incentives and adverse weather. A further contributory factor was crop failures in many key producing countries in 1972/73. In the industrial materials sector capacity utilization was already at a high level before the 1973 surge in demand.

This price boom, which resulted from a unique combination of factors, disturbed a long-term downward trend in commodity prices. This trend has since reasserted itself, although there have been further

marked fluctuations, especially in foodstuffs. (The peak in 1977 was mainly due to steep increases in the price of cocoa and coffee following crop failures.) In 1984 real commodity prices were about 16 per cent below those of 1979 and 35 per cent below 1973, and a further decline occurred in 1985 and 1986.

The long-term decline in real prices has been most marked in the industrial materials sector, especially in metals. Excess capacity has become a feature of many metal markets. This has been largely due to the fact that over-optimistic forecasts of economic growth made in the early 1970s resulted in a major expansion of mining and refining capacity, particularly in the less developed countries. In the ten years to 1983, the less developed countries' primary aluminium production increased by 143 per cent, copper by 52 per cent and zinc by 126 per cent. Although the developed countries' capacity was slightly reduced, the outcome was a substantial degree of overcapacity.

Moreover, predictions of rapid resource depletion leading to rising prices, envisaged in the reports issued by the Club of Rome and other bodies,[5] have not so far been fulfilled. A combination of new discoveries, technological improvements and increases in the efficiency of extraction has meant that economically exploitable reserves of many non-ferrous metals have been relatively static or have actually increased. For example in 1980 copper reserves were equivalent to fifty-two years' consumption compared with thirty-seven years in 1966.

On the demand side, growth rates for many industrial materials have been tempered by technological change. Substitution by synthetic materials has been particularly important in the markets for fibres, rubber and metals. For example cotton's share of the total fibre market declined from 70 per cent in 1950 to less than 50 per cent in 1983, while natural rubber's share of the total elastomer market was halved from 66 to 33 per cent between 1950 and 1983.

The intensity of usage of many metals has declined steadily in the major OECD economies, partly because of substitution. For example since 1970, consumption of tin per unit of gross national product (GNP) has fallen by 45 per cent, nickel by 23 per cent, zinc by 21 per cent, copper by 20 per cent and lead by 14 per cent. (The exception is aluminium, which has increased by 11 per cent.)

The trend of production in foodstuffs has been upwards in recent years. Over the past two decades output has increased by about two-thirds (although the increase per head of world population has been much less). The major impetus to increased food production has been improvements in crop yields. For example the total area under wheat increased by 1.2 per cent a year in the decade to 1982, whereas the yield per acre rose by 2.2 per cent a year. Increased agricultural yields have resulted from improved plant strains, major irrigation projects, greater mechanization of production, the increased use of fertilizers and financial support from national governments and from programmes such as the European Community's Common Agricultural Policy.

Open and perfectly competitive markets

It would take far too long to make a comprehensive comparison between models of open and perfectly competitive markets, but three points may be made.

First, on the one hand there is common ground between the models in that in both product differentiation is limited and price is determined by the interaction of aggregate demand and supply. Similarly, in both models, the individual producer is seen as making a decision on output in the light of this price.

Second, on the other hand there is a divergence of view about the nature of this output decision. In models of perfectly competitive markets it is assumed that a producer can vary his supply by infinitely small amounts in arriving at the profit-maximizing position. In models of open markets it is assumed that such small adjustments are rarely possible. Indeed it may be impossible to adjust supply at all (supply is fixed) during the pricing season. Moreover – and this is an even more important difference – in many open markets output decisions are often made in ignorance as to what demand conditions will be when the production process is completed, and therefore of the price at which output will be sold.

Finally, some economists argue that despite its lack of descriptive realism, the model of perfect competition provides a bench-mark to appraise the efficiency of an economic system. The present author would not, however, agree with this claim since it is difficult to reconcile the assumptions of perfect competition with the conditions required for the introduction of new products and improved methods of production.[6] Although imperfections may sometimes reduce efficiency, there is no reason to think that an economy comprised entirely of perfect markets would be more efficient than one in which some imperfections exist.

Summary

1. Price discrimination denotes that different prices are set for different customers even though the cost of supplying these customers is identical. Profits can be increased by a policy of price discrimination provided that (a) the markets or submarkets supplied have different price elasticities of demand, (b) there is no leakage between the markets.
2. Different cost concepts apply to different types of price and output decision. Application of the concept of incremental cost shows that it may not always be clear whether differential pricing constitutes price discrimination.
3. In open markets there are few or no restrictions on the interplay of market forces. Open markets are characterized by a high level of uncertainty, at the time that production decisions are made, about future price levels, and by extreme difficulty in co-ordinating the activities of producers. In the short run supply tends to be inelastic. Consequently open markets are often subject to much wider price fluctuations than markets in which average cost is the basis of price.
4. The prices of commodities, many of which are sold in open markets, have in recent years been affected by severe imbalances between demand and supply. These price fluctuations have sometimes been accentuated by speculative activity.

Key terms

Price discrimination	Differential pricing
Subdivision of markets	Open markets
Incremental cost	Floor price
Escapable cost	Cobweb
Sunk cost	Speculation
Depreciation	

Notes

1. In practice sunk and fixed cost are seldom identical.
2. There is an analogy with an open economy which is more subject to market forces than a closed economy.
3. Edwards J, *Financial Times*, 13 Oct. 1981.
4. This diagram, and much of the accompanying commentary, appeared in *Barclays Review*, Feb. 1985.
5. Meadows D H *et al.*, *The Limits to Growth*. Earth Island, 1972; Goldsmith E (ed.), *Blueprint for Survival*. Penguin, 1973.
6. This was demonstrated in detail many years ago in Richardson G B, *Information and Investment*. Oxford Univ. Press, 1960.

Essay questions

1. State and illustrate the conditions that must be fulfilled if profits are to be increased by price discrimination.
2. Describe the various ways in which a market might be subdivided by a firm practising price discrimination.

3.   Explain why it may not be easy to decide whether the existence of price differentials indicates that price discrimination is being practised.
4.   Illustrate the type of decision for which the following cost concepts are relevant: marginal cost, incremental cost, escapable cost, opportunity cost.
5.   It has been suggested that all firms should adopt a policy of 'marginal cost pricing'. Discuss the meaning of this term and explain what problems might arise if such a policy were adopted.
6.   'Price discrimination can benefit both producers and consumers.' Discuss.
7.   Explain why many open markets are characterized by frequent price fluctuations.
8.   'Firms act as price takers in both open and perfectly competitive markets.' Discuss.
9.   'Charging half-price fares to schoolchildren at peak periods indicates that bus companies are motivated by considerations of equity rather than profitability.' Discuss.
10. Discuss the statement that in open markets prices are demand determined.

Exercises

7.1 The Road-Ready Tyre Company is a small company producing retread tyres. It normally produces about 1,000 tyres a week at a unit cost of £2.50, which are sold under its own brand name to wholesalers at a price of £3.50. The company has an unexpected opportunity to sell additional tyres under private labels to three retail outlets. Able's Auto Accessories offers to buy 1,000 tyres at £3.25; Baker's Car Accessories offers to buy 1,000 tyres at £3.00, and Charlie's Motor Spares offers to buy 1,000 tyres at £2.75.

The company has sufficient machine capacity to meet these orders. However, it will need to introduce overtime working, which will increase the level of costs. It estimates that the unit cost for the first additional 1,000 tyres will be £2.60, for the next 1,000 £2.70 and for the next 1,000 £2.80.

Which, if any, of these three orders should Road-Ready accept? (Carefully specify your assumptions.)

7.2 An engineering company which usually makes the major components used in the various machines that it manufactures wished to increase its weekly output of one particular component from 200 to 300 units. On this occasion it decided that it should seek a quotation from outside suppliers, and found that the best terms that it could obtain were:

100 units a week – £1.00 per unit
200 units a week – £0.90 per unit
300 units a week – £0.80 per unit

The company estimated its own cost of producing this component as follows:

Direct cost (labour and materials)	£0.50
Factory overhead (100% of direct cost)	£0.50
General overhead (20% of direct cost)	£0.10
Total cost per unit	£1.10

The factory overhead mainly comprised the depreciation of plant and equipment. Since this plant and equipment were used in the manufacture of a large number of different types of component it was not feasible to calculate a precise charge per unit of each component made. Instead factory overhead was levied as a proportion of direct cost. The same principle was applied to the allocation of general overhead, which mainly comprised central administrative expenses.

How many (if any) components should the company buy from the outside supplier if (a) it has sufficient excess capacity to allow it to increase production to 300 units a week, (b) in order to increase production it would have to enlarge its factory and install additional machinery?

7.3 The Johnson Leisurewear Co. make a wide range of sports and leisure wear – anoraks, ski-pants, sweaters, etc. There is a high fashion content in the company's products, which are usually priced towards the top end of the market. Because of the high reputation of its products, Johnson obtains a high volume of pre-production orders, and on the basis of these orders it is usually able to make a fairly accurate estimate of the total demand for any particular article over the forthcoming season. If any articles remain unsold at the end of the season it will dispose of them at a discount; however, the accuracy of its forecasting methods has meant that it has not usually had to make significant markdowns.

At the company's annual showing of the following year's range of products, a new style of anorak was shown, which utilized a new material, designed to give added warmth with no extra weight. This new material also enabled a printing technique to be used which could print in various five-colour combinations.

The new anorak was very well received by the buyers for the stores through which Johnson made most of its sales, and a pre-production order for 25,000 anoraks was placed. The anoraks were to retail at £27, and would cost the retailer £18. This was the largest pre-production order for anoraks ever received, and Johnson decided to make 30,000 articles. However, sales in the shops were by no means as good as had been expected, the main complaint of customers being that the multi-coloured patterns were too 'busy'. None of the retailers who had placed pre-production orders reordered, and other retailers bought only a further 2,000 garments. This left the company with 3,000 unsold garments, which had cost £15 each to manufacture. The marketing manager estimated that sales during the rest of the season, at various prices, would be as follows:

If price to retailer were	Estimated number sold
£18.00	200
£16.50	500
£15.00	600
£13.50	1,000
£12.00	1,300
£10.50	1,700
£9.00	1,900
£7.50	2,500
£6.00	3,000

At what price should Johnson offer the remaining anoraks?

7.4 The most common method of 'pricing' water used by UK domestic consumers is to fix an annual water-rate which is proportional to the rateable value of the premises being supplied. This annual payment is fixed regardless of the actual quantity of water taken by the particular premises. The water-rate is such that the total revenue from all consumers covers the total cost of the water provided by the supplier. Different rates are charged by different supplying authorities. However, within the area supplied by a given authority all domestic consumers occupying premises of a given rateable value pay the same amount.

(i)   What are the economic advantages and disadvantages of this method of pricing water?

(ii) What other methods might be adopted?

(iii) What would be the advantages and disadvantages of these other methods?

7.5   In 1982 London Transport were forced by a House of Lords decision to abandon their cheap fares policy. As a result of this decision fares were doubled, and this was followed by a 5 per cent fall in journeys.

In 1983 London Transport introduced, with the approval of the Courts, a modified package of cheaper fares. Many fares were reduced by a quarter and some, particularly on long Underground journeys, by a half. The 40p fare for central area Underground journeys was extended to cover twice the area (both the City and West End zones). The 40p bus fare was reduced to 30p, but the 20p fare was retained.

Travelcards were introduced, including one giving unlimited travel on buses and tubes throughout greater London, and another allowing a week's unlimited travel in the central area for £4.

Analyse the likely consequences of the cheaper fares (including Travelcards) introduced in 1983, making clear your assumptions.

CHAPTER EIGHT
Factor Markets

Introduction

In several previous chapters we have referred to the factors of production. In particular the demand and supply analysis presented in Chapters 5–7 included illustrations taken from factor markets. However, it is appropriate to devote a separate chapter to factor markets in order to emphasize the special characteristics of these markets. Consequently in this chapter we draw together the references made in previous chapters, and considerably extend the analysis, particularly with respect to the labour market.

The demand for factors of production

Factors of production, or inputs, are required not for their own sake but because they can be utilized in the production of goods and services, i.e. the demand for inputs is a derived demand. In many instances the chain of derived demand is very elaborate. For example the services of coal-miners are demanded because there is demand for coal; coal is itself demanded partly because there is a demand for electricity; one of the uses of electricity is to drive machinery used in the production of a wide range of products.

The marginal productivity theory

The individual firm is often unaware of the full complexity of this chain, and of the changes that may be occurring in it. Its demand for a particular input depends upon the value of the contribution made by that input to the firm's output – the higher the value of the contribution, the greater the demand for the input. If a change in the volume of output could be achieved by a change in the quantity of only a single input, it would be possible

precisely to determine the contribution made by that input. That is to say, it would be possible to measure the marginal physical product (*MPP*) of the input. This is illustrated in Fig. 8.1, where *MPP* shows the changes in the volume of output that would occur as the quantity of the input is varied. As we saw in previous chapters the term 'marginal' denotes a change of a single unit. So for example we see from Fig. 8.1 that an increase from nine to ten units of the factor would lead to an increase of five units in the volume of output, while the employment of a further unit of the factor would increase output by a further four units. The *MPP* of the tenth unit of the input is 5; that of the eleventh unit is 4. The *MPP* would generally be expected to fall as more of one factor is employed in conjunction with a given quantity of other factors.

To convert a marginal product curve into a marginal revenue product curve we multiply the change in the volume of

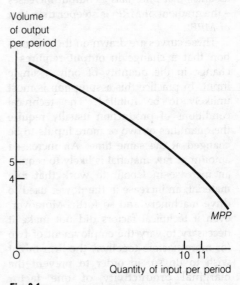

Volume
of output
per period

Fig. 8.1
Marginal physical productivity

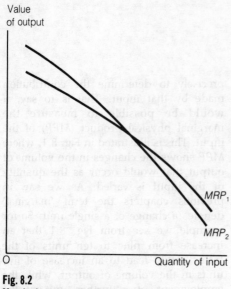

Fig. 8.2
Marginal revenue productivity curves

output by the price of the product. In Fig. 8.2 two marginal revenue product (*MRP*) curves are drawn which might relate to the *MPP* curve of Fig. 8.1. MRP_1 is drawn on the assumption that the price of the product does not change as output changes – the shape of the curve is the same shape as the *MPP* curve. MRP_2 assumes that price falls as output increases – the gradient of MRP_2 is steeper than that of *MPP*.

These curves are drawn on the assumption that a change in output requires a change in the quantity of only a single input. In practice this assumption is most unlikely to be fulfilled. The technical conditions of production usually require the quantities of two or more inputs to be changed at the same time. An increased amount of raw material is likely to require an increase in labour to work that raw material, an increase in the power used to drive machinery and so forth. Moreover, even if technical factors did not make it necessary to vary the employment of two (or more) factors together, the firm might wish to do so, in order to prevent the marginal productivity of one factor declining in the way indicated in Figs 8.1 and 8.2.

In some industries it may be impossible to establish an adequate measure of output. For example in education is it the number of students taught, the number of student hours or the number of students passing examinations with certain grades? A hospital may be able to increase the number of patients treated by reducing the average length of stay, but this could result in fewer patients making a full recovery. Is output the number of patients treated or the number making a full recovery?

The health service also provides a good example of the difficulties of trying to identify the output of a given worker, or even of a group of workers. What are the respective contributions to patient treatment of doctors, nurses, ancillary workers and hospital administrators?

However, although it may be difficult in practice precisely to identify marginal productivity, the theory gives a very useful insight into one of the major determinants of the demand for factors of production.

The supply of factors of production

Whereas a common framework, utilizing the concepts of derived demand and marginal productivity, can be used in analysing the demand for inputs, the supply of the various inputs or factors of production must be discussed separately, since the supply of each factor is subject to a different set of influences.

Land

As we saw in Chapter 2 land can be defined in several slightly different ways. If it is defined as the surface area of the planet, including oceans, lakes and rivers, we can treat it as being fixed in supply. Again, if it is defined as the area of dry land, it is virtually fixed in supply. On the other hand, if the quality of the land, its suitability for economic use, is taken into account, supply is more elastic. As we indicated in Chapter 2, the amount of land suitable for agriculture can be increased by good practice such as irrigation and the application of fertilizer; or decreased, for example, by too intensive farming leading to dust bowls. Land can also be made more suitable for non-agricultural purposes. Marshes can be drained and the terrain made more suitable for the building of factories and offices. (Note that when defined in this way, land includes the result of the application of labour and capital, which makes it difficult to measure the productivity of land alone.)

Finally, under an even wider definition, land would include the natural resources found on or under the surface – minerals, metals, etc. An area of increasing debate in recent years has been the danger of exhaustion of certain natural resources. This danger is clearly greater if we consider only the resources still remaining in the land and sea than if we take into account the recycling of waste or used resources.

Capital

Capital was defined in Chapter 2 as any resource, other than land and labour, that is used in the production and distribution of goods and services. It follows that there are many different types of capital services, e.g. machine-hours, railway passenger-miles. The flow of capital services is usually assumed to be proportional to the stock or volume of capital assets, but this is only approximately so. The flow of services also depends upon the number of hours for which an asset is used and on the quality of the asset – a new machine may yield more services than an older machine.

Labour

As we showed in Chapter 2, the most important determinant of the supply of labour in the long term is the size of the population. Over shorter periods the number of workers is determined by the age and sex structure of the population and also by such institutional factors as

the minimum school-leaving age, the age at which retirement pensions are paid, regulations concerning, and social attitudes towards, the employment of females, etc. The supply of labour is also determined by the number of hours worked per year by each worker. This depends upon the number of holidays and the average length of the working week. It may also be affected by the structure of taxation, as shown in Chapter 20.

The supply of factors of production to particular uses

All factors of production have alternative uses. Because of differences in demand these alternative uses normally offer different rewards. There will be a tendency for factors to move out of the uses which offer the lowest rewards and into those uses which offer the highest rewards. Equilibrium is established, i.e. such movement ceases, when the rewards to be obtained from different uses are equalized, rewards being defined so as to include both monetary and non-monetary components. Note that the non-monetary components may be positive – e.g. status, an interesting job, the ability to control the pace of one's work – or negative – e.g. dangerous or dirty working conditions.

How quickly a system moves towards equilibrium depends partly upon the pace of change on the demand side, and partly upon factor mobility. We briefly discuss the main determinants of the mobility of each factor in turn.

Mobility of land

Although land is physically the least mobile factor it is often highly mobile as between different uses. This is especially true of agricultural land where the farmer can normally choose from among a wide range of alternative crops at the beginning of each planting season.

Mobility is lower when land has been built upon. Changes in use do occur. Factories are demolished and offices and shops are built. Open-cast coal-mining stops and the land is returned to agriculture.

However, such changes take a much longer time and are usually much more costly than is a switch from one crop to another.

Mobility of capital

The mobility of capital depends upon several factors. The first is the number of different uses to which the particular plant or equipment can be put. For example a machine for cutting at the coal-face has a very specific use, whereas a computer can be used for a wide variety of data-processing operations. The second factor is the number of different industries in which the equipment can be used. Although a lorry may be used only for carrying goods, it may be used by firms in many different industries. Finally, physical or geographical mobility is important. Contrast the mobility of a tractor with that of a power station.

Although mobility is clearly a complex matter, there is no doubt that much capital equipment, once built and installed, is highly immobile, i.e. the opportunity cost of such equipment is likely to be low.

Mobility of labour

The ability of an individual to enter a particular occupation depends upon the extent to which his (or her) abilities, experience and training match the requirements of that occupation. The ability required might be strength, intelligence, steadiness of hand, etc. The training might involve an apprenticeship, an extended period in an educational institution, a probationary period 'on the job', etc.

The distribution of abilities in the population is such that the potential supply of labour to different jobs differs. These 'natural' differences in supply may be accentuated by the unwillingness of some potential entrants to meet the cost of education and training. Of the people who have the ability to become doctors only a small proportion apply for admission to medical school, one of the reasons being the very long training period involved. Even if the cost of training is met by the state, the training is not cost-less to the individual. There may be a substantial opportunity cost in terms of the additional income (salary minus grant) forgone during the training period.

In addition to these natural and self-imposed barriers, man-made or institutional barriers to mobility may be imposed. Let us consider further the education and training of doctors. In the UK, as in many other countries, there are sufficient places for only a minority of those who apply for entry to medical school. The decision on the number of places to be made available is taken by the government – not surprisingly in view of the fact that the cost of the facilities is largely met by the state. In its decision the government relies heavily upon the advice of civil servants concerning the country's need for doctors. It also receives advice from many other bodies, not all of whom define 'need' in the same way. For example the Patients Association, one of the representatives of the consumer, is likely to have a different view from that of the spokesmen of the doctors, such as the British Medical Association (BMA). One of the objectives of the BMA is the protection and improvement of doctors' incomes. This might help to explain why in the past the BMA has suggested that the entry to medical schools should be restricted in order to avoid the danger of an 'oversupply' of doctors.

Institutional restrictions on entry are frequently imposed directly by professional organizations and trade unions. Although such barriers may help to maintain the quality of labour, and thus benefit the employer and consumer, the protection of members' interests is usually a more important aim of these restrictions.

If we consider the labour force as a whole, mobility depends to a considerable extent, especially over the longer term, on the movements of those people who leave and enter the labour force. Mobility is enhanced if, upon retirement, people leave contracting occupations while those entering the labour force go into expanding occupations. If it is felt that the mobility arising from this 'natural' process is inadequate, governments may intervene in one way or another.

The determination of price in factor markets

Having discussed the major influences on the demand for and the supply of factors of production we can now examine how the prices of factors are determined.

In Fig. 8.3 the demand and supply curves relate to a given factor market, such as that for a given type of labour. The demand curve indicates the demand for this type of labour by a group of firms engaged in making a particular range of products, and reflects the marginal revenue productivity of this labour. The supply curve indicates the supply of labour to those firms. With demand D_1 and supply S, Q_1 labour is employed at price P_1.

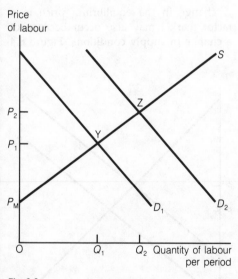

Fig. 8.3
An increase in the demand for labour

The effect of a change in demand

With demand and supply curves of this shape, the price of the factor will change as a result of a change in either demand or supply. For example an increase in

demand to D_2 causes an increase in price to P_2 and an increase in the quantity employed to Q_2. Demand may increase (or decrease) for several reasons.

A change in demand in the product market
As we noted above, the demand for factors is a derived demand, and an increase in the demand for a product causes an increase in the marginal revenue productivity of a factor (or factors) and hence in the demand for that factor.

Substitution
The demand for one factor may increase because it is substituted for another factor whose price has risen. The ease with which one factor can be substituted for another depends very much upon the technical conditions of production and the time-scale involved. For example if the wage rates of bus drivers and conductors increased it might be possible to reduce cost (or at least minimize the increase) by introducing one-man-operated buses, i.e. by substituting capital for labour. However, should a further rise in labour costs occur it would not be possible to reduce the labour content further.

Moreover, the increase in the cost of one factor may, even after substitution, cause the average cost of production to rise. If this increase in cost results in higher product prices, the volume of sales may fall. If this 'price effect' outweighs the substitution effect the demand for *all* factors (including the factor that has become relatively cheaper), is likely to fall.

This process can also operate in reverse. A fall in the cost of an input may induce a producer to substitute this input for others. If the reduction in average cost is passed on in the form of a lower product price, the quantity of the product demanded will increase. If this effect outweighs the substitution effect, the demand for all inputs will increase.

It appears that a rise in the price of labour relative to capital is one of the reasons for the long-term trend towards increasing capital intensity throughout the economy. Begg has estimated that between 1971 and 1981 the ratio of the wage rate to the price of capital goods increased by about 10 per cent. Over this period the real fixed capital per employee rose by a fifth in gas, electricity and water, by about a half in agriculture, forestry and fishing, and by over three-quarters in distribution and services.[1]

A second reason for the increase in capital intensity is technological change. Much investment comprises the installation of capital which embodies labour-saving techniques. This type of technological change may be autonomous, or it may be a response to an increase in the relative cost of labour.

The ultimate in the process of substitution in factor markets is where technological change results in the demand for an input disappearing entirely. Such dramatic changes normally occur only when 'input' is defined very narrowly, for example one metal may be replaced by a newly discovered substitute having superior qualities. Even here substitution in all uses would usually occur only over a long period.

A change in productivity
Another possible reason for an increase in the demand for a factor is an increase in its physical productivity. If we again take labour as an example this could be due to harder or more efficient working.

Transfer earnings and economic rent

In Fig. 8.3 P_M indicates the minimum price that would have to be offered in order to attract any of this factor to this particular use. This minimum price is known as the *transfer earnings* of the factor, i.e. the income that the factor could obtain if it transferred to another use or occupation (a suitable adjustment being made for any non-monetary rewards in the two uses).

The fact that the supply curve slopes upwards indicates that the transfer earnings of different units of the factor differ. As higher rewards are offered in this market

additional resources – resources with higher transfer earnings – are attracted. The total transfer earnings at any point would be given by the area under the relevant portion of the supply curve. For example if Q_1 units were employed, transfer earnings would be OQ_1YP_M. If Q_2 units were employed, transfer earnings would be OQ_2ZP_M.

The income obtained by a factor over and above its transfer earnings is known as *economic rent*. With Q_1 units employed, economic rent would be P_MYP_1. An increase in demand to D_2 would cause an increase in economic rent to P_MZP_2. It is not difficult to understand that the less elastic the supply of a factor, the greater will be the effect on that factor's price of a change in demand. Moreover the greater, as a proportion of the change in its income, will be the change in economic rent.

The effect of a change in supply

A change in the equilibrium price in a factor market may also occur because of a change in supply conditions. Figure 8.4

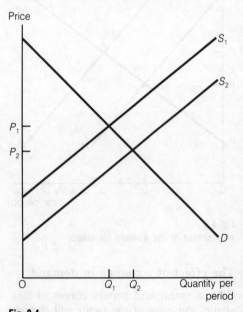

Price

S_1

S_2

P_1

P_2

D

O　　　Q_1　Q_2　　Quantity per period

Fig. 8.4
An increase in the supply of a factor of production

shows that an increase in supply would result in more of the factor being employed at a lower price. An increase in supply might occur for several reasons. For example an increase in the population of working age might lead to an increase in labour supply, new discoveries of mineral deposits to an increase in the supply of raw materials, and technological progress to an increase in the supply of capital goods. In addition to such influences on the total supply of a given input, the supply in one market will be influenced by conditions in other markets. For example if the demand for postmen declines this will lead to an increase in supply to certain other occupations, such as porters and drivers.

The elasticity of supply

The elasticity of supply is defined as the percentage change in the quantity supplied (per period) divided by the percentage change in price. Using symbols this can be expressed as follows:

$$E_S = \frac{\Delta Q}{Q} \div \frac{\Delta P}{P}$$

where Q represents the quantity of the factor supplied per period,
P represents its price and
Δ denotes a small change in the variable.

The shapes of the supply curves in Figs 8.3 and 8.4 indicate that the elasticity of supply of the factor is positive. An aggregate supply curve of this shape would be characteristic of many inputs. However, we have seen that the supply of a particular factor to a particular market may be subject to many influences, and it is therefore appropriate to consider the implications of alternative supply curves.

Figure 8.5 shows a completely (or perfectly) inelastic supply curve, such as might arise if the supply of new qualified people entering an occupation just matched the number leaving through retirement and death. An increase in demand from D_1 to D_2 would have a much greater effect on the income of workers in these circum-

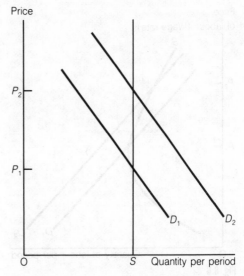

Fig. 8.5
A completely (or perfectly) inelastic supply curve

stances than it would if supply were less inelastic. (The same would also apply, of course, to a fall in demand.)

In practice the supply of labour is unlikely to be completely inelastic, because of the alternative jobs which are open to most people. However, the supply curve for a highly specialized occupation may well have a vertical portion, especially at the upper end in the short term. For example an increase in the demand for airline pilots would be unlikely to cause an increase in the quantity supplied for some time. (Note that in these circumstances the increase in the earnings of existing pilots would entirely comprise economic rent.)

Supply is more likely to be inelastic in the short than in the longer run. It follows that economic rent which is earned in the short run may disappear in the longer run as supply increases. The term *quasi-rent* is applied to such earnings.

A backward-sloping supply curve

In Fig. 8.6 we show a supply curve whose elasticity is positive up to price P_1, but negative at higher prices. As we indicated in Chapter 2, such a curve could indicate that the factor, labour, has a target total

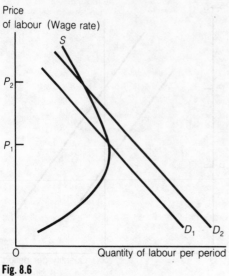

Fig. 8.6
Supply of a factor with a target income

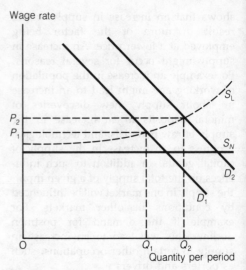

Fig. 8.7
Nationally and locally negotiated wage rates

income. Once this income is achieved, an increase in the price per unit causes less of the factor to be supplied. It has been observed that in dirty or dangerous occupations such as mining, or monotonous jobs such as car assembly, increases in wage rates have sometimes been followed by increased absenteeism.

A consequence of such supply conditions is that once wage rates have reached the level which yields the target income, employers are unable to persuade existing workers to work longer hours by increasing wage rates. (Increases in wage rates may, however, increase the number of workers willing to work for those employers, i.e. total supply would continue to be positively related to price.)

Finally, the supply of a factor may be completely elastic at a given price. This might occur in the market for capital goods where manufacturers' costs are constant at all levels of output, and where the price is fixed for a season.

National and local negotiations

The concept of a pricing season can also be usefully applied to the market for labour. In numerous occupations minimum wage rates are fixed following central negotiations between representatives of

employers and trade unions. In Fig. 8.7 S_N represents the minimum wage for the ensuing period, below which no labour would be supplied. This minimum wage may be supplemented by amounts negotiated at local or plant level. Plant bargaining is sensitive to conditions in the local labour market. The higher the demand for labour, the greater is likely to be the gap between the nationally negotiated minimum rate (S_N) and the locally negotiated rate (S_L), as shown in Fig. 8.7.

Trade unions and labour markets

Trade unions and professional associations may seek to influence labour markets in a number of ways. First, as noted above, they may lay down requirements that must be fulfilled by their members, e.g. in terms of education and training. Such requirements permanently reduce the supply of labour. The result of this reduction, represented in Fig. 8.8 by the shift of the supply curve from S_1 to S_2, is that fewer workers are employed but at a higher wage rate.

Second, as noted above, trade unions may centrally negotiate wage rates. In Fig. 8.9 the free market supply curve, S_F, indicates what supply would be in the absence of central negotiations. With

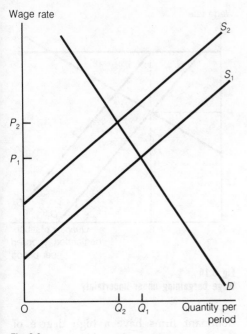

Fig. 8.8
A restriction on the supply of labour

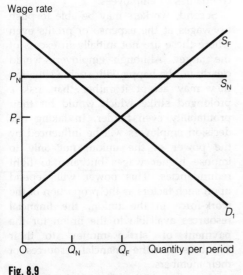

Fig. 8.9
The effect of central wage bargaining

demand D_1, this would yield an equilibrium wage rate P_F. The wage rate negotiated by the union, P_N, is above the free market rate. (We ignore any local negotiations in order to simplify the analysis.)

Consequently the number of workers employed falls from Q_F to Q_N.

Is Fig. 8.9 realistic? Would a trade union push wage rates to the point where the employment opportunities of its members were reduced? Our answers to this question will depend very much upon the assumptions that we make about the negotiation process, and in particular about the information available to the union.

One reason why the union might negotiate a wage rate P_N is that it might misjudge the state of the labour market, believing the demand to be stronger than it actually is. (It must be remembered that wages are often negotiated on an annual basis, so that the negotiators have to try to look up to twelve months ahead.) This may happen, for example, because union and employers fail to foresee a change in government policy designed to reduce the pressure on resources and because central bargaining may cause the market to respond less flexibly to the unforeseen circumstances.[2]

A rather more cynical explanation would be that the union was aware that the higher wage rate might lead to lower employment opportunities but that it was willing to accept this. It might do so if it believed that the reduction in employment opportunities would affect only potential entrants or recent entrants who had little influence within the union.

The third situation is where employers concede higher wages in the belief that they can pass these on in the form of higher prices. If such a belief were justified, an increase in wage rates would be followed by a shift to the right in the demand curve so as to leave the equilibrium employment unchanged. Employers may take this view if they believe that the government is committed to a policy of full employment and to monetary and fiscal policies designed to bring this about. But although these circumstances may make it easier for unions to negotiate higher *money* wages, these are unlikely to be fully reflected in higher *real* wages. Indeed if all employers took a similar view of the economic conditions and all product prices rose to the same extent, the effect of the rise in money wages would be cancelled out. In practice it appears that unionized workers can retain some of the benefits of money-wage increases, as shown below.

Finally, unions may be able to increase wages without a loss of employment opportunities in the short term if technical conditions make it impossible to substitute other factors for labour. But again there is likely to be a bigger effect in the long term, since technical conditions are more likely to change so as to increase the scope for factor substitution.

The above lines of argument can be combined in an explanation that appears to be quite plausible. Drawing the demand curve as a single line, D_1, as we have done in Fig. 8.9, suggests that the factor's marginal revenue productivity, which forms the basis of the demand curve, can be precisely measured. In practice, as we noted earlier in the chapter, this may not be possible, if only because a firm seldom varies the employment of a single factor only. Moreover the quantity of a factor employed is seldom varied by only a single unit. Consequently it may be more realistic to think of the demand curve as a band, bounded by D_1 and D_2 (Fig. 8.10). (This would, of course, imply that there might be more than one equilibrium position.) Given this area of uncertainty the union may believe a claim for higher wages to be in its members' best interests. It may hope that the employer will grant an increase in wages to P_N without reducing employment.

Leaving aside the effect of uncertainty concerning the productivity of labour, let us consider the conditions under which an increase in wage rates is least likely to result in a reduction in employment opportunities for a group of workers, such as the members of a particular union.

First, employers may be earning profits in excess of their target profits. This is most likely to happen when competition in the product market is restricted, e.g. in highly concentrated markets in which the

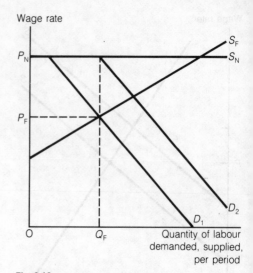

Fig. 8.10
Wage bargaining under uncertainty

dominant firms have a high degree of pricing discretion. In such instances a wage increase may result in some of the excess profits being transferred from companies to employees.

Second, workers may be able to push up wages at the expense of profits even where these are not initially in excess of the target. Although employers would clearly not be happy with such a situation they may accept it rather than risk a prolonged strike which would hit their profitability even harder. In taking this decision employers will be influenced by the power of the union, not only to impose higher wages but also to fight redundancies. This power will depend upon such factors as the proportion of the work-force in the union, the financial resources available to the union for the payment of 'strike money' to their members and the financial resources of their members.

However, although the balance of power between unions and employers may have a crucial effect in the short term, other considerations are likely to be more important in the longer term. If profits remain depressed, companies' investment expenditure is almost certain to fall. This fall in investment will in turn reduce employment opportunities as companies become less competitive in national and/or international markets.

The structure of earnings in the UK

We have discussed various factors which might influence the rewards to factors of production, and especially to labour. We now examine various aspects of the structure of earnings in the UK. We do not go into fine detail since this would involve the consideration of even more explanatory factors. For example if we looked at an individual firm we might find that earnings were affected by the nature of the firm's internal labour market (recruitment and promotion policies), by the aptitude and attitude of individual workers, by group norms, etc. We examine broader aspects of the structure of earnings: the occupational distribution, male–female differentials, the earnings of young workers and the differentials between members of trade unions and non-members.

Occupational earnings

Table 8.1 gives details of average earnings in a number of occupations. It can be seen that earnings are over a third higher in non-manual than in manual occupations. This reflects the fact that overall non-manual occupations require more education and training, which reduces the supply to these occupations.

Of the individual occupations listed, medical practitioners had by far the highest earnings, well ahead of two other groups in the same industry, nurses and hospital porters. This again reflects differences in education and training, as well as in aptitude. In some instances education acts as a screening or signalling device. It helps to identify people who are likely to be capable of undertaking demanding tasks; for example students obtain good grades in examinations partly because they can absorb large amounts of information and work well under pressure. In

Table 8.1
Average gross weekly earnings of full-time males on adult rates

Occupation	Average earnings (£)
Medical practitioners	425
University academic staff	321
Mechanical engineers	286
Scientists and mathematicians	281
Primary teachers	227
Managers – department store, supermarket, etc.	220
Toolmakers, tool fitters, etc.	197
Plumbers, pipe fitters	186
Laboratory technicians	185
Motor vehicle mechanics (skilled)	164
Registered and enrolled nurses, midwives	164
Carpenters and joiners – building and maintenance	160
Painters and decorators	150
Refuse collectors, dustmen	147
Caretakers	136
Hospital porters	126
Salesmen, shop assistants, shelf fillers	126
General farm-workers	121
All non-manual occupations	245
All manual occupations	171
All occupations	208

Source: New Earnings Survey, 1986

addition education may impart specific skills and knowledge which are useful in the student's future profession. This is clearly true of the education of medical students.

University academic staff have a longer period of education and are more highly qualified than another group in the education sector, primary teachers. Other professional groups with high earnings include mechanical engineers, and scientists and mathematicians. Note the lower earnings of laboratory technicians who often support the work of scientists and engineers.

The premium paid for managerial abilities is illustrated by a comparison between the earnings of department store and supermarket managers on the one hand and salesmen, shop assistants and shelf fillers on the other.

In the manual occupations the earnings of craftsmen are considerably greater than those of non-craftsmen. Moreover, there are substantial differences within each group. Compare the earnings of toolmakers and tool fitters, who in many factories are the élite of craftsmen, undergoing a very long training period, with those of motor-vehicle mechanics, carpenters and joiners, and painters and decorators.

Within the non-craftsmen group, refuse collectors and dustmen earn more than other groups such as caretakers and general farm workers. This differential is due partly to the unpleasant nature of the job and partly to the fact that most dustmen benefit from payment-by-result schemes; payments under these schemes accounted for around a quarter of their total earnings.

Male–female differentials

In Table 8.2 the average gross earnings of females are given as a percentage of the earnings of males (the data relate to full-time employees over 18, and excludes

overtime payments). It can be seen that the earnings of women relative to those of men rose appreciably in the early 1970s at the time when the initial effects of the Equal Pay Act were being seen, but since 1975 there has been little change.

The Equal Pay Act, passed in 1970 and implemented from 1975, provided for equal pay where a woman did the same work as a man or where her work was rated as equivalent to his under a job evaluation scheme. The fact that women's earnings are a quarter less than those of men might suggest that the work done by women is not equivalent to that done by men. However, this is not the only explanation. There are differentials in occupations in which it is difficult to believe that women do not do the same (or equivalent) work as men. For example female nurses and midwives earn 10 per cent less than their male colleagues (overtime earnings excluded), while the differential is more than 10 per cent for chefs and cooks, for records and library clerks and as much as 20 per cent for laboratory technicians.

What other factors might explain these differences in earnings? One possibility is that men tend to occupy more responsible, and hence better-paid, jobs within an occupation, even when that occupation is defined narrowly. This could be due to the fact that men have been promoted more often, or have progressed further up the salary scale attached to a particular job. Both these things could happen if women take substantial periods of time off work (i.e. several years) to bring up their families.

Faster promotion for men could also occur because employers, anticipating that women will take more time off work than men, are more willing to provide the training required to prepare employees for promotion (to invest in human capital). It is a moot point as to whether this constitutes discrimination. Some women do not take more time off work than their male colleagues, and it is easy to see why they may feel discriminated against if they are not given the same opportunities for training. On the other hand, it seems

Table 8.2
Women's earnings as a percentage of men's earnings

1970	63.1	1983	74.2
1975	72.1	1984	73.5
1980	73.5	1985	74.1
1981	74.8	1986	74.3
1982	73.9	1987	73.6

Source: Employment Gazette, 1987

reasonable that employers should invest more in training men if the overall return from this investment in human capital is expected to be greater.

To summarize, the differences in earnings shown in Table 8.2 may be due to a combination of three factors: differences in the occupational distribution of men and women, differences in the work done within a given occupation and differences in promotion rates (which may or may not constitute discrimination). Another possible explanation is that employers and/or trade unions practise open discrimination and fail fully to implement the 1970 Act.

Work of equal value
A challenge to the Act itself was successfully mounted by the European Commission which alleged that the Act was

not in accordance with article 119 of the Treaty of Rome which says that men and women should receive equal pay for equal work, i.e. for work of equal value. The European Court ruled against the UK in 1982. Subsequently the Equal Pay (Amendment) Act was passed, and since 1984 any worker has been able to claim equality of pay with a worker of the opposite sex on the ground that their jobs are of equal value.

Other aspects of discrimination

The 1975 Sex Discrimination Act was intended to protect and improve the status of women in other respects. But this Act was also deemed to be inadequate by the European Court. In one case two women employed by Lloyds Bank

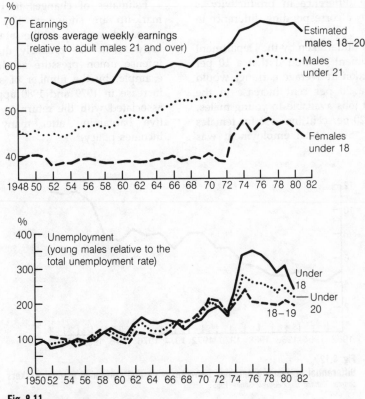

Fig. 8.11
Young males: earnings and unemployment
Source: published in *Financial Times*, 20 Dec. 1983

successfully argued that the bank's occupational pension scheme discriminated in
favour of men. In another case a female
employee of the National Health Service
who had been forced to retire at 62,
successfully argued that the retirement
age should be the same for both sexes.
The UK subsequently introduced legislation to this effect, and it may be that this
will eventually lead to state retirement
pensions being payable to both sexes at
the same age.

The earnings of young workers

Figure 8.11 shows that the earnings of
young workers have risen relative to those
of adult workers. This may be one reason
for the faster rise in unemployment
among young people. Since the
productivity of young workers is often
below that of more experienced workers,
firms will prefer to employ older workers
unless the difference in productivity is
matched by a corresponding difference in
wage rates.

A study undertaken by the Department
of Employment concluded that a 10 per
cent reduction in average earnings would
result in a 20 per cent increase in the
number of jobs available to young males,
and a 15–20 per cent increase for females
under 18.[3] Since total employment was
assumed to be unchanged the younger
workers would benefit at the expense of
older workers.

Trade unions and earnings

We showed above that trade unions might
influence earnings directly via wage negotiations or indirectly by restricting the
supply of labour. The most comprehensive study of the impact of union activity
is probably that undertaken by Stewart.
He found that in 1975 when account was
taken of other influences, e.g. the size of
plant and the degree of monopoly, union
membership was associated with an
average 'mark-up' of 8 per cent.[4] However,
the mark-up for individual industries
ranged from 18 per cent in shipbuilding
to minus 5 per cent in coal and petrol
products, and these mark-ups did not
seem to be related to the density of union
membership.

Estimates of changes in the average
mark-up are shown in Fig. 8.12. The
increased mark-up in the late 1960s and
early 1970s was probably due to more
intense union pressure as denoted, for
example, by the number of strikes. The
increase in 1979 and 1980 appears to be
associated with the return to free collective bargaining after many years of
incomes policy.[5]

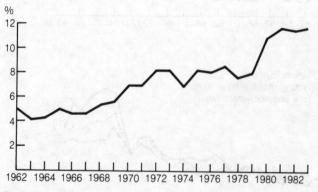

Fig. 8.12
Differential in average earnings between union and non-union manual workers
Source: Midland Bank Review, Spring 1985

Summary

1. A firm's demand for an input depends upon the value of the input's contribution to output, and especially its marginal productivity. As the amount of an input employed increases, its marginal productivity declines; hence the demand curve slopes down from left to right.

2. In practice there are immense difficulties in measuring marginal productivity, since firms seldom vary their employment of a single factor only. Moreover in some industries it may be impossible to establish an adequate measure of output.

3. The supply of each factor of production – land, labour and capital – is subject to a separate set of influences. But the supply of each responds to an increase in potential rewards.

4. The equilibrium price is the price at which the demand for a factor equals its supply. The equilibrium price, and the amount of the factor employed, may change for various reasons. There may be a change in demand for the products in whose supply the factor is used. One factor may be substituted for another because of a change in relative prices. Technological change may lead to investment in labour-saving plant and equipment. The productivity of the factor may change, e.g. labour productivity may change because of changed work practices.

5. The minimum price required to attract a factor to a particular use is known as its transfer earnings. Any income received by the factor in excess of transfer earnings is known as economic rent.

6. The more inelastic is the supply of a factor, the greater will be the impact on its earnings of a given change in demand. Supply is more likely to be inelastic in the short than in the longer run. Economic rent which is earned in the short run may therefore disappear in the longer run. Such earnings are termed quasi-rent.

7. Trade unions and professional associations may influence labour markets in various ways, but especially by specifying criteria for membership and by centrally negotiating wage rates. If they succeed in raising real wages this is likely to be at the expense of employment.

8. In the UK earnings are more than one-third higher in non-manual than in manual occupations, partly because of the greater degree of education and training required for non-manual occupations. Similarly, men's earnings are about one-third higher than those of women. This difference may be due to differences in the occupational distribution of men and women, differences in the work done within a given occupation and differences in promotion rates. Another possible explanation is that employers and/or trade unions practise discrimination.

9. A reduction in the differential in earnings between young and adult workers may be one of the reasons for the faster rate of growth in unemployment among young people.

Key terms

Marginal physical productivity	Quasi-rent
Marginal revenue productivity	Trade unions
Factor mobility	Central wage bargaining
Substitution	Structure of earnings
Transfer earnings	Differentials
Economic rent	Work of equal value
Elasticity of supply	Discrimination

Notes

1. Begg D, Fischer S, Dornbush R, *Economics*. McGraw-Hill, 1984, pp. 288–9.
2. This is a particular example of a general tendency for central bargaining to introduce an element of rigidity into the labour market.
3. Wells W, *The Relative Pay and Employment of Young People*. Department of Employment Research Paper No. 42, 1983.
4. Steward M B, Relative earnings and individual union membership in the UK, *Economica*, 1983.
5. Metcalf D and Nickell S J, Jobs and pay, *Midland Bank Review*, 1985.

Essay questions

1. Assess the usefulness of the marginal productivity theory as an explanation of the demand for factors of production.
2. Why do different wage rates exist in different occupations?
3. Analyse the possible effects of an increase in labour productivity on the demand for (a) labour, (b) other factors.
4. How would you expect a fall in demand for coal to affect the incomes of (a) coal-miners, (b) secretarial staff employed in the mining industry?
5. Explain the relationship between the elasticity of supply of a factor and economic rent.
6. 'The earnings of pop stars are almost entirely economic rent.' Discuss.
7. Analyse the relationship between technological progress and the demand for capital goods.
8. Discuss the ways in which trade unions can influence the supply of labour.
9. In what circumstances are trade unions most likely to be able to achieve an increase in the real incomes of all their members?
10. 'Trade unions can increase the wage rates of their members only at the expense of a reduction in employment.' Discuss.

Exercises

8.1

No. of workers	Expected yield (tonnes)
1	100
2	150
3	180
4	205
5	220
6	225

The above table shows the yield of wheat expected from a farm if different numbers of workers were employed.
  (i) If the farmer expected to obtain a price of £100 per tonne of wheat, how many workers would he employ at an annual wage of (a) £1,000, (b) £2,000?
  (ii) How many would he employ in each case if he expected the price of wheat to be £50 a tonne?

8.2 A beet sugar factory extracts sugar from beet by slicing the beets and washing them in large vats of circulating water. The water is subsequently evaporated, leaving the residue of sugar. The more water used, the greater the quantity of sugar obtained from a given quantity of beet, as shown in the table below.

Water used (000 gallons)	Sugar recovery (%)
500	70
540	71
585	72
635	73
695	74
770	75
860	76
970	77
1100	78

The factory uses 20 tonnes of beet per day, the sugar content of which is estimated as 1 per cent by weight. The value of the raw sugar extracted is £5,000 per tonne. Given that water costs 2p per thousand gallons, and that the fuel cost for evaporation, etc. is 8p per thousand gallons, calculate (a) how much water per day the factory should use; (b) how much sugar per day will be produced.

8.3 In Fig. 8.13 the line labelled 100 indicates the various combinations of two factors, X and Y, which would be required to produce 100 units of a certain product. The price of factor X divided by the price of factor Y is equal to OA/OB.

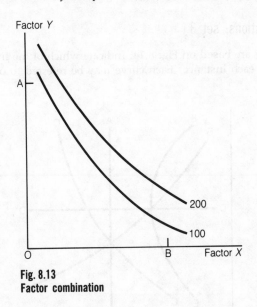

Fig. 8.13
Factor combination

(i) How would you account for the shape of line 100?

(ii) Given the existing prices, profit maximization requires an output of 100 units. Reproduce the diagram, and show what combination of the two factors will be employed.

(iii) The prices of the factors remaining unchanged, a change in demand results in an increase in the profit-maximizing output to 200 units. Indicate what combination of the two factors will now be employed. How would this combination have been affected had factor *Y* become more expensive and factor *X* less expensive?

8.4 What factors might account for the differences in earnings shown in Table 8.3?

Table 8.3
Average hourly earnings, full-time adult males
(excluding effect of overtime)

Occupation	Hourly earnings (p)
Technical sales representatives	627
Other sales representatives and agents	573
Roundsmen and van salesmen	353
Salesmen, shop assistants, shelf fillers	305
Postmen, mail sorters, messengers	375
Ambulance men	435

Source: New Earnings Survey 1986

Objective test questions: set 3

Questions 1–7 are based on Fig. 8.14. Indicate which of the five curves A to E is referred to in each instance. Each curve may be referred to once, more than once, or not at all.

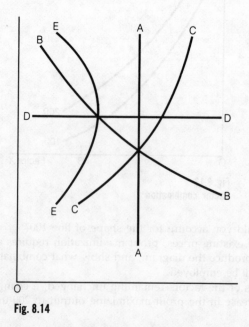

Fig. 8.14

1. A supply curve for labour when workers have a fixed target income.
2. A supply curve for wool sold by auction.
3. A supply curve for a product whose producer enjoys substantial economies of scale.
4. A supply curve when producers maintain a given price regardless of demand conditions.
5. A market demand curve for a Giffen good.
6. A market demand curve for a normal good.
7. A firm's demand curve in a perfectly competitive market.

   Questions 8–11 are based on Fig. 8.15, in which the unbroken lines represent the initial conditions of demand and supply in the market for postmen. The broken lines represent new demand and supply conditions that might apply after the changes listed below have occurred. Starting each time from the initial equilibrium position X, indicate the new equilibrium position A, B, C, D or E. (Each letter may apply once, more than once, or not at all.)

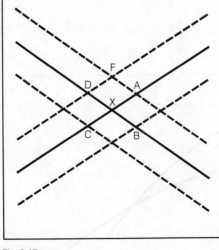

Fig. 8.15

8. An increase occurs in the number of letters posted.
9. Employers offer higher wages in other jobs that could be filled by postmen.
10. The official age of retirement for men is reduced.
11. The number of letters posted remains constant despite an increase in postal charges.

    Questions 12 and 13 relate to Fig. 8.16 in which *D* indicates the demand for, and *S* the supply of, a factor of production.

12. The economic rent obtained by this factor is:
    A   ORTQ;
    B   OPXT;
    C   RPXT;
    D   RPX;
    E   RXT.

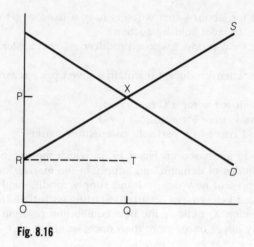

Fig. 8.16

13. The transfer earnings of the factors are:
    A   ORTQ;
    B   OPXT;
    C   RPXT;
    D   RPX;
    E   ORXQ.

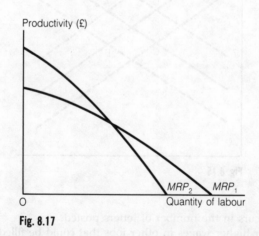

Fig. 8.17

14. Figure 8.17 shows the marginal revenue productivity of labour in a certain firm in two time periods. The shift from MRP_1 to MRP_2 could have been due to the fact that:
    1   the firm substituted capital for labour;
    2   the efficiency of labour increased at all levels of output;
    3   the demand for the firm's products became less price elastic.

15. An increase in the demand for one factor of production could arise following:
    1   an increase in the productivity of that factor;
    2   an increase in the price of the products made by that factor;
    3   a fall in the price of other factors.

16.   The supply curve for labour shown in Fig. 8.18 could reflect the fact that:
   1   fixed workers have a target income;
   2   leisure and income are complementary goods;
   3   higher wages lead to higher productivity.

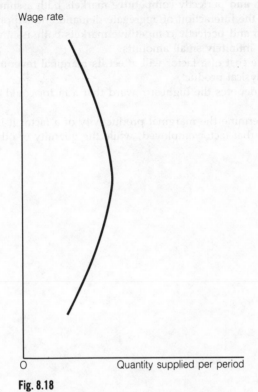

Fig. 8.18

17.   The marginal physical productivity of a factor depends upon both the volume of output and the price at which that output is sold.
      The marginal physical productivity of a factor normally falls as more of the factor is added to fixed quantities of other factors.
18.   An increase in the price of one factor can never cause the demand for another factor to fall.
      A change in the relative prices of factors usually has a substitution effect.
19.   If the total rewards of a factor of production remained unchanged an increase in its transfer earnings would imply a fall in its economic rent.
      The total rewards of a factor of production comprise transfer earnings plus economic rent.
20.   In a perfectly competitive market the firm's marginal revenue curve is horizontal.
      In a perfectly competitive market, market demand is completely elastic.

True/false

1.   In open markets cost has no influence on price.
2.   When a given quantity is supplied regardless of the price, supply is said to be completely inelastic.

3. The demand for all factors of production is a derived demand.
4. The more elastic the supply of a factor the greater will be the change in economic rent following a change in demand for that factor.
5. Price fluctuations increase over time in a divergent cobweb.
6. Models of open and perfectly competitive markets both assume that price is determined by the interaction of aggregate demand and supply.
7. Models of open and perfectly competitive markets both assume that producers can vary output by infinitely small amounts.
8. A change in the cost of a factor will affect its marginal revenue product but not its marginal physical product.
9. Economic rent denotes the highest reward that a factor could obtain in an alternative use.
10. In order to determine the marginal productivity of a factor it is necessary to vary the quantity of that factor employed, while the quantity of other factors remains unchanged.

CHAPTER NINE
Market Failure and Government Intervention

Introduction

In earlier chapters we have discussed various aspects of the price mechanism as it operates in product and factor markets. We have shown that in free market and mixed economies the price mechanism plays an important role in the allocation of resources. However, we have also noted that the price mechanism may have undesirable aspects which lead governments to intervene in order to influence or modify the operation of the mechanism, i.e. in order to remedy *market failure*.

Intervention may occur at various levels. As we show later, macro-economic policy is designed to influence broad economic aggregates such as consumption, investment and aggregate demand. Some macro-economic policies may influence the allocation of resources as between markets, for example by the imposition of indirect taxes, but this is not the primary purpose of these policies.

By contrast micro-economic policies are mainly concerned with the operation of particular markets or even with the activities of certain firms within those markets. The implication of intervention at this level is that the operation of the price mechanism has led to an unsatisfactory allocation of resources in those markets. We expand this point below, but first we refer briefly to the supply-side policies discussed in Chapter 24.

Supply-side measures are designed to increase the quantity of inputs (especially labour) and of output at any given price. Since the effect of these measures can be illustrated by reference to individual markets, a tendency has developed to include the measures within micro-economic policy. Although there is some justification for this approach, the primary purpose of many supply-side

measures, for example reductions in direct tax rates, is to increase *aggregate* supply. We therefore consider most of these measures as part of macro-economic policy. (Macro policy also includes measures whose primary purpose is to influence *aggregate* demand.)

Market failure has numerous aspects, as we shall see. But the thread running through all these aspects is that the price and output resulting from the operation of market forces are considered to be unsatisfactory.

Merit goods

Merit goods are goods whose consumption the government wishes to encourage. Consumption may be encouraged for two reasons. First, the government may believe that it knows better than the consumer what is in his or her interests. Many economists are suspicious of this argument; since a person's desires and motivations can be known only by that person, he or she is in the best position to judge what actions are most likely to be consistent with these desires. However, this need not always be so. It is possible that individuals may lack information about the probable consequences of their actions. For example a person *may* obtain more benefits from education, including the chance of obtaining a more highly paid job, than he anticipates. Again a person may underestimate the benefits likely to follow from receiving medical treatment, including being able to work more effectively and so earn a higher income.

If the government believes itself to be a better judge of the benefits from consumption, it may modify market forces in order to bring about a reduction in the price of the product concerned. (In some instances the government overrides market forces. For example in the UK people up to the age of 16 are compelled to 'consume' education.)

The modification of market forces is illustrated in Fig. 9.1, where ATC denotes the average cost that would be incurred by private sector suppliers of medical facilities. If the supplier added a profit margin CP_1, the supply curve would be S_1, and the equilibrium price P_1. With demand D, quantity Q_1 would be bought.

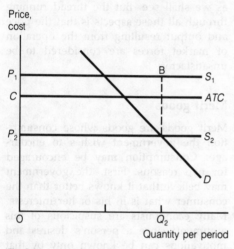

Fig. 9.1
A subsidized merit good

At the lower price P_2, Q_2 would be bought. To achieve this lower price a subsidy of P_2P_1 per unit would be required. In principle this subsidy could be given to private sector producers. In practice, where a large subsidy is required it is more usual for the goods or services to be supplied by public sector producers.

External benefits

The government may also intervene to increase the consumption of a product because it gives rise to external benefits, i.e. benefits which accrue to individuals or groups of individuals other than through market transactions.

External benefits and resource allocation

In Fig. 9.2 the demand curve D_1 incorporates only the private benefits obtained by consumers of a vaccine giving immunity from a certain disease. Given supply S the free market equilibrium price would be P_1 at which Q_1 would be bought. However, D_1 does not take into account any external benefits. For example if some people are inoculated and thus gain immunity, there will be fewer potential carriers of the disease. This will benefit others to whom the disease might have been transmitted. Demand D_2 would take these external benefits into account.

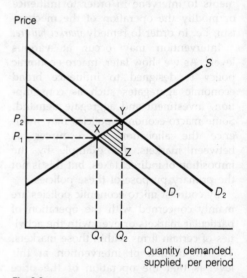

Fig. 9.2
External benefits and equilibrium

With demand D_2 the equilibrium price would be P_2, at which Q_2 would be consumed. The area XYZ indicates the additional *social* (private plus external) benefit that would accrue at the new equilibrium.

In principle the government could attempt to shift the market to the new equilibrium by increasing demand as shown in Fig. 9.2, either by entering the market as a buyer or by subsidizing individual buyers. But in practice governments often modify supply conditions, usually by subsidizing public sector producers, in order to reduce price and hence increase the quantity consumed.

The impact on resource allocation

A lower price affects resource allocation in a number of ways. First, and most obviously, the quantity of resources employed in the industry increases. (This assumes that demand and cost conditions would be the same whether medical services were provided by the public or the private sector. This assumption could, of course, be challenged.) It follows that fewer resources will be available for employment in other industries.

Second, the total amount spent by consumers on medical services will be affected. The effect will depend upon the size of the subsidy and the elasticity of demand for the product. Consequently we cannot say a priori whether total expenditure will increase or decrease. However, it seems clear that the low price charged for medical services in the UK has the effect of reducing expenditure by consumers. This means that the consumers of medical services will have more money to spend on other products.

On the other hand the cost of the subsidy must be met by taxation of one form or another (including National Insurance contributions). The effect of taxation is, of course, to reduce disposable income. Overall, therefore, the subsidy will cause a redistribution of real income and of expenditure.

Whether this redistribution is desirable depends upon the nature of the good or service, upon the form of subsidy and finally, of course, upon one's political and ethical views. In the particular example that we have chosen here the arguments in favour of subsidization are fairly straightforward. In terms of equity it can be argued that some people require more medical services than others – because of accidents or because they are less healthy constitutionally – and that it is unfair that

their ability to obtain these services should depend upon their income. It can also be argued that a healthy community is likely to be more productive – in other words that the provision of medical facilities is a form of investment and that the maximum benefit will be obtained from the investment by making the facilities available free or at low prices.

The critics of subsidies might make a number of points in reply to the above arguments. First, while recognizing that the cost of certain medical facilities, such as those involved in major operations, might be beyond the capacity of some citizens, they would point out that it is possible to subscribe to medical insurance schemes. Under these schemes the benefit payable (and hence the cost of the treatment that can be obtained) is linked to the contributions paid. It is then up to each citizen to decide how he should allocate his income as between medical insurance and other goods and services. To the argument that the incomes of some citizens might be inadequate to permit them to contribute to a medical insurance scheme, the advocates of the free market approach would probably reply that their incomes should be raised by means of a reverse or negative income tax. It might also be necessary to protect the interests of those citizens who were not earning – the unemployed, the retired and children – by paying contributions on their behalf.

With regard to efficiency, while acknowledging the link between health and productivity, the critics of subsidies might point out that there is no reason to think that a subsidized health service would lead to the consumption of medical facilities required to maximize economic efficiency. Indeed it is possible that better facilities would be provided under a free market system. This is an extremely complex issue to which a whole chapter, and indeed a whole book, might be devoted. We can do no more here than point to the fact that the proportion of the national product accounted for by medical services in the UK is only about half that in the USA, and that in some areas of the National Health Service in recent years an increase in spending appears to have been accompanied by an increase in administrative costs but not to an improvement in the service provided to patients.

Demerit goods

Demerit goods[1] are goods whose consumption the government discourages because of the disbenefit caused to the user, for example addictive drugs. In some instances consumption may be forbidden by law, in other instances it may be discouraged by means of heavy taxation (see Ch. 20).

Some economists would argue that if the disbenefit is purely private, state intervention is not justified; a man should be free to smoke himself to death. But in practice consumption often gives rise to external disbenefits or costs, e.g. drug addiction gives rise to crime. The existence of external costs (negative externalities) is a further justification for government intervention.

External costs

External costs are costs incurred by individuals or groups of individuals other than through market transactions. As noted in Chapter 2, increasing attention is being given to external costs arising from pollution of various kinds. External costs also result from the consumption of alcohol and tobacco which cause illness and so require extensive provision of medical facilities; moreover consumption of excessive alcohol by car drivers frequently results in injuries and deaths among passengers, the occupants of other cars and pedestrians.

In Fig. 9.3, which relates to the market for detergents, the demand curve D indicates the quantities that would be demanded at various prices, and thus has the usual meaning; S_1 indicates the quantities that producers would supply at

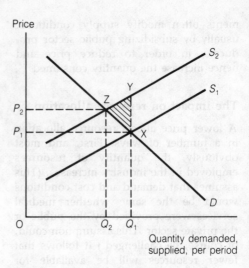

Fig. 9.3
External costs and equilibrium

various prices if they took into account only the costs that they incurred (private costs). The equilibrium output is Q_1. Purchasers are willing to buy this quantity at a price P_1, which covers the producers' private costs.

However, the production of detergents may also give rise to external costs, incurred other than through the purchase of detergents. For example the factories making detergents may discharge wastes into nearby rivers. This pollution may prevent anglers and swimmers from enjoying the amenities of the river and may prevent other factories lying downstream from using the water in their production processes. When pesticides and other chemicals were accidentally released into the River Rhine following a fire in a warehouse in Switzerland, 500,000 fish were killed. Moreover, immediate action was required in order to prevent the chemicals from entering drinking water in German towns bordering the river.

If the government could quantify the external costs and could make the producers bear these costs, i.e. if the costs were internalized, a new supply curve would result. In Fig. 9.3 supply curve S_2 takes social (private + external) costs into account. Price, P_2, is now higher, and the quantity traded, Q_2, is now lower than would be the case if producers took only private costs into account. The area XYZ indicates the external cost that is avoided.

In practice it may be impossible to bring about the exact adjustment in supply that would be required fully to reflect social costs. But governments *are* able to effect reductions in output. Requiring producers to install equipment in order to reduce the quantity of pollution will increase producers' costs and prices, and hence reduce the quantity bought; levying taxes on producers' output will have the same effect. Alternatively the government may limit output by introducing a licensing system.[2]

Public goods

Public goods have two essential characteristics. First, if the good is provided for one citizen, it is provided for all. This is known as non-excludability. Second, the consumption of the good by one person does not impede its consumption by others. This is known as non-rivalness.

The best example of a public good is probably national defence. If the government raises an army to prevent an invasion of its territory, all citizens benefit from this protection. I am made no less safe because my neighbour is made more safe. The services of a police force may also be taken as an example of a public good. However, the growth in recent years of private security organizations such as Securicor suggests that the condition of non-rivalness may not always be met. Presumably the firms who hire Securicor to protect their property feel that the police are so occupied in other duties that they may not be able to offer them sufficient protection.

Other examples of public goods include water-purification plants, barrages and dams to control flooding, and street lighting. The fact that such products are consumed collectively means that it is very difficult to finance their supply through the market. Take as an example

the construction of a barrage to reduce the danger of flooding. Let us assume that everyone likely to be affected by the scheme agrees that the project would be desirable, i.e. that the total benefits would exceed the costs of construction and operation.

On this basis a private firm might hope to raise sufficient money to finance the scheme. However, if it tried to raise the money in advance of the construction it would probably find that many of the potential beneficiaries would refuse to subscribe, even if they felt that their share of the costs would be less than the benefit of the project to them. They might argue that since their contribution was so small a part of the total cost, the project would be likely to go ahead even without their support; this would allow them to benefit from it without incurring any cost. (This is a particular example of a general problem sometimes known as the 'free-rider' problem.)

Faced with this reaction the firm would not undertake the construction of the barrage, since it would have no power to charge individuals for the benefits conferred by the barrage when built. A public authority, on the other hand, could undertake construction since it would be able to recoup the cost by imposing a tax of one kind or another on the beneficiaries.

Cost–benefit analysis

As shown above, free market prices may not reflect costs imposed on, or benefits enjoyed by, the community at large. One use of cost–benefit analysis is to measure (or at least estimate) external costs and benefits and so arrive at a 'price' that would reflect social (private plus external) costs and benefits.

As noted earlier, two important resources, air and the waterways, are frequently used for the disposal of waste products at a negligible cost to the polluter, but at perhaps considerable cost to the community as a whole. In other words these resources are underpriced.

Consequently there has been a strong trend in many countries towards greater government intervention, of one form or another, designed to reduce pollution. However, in recent years increasing attention has been given to the costs of intervention. It was estimated that the total cost to US business of complying with clean air and water rules would rise, in constant prices, from $19bn. in 1977 to $52bn. in 1986. If these additional costs are passed on as higher prices, they are ultimately borne by the consumer. In the USA a study by the Environmental Protection Agency estimated that federal anti-pollution laws would cause the 1986 consumer price index to be 3.6 per cent higher than it would have been in the absence of federal anti-pollution laws.

When the British government announced that lower limits for lead in petrol were to be introduced, as part of a programme to reduce the dangers to health, particularly of young children, from lead pollution, it was estimated that to meet the new requirements would cost the oil industry £200m. a year in additional crude oil and new equipment, and that the price of petrol would rise by 4p to 5p a gallon as a result.

Cost–benefit analysis and investment decisions

Cost–benefit analysis can also be used in investment decisions. It is possible that a decision which would not yield a satisfactory return at market prices would do so if all the external effects were taken into account. If a private producer is involved in the decision, the state might provide a subsidy to the investment.

If the investment is undertaken by a public sector producer the shortfall on revenue may be made up from the revenue obtained from that producer's other activities, or by a government subsidy. As an example consider the decision to build the Victoria Line on the London Underground system. This line was not expected to yield a private profit. However, an analysis undertaken after the decision had been made, suggested that the building of the line would increase total welfare, i.e. that a 'social profit' would result when external effects were taken into account. These effects included benefits both to users, which were not reflected in higher prices, and to non-users, such as a reduction in road congestion as some drivers and passengers switched from road to rail.

Some potential public sector investment projects, such as the building of a motorway, have no private benefits as measured by prices, since the 'product' is supplied free. In these instances cost–benefit analysis attempts to measure external benefits, to compare these with total cost and thus to arrive at a social rate of return.

Sometimes cost–benefit analysis may suggest that an investment project which would yield a satisfactory private profit ought not to be undertaken because of the external costs that would be involved. These costs might include a risk to health or life, pollution of various kinds and congestion.

Finally, cost–benefit analysis may be applied to alternative investment projects, such as the siting of the third London airport. The Roskill Commission, set up to advise the government, evaluated the costs and benefits attaching to four alternative sites. The costs examined again related both to users (in particular the time taken to get from the airport to central London) and non-users (especially aircraft noise).

Price controls

Governments might feel that the profits earned in a market are too high, causing price to be too high and, consequently, output to be too low. In this situation intervention might take the form of price controls. A product whose price has been frequently controlled is rented accommodation.

There are well-documented examples of high profits being earned by landlords, some of whom have resorted to dubious practices, including threats of violence against tenants.[3] However, there is little evidence that overall the returns earned by owners of property to let are above those yielded by other forms of investment. The tendency of governments to impose controls on the price of rented property probably owes more to the feeling that since it is a basic necessity, everyone should be able to enjoy at least a minimum standard of housing. Consequently, when the price of rentals rise, they are sometimes judged to be 'excessive'.

There is no doubt that some families, especially in London and south-east England, find it extremely difficult to obtain adequate housing. However, it does not follow that price controls are the best solution to the 'housing problem'. In fact it seems entirely possible that control will make the problem worse. The imposition of controls implies that the profitability of suppliers will be reduced, and this will tend to reduce the supply of houses, especially if only normal profits are being earned initially. So we find that in 1969 in New York City, about five times as many apartment units were abandoned by landlords as were built or rehabilitated in that year.[4] It is clearly possible that the benefit derived by some tenants from rent controls was outweighed by the distress of prospective tenants who could not obtain accommodation.

The UK housing market has had a not dissimilar experience. The control of privately rented accommodation was probably the main reason for the decline in the number of rented dwellings from 55 per cent of the housing stock in 1945 to 14 per cent in 1972 and 11 per cent in 1986. A reduction in rented accommodation tends to be a particular disadvantage to people setting up home for the first time, for example after getting married, and to people seeking to move to find a job.

This situation is illustrated in Fig. 9.4. In the absence of controls the equilibrium price would be P_1, Q_1 houses being

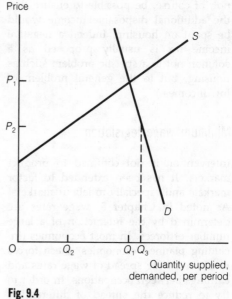

Fig. 9.4
The effect of price control

rented. If the government imposes a price ceiling P_2 only Q_2 houses will be made available for rent, leaving an unsatisfied demand of Q_2Q_3.

It may be possible to fill the gap left by private builders or landlords by expanding the activities of the public sector – in the UK this means mainly the local authorities. However, the provision of council houses is by no means an unmixed blessing. There is no guarantee that public housing will always be allocated to those in greatest need. Indeed subsidized rents provide an incentive to existing occupiers to stay put, even when their family and financial circumstances have become far more favourable than those of people on the authorities' 'waiting lists'.

It is conceivable that a better solution to the housing problem might be to improve the financial position of those people who cannot afford accommodation at free market prices. This might be done by altering the pattern of assistance available from the building societies, in such a way as to favour first-home buyers more strongly. Another solution might be to improve the incomes of the lowest paid by means of a negative income tax. (It would not, of course, be possible to ensure that the additional disposable income would be spent on housing. Indeed a negative income tax is usually proposed as a solution not to a specific problem such as housing, but to the general problem of low incomes.)

Minimum wage legislation

Intervention is not confined to product markets. It has been extended to factor markets and especially to labour markets. As noted in Chapter 8, wage rates are determined by the interaction of a large number of forces. In most economies (including planned economies) these forces result in a wide spread of wage rates and earnings between occupations. In order to try to reduce the spread of differentials some countries have introduced legislation specifying minimum wage rates. However, there are reasons for believing that this attempt to protect the lower-paid from the consequences of the operation of market forces may not succeed.

One possible outcome is that higher-paid workers negotiate pay rises which restore the differentials *vis-à-vis* the lower paid. If producers pass on the increased costs in the form of higher prices, the real incomes of the lower-paid will not have been improved.

Alternatively, if the lower paid do obtain an increase in real incomes this may be at the expense of the number of such workers employed. This is most likely to happen if the wage differentials are due to differences in productivity. If the wages of the lower-paid workers are increased, and there is not a corresponding increase in productivity, employers will dismiss workers, preferring to use more skilled workers or to substitute capital for labour.

Moreover, this response may occur even when there is a 'non-economic' reason for the differential. For example if employers have a prejudice against coloured workers they will employ such

workers only if they are allowed to pay them lower wages than white workers. Legislation which prevents this may lead employers to substitute white for coloured labour. In 1959 the minimum hourly wage in the USA was raised from 75 cents to $1. Subsequently a Department of Labor survey of twelve industries affected by the new minimum found that employment had decreased in all but one. The workers whose employment prospects were most affected by the legislation were black teen-agers.[5] A survey of thirty studies of the US economy arrived at the conclusion that a 10 per cent increase in the minimum wage would reduce teenage employment by from 1 to 3 per cent.[6]

This process is illustrated in Fig. 9.5. In the absence of government intervention the equilibrium wage would be W, Q workers being employed. If the government imposes a minimum wage of X, the number employed falls to R. (We showed in Chapter 8 that a wage increase might not always lead to a reduction in employment, especially when a trade union can prevent redundancies. However, we suggested that a reduction in employment was likely to occur, especially in the longer term.)

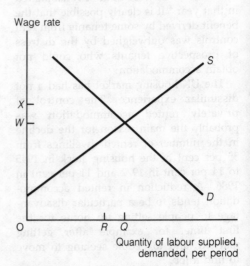

Wage rate

Quantity of labour supplied, demanded, per period

Fig. 9.5
The effect of minimum wage legislation

Limiting price fluctuations

We showed in Chapter 7 that large price fluctuations are far more likely to occur in open markets than in markets in which individual producers have a greater measure of influence on price. Sir Sydney Caine has recently given some examples of these fluctuations:

In 1968 the price in New York of sugar sold on the free world market was below 3 cents per lb; in 1974 it rose above 65 cents; in July 1978 it was under 7 cents. Coffee sold for under 20 cents per lb in 1947, over 150 cents in 1954, 35 cents in 1963, as much as 340 cents in 1977 and in July 1978 was quoted at about 150 cents. . . . Within four months in 1974 the price of copper fell from £1,400 per ton to £586.[7]

Fluctuations of this magnitude cause substantial fluctuations in producers' incomes. Since living standards are very low in many of the producer countries, reductions in income may have serious consequences in terms of sickness and even death. Moreover the fluctuations are a disincentive to investment by producers.

Price fluctuations can also be a disadvantage to consumers, and especially to the users of raw materials, who find it more difficult to plan their operations. To try to avoid the worst price fluctuations consumers may turn to synthetic substitutes, to the detriment of the producers of the natural product. In the 1970s the very high price of sisal caused many industrial consumers to substitute polypropylene. Producers of polypropylene responded to the increased demand by increasing their supply. This not only gave them a substantial share of the market but also caused a dramatic drop in the price of sisal.

It is therefore not surprising that numerous attempts have been made to reduce price fluctuations, especially by establishing buffer stock schemes.

Buffer stock schemes

Fluctuations in supply

A buffer stock scheme is operated by a central agency, national or international. This agency enters the market – as a buyer or seller – in order to maintain the target price, denoted by P_T in Fig. 9.6. Given consumers' demand D, the target price would be achieved with an output of Q. If output is above Q, say T, the equilibrium price would fall to P_L. To prevent this happening, the central agency will buy QT at price P_T, and add this to the buffer stock, i.e. the quantity supplied to the market is reduced. Conversely if, when output is R, the agency wishes to prevent price from rising to P_H it will release from the buffer stock RQ, which it will sell at P_T, i.e. the quantity supplied to the market is increased. (An alternative way of illustrating the agency's operations, namely via a modification of the demand curve, is presented below; see Fig. 9.7.)

Considerable difficulties may arise in operating a buffer stock scheme. If, as we have assumed so far, the only purpose of the scheme is to eliminate price fluctuations, the agency must be able to forecast what the average free market price would be over a number of years. This average

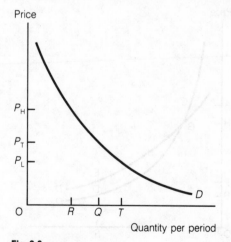

Fig. 9.6
The stablization of price

is the target price set by the agency. Unless it sets an appropriate target price, the agency's sales and purchases will not balance out over the years.

Furthermore, even if the agency is able to forecast the average free market price and thereby set an appropriate target price, the cost of holding stocks may be substantial. Indeed one of the major obstacles to an extension of buffer stock schemes has been the difficulty of reaching agreement on their financing. The richer nations have been unwilling to accept the share of the burden suggested by the poorer nations.

While a buffer stock scheme of the type illustrated in Fig. 9.6 eliminates fluctuations in price, it does not eliminate fluctuations in producers' income. Indeed, if price is maintained at a constant level regardless of output, the producers' income will change in line with output.

In order to reduce fluctuations in income following changes in output, the elasticity of demand must be brought closer to unity. Indeed if demand is of unitary elasticity revenue is the same at all prices. A demand curve having this property is a rectangular hyperbola, shown as D_1 in Fig. 9.7. Revenue at output Q (OQCA) equals revenue at output R

(ORDB). If, without the buffer stock scheme, the demand curve had been D_2, revenue at output R (OREF) would have been greater than at output Q (OQGH).

Fluctuations in demand

The schemes considered above are designed to modify fluctuations in prices or incomes arising from fluctuations in supply. Fluctuations in supply frequently characterize agricultural markets, especially foodstuffs. In markets for many industrial raw materials the main cause of fluctuations in price is fluctuations in demand.

Since open markets are sometimes supplied by a large number of small producers, it may be very difficult to adjust supply in line with demand. Figure 9.8 illustrates the extreme case where, in the absence of intervention, there would be no adjustment of supply, i.e. Q would be supplied regardless of the state of demand. If consumers' demand were at D_1, then in order to maintain the target price, P_T, the agency would be required to buy RQ, thus reducing the quantity supplied to the market to R. Conversely, with demand at D_2 the agency would be required to release QT from stock, increasing the amount supplied to the

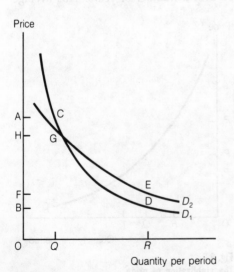

Price

Fig. 9.7
Stabilization of producers' income

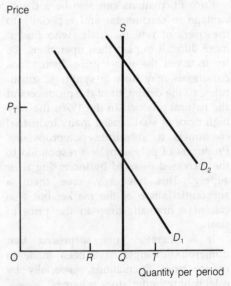

Price

Fig. 9.8
Stablization of price and income

market to T. (Note that in this instance, since the quantity supplied by producers is constant from one period to the next, stabilization of price also implies stabilization of producers' income.)

Cartels
Price fluctuations used to occur in the market for diamonds because of the difficulty of ensuring that supply varied in line with demand. The difficulty was overcome by the creation of a cartel, a unified selling organization, in 1930. The Central Selling Organization (CSO) now undertakes the marketing for all major producers in the Western world. It buys diamonds from the producers at a contracted price – the contracts being reviewed from time to time – and regulates supply in accordance with the state of demand.

Several factors help to account for the success of the cartel. First, the CSO is run by the dominant producer, De Beers, which accounts for more than a fifth of the total world output. Second, the demand for diamonds has increased substantially, the annual sales of the CSO having risen from £3m. in 1930 to over £1bn. by the mid 1970s. Third, the CSO engages in other marketing activities, e.g. advertising, in which there are economies of scale. Finally, the CSO's policy is never to reduce prices, a policy that is appropriate for a product bought for purposes of conspicuous consumption.

Buffer stock schemes in practice

We noted above that the central agency may find it difficult to identify and set an appropriate intervention price, and to obtain the funds needed to finance purchases on the scale required to support this price. A good example of these difficulties is provided by the Tin Agreement which collapsed in 1986.

The International Tin Council was established by the United Nations in 1956 as an agency to stabilize prices. In 1985, having accumulated stocks of 85,000 tonnes of tin, it ran out of money. Indeed it defaulted on debts of £900m. owed to

banks and metal traders. It is clear that the price at which the Council had bought tin was too high given the underlying demand and supply conditions. When trading was suspended in October 1985 the price was £8,140 a tonne, compared to the fixed price of £6,250 set by the London Metal Exchange in 1986 after the collapse of the Tin Agreement, and a price of £5,000 ruling in other markets.

The critics of international commodity agreements received support from an unexpected source in 1985, in the form of a report from the United Nations Conference on Trade and Development (UNCTAD), under whose tutelage many agreements were established. Most of the agreements involve buffer stock schemes and/or export quotas. The report reviewed the operation of ten agreements covering seven commodities and found that they had had mixed success in stabilizing prices in the short term. (Ironically the Tin Agreement was deemed to be one of the more successful ones at the time.) Moreover the agreements had done little or nothing to meet the longer-term objectives of improving the export earnings and competitive capacity of developing countries.

Other forms of intervention

As the UNCTAD report made clear many commodity agreements are intended not only to reduce price fluctuations but also to increase producers' incomes. This latter aim is even more important in some other forms of intervention.

Production quotas

If demand is price inelastic, producers may agree to restrict their output by means of production quotas, and raise their price in order to increase their revenue. This policy was successfully implemented in the 1970s by the members of the Organization of Petroleum Exporting Countries (OPEC). However, a number of

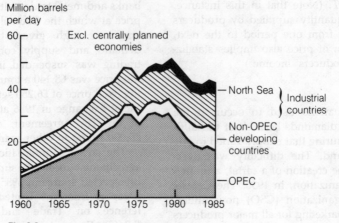

Fig. 9.9
World oil production
Source: Financial Times, 11 April 1986

subsequent factors combined to weaken OPEC's influence.

The steep rise in price encouraged the development of alternative sources of supply. The market share of OPEC, after rising from a third in the early 1950s to nearly two-thirds at the time of the first price shock in 1973–74, fell again to around one-third (Fig. 9.9). Moreover demand became far more elastic as time progressed, as some consumers turned to other fuels and as consumers became more efficient in their use of fuel. In OECD countries oil consumption per unit of output fell by nearly 40 per cent, and total oil consumption by almost 20 per cent, between 1973 and 1985.

Faced with this change in the balance between demand and supply, OPEC found it impossible to maintain discipline among its members. Several countries exceeded the production quotas that had been agreed to support the price. Iran, Iraq and Libya exceeded their quotas in order to finance military expenditure, and Nigeria to support its ambitious programme of economic development. Prices gradually weakened and eventually collapsed in 1986. (However, even then prices in real terms were still more than twice as high as in 1973.)

Land banks

Another way of trying to restrict supply and hence bring about an increase in price is by reducing the capacity of the industry. In agriculture this means reducing the land under cultivation, either by government edict or by paying compensation to farmers. The expense of compensation payments has meant that this policy has been mainly confined to richer countries such as the USA and Japan.

The justification advanced for the adoption of this policy in the USA is that higher prices are required to improve the living standards of the poorer farmers – usually those owning small farms. While the policy may have this effect, it is likely to be of even greater benefit to the richer farmers with big farms. They have more land to withdraw from cultivation and therefore qualify for bigger compensation payments. Lee and McNown quote the finding of C L Schultze that in the late 1960s 40 per cent of the additional income received by farmers as a result of government intervention went to only 7 per cent of the farms. In 1970 nine farms received subsidy payments of more than $1m. each. The average income of these recipients was, of course, substantially above that of the taxpayers who ultimately met the cost of the compensation payments.[8] It was estimated that the cost to the US government of the 25 per cent reduction in cotton and grain acreage in 1982 was $15bn. There was also a cost to consumers in the form of higher prices.

In 1987 the European Community agreed a scheme under which national governments, with the help of Community funds, would pay farmers to take cereal-growing land out of production. The UK government subsequently announced that British farmers would receive £200 a hectare a year if they agreed to take at least 20 per cent of their land out of production for five years.

Deficiency payments

Under this system producers receive a guaranteed price for their produce, governments giving subsidies to top up the market price as required. This system operated in the UK before she joined the European Community.

The effects of agricultural protection

The World Bank has constructed a model of supply and demand for grains, livestock products and sugar, which account for roughly three-quarters of world agricultural trade. The model was used to estimate the effects of agricultural protection by comparing the current system of protection with more liberal regimes. The results show that reducing protection would cause a market transfer of income away from farmers in industrial countries, but that this would be more than offset by gains to consumers and taxpayers as a result of overall gains in economic efficiency. The estimated efficiency gains if both industrialized and developing countries were to reduce protection were: to industrialized countries $46bn., to developing countries $18bn., to East European non-market economies minus $23bn., giving a total gain of $41bn.[9]

The World Bank report gave a number of specific examples of how protection causes the rewards to producers to become out of line with market prices. Japanese farmers receive three times the world price for their rice; so much rice is grown that some is sold for animal feed at half the world price. The US government subsidizes irrigation and land-clearing projects and then pays farmers not to grow crops on the land. Finally, two results of the Common Agricultural Policy (discussed in more detail below): Community farmers received 18 cents a pound for sugar in 1985; some of this sugar was then sold for 5 cents on the world market, while the Community was at the same time importing sugar at 18 cents. In some extreme cases, Community farmers have paid more to import feed for their cows than they would have received on the world market for their milk.

The Common Agricultural Policy

Price stabilization and the protection of producers' living standards are the two main objectives of the European Community's Common Agricultural Policy (CAP). Another important objective is to encourage structural improvements in farming. However, at present expenditure on structural aspects is only about 6 per cent of total Community expenditure on farming.[10]

The main features of the CAP price-support mechanism are as follows. First, a target price is set, which reflects the price which the market is intended to reach in the area where the product is in shortest supply, and which takes account of the estimated costs of production, transport and storage. Second, a threshold price is set which, when transport costs are added, will equal or slightly exceed the target price. If world prices are below the threshold price, an import levy equal to the difference is imposed. (See the right-hand column of Fig. 9.10.)

If supply exceeds demand at the target price, support buying becomes necessary.

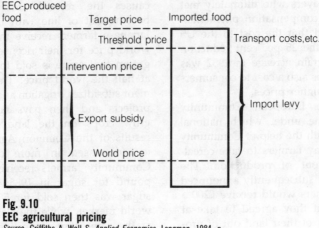

Fig. 9.10
EEC agricultural pricing
Source: Griffiths A, Wall S, *Applied Economics*, Longman, 1984, p. 461

However, the excess supply is bought not at the target price but at a slightly lower intervention price. This is shown in the left-hand column of Fig. 9.10. (In fact separate target and intervention prices are then set for each area of the Community. There are eleven such areas in the UK.) This column also shows that export subsidies are given for Community output sold into other markets. These subsidies are usually sufficient to bridge the gap between the intervention price and the world price.

The effects of the CAP

The guarantee to support prices at a fixed level has made it impossible to control spending, and annual expenditure has increased from about £8bn. to about £19bn. in the past seven years. This in itself has been sufficient to give rise to demands for the reform of the system. But the system can also be criticized on other grounds. A number of studies have shown that the CAP has reduced the level of economic welfare not only in the world as a whole but also within the European Community. The CAP has, of course, led to an increase in European agricultural output, but also to reductions in the output of the manufacturing and service

sectors. Overall, real incomes in Europe are lower than they would otherwise have been, and unemployment is estimated to have been increased by 1 million.[11] (The UK, with a small agricultural sector, suffered particularly badly in this respect, with an estimated increase of 16 per cent in the unemployment rate.)

These effects result from the operation of several mechanisms. First, artificially altering the balance of trade in agricultural products has caused a rise in the exchange rate of European countries which has made their other products less competitive. Second, the prices of commodity raw materials have been increased to between one and a half and five times world prices, imposing additional costs on industry. Third, higher real returns would have been obtained from investing in other industries. Finally, the CAP appears to have been of limited help to agricultural employment because it favours large, capital-intensive farms rather than small labour-intensive units.

One of the most obvious effects of the CAP is that support buying by the European Commission has resulted in mounting stocks of some foods, including over 1 million tonnes of butter, 800,000 tonnes of beef and 15 million tonnes of grain. Stocks of this size are clearly a political embarrassment, especially at times when people are dying from starvation. They are also a considerable financial burden. In 1985 the storage costs for butter, beef and grain amounted to almost £2bn., more than £7 for every man, woman and child within the Community. Total storage costs were projected at 15 per cent of the 1986 farm budget.

The Commission has tried to reduce stocks by various means. For example *ad hoc* measures to reduce the butter mountain have included cut-price sales to Russia, special offers to retirement pensioners and feeding butter to veal calves.[12]

The dilemma facing the Community is that special cut-price deals to reduce stocks might depress world prices and so increase the export subsidies paid to farmers making 'normal' export sales. (The same would also apply to a policy of giving away surplus stocks.) Exports from the Community also reduce the incomes of overseas producers, including many in low-income, less developed countries.

Despite these disadvantages and criticisms, the CAP is strongly supported by the governments of most Community members, who are aware of the importance of the farmers' votes. Agriculture is a more important source of employment in all other member countries than in the UK. For example in 1986 it accounted for over 8 per cent of the total labour force in France and Denmark, and 13 per cent in Italy, compared to less than 3 per cent in the UK. It is believed that the CAP has maintained farmers' incomes at a level above what they would otherwise have been, although farmers in most countries have failed to share in the improvements in living standards achieved by other workers.

Moreover, important structural changes have occurred. There has been a reduction of almost a third in the number of farm units since 1960, and a consequent increase in the average farm size. In the period 1973–82 employment in agriculture fell by over a fifth, and labour productivity increased by 50 per cent.

Stabilization schemes for industrial products

Stabilization schemes for industrial products are relatively rare since fluctuations in the balance between demand and supply tend to be much less pronounced than in the markets for primary products. But fluctuations do occur and this has sometimes led to government intervention. For example the European Commission imposed minimum prices for certain steel products, these prices being supported by reductions in production capacity. It is interesting to reflect that this restriction on price would have been illegal if it had been taken by a group of private producers (see Ch. 10).

The time dimension of the price mechanism

The rapid reallocation of resources in response to the signals generated by the price mechanism is said to be a main advantage of market and mixed economies. But doubts have been expressed by some economists about the ability of these economies to anticipate and adjust to future changes in demand and supply. It is argued that the price mechanism may not give sufficient advanced warning of these changes and that the adjustment process may therefore be slower than would be desirable. (A neat way of expressing this is that there may not be a satisfactory market in future goods.) This argument has been advanced most frequently in connection with energy supplies.

Energy supplies

Unlike many other material resources, the resources from which energy is obtained cannot usually be recycled (some nuclear fuels are an exception to this generalization). This might suggest that governments would be justified in controlling, or at least influencing, the rate at which these resources are utilized, and in subsidizing the search for alternative energy sources.

Particular concern has been expressed about the possible exhaustion of oil supplies, and various alternative sources of energy are being investigated including wave and wind power. Very substantial expenditure would be required for some of the proposed projects, e.g. several billions of pounds to finance a barrage across the Severn Estuary in order to generate electricity from tidal power. Since the construction period would be around twenty years, government involvement might well be necessary.

However, some economists are dubious about the alleged benefits of government involvement. They point to the fact that any forecasts of future supply (and demand) are subject to very large margins of error. Forecasters usually fail to predict technological changes that have a major impact on supply. Also they may underestimate the impact of price increases on demand, as happened with the OPEC-inspired increases in oil prices. (The rate of technological change may increase in response to price changes. For example, following the steep rise in the price of oil, Shell and Esso announced in 1981 the development of a new method of extracting oil from below the sea. Using robots which are able to operate at much greater depths than divers, it promised to lead to a substantial increase in oil production.)

Conservation of other resources

Concern has also been expressed about the possible exhaustion of other resources. It is sometimes claimed that resources will be used up more quickly, i.e. that conservation will be less likely, under a system of private than of collective property rights. The validity of this argument depends very much upon the form in which the collective rights exist. If they are vested in the government it will certainly have the *power* to control the utilization of resources, although it is by no means certain whether or how it will use this power.

If collective rights are not vested in a central authority, it seems that resource utilization and depletion are likely to occur *more* quickly than when there are private ownership rights. For example if a forest is privately owned the owner will take into account the cost of depleting the forest and is likely to try to regenerate it by planting new trees as mature ones are felled. If, on the other hand, the forest is collectively owned, each person will exercise his rights as fully as possible. Furthermore he will have little interest in regeneration since he cannot be sure that a private cost to him (planting new trees) will result in a private benefit, since these trees may be felled by someone else.

Conservation, substitution and recycling

The fear that, in the absence of government intervention, certain resources might soon become exhausted is sometimes expressed in very strong terms. Note, for example, the following passage: 'Present reserves of all but a few metals will be exhausted within fifty years if consumption rates continue to grow as they are.' Further, 'if current trends are allowed to persist . . . the breakdown of society and the irreversible disruption of the life support systems on this planet are inevitable'.[13]

While the increase in the world's population and in the level of economic activity have certainly led to a tremendous increase in the rate of utilization of resources, statements such as these appear to give too little weight to certain fundamental aspects of the price mechanism.

First, if the pressure of demand causes an increase in the price of resources, producers will have an additional incentive to search for new supplies. A good example of this process is the impetus given to the development of North Sea oil by the increase in the price of OPEC oil. (Estimates of reserves at a given point in time normally refer to 'proven' reserves, and may be far below the absolute level.)

Another example is the development of techniques for mining the ocean floor for such minerals as nickel, cobalt, manganese and copper.

Second, as one resource becomes more expensive, there is an incentive to develop substitutes. Sometimes the source of the substitute may be most unlikely. For example in textiles we have seen natural fibres, such as wool, cotton, flax and jute, supplemented by a range of artificial fibres produced by the chemical industry . Many more such examples will undoubtedly result from the rapid spread of bio-technology.

Finally, as reserves in the ground dwindle it becomes more worth while to recycle material that would previously have been wasted. In the UK we recycle more than half the iron and steel used, over a third of the copper and over a quarter of the aluminium, paper and glass.

This does not mean, of course, that we should be complacent about the possible exhaustion of reserves. But it does suggest that the economic system may be able to adjust to potential shortages rather more easily than is sometimes suggested. There are two areas in which intervention to modify or supplement the price mechanism is most likely to be required. The first, as noted above, is where there is a long lead time in the process of design and production. The second is where there are important economies of scale, including economies of information and standardization. For example the government may facilitate an increase in recycling by providing the physical facilities, by bringing together suppliers and potential users of recycled materials, and by establishing technical specifications designed to encourage standardization of product.

Finally, from a purely nationalistic viewpoint, government intervention may also be required to reduce political risks. The UK imports large quantities of many minerals, including her entire consumption of nickel, zinc, manganese, chromium and platinum. Consequently, she is very vulnerable to an interruption of supply caused, for example, by the outbreak of war or revolution in supplier countries. It has been suggested that to reduce these risks the UK should follow West Germany in subsidizing the exploration of alternative sources of supply, and introduce a stockpiling system.

Government intervention, investment and economic growth

We noted in Chapter 2 that there may be a link between investment (expenditure on capital goods) and economic growth. Since economic growth is usually an aim of government policy, governments may try to increase the volume of investment. The various measures that might be adopted are considered below. But first we examine the implications of intervention.

In Fig. 9.11 the production possibility frontier (boundary or curve) AB, indicates the economic capacity of the country concerned. It shows all the combinations of consumption and capital goods that could be produced in a given period. One possibility would be an output of G

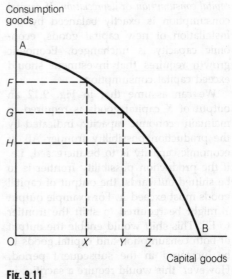

Fig. 9.11
A production possibility frontier

consumption goods (e.g. food) and Y capital goods (e.g. machines). Another possibility would be an output of H consumption goods and Z capital goods.

The frontier is concave to the origin because some resources are better suited to the production of capital goods and some to the production of consumption goods. As the output of one product is increased it is necessary to employ resources that are less efficient (in that use) than those already employed. Consequently the greater the initial output of a product, the more of the other product must be forgone for a given increase in the output of the first product. Whereas an increase of HG consumption goods would require a reduction of ZY capital goods, an increase of GF (= HG) consumption goods would require a larger reduction (YX) of capital goods than previously.

Economic growth

Economic growth can be defined as an expansion of economic capacity, represented by an outward shift of the production possibility boundary. (An alternative definition of economic growth is given in the appendix to this chapter.)

Every year some capital goods wear out or become obsolete, a process known as *capital consumption* or *depreciation*. If capital consumption is exactly balanced by the installation of new capital goods, economic capacity is unchanged. Economic growth requires that investment should exceed capital consumption.

We can assume that in Fig. 9.12 an output of X capital goods is required to maintain economic capacity, indicated by the production possibility frontier AB. If economic capacity is to be increased, i.e. if the production possibility frontier is to be shifted outwards, the output of capital goods must exceed X. For example output Y might be required to shift the frontier to EF. This shift would enable the output of both consumption and capital goods to be increased in the subsequent period. However, this would require a sacrifice in consumption of KJ in the current period.

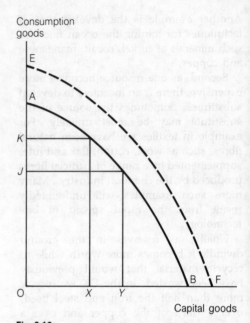

Fig. 9.12
Investment and the production possibility frontier

The effect of diverting resources from the consumption to the capital goods industries is illustrated in a slightly different way in Fig. 9.13. Line A shows the rate of increase in consumption that could be achieved with a given rate of investment. Line B shows the rate of increase with a higher rate of investment, i.e. when, in each period, a higher proportion of resources is devoted to the capital goods industries. Consumption grows more slowly at first and subsequently more quickly. In period X the volume of consumption is identical for the two growth paths; thereafter the volume of consumption per period is greater for path B. However, the total volume of consumption since period O becomes identical only in period Y; thereafter it is greater for path B.[14]

Given the importance of the time dimension, the choice of investment rate is not an easy one. It has been argued that planned or command economies have frequently depressed current levels of consumption more than was justified, i.e. have directed too many resources into the capital goods industries. One's reaction to

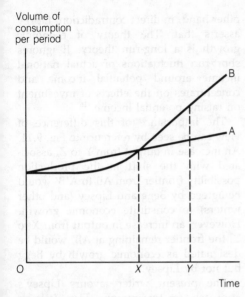

Volume of
consumption
per period

Fig. 9.13
Alternative consumption growth paths

this argument will clearly depend partly upon one's view about the relationship between successive generations of citizens. It will also depend upon the current level of consumption. A reduction in current consumption is far more feasible in highly industrialized countries than in underdeveloped countries where many people are living at subsistence level.

Measures to increase investment

Some government measures which influence the aggregate level of investment are examined in later chapters as part of our discussion of macro-economic policies. We confine our attention here to measures directed towards specific markets or industries rather than to the economy as a whole.

Planning
In command economies planning is *mandatory*, i.e. the planning authorities allocate to the capital goods industries whatever proportion of national resources they desire. In mixed economies, on the other hand, reliance has to be placed on *indicative planning*.

Indicative planning usually involves much less detailed plans than are drawn up in command economies. A more important difference, however, is that the plans are merely targets, not instructions which must be followed. The government does not have the power to discipline any producer who chooses to disregard the plan.

Nevertheless it is hoped that the planning process will identify obstacles to improvement in the performance of particular industries, and suggest ways of overcoming these obstacles. This often requires increasing the rate of investment.

In the UK the central planning forum is the National Economic Development Council, and the detailed work is undertaken by sector working parties and, in a few instances, economic development committees. They have identified imports that could be replaced by domestic production, researched opportunities in overseas markets, suggested improved ordering procedures, and studied possible applications of advanced technology, especially micro-electronics.

Subsidies for investment

Where an apparent shortfall in investment has been identified, the government has provided various forms of subsidy. For example between 1975 and 1985 £440m. was provided to support innovation in the 'sunrise industries': micro-electronics, fibre-optics, biotechnology, etc. The government-funded British Technology Group helps inventors and researchers to market their innovations, providing finance where necessary. The government also assists research and development through work undertaken in government laboratories and, indirectly, through the financing of work in universities, etc. About one-half of total expenditure on research and development is funded by the government.

The external benefits of research and development
Government support implies a belief that R & D conveys benefits to parties other

than those to whom the support is given. By definition the returns to expenditure on research are uncertain, and in the absence of government support less expenditure would be undertaken, causing a reduction in the rate of innovation. Consumers would therefore be denied the benefits of new processes and products.

The patent system

The existence of external benefits is a major justification of the patent system. Unless the profits derived from R & D activity are protected, firms will be much less likely to engage in such activity.

If we adopted a short-term view the patent system might appear to operate against the public interest. Once a new process or product has been developed, the interests of consumers would be best served by allowing free dissemination of the knowledge involved, i.e. allowing any producer to copy the innovation. But this prospect would reduce the chance of the innovation being made! The patent system is a compromise between these two conflicting requirements, and there is no guarantee that the right balance will always be struck.

Other aspects of government intervention

Government competition policy and policy towards public ownership are also influenced by perceptions of market failure. Since these are important topics in their own right they are discussed separately in the following two chapters.

Appendix

There is, unfortunately, no universally accepted definition of economic growth. On the one hand Begg says that 'economists usually take economic growth to mean the percentage annual change in the national income of a country'.[15] On the

other hand, in direct contradiction, Lipsey asserts that 'The theory of economic growth is a long-run theory. It ignores short-run fluctuations of actual national income around potential income and concentrates on the effects of investment on raising potential income.'[16]

The importance of this difference of view can be seen by reference to Fig. 9.14. An increase in output from Y to Z, associated with the shift in the production possibility frontier from AB to A'B' would be agreed by Begg and Lipsey (and other writers) to constitute economic growth. However, an increase in output from X to Y, the frontier remaining at AB, would be designated as economic growth by Begg but not by Lipsey.

The present writer favours Lipsey's approach, for two reasons. First, it is an accurate description of growth theory. Second, it draws attention to the fact that circumstances can affect the significance of a given change in output. The move from X to Y may well represent a very welcome improvement in living standards. But since it results from an increase

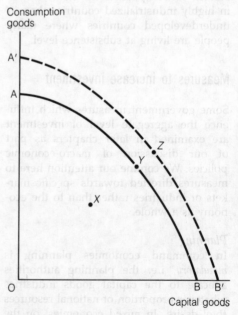

Fig. 9.14
Economic growth and increases in output

in the level of utilization of the existing economic capacity it is essentially a short-term phenomenon. The process must come to an end when capacity is fully utilized, i.e. when the frontier is reached. The favourable trend in output may draw attention away from the need to adopt policies to increase economic capacity.

Summary

1. Market failure is said to occur when the price and output resulting from the operation of market forces are considered to be unsatisfactory.

2. A government might intervene in the process of resource allocation in order to encourage the consumption of a product, e.g. by subsidizing its production. It may do so either because it feels that it is a better judge than consumers of the private benefits derived from consumption or because consumption gives rise to external benefits.

3. A government might discourage the consumption of other products, e.g. by imposing taxes. It might do so because of the private or external costs arising from consumption.

4. Subsidies may be given to private producers. Alternatively a product might be supplied by a public sector producer at a price below cost, the loss being met out of taxation.

5. Public goods are characterized by non-excludability and non-rivalness. Because of these two characteristics they are supplied by public sector producers.

6. Cost–benefit analysis can in principle help governments to decide whether they should intervene in the process of resource allocation. It does this by imputing values to external costs and benefits, in order to arrive at a 'price' that would reflect social (private plus external) costs and benefits.

7. In some markets, e.g. for rented accommodation, intervention takes the forms of price controls. Although these controls may benefit existing consumers of the product, they often lead to a contraction of supply, to the disadvantage of other potential consumers.

8. Minimum-wage legislation may benefit existing workers but may lead to a fall in total employment in the occupations or industries affected.

9. Large price fluctuations can operate to the disadvantage of both the producers and consumers of the products concerned. Consequently many attempts have been made to reduce these fluctuations, especially by the operation of buffer stock schemes. However, it has often proved difficult to agree on a viable target price, and many schemes have been ineffective.

10. Other forms of intervention, specifically designed to benefit producers, are production quotas (often associated with target prices), land banks and financial assistance for investment projects.

11. Price stabilization and the protection of producers' living standards are the two main objectives of the European Community's Common Agricultural Policy. In achieving these objectives the CAP has in effect transferred income to European farmers from European consumers and from overseas farmers.

12. It is sometimes claimed that government intervention is justified because current market prices give inadequate weight to possible future developments such as the depletion of resources. However, there is no guarantee that a government, or any central organization, will be able to 'out-guess' the market, especially when the possibility exists of recycling resources.

13. Sustained economic growth involves an expansion of economic capacity, which often requires an increase in investment. This may in turn require a reduction in the rate of growth of consumption.

Key terms

Market failure	Price controls
Resource allocation	Minimum wage legislation
Merit good	Buffer stock schemes
Demerit good	Production quotas
External benefits	Land banks
External costs	Common Agricultural Policy
Subsidies	Time
Indirect taxes	Recycling
Public goods	Economic growth
Cost–benefit analysis	Planning

Notes

1. The term 'merit bad' is sometimes used, for example in Begg D, Fischer S and Dornbusch R, *Economics*. McGraw-Hill, 1984, p. 355.
2. The advantages and disadvantages of various corrective mechanisms are discussed in Day J and Hodgson D, Pollution control policy issues, *Economics*, XXI (Summer 1985).
3. The practices of one landlord gave birth to a new word, 'Rachmanism'.
4. Lee D R and McNown R F, *Economics in Our Time: Concepts and Issues*. Science Research Associates, Ch. 3.
5. Lee D and McNown R, op. cit., Ch. 3.
6. Brown C, Gilroy C and Kohen A, The effect of the minimum wage on employment and unemployment, *Journal of Economic Literature*, 1982. For another useful review of previous studies see Forrest D, *Low Pay or No Pay: A Review of the Theory and Practice of Minimum-Wage Laws*. Institute of Economic Affairs, 1984.
7. Caine S, *The Price of Stability?* Institute of Economic Affairs, 1983.
8. Lee and McNown, op. cit., Ch. 3.
9. World Bank, *World Development Report 1986*. Oxford Univ. Press, 1986.
10. El-Agraa A M, The CAP: theory and practice, *The Economic Review*, Sept 1984 pp. 9–14.
11. Bureau of Agricultural Economics and Centre for International Economics, Canberra, *Effects of EC Agricultural Policies*. 1987.
12. This last measure inspired a cartoon in the *Financial Times*, 27 June 1986, in which a farmer is saying: 'I'm not so much a dairy farmer – more a butter recycler.'
13. Goldsmith E (ed.), *Blueprint for Survival*. Penguin, 1973.
14. Even then we cannot conclude that path B is to be preferred, since society may value consumption in one period more highly than consumption in a later period.
15. Begg, Fischer and Dornbush, op. cit., p. 28.
16. Lipsey R G, *An Introduction to Positive Economics*, 6th edn. Weidenfeld and Nicolson, 1983, p. 638.

Essay questions

1. Explain why price control has often been felt to be more necessary in open than in other markets.
2. Show how buffer stocks may be used to stabilize (a) prices, (b) producers' incomes.
3. Discuss the conditions required for a successful price stabilization scheme.
4. Evaluate the case for the provision by the state of (a) free education, (b) subsidized medical services, (c) subsidized television sets for retirement pensioners.
5. Discuss the possible consequences of a government policy which controlled the rents of private rented accommodation and subsidized the rents of council houses.
6. Analyse the possible consequences of the introduction into the UK of minimum wage legislation.
7. Explain the statement that cost–benefit analysis may be used to adjust for imperfections in the market mechanism, and discuss the factors which are likely to limit its application.
8. How would you expect a market system to adjust to the approaching depletion of a natural resource? Under what circumstances might government intervention in the adjustment process be justified?
9. Explain with examples the statement that government intervention may be designed to increase, decrease or stabilize the price of particular products.
10. 'Changes in market prices are signals which lead to the re-allocation of resources in the public interest.' Discuss.
11. Explain the distinction between private cost and external cost and show how these concepts may be applied to traffic congestion.
12. Evaluate the case for governments subsidizing investment.

Exercises

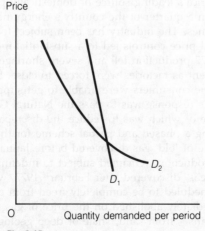

Fig. 9.15
Alternative demand curves

9.1   In Fig. 9.15 the two demand curves indicate the demand for the current output of
      a product (a) when a buffer stock scheme exists, (b) when there is no interference
      with market forces.
      (i)   Indicate which demand curve applies in each situation.
      (ii)   Use the diagram to show the possible effects of the buffer stock scheme on
             (a) fluctuations in price, (b) fluctuations in producers' income.
      (iii) Indicate the range of output which would cause the size of the buffer stock
             to increase, and discuss the problems which would arise if this level of
             output were maintained.

9.2   The following measures were proposed by President Carter during the period
      1977–79. (Some became law; others did not.) Say in two/three sentences why you
      agree or disagree with each of the proposals.
      (i)   Federal controls on the price of newly discovered gas to be lifted in 1985.
             Meanwhile the price of new gas to be raised each year; industry, not
             consumers, to bear the brunt of the increases.
      (ii)   Industries should convert from oil to gas, but many exemptions and
             provisions for 'hardship cases'.
      (iii) State utility regulating agencies to consider schemes promoting energy
             saving, such as ending discounts for big volume users.
      (iv)   Taxes to be levied on fuel-inefficient cars, starting with $200 tax on cars
             getting less than 15 mpg in the 1980 model year, and rising to a minimum
             of $400 on cars getting less than 25 mpg by 1985.
      (v)   Subsidies to householders for home insulation improvements, and
             installation of solar heat.
      (vi)   The imposition of a 'windfall tax' on the oil companies (windfall denoting
             that profits had increased because of higher oil prices rather than greater
             efficiency).
      (vii) Creation of an energy security corporation to direct the development of oil
             substitutes (synthetics) from coal liquids and gases, oil-shale and biomass
             (vegetable, sugar, alcohol, woodchips); the corporation's activities to be
             funded from the windfall profits tax.

9.3   Natural gas is America's leading source of domestically produced energy,
      providing more than a quarter of the country's energy needs, and heating more
      than half of US homes. The industry has been subject to government regulation
      since the 1930s, and price controls led to a substantial increase in consumption. In
      the winter of 1976/77 production fell and severe shortages developed which
      caused unemployment as factories were forced to close. Schools using gas heating
      also closed and some consumers were unable to get supplies to heat their homes.
         The government's response was to pass the Natural Gas Policy Act, the
      underlying objective of which was to reduce the discrepancy between gas and oil
      prices by introducing a phased and partial scheme for the deregulation of natural
      gas prices. The price of 'old' gas discovered before January 1977 (which accounted
      for two-thirds of production) remained subject to indefinite government control.
      The price of 'new' gas, discovered after February 1977, was allowed to rise fairly
      rapidly and was scheduled to be completely freed from controls by 1985. Finally,
      controls were immediately abolished on the price of gas produced via
      unconventional means – from sand, shale or deep geological formations ('deep
      gas').
         Discuss the likely consequences of these provisions of the Natural Gas Policy
      Act.

9.4 Figure 9.16 shows the production possibility frontier (boundary) for an economy at a given point in time.
   (i) Account for the shape of the curve.
   (ii) Compare positions A and B in terms of
       (a) current living standards and (b) future living standards.
   (iii) Why might the combination of goods represented by point X be produced?
   (iv) Show the effect of a change in technology which resulted in the country becoming less efficient in the production of consumption goods and more efficient in the production of capital goods.

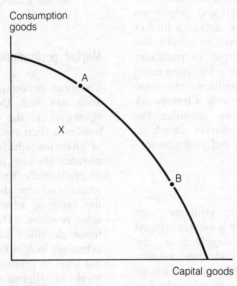

Fig. 9.16
A production possibility frontier

9.5 In 1983 the Severn Trent Water Authority introduced a Bill into Parliament that would enable it to spend £6.4m. on lowering the watercourse of the River Soar in Leicestershire´and Nottinghamshire. The scheme would increase the rate at which the river drains its flood-plain.
   Some villages would receive improved flood protection (although this could be provided independently for a few hundred thousand pounds), and motorists on some roads would be spared some inconvenience in winter. But the main impact would be on farm production. It was expected that milk production would rise a little and that the production of beef and lamb would fall somewhat. Oil-seed rape production was expected to rise tenfold to 335 tonnes, and wheat production more than threefold to 5,340 tonnes, much of it from land never previously ploughed.
   Approximately one-third of the cost of the scheme would be provided by the central government and the rest from the ratepayers. Applying a discount rate of 5 per cent, the Authority concluded that the scheme would yield a positive net benefit.
   Present the case (a) for, (b) against, allowing the scheme to proceed.

CHAPTER TEN
Competition Policy

Introduction

In Chapter 9 we showed that governments may intervene in the market process because they think that price in a given market is too high and output too low. In this chapter we discuss a further set of measures designed to modify the level of price and output in particular markets, in this instance by influencing the nature of competition in those markets. In order to provide a framework for this discussion we consider the relationship between market structure, conduct (or behaviour) and performance.

Market structure

The aspects of market structure with which competition policy is most concerned are the number of suppliers in the industry or market, and their relative market shares. It is believed that highly concentrated industries (a relatively few firms account for a high share of total output) may give more opportunity for undesirable conduct than less concentrated industries.

Market conduct

Market conduct refers to the behaviour of firms, especially important aspects of behaviour being:

(a) whether or not existing firms seek to prevent new firms from entering the industry;
(b) how sensitive prices are to changes in the balance between supply and demand.

Market performance

The most important elements of performance are first the level of *productive efficiency*, i.e. the extent to which firms minimize their costs, and second a group of elements which together indicate the *allocative efficiency* of the system – the rate of profitability, the rate of innovation, in terms of new products and processes, and the ratio of advertising expenditure to sales revenue. (This last factor is sometimes classified as a conduct element.) When we look at the economy as a whole, the level of productive efficiency and the level of allocative efficiency together determine the level of *economic efficiency*.

One possible relationship among the above three elements is illustrated in Fig. 10.1, which indicates that structure influences conduct, which in turn influences performance. This might suggest that it would be sufficient if policy was concerned only with structure and conduct, or even with structure alone. However, there are several arguments against such an approach.

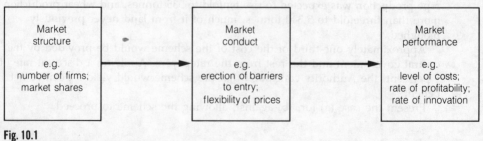

Fig. 10.1
Structure, conduct, performance

First, highly concentrated markets may have desirable as well as undesirable features. Considering first the undesirable features, larger firms may be in a better position to prevent potential new suppliers from entering the industry. Furthermore, if existing firms are protected from new entry they may earn abnormally high profit margins. Alternatively, being sheltered from competition, they may allow their costs to rise. In either event their performance would be judged to be undesirable.

On the other hand, the concentration of output in the hands of only a few firms may enable these firms to enjoy economies of scale (see Ch. 5) and so lower costs of production, i.e. productive efficiency would be high. Even if the profitability of these firms is above average, their prices could actually be lower than if the industry were less concentrated. Furthermore, these firms may use at least some of their additional profits to invest in R & D, which may result in a high rate of innovation. (Note that the patent system, established by law, is designed to ensure that firms enjoy the benefits of their expenditure on R & D.) In these respects, therefore, the performance of the industry could be considered to be satisfactory.

We also explained in Chapter 5 why it is difficult to specify a clear link *in principle* between structure, conduct and performance. We showed that some economists believe that higher than average profits in concentrated industries are due to the fact that competition is less intense, giving suppliers greater discretion in setting prices. In other words market structure, via conduct, influences performance. Other economists, however, emphasize the fact that some firms are more efficient than others, and that this superior efficiency enables these firms to earn above-average profits and to achieve a high market share. In other words performance influences market structure.

This second interpretation might suggest that good performance is more likely to be associated with high concentration resulting from the internal growth of firms than from mergers. Most studies of mergers have revealed that on the whole the performance of merged companies has been no better than that of non-merging companies.[1]

Contestable markets

The recently developed theory of contestable markets also leads to the conclusion that a policy that concentrated on the existing number of suppliers might be aiming at the wrong target. The main feature of a contestable market is that firms may freely enter and leave it.

The key element for efficiency is, therefore, the existence of a pool of *potential* entrants rather than the size or number of the incumbents *per se* – it is the threat of entry which acts as the constraint on exploitation. Competitors will survive in such markets only if they are the most efficient (irrespective of size) and do not attempt to exploit their situation.[2]

Moreover the threat of being taken over is a constant spur to efficiency. As the *Financial Weekly* put it, it 'sticks pins into indolent corporate posteriors and forces companies to implement much-needed reforms'.

These considerations help to explain why UK competition policy is concerned with market structure, conduct and performance. Giving attention to three factors rather than one has meant that policy has proceeded on a pragmatic, case-by-case approach, rather than through the application of simple rules.

We begin our examination of policy by considering legislation relating to mergers and monopolies.

Legislation relating to mergers and monopolies

The Monopolies and Mergers Act 1965

This Act represented the first serious attempt in the UK to control mergers. Any proposed merger that would result in at least one-third (subsequently one-quarter) of the market being in the hands of a single supplier, or that would involve the acquisition of assets above £5m. (subsequently £30m.) could be referred to the Monopolies and Mergers Commission (MMC). If it appeared from the MMC's report that the merger was likely to operate against the public interest, the Secretary of State was empowered to stop the merger, break up a merger that had already taken place or lay down the conditions on which the merger could proceed.

The Fair Trading Act 1973

This Act established a new office and officer: the Office of Fair Trading and its Director-General. Both the Director-General and the relevant Minister (the Secretary of State) can make monopoly references to the MMC. Merger references can be made only by the Minister (although he seeks the advice of the Director-General).

The market-share criterion for reference to the MMC was reduced to 25 per cent. It also became possible to investigate export and local (geographical) monopolies. Moreover the Act provided for the investigation of 'complex monopolies', situations in which, although no one firm has 25 per cent of the market, several firms which together have 25 per cent so conduct their affairs as to prevent, restrict or distort competition.

The Act also laid down criteria by which the public interest might be determined. These criteria, which related to both conduct and performance, included: maintaining and promoting effective competition in the supply of goods and services; promoting the interests of consumers, purchasers and users of goods and services; promoting the reduction of costs, the development and use of new techniques and products, and the entry of new competitors; maintaining and promoting a balanced distribution of industry and employment.

The first stage in implementing the legislation with respect to **mergers** is the decision as to which proposed mergers should be referred to the MMC. The criteria laid down in the Act, and especially the size of the assets acquired, were such that a very large number of mergers came within the scope of the legislation – more than 2,500 during the period 1965–84. Because of the size and composition of the MMC – most members serve in a part-time capacity – it cannot be expected to investigate more than a small fraction. Of the 2,500 only 79 were referred.

In deciding which mergers to refer, it is inevitable that conduct and performance variables should be taken into account. Indeed the Office of Fair Trading, which in 1973 was given responsibility for administering policy (see below), indicated that product sectors would probably be considered most worthy of investigation if they achieved 'high marks' in terms of four conduct and four performance indicators.

The four conduct indicators were: complaints, from both trade and consumer sources, evidence or accusation of either price leadership or parallel pricing, the ratio of advertising expenditure to sales (sometimes treated as a performance indicator as noted above) and the degree of merger activity in the field concerned. The four performance indicators were the ratio of capital employed to turnover (a high ratio possibly indicating inefficiency), changes in profit margins, return on capital employed and the movement of prices in a particular product sector relative to the general rate of inflation.

The importance of this initial decision, and thus of the criteria taken into account, can be seen from the fact that whereas about 97 per cent of proposed mergers have been allowed to proceed without reference to the MMC, only about 30 per cent of those referred have subsequently come to fruition. Some proposed mergers are abandoned following an adverse report by the MMC, others before an investigation gets under way.

This takes us to the second stage of the implementation of the legislation, namely the findings of the MMC, and the action taken following those findings. The MMC is invariably asked to consider proposed rather than past mergers, and thus has to predict what the effect of the merger is likely to be. In its prediction, while the MMC takes into account what economic theory has to say about the effects of an increase in the level of market concentration, it also considers the facts appertaining to a particular merger, and its conclusions are likely to be strongly influenced by its findings about the past conduct and performance of the firms concerned.

When the MMC considers existing **monopolies** it must clearly be concerned with past conduct and performance. In its report, *Building Bricks*, issued in 1976, the MMC noted that the profits of the London Brick Company (LBC) were not excessive and that its prices were reasonable. Indeed one of the reasons for the company's monopoly position was that its prices were so low that other, less efficient, producers had left the market. The only change in policy recommended by the MMC was the LBC's policy of subsidizing the cost of transport to its more distant customers should be abandoned, since it represented unfair competition.

When it investigated the market for petfoods the MMC found that Pedigree Petfoods, with a 50 per cent share of the market, had achieved a rate of return on capital of 46.7 per cent, compared to the 19.2 per cent earned by Spillers, who had 30 per cent of the market. However, the real price of petfoods had declined over the previous decade and the MMC concluded that the main reason for Pedigree's very high rate of return was their superior efficiency, and the high profits were not therefore a cause for criticism.

The MMC has accepted other reasons as justifying high profits. Pilkington's rate of return, roughly twice the manufacturing average, was largely due to the develop-

ment of the float-glass process on which they had spent £4 million despite apparently poor commercial prospects. Rank Xerox had achieved a market share of 96 per cent in plain paper copiers. Its return on capital of over 40 per cent brought only mild criticism, high profits being regarded as reward for the risk involved in developing a new product. The MMC noted that Rank's market share was under attack from competitors, and in fact both market share and profitability have subsequently declined substantially.[3]

On the other hand, in other instances the MMC has concluded that high profits have resulted mainly from the exploitation of a dominant position. In such situations one 'solution' would be to split the company concerned into a number of smaller units having less market power, i.e. to change the structure of the industry. The disadvantage of this approach is that it might lead to an increase in costs, because of the disruption caused and because of the loss of economies of scale.

In fact the MMC has never recommended this approach, preferring instead that prices and profits should be controlled by the appropriate government department, i.e. that action should be taken relating to conduct and performance. Industries in which price controls have been recommended include detergents (Unilever and Procter and Gamble), breakfast cereals (Kelloggs), pharmaceuticals (Hoffman-La Roche), and colour films (Kodak).

The Competition Act 1980

This Act enlarged the scope of monopoly legislation in two significant respects. First, it provided for the investigation of bodies such as nationalized industries and other enterprises operating in markets where competition is limited by statute or other special circumstances. The Secretary of State may direct the MMC to examine questions of efficiency and costs, standards of service or possible abuses of monopoly power.

The second provision of the Competition Act relates to certain anti-competitive practices which fell outside the scope of previous legislation, or which could be investigated only in a very cumbersome manner. The Competition Act made it possible for specific practices by named individual firms to be investigated without requiring a full investigation of all major suppliers in the market. A preliminary investigation is undertaken by the Office of Fair Trading (OFT); on the basis of the findings the Director-General decides whether or not to refer the matter for a fuller investigation to the MMC. Should the MMC find a practice to be against the public interest the Minister may act to control it. Examples of anti-competitive practices are: arrangements under which a distributor agrees to sell the products only of a specificed manufacturer; the refusal to supply one product unless the distributor buys other products from the same manufacturer; selling below cost in order to force competitors out of business.

Legislation of the European Community (EC)

Competition policy is central in promoting the Common Market, one of the founding principles of the European Community. The policy is based on articles 85 and 86 of the Treaty of Rome. Article 86 states that any abuse of a dominant position within the Common Market or in a substantial part of it shall be prohibited. This is tougher than the corresponding UK legislation. Practices deemed to constitute abuse include: imposing unfair purchase or selling prices; limiting production, markets or technical development to the prejudice of consumers; applying dissimilar conditions to equivalent transactions with other trading parties.

As an example of practice that would be allowed under UK but not EC legislation, consider 'dual pricing'. British producers selling abroad have sometimes found it desirable to allow their overseas distributors higher margins because, for example, tougher competition from domestic products requires the overseas distributors to undertake more promotional activities than their counterparts in the UK. The higher margins to distributors would imply higher consumer prices abroad than at home. For example the Distillers Company sold whisky at higher prices in France than in the UK, and to support the higher price tried to restrict 'parallel imports' via unofficial distributors at lower prices. This restriction was, however, ruled to be illegal by the EC on the grounds that it distorted competition.

BL (later Austin-Rover), the state-owned UK car manufacturer, was fined over £200,000 because it was alleged to have sought to deter British importers from buying new Austin Metros on the Continent at lower prices than in the UK. A higher fine would have been imposed had not BL co-operated with the European Commission's investigations. It agreed to make available to continental dealers right-hand-drive cars, which could then be resold in the UK.

The European Commission also has the power to act against proposed mergers. However, as yet it has been very reluctant to use this power, although the present Commissioner with responsibility for matters pertaining to competition, Peter Sutherland, is seeking a more active role.

The effectiveness of monopoly and merger policy

As we saw above, only some 3 per cent of the mergers that come within the scope of the legislation are referred to the MMC. Some of these subsequently proceed, and it appears that legislation does not prevent more than 2 per cent of proposed mergers from going ahead. It is therefore not surprising that the trend to an increase in market concentration, shown in Table 10.1, has continued.

A number of studies have suggested that of the increase in concentration about

Table 10.1
Five-firm concentration ratio for selected product groups

Product group	Concentration ratio (%)	
	1963	1977
Biscuits	65.5	79.7
Bread	71.4	81.2
Pharmaceuticals	53.9	63.2
Raincoats	22.3	54.7
Washing machines	85.2	96.2

Source: Business Monitor PO 1006

half can be explained by mergers and half by internal growth.[4] Merger activity tends to be cyclical, peaks in expenditure on acquisitions and mergers having occurred in 1968, 1972 and 1986 (Fig. 10.2). The increased rate of merger activity was no doubt one of the factors which led the government to announce in June 1986 that a review of competition policy was to be undertaken.

£bn.
1980 prices

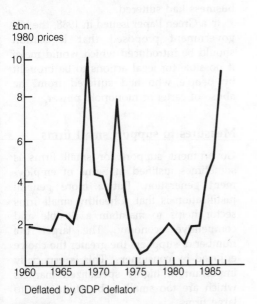

Fig. 10.2
Expenditure on acquisitions by UK industrial and commercial companies
Source: Bank of England Quarterly Bulletin, Aug. 1987

In 1984 the government emphasized that the effect on competition was the predominant criterion in deciding which bids to refer to the MMC. (In sixteen of the next twenty cases referred to the MMC, competition was the major issue.) This has led to an increase in the proportion of conglomerate or diversifying mergers.[5] In 1985 diversifying mergers accounted for over half by value of all mergers falling within the legislation. In no previous year had they accounted for as much as a third.

An increasingly important feature of merger activity in recent years has been the subsequent divestment (selling-off) of parts of the acquired company. In some instances this has occurred to avoid reference to the MMC. In 1986 United Biscuits agreed that in the event of a successful bid for the Imperial Group it would sell Golden Wonder, its crisps business, in order to reduce its market share. Similarly Guinness, bidding for Distillers, promised to sell sufficient whisky interests to reduce its market share to 25 per cent. In other instances divestment has been part of a reorientation of a company's activities and assets.

Diversification

Although some conglomerates, such as BTR and Hanson Trust, are very efficient, a policy of diversification is not always successful.

Professor Constable has shown that diversified companies are generally less profitable than successful non-diversified companies.[6] (An important feature of BTR and Hanson's policy is that they sell parts of acquired businesses which do not fit with their 'core' activities.) Diversified mergers cause an increase in overall, if not in market, concentration. Constable shows that overall concentration is higher in the UK than in the USA, West Germany, France or Japan. He concludes, as did Professor Prais in an earlier study,[7] that this high degree of concentration is one of the reasons for the UK's relatively poor economic performance.

Alternative approaches

The current attitude to mergers is benign in the sense that a merger will be allowed to proceed unless the MMC finds that it is *expected* to operate against the public interest. The probability of a merger being allowed to proceed would be reduced if the *possibility* of its operating against the public interest was sufficient grounds for its being blocked.

Another approach would be the incorporation in competition policy of non-discretionary rules. For example it might be stipulated that no merger would be allowed which involved the biggest five firms in any market; or which brought the market share of the merging firms up to, say, 25 per cent. The term 'non-discretionary' refers to the fact that the rules are applied automatically, and not at the discretion of, say, the Director-General of Fair Trading or a government minister.

There is no doubt that such rules could substantially reduce the pace of merger activity. Moreover the cost of administering the policy would probably fall. However, a non-discretionary approach has the disadvantage that it could prevent changes in structure which, even if they could be shown to be *generally* undesirable, might be desirable in particular instances, e.g. because they afforded the opportunity of sharing scarce and expensive research facilities.

Moreover there are technical problems which mean that the implementation of policy may not be as straightforward as it seems at first sight. For example, even if it were possible to agree on the appropriate limitation on market share, say 25 per cent, it might not be possible to arrive at a satisfactory definition of 'the market'. When the proposed merger between British Sidac and Transparent Paper was referred to the MMC it was decided that the relevant market was cellulose film, and that, had the merger proceeded, the resulting company would have been a monopoly in terms of the 1965 Act. On the other hand, had the market been defined as 'all flexible packaging materials', no monopoly would have been found to exist. Other problems of definition exist, such as the inclusion or non-inclusion of imports and exports, the time period over which market share should be measured, etc.

Given these disadvantages, some economists have advocated an approach which is a compromise between the discretionary or pragmatic and non-discretionary approaches. Mergers falling into certain categories would be forbidden unless the parties to the merger could convince an independent body that the net effect of the merger was likely to be beneficial. This approach would put the control of mergers on a roughly similar basis to that applying to restrictive practices.

Monopoly policy could also be strengthened by imposing penalties for the abuse of monopoly power. In the USA the American Telephone and Telegraph Co., being found guilty of illegally impeding the growth of a competitor, was ordered to pay a fine of $600m. They also faced a potential claim of $1.8bn. (triple damages) from the competitor whose business had suffered.

In a Green Paper issued in 1988, the UK government proposed that legislation should be introduced which would make it possible for legal actions to be brought by people who had suffered from the abuse of cartel or monopoly power.

Measures to support small firms

Government support for small firms is sometimes justified in terms of employment generation. But a more general justification is that a healthy small-firms sector helps to maintain a flexible and competitive economy. The larger the number of suppliers the greater the choice enjoyed by consumers. This is especially important in highly specialized markets which are too small to be of interest to large firms.

There is considerable controversy about the relationship between size of firm and research, development and innovation. Most of the evidence suggests that the proportion of resources devoted to R & D increases with the size of the firm. Galbraith argued that the modern industry of a few large firms is an almost perfect instrument for inducing technological change, and in Chapter 5 we gave examples of the large amount of money that is required to finance R & D in some industries. On the other hand many products and processes of great commercial significance have originated in small firms, including the tufting of carpets, the ultrasonic detector, solid-state laser machining and the use of lasers for drilling, printed circuit boards, glass-reinforced plastic lifeboats, four-wheel drive for private cars, and polyurethane coatings for leathers.

The measures adopted to support small firms include certain forms of regional assistance not available to large firms, a concessionary rate of corporation tax on small profits, the introduction of specialist sources of finance and granting exemptions from certain obligations placed on larger firms, e.g. with respect to workers' rights. Some of these measures are discussed at greater length in Chapters 12, 16 and 20.

Legislation relating to collective restrictive practices

The Restrictive Trade Practices Act 1956

This Act required all restrictive agreements to be registered with the Registrar of Restrictive Trading Agreements. A restrictive agreement is defined as any agreement between two or more persons carrying on business in the production or supply of goods, under which restrictions are accepted by the parties in respect of the prices to be charged, the terms or conditions of sale, quantities or types to be produced, the process of manufacture, the persons or areas to be supplied or the persons or areas from which the goods are to be acquired.

The emphasis here is clearly on conduct, and the Act was based on the presumption that certain types of conduct are undesirable. However, the Act also recognized that performance is important, and it made provision for these potentially undesirable forms of conduct to be continued, provided that it could be shown that in practice they led to an improvement in performance.

The decision as to whether or not an agreement should be permitted is made by the Restrictive Practices Court, also established by the 1956 Act. The parties to an agreement can attempt to justify it only on certain specific grounds. These 'gateways' are:

(a) that the restriction is reasonably necessary to protect the public against injury;

(b) that the removal of the restriction would deny to the public, as purchasers, consumers or users of any goods, specific and substantial benefits;

(c) that the restriction is reasonably necessary to counteract measures taken by a person, not party to the agreement, with a view to restricting competition;

(d) that the restriction is reasonably necessary to enable fair terms to be negotiated with a large supplier or purchaser;

(e) that the removal of the restriction would be likely to have a serious and persistent adverse effect on unemployment in areas in which the industry is concentrated;

(f) that the removal of the restriction would be likely to cause a substantial reduction in export business;

(g) that the restriction is reasonably required for the purpose of supporting other restrictions in the agreement which are in the public interest;

(h) that the restriction does not directly or indirectly restrict or discourage competition to any material degree in any relevant trade or industry and is not likely to do so. (This last clause was added by the Restrictive Trade Practices Act, 1968.)

The three gateways that have received most prominence in the cases heard by the Court are (b), by far the most important, (e) and (f), all of which refer to aspects of an industry's performance.

Since the passing of the 1956 Act around 5,000 agreements have been registered. However, the vast majority were ended by the parties themselves. During the first twenty years of this legislation only thirty-seven agreements were contested before the Court, and of these only eleven were upheld as being in the public interest. The very high rate of abandonment can be explained mainly by the fact that the Court approved of very few of the early agreements that it considered – only one of the first seven.

The Fair Trading Act 1973

As noted above this Act established the Office of the Director-General of Fair Trading who assumed responsibility for the implementation of restrictive practices legislation. The Fair Trading Act also enabled the provisions of the 1956 Act to be extended to firms supplying commercial services, such as hairdressers, estate agents and travel agents. This extension was achieved by the Restrictive Trade Practices (Services) Order 1976, under which registration with the OFT is required for agreements relating to:

(a)   the charges made, quoted or paid for services;
(b)   the terms or conditions on which services are supplied or obtained;
(c)   the extent or scale on which services are supplied or obtained;
(d)   the form or manner in which services are supplied or obtained;
(e)   the persons, areas or places to, in, or from which services are supplied or obtained.

By the end of 1985, over 1,000 service agreements had been registered. If the Director-General of Fair Trading considers that a registered agreement restricts competition he may refer it to the Restrictive Practices Court. Thus the distinction between goods and services, which was

introduced by the 1956 Act but which made little economic sense, was swept away.

As an example of the impact of the Order we can note that when the first batch of agreements were registered it was found that the Association of British Travel Agents had dropped its recommendation to members to charge a standard 10 per cent commission on holidays sold, and that it had withdrawn its advice on minimum charges to be made for other services such as the sale of travellers' cheques.

If the Director-General is satisfied that the restrictions in a registered agreement are 'not of such significance as to call for investigation by the Court' the agreement need not be referred (the so-called section 21(2) procedure). In recent years reference to the Court has been very much a 'long stop', being used only when the OFT is unable to persuade the parties to an agreement to remove any restrictions considered to have significant adverse effects upon competition or customers.

The Restrictive Trade Practices Acts 1976, 1977

The Acts discussed above were subsequently replaced in consolidated form by the Restrictive Trade Practices Act 1976. This Act, as amended slightly by the Restrictive Trade Practices Act 1977, currently contains the whole of the law on collective restrictive practices (although new legislation is promised in the near future).

The legislation of the European Community

Article 85 of the Treaty of Rome deals with agreements and practices which hinder the free play of competition: 'Agreements between undertakings, decisions by associations of undertakings, concerted practices which may affect trade between member states and which have as their objective the prevention, restriction or distortion of competition within the Common Market shall be prohibited as incompatible with the Common Market.' An agreement may be exempted from this prohibition if it contributes to improving the production or distribution of goods, or to promoting technical or economic progress, while allowing consumers a fair share of the resulting benefits.

Article 85 is similar to UK restrictive practices legislation in its emphasis on conduct and performance, and the requirement to weigh possible benefits and detriments. But the European Community policy is tougher: it covers a wider range of agreements, imposes heavier penalties (fines up to 10 per cent of the company's turnover in the previous year as well as the annulment of the agreement) and has more limited conditions for exemption (gateways).

In 1986 the European Commission imposed the heaviest fines to date on ten European chemical producers who had conspired to fix prices and production quotas for polypropylene. The biggest fine, 11m. European Currency Units (ECUs) (£7m.), was imposed on an Italian producer, while the fine of 10m. ECUs on ICI was the heaviest ever imposed on a British company.

Resale price maintenance

The collective restrictive agreements considered above are horizontal, i.e. agreements made between a group of manufacturers or between a group of retailers. Competition may also be inhibited by vertical arrangements. We have already noted some of the arrangements that might be investigated under the Competition Act, e.g. arrangements under which a distributor agrees to sell the products of only a single manufacturer. Agreements whereby a manufacturer seeks to enforce the price at which distributors sell his products are subject to the provisions of the Resale Prices Act.

The Resale Prices Act 1964

The background to this Act was a rapid increase in the market share of multiple retailers, largely due to their policy of reducing prices in order to achieve a higher volume of turnover. The ability of manufacturers to prevent distributors from reducing prices inhibited the growth of such firms. The 1964 Act was, therefore, seen as a way of trying to improve market performance and economic efficiency in retailing.

Specific grounds for the justification of an agreement were again laid down, namely that in the absence of resale price maintenance (RPM) the public would suffer in one of the following ways:

(a) the quality and variety of goods available for sale would be substantially reduced;

(b) the number of retail establishments in which the goods were sold would be substantially reduced;

(c) the retail prices of the goods would increase;

(d) goods would be sold under conditions likely to cause danger to health in consequence of their misuse by the public;

(e) any necessary services provided in connection with the sale of goods would cease to be provided, or would be substantially reduced.

Even if a manufacturer succeeds in justifying RPM on one of these grounds, he has then to show that this advantage of RPM outweighs the disadvantage of restricting the freedom of distributors. Only the manufacturers of books, maps and certain medicaments have satisfied the Court in this respect.

The Resale Prices Act 1976

This Act, which replaced the 1964 Act, forbids manufacturers from trying to get round the intention of legislation by refusing to supply dealers who undercut recommended prices. One manufacturer who fell foul of this Act was Hotpoint, who had refused to supply electrical appliances to Comet.

A similar policy pursued by Britain's largest cycle manufacturer, TI Raleigh, was declared anti-competitive by the

Director-General under the terms of the 1980 Competition Act, and referred to the MMC. This followed complaints from discount retailers like Argos and Tesco that the company had refused to supply bicycles while they maintained cut-price policies. The Director-General's initial report found that Raleigh's dominant market share of 45 per cent meant that its refusal to supply certain outlets could adversely affect their selling power and standing, and deprive consumers of potentially lower prices. Raleigh, supported by their trade association, claimed that the initial report only considered the matter of competition, to the exclusion of broader issues of public interest such as road safety. However, the report of the MMC declared that the policy was against the public interest, and the Director-General sought an undertaking from TI Raleigh to modify the practice.

The effectiveness of restrictive practices legislation

The fact that very few of the agreements registered under the Restrictive Trade Practices Act have survived might suggest that the legislation has been effective. However, a number of unregistered agreements on market sharing and collusive tendering have been discovered in industries as disparate as blacktop, telephone cables, concrete pipes, copying equipment, gas boilers, bread manufacturing and ferry services. This suggests that the OFT's powers of investigation need to be strengthened. For example the Director-General has to have evidence of a cartel before he can require the parties to disclose details of the price-fixing agreement. The OFT does not have the power given to the European Commission to seize documents during unannounced visits to companies. However the government has declared its intention to set up a new authority, under the OFT, with extensive powers to enter and search business premises for evidence of covert price-fixing and anti-competitive agreements.

Furthermore the deterrents against secret agreements could be strengthened. At present if a secret agreement is discovered it merely becomes void, and unlawful for the parties to enforce it. Only if the Restrictive Practices Court grants the OFT an injunction against any similar agreement operating in the future and the same parties are found to be colluding again, is a criminal offence committed. Any person suffering loss because of the operation of an unregistered agreement can bring an action for damages, but in only one instance has the threat of such an action resulted in the payment of substantial compensation; the Post Office obtained £9m. in an out-of-court settlement from four cable manufacturers who had operated an unregistered price agreement.

The 1988 Green Paper, referred to above, proposed that fines of up to 10 per cent of the turnover of a company or professional practice should be levied against those found in breach of restrictive practices legislation. New legislation would also make it easier for private actions to be brought, as noted above.

A more radical approach would be to declare collective restrictive agreements illegal *per se*, as happens in the USA, in West Germany and under European Economic Community (EEC) legislation. Participation in such an illegal agreement is usually punished by the imposition of a fine, as noted above. But the US courts have also been known to impose short prison sentences.

Perhaps even more important are the provisions for private actions for damages. For example in the USA anyone suffering from a collective restrictive practice, for example to raise prices, can sue the offending parties for triple damages, which may run into many millions of dollars. In the UK it is possible in principle to bring private actions, but extremely difficult in practice. In March 1987 the Restrictive Practices Court found that more than 200 firms supplying stone, sand, gravel, asphalt and coated macadam to county councils had been party to price fixing and other restrictive practices. But the Association of County Councils advised councils not to sue for damages. The Association found it difficult to know what the price would have been without the agreement, information that would be required as the basis for any claim.

Attention also needs to be given to the type of agreements that might be covered by legislation. The need for a review of the situation is illustrated by the agreement between Cadbury Schweppes and J. Lyons and Co., two major processors of citrus concentrates. Cadbury Schweppes agreed to buy 43 per cent of its sales from Lyons or to pay a penalty if less was ordered. The Director-General of Fair Trading argued that Cadbury Schweppes was effectively restricted from manufacturing or purchasing from other sources more than 57 per cent of its sales without penalty. An agreement to this effect would have been registrable. However, the Court decided not to treat the agreement as registrable even though it was admitted that its effect had been to determine the market shares of the companies concerned. Thomas Sharpe, a prominent barrister and economist, has argued that 'for many parties registration is an election. The agreement, being voluntary, can be structured in such a way that in many instances it need not be registered.'[8]

Summary

1. Competition policy is concerned with market structure, conduct (behaviour) and performance. United Kingdom policy has been conducted on a pragmatic, case-by-case approach, partly because it is difficult to specify a clear link in principle between structure, conduct and performance. The existence of large firms and high levels of market concentration may have advantages and disadvantages.
2. Only a small proportion of proposed mergers are referred to the MMC. In the decision as to which mergers should be referred, the potential effect on competition is paramount.
3. In reporting on monopolies the MMC has paid attention to various aspects of performance, including profitability, the trend of prices, the rate of innovation and the level of efficiency.
4. Economic theory suggests that collective restrictive practices may give rise to the disadvantages of monopoly, but without the accompanying advantages. Consequently the legislation is more stringent than legislation relating to mergers. The grounds on which firms can attempt to justify restrictive agreements are closely specified. Strict interpretation of these 'gateways' by the Restrictive Practices Court has led to the abandonment of most of the registered agreements. (However, in some instances the firms have been able to achieve the same objectives through non-registrable agreements.)
5. Resale price maintenance is adjudged to restrict increases in efficiency, especially in the distributive trades. Consequently the producers of only very few products have been allowed to enforce the price at which their products are sold.
6. Although the scope of competition policy has been extended in recent years, numerous suggestions have been made for further changes in order to increase the policy's effectiveness.

Key terms

Structure–conduct–performance
Concentration

Director-General of Fair Trading
Treaty of Rome

Mergers
Monopolies and Mergers Commission
Restrictive Practices Court

Collective restrictive practices
Resale price maintenance

Notes

1. See, for example, Meeks G, *Disappointing Marriage: A Study in the Gains from Merger*. Cambridge Univ. Press, 1977; Firth M, The profitability of takeovers and Mergers, *Economic Journal*, 1979; Cowling K *et al.*, *Mergers and Economic Performance*. Cambridge Univ. Press, 1980. A more favourable verdict is contained in Franks J R and Harris R S, Shareholder wealth effects of corporate takeovers; the UK experience 1955–85. Paper presented at the IFS Conference on Merger Policy, July 1986.
2. Button K J, New approaches to the regulation of industry, *The Royal Bank of Scotland Review*, 1985.
3. These and other cases are reviewed in Ferguson P R, The Monopolies and Mergers Commission and economic theory, *National Westminster Quarterly Review*, Nov. 1985.
4. Hannah L and Kay J, *Concentration in Modern Industry*. Macmillan, 1977; Cowling *et al.*, op. cit.
5. Company profitability and finance, *Bank of England Quarterly Bulletin*, June 1986, p. 233.
6. Constable J, Diversification as a factor in UK industrial strategy, *Long Range Planning*, **19** No 1 (1986). However, a paper presented by Hughes A, at the IFS Conference on Merger Policy in July 1986 showed that in the UK diversifying mergers tended to be more successful than horizontal mergers.
7. Prais S J, *The Evolution of Giant Firms in Britain*. Cambridge Univ. Press, 1976.
8. Sharpe T, British competition policy in perspective, *Oxford Review of Economic Policy*, **1** (1985).

Essay questions

1. Explain the meaning of market structure, conduct and performance and discuss the possible relationships among them.
2. Outline the major elements of market structure and discuss the possible implications of each element.
3. Explain how competition policy may influence the level of economic efficiency.
4. 'Since high levels of concentration facilitate undesirable conduct, competition policy should try to prevent any increase in concentration.' Discuss.
5. Outline the main provisions of UK legislation concerning (a) monopolies, (b) mergers, (c) collective restrictive practices, and discuss the major objectives of this legislation.
6. Why have UK governments adopted a much tougher line towards collective restrictive practices than towards mergers?
7. Outline the main provisions of the 1973 Fair Trading Act and explain how these provisions might benefit consumers.
8. Discuss the view that the most effective form of competition policy would be to control the prices of large firms.

9. Discuss the view that the most effective form of competition policy would be to control the profits of large firms.
10. Discuss the advantages and disadvantages of a competition policy which incorporates non-discretionary rules.

Exercises

10.1 All of the practices below were identified in reports of the MMC. Discuss the advantages and disadvantages of each practice.
  (i)   Supply restrictions to retailers: the MMC's report on infant milk foods found that their distribution by the two major manufacturers – Glaxo and Cow and Gate – was mainly restricted to chemists and clinics.
  (ii)   Restrictions on the sale of competitors' goods: in its report on asbestos products the MMC showed that the dominant manufacturer, Turner and Newall, had concluded agreements with certain customers which restricted them from buying asbestos textiles, packing and jointing products from its competitors.
  (iii) Full line forcing: in a report on metal containers the MMC found that Metal Box offered substantial discounts for customers buying all their requirements from that company.
  (iv)   Tie-in sales: the report on colour film drew attention to the practice of including the price of processing in the price of colour film.
  (v)   Patent licensing policy: the report on photo-copying machines found that both Xerox and Rank Xerox had accumulated large numbers of patents to protect their inventions.
  (vi)   Discriminatory pricing: the MMC's report on cellulosic fibres found that Courtaulds, the main producer, would supply fibres at cheaper rates to certain customers, often subsidiaries or associated companies of Courtaulds.
  (vii) Special terms or prices: in its report on discounts to retailers the MMC found 'relatively few suppliers who do not negotiate with, or grant to, some of their customers special terms or prices'.

10.2 The passage below was taken from the statement circulated to shareholders by the chairman of the London Brick Company. Discuss the chairman's comments concerning (a) the policy of raising prices in a recession, and (b) the policy of accepting lower margins on bricks delivered over longer distances.

The Monopolies Commission were satisfied that the Company had not used its monopoly position to make excessive profit out of fletton brickmaking. The report showed that in terms of capital employed on an historic basis, at no time over the last 20 years had the return exceeded 30 per cent and that the average level of Group profit had been 23 per cent. In a significant passage the Commission stated that they were struck by the consistency of the Company's profit record.

This suggests that the risks attached to LBC brickmaking activities are less than might be inferred from the vagaries of the brickmaking industry. The evidence indicates that LBC has not exploited its market power to raise prices at times when demand for bricks has been strong but has been able to use its market power to raise its prices in a recession so as to recover its profitability. Use of market power in this way is, I would contend, wholly legitimate. Not only does it safeguard the livelihood of those engaged in the industry and protect the interests of stockholders, but it ensures that the industry remains viable and that the customer continues to receive an efficient service in the supply of fletton bricks.

The one practice operated by the Company which was felt by a majority of the Commission to be against the public interest lay in the field of distribution. The practice related to the treatment of delivery charges in the compilation of the Company's delivered prices for bricks at distant points and whilst rather unimportant in commercial terms, is interesting in the broader context of seeking to decide where the common interest lies.

Before the war when London Brick was seeking to expand its markets throughout the country, a policy was adopted of seeking a lower return on the price of bricks delivered longer distances from the works from those delivered nearer home. This was unashamedly designed to establish wider markets for the fletton brick at a time when the 'fletton' was not nationally accepted and when a few pence off the price could mean the difference between winning or losing an order. Those days have long since gone and for some years the sale of LBC bricks has been firmly established throughout the country at prices considerably below those of its competitors. The practice however of accepting some lower margin on bricks delivered over longer distances and balancing this by rather higher margins on bricks delivered nearer home has been maintained for rather different reasons. It was believed that, as fletton bricks are a basic material for building and particularly used in low cost housing, it was in the interest of both our builder and local authority customers engaged in brick construction to apply some element of levelling in the prices charged throughout the country. Secondly, it was felt that through maintaining a large volume of business at distant points we would gain the same additional benefit of economy of scale, both in our production and perhaps more important in our methods of distribution.

10.3 The following data were taken from the MMC's *Report on Household Detergents* (HMSO, 1966). It refers to the activities of Unilever and Procter and Gamble, whose sales of household detergents in 1964 were roughly equal, and who together accounted for some 90 per cent of total supplies.

Breakdown of retail price of 'typical' packet of detergent (index nos.)

	Unilever	P. & G.
Factory cost	46	43.5
Research, administration, distribution	7.5	7
Selling cost	23	23
Total manufacturer's cost	76.5	73.5
Manufacturer's profit	7.5	10.5
Manufacturer's price	84	84
Retailer's margin	16	16
Retail price	100	100

Indices of sales, manufacturer's prices and costs: all detergents 1964
(1954 = 100)

	Unilever	P. & G.
Sales tonnage	115	148
Manufacturer's price	118	105
Costs other than selling expenses (per ton)	113	97
Selling expenses (per ton)	88	99
Total costs (per ton)	103	97

Profits as a percentage of capital employed (replacement cost basis)

	Unilever	P. & G.	Manufacturing industry average
1959	n.a.	29.3	12.2
1960	34.3	36.2	13.1
1961	12.9	34.8	11.1
1962	14.8	42.4	9.9
1963	26.9	40.3	10.8
1964	17.6	36.9	n.a.
1965	16.4	37.0	n.a.

n.a. = not available.

In the light of these data, evaluate the heavy selling expenses incurred by the manufacturers of detergents from the viewpoint of (a) the two manufacturers, (b) consumers.

10.4 The table below gives the price (net of taxes) of an Austin Metro 1000L in various countries in autumn 1983.
  (i)   How would you account for these price differentials?
  (ii) How might distributors react to these price differentials?
  (iii) What policies might BL (Austin-Rover) have adopted in order to try to ensure that the price differentials were not eroded?
  (iv) Evaluate the likely consequences of the differentials for consumer welfare.

Austin Metro 1000L prices

	Belgium	France	W. Germany	UK
In ECUs	3,978	4,236	4,318	5,938
In £s	2,296	2,445	2,492	3,427

10.5 In 1986 the MMC reported on the proposed take-over of Plessey by GEC. Together the two companies supply between 25 and 30 per cent of the total UK output of electronic capital equipment and components, and larger proportions of some important segments of the telecommunications and defence electronics markets. Both companies were judged to be generally successful, financially sound and profitable.

  In international terms, GEC was the fourteenth and Plessey the twenty-first largest supplier in the markets concerned. Even after a merger the combined sales would be considerably smaller than those of the world's leading companies. Plessey's overseas sales in 1984–85 were equivalent to 17 per cent of the group's UK sales.

  In the five years to 1984–85 Plessey's spending on R & D increased by over 200 per cent. GEC and the Department of Trade and Industry told the MMC that the merger could eliminate duplication in R & D. But the Ministry of Defence, a major customer, feared the elimination of separate research teams seeking alternative solutions.

  In telecommunications equipment the two companies together supplied about 50 per cent of the market. Both companies had excess System X public exchange capacity, due to a failure to achieve export targets.
  (i) On the basis of the above information, do you think GEC should have been allowed to proceed with its bid?
  (ii) What additional information might the MMC have sought during its investigation?

CHAPTER ELEVEN
Nationalization and Privatization

Introduction

Nationalization and denationalization or privatization usually involve a change in the ownership of assets. We examine the theoretical arguments that have been advanced to justify a change in ownership and some of the consequences. But we begin by defining nationalized industries.

Nationalized industries

The essential features of nationalized industries are that:
(a) their assets are in public ownership and vested in a corporation which is primarily engaged in industrial or other trading activities;
(b) their revenue is mainly derived from these trading activities, i.e. from the sale of goods and services;
(c) their boards are appointed by a government minister, but board members and employees are not civil servants.

Examples of nationalized industries that readily come to mind are British Rail, the Post Office and British Coal. At the end of 1987 nationalized industries accounted for 5.5 per cent of UK output (as compared to 9 per cent in 1979) and almost 4 per cent of employment.

Publicly owned enterprises which are not nationalized industries include public corporations which do not derive most of their revenue from the sale of goods and services, e.g. the British Broadcasting Corporation whose main source of revenue is licence fees, and central government trading bodies which may derive their revenue from sales but do not have independent boards, e.g. Her Majesty's Stationery Office.

The reasons for nationalization

Industries may be nationalized for political or ideological reasons, but we confine our attention to economic motives, as far as possible. An industry might be nationalized in order to prevent the earning of above-average profits. This is especially relevant in a 'natural monopoly' where, because of economies of scale, the market can be supplied at lowest cost by a single firm.

A reduction in profits following nationalization would imply a redistribution of real income, towards either consumers via a price reduction, or workers via wage increases. Countries may nationalize foreign-owned assets to ensure that profits are retained within the country. This entails redistribution of income at the international level.

Bringing the assets of an industry under unified control may make it easier to organize production in such a way that economies of scale can be enjoyed. Economies of scale were discussed in detail in Chapter 5, and it is sufficient to note here that two particular types of economy may in principle be expected to follow from nationalization. The first is the reduction in cost per unit of output that can be obtained by concentrating production in fewer and bigger plants and/or organizations. The second is the reduction in cost that can arise from the closer integration of different operations. So, for example, in the steel industry the siting in close proximity of plants producing ingots and plants rolling those ingots allows savings in fuel and transport costs.

Economic efficiency can also be increased by eliminating the overlapping activities of competing suppliers. The supply of such services as electricity and water requires the provision of physical 'channels of supply' – pipes, conduits, etc. – and it is clearly more economical to provide one set of channels for a given area than several.

An industry may be nationalized in order to ensure an adequate supply of goods and services. The public provision of merit and public goods was examined in Chapter 9 and so need not be discussed here. A quite different argument relates to the concepts of linkages and bottlenecks. This argument may be illustrated by reference to the steel industry. The demand for steel tends to be highly cyclical. Consequently if the industry were in private hands producers might play safe by restricting the expansion of capacity so as to ensure, as far as possible, a high degree of capacity utilization. They might risk a loss of potential profits should demand turn out to be higher than expected, in order to minimize the possibility of losses due to demand turning out to be less than expected.

While such a policy might be sensible from the steel producers' point of view, it might mean that producers in other industries are unable to meet the peak demand for such products as cars and washing machines, because of a shortage of steel.

Private sector producers might be unwilling to supply certain parts of the market, for example remote geographical areas, because of the high costs involved. This is especially likely to happen where substantial costs have to be incurred before supply can take place, e.g. in electricity distribution. Under nationalization, supplies to these areas can be subsidized out of the revenue derived from the more profitable parts of the market (cross-subsidization), or out of general taxation.

Finally, an industry might be nationalized in order to maintain employment above the level that would result from the free operation of market forces. This implies that additional cost will be incurred. If the industry is to avoid making a loss, a subsidy is likely to be required. This subsidy is in effect an alternative to the payment of unemployment benefits.

The performance of the nationalized industries

It is difficult to evaluate the performance of the nationalized industries as a whole, if only because the economic circumstances facing the various industries differ enormously, resulting in a wide variety of outcomes. For example Pryke found that between 1968 and 1978 real unit costs fell by 40 per cent in telecommunications and by 46 per cent in gas, but rose by 52 per cent in bus transport and by 81 per cent in coal-mining.[1]

Given these disparities it might seem sensible first to try to evaluate the performance of individual industries, leaving overall comparisons until later. Where there is competition between publicly owned and privately owned producers, the performance of the two can be compared.

The performance of publicly and privately owned producers

Pryke compared performance in three markets: air transport (British Airways with British Caledonian), sea transport (Sealink UK with European Ferries), and the retailing of household appliances (British Gas Corporation and Electricity Board Showrooms with Currys and Comet).[2] Pryke concluded that in terms of a number of indicators, privately owned concerns showed the better performance.

For example European Ferries' turnover was 80 per cent greater than that of Sealink on the routes on which they competed. Comet had increased their share of all sales by electrical shops from a negligible figure in 1971 to 9 per cent in 1980, whereas in the same period the electricity boards failed to increase their market share of 18 per cent. Productivity and operating profits were higher in

British Caledonian than in British Airways, and in European Ferries than in Sealink.

Pryke's study has been criticized on two grounds. The first is that it ignored some of the factors that might affect performance, e.g. the different range of routes operated by the two ferry companies. Second, Pryke compared the nationalized organizations with the best of private sector organizations.[3] Other private sector ferry operators have been much less successful than European Ferries. For example P. & O. Ferries made losses for several years before selling their operations to European Ferries. (Moreover the profitability of European Ferries has declined since Pryke's study.) 'The implication is that private firms are not necessarily intrinsically more efficient, but that market pressures are more effective at weeding out poorly performing firms in the private sector than in the public.'[4]

The criteria used by Pryke to evaluate performance were normal commercial criteria. But, as we noted above, it is sometimes argued that one of the objectives of a nationalized industry should be to protect the interests of the workers. In this context it was interesting to note the reactions of the trade unions to the privatization of Sealink. The unions threatened to strike in order to try to prevent the privatization, since privatization would pose a threat to their jobs and conditions of service. The reactions of the unions supports Pryke's hypothesis that private ownership is conducive to superior commercial performance.

Other comparative studies

Local authority refuse services have recently been thrown open to competitive tender in parts of the UK. A study by the Audit Commission found a considerable diversity in the performance of public suppliers. The Commission's analysis implied that in some areas an efficient private supplier would substantially undercut the local authorities. On the other hand the Commission found that costs in the most efficient 25 per cent of local authorities were as low as those of the best private contractors.[5]

When the Commission studied municipal housing it found a number of chronic deficiencies that would have been much less likely to have persisted in the private sector. These deficiencies included supplying the wrong product (e.g. deck-access, system-built tower blocks), very high administrative costs (approaching £10 per dwelling per week in some Inner London boroughs), and more than 100,000 empty properties (about a quarter of which had been empty for more than a year), despite long waiting lists for housing.

Other empirical studies of the relative performance of private and public enterprises have been summarized by Yarrow, by Borcherding *et al.* and by Millward.[6] The evidence of these studies is mixed. But there is a tendency for performance to be better in private than in public sector organizations in markets that are competitive. The importance of the environment in which the organization operates is considered again when we discuss privatization.

Productivity

A study by the Treasury, published in 1987, showed that since 1980/81 productivity (output per head) had increased by 45 per cent in the nationalized industries, as compared to 38 per cent in manufacturing and 21 per cent in the economy as a whole. This higher rate of productivity increase had been achieved despite the fact that output increased by less (3 per cent) in the nationalized industries than in manufacturing (13 per cent) and the economy as a whole (more than 20 per cent). However, employment in the nationalized industries had fallen by almost a third, as compared to a fifth in manufacturing and 5 per cent in the whole economy (excluding the North Sea oil industry and the non-trading public sector).

These differences in performance are due partly to the fact that as the economy emerged from recession, demand remained relatively depressed for such basic industries as coal, and partly to the greater financial discipline exerted by the government. The external finance limit for the industries (see below) was reduced from £3.2bn. in 1980/81 to £1.2bn. in 1986/87.

Profitability

As a whole the nationalized industries have consistently earned lower profits than private sector companies. Indeed in the absence of subsidies, the nationalized industries would have earned a negative real rate of return in most years.

It might be argued that low profitability is desirable as an indication that 'fair' prices have been set. However, low profits can also arise because of inefficiency, and on the whole prices (and wages) have tended to rise more quickly in the nationalized industries than in private sector firms.[7]

Whatever the cause of low profitability, its consequence is that nationalized industries have been unable to finance as much of their capital expenditure as private sector firms. However, in the 1980s the Conservative government required the nationalized industries to set prices that would enable a higher level of self-financing to be attained (see below).

The control of the nationalized industries

The Nationalization Acts lay down responsibilities only in the most general terms, e.g. that the industry should provide a service 'with due regard to efficiency, economy and service'. Consequently far greater importance attaches to the influence exercised by the government of the day. We discuss this influence with reference to pricing and investment decisions.

The pricing policies of the nationalized industries

Guidelines for pricing policies were laid down in a White Paper issued in 1967. The major guidelines were as follows:

(a) '. . . nationalized industries' revenues should normally cover their accounting costs in full';

(b) '. . . pricing policies should be devised with reference to the costs of the particular goods and services provided. Unless this is done, there is a risk of undesirable cross-subsidization and consequent misallocation of resources';

(c) '. . . in addition to recovering accounting costs, prices need to be reasonably related to costs at the margin and to be designed to promote the efficient use of resources within industry. Where there is spare capacity . . . or excess demand, short-run marginal costs are relevant . . . In the long run, the main consideration is . . . long run marginal costs.' (This guideline was emphasized in a later White Paper, published in 1978.)

Guidelines (a) and (c) may be compatible in principle, but are frequently incompatible in practice. Figure 11.1 refers to an industry whose average cost continues to fall as output increases. In this situation, at price P_1 revenue covers average cost but the price exceeds marginal cost. Conversely, although price P_2 equals marginal cost, revenue does not cover average cost. In other words it is impossible in this situation (whatever the demand conditions) to set a price which meets both guidelines (a) and (c). (If price is set equal to marginal cost the result is, of course, that the industry makes a loss and requires a government subsidy.)

It may be possible to reconcile these objectives by means of a two-part tariff, comprising a charge per unit consumed and a standing charge (to meet the organization's fixed costs). In Fig. 11.2 D

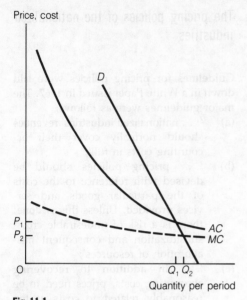

Fig. 11.1
Nationalized industry price with falling average cost

indicates the number of units that would be purchased at various unit charges. At price P, Q is bought and price equals marginal cost. In order to meet fixed costs a standing charge has to be levied to yield revenue $OQ(YZ)$. Two-part tariffs are used in the gas, electricity and telecommunications industries, although the standing

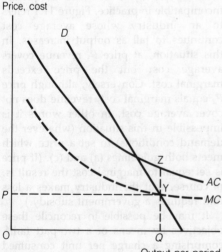

Fig. 11.2
A two-part tariff

charge is sufficient to cover only part of the organization's fixed costs.

Investment decisions

The investment programmes of the nationalized industries are influenced by three sets of measures.

Target rates of return[8]

The industries have been expected to invest only in projects which promise to yield more than the test discount rate (TDR) (set at 10 per cent in 1969). The TDR is intended to approximate to the average rate of return achieved on low-risk projects in the private sector, and in principle is a sound guideline to the allocation of resources. It is, however, a guideline that is often difficult to follow in practice, since many individual projects must be undertaken since they form part of a much bigger investment programme determined by prior strategic decisions, for example to install sufficient generating capacity to meet the peak demand for electricity.

In order to overcome this problem the government specified a required rate of return (RRR) on investment which was intended to give more weight to investment programmes as a whole rather than to individual projects. The RRR is 5 per cent in real terms before tax, a good approximation to the average rate of return earned by private sector firms.

Financial targets

When the RRR was introduced, it was suggested that it could be translated into a financial target by which the industry's performance as a whole could be judged. In specifying these financial targets the government takes account of the industries' economic circumstances. Since these differ, the financial targets also differ. It is not unknown for the target of an industry facing very difficult circumstances to be expressed in terms of a maximum loss.

External finance limits

Each year the government specifies the maximum amount of external finance that can be raised by each industry. Any industry that is in danger of exceeding the limit is expected to seek to improve its efficiency rather than to gain additional revenue via higher prices. The industries' ability to borrow was severely limited by the Conservative government in the mid 1980s. The intention was to increase the proportion of capital spending financed from internal sources from 45 per cent in 1983–84 to 98 per cent by 1986–87. The total external finance limit for 1987–88 was £692m. British Coal and British Rail were each allowed to borrow more than £700m. On the other hand the electricity industry (in England and Wales) had a negative limit of £1.3bn., i.e. it was expected to pay this amount to the government.

Privatization

Privatization, like nationalization, can be undertaken for both economic and political motives. An important economic factor, mentioned above, is to avoid the inefficiency that can arise when suppliers are sheltered from market forces. An obvious political factor in the UK was the election in 1979 of a Conservative government determined to reduce the size of the public sector. However, the 1980s has seen privatization programmes in countries with governments of widely differing political complexions, including France, Spain, Brazil, Bangladesh and even – on a very limited scale – Cuba and China.[9]

Privatization defined

Two aspects of privatization can be distinguished, both of which lead to a switch of resources from the public to the private sector. The first is a transfer of ownership to the private sector, i.e. the opposite of nationalization. The second is opening to private sector suppliers markets that were previously reserved for public sector suppliers. For example many local authorities have given contracts for services such as refuse collection and hospital cleaning to private contractors. The Conservative government permitted private sector suppliers to compete in part of the market for telecommunications equipment. In 1982 a licence was granted to Mercury, owned by Cable and Wireless, BP and the Barclays Bank group, to operate a rival telecommunications network, prior to the privatization of British Telecom (BT).

In the early years most of the privatization programme was implemented by the local authorities, through the contracting out of services and the sale of council houses. Between 1979 and 1983 nearly 600,000 housing units were sold, more than in the whole of the 1945–79 period. Receipts rose from around £300m. in 1979 to nearly £2bn. in 1982.

Since 1984 the emphasis has swung towards the sale of large public enterprises. When BT was sold for almost £4bn., it was at the time the largest share offer anywhere in the world, and this record was subsequently broken by the sale of British Gas for around £5.5bn., and of the government's remaining stake in BP for over £6bn. Sales on this scale can meet a number of objectives.

The objectives of privatization

The objectives of privatization appear to have included to:

(a) increase producers' exposure to competition and so provide an incentive to increased efficiency;
(b) reduce the public sector borrowing requirement;
(c) widen share ownership;
(d) allow firms to compete more freely for funds in the capital market;
(e) ease problems of pay determination in the public sector;
(f) redistribute income and wealth;
(g) free producers from detailed government intervention.[10]

Conflicts inevitably arise between various objectives. For example, exposing producers to competition, in line with the first objective, is likely to make their shares less attractive, and so reduce the goverment's receipts from the sale, i.e. it militates against the second and third objectives. In fact the government has not increased the amount of competition as much as it might in a number of instances. It could, for example, have split BT and British Gas into a number of regionally based competing units. Additional competitors to BT, other than Mercury, could have been licensed. Some economists have criticized the policy adopted on the ground that it simply substituted a privately owned for a publicly owned monopoly. On the other hand the government decided that the National Bus Company should be split into seventy-one units, including engineering companies, even though it was thought (wrongly in the event) that this might

reduce the value put on an issue by as much as a half.[11]

The decision to confirm BT's monopoly status (except for the limited competition offered by Mercury) was accompanied by the establishment of a regulatory body, the Office of Telecommunications (OFTEL), responsible for preventing anti-competitive behaviour. Moreover a pricing formula was agreed whereby the maximum price increase allowed on a basket of BT's outputs (services where little or no competition exists and accounting for about half of the company's revenue) is $4\frac{1}{2}$ per cent less than the change in the retail price index. In addition BT is required to provide a number of 'public service' facilities, including public phone boxes and emergency services. A similar regulatory structure and pricing formula has been adopted for British Gas.

Summary

1. Nationalization has been justified on the grounds that it can help to prevent the earning of monopoly profits, redistribute income, increase economic efficiency, ensure an adequate supply of goods and services and maintain employment.
2. There are vast differences in the performance of different nationalized industries. Moreover, when a comparison is made between publicly and privately owned suppliers of given products, the results are not unambiguous. However, it appears that poorly performing firms are less likely to survive in the private than in the public sector.
3. The activities of the nationalized industries are constrained by a range of mechanisms. Two areas in which governments frequently intervene are decisions relating to price and investment.
4. A major motive for privatization is to avoid the inefficiency that can arise when suppliers are sheltered from market forces. Privatization may involve the transfer of assets from the public to the private sector. Alternatively, it may involve opening to private sector suppliers markets that were previously reserved for public sector suppliers.
5. In transferring assets to private ownership there may be a trade-off between raising revenue for the government and increasing competition. The UK programme of privatization has been criticized as putting too much emphasis on the first objective.

Key terms

Monopoly profits   Two-part tariff
Efficiency   Test discount rate

Linkages and bottlenecks   Required rate of return
Subsidies   External financing limits
Cross-subsidization   Exposure to competition
Marginal cost pricing   RPI$-x$ pricing formula

Notes

1. Pryke R, *The Nationalized Industries: Policies and Performance since 1968*. Martin Robertson, 1981.
2. Pryke R, The comparative performance of public and private enterprise, *Fiscal Studies*, 1982.
3. Marshall D, The nationalized industries. In Griffiths A and Wall S, *Applied Economics*. Longman, 1986.
4. Kay J A and Thompson D J, Privatization: a policy in search of a rationale, *Economic Journal*, March 1986.
5. Audit Commission, *Securing Further Improvements in Refuse Collection*. HMSO, 1984.
6. Yarrow G, Privatization in theory and practice, *Oxford Review of Economic Policy*, 1986; Borcherding T E, Pommerehne W W and Schneider F, Comparing the efficiency of private and public production: the evidence from five countries, *Zeitschrift für Nationalökonomie* (Journal of Economics), Suppl. 2 (1982); Millward R, The comparative performance of public and private ownership. In Roll E (ed.) *The Mixed Economy*. Macmillan, 1982.
7. Pryke, op. cit., 1981.
8. The calculation of the rate of return is explained in Chapter 16.
9. Privatization overseas, *Economic Progress Report*, March–April 1986; Aylen J, Privatization in developing countries, *Lloyds Bank Review*, Jan. 1987.
10. This list of objectives follows that presented in Yarrow, op. cit.
11. Fisher A, Mr Ridley drives on despite the doubters, *Financial Times*, 26 Feb. 1986.

Essay questions

1. What do you think should be the objectives of nationalized industries? How (if at all) do you think these objectives should differ from those of non-nationalized concerns?
2. 'All commercial institutions should be subject to discipline of one kind or another, either the discipline of the market-place, or discipline imposed by higher authority. The trouble with nationalization is that it removed the first source of discipline, without introducing the second.' Discuss.
3. Outline the various objectives which nationalization might be designed to achieve, and show why conflicts may arise between these objects.
4. 'Although nationalization may in principle contribute to an increase in economic efficiency, the performance of the nationalized industries indicates that it does not do so in practice.' Discuss.
5. To what extent are the financial results of the nationalized industries an indicator of their efficiency?
6. Show how nationalization may lead to a redistribution of real income.
7. Outline the major objectives of nationalization and discuss what alternative measures (if any) might enable these objectives to be achieved.
8. What factors should be considered by (a) a private sector producer and (b) a public corporation in making an investment decision?

9. Discuss the relative merits of the public regulation of, and the public ownership of, a monopoly.
10. Compare the effects of privatization by selling shares to investors with privatization by a free distribution of shares to all citizens.

Exercises

11.1 Below is a list of policies each of which may be assumed to result in a loss to the nationalized industry adopting that policy. State in each case whether you think that the policy should be adopted, and if so, who should bear the loss. Explain the reasoning underlying your answers.
   (i) The provision of air services to the Highlands and Islands of Scotland.
   (ii) The building of an underground railway line in London, which would reduce the amount of rush-hour congestion.
   (iii) The operation of unprofitable coal-mines in areas of high unemployment.
   (iv) The purchase of coal produced in the UK, rather than cheaper imported coal, to fuel electricity-generating stations.
   (v) The movement of steel by rail rather than by road transport, which would be less expensive.

11.2 Table 11.1 shows the financing of the nationalized industries in 1983–84, and the government's plans for the next three years.
   (i) How would you explain the government's plans as shown in Table 11.1?
   (ii) Discuss the likely impact of these plans on (a) the nationalized industries, (b) private sector producers, (c) consumers.

Table 11.1
Nationalized industries' capital spending and financing*
(£m., cash basis)

	1983/84	1984/85	1985/86	1986/87
Capital spending	5,218	5,330	4,869	4,867
To be financed from:				
Internal resources	2,341	3,039	3,724	4,775
External funds	2,877	2,291	1,145	92

* Excluding BT, British Airways and Enterprise Oil.
Source: Public Expenditure White Paper

11.3 The passage below is based on an article in the *Financial Times*, 11 April 1986. What policy do you think the government should adopt towards coal prices? Explain your decision.

Differences emerged yesterday between the Department of Energy and the Treasury about the extent to which electricity consumers should be allowed to benefit from the fall in oil prices. Last week the Central Electricity Generating Board said it would save the equivalent of up to £500m. in a full year if it switched from burning coal to oil in its power stations. This would be enough to

Table 11.2
Financial results of the major nationalized industries

	Electricity Council 1986 (£m.)	1985 (£m.)	British Gas 1986 (£m.)	1985 (£m.)	Post Office 1986 (£m.)	1985 (£m.)	British Steel 1986 (£m.)	1985 (£m.)	British Rail 1986 (£m.)	1985 (£m.)	British Coal 1986 (£m.)	1985 (£m.)	British Shipbuilders 1986 (£m.)	1985 (£m.)
Turnover	10.743	9.942	7.687	6.914	3.248	3.208	3.735	3.736	3.145	3.558*	5.340	2.018	173	171
Historic cost pre-tax profit (loss)	1.445	(593)	1.101	992	224	173	42	(378)	(12)	(288)*	(48)	(2.222)	(182)	(109)
CCA pre-tax profit (loss)†	414	(1.708)	782	712	152	144	79	(497)	(97)	(380)*	(429)	(2.459)	(182)	(110)
CCA net assets (deficiency of assets)	36.727	35.345	18.183	16.629	1.641	1.462	2.868	2.276	2.666	2.478	2.450	2.635	(43)‡	†320
External financing limit (EFL)	(1.128)		(176)		(70)		414		918	929	929		75	
Outcome against EFL	(467)		(190)		(75)		411		910		429		73	
Capital expenditure	1.262	1.309	572	812	129	155	220	210	263	206*	660	363	15	8
Employees	131,466	133,718	89,747	93,118	179,753	177,381	54,200	64,500	173,760	180,669	179,645	221,298	10,013	40,785

* Fifteen-month period.
† CCA = Current cost accounting.
‡ Historic cost figures.
Source: Financial Times, 11 Aug. 1986

cancel out the 5 per cent rise in electricity tariffs announced recently. The NCB has offered price reductions which would save the CEGB £100m. off its existing coal bill. Mr Peter Walker, Energy Secretary, appears to be in favour of letting electricity consumers benefit to the maximum extent possible from cheaper oil. He does not believe, however, that too much pressure should be put on the NCB at a time when morale is recovering from the coal strike and capacity is being reduced. The Treasury is unwilling to sanction any extra subsidy to the NCB to compensate for lower coal prices.

11.4 (i) With reference to Table 11.2 discuss the performance of the nationalized industries.

(ii) The profit of British Gas is struck after deducting a gas levy of £525m. British Rail's loss is arrived at after crediting government grants of £914m. relating to its public service obligations. British Coal's loss is struck after crediting social grants of £513m. Evaluate the case for making these adjustments.

11.5 British Telecom and British Gas are subject to the retail price index (RPI) − x pricing formula, whereby any increase in their average price must be less than the increase in the RPI. In an article in *Lloyds Bank Review*, 1983, Beesley and Littlechild argued that this should be

a temporary safeguard, not a permanent method of control. . . . A preferable alternative to detailed regulation of costs, profits or prices is greater reliance on competition policy. Predatory competition should be discouraged, both to curb monopoly power and to allow new ownership structures to emerge after privatization. . . . Certain practices (e.g. price discrimination, refusal to supply, full-line forcing) should be explicitly prohibited if they are used by the dominant incumbent to eliminate or discipline specific competitors. Parties adversely affected should be able to sue in the Courts, perhaps for triple damages.

Evaluate the arguments presented by Beesley and Littlechild.

CHAPTER TWELVE
Regional and Urban Policy

Introduction

This is the final chapter concerned with government policies which affect individual markets or sectors of the economy. Previously we have distinguished markets and sectors in terms of the products demanded and supplied. In this chapter the basis of our distinction is geographical. Our main concern is the inequalities between regions, and especially regional differences in levels of unemployment and income.

We examine below the measures that governments have taken in an attempt to reduce these inequalities. But since government intervention is not favoured by all economists, we first consider the alternative approach, in which reliance is placed on the elimination of inequalities through the operation of market forces.

The free market approach

The ideological view underlying this approach is that economic units should be free to make their own decisions. The argument is advanced that if workers are dissatisfied with the employment opportunities, and the associated standard of living, in a given area they will seek work in other areas. In this way the unemployment differentials will be reduced and eventually disappear. If workers do not move, this would be taken as an indication that the area has advantages which outweigh the limited employment opportunities, so that again, it is argued, there is no case for government intervention.

Similarly, if firms are left free to make their own location decisions they will establish plants in areas of high unemployment in order to take advantage of the excess labour supply, and of the lower wage rates with which (in the absence of union monopoly power) this will be associated. If firms do not establish plants in these areas it indicates that they consider the advantages of a plentiful labour supply to be outweighed by other economic disadvantages, and so again there is no case for government intervention.

To summarize, this suggests that market forces are likely to lead to the elimination of unemployment differentials; furthermore if this does not occur it indicates that workers and firms consider that the costs involved in eliminating the differentials would outweigh the benefits. Hence the government should not attempt to influence the location decisions of workers and firms.

An evaluation of the free market approach

An evaluation of the free market approach must take into account institutional factors, the nature of the costs and benefits involved in decisions, and the time-scale likely to be involved in the solution. It should also, of course, take into account the costs of alternative solutions, a point considered later in the chapter.

Institutional factors

An important plank in the free market platform is the assumption that the labour market is highly sensitive to market forces, and in particular that differential rates of unemployment will be reflected in differential wage rates. In practice the spread of collective bargaining, often on an industry or occupation-wide basis, has reduced the sensitivity of wage rates to local unemployment rates. (Incidentally, even if wage rates are lower in some areas than others it does not follow that labour costs will be lower, since differences in wage rates may be balanced or even outweighed by differences in labour productivity.) Another important institutional factor is the availability of unemployment and other social security benefits. The narrower the gap between benefits and earnings, the greater the interference with the operation of market forces. We are not concerned with whether this interference is or is not desirable. We merely point out that a 'pure' free market solution to the regional problem is in fact ruled out.

The costs and benefits
It is impossible to identify and measure all the costs and benefits associated with location decisions, if only because subjective judgements are involved, at least on the part of workers. Nevertheless the free market approach can be challenged on the grounds that it ignores two important types of cost.

First, the approach takes account only of internal or private costs, and ignores external costs – costs incurred by people not party to the decision. When a firm considers the cost of establishing a plant in alternative locations it is likely to take account only of the costs which affect its own profitability; it does not consider how its decision may affect the profitability of other firms. And yet it is not difficult to show that external costs are likely to arise. The arrival of a firm of any size in an area adds to the pressure in the labour market which may make it more difficult and/or expensive for other employers to attract and retain labour. Similarly, added pressure will be put on the transport network, which may result in more congestion, delays in the delivery of goods, etc.

Again, the movement of workers into an area is likely to put additional pressure on communal facilities – medical, educational, recreational, etc. – to the detriment of people already living in that area.

It should be said that external effects, or externalities, are not always adverse. External benefits (external economies) may also arise. The establishment of one firm may reduce the costs of other firms

in the area, either directly or indirectly. The new firm may be able to supply components at a lower price than alternative suppliers located in other, more distant, areas. An indirect benefit may arise if the establishment of new firms justifies the creation or development of facilities, such as an airport or a technical college, that benefit all firms in the area. Similarly the migration of workers to an area may justify the development of social facilities such as a theatre or sports complex. (However, this migration is equally likely to reduce the viability of such enterprises in their 'home' areas.) We cannot therefore conclude that the external effects of every location decision will on balance be adverse. However, the fact remains that total welfare is affected by external effects, and any approach which neglects such effects is to some extent inadequate.

An allied but slightly different point concerns what we may call removal costs. These are simply the costs incurred when people move their residence or firms change their location – the costs of searching for a new home or site, of moving furniture or machines, etc. Although existing 'residents' – firms or families – may be adversely affected by an inflow of firms or workers, they may still be better off than they would be if they uprooted themselves and moved to another area, because of the removal costs that they would then incur. However, the fact that they stay does not mean that they have not suffered additional costs on account of the inflow.

A final set of costs which should be mentioned here, are partly internal and partly external. These include the disruption of family life that may occur when workers move, the increase in vandalism and crime that may result when people move into an area whose recreational facilities are inadequate, and mental illness suffered by people living alone in large cities. Since these factors often give rise to monetary costs – such as the cost of preventing or repairing the effects of vandalism, and an increase in expenditure on social services – they are of considerable economic importance.

The time-scale

Advocates of the free market approach seldom indicate how long they believe it would take for the problem to be solved – for regional unemployment differentials and differences in income to be eliminated. We clearly could not expect a precise time-scale to be provided, but an approximation would be useful since there is a danger that any solution which required a long period for its implementation would be unacceptable.

There are in fact several reasons for believing that the free market solution *would* require a long period. First, the differential rates of unemployment have arisen mainly because of the decline in long-established industries – coal-mining, slate-quarrying, shipbuilding, cotton textiles, etc. – which were highly concentrated geographically. The areas affected had a comparative advantage in these industries. On the other hand they may have a comparative disadvantage in many of the new industries that have become established more recently – light engineering, electronics, etc. The requirements of these new industries for labour, factory sites and access to markets were often met more easily in the south of England than in the more traditional industrial areas in the north of England, Scotland and Wales.

The second reason is the operation of the 'local multiplier'. This means that prosperous areas, to which workers move, become even more prosperous; depressed areas, from which workers move, become even more depressed. In terms of unemployment, the emigration of workers can be self-defeating. As some unemployed workers leave an area, additional unemployment may result from the loss of their purchasing power. These changes in the purchasing power of particular areas may also influence the subsequent location decisions of some firms. Other things being equal, the bigger the market the more attractive the area.

Third, of the workers who emigrate, a relatively high proportion tend to be, for obvious reasons, young and potentially more adaptable. These are the types of workers who are required by many employers, and their loss may make the area less attractive to potential new employers.

Finally, the free market approach will take longer to eliminate regional inequalities the less sensitive firms are to these inequalities, and especially to cost differentials. The approach assumes that firms undertake an extensive evaluation of alternative locations in order to discover the location at which profitability will be maximized. (This evaluation will take into account both costs and revenue.) In fact numerous studies have shown that the degree of search undertaken by firms is often very limited. Firms tend to set certain minimum requirements and to choose the first location which meets these requirements.

It would appear then that we may not be justified in leaving a solution of the regional problem to the operation of market forces, and that the case for intervention should be considered. Let us now therefore examine the policies that governments might adopt in order to modify the operation of market forces.

Government intervention

The first distinction is between policies designed to induce workers, and especially the unemployed, to move to areas of relatively low unemployment and those designed to induce firms to move to areas of high unemployment.

The first of these approaches implies the provision of incentives – financial assistance, training facilities – and/or information. The second approach may involve incentives of various kinds and/or restrictions, for example on where a new plant can be built. Restrictions are likely to represent the greatest degree of interference with the free play of market forces, although this depends, of course, upon the nature and scale of the restrictions and of the incentives offered.

We discuss below the actual policies in force in the UK. As a preliminary to this discussion we present a classification of the types of incentive that might in principle be offered to firms which create employment in areas of high unemployment.

Government incentives to firms

1. Subsidies related to the total costs and/or revenue of the firm.
2. Subsidies related to the cost of capital inputs – buildings, plant and equipment.
3. Subsidies related to the cost of labour.
4. The provision of advice and facilities, especially factories, for individual firms. Factories may be made available to rent or purchase. If they are provided at less than the market price, this measure is very similar to item (2).
5. The provision of facilities that might benefit more than one firm, e.g. central training facilities, an improved communications network.

The term 'subsidy', as used above, may refer to: tax relief (1), a low-cost loan (2) or a grant (2 and 3). A further distinction can be made between assistance available only to firms which move to an area and assistance available to all firms in an area, including those already established there. Finally, other conditions may be specified for the provision of assistance, e.g. that the assisted project creates a certain amount of additional employment.

Having examined the types of incentive that might be offered, we now outline the pattern of assistance in the UK. We shall

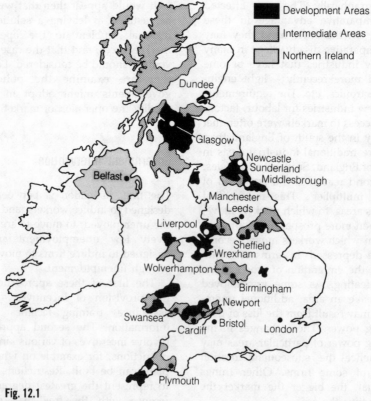

Development Areas

Intermediate Areas

Northern Ireland

Dundee

Glasgow

Newcastle
Sunderland
Middlesbrough

Belfast

Manchester
Leeds

Liverpool

Sheffield
Wrexham

Wolverhampton

Birmingham

Newport

Swansea

Cardiff   Bristol   London

Plymouth

Fig. 12.1
The Assisted Areas
Source: Department of Trade and Industry

Table 12.1
The main regional incentives in Great Britain*

Type of incentive	Development Areas	Intermediate Areas
Building, machinery and equipment grants	15%	Nil
Grants towards starting-up costs	Assistance on a discretionary basis related to the employment, location and capital requirements of the project	
Training grants	40% of basic wages and training costs	
R & D grants	Up to 33⅓%; maximum £5m.	
Factory rents	Subsidies of varying magnitude	

* The levels of assistance are considerably higher in Northern Ireland.
Source: British Business 1984

see that all except the first of the above types of incentive are available.

The pattern of assistance

Regional assistance has been provided for over fifty years. But the present pattern of assistance dates from April 1988. The areas in which assistance is available are shown in Fig. 12.1 and the forms of assistance are listed in Table 12.1.

This pattern of assistance differs from the previous one in a number of respects. Regional Development Grants (RDGs), which were available automatically to firms meeting the required conditions, were abolished (although existing commitments were honoured). Previously, RDGs were the main source of regional aid and the money released by their abolition was used to boost other forms of regional aid.

The greater emphasis on Regional Selective Assistance meant that the government (the Department of Trade and Industry) gained more control over the allocation of assistance. It seemed likely that this would result in less money being given to large British firms, who would probably invest even without government assistance, and more being given to small firms and overseas companies. Small and medium-size firms would also benefit from three new forms of assistance not listed in Table 12.1. Investment and Innovation Grants are available only in the Assisted Areas, and Enterprise Initiative Grants are

paid at a higher rate in Assisted Areas and Urban Development Areas (two-thirds of cost) than elsewhere (one-half).

The effect of these changes was expected to be an increase in spending on regional aid from £478m. in 1987/88 to £513m. in 1989/90.

The European dimension of regional policy

As noted in Chapter 25, UK membership of the European Community has given access to various European instruments of regional development. The European Regional Development Fund (ERDF) aids industrial and infrastructure projects. The money goes to the central government and local authorities and is thus not of direct benefit to firms. However, it does allow spending on regional policy to be higher than it would otherwise be. Since the inception of ERDF in 1975 over £2bn. has been allocated to the UK.

The European Investment Bank provides medium and long-term loans of up to 50 per cent of the capital costs of industrial projects in the Assisted Areas. The loans are provided at rates of interest below the commercial rate.

Loans are available from the European Coal and Steel Community (ECSC) for projects which contribute to improving efficiency, productivity or marketing in the coal and steel industries, and for projects providing new employment opportunities in coal or steel closure areas. The ECSC will lend up to 50 per cent of the capital cost of the project at a concessionary rate of interest.

The effectiveness of assistance

Moore, Rhodes and Tyler estimated that the cost of the 600,000 manufacturing jobs created during the period 1961–81 was £40,000 per job (in 1982 prices).[1] The main reason for this high cost was that RDGs, which were automatically available, were most attractive to capital-intensive industries. Of the £4.4bn. paid out in RDGs in the period 1973–84 no less than a quarter went to the chemical industry, and a third to chemicals, coal and petroleum.

Relatively few jobs were created by some of the projects funded in industries

such as chemicals and steel. Indeed Moore and his colleagues found evidence that in some industries capital subsidies had encouraged companies to install equipment at the expense of labour. On the other hand industries such as mechanical engineering, electrical engineering, vehicles and clothing, which received a much smaller share of overall expenditure, generated about 50 per cent of all new jobs. The cost per additonal worker in clothing was estimated by Rhodes to be £10,000, compared to £367,000 in metal manufacture.

Regional aid has been largely concentrated on the manufacturing sector. This bias towards manufacturing has proved especially unfortunate in view of the shift of employment from manufacturing to the service sector.[2]

Moreover, within the manufacturing sector, regional policy was associated with the establishment of many branch plants in the Assisted Areas. These plants, exter-

Table 12.2
Regional redundancy rates

Region	Redundancies per 1,000 employees in manufacturing	
	Average 1977–79	Average 1980–82
South East	9.0	34.2
East Anglia	12.9	37.6
South West	12.8	51.3
West Midlands	10.6	57.2
East Midlands	8.6	53.4
Yorkshire and Humberside	17.5	74.9
North West	25.5	77.1
North	28.6	76.4
Wales	19.8	104.2
Scotland	33.8	77.5
Great Britain	16.9	58.8

Source: Department of Employment, *Employment Gazette*, June 1983

Table 12.3
Gross domestic product per head as percentage of UK average

Region	GDP per head (UK = 100)	
	1975	1985
Greater London	125.7	125.8
Rest of South East	103.5	107.7
East Midlands	96.1	95.7
East Anglia	92.8	100.8
Scotland	97.1	97.3
North West	96.3	96.0
South West	90.3	93.8
West Midlands	100.1	92.3
Yorkshire and Humberside	94.1	91.8
Wales	88.7	88.8
Northern Ireland	80.2	74.8

Source: Economic Trends, Nov. 1986

nally owned and controlled, and frequently involved in the standardized manufacture of products in a fairly advanced stage of the product life-cycle, became only weakly integrated in the local economy. Consequently their multiplier impact was limited. Moreover they were very vulnerable in times of economic downturn. One indication of this vulnerability is the differentials in redundancy rates shown in Table 12.2.

Regional gross domestic product

Gross domestic product (GDP) per head (a measure of living standards) has grown more rapidly in London and the South East than in other regions. This is reflected in the differences in regional GDP shown in Table 12.3.

Regional household income and expenditure

Table 12.4 presents two other indicators of living standards, based on the Family Expenditure Survey. These figures again suggest that London and the South East are more prosperous than other regions. (However, it should be remembered that no allowance is made in Table 12.4 for possible differences in the cost of living.)

Regional unemployment

Overall there has been relatively little change in the pattern of regional unemployment. With the exception of the West Midlands, every region with below-average unemployment in 1971 continued to enjoy below-average unemployment; conversely every region with above-average unemployment in 1971 continued to suffer above-average unemployment (Table 12.5).

If we consider changes in GDP and unemployment together, it is very difficult to find evidence that regional policy has caused regional disparities to diminish. Indeed as a broad generalization we can say that the areas which have shown the

Table 12.4
Average household income and expenditure, by region (1985 and 1986)

Region	Income (£ per week)	Expenditure (£ per week)
Greater London	268	201
Rest of South East	260	212
South West	233	178
East Anglia	225	174
East Midlands	217	161
Scotland	210	161
West Midlands	209	160
North West	204	160
Wales	203	158
Yorkshire and Humberside	193	149
Northern Ireland	193	165
North	188	147
United Kingdom	225	174

Source: Employment Gazette, various years

Table 12.5
Regional unemployment

Region	Unemployed (%)	
	1971	*1987*
United Kingdom	3.5	10.3
South East	2.0	7.2
East Midlands	2.9	9.3
West Midlands	2.9	11.6
East Anglia	3.2	7.2
South West	3.3	8.2
Yorkshire and Humberside	3.8	11.8
North West	3.9	13.2
Wales	4.4	12.9
North	5.7	14.7
Scotland	5.8	13.4
Northern Ireland	7.9	18.9

Source: Employment Gazette, various years

greatest increase in relative prosperity, the South and East, are those which received least regional assistance.

What we cannot know is the extent to which there would have been a further widening of regional disparities in the absence of regional policy.

The evaluation of policy

Even if we focus on a single aspect, the number of new jobs created, it is difficult to give a precise measure of the benefits of regional policy. We quoted above a figure of £40,000 per new job created. But some of these jobs might have been diverted from non-Assisted Areas, and therefore would not have been a benefit to the country as a whole.

Furthermore, it is impossible to judge (a) how many potential new jobs in non-Assisted Areas did not come to fruition because of the controls on development that used to operate, and (b) how many jobs were located in high-cost areas because firms were not allowed to build or expand in their preferred, lower-cost areas. (If higher costs lead to higher product prices, output and employment will be reduced.)

The possible detrimental effects led to many controls on regional development being abandoned in the 1980s. This meant, of course, that more reliance had to be put on the incentive effect of financial assistance.

Urban policy

A major shift of emphasis in government policy occurred in the late 1970s when inner-city problems, traditionally diagnosed as environmental and social deprivation, were seen to be linked to local economic decline, and in particular to the rapid erosion of manufacturing in the conurbation cores. Inner-city problems were by no means confined to the Assisted Areas, and the urban programme became the responsibility of the Department of the Environment, working with local authorities in the areas designated under the Inner Urban Areas Act. One result of the shift of administrative responsibility has been an increase in the number of types of agencies providing assistance. These range from the Urban Development Corporations covering the London and Merseyside docklands to a multiplicity of agencies sponsored by local authorities and other bodies operating on a local scale.

Administrative responsibility has been further diffused by the increasing involvement of the European Commission in regional affairs. The ERDF has a non-quota section which earmarks resources for small areas affected by other EEC policies towards restructuring e.g. in steelmaking and textiles. This has given rise to a new set of policy instruments, often focusing on smaller firms and not confined to the Assisted Areas. (Many of these policy instruments are similar to the local initiatives mentioned above.) Financial assistance on a regional basis is available from the quota section of the ERDF, the UK being one of the main beneficiaries of this form of assistance. Finally the European Social Fund has significant resources for spending in the Assisted Areas related to manpower training.

Enterprise zones

The political philosophy underlying enterprise zones is that a reduction in government interference – minimizing planning restrictions and granting financial concessions (a rates 'holiday' and exemption from development land tax) – would facilitate the growth of companies.

A report on the operation of the first eleven zones to be established found that by May 1983 just over 8,000 jobs had been created at a cost of £133m.[3] This worked out at a cost of approximately £16,500 per job, well over the limit for regional assistance imposed in 1984. However, almost 60 per cent of the cost comprised expenditure on infrastructure, much of which would have been required anyway. (The remaining costs were building allowances and rate relief.) On the other hand, there is some doubt as to what was the *net* increase in jobs as a result of the creation of the enterprise zones. Most of the firms that relocated moved only a short distance – 86 per cent had remained within the same county. This might suggest that growth was rerouted rather than stimulated, at least in some instances.

Enterprise boards and agencies

Two other types of agency whose main objective is to stimulate economic activity at the local level are the enterprise boards and enterprise agencies. The enterprise boards are financed under section 137 of the Local Government Act which enables county and borough councils to spend the product of a 2p rate for any purpose they choose. This money is often used in conjunction with private sector finance in a variety of ways – to finance new firms, management buy-outs, the establishment of co-operatives, etc.

Enterprise agencies are more numerous (over 250) and have a much more limited role than enterprise boards. Essentially they are offices whose main function is to give advice to people engaged in, or wishing to establish, small businesses.

Inner-city Compacts

In 1988 the government announced that the Manpower Services Commission and the Department of Employment would provide financial and organizational support to help set up twelve inner-city Compacts. Compacts are agreements between industry and schools and colleges by which employers aim to guarantee jobs to local school-leavers in return for agreed standards of achievement and commitment.

Changes in the structure and organization of industry

Various changes have occurred in the structure and organization of industry that have reduced the effectiveness of traditional regional policy weapons. An important factor underlying the use of these traditional weapons was the association between structural decline in particular industries and employment decline in the areas in which those industries were concentrated. But this has become a less important cause of regional differences in the rate of employment change.[4]

A second important change affecting the nature of the regional problem is a massive shift in the location of manufacturing from conurbations and cities to small towns and rural areas.

Third, it has been suggested that regional uneven development based on industrial specialization by *sectors* (e.g. coal, steel, textiles) has been supplanted to a large degree by regional differentiation based upon specialization by corporate *functions* (e.g. management, research and development, component manufacture, assembly-line production) The more peripheral regions of the UK are characterized by relative dependence upon routine, branch plant production activities. In contrast, the core region of the South East is distinguished by the concentration there of financial and business services and by its specialization in corporate planning and control functions and in research and development.[5]

Summary

1. The main aim of regional policy has traditionally been to reduce regional inequalities, although more stress has recently been put on increasing economic efficiency.
2. Institutional factors may seriously impede the free market 'solution' to regional unemployment differentials.
3. Most government assistance has aimed at increasing employment opportunities in

areas of very high unemployment, although some assistance has been provided to encourage workers to move out of these areas.

4. In the assistance provided to employers there has recently been a change of emphasis from automatic to selective assistance, in order to increase the cost-effectiveness of aid. Government assistance appears to have done little to reduce regional inequalities, although without this assistance the inequalities might well have increased.

5. Increased attention and assistance have recently been given to areas in conurbations affected by the shift of manufacturing to small towns and rural areas.

Key terms

Development Areas	Regional income
Intermediate Areas	Regional expenditure
Regional Selective Assistance	Regional unemployment
Investment Grants	Enterprise zones
Innovation Grants	Enterprise boards
Enterprise Initiative Grants	Enterprise agencies
Regional GDP	

Notes

1. Moore B, Rhodes J and Tyler P, *The Effects of Government Regional Policy*. HMSO, 1986.
2. The undesirable consequences of this policy are examined at length in McErnery J H, *Manufacturing Two Nations*. Institute of Economic Affairs, 1981. From 1984 the service sector has received greater equality of treatment with manufacturing.
3. Roger Tym and Partners, written and published by, *Monitoring the Enterprise Zones: Year Three Report*. 1984.
4. Fothergill S and Gudgin G, *Unequal Growth: Urban Regional Employment Change in the UK*. Heinemann, 1982.
5. Regional Studies Association, *Report of an Inquiry into Regional Problems in the United Kingdom*. Geo Books, 1983, p. 46.

Essay questions

1. 'Since businessmen know most about the costs and benefits of alternative locations governments should not attempt to influence their location decisions.' Discuss.
2. 'There are several different regional problems which require different solutions.' Discuss.
3. Evaluate the free market approach to the problem of regional inequalities.
4. Discuss the view that the objective of government regional policy should be to take workers to the work rather than work to the workers.
5. Discuss the major components of the government's current regional policy and explain the objective of each component.
6. Discuss the various criteria by which regional policy might be evaluated.
7. What difficulties arise in trying to measure the success of regional policy?
8. 'Regional policy inhibits the allocation of resources in accordance with the principle of comparative advantage and should therefore be abandoned.' Discuss.

9. Explain what information would be required in order to enable the costs of regional policy to be measured.
10. 'Regional policy may redistribute the nation's wealth, but it cannot increase it.' Discuss.

Exercises

12.1 Critically evaluate the arguments advanced in the passage below.

The essence of the free market approach to the 'regional problem' is that firms and individuals should be allowed to make to make their own decisions. Firms' location decisions should not be subject to government interference either in the form of inducements to locate in certain areas or the imposition of controls on development in other areas. Similarly individuals should have a free choice, again 'unbiased' by government inducements, as to where they seek work.

Under these conditions the forces of demand and supply will operate so as to bring about an efficient allocation of resources. If the costs of congestion in high-growth areas cause firms' costs to become higher than they would be in other areas, this will prove a disincentive to further growth in the former areas. If social costs bear so heavily on workers in high-growth areas as to outweigh the advantages of working in those areas, workers will be more ready to look for work in other areas. To counteract this tendency employers in high-growth areas will have to increase wages in order to retain workers.

Conversely if, in the low-growth areas, the costs to workers, in terms of poor employment prospects, are greater than the advantages of living in those areas, workers will move to other areas to find employment. Thus eventually the 'excess' unemployment will disappear.

Table 12.6
Regional performance

Region	GDP per head, 1985 £	Personal disposal income per head, 1985 £	Real personal disposable income growth per head, 1975–85 %	Unemployment % of working population Jan. 1987	Long-term unemployed % of unemployed Jan. 1987
South East	5,831	4,725	19.92	8.5	36.2
East Anglia	5,118	4,244	26.21	9.3	33.5
Scotland	4,942	4,181	20.86	15.1	39.2
North West	4,877	4,074	16.95	14.3	44.3
East Midlands	4,861	4,066	18.46	11.4	39.2
South West	4,763	4,152	21.34	10.4	32.7
North	4,717	3,919	18.24	16.9	44.3
West Midlands	4,690	3,997	10.24	13.8	46.3
Yorkshire and Humberside	4,662	3,923	17.70	13.8	42.0
Wales	4,509	3,778	14.27	14.3	40.6
Northern Ireland	3,799	3,538	18.67	19.3	50.0

Source: Economic Trends, Employment Gazette

12.2 What factors might account for the differences in GDP per head, shown in Table 12.6? To what extent are these data likely to be indicators of differences in living standards in different regions?

12.3 Drawing on the data presented in Table 12.6, and on any other data with which you are familiar, evaluate the success of regional policy.

12.4 Over the first half of this century the dominant feature of internal migration was a drift from Scotland, Wales and the north of England towards the Midlands and the South East. Although a general north-to-south shift remains evident, since the 1960s this has been accompanied by an increasing tendency for migration to take the form of movements away from densely populated city areas towards the outer suburbs and country. Between 1971 and 1981 the combined population of eight major cities (Inner London, Birmingham, Leeds, Liverpool, Manchester, Newcastle, Sheffield and Glasgow) fell by 14 per cent, while the population of predominantly rural areas increased by 10 per cent.

The most rapidly growing regions over the last twenty years have been those without large conurbations, such as East Anglia and the South West. In contrast, the population of the South East actually fell in the 1970s as a result of London's loss of population which was not completely offset by the growth of the outer South East area.

(i)   What factors might explain the changes in the distribution of population identified in the above passage?

(ii) Discuss the implications of these changes for government regional policy.

Objective test questions: set 4

1. If the government controls the price of a product at a level below the free market price the effect will be:
    A   an increase in the quantity demanded and no change in the quantity supplied;
    B   a fall in the quantity supplied and no change in the quantity demanded;
    C   an increase in the quantity demanded and supplied;
    D   a fall in the quantity demanded and supplied;
    E   an increase in the quantity demanded and a fall in the quantity supplied.

2. The CAP has benefited:
    A   European consumers as a whole;
    B   European producers as a whole;
    C   non-European consumers as a whole;
    D   non-European producers as a whole;
    E   none of the above.

3. A collective restrictive agreement may be justified before the Restrictive Practices Court on any of the following grounds except that the removal of the restriction would:
    A   lead to an increase in merger activity;
    B   deny to the public specific and substantial benefits;
    C   cause a substantial reduction in export business;
    D   have a serious and persistent adverse effect on unemployment;
    E   reduce protection to the public against injury.

4. In Great Britain all of the following types of regional incentive are available except:
    A   subsidies related to the total cost of the firm;
    B   subsidies related to the cost of capital inputs;
    C   subsidies related to the cost of labour;
    D   the provision of factories to rent;
    E   the provision of factories to purchase.

5. An increase in government subsidies to a nationalized industry implies a redistribution of real income:
    A   from consumers to employers;
    B   from employees to consumers;
    C   from employees to taxpayers;
    D   from consumers to taxpayers;
    E   from taxpayers to consumers.

6. The Restrictive Trade Practices Act makes it more difficult:
    1   for firms to sustain collective restrictive agreements;
    2   for individual manufacturers to enforce RPM;
    3   for firms to merge.

7. Resale price maintenance may be justified under the Resale Prices Act on the grounds that in its absence:
    1   the retail prices of the goods would increase;
    2   the number of retail establishments in which the goods were sold would be substantially reduced;
    3   the quantity and variety of goods available for sale would be substantially reduced.

8. Which of the following constitute(s) an external cost?
    1   A firm's average cost of distribution increases as it extends its geographical market.
    2   Government expenditure on regional policy increases.
    3   A factory discharges highly toxic materials into a river used by anglers.

9. Which of the following might result from the introduction of a minimum wage for young workers at a level in excess of the wage currently paid to these workers?
    1   The total income of all young people of working age falls.
    2   Firms substitute older for younger workers.
    3   Firms substitute capital for young workers.

10. Productive efficiency increases when:
    1   the cost of producing the existing mix of goods and services falls;
    2   the profits derived from producing the existing mix of goods and services increase;
    3   new goods and services are introduced.

11. The free market approach to the regional problem takes account of:
    1   social costs;
    2   external costs;
    3   internal costs.

12. Examples of external economies include:
    1   central training facilities available to all the firms in the area;
    2   improved public transport facilities;
    3   the take-over by a firm of a supplier.

13. The Competition Act 1980 provided for:
    1 the investigation of nationalized industries by the MMC;
    2 an increase in government assistance to small firms;
    3 the exemption from UK legislation of any restrictive practices approved by the European Community.

14. Firms establishing plants in Assisted Areas after April 1988 may qualify for:
    1 Regional Development Grants;
    2 Regional Selective Assistance;
    3 European Regional Development Fund loans.

15. Which of the following is/are an example of privatization?
    1 Government subsidies to private sector producers.
    2 Opening to private sector suppliers markets previously reserved for public sector suppliers.
    3 Transferring the ownership of assets from the public to the private sector.

16. Which of the following might follow from a programme of privatization?
    1 Increased competition.
    2 Wider share ownership.
    3 An increase in the public sector borrowing requirement.

17. A pragmatic, case-by-case approach to competition policy is most likely to be adopted when a clear link can be established between market structure, conduct and performance.
    Market performance may affected by either market structure or conduct.

18. Under the Restrictive Trade Practices Act collective restrictive agreements are forbidden.
    The Restrictive Trade Practices Act is based on the presumption that collective restrictive agreements are against the public interest.

19. A fall in the profits of an industry following nationalization would indicate that consumers have benefited from nationalization.
    The nationalization of an industry may result in a redistribution of real income.

20. Any buffer stock scheme which reduces price fluctuations also reduces fluctuations in producers' incomes.
    Producer's incomes are affected by fluctuations in the prices of their products.

True/false

1. The spread of collective bargaining has reduced the sensitivity of wage rates to local unemployment rates.
2. Regional Development Grants towards the cost of new buildings and works are available in all the Assisted Areas.
3. Merit goods are characterized by non-excludability and non-rivalness.
4. Costs incurred by individuals other than through market transactions are known as external costs.
5. European consumers have benefited overall from the CAP.
6. Economic growth can be defined as an expansion of economic capacity.
7. A two-part tariff can enable a firm to set price equal to marginal cost and cover its total costs.
8. Privatization always leads to an increase in competition.
9. Resale price maintenance is forbidden under the Resale Prices Act.
10. Collective restrictive agreements in all service industries must be registered with the Restrictive Practices Court.

CHAPTER THIRTEEN
The Measurement of Economic Activity and the Standard of Living

Introduction

In Chapter 3 we presented a highly simplified representation of a national economy. We showed that the owners of resources supply inputs to producers in return for rewards or income of various kinds, and that these resources are transformed into a flow of outputs supplied to consumers in exchange for payment. In many countries, including the UK, economic statisticians measure three of these four flows. They measure the level of economic activity in terms of the value of incomes, output and expenditure.

The UK national accounts are examined below. But first a simplified model is presented in order to demonstrate the principles that underlie the construction of these accounts.

Value added

In converting inputs to outputs, producers add value to the goods and services that they supply. Value added is defined as sales receipts (or the value of sales) minus the cost of bought-in materials. Table 13.1 illustrates the value that might be added during the processes involved in the production and sale of £1m. of frozen peas.[1]

In order to simplify the analysis it is assumed that at the beginning of the period farmers have already prepared the land and have acquired all the seed, equipment, etc. that they need. Consequently they do not need to buy any materials during the period under consideration. They grow peas which they sell to manufacturers for £300,000. Since it is assumed that the cost of bought-in materials is zero, all of this £300,000 constitutes value added.

The manufacturers process and pack the peas and sell them to retailers for £750,000. The value added at the manufacturing stage is therefore £450,000 (£750,000 minus £300,000). The retailers store and display the peas and then sell them to consumers for £1m. The value added by the retailers is therefore £250,000 (£1m. minus £750,000). Note that the value of the final output of sales, £1m., equals the sum of the value added at the various stages of the process of production and distribution.

This example is simplified in that it ignores many of the inputs required to produce frozen peas. For example, farmers might buy fertilizers, tractors, etc. and the manufacturers would probably buy not only peas but also packaging materials, equipment for freezing, etc. Nevertheless, although highly simplified, the example does illustrate the principle that underlies the output approach to the measurement of economic activity in the national accounts.

Income

The value added at each stage of production is available as payments to the

Table 13.1
Value added in production (£)

	Cost of bought-in materials	Sales receipts	Value added
Farming	—	300,000	300,000
Manufacturing	300,000	750,000	450,000
Retailing	750,000	1,000,000	250,000
			1,000,000

Table 13.2
The distribution of value added (£)

	Value added	Wages	Profit
Farming	300,000	200,000	100,000
Manufacturing	450,000	300,000	150,000
Retailing	250,000	150,000	100,000
	1,000,000	650,000	350,000

factors of production used at that stage. Continuing to simplify, it is assumed for the moment that there are only two factors: labour, which receives wages, and capital, which receives profit. The distribution of value added between wages and profit is shown in Table 13.2.

Expenditure

Expenditure is the third approach to the measurement of economic activity that was noted in the introduction to this chapter. In fact in this example all final expenditure is undertaken by a single group, consumers.

Capital consumption

As mentioned above, producers (farmers, manufacturers and retailers) would in practice require inputs in addition to those specified in our example. Among these other inputs would be capital assets of various types: tractors, freezing equipment, shelves and other fitments, etc. An important characteristic of capital assets is that they provide a flow of services, or inputs, over a considerable length of time. For example, freezing equipment might, given normal use, be expected to last for ten years. It follows that as equipment is used for, say, a year, its residual value falls. This fall in value can be seen as the cost of using the equipment, a cost that should be charged to the firm's operations in that year. This charge is known as depreciation or capital consumption. (The

first term is normally used in company accounts, the second in the national accounts.)

If a firm is to continue in existence it will, of course, have to renew its assets as they wear out. In order to finance future purchases it sets aside from its income an annual depreciation charge or allowance. These depreciation allowances are not then available to be allocated in other ways, for example as dividends paid to shareholders.

Profit

In the above example a single category of profit was identified. In drawing up the national accounts it is necessary to distinguish between gross and net profits, where:

Gross profit minus depreciation equals net profit

Stock appreciation

A further complication can arise in the construction of the national accounts because of the existence of stocks of raw materials, components, semi-finished goods, etc. The prices at which these stocks could be sold may vary over time, and producers normally allow these price changes to affect their declared profit. So if a retailer had 1,000 bags of frozen peas at both the beginning and the end of the year, and the price of a bag of peas had increased during the year from £1.00 to £1.20, this would give rise to a profit of £200 (1,000 × 20p). This contribution to profit is due entirely to the increase, or appreciation, in the value of a given quantity of stock.

While this treatment of stock appreciation may be appropriate for an individual producer, or indeed for producers as a whole, it is not appropriate when constructing a set of national accounts. The nation as a whole does not gain any benefit from an increase in the price of stocks. Consequently stock appreciation is not included in calculations of national income and output; an adjustment is made to company data that include stock appreciation.

Expenditure taxes

The earlier example assumed that no tax was imposed on the frozen peas sold to consumers. In practice there are, of course, many products that are subject to expenditure taxes. As these taxes are passed on – either partially or fully – to consumers in the form of higher prices, they affect the value of expenditure. The national accounts include expenditure data adjusted to take account of expenditure taxes.

The non-market sector

The output of government or non-market sector comprises goods and services that are supplied at either a zero price or a price not related to the cost of supply, e.g. education and medical services. Since this output yields a benefit to consumers, it must be included in the national accounts. However, sales receipts, if any, would be a misleading indicator of the value added. A better indicator is the incomes of the factors of production. (We showed above that total factor incomes equal total value added.)

Since the government is a non-profit-making institution, profit does not, of course, enter into the calculation of factor incomes. However, this does not mean that the recorded value added (income) is necessarily lower than the figure that would have applied had the services been provided through the market. The value of consumption through the market might have been either higher or lower.

The value added of dwellings

There is one final point that needs to be made before we examine a set of national accounts. All domestic dwellings yield a benefit to their occupiers, a benefit which can be seen as the value added of those dwellings. However, the price of occupation may not reflect that benefit. Owner-occupied dwellings are, of course, occupied without payment of rent, while many dwellings owned by local authorities are let at subsidized rents. Since the total benefit to occupiers is adjudged to be substantial, it is felt necessary to make an adjustment for this 'under-pricing'. The 'imputed' output of dwellings is an estimate of the value added that would accrue if all dwellings were let at commercially determined rents.

The UK national accounts

Having examined the principles underlying the construction of the national accounts we now examine a subset of those accounts for one year. We begin by considering the flow of expenditure.

Total final expenditure

The left-hand diagram in Fig. 13.1 shows the composition of total final (aggregate) expenditure at market prices in 1986. We briefly examine each of the five components beginning with the most important, consumers' expenditure.

Consumers' expenditure

Accounting in 1986 for 49 per cent of final expenditure, this category includes almost all the items bought by consumers – food, drink, heat and light, consumer durable goods, travel, entertainment, etc. There is one exception, one item which one might expect to be included under this heading but is not; that is consumers' expenditure on the purchase of new dwellings, which is classified as part of gross fixed capital formation.

General government consumption

This category is similar to consumers' expenditure in so far as it refers mainly to goods or services that are 'consumed' by households. However, there is an

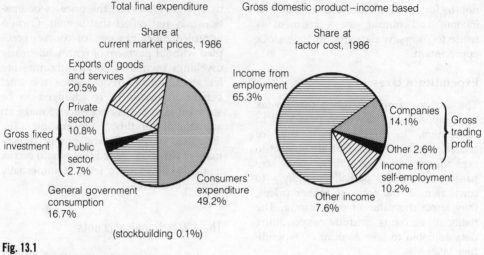

Fig. 13.1
Shares of expenditure and income
Source: Economic Trends

important difference between the two categories. As noted above, most of the government's current expenditure consists of goods or services which are provided either free or below cost, and are valued in the national accounts at their cost of production – the amount paid for materials, wages, salaries, etc. Incidentally, one should not think of the government as meaning only the central government. Over one-third of government consumption is accounted for by the expenditure of local authorities.

Gross fixed investment

Gross fixed investment or capital formation is the major component of investment expenditure, which approximates to the 'capital' input identified in Chapter 2. Producers are responsible for most fixed capital formation, followed by the government and by households. Major items include buildings of various kinds – factories, offices, shops, hospitals, schools, dwellings – plant and equipment, vehicles, ships, transport and communication facilities. The importance of capital formation in preserving future living standards was emphasized in Chapter 2, and we can

see that in 1986 this category accounted for over 13 per cent of total expenditure.

Value of physical increase in stocks and work in progress

The second component of investment expenditure, this is much less important than fixed capital formation. Changes in both categories may occur in line with producers' plans. However, changes in stocks may also be unplanned. For example, if firms produce to meet a level of demand greater than actually occurs, stocks are likely to rise, at least until producers have had time to revise their production levels. In 1986 the value of stocks increased slightly.

Exports of goods and services

One of the main purposes of measuring the flow of expenditure is that it provides an indication of the pressure of demand on the country's resources. Consequently we include exports, i.e. the expenditure by overseas residents on British goods and services, since this involves the utilization of our resources. It can be seen from Fig. 13.1 that exports constitute the second largest flow of expenditure.

Total final expenditure and gross domestic product

The sum of the above items gives total final expenditure at market prices which, as shown in Table 13.3, amounted in 1986 to £476bn. However, not all of this expenditure resulted in the utilization of domestic resources. To obtain a measure of resource utilization we have to subtract two items, imports and expenditure taxes.

Table 13.3
Gross domestic product (1986)

	£bn.
1. Consumers' expenditure	234.2
2. General government final consumption	79.4
3. Gross domestic fixed capital formation	64.2
4. Value of physical increase in stocks and work in progress	0.6
5. Exports of goods and services	97.8
Final expenditure on goods and services at market prices	476.2
6. Less imports of goods and services	−101.3
Gross domestic product at market prices	374.9
7. Less taxes on expenditure (net of subsidies)	− 55.8
Gross domestic product at factor cost (GDP)	319.1

Source: United Kingdom National Accounts

Imports of goods and services

Imports amounted to £101bn., over one-fifth of total expenditure. We subtract imports from expenditure because purchases of goods and services from abroad involve the utilization of other countries' resources (just as purchases by overseas residents of UK goods and services involve the utilization of UK resources).

Expenditure taxes

Subtracting imports gives GDP at market prices of £375 billion. However, of this figure £56bn. represented expenditure taxes (net of subsidies). These taxes accrue, of course, to the government and not to producers, and so do not directly involve the utilization of resources. When we subtract this figure we arrive at GDP at factor cost (£319bn.). GDP at factor cost measures the rewards accruing to factors of production and is a better indicator of the utilization of the nation's resources.

Figure 13.2 shows the sources and destinations of the various expenditure flows that we have discussed. In Fig. 13.2 four sectors are identified: households (consumers), UK producers, the government and the overseas sector (producers and consumers). It may help you to understand this rather complex network if you take each of the flows listed in Table 13.3 and trace it from source to destination in Fig. 13.2.

The usefulness of measures of expenditure

The classification of expenditure presented in Table 13.3 has several advantages. It makes it possible to monitor changes in consumption, the most important element of the current standard of living, and in investment, a primary determinant of future living standards. It also helps in the analysis of the likely effects of changes in the many factors, including government policies, which influence expenditure, since a change in a given factor will have different effects on different forms of expenditure. For example, a change in the rate of tax on personal incomes is likely to have the greatest effect on consumers' expenditure, whereas the introduction of investment grants would be most likely to affect fixed capital formation. This point has become more important as the involvement of government in economic management has increased, and will be discussed at length in future chapters.

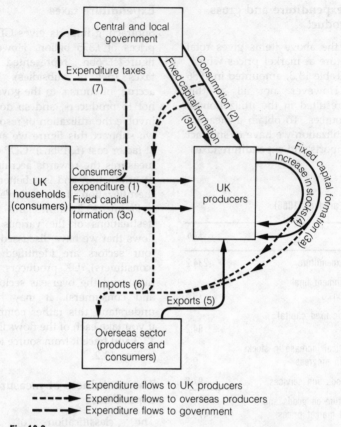

Expenditure flows to UK producers
- - - - → Expenditure flows to overseas producers
- - - - → Expenditure flows to government

Fig. 13.2
The flow of expenditure

Finally, as we said above, the total of the various expenditure flows, GDP at factor cost, indicates the overall utilization of the nation's resources in the period in question. We also pointed out above that statisticians provide measures of other flows, i.e. measure economic activity in other ways. In the following sections we briefly examine these alternative measures.

The flow of output and gross domestic product

Table 13.4 incorporates the output approach to the measurement of economic activity, showing the contribution to GDP of the various industries or sectors of the economy. Manufacturing's share of GDP fell from one-third in 1970 to one-quarter

today. There has been a corresponding increase in the relative share of the service sector, and especially of banking, finance, insurance and business services.

The flow of incomes, gross national product and national income

Table 13.5 presents the final method of classifying GDP, namely in terms of the types of income received by the owners of resources. (The right-hand diagram in Fig. 13.1 presents a simplified version of the same information.) This table also shows the various adjustments to GDP that are required in order to arrive at a measure of the *national income* or *net national product*. These adjustments could, of course, be made to the GDP figures in

Table 13.4
Gross domestic product by industry (1986)

	£bn.
Agriculture, forestry and fishing	5.9
Energy and water supply	24.4
Manufacturing	79.1
Construction	20.1
Distribution, hotels and catering; repairs	45.8
Transport	14.8
Communication	8.9
Banking, finance, insurance, business services and leasing	51.5
Ownership of dwellings	18.9
Public administration, national defence and compulsory social security	23.6
Education and health services	29.5
Other services	21.0
Less adjustment for financial services	−17.4
Gross domestic product (income-based)	326.0
Residual error	− 7.0
Gross domestic product (at factor cost)	319.1

Source: United Kingdom National Accounts N.B. apparent discrepancies in figures due to rounding.

Table 13.5
National income (1986)

	£bn.
Income from employment	209.4
Income from self-employment	34.0
Gross trading profits of companies	48.9
Gross trading surplus of public corporations and government enterprises	8.2
Rent	22.5
Imputed charge for consumption of non-trading capital	3.0
Gross domestic product (income-based)	326.0
Residual error	− 7.0
Gross domestic product (at factor cost)	319.1
Net property income from abroad	4.7
Gross national product (at factor cost)	323.8
Less capital consumption	− 46.0
National income (net national product)	277.8

Source: United Kingdom National Accounts

Table 13.3 or 13.4, but it is conventional to make them to the incomes table.

The first adjustment is for net property income from abroad. This represents rent, interest, profits and dividends received by UK residents from abroad, minus the corresponding payments made abroad. In 1986 the UK had a modest surplus on these items; GNP was more than GDP. GNP is yet another possible indicator of the standard of living, although it is inferior to GDP as a measure of the utilization of domestic resources.

Second, a substantial sum is deducted for capital consumption. As we noted above, the nation's capital stock − factories, machines, roads, hospitals, etc. − gradually wears out with use. If our productive or economic capacity is to be maintained, this capital consumption has to be made good. In other words, part of the gross capital formation that takes place in any year is required to maintain the existing productive capacity; only the remainder (net investment) represents an addition to capacity. A comparison of Tables 13.3 and 13.5 shows that in 1986 capital consumption amounted to more than two-thirds of gross fixed capital formation.

Since capital consumption is allowed for in the calculation of national income, changes in national income provide a good indicator of *sustainable* changes in living standards. However, since resources are utilized by all capital formation, including that required to balance capital consumption, national income is a less good measure of resource utilization than either GDP or GNP.

Errors in measurement

The hypothetical example presented in Tables 13.1 and 13.2 showed that in principle all three methods of measuring economic activity should give the same answer. It can be seen that in practice although the estimates of GDP obtained by the three methods are identical, this happens only because a 'residual error' figure is included in Tables 13.4 and 13.5. This reflects the fact that the methods of data collection are imperfect.

A source of error that has received increasing attention of late has been the under-recording of incomes. A former chairman of the Inland Revenue estimated in 1981 that as much as 7.5 per cent of GDP – £3bn. to £3.5bn. – was lost to the Exchequer through the 'black economy': unreported income sources ('moonlighting') and underestimates of declared earnings, although subsequently a study published by the Institute of Fiscal Studies arrived at a lower figure of 3–5 per cent of GDP. If the relative size of the black economy expands, measures of economic activity based on estimates of income will underestimate the growth, or overestimate the decline, in economic activity.[2]

A composite measure of gross domestic product

Statisticians in the UK present a composite measure, an estimate of GDP which is an average of the three separate estimates. This reduces the chances of error that could arise from using a single estimate.

Index numbers showing average changes in GDP for the period 1976–86 are presented in the top line of Table 13.6. Since adjustments have been made for changes in prices the data indicate changes in real GDP. It can be seen that GDP rose by more than a fifth over the decade. However, this growth did not occur evenly; indeed GDP fell in two of the ten years.

Gross national disposable income

Table 13.6 also includes average estimates (again in index number form) of gross national disposable income. These estimates are derived from GNP at market prices. An adjustment is made to GNP to allow for changes in the terms of trade, i.e. the ratio of the average price of our exports to the average price of our imports. This adjustment means that there is frequently a divergence between the two series. However, it can be seen that they tend to move in the same direction.

Gross domestic product and the standard of living

A good indicator of the standard of living is the volume of goods and services consumed per head in a given time period. Output (GDP) can often be taken as a reasonable approximation to consumption. However, the relationship

Table 13.6
Gross domestic product and gross national disposable income (average measure, constant market prices, 1980 = 100)

	1976	1977	1978	1979	1980	1981	1982	1983	1984	1985	1986
Gross domestic product	94	96	100	103	100	99	100	104	106	110	114
Gross national disposable income	92	94	99	102	100	99	101	105	108	111	115

Source: United Kingdom National Accounts

between GDP and the standard of living or economic welfare[3] is complex and is probably most easily explained if approached through a question that, in one form or another, is a favourite of examiners: 'Why may an increase in GDP *not* imply an improvement in the standard of living?' In answering this question several sets of factors need to be considered.

Nominal versus real changes

We have shown that GDP is a record of the *value* of economic activity. Therefore GDP will increase if an increase occurs in either the volume of transactions, i.e. the number of items bought, or in their prices (or in both). But these two alternatives have very different implications for the standard of living. An increase in the prices of goods and services does not benefit the standard of living. (Indeed, unless factor incomes increase at the same rate, the average standard of living will fall.) On the other hand, an increase in the volume of transactions implies an improvement in living standards (other things remaining equal).

Table 13.7 shows GDP for the later part of the period covered by Table 13.6. Nominal GDP, i.e. GDP measured at current prices, increased every year, rising by 63 per cent over the period as a whole. However, after correcting for price changes we see a very different picture. The increase in real GDP, i.e. GDP measured at current prices, over the period as a whole was much more modest, 13 per cent.

The GDP deflator (used in adjusting nominal GDP to real GDP), takes into account changes in prices of all final goods and services produced in the UK. It has therefore a broader coverage than the retail price index, another common means of measuring price changes. However, the broad coverage gives rise to problems since the composition of output constantly changes as new products are introduced to the market and existing products are modified.

There are other factors which reduce the validity of GDP as an indicator of living standards. Some of the factors are briefly discussed in the following sections.[4] (The illegal unrecording of economic transactions was discussed earlier in this chapter.)

An extension of consumer choice

The satisfaction of consumers is influenced not simply by the volume of goods and services that they buy, but also by the degree of choice that they are offered. Choice refers here both to the range of different products and to differences in style and quality within a given product. A large amount of research and development effort in highly developed countries is devoted to the widening of the consumer's choice in both respects.

The increase in welfare that results from this activity is sometimes very great, as when a new life-saving drug is discovered. In other instances the benefits may appear to be negligible as, for example, when another brand of toothpaste is marketed. However, appearances can be deceptive; the new toothpaste might well have a distinctive characteristic – colour,

Table 13.7
Nominal and real GDP (market prices)

	1980	1981	1982	1983	1984	1985	1986
At current prices (£bn.)	231	254	276	301	320	352	375
At current prices	100	110	120	131	139	152	163
At constant prices	100	99	100	104	106	110	113

Source: United Kingdom National Accounts

flavour or texture – that encourages teeth-cleaning (especially by young children).

Work, leisure and consumption

Work undertaken at the Technical Change Centre suggests that when one takes a long historical perspective, around one-third of the potential benefit derived from increases in productivity has taken the form of an increase in leisure, as represented by later entry into, and earlier retirement from, the labour force, a shorter working week and longer holidays.

These trends are continuing, at least for men. The activity rate (i.e. the percentage of the population in the civilian labour force) for males aged 16 or over fell from 81 per cent in 1971 to 73 per cent in 1986. Especially steep falls were recorded in the oldest age-groups. The activity rate for men aged 70 or over fell from 11 to 5 per cent, for men aged 65–69 from 30 to 13 per cent, and for men aged 40–64 from 83 to 53 per cent.

The activity rate for females has run counter to the trend for males. Between 1971 and 1986 the activity rate increased in all age-groups from 16 to 59, and the overall increase for all ages was from 44 to 49 per cent.

The average length of the working week fell by 10 per cent between 1961 and 1981, although it has increased slightly since then as economic activity has revived. Moreover, there has been a substantial increase in the proportion of part-time work, especially for females. The percentage of women working less than sixteen hours a week increased from 4 to 16 per cent between 1951 and 1981, and a further increase has occurred since then.

The role of women

We noted in the previous section the tendency for a higher proportion of women to take paid employment. They must value the income they receive, or the resultant consumption, more highly than the leisure they forgo; otherwise they would not seek work.[5]

However, it can be argued that by counting only the additional output (and income and consumption) that occur when more women take paid employment the increase in GDP is overestimated. Against this benefit should be offset the reduction in the services provided within the home and in unpaid work, e.g. for charities, outside the home. The non-inclusion of these 'voluntary' services in the national income accounts is purely a matter of convention.

Military expenditure

Expenditure on the purchase of weapons and equipment and on the pay of the armed forces and the civil servants concerned with defence is included in the calculation of GDP, the assumption being that this expenditure yields the same benefits as would an equivalent sum spent on, say, private consumption. While military expenditure may be vital to the preservation of living standards, it can easily be shown that an increase in military expenditure does not necessarily imply an improvement in living standards.

Two nations spending most on defence are the USA and the USSR. If both were to double their military expenditure in order not to fall behind in the arms race, that would not in itself change living standards. Neither group of citizens (much less the citizens of other countries) would be more safe than previously. But the recorded GDP of both countries would increase. Alternatively, if the increased output of military goods was produced by resources transferred from the consumer goods sector, current living standards would fall, although GDP would not change.

Public sector spending

It has been argued that the national accounts overstate the benefit derived from spending by the public sector (including military spending) for several reasons. First, there is no guarantee that the mix of goods and services produced by the public sector is what would be produced if resources were allocated through the market mechanism.

Second, goods and services may be produced less efficiently by public sector producers. Consequently even in the absence of a profit margin, the real costs to consumers may be higher.

Finally, much public expenditure comprises the cost of the administration and infrastructure required to monitor and control a modern dynamic economy. Mishan gives as examples expenditure on regulating, rate-setting and conciliating agencies, on tax collecting and on the police.[6] He argues that this expenditure should be seen as an input cost for the economy as a whole, and the services produced as intermediate goods. (As shown above the cost of intermediate goods is not part of the value added by the sector purchasing those inputs.)

Changes in the environment

We noted in Chapter 9 that the production of goods and services may be accompanied by the output of economic 'bads', giving rise to various forms of external cost. Information is available on changes in the incidence of some of these bads.[7]

Looking first at river pollution, we find that areas classified as poor or grossly polluted accounted for less than 7 per cent for non-tidal rivers in 1980, as compared to 9 per cent in 1970, and 16 per cent for tidal rivers as compared to 28 per cent. Since in the polluted rivers the degree of pollution had also fallen, there had clearly been a reduction in pollution overall. One result of this which received considerable publicity was the return of salmon to the River Thames, now claimed to be the cleanest river in a major European capital. (A new classification of pollution has been used in the 1980s, a decade in which there appears to have been little change.)

Between 1951 and 1986 the emission of smoke from coal combustion fell from 2.42 to 0.27 million tonnes, and the emission of sulphur dioxide (one of the contributors to acid rain) from fuel combustion from 4.77 to 3.74 million tonnes.

Despite an increase of about a fifth in petrol consumption since the early 1970s, emissions of lead fell by 60 per cent between 1971 and 1986. Moreover, there has been a slight fall in the number of deaths from road accidents, another hazard accompanying road travel.

Partly because of difficulties in measuring noise, there are no statistics to show how noise levels have changed over the country as a whole. However, the number of complaints made to Environmental Health Officers in England and Wales about noise increased more than threefold between 1975 and 1986.

Economic bads and the standard of living

In analysing the relationship between economic bads and the standard of living a distinction should be made between two alternative situations.

The first is where producers ignore the costs arising from their output of bads. In this situation the production of bads will vary as the output of goods varies. By definition an increase in the output of bads worsens living standards; conversely a reduction in output improves living standards. The only important qualification to this principle is if the effects of the output of bads are cumulative, as it appears to be with for example, acid rain and lead. If this is so the effect of pollution could increase from one period to the next even when the current output of the pollutants declined.

Since in this first situation the costs of producing bads is not included in the national accounts, an increase in the output of bads means that GDP will overstate the level of economic welfare. Conversely, a reduction in output means that economic welfare will be understated. In the light of the evidence presented above it might be concluded that overall the output of bads has declined in the UK. (Although there are, of course, other aspects of environmental change on which information was not provided.) However, this does not mean that the improvement in the standard of living was necessarily greater than indicated by the increase in real GDP, since in practice producers do take at least some of the costs of producing bads into account in their production decisions, i.e. the second of the two situations is the relevant one.

Cost may be taken into account (internalized) either as a result of government intervention or because producers wish to be 'good citizens'. Internalizing costs causes the cost of production to increase. Estimates were given above of the increase in the price of electricity if power stations were to be modified to reduce emissions of sulphur dioxide to the extent required by the European Commission, and of the higher prices of petrol containing less lead.

An increase in production costs leads to an increase in the price of the product and a reduction in the quantity traded, and hence nominal GDP could increase, decrease or remain unchanged. But even if nominal GDP increased, real GDP would not. The increase in the price of the product would increase the size of the GDP deflator, and thus cause a bigger adjustment to be made when nominal GDP is converted to real GDP.

On the other hand, when government incurs costs in order to reduce pollution, e.g. building effluent treatment plants, producers' costs are not increased, and so the costs of maintaining or improving environmental standards are not recorded.

Gross domestic product per head

In some less developed countries population is increasing by more than 2 per cent a year and this may, of course, mean that GDP per head grows much less quickly than aggregate GDP. In fact even to maintain existing living standards has proved difficult in some instances (see Ch. 25).

In countries where population is changing very slowly, as in the UK, changes in aggregate GDP are a more reliable guide to changes in average living standards. However, even here an increase in GDP does not imply an improvement in the living standards of all citizens, since there may be considerable variations around the average. Indeed a problem of increasing importance in the UK in recent years has been the growing gap in living standards between people in paid employment and the unemployed.

Moreover, economic bads do not have an equal impact on all members of the community. For example, there is evidence to suggest that people living in areas of heavy traffic have above-average amounts of lead in the blood. The problems to which this can give rise include anaemia, mental retardation and hyperactivity and other behavioural problems in children.[8]

Social indicators

The deficiencies of GDP as a measure of the standard of living have led to a search for alternative measures. In 1971 the OECD put its authority behind the idea of constructing accounts incorporating a number of social indicators. As yet little progress has been made in developing such accounts, and most economists would assert that real GDP per head is the best indicator available at present.

Many of these social indicators proposed by the OECD relate to health,[9] and the length of expectation of life might be seen as a summary measure of a nation's health. It is sometimes said that the pressures of modern industrial society can lead to an early death. If this is so, the effect must be outweighed by the benefits of modern society, since as societies have developed, life expectancy has increased. In the UK a boy born in 1901 could expect to live to 48 and a girl to 52. Today the corresponding figures are 71 and 77.

Summary

1. In converting inputs to outputs, producers add value to the goods and services that they supply. Value added is defined as sales value minus the cost of bought-in materials. The aggregate of the value added by all producers and distributors constitutes a measure of economic activity by the output approach.
2. Value added is available as payments to factors of production. By aggregating the value added that is distributed to each factor we obtain a measure of economic activity by the income approach.
3. Aggregate value added equals total expenditure (and can provide a measure of economic activity by the expenditure approach).
4. In the national accounts final expenditure at market prices comprises consumers' expenditure, government consumption, gross fixed investment, stockbuilding and exports.
5. Final expenditure at market prices, minus imports and minus expenditure taxes (net of subsidies) equals GDP at factor cost. Gross domestic product at factor cost is a good indicator of resource utilization.
6. Gross domestic product at factor cost, plus net property income from abroad, minus capital consumption, equals national income (net national product). National income is a good indicator of sustainable changes in living standards.
7. Because of rising prices, nominal national income has risen much more rapidly than real national income.
8. Gross domestic product and national income are useful indicators of living standards. However, their usefulness is limited by various factors, including changes in leisure, the changing role of women, military expenditure, public sector spending and changes in the environment.

Key terms

Value added	Final expenditure
Capital consumption (depreciation)	Gross domestic product
Profit	National income
Stock appreciation	Gross national disposable income
Expenditure taxes	Nominal and real changes in income
Subsidies	The standard of living
The non-market sector	Economic bads

Notes

1. The tables in this section originally appeared in Livesey F, National income in Atkinson G J B, *Developments in Economics*, vol. 2. Causeway Press, 1986. The use of value added in the construction of the national accounts is discussed in detail in Jackson D, *Introduction to Economics: Theory and Data*. Macmillan, 1982.
2. The term 'black economy' is perhaps unfortunate in view of possible racial overtones. It does not, of course, imply that black workers are more likely to have undeclared earnings than workers with fairer skins. Many other terms, including the informal, underground, hidden, parallel and irregular economy, are noted as part of a discussion of the under-recording of income in various countries in Smith A, The informal economy, *Lloyds Bank Review*, July 1981.

3.   The terms 'standard of living' and 'economic welfare' are often used interchangeably, although some writers prefer the former and others the latter term.

4.   The most trenchant criticisms of GDP or GNP as an indicator of economic welfare have probably been expressed by E J Mishan. For example in an article entitled, GNP – measurement or mirage?, *Lloyds Bank Review*, Nov. 1984, on which the following sections draw, Mishan concluded that a corrected estimate of the rise in per capita real income over the last fifty years in any of the Western countries would be significantly smaller than that derived from conventional statistics, and *could possibly be negative* (my italics).

5.   For some people additional leisure may, beyond a certain point, induce boredom and have a negative value.

6.   Many private sector services are required only because of the growing complexity of the economic system. Mishan op. cit. notes that many of the services provided 'by banks, by labour unions, by employment agencies, welfare agencies, travel agencies, by lawyers and accountants, by marriage bureau and computer-dating services, by race-relations organizations and sex-advice clinics, were not needed in a more traditional society of small towns and villages'.

7.   A convenient source of information is *Social Trends*, published annually by HMSO.

8.   Day J and Hodgson D, Pollution control: The cases of acid rain and lead in petrol, *Economics*, Autumn 1985.

9.   A list of social indicators for various OECD countries is given in Culyer A J, *Economics*. Blackwell, 1985, p. 424.

Essay questions

1.   Outline three different methods of measuring the level of economic activity and explain why they should in principle give the same answer.

2.   Explain why a change in the value of consumers' expenditure may be an imperfect indicator of a change in the standard of living.

3.   'Since an increase in our consumption of imports means an increase in our living standards, imports should not be excluded from the calculation of national income.' Comment.

4.   Define capital consumption and explain its significance.

5.   Explain what each of the following terms measures: (a) gross domestic product; (b) gross national product; (c) (net) national income.

6.   Explain why it is possible, between one year and another, for gross national product and gross national disposable income to move in different directions.

7.   Explain why it may be important but difficult to measure the incidence of economic bads.

8.   'Changes in national income are a poor indicator of a country's economic progress.' Discuss.

Exercises

13.1   Calculate from Table 13.8 each of the following; (a) gross domestic product at market prices; (b) gross domestic product at factor cost; (c) gross national product at factor cost, (d) (net) national income.

Table 13.8
The national accounts of Brittanica

	£bn.
Consumers' expenditure	70
General government final consumption	10
Gross domestic fixed capital formation	15
Value of physical increase in stocks and work in progress	5
Exports of goods and services	9
Imports of goods and services	11
Taxes on expenditure	6
Subsidies	2
Net property income from abroad	3
Capital consumption	5

13.2 At the beginning of 1989, Mr A L L Go, a senior economist in Europa, a prominent Western industrialized nation, paid a visit, for cultural and educational purposes, to a number of underdeveloped nations.

One evening found him engaged in an informal after-dinner discussion with a group of officials who were anxious to benefit as much as possible from the experience of Mr Go and his colleagues. They said they understood that 1988 had on the whole been a good year for Europa. 'It certainly has,' replied Mr Go, 'last year expenditure went up by around 7 per cent in real terms. Almost all sectors of the economy expanded, but the leader was construction. You know, some of our cities have become pretty snarled up with traffic – workers always arriving late, goods often delayed and so forth, and several of the big companies have wanted to move to the outskirts for some time. However the government had always refused to release any green-belt land for building. It reversed this policy in 1987 and the building boom got under way in 1988.

'Of course we are putting more into our buildings these days. Double glazing and air-conditioning are standard in new houses – although I must admit that with the rise in prices, new houses are getting beyond the reach of most people.'

At this point Mr Go's host interrupted him to ask why they needed air-conditioning and double glazing.

'Well, I suppose that when people have sufficient of the necessities of life – food, shelter and so forth – they are willing to pay more for comfort, and these things certainly make life more comfortable. I know that the climate in our two countries isn't all that different, but one seems to notice the extremes more, and especially the heat, in large cities. Also we can't just open a few windows, as you do, because of the noise. This is getting an increasing problem, especially with the growth of jet travel. I reckon that the building of our new airport was worth at least £2 million in sales to the double glazing manufacturers.'

'Your cities do not seem to be particularly pleasant places in which to live,' said his host. 'Oh, I don't know. There's plenty by way of entertainment. I could go to a different cinema or theatre every night of the week and never see the same film or play twice. All the same, most people do seem to feel the need to get away from the city fairly often. The second cottage in the country is becoming increasingly common, and of course most families have a car (three or four in some families), and they get away for the day whenever they can.

'I suppose that the vehicles industry is also doing well,' asked his host. 'They have expanded considerably during the past decade, but 1988 was rather a flat year. Money expenditure was up by about 10 per cent, but this was almost entirely due to higher car prices – the manufacturers seem to have gone in for chrome in a big way this year. Also they have had to meet the cost of engine modifications to reduce pollution, and safety modifications to cut down on the number of accidents.'

'Do your drivers have a bad safety record then?'

'I don't think that we are any worse than any other country with the same

Table 13.9
Time necessary to pay for goods and services

	1971		1985	
	h	m	h	m
Large white loaf		9		7
1 lb rump steak		54		47
500 g butter		20		17
1 pint fresh milk		5		4
1 dozen medium eggs		22		14
100 g instant coffee		22		24
125 g tea		9		9
1 pint beer		13		12
1 bottle whisky	4	17	2	11
20 cigarettes		22		22
Weekly gas bill	1	23	1	20
'Electricity'	1	04	1	06
1 gallon 4-star petrol		33		34
1 cwt coal	1	19	1	32
Weekly phone bill		50		38*
Car licence	39	59	27	46
Colour TV licence	19	40	16	07
Cinema admission		29		31
LP record	3	16	1	37
100-mile rail trip (2nd class single)	3	05	3	27*

Note: All calculations for married man on average hourly male earnings with non-earning wife.
Source: Social Trends, 1987
* 1984.

number of cars as ourselves. Certainly the number of accidents has gone up much less than the number of cars on the road. However, what with road accidents and the increasing number of deaths from bronchitis and cancer – it seems fairly clear that these are connected with the increasing consumption of cigarettes and with air pollution – we have had to expand medical services generally, and in particular the number of hospital beds available.'

'And that I suppose, gives another boost to the construction industry,' said his host, neatly completing the circle of the conversation.

Discuss the meaning of an increase in the national income with particular reference to the above passage.

13.3 What can be deduced from Table 13.9 about changes in the standard of living?

13.4 In 1986 Austin-Rover was ordered by Oxford Magistrates' Court to pay £76,000 costs after being found guilty of failing to comply with an abatement notice served on it by Oxford City Council to reduce paint fall-out emission. Moreover, following the court's decision, it was believed that about 100 residents affected by the pollution might proceed with civil actions against Austin-Rover. They had complained that paint fall-out on their homes, gardens and cars was making their lives a misery.

Company officials said that they had done their best to cut pollution, spending more than £500,000 on new filters. But after the judgment they agreed to install new filters and baffles which were likely to cost a further £500,000.

(i) Outline the costs incurred by residents affected by the pollution.

(ii) What might be the subsequent impact of these costs on GDP?

(iii) Discuss the possible consequences, other than on the residents, of the court's decision.

(iv) What information would be required in order to assess the net change in economic welfare following the court's decision?

13.5

Table 13.10
Index numbers of output at constant factor cost 1980 = 100

	Weight per 1,000	1976	1977	1978	1979	1980	1981	1982	1983	1984	1985	1986
Agriculture, forestry and fishing	22	75.3	85.1	91.5	90.1	100.0	102.6	111.2	105.2	122.5	118.8	118.8
Production												
Energy and water supply	95	60.9	74.8	85.0	100.5	100.0	103.8	110.0	115.9	110.2	120.1	125.4
Manufacturing	266	107.0	109.0	109.7	109.5	100.0	94.0	94.2	96.9	100.8	103.8	104.7
Total production	361	95.3	100.2	103.2	107.1	100.0	96.6	98.4	101.9	103.3	108.1	110.2
Construction	63	98.7	98.4	105.1	105.8	100.0	89.9	91.6	95.3	98.6	99.8	102.1
Distribution, hotels and catering; repairs	128	99.6	99.0	104.8	107.9	100.0	98.4	100.3	104.6	109.5	114.8	120.4
Transport and communication	72	91.6	94.2	96.6	101.3	100.0	100.2	99.2	102.1	106.4	112.1	116.7
Other	354	91.1	92.8	94.9	97.6	100.0	101.1	102.8	105.6	109.6	112.9	116.9
Gross domestic product (output-based)	1000	93.8	96.5	99.8	103.0	100.0	98.4	100.1	103.3	106.7	110.7	114.0

Source: United Kingdom National Accounts

With reference to Table 13.10:

(i) Identify the major changes in output between 1976 and 1986 and give a brief explanation of these changes.

(ii) Say what you understand by the term 'weight per 1,000' and indicate its significance.

(iii) Identify the sectors which show the greatest fluctuations in output, and explain these fluctuations.

(iv) What conclusions do you draw from the data about changes in living standards over the period?

(v) What other information would you have found helpful in answering (iv)?

Objective test questions: set 5

1. All the following are part of a country's stock of capital except:
   A   factories;
   B   hospitals;
   C   machinery;
   D   stocks of components;
   E   money.

2. Economic capacity is likely to increase in all of the following situations except:
   A   capital consumption exceeds gross investment;
   B   the quality of the labour force increases;
   C   the size of the labour force increases;
   D   the quality of capital increases;
   E   the quality of land increases.

3. In the national income accounts consumers' expenditure includes expenditure on all of the following except:
   A   school fees;
   B   private legal services;
   C   consumer durables;
   D   new houses;
   E   travel.

4. In an economy whose resources are fully utilized, the most likely effect on the output of consumption goods of an increase in the current output of capital goods is:
   A   a reduction in both the current and subsequent periods;
   B   an increase in both the current and subsequent periods;
   C   a reduction in the current and an increase in subsequent periods;
   D   an increase in the current and a reduction in subsequent periods;
   E   no change in the current and an increase in subsequent periods.

5. Value added is defined as:
   A   cost of bought-in materials plus labour;
   B   cost of bought-in materials plus labour plus capital consumption;
   C   sales receipts minus cost of bought-in materials;
   D   sales receipts minus cost of labour;
   E   sales receipts minus capital consumption.

6. To convert GNP at market prices to gross national disposable income an adjustment is made for changes in:

A   capital consumption;
B   the terms of trade;
C   expenditure taxes;
D   income taxes;
E   imports and exports.

Questions 7–10 relate to the table below.

	£m.
Consumers' expenditure	1,300
General government consumption	300
Gross domestic fixed capital formation	250
Change in the value of stocks	0
Exports of goods and services	350
Imports of goods and services	400
Taxes on expenditure (net of subsidies)	150
Net property income from abroad	100
Capital consumption	200

7.   Gross domestic product at factor cost (£m.) is:
    A   1,600;
    B   1,650;
    C   1,800;
    D   1,900;
    E   1,950.

8.   Gross domestic product at market prices (£m.) is:
    A   1,650;
    B   1,700;
    C   1,800;
    D   1,900;
    E   1,950.

9.   Gross national product at factor cost (£m.) is:
    A   1,650;
    B   1,750;
    C   1,850;
    D   1,900;
    E   1,950.

10.   (Net) National income (£m.) is:
    A   1,550;
    B   1,600;
    C   1,650;
    D   1,700;
    E   1,750.

11.   In order to convert GDP at market prices to GNP at factor cost it is necessary to:
    1   add net property income from abroad;
    2   subtract taxes on expenditure (net of subsidies);
    3   subtract capital consumption.

12.   National income can be estimated by aggregating the flow of:
    1   expenditure;
    2   incomes;
    3   output.

13.   In order to obtain an estimate of national income, one would subtract from GNP at factor cost:
  1   expenditure taxes;
  2   net property income from abroad;
  3   capital consumption.

14.   The flow of labour inputs in a given period is likely to be influenced by:
  1   the age structure of the population;
  2   the sex structure of the population;
  3   the average number of hours worked per worker.

15.   Fixed capital includes:
  1   stocks of raw materials;
  2   stocks of work in progress;
  3   machinery.

16.

	Price index	Index of volume of output
Year 1	100	100
2	120	90

From the above data we can conclude that between year 1 and year 2:
  1   nominal GDP increased;
  2   real GDP increased;
  3   economic welfare increased.

17.   An increase in real national income might not be accompanied by an improvement in the average standard of living because the increase might have resulted from an increase in:
  1   prices;
  2   military expenditure;
  3   population and the work-force.

18.   In each year in the last decade nominal national income has increased by more than real national income in the UK.
    In each year in the last decade prices have risen in the UK.

19.   Provided that the distribution of income does not change, an increase in the average standard of living implies an increase in the living standards of every citizen.
    A change in the distribution of income is likely to affect the relative living standards of different citizens.

20.   An increase in expenditure in UK exports implies an increase in the UK's GNP.
    GNP is defined as GDP plus exports minus imports.

True/false

1.   Gross domestic product at market prices must always exceed GDP at factor cost.
2.   Gross national product at market prices must always exceed GDP at market prices.
3.   National income can never exceed GNP.
4.   Gross national product can never exceed gross national disposable income.
5.   Other things remaining equal, an improvement in a country's terms of trade implies an increase in its gross national disposable income.
6.   Education and training can be considered as either investment or consumption.

7. Stock appreciation is excluded from national income.
8. Nominal GDP increases as a result of an increase in either the volume of transactions or their average price.
9. If gross investment is greater than zero, productive capacity will increase.
10. Gross domestic product is usually a better indicator than GNP of the level of utilization of domestic resources.

CHAPTER FOURTEEN
Consumers' Expenditure

Introduction

As we saw in Chapter 13, consumers' expenditure is the most important element in total expenditure. It accounts for almost half of final expenditure and 60 per cent of GDP at market prices. It is therefore appropriate to begin our detailed examination of expenditure by considering consumers' expenditure.

Consumers' expenditure and consumption

For much of the time we shall use the term 'consumption' as being synonymous with consumers' expenditure. However, strictly speaking this is not so. Consumers' expenditure occurs when goods and services are exchanged for money (or a promise to pay). These goods and services are purchased not for their own sake, but for the benefits that they yield in use. Food provides nutrition, a car provides transport and so forth. Consumption occurs when these benefits are enjoyed, e.g. when a meal is eaten and a series of car journeys is undertaken. Consumption can also be defined as destruction in use. Once food is eaten (and assimilated) it yields no further benefits; its destruction is complete. On the other hand, one journey constitutes only a very small part of the benefits, of the destruction, of the car (unless of course the car crashes!).

To obtain an estimate of consumption, as defined above, would be very difficult. Consequently in the national accounts, consumers' expenditure is used as a proxy for consumption.

The determinants of consumption

The level of income

Numerous studies have found that income is the most important determinant of consumption. Indeed whenever you hear an economist use the term *consumption function* you can be sure that he is speaking of consumption as a function of income, i.e.

$$C = f(Y)$$

where C denotes consumption,
  Y denotes income,
  f indicates that consumption is a function of, depends upon, income.

It does not require a great deal of insight to reach the conclusion that consumption depends to a large extent upon income; we need only consider our own experience. But much more effort is required to identify the precise relationship between income and consumption, and in particular to identify the change in consumption associatied with a given change in income.

To illustrate this point let us consider Fig. 14.1 which shows the changes that have occurred in two measures of income and in consumers' expenditure.

If we first consider GDP as our measure of income, we find that income and expenditure moved in the same direction. In five of the seven years in which GDP increased, an even bigger percentage increase occurred in expenditure. In both of the years in which GDP fell, expenditure also fell, but by a smaller percentage (Fig. 14.1).

When we consider the other measure of income, personal disposable income, we find that income and expenditure move in the same direction in every year except one (1980). Of these eight years,

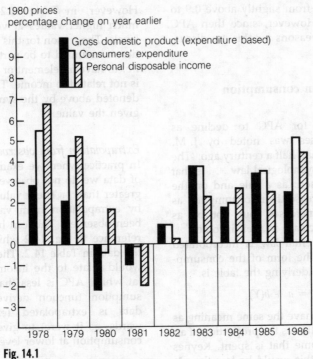

Fig. 14.1
Income, product and spending per capita

the bigger percentage change occurred in income in four, and in expenditure in the other four. There is no evidence of a stable empirical relationship that would constitute a sound foundation for analysis. In order to build this foundation we have to concentrate on the longer-term behaviour of income and consumption.

The average propensity to consume
The average propensity to consume (APC) is the proportion or percentage of income that is spent in a given period.

$$APC = \frac{C}{Y}$$

where C is consumption,
Y is income.

In Table 14.1 personal disposable income is the income measure and, as usual, consumers' expenditure is used as a proxy for consumption. It can be seen that in the early part of the period the personal sector[1] spent a lower proportion of its income as income increased. In the

Table 14.1
Average propensity to consume

	Personal disposal income (£bn. 1980 prices)	Consumers' expenditure (£bn. 1980 prices)	Average propensity to consume
1964	107,390	98,864	92.1
1968	115,793	107,498	92.8
1972	133,093	121,464	91.3
1976	142,500	125,307	87.9
1980	161,185	136,995	85.0
1981	157,263	136,598	86.9
1982	157,564	137,614	87.3
1983	161,301	143,977	89.3
1984	165,671	147,056	88.8
1985	170,124	152,501	89.6
1986	177,355	161,277	90.9

Source: Economic Trends

1960s APC fell from slightly above 0.9 to 0.85 in 1980. However, since then APC has risen (the reasons for this are discussed below).

The Keynesian consumption function

The tendency for APC to decline as income increases was noted by J. M. Keynes more than half a century ago: 'The fundamental psychological law . . . is that men are disposed, as a rule and on the average, to increase their consumption as their income increases, but not by as much as the increase in their income.'[2]

This fundamental law is incorporated in Table 14.2. The form of the consumption function underlying the table is:

$$C = a + b(Y)$$

where C and Y have the same meaning as above, and b indicates the proportion of an increase in income that is spent. Keynes suggested that this would be less than 1, and in Table 14.2 we have assumed a value of 0.7. We assume that $a = 10$, and we can then work out the level of consumption associated with any given level of income.

It can be seen that when income is in the range 40–70, APC assumes a similar range of values to those in Table 14.1.

However, in Table 14.2 APC assumes much higher values at very low income levels. The reason for this is the consumption is assumed to be partly autonomous, i.e. to have an element or component that is not related to income. This element was denoted above by the symbol a, and was given the value 10.

Extrapolation from observed values

In practice when we examine time series of data we do not observe values of APC greater than 1. These values are obtained by extrapolation from values that have been observed. This can be illustrated by reference to Fig. 14.2 which is based on the data in Table 14.2. The observed data would relate to the income range 40–70 (at which APC is less than 1). The consumption function derived from these data is extrapolated (extended backwards, as it were) to give the values of consumption at lower levels of income.

Cross-section analysis

It may not be entirely satisfactory that the consumption function should relate to situations that have not been observed in

Table 14.2
A hypothetical consumption function

Income	Consumption	Average propensity to consume
0	10	—
10	17	1.7
20	24	1.2
30	31	1.03
40	38	0.95
50	45	0.9
60	52	0.87
70	59	0.84

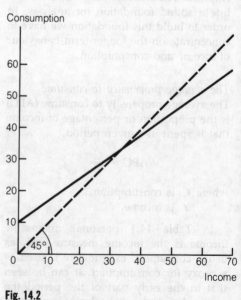

Fig. 14.2
A consumption function: $C = 10 + 0.7(Y)$

Table 14.3
A cross-section analysis of consumption

Disposable income per person (£ per week)	Expenditure per person (£ per week)	Average propensity to consume
35.38	37.59	106.3
33.35	38.10	114.2
35.82	40.08	111.9
40.70	44.24	108.7
44.80	45.14	100.8
49.55	51.07	103.1
54.60	51.81	94.9
60.15	57.10	94.9
74.15	61.62	83.1
73.19	66.05	90.2
78.97	74.60	94.5
75.09	72.36	96.4
92.43	77.57	83.9
104.41	89.31	85.5

Source: *Family Expenditure Survey*, 1984

practice. It is therefore reassuring that cross-section analysis reveals situations in which a low income is associated with an APC greater than 1 (Table 14.3).

The marginal propensity to consume
We noted above that economists are especially interested in the response of consumption to a change in income. This response is measured by the marginal propensity to consume (MPC), defined as:

$$\text{MPC} = \frac{\Delta C}{\Delta Y}$$

where Δ denotes a change in the variable concerned. In the formula given earlier, MPC was denoted by the symbol b.

The MPC for any given change in income can be derived from Table 14.1. So for example the increase in income between 1983 and 1984 of £345bn. was

associated with an increase in consumption of £238bn., indicating an MPC of 0.69.[3]

This is very close to the value of b (0.7) assumed in the hypothetical consumption function discussed above. However, as Fig. 14.1 revealed, and as would also be seen if more calculations were performed on Table 14.1, the MPC tends to vary considerably from one year to another. In the consumption function $C = a + b(Y)$, b is the best overall estimate of the MPC for whatever period is being studied.

An assessment of the Keynesian theory of consumption

We have shown that the Keynesian theory of consumption emphasizes the relationship between consumption and current (disposable) income. But we have also shown that when annual changes are examined, the relationship is far from stable; substantial variations occur in the MPC. Moreover, further studies have suggested that the short-run response to a change in income is not as great as the long-run response, i.e. MPC has a lower value in the short run.

This is illustrated in Fig. 14.3 where C_s and C_L represent the short- and long-run consumption functions. When income

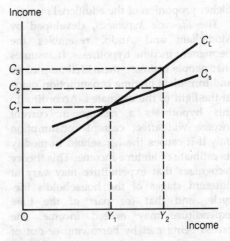

Fig. 14.3
Short- and long-run consumption functions

increases from Y_1 to Y_2 consumption first increases from C_1 to C_2 in accordance with the short-run consumption function. Subsequently, if the higher level of income persists, consumption increases further to C_3. Similarly if income were to fall, the decline in consumption would be greater in the long than the short run.

Cross-section studies have also revealed lower propensities to consume than those found in time-series studies of long-run consumption functions. Since Keynesian theory did not provide a ready explanation of these facts, alternative theories, more in accordance with the data, were developed.

Post-Keynesian theories of consumption

There are three major alternative theories, each of which will be discussed briefly. The *permanent income hypothesis* was developed by Milton Friedman, who argued that consumption depends upon average long-run ('permanent') income. Consumption will not respond fully to a change in income (e.g. from C_1 to C_3 in Fig. 14.3) unless people believe that the change in income will be maintained. If they believe the change to be only temporary, the response will be less (e.g. consumption will increase from C_1 to C_2 in Fig. 14.3) and consumers will save a higher proportion of the additional income.

The *life-cycle hypothesis*, developed by Modigliani and Ando, resembles the permanent income hypothesis. It assumes that people estimate their lifetime income and formulate lifetime consumption plans in the light of the estimates. According to this hypothesis a change in current income will affect current consumption only if it causes the household to modify its estimate of lifetime income. This theory recognizes that expenditure may vary at different stages of the household's life-cycle, and that for part of the time expenditure may exceed income, the excess being met by borrowing or out of savings. Consequently this theory draws

attention to a range of factors not so far considered, including the availability of credit and rates of interest. These factors are discussed further below.

Both of these theories could explain data that cannot be explained by the Keynesian theory, and they might therefore be considered to have improved upon that theory. However, it would be extremely difficult to subject either the permanent income or the life-cycle hypothesis to a rigorous test since they both incorporate individuals' expectations for a long period ahead. To understand the difficulties involved in such a test, try to estimate your own lifetime earnings. Even if you are currently in employment, or if you know the salary or wage at which you are likely to start work, you will not find it an easy task.

The final theory is Duesenberry's *relative income hypothesis*. This theory assumes that current consumption is determined by the individual's income relative to his or her previous peak income and to other people's consumption.

The peak income becomes important when income falls. In Fig. 14.4 C_L is the long-run consumption function and C_s is a short-run function (of which there might be several). If income falls from Y_1 to Y_2 consumption falls from C_1 to C_2 in accord-

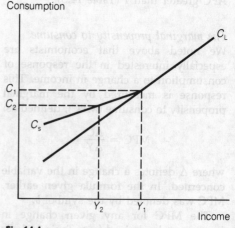

Fig. 14.4
A fall in income and consumption

ance with the short-term function C_s. If income subsequently returns to Y_1, consumption returns to C_1. Any further increase in income leads to an expansion of consumption in line with the long-run function C_L.

The relative income hypothesis also provides a possible explanation of the fact that many cross-section studies reveal that APC falls as income increases. It suggests that low-income groups spend a higher proportion of their income, or even borrow to finance an excess of expenditure over income, because they wish to move closer to the average consumption pattern. Conversely, households with above-average income spend a lower than average proportion of their incomes.

Other determinants of consumption

As noted in our discussion of post-Keynesian theories, consumption may be influenced by other factors in addition to income. We now briefly discuss a number of these factors.

The saturation of markets: secular stagnation

It has been recognized that as people become more wealthy they may spend a lower proportion of their income. This seems particularly likely when it is understood that wealth includes stocks of consumer durable goods such as cars, refrigerators and washing-machines. As the proportion of households having such goods increases, i.e. as markets become saturated, sales decline. The significance of any decline in the sales of durables is increased by the fact that consumers usually spend a smaller proportion of their income on food as income increases.

If a fall in the consumption ratio is not balanced by an increase in other forms of spending, the economy will tend to stagnate.

Long-term or secular stagnation may seem a remote possibility when one considers the creation of new markets by the introduction of such products as combined fridge-freezers, video-recorders and personal computers. There is also a tendency for consumers in advanced societies to spend a higher proportion of their income on services: travel, leisure activities, etc. Moreover when one takes a purely domestic viewpoint one sees that for many products consumption per head is lower in the UK than in other countries such as the USA. However the fact remains that the consumption ratio has fallen and this may be partly due to the saturation of markets.

Price increases

There are a number of recorded instances, such as the hyperinflation experienced by Germany after the First World War, of consumers responding to rapid price increases by increasing the consumption ratio. Whenever prices are rising at a rate in excess of the rate of interest on savings, consumers can maximize the volume of goods obtained from a given income by spending that income as soon as it is received.

On the other hand there is some evidence that more modest price increases can cause consumers to increase their savings in order to restore the real value of their wealth (the 'real wealth' effect). Moreover price increases reduce consumers' liquidity which in turn is likely to lead to a fall in spending and an increase in saving.

When the UK's annual rate of inflation approached 25 per cent in 1975 fears were expressed that the propensity to consume might increase and thus add to the inflationary pressure. After all when prices rise at that rate the value of money is halved in just over three years. The propensity to consume did increase in 1975, but this was probably due mainly to the fall in disposable income, noted above. As disposable income continued to fall over the following two years, the propensity to consume continued to increase, even though the rate of inflation moderated.

Unemployment

Another possible explanation of the fall in propensity to consume in the latter part of the 1970s is that the threat of increasing unemployment caused workers to put more aside for a rainy day, i.e. in case of redundancy.

Unemployment itself tends to reduce absolute consumption. However, it is not clear what is most likely to happen to the propensity to consume. The average propensity to consume of the unemployed probably increases as their incomes fall. But this may be offset by a fall in the propensity to consume of those in work whose real income rises.

Taxation and government expenditure

Real disposable income is affected by changes in taxation (in particular rates of personal taxation and expenditure taxes) and in government spending (e.g. the level of social security payments). Consequently we would expect changes in these factors to lead to changes in the propensity to consume.

The distribution of income and wealth

In the long term consumption may be influenced by changes in the distribution of income and wealth. This is especially likely if income and wealth are redistributed in favour of the poorer members of the community whose propensity to consume is above average.

The propensity to save

The marginal propensity to save (MPS) relates a change in saving to a change in income:

$$\text{MPS} = \frac{\Delta S}{\Delta Y}$$

If we make the simplifying assumption that all income is either consumed or saved, it follows that the MPC plus the MPS must equal 1.

The average propensity to save (APS) expresses the relationship between total saving and income:

$$\text{APS} = \frac{S}{Y}$$

It follows that APC + APS = 1.

The savings ratio

The personal savings ratio is defined in the national accounts as the proportion of personal disposable income allocated to saving.[4] It is therefore very similar to the APS.

The determinants of saving

Given the relationships set out in the previous sections, we could explain saving in terms of the various factors that influence consumption, although with the opposite signs. For example, the increases in the personal savings ratio in 1972–73 and 1978–79, shown in Fig. 14.5, appear to be mainly due to the unexpectedly big increases in *personal disposable income*.

In other periods changes in income appear to have much less influence. For example, in the 1980s the savings ratio has fallen despite a substantial increase in disposable income and in *real interest rates*, factors which, as shown above, we would usually expect to lead to an increase in saving. It appears that their influence was outweighed by a third factor, the fall in the *inflation rate*.

We noted above that inflation can cause consumers to increase their consumption (reduce saving) in order to 'beat' future price increases. Alternatively, by reducing the real value of existing savings, it can cause consumers to increase their savings ratio. With the high inflation rates of the 1970s, the second effect seems to have predominated. Subsequently, as inflation moderated in the 1980s, the savings ratio fell back to its earlier level (Fig. 14.6).

Consumer expenditure annual change

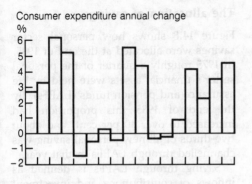

Personal savings ratio annual change

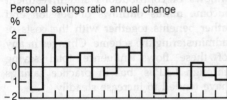

Personal disposable incomes annual change

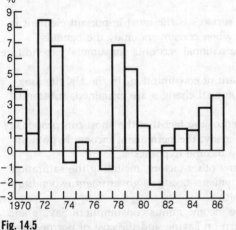

Fig. 14.5
Personal disposable income, consumer expenditure, personal savings ratio
Source: Economic Progress Report, Nov.–Dec. 1986

Personal sector savings ratio

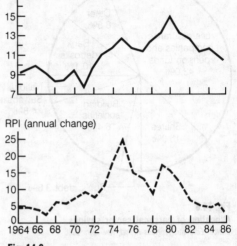

RPI (annual change)

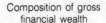

Fig. 14.6
Retail price index and the savings ratio
Source: Economic Progress Report, Nov.–Dec. 1986

Composition of gross financial wealth

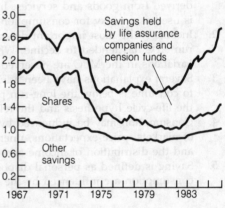

Fig. 14.7
Personal sector financial wealth
Source: Economic Progress Report, Nov.–Dec. 1986

The prolonged rise in *stock market prices* in the first part of the 1980s led to a substantial increase in the real value of shares held by individuals, both directly and via life assurance companies and pensions funds, as shown in Fig. 14.7.

Another factor affecting savings is the *availability and cost of credit*. In the mid 1980s consumer credit rose rapidly. Credit growth in 1986 was the highest of the decade at 13.2 per cent in real terms. This helped to explain why consumption increased more rapidly than income and the savings ratio fell. The rapid rise in consumer credit was partly due to the spread of new credit mechanisms, e.g. credit cards.

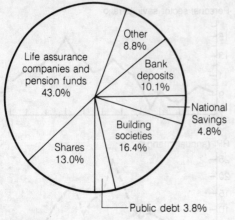

Fig. 14.8
Allocation of personal sector savings
Source: Economic Progress Report, Nov.–Dec. 1986

The allocation of savings

Figure 14.8 shows how personal sector savings were allocated at the end of 1985. In 1975 roughly a quarter of the personal sector's financial assets were held by life assurance and pension funds (LAPFs). By the end of 1985 this proportion had increased to over 40 per cent, and about two-thirds of all new personal saving was channelled through LAPFs in that year.

Saving through LAPFs is defined as inflows of contributions and investment income minus outflows of pension and other benefits together with the costs of administering the scheme. Changes in any of these flows influence total saving through LAPFs, but in practice savings have tended to increase steadily.

Summary

1. Consumers' expenditure on goods and services is the most important element in total expenditure. Consumption occurs when consumers enjoy the benefits derived from goods and services. In the national accounts consumers' expenditure is used as a proxy for consumption.
2. Income is the most important determinant of consumption. In the UK the long-run APC has tended to decline. When annual changes are examined, substantial variations in the MPC are observed.
3. Several explanations have been advanced of the fact that the short-run propensity to consume is below the long-run propensity: the permanent income hypothesis, the life-cycle hypothesis and the relative income hypothesis.
4. Consumption may be influenced by many other factors, including the saturation of markets, price expectations, unemployment, taxation, government expenditure and the distribution of income and wealth.
5. Saving is defined as personal disposable income minus consumption. Saving and consumption are influenced by the return on saving and the cost of borrowing.

Key terms

Consumption function
Average propensity to consume
Marginal propensity to consume

Average propensity to save
Marginal propensity to save
Savings ratio

Notes

1. The personal sector comprises households, unincorporated businesses, charitable bodies and other non-profit-making institutions.

2.   Keynes J M, *The General Theory of Employment Interest and Money*. Macmillan, 1936, p. 96.
3.   Strictly speaking the changes in income should be much smaller than in Table 14.1.
4.   The inclusion of unincorporated businesses in the personal sector is particularly significant when savings are considered. For example, in 1982 the personal sector savings ratio was 10.8 per cent but the household savings ratio was only 2.5 per cent. The difference was mainly undistributed profits by unincorporated businesses. In 1983 the household savings ratio was estimated to be zero (*Lloyds Bank Economic Bulletin*, Feb. 1984).

Essay questions

1.   Discuss the major determinants of the aggregate level of consumption.
2.   Explain what is meant by the term 'consumption function' and show why the value of the function in the short run may differ from that in the long run.
3.   Discuss the possible effects of inflation on the propensity to consume.
4.   'Since it is impossible to test the permanent income hypothesis and the life-cycle hypothesis, they are not useful concepts.' Discuss.

Exercises

14.1   (i)   Assuming that the country referred to in the table below has a constant MPC, calculate the level of consumption when GNP is (a) zero, (b) £6bn.

A hypothetical consumption schedule	
GNP (£bn.)	Consumption (£bn.)
1	1.5
2	2.0
3	2.5

   (ii)   Calculate the APC when GNP is £5bn.
   (iii) Substitute the appropriate values of a and b in the following equation: $C = a + b \text{ (GNP)}$.
   (iv)   What economic concept does the term b denote?
   (v)   What is the MPS in this economy?

14.2   What factors might explain the changes in consumer expenditure shown in Fig. 14.5?

14.3 (i) Explain what you understand by the savings ratio.
(ii) What factors might have caused the changes in the savings ratio shown in Fig. 14.9?
(iii) Assess the possible consequences of these changes.

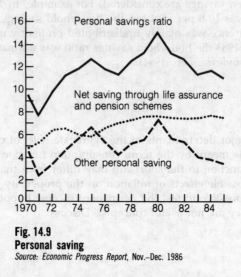

Fig. 14.9
Personal saving
Source: *Economic Progress Report*, Nov.–Dec. 1986

14.4 Figure 14.10, taken from *Social Trends*, shows the flow of household incomes, taxes and benefits. With reference to this diagram show the probable effect on consumption of an increase in (a) real wage rates, (b) the standard rate of VAT, (c) the level of retirement pensions, (d) prescription charges, (e) dividend payments, (f) the standard rate of income tax.

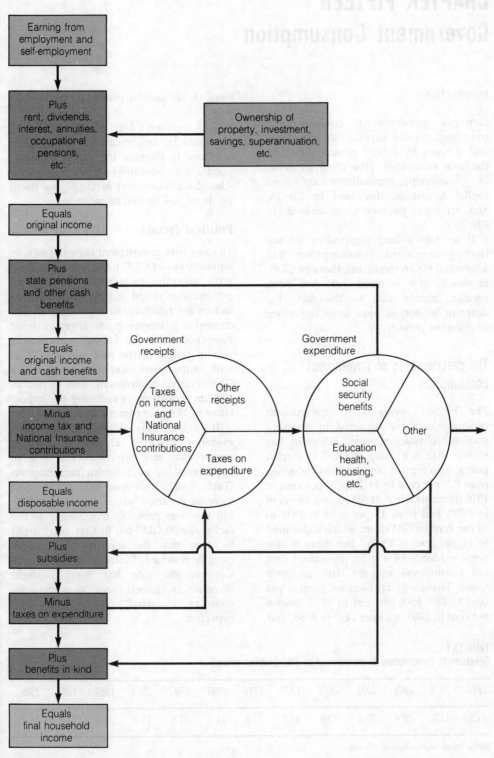

Fig. 14.10
The flow of household incomes, taxes and benefits

CHAPTER FIFTEEN
Government Consumption

Introduction

General government consumption comprises current expenditure on goods and services by central government and the local authorities. (The other elements of government expenditure are fixed capital formation, discussed in Ch. 16, and transfer payments, discussed in Ch. 20.)

If we take a long perspective we see that government consumption has accounted for an increasing share of GDP. However, the increase has not been regular, mainly due to the fact that different influences have been important in different periods.

The determinants of government consumption

The biggest increases in government consumption have occurred in times of war, for obvious reasons. Feinstein has shown that as a share of GDP at market prices, government consumption increased from 8.7 per cent in 1913 to 37 per cent in 1916 (from which it declined to 8 per cent in 1920) and from 13 per cent in 1938 to 49 per cent in 1944 (from which it declined to 16 per cent in 1948).[1] But there is also some evidence of a mild, persistent (but not continuous) upward drift at other times. There was an increase from 5 per cent in 1870 to 8 per cent in 1913, from 8 per cent in 1920 to 13 per cent in 1938, and

from 16 per cent in 1948 to 21 per cent in 1986.

This upward drift can probably be explained by an increasing acceptance of the need to increase the supply of merit goods, e.g. education, medical services. Also the relative cost of supplying these products has tended to increase.

Political factors

The fact that government consumption as a percentage of GDP has risen in the long term despite numerous changes of government might suggest that political factors are relatively unimportant. In this context it is interesting to compare what happened when a Labour government was in power in the mid and late 1970s with subsequent experience under a Conservative government, first elected in 1979 on a platform of reducing the importance of the government sector.

It is extremely difficult to find any evidence that the change in political power had any effect on the relative importance of government consumption (Table 15.1). It is true that the biggest increase occurred under Labour in 1975. But this was probably due mainly to the fact that real GDP fell in that year; it can be seen that the increase was subsequently reversed. Moreover the period of Conservative rule has seen a slight increase in government consumption, contrary to what might have been expected.

Table 15.1
Government consumption as percentage of GDP (market prices)

1974	1975	1976	1977	1978	1979	1980	1981	1982	1983	1984	1985	1986
19.9	21.8	21.4	20.2	19.9	19.8	21.3	21.8	21.8	21.9	21.8	21.2	21.2

Source: United Kingdom National Accounts

The pattern of government consumption

Table 15.2 shows that there have been marked changes in the relative importance of the major areas of government consumption. The percentage of consumption accounted for by military defence fell substantially in the early part of the period, probably due mainly to a reduction in the UK's overseas commitments. The subsequent halting of this downward trend reflects the greater priority given to defence by the Conservative government elected in 1979.

The trend of spending on education has been almost the reverse. Education's share of consumption increased in the earlier part of the period, probably because a rise in the birth-rate had led to an increase in the numbers at school and in college. (Raising the school-leaving age also had an impact.) Subsequently, as school rolls began to decline, the increase in education's share came to an end and is now declining.

The third major area of spending, the National Health Service, showed a modest but steady increase in relative importance

Table 15.2
The pattern of government consumption (%)

	1966	1979	1986
Military defence	32.7	23.7	23.6
Education	18.0	21.4	20.3
National Health Service	19.6	22.7	23.7
Other	29.7	32.2	32.4
Total	100	100	100

Source: United Kingdom National Accounts

throughout the period. This was also due partly to the increase in the birth-rate. It was also affected by the substantial rise in costs, reflecting an increase in the numbers working in the National Health Service, and the discovery and development of potent, but often expensive, drugs. (This can be seen as a parallel with the introduction of new products which provide a stimulus to consumers' expenditure, referred to in Chapter 14.) Finally it reflects a commitment of both Labour and Conservative governments to try to improve the standard of health care.

Summary

1. General government consumption comprises current expenditure on goods and services by central government and the local authorities. Government consumption has accounted for an increasing share of GDP, the main increases having occurred in times of war.
2. There is little evidence that changes in political power have affected the relative importance of government consumption. However, political factors have had more influence on the pattern of consumption.
3. The pattern of government consumption has been strongly influenced by demographic factors.

Key terms

Current expenditure on goods and services
The distribution of government expenditure

Notes

1. Feinstein C H, *National Income, Output and Expenditure of the United Kingdom, 1855–1965*. Cambridge University Press, 1972.

Essay questions

1. What are the major determinants of government current expenditure on goods and services?
2. Why has government current expenditure on goods and services tended to grow more rapidly than consumers' expenditure in the post-war period?
3. 'The increase in the relative importance of government current expenditure on goods and services is to be welcomed as an indicator that society is becoming more responsible.' Discuss.

Exercises

15.1 Discuss the reasons for the change in the relative importance of government expenditure, as shown in Table 15.1, and assess the implications of this change.
15.2 (i) Discuss the reasons for the changes in the pattern of government expenditure, shown in Table 15.2.
    (ii) What future changes in the pattern would you expect to occur?

CHAPTER SIXTEEN
Investment

Introduction

Investment, which in 1986 accounted for 13.7 per cent of final expenditure, and 17 per cent of GDP at market prices, comprises two components. These are gross domestic fixed capital formation and the value of the physical increase in stocks and work in progress. Of these two components fixed capital formation is by far the larger in value and will be discussed first.

Gross domestic fixed capital formation

Table 16.1 shows the amount spent, on the assets listed, by the private sector, (private sector producers and households), the public corporations (public sector producers), e.g. British Coal, British

Rail, and general (central and local) government. We examine the major determinants of the expenditure of each of these groups in turn. But most attention will be paid to expenditure by private sector producers.

Expenditure by private sector producers

Private sector producers have increased their share of spending on fixed investment in recent years and in 1986 the private sector as a whole accounted for 80 per cent of the total. The major items of expenditure are plant and machinery, new buildings and works, vehicles, ships and aircraft. Expenditure on these items leads to an increase in economic capacity. However, part of this expenditure is required to replace existing plant, equipment, etc. that wears out or becomes

Table 16.1
Gross domestic fixed capital formation, by sector and type of asset

Sector	1986		
	£m.	%	% change 1976–86 (constant prices)
Private sector	51,376	80	+45
Public corporations	5,555	9	−47
General government	7,296	11	−33
	64,227	100	+10
Type of asset			
Plant and machinery	24,605	38	+36
Vehicles, ships and aircraft	6,605	10	− 4
Dwellings	14,082	22	− 3
Other new buildings and works	18,935	29	+ 2
	64,227	100	+10

Source: United Kingdom National Accounts

obsolete. As we saw in Chapter 13, this estimated reduction in capacity is entered in the national accounts as capital consumption. (As noted in that chapter the term 'depreciation' may also be used, especially with reference to the activity of individual firms.) We denote the amount of investment required to compensate for capital consumption as *replacement invest-ment*, and the remainder, which represents an increase in the capital stock, as *net investment*. Summarizing:

Gross investment = Replacement invest-ment + Net investment

In examining the determinants of expenditure we shall occasionally distinguish between replacement and net investment. When we simply use the term 'investment' (or fixed capital formation) it should be understood to refer to both together, i.e. to gross investment.

The motives for investment

Businesses may invest for many reasons – to increase capacity and thus facilitate an increase in sales, to improve the quality of the product and thus improve its market share, to reduce the cost of production, etc. Most of these reasons have as a common element a desire to increase profitability (including preventing the fall in profitability that might occur if the investment were not undertaken, a motive which is especially important in relation to replacement investment). Consequently it is appropriate to relate the volume of desired investment to the expected profitability or, more precisely, rate of return. (The rate of return is defined in the appendix to this chapter.) This relationship can be expressed by means of an investment demand schedule.

The investment demand schedule

If we consider private sector producers as a whole there will be, for any given period, a range of investment opportuni-ties with differing potential rates of return. There will be a few projects that

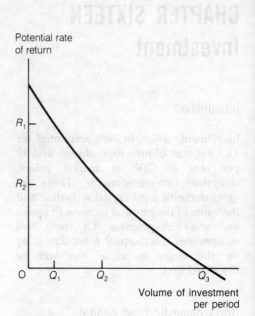

Fig. 16.1
An investment demand schedule

appear likely to yield very high returns and far more with potentially lower yields. This situation is illustrated in Fig. 16.1.

The investment projects within the range OQ_1 have prospective yields of at least R_1. The projects within the range Q_1Q_2 have lower yields, between R_1 and R_2. The prospective yield continues to fall until finally, if investment were pushed to Q_3, no further project with a positive rate of return would remain. (As we shall see in the appendix, investment would only be pushed to this point if investment funds were available at zero cost.)

Factors influencing the yield from investment

The potential yield from any given volume of investment is likely to change from one period to another. Such changes would be represented by shifts of the investment demand schedule. If the potential yields from investment increased, the schedule would shift to the right; if they decreased it would shift to the left. The factors most likely to cause such shifts are discussed in the following sections.

The level of gross domestic product

As we showed in Chapters 12 and 13, a higher GDP implies higher expenditure, incomes and output. Consequently the higher the GDP the greater will tend to be the volume of investment with any given prospective yield. In other words the higher the GDP the further to the right the investment demand schedule will tend to be. This is illustrated in Fig. 16.2 which shows demand schedules relating to two time periods. In period t_1 GDP is Y_1. In period t_2, GDP is higher at Y_2.

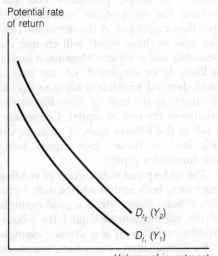

Fig. 16.2
The investment demand schedule at different levels of GDP

The effect of a change in GDP: the acceleration principle

Figure 16.2 simply indicates that investment demand is higher the higher the level of GDP. It says nothing about the effect of a change from one level of GDP to another. There is, however, reason to believe that the process of change itself has an effect on investment. This response of investment to a change in the level of GDP is known as the acceleration principle.

The operation of this principle can be illustrated by means of a simple example.

Let us assume that for a number of years consumers purchase 20,000 kitchen tables a year. These tables are produced on 10 machines, each having a capacity of 2,000 tables a year. These machines have an average life of ten years and the producers have to replace one machine each year. (Since gross investment equals depreciation, net investment is zero.)

Consider now the effect of a 10 per cent increase in consumers' demand as part of a 10 per cent increase in GDP between year t_1 and year t_2. In year t_2 consumers wish to buy 22,000 tables. In order to meet this demand, and thereby increase their profits, producers require eleven machines. In this year they will therefore buy two machines, one for replacement, as in year t_1, and one to increase their capacity (net investment). A 10 per cent increase in GDP and in consumers' expenditure has led to a 100 per cent increase in investment expenditure.

The accelerator is the link between the change in consumption, output or sales and the level of net investment. The acceleration principle can be expressed formally as follows:

$$I = a(\Delta C)$$

where I is net investment,

C is consumers' expenditure,

a is the accelerator coefficient,

Δ denotes a small change in the variable.

A more general formulation of the principle is

$$I = a(Y_{t_2} - Y_{t_1})$$

where $Y_{t_2} - Y_{t_1}$ is the change in output, sales or, more generally, GDP, between one period and another.

The value of the accelerator depends upon the desired ratio of the capital stock to output. (Indeed the 'incremental capital–output ratio' is another term for the accelerator coefficient.) Let us assume that for the economy as a whole £5 of capital is required to produce £1 of output a year. In this instance the accelerator coefficient would be 5. Let us apply this to the 'kitchen table industry' considered above. If the price of each table was £40, the value of the increase in output would be £80,000 (2,000 × £40). This would imply a price for the additional machine of £400,000 (5 × £80,000).

Note that the value of the accelerator may not be the same for decreases as for increases in GDP. This can be illustrated by developing the above example. Assume that in year t_3 GDP fell to its level in year t_1 and that consumers' demand for tables fell to 20,000. Since producers now have eleven machines they would not need to replace the one that wears out. The required output of 20,000 tables could be made on the remaining 10 machines. Consequently investment in year t_3 would be zero.

A dampened accelerator

The acceleration principle may not operate in quite so violent a manner as indicated in the above section, for a number of reasons. First, the producers of consumer goods (tables) may have some excess capacity which enables them to meet at least modest increases in demand without further (net) investment. Second, if they are working at full capacity they may be cautious in their response to increases in demand. At least some producers may refuse to increase capacity until they are convinced that the increase in demand is permanent. In the meantime they may ration their customers by one means or another, including raising the price of tables. Finally, even if the manufacturers of tables do wish to increase their capacity immediately they may not be able to do so if there is a shortage of capacity in the capital goods sector – in those firms which make the woodworking machines.

Lags

In the Treasury model of the economy a 1 per cent increase in manufacturing output results in a 2 per cent increase in investment five quarters later; for private non-manufacturing output the figure is 4.5 per cent, again five quarters later. The existence of lags reduces the simplicity of

the principle. (In addition some of the many other factors which influence investment may also be changing.[1]) Nevertheless experience shows that investment expenditure is more volatile than some other forms of expenditure, and this seems likely to be at least partly due to the operation of the acceleration principle.

Substitution: the cost and availability of other inputs

When deciding which method of production to adopt, producers take into account the costs of the various inputs that they might use. A change in the relative cost of these inputs will change the desirable mix of inputs. More fixed capital is likely to be employed, i.e. the investment demand schedule is likely to shift to the right, as the costs of other inputs rise relative to the cost of capital. Conversely, a fall in the relative costs of other inputs will lead to these other inputs being substituted for capital.

The widespread introduction of vending machines, both within and outside factories, offices, shops, etc. is a good example of the substitution of capital for labour. Another familiar, if less visible, example is the introduction of automatic telephone equipment which reduces the number of operators required.

Technological change

The above examples indicate that technological change may be stimulated by changes in the relative costs of inputs. In other instances technological change has resulted in better and more efficient machines that have been capital-saving rather than labour-saving. This again influences the rate of investment, although the exact nature of the effect is not easy to predict.

Business expectations

Although producers may attempt to make accurate estimates of the yield from investment, the future is always subject to uncertainty. Consequently subjective factors invariably have some influence.

Since an investment demand schedule relates investment to the prospective or expected yield, a change in business expectations will cause the schedule to shift. If producers become more optimistic the schedule will shift to the right. If they become less optimistic it will shift to the left.

The availability and cost of finance

So far we have considered the factors which influence the *desired* expenditure on investment and thus the demand for investment funds. The amount of investment undertaken in a given period depends also upon the supply of investment funds, and we now turn our attention to the supply side, i.e. we examine the factors influencing the availability and cost of finance.

The level of gross domestic product

In Chapter 14 we saw that the balance of evidence from a number of studies suggests that (except during a hyper-inflation) APC either remains constant or declines as GNP and GDP increase. If we continue to make the assumption that income not spent on consumption is saved, it follows that the volume of savings will rise in line with, or perhaps faster than, GDP. This parallels the increase in the demand for investment funds that normally accompanies a rise in GDP. We discuss below the various processes by which these savings are made available to the firms who wish to undertake investment, but first we discuss briefly other determinants of the volume of savings. (As we shall see, saving is undertaken by other institutions, in addition to households.)

Government economic policy

In many modern economies, including the UK, the government's fiscal and monetary policies have an important influence on the supply of money. Since these policies are discussed in detail in Chapters 20 and 21 it is sufficient here to outline the policies that have especially important impli-

cations for the supply of finance for investment. Policies which would tend to lead to an increase in the supply of such finance include:

1. A reduction in taxation – especially important would be a reduction in the taxation of company profits.
2. The operation of a budget deficit, i.e. the government spends more than it raises in taxation. (There could clearly be a connection here with the previous point.)
3. Making it easier for banks and other financial institutions to create money to lend – this might be achieved by various forms of monetary policy.

Changes in the disposition of savings

Private sector producers are only one of several groups of institutions seeking investment funds. As shown in Chapter 14, the success of these producers in obtaining funds is influenced by the attractiveness of the prospective returns they offer to savers – in terms of yield, security and liquidity – by comparison with what is offered by other institutions such as building societies, local authorities and the central government.

As we noted above, a budget deficit would normally tend to increase the supply of money. However, the investment funds available to private producers may not increase if the government, in order to borrow sufficient money to cover its deficit, offers a rate of return that private producers find difficult to match (see Ch. 21).

Having discussed the factors that influence the volume of savings likely to be made available to finance investment by private sector producers, we examine the ways in which this finance might be transferred from savers to investors.

The sources of finance

There are two main routes by which the savings of households are made available to producers. First, savers can directly supply finance to producers in the form of either long-term loans (by buying debentures) or permanent, equity, capital (by buying shares). Second, households can deposit their savings with banks and other financial institutions who in turn make the money available to producers, again in the form of either loans (short, medium and long term) or permanent capital.

In addition the government may provide financial assistance of various kinds. The government itself obtains the money either by taxation – which could be seen as a form of forced saving – or by borrowing from households, and thus acting as a financial intermediary.

Finally, firms themselves save, i.e. retain and plough back earnings which could otherwise have been distributed to shareholders and thus been available for consumption. This is known as internal finance. As we show later, internally generated funds are considerably more important than the total of funds from all external sources.

Sources of external finance

We now examine the sources of external finance in greater detail. First we look at the various sources available to different legal forms of business.

Unincorporated businesses: sole traders and partnerships

There are about 1.25 million unincorporated businesses in the UK, making this the most important form numerically. However, they are mainly very small, and together account for only about one-tenth of the capital expenditure undertaken by all businesses.

External finance for one-man businesses (sole traders), which are particularly common in retailing, farming and the building trades, is largely short term, comprising bank loans, trade credit, hire-purchase finance, etc. Longer-term credit may sometimes be obtained by means of a mortgage on land or buildings. (Perma-

nent capital is restricted to the savings of the owner and the earnings retained in the business, i.e. to internal finance.)

Sources of finance for partnerships, which are very common in the professions – law, accountancy, medicine, etc. – are similar to those for the one-man business. But a partnership usually has more permanent capital since it can have up to twenty partners – more for solicitors and accountants.

Joint-stock companies

There are about 750,000 companies registered in the UK. They are of two types: private companies, which are the most important numerically (over 98 per cent of the total), and public limited companies (often abbreviated to plcs or PLCs, and not to be confused with public corporations), which are more important in terms of aggregate size. In addition to having access to all the sources of finance available to unincorporated businesses, joint-stock companies are able to raise permanent capital by the issue of shares.

The two main types of share are preference and ordinary shares. Preference shares usually attract a fixed rate of dividend which is paid in full before holders of ordinary shares receive anything. (Preference shareholders are, however, paid after the holders of debentures – issued in return for long-term loans – and usually receive a slightly higher payment in compensation.) Ordinary shares generally do not carry a fixed rate of dividend, and holders receive a share of profits only after all other claims have been met. Similarly, ordinary shareholders have the last claim upon the assets of the firm following bankruptcy or liquidation. Consequently, ordinary shares constitute a risky form of investment. On the other hand, ordinary shareholders tend to receive the greatest rewards when the business flourishes and profits are high.

Public limited companies must have a minimum nominal share capital of £50,000, of which at least a quarter must be paid up. The securities issued by PLCs, unlike those issued by private companies, can be freely traded. This provides an additional incentive to make funds available to PLCs.

The Stock Exchange

Most transactions in the securities issued by PLCs take place on the Stock Exchange. The UK Stock Exchange also provides a market for UK government (gilt-edged) securities, for other public sector securities and for securities issued by a number of foreign companies and governments.

Stock Exchange member firms, whether broker-dealers or market-makers, are able to act in a dual capacity. They can deal direct with investors, buying and selling securities from their own book, or they can act as agent on behalf of a client. (Many member firms are part of financial services conglomerates, a number of which include a UK or foreign bank.)

The new issue market

As noted above, transactions on the Stock Exchange are confined to securities that have already been issued. New issues, i.e. the raising of additional finance by companies, may take several forms.

Public issue by prospectus

Here the company offers, directly to the general public, a fixed number of shares or debentures at a stated price. A prospectus must be issued, setting out the nature of the company's business, and giving details of its past turnover, profits, etc.

Offer for sale

This is similar to the public issue, but the company sells the securities to an issuing house (usually a merchant bank), which in turn offers them to the general public.

Placing

The securities are again acquired by an issuing house, which now places them with its clients and with jobbers. In order to reduce the possibility that the institutions with whom the securities are placed may make substantial profits when the securities are subsequently traded on the Stock Exchange, the authorities stipulate that a minimum quantity be initially placed with jobbers.

Offer for sale by tender

This form tends to be used when investors' attitudes are very volatile, making it difficult to assess the appropriate issue price. A minimum price at which a tender will be accepted is stated. If investors believe that the securities are worth more than this minimum they will put in a higher offer in order to try to secure an allocation.

Rights issue

Rights issues are confined to existing shareholders who are offered additional shares in proportion to their holdings. The new shares are issued at a price below the current market price, and this can be seen as a reward to shareholders. A compensating benefit to the company is that the administration costs are lower than for alternative methods. Even though the shares are initially available only to existing shareholders it is possible to raise substantial sums in this way. In 1985 existing shareholders in both Hanson Trust and Barclays Bank subscribed over £500m., and in 1988 Barclays raised over £900m.

Rights issues should not be confused with bonus or scrip issues. These also involve the issue of additional shares to existing shareholders, but since they are issued free, no new finance is raised.

Underwriting

Since companies issuing securities normally plan in advance the uses to which they will put the funds raised, it is important that they should obtain these funds. Although they set a price for the securities at which they expect the public to buy, it is difficult to predict reactions, since conditions in the market may change during the period between setting the price and the day of issue.

To insure against the consequences of the issue not being fully subscribed, it is arranged that one or more underwriters – substantial financial institutions such as insurance companies – will take up any securities not bought by the general public. Where an issue is undersubscribed it is probable that trading in the securities will open at a price below the market price. In order to compensate for this risk the underwriters charge a small commission related to the total value of the issue.

The Unlisted Securities Market

In the mid 1970s the flow of new companies to the Stock Exchange all but ceased, implying that a vital part of the market system for channelling savings into new businesses was no longer working.

In addition to the worsening economic situation two other factors were felt to be responsible for the reduction in the number of companies seeking a Stock Exchange listing: the costs involved and the requirement that a minimum of 25 per cent of the shares be made available to the general public. To overcome these obstacles the Stock Exchange introduced the Unlisted Securities Market (USM) in 1980.

The USM requires a minimum of only 10 per cent of shares to be made available to the general public, and a company can come to the market with only three instead of five years' trading (or even less for well-researched high-technology companies). By August 1987 around 500 firms had entered the USM (considerably more than the number of entrants to the main market over the same period). Some of these firms had graduated to the main market, others had been absorbed through mergers or acquisitions and a few had failed. This left the shares of 366 companies being traded, with an estimated market value of more than £8bn. This gives an average market capitalization of almost £22m., but this figure conceals a wide range of company sizes.

The costs of USM entry depend upon a number of factors, including the method of entry (e.g. offer for sale, placing) and the amount raised. On average companies pay about 2.5 per cent of their market capitalization in flotation expenses, which is about a quarter to a third less than the costs that firms of comparable size might incur in joining the main market.

The Third Market

Firms that are too small or speculative to enter the USM may apply to have their shares traded on the Third Market, established in 1987. In order to enter the Third Market a company must produce accredited accounts for at least one year (or as a 'greenfields' company prove that it required capital to finance a viable project), be incorporated in the UK with at least three directors and be sponsored by a Stock Exchange member firm.

The shareholders

A feature of modern capitalism is that an increasing proportion of company securities is held by institutional investors: pension funds, life assurance and insurance companies, investment trusts, unit trusts, etc. Between 1963 and 1981 the proportion of shares held by UK financial institutions increased from 21 to 58 per cent. By contrast the proportion held by personal investors decreased from 54 to 28 per cent. (The remaining shares are held by industrial and commercial companies, charities, etc.)

There is evidence that more recently this decline in personal shareholdings has been reversed. A survey sponsored by the Treasury and the Stock Exchange found that share ownership had roughly trebled from 7 per cent of the adult population in 1979 to nearly 20 per cent at the beginning of 1987.

Most of this change was due to two government initiatives. The first was the privatization programme (discussed in Ch. 11). Six and a half million, more than three-quarters of shareholders, were found to have shares in privatized companies (including the Trustee Savings Bank). The second initiative was the granting of favourable tax treatment for employee share schemes. One and a half million people hold shares in the company for which they work.

At the beginning of 1987 the proportion of the population holding shares in the UK was approaching the level in the USA and was considerably greater than in many other countries, including Japan and France. However, the spread of share ownership occurred during a prolonged 'bull market' and there was some doubt as to how the new shareholders would react to a steep fall in share prices, such as occurred in October 1987. Of the 6.5 million shareholders in recently privatized companies, 3.5 million did not hold shares in any other companies. The reaction to the fall in prices was encouraging, at least in the short term. A further survey undertaken by the Stock Exchange found a total of nine million shareholders at the beginning of 1988.

As noted above, institutional investment has the advantage that it enables the individual saver or investor to spread his risks. However, there may also be disadvantages. It has been suggested that institutional investors prefer not to become involved in the formulation of company policy. They may even be reluctant to intervene in order to influence policy in companies whose financial or economic performance is poor, preferring either to sell their holdings for reinvestment elsewhere or, if the holdings are so large that they could sell only at an unattractive price, simply to wait in the hope that the companies' performance will eventually improve. When large shareholders, which increasingly means institutions, behave in this way, it is said that a divorce has occurred between ownership and control. One result of this divorce may be that boards of directors become less concerned to increase profits than they would be if they were themselves major shareholders.

A second aspect of institutional shareholding to which increasing attention has recently been given is the increase in the volatility of share prices that may result when buying or selling orders are large. A vicious circle may emerge here; the volatility may deter potential small inves-

tors, which will result in a further increase in the relative importance of institutional investors, and thus lead to further increases in volatility.

Finally, institutions may be less ready to take risks, which can make it difficult for smaller, more adventurous firms to raise the capital required to develop their businesses. Also, institutions have often been unwilling to deal in small quantities of shares.

The relative importance of the various sources of finance

Table 16.2 shows the overwhelming importance of internally generated funds (undistributed income). In all but two of the years covered by Table 16.2, internal funds provided more than half the companies' capital requirements. Moreover there is no evidence of a decline in their importance. Bank borrowing is by far the most important source of external finance, accounting for over half of external funds, and almost a fifth of funds from all sources. United Kingdom capital issues are much less important overall. However, new capital may be very important to fast-growing companies.

Table 16.2
Sources of funds of industrial and commercial companies,1963–86

	£bn.	%
Internal funds	258	66
Bank borrowing	72	18
Other loans and mortgages	10	3
UK capital issues*	28	7
Overseas†	20	5
Net credit	3	1
Total	391	100

Source: Financial Statistics
* Issues of ordinary shares, preference shares and debentures.
† Overseas capital issues, overseas direct investment in securities, and intra-company investment by overseas companies.

The needs of small and medium-sized firms

If the outcome of every proposed investment project were certain, the ability of a firm to raise sufficient funds to finance any project would depend upon the prospective yield from that project and not upon the size of the firm. In practice the yields of all investment projects are uncertain, a factor which militates against the small firm with respect to a given project.

To see why this is so, consider the following simple example. Assume that a firm has accumulated reserves of £1m. and that it is considering investing this in a project whose profitability, i.e. the excess of total revenue over total cost, is estimated as shown in Table 16.3. The most likely outcome (probability 0.5) is a profit of £200,000. There is a reasonable chance (probability 0.25) that a profit of £500,000 may result, but an equal probability that a loss of £100,000 may be incurred. The weighted probable outcome is:

$$(£500,000 \times 0.25) + (£200,000 \times 0.5) + (-£100,000 \times 0.25)$$
$$= £125,000 \quad + £100,000 - £25,000$$
$$= £200,000$$

If the firm were certain that it could obtain a profit of £200,000 it would undertake the project. However, the presence of uncertainty requires it to consider the implications of outcomes other than the most probable and in particular the possibility of making a loss. Since the whole of the firm's reserves would be required for

Table 16.3
Estimated profitability of a hypothetical investment project

Profit (£)	Probability
500,000	0.25
200,000	0.5
−100,000	0.25

this project, a loss might lead to bankruptcy. This danger would not be thought to be compensated by the chance of obtaining a profit of £500,000.

A firm with larger reserves, on the other hand, would be able to take the risk. If it considered that the weighted probable profit of £200,000 represented an adequate return it would go ahead with the investment. For this firm the possibility of a loss, which would *not* now involve bankruptcy, would be counterbalanced by the possibility of a larger profit.

When firms rely on external finance the situation becomes more complex, but the same principle applies. Investors, and especially those buying ordinary shares, are likely to steer clear of companies which may go bankrupt if things go badly, even if those same companies might do very well under more favourable conditions. Investors are likely to believe that such situations are more characteristic of small than large companies.

In order to compensate for the additional risk, investors may require higher returns (interest or dividends), from small companies, i.e. the cost of capital will be higher for small than for large companies. (Furthermore, administrative costs tend to be higher for small than for large *issues*, although as noted above, administrative costs are usually less on the USM and the Third Market.) Some small companies may be unable to offer the returns required to elicit sufficient finance from the usual sources (including such institutions as merchant banks), especially if they wish to expand rapidly. In order to overcome these problems a large number of institutions catering for the needs of small and medium-sized firms have been established.

Specialist sources of finance

Investors in Industry (3i) is the name adopted in 1983 by Finance for Industry, a holding company formed in 1973. 3i is owned by nine London and Scottish banks (85 per cent) and the Bank of England (15 per cent). Of the various subsidiaries of 3i the most important for small firms is the Industrial and Commercial Finance Corporation (ICFC) which will commit up to £2m. in any one financing project and whose portfolio comprises around £500m. of investments in about 4,000 companies.

The *Business Expansion Scheme* (BES) grew out of the Business Start Up Scheme, which was introduced in 1981. The BES permits investors to offset the cost of buying shares against their marginal rate of tax. They can also sell their shares free of capital gains tax. To qualify for relief investors must invest at least £500 and may not invest more than £40,000 in any tax year. They must also retain the shares for at least five years. Investment can be made directly in the company concerned or via a fund. Finance has been provided for established businesses, start-up businesses and management buy-outs. The average investment made by BES funds has been estimated at £150,000, and about a third of BES companies are thought to raise less than £50,000.

The tax incentives offered to investors are intended to compensate for the high risks attached to this form of investment; it was estimated that one-fifth of the BES companies financed in 1983–84 went bankrupt within the next two years.

The *Loan Guarantee Scheme* (LGS) was also introduced in 1981, initially for three years and subsequently renewed. By January 1986 the LGS had helped 13,000 businesses with government guarantees totalling £554 million.

The rationale of the LGS is that some worthwhile projects might fail to find adequate finance because of the absence of a 'track record'. Under the scheme the government provides to the lender a guarantee of up to 70 per cent of the loan. A premium of 2.5 per cent over normal business lending rates is charged on loans, intended to compensate for possible losses. The need for a premium can be seen from the fact that 40 per cent of the companies that used the LGS in the year to May 1982 foundered within the next

three years. By April 1987 business failures had cost the government more than £100m.

The main objective of *Local Enterprise Boards* is to preserve and create jobs, and it is therefore not surprising that they are most active in the more depressed parts of the country. They are funded by local authorities, but use this funding as a lever to attract private capital to finance projects. Most of this finance is used to support smaller businesses: funding between £10,000 and £100,000 is typical.

The term *venture capital* has been used to describe a way in which investors support entrepreneurial talent with finance and business skills to exploit market opportunities, and thus to obtain long-term capital gains. It is in essence concerned with venture capital companies that have managers with the necessary industrial and commercial – as well as financial – expertise to give active, involved help to companies across a range of problems, over a long period.[2]

Although this description emphasizes the provision of non-financial as well as financial support, some of the institutions discussed earlier in this section would consider themselves part of the venture capital market. For example 3i Ventures (formerly known as Technical Development Capital) is the venture capital arm of Investors in Industry.

It is estimated that the number of specialist venture capital organizations operating in the UK increased from less than 20 in 1979 to more than 100 today. Venture capital funds account for a higher percentage of GDP in the UK than in any other country in the European Community and in the USA.

The spread of sectors obtaining venture capital has gradually widened and now includes companies involved in computers and automation, in the electronics industry, medical goods, etc.

The institutions providing venture capital range from the banks (an estimated 32 per cent share in 1985), through insurance companies (11 per cent) and pension funds (9 per cent) to universities (0.1 per cent).[3]

Other sources of finance

There are numerous other schemes and institutions, in both the public and private sectors, part of whose remit is to provide finance for smaller firms. These include development agencies, enterprise agencies, the Enterprise Allowance Scheme and the Council for Small Industries in Rural Areas.

The volume of investment

As we noted above, the volume of investment undertaken in a given period depends upon both the demand for investment funds, which reflects the expected return from investment projects, and the supply of such funds. (Remember that we have assumed there to be adequate capacity in the capital goods industries.) The interaction of these two sets of forces is illustrated in Fig. 16.3.

As before, the investment demand schedule, D, indicates the demand for investment funds. The supply of funds, S, is positively related to the rate of interest. At the equilibrium point the return, R, from the last unit of investment undertaken equals the cost of the funds required for that investment. The total amount of investment undertaken is Q. The yield from any further investment would be less than the cost of the funds required for that investment.

Earlier in the chapter we noted that one of the motives for investment was to prevent the fall in profitability that would occur if obsolete and worn-out plant and equipment were not replaced. If this was the only motive for investment, Q would represent replacement investment. But in practice the dynamic nature of economic systems gives rise to other motives for investment, as noted above. This means that in practice Q would comprise partly replacement and partly net investment.

The demand and supply schedules in Fig. 16.3, which may apply only for a single period, incorporate the many factors discussed in this chapter. We can draw together the various points discussed by considering the effect of a change in

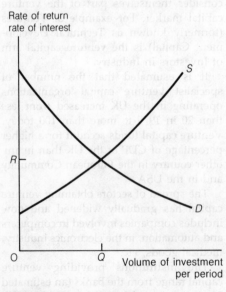

Fig. 16.3
The market for investment funds

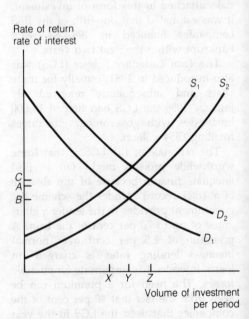

Fig. 16.4
Change in the market for investment funds

these factors. We do this with reference to Fig. 16.4. This figure shows an increase in demand and supply; in practice, of course, both demand and supply may either increase or decrease from one period to another.

An increase in demand

An increase in demand, represented by a shift of the demand curve from D_1 to D_2, occurs because of an increase in the prospective returns or yields of investment projects. This could be due to: an increase in national income and hence in demand; the impact of technological change in the form of new products or processes; an increase in the cost of other inputs, and especially labour, for which capital is substituted; an improvement in business confidence – this might relate to some of the other factors, but it is identified separately to emphasize the fact that the demand curve reflects *prospective* yields, and also because it is known that in practice the level of business confidence affects investment decisions. Finally, we should note that if the capital stock increases over time, this will eventually lead to an increase in the level of replacement investment (assuming a constant rate of depreciation per unit of capital stock).

An increase in supply

An increase in the supply of investment funds, represented by a shift of the supply curve from S_1 to S_2, may occur because of an increase in the total money supply within the economy. (The factors affecting the money supply are discussed in Ch. 21.) A higher level of national income is also likely to mean an increase in the level of savings and hence in the supply of funds for investment (as well as an increase in demand, as noted above).

We saw in Chapter 14 that considerable changes can occur in the relative proportions of income allocated to consumption and saving. It follows that in principle the level of saving could increase even if national income did not change. This would increase the supply of investment funds. But it would also be likely to cause a fall in the demand for these funds because of the fall in consumption.

We saw earlier that the saving of companies, i.e. undistributed income, forms a major source of funds for investment. It follows that increased company profitability in one period may lead to an increased supply of investment funds in a subsequent period. (An increase in profits in one period may also lead to an increase in business confidence and hence to a higher demand for investment funds.)

The interaction between monetary and real variables

One further point may be made with respect to Fig. 16.4. If, given demand D_1, supply increases from S_1 to S_2 this leads to a fall in the rate of interest (a monetary variable) from A to B. This causes the volume of investment (a real variable) to increase from X to Y. If this higher level of investment caused an increase in national income (another real variable) this might cause the demand for investment to shift from D_1 to D_2. This would cause the interest rate to rise from B to C. There can, therefore, be a complex pattern of interaction between monetary and real variables.

Expenditure on other forms of investment can also be explained in terms of the interaction of the demand and supply of investment funds, although each form of investment is particularly sensitive to certain factors which may be less important for other forms. We now briefly examine these remaining forms, beginning with the second element of fixed capital formation, investment in dwellings, almost all of which is undertaken by households.

Expenditure by households on new dwellings

Expenditure on dwellings accounts for over a fifth of total investment. The most important determinant of the long-term demand for new dwellings is the rate of change in population and, more specifically, in the formation of new households. Other factors which may be important in the long term are changes in multiple occupancy (the sharing of a dwelling by two or more households) and in the ownership of second homes, for example for holidays. Finally, demand is influenced by the relationship between people's ideas of what constitutes an adequate standard of housing and the quality of the existing housing stock. Expectations normally rise as average incomes rise, and this causes an increased reluctance to live in old houses or houses without such amenities as indoor sanitation.

The most important influence on demand in any particular year is the availability of mortgage funds. A high proportion of house-purchase transactions are partly financed by money borrowed from institutions, and in particular from the building societies. There is a close relationship between the real level of building society mortgage advances and the number of dwellings started in a given year.

The number of dwellings started (and completed) in any year can also be affected by the capacity of the construction industry. When the demand for new houses is very high, potential buyers may have to wait longer before obtaining possession. Supply constraints have occurred from time to time in the UK. However, in general the number of dwellings built has been determined primarily by demand conditions.

Expenditure by the public corporations

Table 16.1 shows that in 1986 public corporations accounted for 9 per cent of total gross fixed capital formation. The investment expenditure of the public corporations is similar to that of the private sector in that much of the expenditure (a) is on plant, equipment and ve-

hicles, and (b) can be ranked in terms of the prospective rate of return. The major difference from the private sector is that the public corporations do not usually have to compete for funds on the open market. If they are unable to finance their operations out of retained earnings, the shortfall is made good by the government. (Government's influence on the public corporations' investment was outlined in Ch. 11.)

General government expenditure

Table 16.1 shows that investment spending by government fell by a third between 1976 and 1986 and that by 1986 it accounted for only 11 per cent of the total. The bulk of government investment is undertaken by the local authorities, and the decline reflects reduced spending in several areas, especially housing and schools.

The local authorities' demand for investment funds tends to be determined by the concept of social need rather than prospective financial return. Moreover the bulk of the funds are raised not on the open market but either from the rate-payers, or as grants and loans from the central government (see Ch. 20). However, this does not mean that economic or financial factors are ignored. The local authorities have come under increasing pressure from the central government to limit their spending. The use of scarce funds implies that the authorities should try to ensure that a given level of service, a given output, is provided at minimum cost. Hence careful consideration should be given to the savings in costs that might result from capital expenditure.

Value of the physical increase in stocks and work in progress

This item is more important in the private than the public sector and changes in stocks are often due to the same factors as affect expenditure on fixed capital by private producers. On the demand side many of the forces which stimulate expenditure on fixed capital – an increase in GDP, the introduction of new products, etc. – lead to an increase in the value of stocks. Similarly, the acceleration principle can again be applied to investment in stocks. The major difference between the two elements is that whereas fixed capital formation is always planned, a change in stocks may sometimes be unplanned, as when production takes place in anticipation of a demand that does not arise. Also while in practice net fixed investment has always been positive, stock building has occasionally been negative.

Levels of stocks and work in progress are sensitive to changes in the cost and availability of funds; indeed some studies have found that one of the earliest reactions to an increase in interest rates is a reduction in stock levels.

Appendix: the measurement of the rate of return and of the cost of investment funds

The rate of return or marginal efficiency of capital

When calculating the yield of an investment project, firms may use one of several methods. The method that has probably the most to commend it in terms of its underlying economic logic is the internal or discounted cash flow (DCF) rate of return method. This method takes account of the fact that a given sum of money received at different points in time has different values. It is better to receive money this year than next year, because the money can be put to work for a year in one way or another. In order to take this into account, a discount factor is applied to money which is expected to be received in future years. The use of a discount factor explains why this method is usually known as the discounted cash flow method.

In order to calculate the expected rate of return of a project the firm must be able to estimate first the initial cash outflow required (CO) – this will usually consist of expenditure on plant, equipment, etc. – and second the net cash inflows (NCI) arising in future years as a result of the initial expenditure – these inflows will usually comprise revenue from additional sales, minus other costs incurred, e.g. for labour, materials and power. (However, note that the NCI can also be increased by an investment which simply leads to a reduction in the costs of production.) Having obtained these estimates the firm can calculate the rate of return by applying the following formula:

$$CO = \sum \frac{NCI}{(1 + r)^n}$$

In the above formula r is the internal rate of return, sometimes known as the marginal efficiency of capital; n indicates the number of years over which the return is calculated. If the investment relates to the purchase of an additional machine the firm might expect this to yield revenue, for, say, ten years. In this instance, 'exploding' the formula gives us:

$$CO = \frac{NCI_1}{(1 + r)^1} + \frac{NCI_2}{(1 + r)^2} + \frac{NCI_3}{(1 + r)^3}$$
$$+ \ldots + \frac{NCI_{10}}{(1 + r)^{10}}$$

where NCI_1 refers to the cash inflow in year 1, NCI_2 to year 2, and so forth.

A more simple example, but one which applies exactly the same principle, would be the purchase by a farmer of young beef cattle for fattening and subsequent resale in a year's time. This gives us the simplest possible form of the formula:

$$CO = \frac{NCI_1}{(1 + r)}$$

If the cattle cost the farmer £100,000 and he estimates that, after meeting all his other costs, he will receive £120,000 when he sells them in a year's time, the rate of return is 0.2 or 20 per cent. This can easily be seen by substituting the relevant values in the formula:

$$£100,000 = \frac{£120,000}{1.2}$$

This means that if the farmer obtained finance at a cost of 20 per cent per annum and invested it in the purchase of cattle he would be just as well off as if he had not done so. (Technically, the net present value of the project equals zero.) If he could obtain finance for less than 20 per cent the investment would leave him better off; if he had to pay more than 20 per cent he would be worse off and should not undertake the investment.

We consider in a moment how the cost of finance might be calculated, but first, in order to consolidate understanding of the discounting procedure, let us assume that our farmer has to keep his cattle for two years before reselling them at a price which leaves him with £120,000 after meeting all his other costs. The rate of return would now be approximately 0.095 or 9.5 per cent. (We make the simplifying assumption that all the farmer's other costs are incurred in year 2.)

$$CO = \frac{NCI_2}{(1 + r)^2} \qquad £100,000 = \frac{£120,000}{(1.095)^2}$$

It would now pay the farmer to invest only if he could obtain finance at a cost of 9.5 per cent a year or less. This example shows why it is so important to take the time pattern of cash flows into account.

The cost of investment funds

If one considers firms' investment programmes over a number of years one normally finds that the expenditure is funded by three broad types of finance – money borrowed, for example by the issue of debentures, permanent (equity) capital obtained by the issue of shares, and retained earnings. The cost of these three types of finance will vary over time and also, as noted earlier in the chapter, from one firm to another. However the general rule is that, after taking tax considerations into account, borrowed money is cheapest and equity capital the most expensive, with retained earnings coming in between. (Attaching a cost to the use of retained earnings can be justified in terms of the concept of opportunity cost – if these earnings were not used to finance investment within the firm they would be available for use in some other way, e.g. to be loaned at interest.)

One might expect firms to finance as much of their investment as possible by the cheapest type of finance, borrowed money. In practice, however, considerations of risk, both to borrower and lender, will limit the use made of this source of funds.

In order to calculate its cost of capital the firm must estimate the cost of each type of finance and the amounts of each type that it would expect to use, taking one year with another. If it estimated the costs to be: borrowing 8 per cent, permanent (equity) capital 12 per cent and retained earnings 10 per cent, and it planned to finance investment thus: 25 per cent borrowed money, 25 per cent new permanent capital, 50 per cent retained earnings, then its overall cost of capital would be:

$$(0.25 \times 8\%) + (0.25 \times 12\%)$$
$$+ (0.5 \times 10\%) = 10\%$$

The rate of return and the cost of finance compared

Calculating the rate of return and the cost of finance in the ways described in this appendix makes it easy to compare the two. As we have said, the guideline is that investment should be undertaken only where the rate of return is at least equal to the cost of finance, i.e. where the net present value of the project is zero or (preferably) positive. In practice it has been found that firms usually prefer to work with a 'safety net', i.e. they invest only if they expect the rate of return to exceed the cost of capital, often by several percentage points. This allows for the possibility that their estimates of costs and revenue may turn out to have been too optimistic.

Furthermore, it is known that other methods of 'investment appraisal' are used. For example projects may be ranked in terms of the length of time likely to elapse before the sum of the NCIs equals the initial CO. The shorter the 'payback' period, the higher the project is ranked. The payback method has most to recommend it when future economic conditions are very uncertain and the firm wishes to limit its risks. (When the DCF method is used, a very high discount factor becomes appropriate in such circumstances.)

Summary

1. An investment demand schedule indicates the volume of investment projects with given prospective yields. Current prospective yields are influenced by the level of GDP, changes in GDP, the cost and availability of other inputs, technological change and business expectations.
2. The accelerator is the link between the change in consumption, output, sales or, more generally, GDP, and the level of net investment. The value of the accelerator may not be the same for decreases as for increases in GDP.
3. The prospective yield influences the desired expenditure on investment and thus the demand for investment funds. The amount of investment undertaken also depends upon the supply of investment funds. This in turn is influenced by the level of GDP, by government economic policy and by the disposition of savings.
4. In order to maximize profits the return from the last unit of investment undertaken should equal the cost of the funds required for that investment. A change in the equilibrium level of investment will result from a change in either the demand for or the supply of investment funds.
5. Savers may directly supply finance to producers by buying debentures (long-term loans) or shares (permanent capital). Alternatively, households may deposit their savings with financial institutions which make the money available to producers. Other sources of external finance include short-term loans, trade credit and government financial assistance.
6. Firms retain and plough back earnings which could have been distributed as dividends. This internal finance exceeds the total of funds from all external sources.
7. Most trading in the securities issued by PLCs takes place on the Stock Exchange. The alleged failure of the main market to meet the needs of smaller companies led to the establishment of the USM and the Third Market. Numerous other institutions – some with government backing – have been established to meet the financial needs of small companies.
8. The most important long-term determinant of the demand for dwellings is the rate of change in the formation of new households. In the short term, demand is very responsive to changes in the availability and cost of mortgage finance.

Key terms

Gross domestic fixed capital formation
Stocks and work in progress
Investment demand schedule
Stock Exchange
Shareholders
Equilibrium rate of return

Supply schedule of investment funds	Equilibrium level of investment
Acceleration principle	DCF rate of return
Incremental capital–output ratio	Marginal efficiency of capital
Sources of finance	Cost of capital

Notes

1. See Robins P, The accelerator principle – development and evidence, *Economics*, Spring 1984.
2. *Economic Progress Report*, Sept.–Oct. 1985.
3. *Financial Times*, 3 Dec. 1985 (drawing on figures produced by the European Venture Capital Association).

Essay questions

1. What are the major determinants of investment spending by (a) private sector producers, (b) public sector producers, (c) central and local government?
2. Assess the relative contribution to economic growth of the investment expenditure of (a) private sector producers, (b) public sector producers, (c) central and local government.
3. Explain the statement that the amount of investment undertaken is determined by the interaction of the demand for and the supply of investment funds.
4. Discuss the factors which might cause a change in the demand for investment funds.
5. Explain why the value of the accelerator is unlikely to be the same for an increase as for a decrease in GDP.
6. 'The operation of the accelerator may amplify but not initiate fluctuations in economic activity.' Discuss.
7. What factors would tend to reduce the supply of investment funds?
8. What do you understand by the term 'divorce between ownership and control'? Discuss the factors encouraging this 'divorce' and assess their implications.
9. 'An increase in the demand for investment funds causes a rise in the rate of interest.' 'At higher rate of interest less investment is undertaken.' How may these apparently conflicting statements be reconciled?
10. Show how the rate of return may be calculated and explain the relationship between the rate of return and the investment demand schedule.

Exercises

16.1 The information below relates to four pairs of hypothetical companies. Say, in each case, for which company you would expect the cost of finance to be higher, and briefly justify your answers.
   (i)   Company A has assets of £3m. and manufactures a wide range of foodstuffs.
         Company B has assets of £200,000 and manufactures components for the vehicles industry.

(ii) The profits of the two companies, which have the same volume of assets, over the past five years have been as follows:

	Company A (£000)	Company B (£000)
Year 1	500	500
2	550	700
3	450	300
4	500	700
5	500	300

(iii) The profits of the two companies over the past five years have been as follows:

	Company A (£000)	Company B (£000)
Year 1	200	30
2	220	50
3	160	90
4	220	130
5	200	180

(iv) Company A plans capital expenditure of £500,000 and will obtain the necessary finance by the issue of debentures. Company B plans capital expenditure of £3m. and will obtain the necessary finance by an equity rights issue.

16.2 Discuss (a) the causes, and (b) the consequences of the changes in investment spending shown in Fig. 16.5 on the following page.

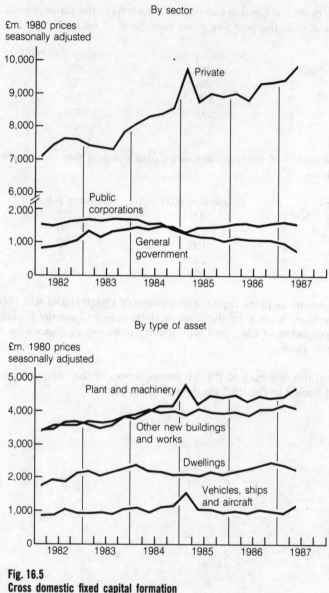

Fig. 16.5
Cross domestic fixed capital formation
Source: Economic Trends

16.3 With reference to Fig. 16.6 on the following page discuss the relationships between manufacturing investment and output.

16.4 The table below on the following page shows the changes that have occurred in manufacturing output and investment.
   (i) Discuss the relationship between output and investment.
   (ii) What factors, other than changes in output, might have influenced the level of investment?

Output and investment in manufacturing (1980 = 100)

	Output	Fixed capital formation
1981	94.0	75.5
1982	94.2	72.5
1983	96.9	73.8
1984	100.8	88.7
1985	103.7	99.2
1986	104.8	97.7

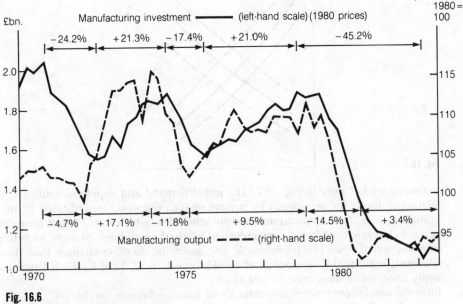

Fig. 16.6
Manufacturing output and investment
Source: Lloyds Bank Economic Bulletin, Jan. 1984

Objective test questions: set 6

1. An investment demand schedule shows, for a given period,
   A   the amount of investment undertaken;
   B   the amount of investment expected to yield given rates of return;
   C   the number of shares demanded by investors;
   D   the number of shares and other securities demanded by investors;
   E   the relationship between the demand for investment funds and the cost of capital.

2. Which of the following would be least likely to cause an investment demand schedule to shift to the right?
   A   An increase in GDP.
   B   The development of a large number of new products.
   C   A rise in the price of labour.
   D   A fall in the productivity of labour.
   E   A rise in the cost of investment funds.

3. A public company can raise additional finance by all of the following methods except:
   A a public issue by prospectus;
   B an offer for sale;
   C a Stock Exchange placing;
   D a bonus issue;
   E a rights issue.

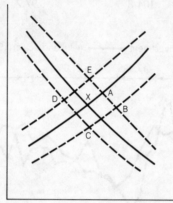

Fig. 16.7

Questions 4–7 refer to Fig. 16.7. The initial demand and supply schedules relating to funds for investment by private sector producers, are indicated by the unbroken lines. New demand and supply schedules, which might result from the various changes listed below, are indicated by the broken lines. Starting each time from the initial point of equilibrium X, and assuming no other changes than those specified, indicate the new points of equilibrium A, B, C, D or E. (Each letter may apply once, more than once, or not at all.)

4. Businessmen become more optimistic about future economic conditions.
5. Technological progress results in new products being introduced on to the market; the rates offered to depositors by building societies increase.
6. Gross domestic product falls substantially.
7. New institutions are established to supply funds for investment by medium-sized companies; technological progress leads to the introduction of more labour-saving equipment.

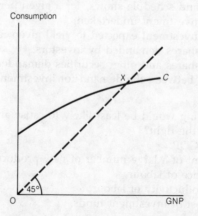

Fig. 16.8

8.   Figure 16.8 indicates that:
     1   APC falls as GNP rises;
     2   MPC falls as GNP rises;
     3   APC = 1 at point X.

9.   The permanent income hypothesis implies that:
     1   when income rises the long-run MPC exceeds the short-run MPC;
     2   when income falls the short-run MPC exceeds the long-run MPC;
     3   MPC can never equal APC.

10.

GNP (£m.)	Consumption (£m.)
1,000	850
2,000	1,350
3,000	1,850
4,000	2,350

From the above table we can deduce that:
     1   within the income range £2,000m. to £3,000m., MPC = 0.5;
     2   when GNP is £2,000m., APC = 0.5;
     3   as income rises APC and MPC decline.

11.   General government final consumption includes:
     1   the payment of teachers' salaries;
     2   expenditure on building a new school;
     3   transfer payments.

12.   The effect of the accelerator will tend to be dampened if:
     1   producers of consumer goods have excess capacity;
     2   producers of capital goods are working at full capacity;
     3   some producers feel that the increase in demand is temporary.

13.   Which of the following sources of finance is/are available to private companies?
     1   Bank loans.
     2   Shares, which can be traded on the Stock Exchange.
     3   Debentures, which can be traded on the Stock Exchange.

14.   Assume a consumption function of the form $C = a + b\,(Y)$, where Y represents GNP. If a is positive and $b = 0.5$ we can conclude that:
     1   APC = MPC;
     2   the change in total consumption will be less than the change in GNP;
     3   MPS = 0.5.

15.   Fixed capital formation is undertaken by:
     1   producers;
     2   government;
     3   households.

16.   A fall in the MPC implies that the APC also falls.
      APC and MPC are always equal.

17.   Redistribution of income and wealth from the poorer to the richer members of a community is likely to cause a fall in the overall propensity to consume.
      The propensity to consume of richer people tends to be less than that of poorer people.

18.   The rate of change in investment will be greater than the rate of change in GDP whenever the accelerator coefficient exceeds zero.
      The accelerator coefficient is the incremental capital–output ratio.

19   The level of fixed capital formation and of stocks of work in progress always rises
      when GDP rises.
          Both fixed capital formation and stocks of work in progress are forms of
      investment.
20.   A change in the productivity of labour may affect the demand for both labour and
      capital.
          An increase in the demand for one factor of production implies a fall in the
      demand for other factors.

True/false

1.   If we assume that all income is either consumed or saved it follows that APC +
      APS = 1.
2.   The amount of investment required to compensate for capital consumption is
      known as net investment.
3.   The acceleration principle states that the higher the level of GDP the higher is the
      level of investment.
4.   Stock jobbers act as agents for investors in the buying and selling of securities.
5.   If the rate of return of an investment project is greater than the cost of capital the
      net present value of the project is positive.
6.   The MPC denotes the proportion consumed of a small increase in income.
7.   The APS denotes the change in saving that occurs as a result of a small change in
      income.
8.   The value of the MPC is indicated by the gradient of the consumption function.
9.   In the national accounts only some transfer payments are included in the
      government's expenditure on goods and services.
10.   Expenditure on new houses forms part of investment.

CHAPTER SEVENTEEN
International Trade and the Balance of Payments

Introduction

In Chapter 13 we identified four major flows of expenditure which give rise to the utilization of domestic resources. Chapters 14–16 have each been concerned with one of these flows, and in this chapter we discuss the fourth and final flow – expenditure on exports (and also on imports) of goods and services.

We begin by considering why international trade might arise. We then examine some of the major implications of international trade – and in particular of an imbalance between imports and exports. Finally we discuss changes in the UK's overseas trade and balance of payments in recent years. The starting-point, the key to international trade, is the principle of comparative advantage.

The principle of comparative advantage

We saw in Chapter 2 that an economy can be considered as a bundle or collection of resources which can be transformed into alternative combinations of products, and that these alternative combinations can be represented by a production possibility frontier.

Figure 17.1 shows the production possibility frontiers for two hypothetical countries. Country A could allocate its resources so as to produce, in a given period, either 10,000 units of food or 5,000 machines or any combination of food and machines lying on the line AA. The fact that the production possibility frontier is a straight line indicates that the opportunity cost of producing one product, in terms of the other, is constant. The oppor-

tunity cost of one machine is two units of food, i.e. for every additional machine produced, two units of food must be sacrificed. (As we showed in Ch. 2 the opportunity cost ratio may often not be constant. Production possibility frontiers are more likely to be concave to the origin. We have assumed a straight line frontier merely in order to simplify the analysis.)

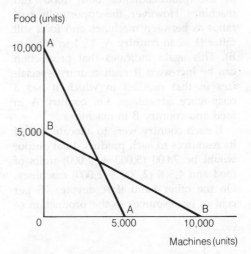

Fig. 17.1
Alternative production possibility frontiers

The resources with which country B is endowed would permit it to produce 5,000 units of food or 10,000 machines, or any combination lying on the line BB. For B the opportunity cost of producing one additional machine is 0.5 unit of food, i.e. for every additional machine produced, 0.5 unit of food must be sacrificed.

To summarize, the opportunity cost ratios as between machines and food are 1 : 2 in country A and 1 : 0.5 in country B. In these circumstances it is easy to see that total production will be greater if each country specializes in that product in which it has a comparative advantage, i.e. country A in food and country B in machines. A can produce 10,000 units of food and B 10,000 machines, whereas if there were no specialization, if each country allocated half its resources to each product, total production would be 7,500 (5,000 + 2,500) units of food and 7,500 (2,500 + 5,000) machines.

We examine below the conditions which must be fulfilled in order for specialization to occur, but first let us consider the situation represented in Fig. 17.2. In contrast to the previous situation, country A has an *absolute* advantage in the production of both food and machines. However, the opportunity cost ratios as between machines and food still differ (1 : 2 in country A, 1 : 1 in country B). This again indicates that production can be increased if each country specializes in that product in which it has a *comparative* advantage, i.e. country A in food and country B in machines.

If each country were to allocate half of its resources to each product, total output would be 7,000 (5,000 + 2,000) units of food and 4,500 (2,500 + 2,000) machines. On the other hand if A devotes 75 per cent of its resources to the production of

food and the remaining 25 per cent to machines, while B specializes entirely on machines, total output will be 7,500 units of food and 5,250 (1,250 + 4,000) machines. The output of both food and machines has increased.

Only if opportunity costs were identical, i.e. only if a situation of comparative advantage did not exist, would specialization fail to lead to a greater total output.[1]

The conditions for international trade

As we have seen, if international specialization and trade are to lead to increased production, opportunity cost ratios in different countries must differ. Given that this condition is fulfilled, trade will take place provided that the countries can agree on a rate at which the products should exchange. This rate of exchange must lie between the two domestic opportunity cost ratios.

In the second situation considered above, the rate of exchange of machines for food must lie between 1 : 1 and 1 : 2. The countries might, for example, agree that one machine should exchange for 1.5 units of food. Country A, which specializes in the production of food, would then obtain one machine in exchange for each 1.5 units of food sold, whereas to produce one more machine it would have to sacrifice the production of two units of food. Conversely, country B would obtain 1.5 units of food for each machine it sold, whereas if it produced its own food it would obtain only one unit of food for every machine forgone.

Production possibility frontiers, adjusted to take account of the possibility of trading at this rate of exchange, are shown by the broken lines, A' and B' in Fig. 17.3.

Today most international trade ·does not, of course, take place on a barter basis as in the above example. Instead transactions are undertaken in terms of internationally accepted currencies. In these circumstances the condition for inter-

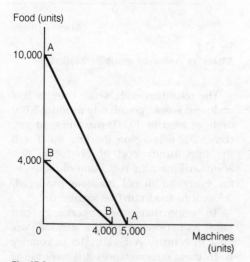

Food (units)

10,000 — A

4,000 — B

0   4,000   5,000   Machines (units)

Fig. 17.2
Alternative production possibility frontiers

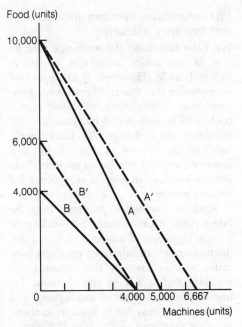

Food (units)

10,000

6,000

4,000

B′ A′

B A

0   4,000 5,000 6,667

Machines (units)

Fig. 17.3
Production possibility frontiers with trading

national trade can be specified as follows. Specialization and trade will occur provided that the exchange rates of currencies lie between the limits set by the international (non-trading) price ratios for different products.

In order to demonstrate this point let us recast in monetary terms the data relating to the second situation considered

above. The opportunity cost ratio within a country will be reflected in the domestic price ratio. This is illustrated in the first line of Table 17.1.[2] Since country A can produce, with a given quantity of resources, twice as many units of food as machines, the price of food ($2 per unit) is half that of machines ($4). In country B, with an opportunity cost ratio of 1 : 1, food and machines have the same price (£1).

The international, non-trading, price ratios are £1 = $2 (for food) and £1 = $4 (for machines). Provided that the exchange rate is between these limits, trade will occur. If, for example, the exchange rate were £1 = $3 import prices would be as shown in the second line of Table 17.1. At these prices producers in country B would be able to sell machines (but not food) in A, and producers in A would be able to sell food (but not machines) in B.

Table 17.1 also illustrates the situation where the exchange rate lies outside the limits set by the international, non-trading, price ratios. In line 3 we assume an exchange rate of £1 = $5. At this rate producers of both food and machines in country A would be able to export to country B at prices below those charged by domestic producers. However, producers in B would be unable to sell either food or machines in A. In line 4, with an exchange rate of £1 = $1, the

Table 17.1
Alternative exchange rates and international trade

	Price in country			
	A		B	
	Food ($)	Machines ($)	Food (£)	Machines (£)
Domestic prices	2	4	1	1
Import prices at exchange rate				
£1 = $3	3	3	0.67	1.33
£1 = $5	5	5	0.4	0.8
£1 = $1	1	1	2	4

situation is reversed. Producers in B would be able to sell both food and machines in country A, but producers in A would be unable to sell either in country B.

This simple example illustrates the significance of exchange rates for international trade and the implications of changes in exchange rates are discussed in greater detail below. But for the moment we continue to examine the conditions that must be fulfilled if international specialization and trade are to occur.

In the above example we made no reference to transport costs. In fact transport costs should not be so high as to outweigh the price advantage enjoyed by exporters over domestic producers. In Table 17.1, with an exchange rate of £1 = $3 international trade would cease if transport costs were more than $1 (or £0.33) per unit. In practice transport costs differ from one product to another, tending to be highest in relation to the price of the product for products with a low price–volume ratio. Consequently they inhibit trade in some products (e.g. bricks, cement) far more than others (e.g. watches, jewellery).

The second condition is that international trade should not be seriously inhibited by artificial barriers to trade. Especially important barriers are tariffs, which in effect are taxes on imports, and quotas, which regulate the volume or total value of imports. These barriers are imposed by governments and are therefore examined during our discussion of international economic policies in Chapter 25.

To conclude this outline of the conditions for international specialization and trade, one final point should be made. The example above related to a two-product, bilateral (two-country) trading situation, whereas in practice international trade is conducted on a multi-product, multilateral basis. The wider the basis for trade, the greater is likely to be the scope for the application of the principle of comparative advantage, and thus for an increase in total economic welfare.

The interaction between product and currency markets

We have identified the exchange rate as one of the major influences on international trade. However, it is important to recognize that this relationship is a two-way one. The pattern of international trade can be influenced by, but can also influence, the exchange rate. For example consider an increase in the volume of a country's exports relative to imports. This relative increase in exports may occur for various reasons.

First, technological progress may be faster than in other countries, leading to a more rapid rate of innovation. The introduction of new or improved products may cause an increase in the demand for exports, and a fall in the demand for imports. Second, costs of production, and hence prices, may fall in relation to those in other countries, increasing the attractiveness of this country's products *vis-à-vis* those of other countries. Finally, the emergence of unfavourable domestic economic conditions may induce producers to put more resources into exporting. The changed conditions may be short term, e.g. a government may freeze domestic prices and thus cause a reduction in domestic profit margins if costs rise. A longer-term change in conditions would be implied by a reduction in the growth rate of GDP relative to growth in other countries. This should also induce exporters to put more resources into exporting. (However, it is possible that factors which may cause a slow rate of growth – a lack of innovation, outdated working methods, etc. – may also inhibit exports.)

Whatever the cause this increase in the volume of exports relative to imports is likely to cause a rise in the external value of the country's currency, i.e. in the exchange rate. Moreover the interaction between the two types of market is unlikely to end there. If a change in the pattern of trade causes the exchange rate to alter, this will in turn cause a change in the relative profitability of importing and exporting, and hence in the pattern of trade.

Again, consider a change in the exchange rate arising from an international monetary flow not directly connected with trade flows. For example an increase in domestic interest rates may lead to an inflow of investment funds from abroad and hence in a movement of the exchange rate. This movement will influence the pattern of international trade and changes in this pattern may cause further movements in the exchange rate.

Gross domestic product and international trade

Provided that the conditions for international trade, outlined above, continue to be fulfilled we would expect an increase in GDP to be accompanied by higher levels of both imports and exports. If we were to consider a single country the higher level of imports would be attributed to the increase in expenditure, by both consumers and producers, some of which is satisfied by importing goods from abroad. On the export side, the increase in exports would reflect the increase in that country's economic capacity, not all of which is absorbed by additional domestic expenditure.

In practice we cannot, of course, confine our attention to a single country when we are considering international trade. Part of the explanation of the increase in imports is that overseas countries have expanded their economic capacity and are therefore able to satisfy part of our increased demands. Similarly the ability to increase exports depends upon the increase in the GDP, and hence the expenditure, of overseas countries. In fact experience shows that as the world economy expands, international trade tends to expand more rapidly, reflecting a greater degree of specialization between countries.

Specialization may occur between industries as in the hypothetical examples above, or within industries. Intra-industry or intra-product trade has increased in importance in recent years and is discussed further below.

Table 17.2
Imports of goods and services (% of domestic demand)

	1960	1970	1980	1983
Canada	18.4	21.1	27.5	23.3
USA	4.4	5.5	10.9	9.3
Japan	10.4	9.7	14.7	12.3
France	13.2	15.9	23.6	23.9
West Germany	16.9	19.5	27.5	28.6
Italy	14.2	17.3	27.2	25.8
Netherlands	47.2	45.8	52.7	56.9
UK	22.1	22.6	25.9	25.9

Source: *Economic Progress Report* June–July 1985

For all the countries listed in Table 17.2, imports have increased as a percentage of domestic demand. If we were to examine export trends we would see the same picture. This is not surprising since one country's imports are another country's exports.

International trade and resource utilization

We would expect a deficit in payments for imports over exports to be associated with a lower level of domestic resource utilization, and a surplus with a higher level. But when changes occur in relative prices the analysis is more complicated. It is no longer possible to draw such firm conclusions about the relationship between an imbalance (whether surplus or deficit) and resource allocation.

For example, let us examine the possible consequences of an increase in the relative price of imports. This increase is likely to cause some switching of expenditure from imported goods to domestic substitutes, and thus an increase in the utilization of domestic resources. However, although total expenditure on imports may fall, this is by no means certain to happen. Indeed in the past large increases in the prices of fuels and basic materials have resulted in a substantial increase in the UK's expenditure on imports and in the gap between expenditure on imports and exports.

We can see, then, that when there is a change in relative prices, the simple rule that we gave above may no longer apply. A deficit (or an increase in the deficit) in payments for imports over exports need not imply a lower level of domestic resource utilization in that period.

The international economic transactions of the United Kingdom

Having discussed the factors which exert a major influence on international economic transactions (including, of course, the flow of trade), we now examine the pattern of transactions of the UK. Starting with the broadest categories, we see from Table 17.3 that in most years the value of imports of goods exceeds the value of exports, whereas the reverse applies in services.

Within the goods category (visible trade) there is again considerable specialization, as shown in Table 17.4. The UK's lack of many foodstuffs and basic materials is reflected in the fact that they account for a much higher proportion of imports than of exports. An even bigger disparity used to exist in fuels, as shown

Table 17.3
UK international trade in goods and services (£m., current prices)

	Exports of goods minus imports	Exports of services minus imports
1976	−3,930	2,245
1977	−2,284	3,038
1978	−1,542	3,478
1979	−3,449	3,818
1980	1,360	3,868
1981	3,360	3,820
1982	2,331	2,604
1983	− 835	3,651
1984	−4,384	3,827
1985	−2,178	5,705
1986	−8,463	5,382
1976–86	−20,014	41,436

Source: Central Statistical Office, *United Kingdom Balance of Payments*

by the 1976 data. However, the development of North Sea oil and gas has turned the deficit on this item into a surplus. The UK's status as an industrial nation used to be reflected in the fact that manufac-

Table 17.4
Pattern of the external trade of the UK (percentages)

	Exports		Imports	
	1976	1986	1976	1986
Food, beverages and tobacco	6.6	7.5	15.9	11.4
Basic materials	3.2	2.8	10.4	5.4
Fuels	5.0	11.9	17.9	7.4
Manufactures	82.0	74.8	54.0	73.8
Other	3.2	3.0	1.7	2.1
	100	100	100	100

Source: Monthly Digest of Statistics

tures accounted for a much bigger percentage of exports than imports. But it can be seen from Table 17.4 that this situation has now changed, with manufactures accounting for roughly equal proportions of each. This is partly due to the fact that the development of North Sea oil and gas led in the early part of the 1980s to a rise in the sterling exchange rate, which reduced the competitiveness of other sectors, including manufacturing.

When we examine smaller categories we find many further examples of specialization. For instance within manufactures the UK has a fairly healthy surplus in chemicals, metal products and industrial machinery, but a deficit in paper manufactures, clothing and footwear. Although the UK has a deficit in food, beverages and tobacco taken together, she has a surplus in beverages (but a deficit in some individual beverages, e.g. wine).

The surpluses on services, shown in Table 17.3, arise mainly from the UK's expertise in commercial and financial services: insurance, banking, brokerage, etc. (Services is only one of three items which constitute the invisible balance. The UK has a consistent and fairly stable deficit on transfers, which partly offsets the surplus on services. The third item, interest, profits and dividends, has usually been in surplus in recent years, but the balance fluctuates markedly. The overall result is that the invisible balance is invariably in surplus (see Table 17.7 below) but this overall balance is sometimes greater than, sometimes less than, the surplus on services.)

The terms of trade

We noted above that the volume and pattern of international trade is influenced by changes in relative prices. The prices of one country's products, in relation to those of another country, may change because of a change in either the ratio of the costs of production in the two countries or in the exchange rate. The terms of trade is a summary measure which takes into account both of these factors. It expresses the relationship between the average price of our exports of goods and of our imports of goods. In each case the average price is a weighted average, the weights being the relative importance of different categories of goods in the base year.

The terms of trade are expressed as an index with a value of 100 in the base year. If the average price of our exports increases in relation to the price of our imports the index rises; if the average price of our exports falls in relation to the price of our imports the index falls.

Table 17.5
UK terms of trade (1980 = 100)

| | Unit value (price) indices of visible trade | | Terms of trade |
	Exports	Imports	
1976	61	71	86
1977	72	82	88
1978	79	85	93
1979	88	91	96
1980	100	100	100
1981	109	108	101
1982	116	117	100
1983	126	128	99
1984	136	140	98
1985	144	145	99
1986	137	134	102

Source: Economic Trends

Table 17.5 shows that between 1976 and 1981 the average price (unit value) of UK exports of goods rose more than the price of imports, causing a rise in the index. Since 1981 there has been relatively little change.

A rise in the index is said to constitute an improvement in the terms of trade since a bigger volume of imports can then be purchased with the proceeds of a given volume of exports. But the increase in relative prices may cause a fall in the volume of exports relative to imports. The net effect on the balance of payments (see below) could therefore be either favourable or unfavourable. The effect on employment is likely to be unfavourable.

A fall in the index is said to constitute a deterioration in the terms of trade, since a smaller volume of imports can then be purchased with the proceeds of a given volume of exports. But again the effect on the balance of payments could be either favourable or unfavourable, while the effect on employment is likely to be favourable.

International trade competitiveness

Changes in a country's competitiveness in international trade can be measured, or at least estimated, in several ways, as shown in Fig. 17.4.

Import price competitiveness is plotted in the top chart. This reflects the relationship between the prices of imports of a sample of manufactures and the corresponding wholesale domestic prices. The chart shows that imports became less competitive, implying an increase in their relative price. The main reason for this was the fall in the sterling exchange rate (see Table 17.6 below). The bottom chart

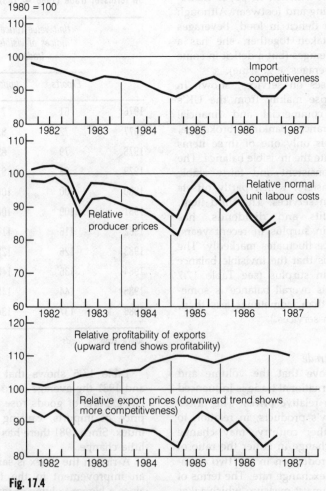

Fig. 17.4
Measures of UK trade competitiveness
Source: Economic Trends

shows that UK exports became more competitive, implying a fall in their relative price. This again reflects the fall in the sterling exchange rate.

The bottom chart also gives an estimate of the relative profitability of exports, based on the relationship between export prices and domestic prices, i.e. it is a comparison of the revenue that would be received if a given volume of goods was sold abroad or at home. We can say that relative export prices indicate the potential for exporting, while relative profitability indicates the incentive.

The middle chart presents information on changes in relative labour costs, and shows how these changes are reflected in changes in relative producer prices. It can be seen that since 1981 the UK's relative costs have tended to decline, although the situation was reversed in 1985. This fall in relative costs is again a reflection of the fall in the sterling exchange rate.

The sterling exchange rate index
The exchange rate for sterling is often quoted in relation to a certain key currency such as the dollar. However, this can give a misleading picture of the overall strength (or weakness) of the pound, since it might be moving up against one currency and down against others. The sterling exchange rate index (or sterling index for short) measures the overall change in the value of sterling against other currencies as a whole. The index is calculated by taking a weighted average against seventeen other currencies, the weights reflecting the importance of the individual currencies to UK trade.

Table 17.6 shows changes in the sterling index and also, by way of comparison, changes in the value of sterling in terms of two key currencies, the dollar and the Deutschmark.

The real exchange rate
The real exchange rate measures the relative prices of goods from different countries in terms of a common currency. Taking a two-country situation as an example, the UK's real exchange rate, with respect to the USA, would be defined as:

$$\frac{\text{£ prices of UK goods}}{\text{\$ prices of US goods}} \times \text{\$/£ exchange rate}$$

The formula applies to the prices of all goods, but we can illustrate it by considering one product, bicycles. We assume that bicycles can be produced and sold for £100 in the UK and for $300 in the

Table 17.6
Sterling exchange rates

			Annual averages
	US dollars/£	D-mark/£	*Sterling exchange rate index (1975 = 100)*
1979	2.12	3.89	87.3
1980	2.33	4.23	96.1
1981	2.03	4.56	95.3
1982	1.75	4.24	90.7
1983	1.52	3.87	83.3
1984	1.33	3.79	78.8
1985	1.30	3.78	78.7
1986	1.47	3.18	72.9

Source: Economic Trends

USA. At an exchange rate of $2/£, the rate ruling in 1981 (Table 17.6 but rounding here to simplify the arithmetic) the relative price would be 1 : 1.5. In terms of sterling the British bicycle would sell at £100, and the American bicycle at £150; in terms of dollars the British bicycle would sell at $200 and the American at $300.

The real exchange rate will change if a change occurs in either the nominal exchange rate or domestic prices. Taking the exchange rate first, consider the effect of the move to the 1984 exchange rate of $1.33/£. The above formula tells us that this fall in the $/£ exchange rate (i.e. the depreciation of sterling) would cause the real exchange rate to fall also.

This fall in the real exchange rate would make British goods more competitive. To demonstrate this we can recalculate the relative prices of bicycles. In sterling British bicycles would sell at £100 and American bicycles at £225; in dollars British bicycles would sell at $133, American bicycles at $300. (In both instances the relative price is 1 : 2.25.)

Consider now a change in relative prices. The formula tells us that, for example, an increase in the relative price of British goods would cause the real exchange rate to rise, a rise that will cause British goods to become less competitive. Let us assume that the domestic price of British bicycles increased from £100 to £150, while the price of the American bicycles remain at $300. At the initial nominal exchange of $2/£ the relative price would change from 1 : 1.5 to 1 : 1. Both bicycles would sell at £150 or $300.

Non-price competitiveness

All the measures discussed above relate to price competitiveness, and price is obviously an important element in competitiveness. But there is reason to believe that non-price forms of competition are increasing in importance. These forms include quality, product design, before- and after-sales service, early delivery times and reliability in achieving delivery schedules. Non-price competition may be especially important in explaining the growth of intra-industry trade.

The balance of payments

We have concentrated so far on exports and imports of goods and services, and the corresponding monetary flows, because they directly involve the utilization of resources, and so are comparable with the expenditure flows discussed in the previous three chapters. However, we have also mentioned other international monetary flows, which do not correspond to flows of goods and services. Since these other flows also have important implications, albeit indirect, for the utilization of resources, it is appropriate that they should be examined in somewhat greater detail.

These various types of international financial flows are brought together in the UK balance of payments accounts, a summary version of which is presented in Table 17.7. For all items a net figure is presented, i.e. a flow of money into the UK is offset against any corresponding outflow.

The first two items relate to the flows to which we gave most attention above. The *visible balance* comprises expenditure on goods. This balance is almost always negative, there having been a surplus is only ten years since 1800. The surpluses earned in 1981 and 1982 reflected the development of North Sea oil.

Services and transfers – which include trade in services, discussed above, and transfers such as military and economic assistance provided by the government to other countries – together with interest, profits and dividends, comprise the *invisible balance*. This is invariably positive, the size of the surplus frequently being sufficient to outweigh the deficit on visible trade, giving a surplus on *current account*.

The behaviour of the current account receives a great deal of attention and

Table 17.7
Summary balance of payments

	1982	1983	1984	1985	1986
Visible balance	2,331	−835	−4,384	−2,178	−8,463
Invisible balance	1,704	4,173	5,858	5,097	7,483
Current balance	4,035	3,338	1,474	2,919	−980
Net transactions in UK assets and liabilities	−2,262	−4,742	−6,916	−7,421	−10,747
(Of which, change in official reserves (additions to − drawings on +))	(+1,421)	(+607)	(+908)	(−1,758)	(−2,891)
Balancing item	−1,773	1,404	5,442	4,502	11,727

Source: Central Statistical Office, *United Kingdom Balance of Payments*

publicity. This is partly due to the fact that the current balance is the best indicator of the extent to which the UK is 'paying her way' internationally. If the current balance is seriously in deficit for any length of time, the government will be obliged to take remedial action. (The various policies which might be adopted are discussed in subsequent chapters and especially in Ch. 25.)

Table 17.7 shows that the UK had a steadily increasing negative balance (outflow of money) on *net transactions in UK assets and liabilities* (the capital account). We have identified separately one of the capital account items, the *change in official reserves*. These are official holdings of gold and convertible currencies, special drawing rights, and changes in the UK reserve position with the International Monetary Fund (IMF). Over the period covered by Table 17.7, these reserves increased, and by the end of 1986 they amounted to £17.4bn.

In principle the balance on the capital account should equal the balance on the current account (but with opposite signs). The reason it does not do so is because there are a substantial volume of unrecorded transactions, the *balancing item*. The balancing item fluctuates considerably from one year to the next, and this makes it very difficult to gain an accurate picture of the state of the balance of payments.

UK external assets and liabilities

Capital outflows and inflows give rise to external assets and liabilities. Table 17.8 shows that in 1986 UK external assets exceeded external liabilities by £114bn. (an increase of £37bn. over 1985). The UK had borrowed more than it had loaned overseas. However, this deficit was outweighed

Table 17.8
UK external assets and liabilities

	£bn.
Non-bank portfolio investment	
Assets	+111.3
Liabilities	− 24.5
Direct investment	
Assets	+ 94.6
Liabilities	− 48.6
UK banks' net liabilities	− 22.9
Public sector	
Reserves (assets) less official foreign currency borrowing	+ 8.5
British government stock (liabilities)	− 13.7
Other net public sector assets	+ 8.1
Other net assets	+ 1.6
Total net assets	114.4

Source: Bank of England Quarterly Bulletin, Nov. 1987

by surpluses on direct investment (e.g. when a British company builds a factory overseas) and on portfolio investment (e.g. when British companies and individuals buy shares in overseas companies). This surplus of assets over liabilities should lead to a net inflow (of dividends, etc.) on the current account in future years.

The benefits and costs of overseas investment

Overseas investment on the scale seen in the first half of the 1980s has given rise to considerable controversy.[3] Institutions and individuals invest overseas because they believe that they will obtain a higher return than would be obtained by investing in their own country. Only time will tell whether this belief will be borne out in future, but there is some evidence that this has been so in the past.

The higher return is clearly a private benefit to the investors concerned. This benefit may in fact be spread quite widely around the economy; as we showed above, the most rapid rise occurred in purchases of overseas securities by financial institutions such as insurance companies and pension funds. These institutions gather together the savings of millions of individuals who forgo current consumption. The higher the return on investments the greater will be the increase in future income, e.g. in the form of pensions, and thus in consumption opportunities.

Looking at the situation from a national viewpoint one sees a similar picture. The build-up of external assets will lead to an increase in future income. This may comprise higher receipts in interest, profits and dividends, which benefit the balance of payments current account and allow a higher level of purchases of foreign goods and services. Alternatively or additionally it may comprise income from capital gains, which benefits the capital account.

The main justification for restricting overseas investment is that it provides jobs overseas rather than in the UK. Such investment is, therefore, argued to be inappropriate when unemployment is as high as it is at present. Two points can be made to counter this argument. First, some direct investment overseas can lead to additional employment in the UK, as when extensions to factories overseas allow more British components to be imported. More generally it is argued that the best way of boosting investment in the UK is to improve the returns on such investment. (However, experience shows that this is easier said than done.)

Appendix: the determination of exchange rates

The behaviour of exchange rates has received increasing attention as a move has occurred away from fixed and towards floating rates. In this appendix we present a more rigorous analysis of the determination of exchange rates than was given in the main body of the chapter.

The basic determinant of the rate at which one currency exchanges for another is the balance between the demand for and the supply of two currencies. We can illustrate this by considering the position of sterling in relation to the dollar. This illustration relates to transactions which affect the current account. But it is important to remember that capital flows can also affect exchange rates. This is discussed further below.

The demand for sterling

Pounds are demanded by American importers to pay for products purchased from the UK. The lower the value of sterling in relation to the dollar, the greater will be the volume of our exports, and so the greater the number of pounds demanded.

To understand why this is so, consider a British company exporting bicycles which it sells on the domestic market for £100. If it wishes to obtain the same revenue per unit from export sales, and the current rate of exchange is £1 = $2, it will set a price of $200. If now the exchange rate falls to £1 = $1.50 it need set a price of only $150 in order to obtain a revenue per unit of £100. As the price is reduced the volume of sales, and therefore the demand for sterling, is likely to rise. If, for example sales increase from 1,000 bicycles to 1,200 a month, the monthly demand for sterling from US importers will rise from £100,000 to £120,000.

Changes in exchange rates are not always fully reflected in export prices. If the country's exports represent a very small part of international trade in the product concerned, exporters may have to accept the going price, acting as price takers (see Ch. 7). On the other hand, if the country accounts for a more substantial part of trade, exporters may be able to exert an influence on price, i.e. to act as price makers.

Overall a change in exchange rates is likely to have some effect on prices, and consequently on the volume of exports. The relationship between the exchange rate and the quantity of the currency (sterling) demanded can therefore be represented by a demand curve, of the form shown in Fig. 17.5. (In the very unlikely event that no change occurred in the quantity of exports demanded, the demand schedule for sterling would be vertical.)

The supply of sterling

The change in the exchange rate will also be reflected in the price of our imports from the USA. For example assume that an American manufacturer of golf balls which sell at $3.00 in the USA, sells these for £1.50 in the UK when the exchange rate is £1 = $2. If now the exchange rate alters to £1 = $1.50 he will have to adjust the UK price to £2 if he is to continue to obtain $3.00 per ball from UK sales.

The effect of this price change on the sterling revenue of this firm, and thus on the supply of sterling to the international currency market, will depend upon the PED for golf balls. There are three alternative situations, three alternative responses to the increase in import prices. First, if demand is elastic (PED > 1) the revenue of the exporter, and hence the supply of sterling to the currency market, will fall. This situation is represented by the supply curve S_E in Fig. 17.6. Second, if demand is of unitary elasticity (PED = 1) revenue

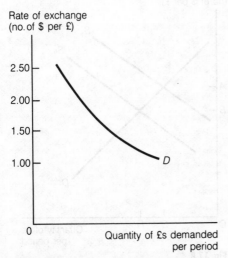

Fig. 17.5
The exchange rate and the demand for sterling

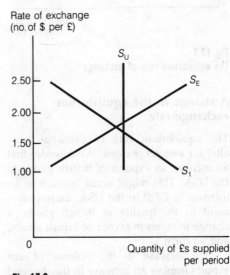

Fig. 17.6
The exchange rate and the supply of sterling

and hence the supply of sterling will be unchanged (supply curve S_U). Finally, if demand is inelastic (PED < 1) the revenue and hence the supply of sterling will increase (supply curve S_I).

The equilibrium exchange rate

The equilibrium rate of exchange is the rate at which the demand for sterling equals the supply, i.e. the rate at which the demand and supply curves intersect. In Fig. 17.7, which assumes that the supply curve is upward sloping, the initial equilibrium rate is A, the quantity of sterling traded being Q.

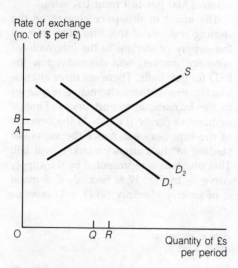

Rate of exchange
(no. of $ per £)

Fig. 17.7
The equilibrium rate of exchange

A change in the equilibrium exchange rate

The equilibrium rate of exchange may alter for various reasons. We consider first an increase in exports of British goods to the USA. This might occur because of an increase in GDP in the USA, an improvement in the quality of British goods, a change in tastes in favour of British goods, and so forth.

This increase in the volume of our exports implies an increase in the demand for sterling, as indicated by the shift of the

demand curve to D_2 in Fig. 17.7. The new equilibrium rate of exchange is B, the quantity of sterling traded being R. Note that this increase in the exchange rate implies a rise in the dollar price of UK goods. Consequently, although the level of exports, and thus the volume of sterling traded, is higher than it was initially, it is not as high as it would have been had the exchange rate not risen. (We can say that the initial income or quality effect is partly offset by the price effect.)

The converse of this situation is illustrated in Fig. 17.8. Here the UK's demand for imports is assumed to rise because of an income or quality effect. This causes the supply curve of sterling to shift to the right, from S_1 to S_2, and the equilibrium exchange rate to fall from A to B. This fall in the exchange rate implies a rise in the price of imports and a fall in the price of exports. These price effects will partly offset the initial income or quality effect. (We are, of course, assuming here a system of freely floating exchange rates. If the authorities were unwilling to allow the exchange rate to fall, they could purchase QR pounds in exchange for dollars through the Exchange Equalization Account.)

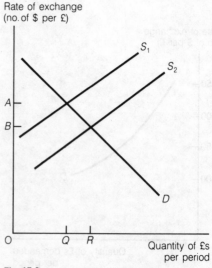

Rate of exchange
(no. of $ per £)

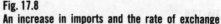

Fig. 17.8
An increase in imports and the rate of exchange

We now turn to the situation where the initial change represents a price and not an income or quality effect. Let us assume that the rate of inflation is higher in the UK than in the USA with the result that the prices of British goods rise, relative to the prices of American goods, in both markets. In fact we can assume, for the sake of simplicity, that the rate of inflation in the USA is zero.

As the UK's exports become dearer, their volume falls. The effect on the total value of exports, and thus on the demand for sterling, depends upon the elasticity of demand for exports. If demand is elastic the value of exports *at any given exchange rate* will fall, i.e. the demand curve for sterling will shift to the left (from D_1 to D_2 in Fig. 17.9). If demand for exports is inelastic, the demand curve for sterling will shift to the right (D_3). Finally, if demand for exports is of unitary elasticity, the demand curve for sterling will remain at D_1.

We have assumed that the rate of inflation in the USA is zero; consequently there will *initially* be no tendency for the price of imports to change. Nevertheless the volume of imports is likely to rise as expenditure is switched from the dearer domestically produced goods. Conse-

quently the total value of imports, and thus the supply of sterling, *at any given exchange rate*, will rise, i.e. the supply curve for sterling will shift to the right.

The possible effects on the exchange rate, via changes in both exports and imports, are illustrated in Fig. 17.10. With the initial demand for and supply of sterling represented by D_1 and S_1, the equilibrium exchange rate is *A*. As UK prices rise, the supply curve shifts to S_2. If the demand for UK exports is elastic, the demand curve shifts to D_2 and the exchange rate falls from *A* to *B*. If the demand for exports is inelastic the demand curve shifts to D_3. This implies a smaller fall in the exchange rate, to *C*. Indeed the exchange rate may be unchanged, or it could even rise.

Of these three possibilities, the most likely reaction to a rise in the prices of UK goods is a fall in the sterling exchange rate. Indeed the *purchasing power parity theory*[4] suggests that the exchange rate would alter so as to compensate exactly for the change in relative prices. Although experience has shown that an exactly compensatory change seldom occurs, changes tend to be in the direction

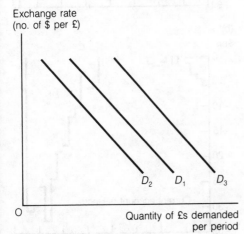

Exchange rate
(no. of $ per £)

Fig. 17.9
The elasticity of demand for exports and the demand for sterling

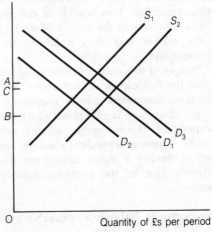

Rate of exchange
(no. of $ per £)

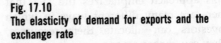

Fig. 17.10
The elasticity of demand for exports and the exchange rate

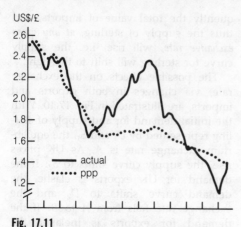

US$/£

Fig. 17.11
Purchasing power parity theory and exchange rates
Source: IMF; Economic Dept. estimates published in *Midland Bank Review*, Winter 1985

predicted by this theory. Figure 17.11 compares actual changes in exchange rates with those predicted.

As noted at the beginning of this appendix the exchange rate may be influenced by transactions on the capital as well as the current account. These transactions may themselves be indirectly influenced by current account changes. For example a UK current account deficit may be seen as indicating that a fall in the exchange rate is likely, and this possibility may persuade overseas investors to sell British securities. This would, of course, cause an increase in the supply of sterling to the market and thus a fall in the exchange rate.

Changes of this nature can be analysed within the framework set out above. But a different framework may be required to analyse changes in capital flows which are independent of changes in the current account. These independent changes are seen as having a major impact on the exchange rate in the portfolio balance approach.

The portfolio balance approach

This approach emphasizes the fact that there are many different ways in which investors can allocate their resources. They can choose among a range of assets,

e.g. money, bonds, and they can also choose the currency in which the assets are denominated. For example, they may buy dollar bonds issued by the US government or sterling bonds issued by the UK government. These allocation decisions take into account the rewards and risks associated with the various types of assets and currencies. With this in mind let us consider the situation portrayed in Fig. 17.12.

The top chart shows that the value of the dollar (measured on the left-hand scale) rose strongly in the first half of the 1980s, and it appears that this was due to the preferences of investors for assets

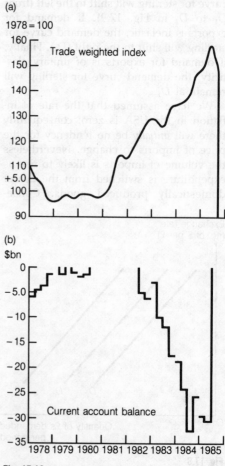

(a)
1978 = 100

Trade weighted index

(b)
$bn

Current account balance

1978 1979 1980 1981 1982 1983 1984 1985

Fig. 17.12
The exchange rate index and current account of the USA

denominated in dollars rather than in other currencies. These preferences were a response to a combination of interest rates that were historically high by US standards and the rapid growth of the US economy.

The bottom chart measures (on the left-hand scale) the US current account balance. It can be seen that this deteriorated sharply after 1981, and it is likely that the main reason for this was the rise in the dollar exchange rate which weakened US competitiveness in international trade.

The differences between the two

approaches explained in this appendix are now clear. The first approach, which concentrates on the effect of current account transactions on the exchange rate, would have been unable to explain recent US experience. This can, however, be explained by the second approach which emphasizes the effect of changes in the exchange rate on the current account.

On the other hand there are, of course, many instances where the first approach does apply, i.e. where a change in the current account, perhaps bolstered by a consequential change in the capital account, causes a change in the exchange rate.

Summary

1. In the international economy a situation of comparative advantage exists whenever the opportunity cost ratios (of producing different products) vary between different countries. In order to maximize total output, each country should specialize in those products in which it has a comparative advantage *vis-à-vis* other countries.

2. In order for international trade to take place, the rate of exchange must lie between the domestic opportunity cost ratios, or between the limits set by the international (non-trading) price ratios for different products.

3. An increase in exports involves an increase in the utilization of domestic resources; an increase in imports involves an increase in the utilization of resources in other countries. If, at a given level of prices, the volume of exports equals the volume of imports, the net effect on the utilization of domestic resources is zero.

4. A reflection of international specialization is the fact that in most years the UK has had a surplus on trade in services and a deficit on trade in goods. Further specialization can be observed within each of these categories.

5. The terms of trade expresses the relationship, in index number form, between the average price of a country's exports of goods and of its imports of goods. A rise in the index is likely to have an unfavourable effect on employment, but the effect on the balance of payments might be either favourable or unfavourable.

6. In the 1980s the surplus on the UK's invisible trade has exceeded the deficit on the visible trade, yielding a positive current balance. But this has sometimes been outweighed by the outflow on investment and other capital transactions. This outflow is reflected in the strong growth in the UK's net external assets.

7. The rate of exchange between two currencies is determined (in the absence of government intervention) by the balance between the demand for and the supply of the two currencies.

8. The equilibrium rate of exchange is that at which the demand for a currency equals its supply. The equilibrium rate of exchange may change because of a change in exports and imports.

9. The rate of exchange may also be affected by other transactions giving rise to international currency flows. A change in the exchange rate may in turn affect exports and imports and hence the current balance.

Key terms

Principle of comparative advantage
Opportunity cost ratios
Non-trading price ratios
Utilization of resources
Terms of trade
Sterling exchange rate index
Real exchange rate

Current balance
Balance of payments
Official reserves
Net overseas assets
Equilibrium exchange rate
Elasticity of demand
Portfolio balance approach

Notes

1. If specialization leads to greater economies of scale (see Ch. 5) production may increase even if the *initial* opportunity cost ratios are identical. However, following specialization the *final* ratios will differ.
2. In practice the correspondence between the two ratios may not be as exact as assumed here.
3. A fuller account of the controversy is given in James S, Exchange controls, investment and the balance of payments, *Economics*, Summer 1986.
4. The purchasing power parity theory considers the equilibrium exchange rate between two currencies to be that at which they have equivalent domestic purchasing power, e.g. if a given basket of goods costs $20 in the USA and £10 in the UK, the equilibrium rate of exchange would be $2/£.

Essay questions

1. Discuss the conditions which are favourable to international specialization and trade.
2. Show by means of a numerical example how economic welfare can be increased by means of international specialization and trade in accordance with the principle of *comparative* advantage. Indicate what factors might prevent trade taking place in accordance with this principle.
3. 'The pattern of international trade can be influenced by, but can also influence, the exchange rate.' Discuss.
4. Discuss the implications of a balance of payments deficit for the utilization of domestic resources.
5. What costs might be incurred by a country which experienced a substantial deficit on the balance of payments current account?
6. Explain what factors would determine a country's exchange rate in the absence of government interference.
7. Define the equilibrium rate of exchange and explain what might cause a change in its value.
8. Discuss the possible effects of a substantial rise in the price of UK exports.
9. How might a marked fall in import prices affect the UK economy?

Exercises

17.1 The production possibilities in countries X and Y in three alternative situations are as follows.

Situation	Country X	Country Y
A	100 fish, or	60 fish, or
	10 rabbits	12 rabbits
B	120 fish, or	60 fish, or
	24 rabbits	20 rabbits
C	100 fish, or	50 fish, or
	20 rabbits	10 rabbits

(i)   In which of these three situations could total output be increased as a result of international specialization and trade?

(ii)   In situation B, calculate the difference in output between the following alternatives: (a) each country allocates half its resources to fishing, and half to hunting; (b) X allocates eleven-twelfths of its resources to fishing and one-twelfth to hunting, while Y specializes completely in hunting.

(iii)   Assume that domestic costs are as follows: in X one fish costs one 'single' (s), one rabbit costs 5s; in Y one fish costs one 'double' (d), one rabbit costs 3d. At which of the following exchange rates would international specialization and trade take place: 1s = 0.5d, 1s = 0.8d, 1s = 1.5d?

17.2   Read the following passage, taken from *Lloyds Bank Economic Bulletin*, Jan. 1986, and then answer the questions below:

Mr Nigel Lawson . . . told the House of Lords that 'the balance on non-fuel trade, including in particular trade in manufactures, will tend to improve, in part responding to a fall in the real – and I emphasize the word real – exchange rate'. While the Chancellor hoped that this would occur through a fall in relative unit labour costs, it is more likely that the nominal exchange rate will have to fall if the real exchange rate is to come down. This implies a change in the present policy of keeping the exchange rate up in order to hold inflation down, if the deficit in trade in manufactures is to be reversed.

(i)   Define (a) the nominal exchange rate, (b) the real exchange rate, (c) relative unit labour costs.

(ii)   Identify two possible causes of a change in the real exchange rate.

(iii)   Explain why the balance on non-fuel trade might improve following a fall in the real exchange rate.

(iv)   Why should a policy of keeping the exchange rate up hold inflation down?

17.3   Indicate which of the factors listed below would cause a change in (a) visible trade, (b) invisible trade, (c) investment and other capital transactions, and whether each factor would have a favourable or unfavourable effect on the UK's balance of payments.

(i)   ICI increases its exports of chemicals to Belgium.

(ii)   Encouraged by the success of this venture, ICI builds a factory in Belgium from which to supply the Belgian market.

(iii)   Having lost some of its Belgian market to ICI, German chemical manufacturers retaliate by stepping up exports to Britain.

(iv)   A British shipping line wins a contract to transport these chemicals from Hamburg to London.

(v)   In order to try to reduce political unrest, the UK makes a long-term loan to three underdeveloped countries.

(vi)   The initial interest payments on these loans are made by the three countries.

(vii) A US company buys out the minority British holding in its UK subsidiary.

(viii) The number of British troops stationed in Europe is reduced.

(ix) Increasing unemployment in the USA leads to a reduction in the number of American tourists visiting Britain.

(x) Cliff Richard and the London Symphony Orchestra both have successful American tours.

17.4 In a period in which the pound depreciated by more than a quarter against the US dollar and by over 20 per cent against the weighted average of leading trading currencies, companies were asked what effect the fall in the pound was having on the pricing and volume of their business.

The principal conclusions were that:

1. Most exporters either cannot, or do not want to, reduce foreign currency prices to reflect the decline in sterling.

2. Companies do, however, feel that they can hold foreign prices for some time to come and this should make them progressively more competitive.

3. Almost all industries fear that increased raw material import prices could cancel out what competitive advantage has been gained.

   (i) How would you explain companies' pricing policies?

   (ii) Given the conclusions presented in the passage, discuss the probable effects of the depreciation of sterling.

Table 17.9
Volume and unit value indices of exports and imports (1980 = 100)

	Volume indices		Unit value indices	
	Exports	Imports	Exports	Imports
1976	85	90	61	71
1977	92	91	72	82
1978	95	96	79	85
1979	99	106	88	91
1980	100	100	100	100
1981	99	96	109	108
1982	102	102	116	117
1983	104	110	126	128
1984	112	122	136	140
1985	119	126	144	145
1986	123	134	137	134

Source: Monthly Digest of Statistics

17.5 (i) What factors might have caused the changes in exports and imports shown in Table 17.9?

   (ii) Calculate the terms of trade for (a) 1976, (b) 1986.

   (iii) Discuss the implications of the change in the terms of trade between 1976 and 1986.

CHAPTER EIGHTEEN
Aggregate Expenditure

Introduction

We have already discussed, in Chapter 13, the flow of total or aggregate expenditure in the UK. Following this discussion we examined, in the following four chapters, the determinants of each of the four major expenditure flows. We now put together the pieces and consider once more the overall picture, i.e. we are again concerned with aggregate expenditure. However, the focus of our attention in this chapter is quite different from what it was in Chapter 13. We shall be concerned here with the concept of the equilibrium level of national income and with changes in that level. We shall also explore, towards the end of the chapter, what might be meant by the optimum level of expenditure.

A note on definitions
In Chapter 13 we presented several alternative measures of economic activity: GDP, GNP and national income. We showed that GDP, the sum of $C + I + G + (X - M)$, is a good indicator of current living standards, and it is the measure of economic activity used in this chapter. However, 'In their theories, economists usually use the generic concept of national income (indicated by the symbol Y)',[1] and we follow this convention, remembering that 'Usually Y may be thought of as interchangeable with constant price GDP, i.e. total real output.'[2]

Equilibrium national income

The general meaning of equilibrium is that the plans of all transactors – consumers, suppliers, etc. – are fulfilled. If all plans are fulfilled at a given level of national income, national income will remain at that level for as long as these plans do not

change. In other words that is the equilibrium national income.

National income attains equilibrium when *planned* expenditure in one period $(t + 1)$ equals national income in the previous period (t). This is illustrated in Fig. 18.1. From a national income (Y) of £100m. in period t, expenditure (E) of £100m. in period $t + 1$ is planned. Assuming that producers are able to supply the goods and services required, these expenditure plans will be fulfilled. Consequently national income in period $t + 1$ will again be £100m. and this process, the circular flow of income, will continue at that level. Furthermore, provided that the price level is unchanged, the real level of economic activity will be unchanged.

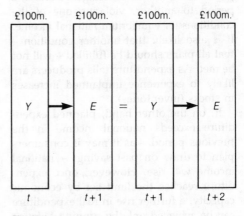

Fig. 18.1
Equilibrium national income

A changing level of national income

What happens when the conditions for equilibrium are not fulfilled, i.e. when $E_{t + 1}$ does not equal Y_t? Let us consider first the situation when planned expenditure is less than the national income of the previous period. In Fig. 18.2 planned expenditure is assumed to be 80 per cent of national income in the previous period.

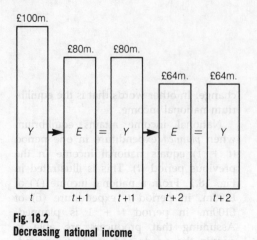

Fig. 18.2
Decreasing national income

It can be seen that national income declines from £100m. in period t to £80m. in period $t + 1$ and to £64m. in period $t + 2$. (With an unchanged price level a corresponding decline in the real level of economic activity would occur.) Note that planned expenditure changes from one period to another, violating one of the conditions for equilibrium national income. It is also likely that another condition – that all plans should be fulfilled – will not be met. As expenditure falls producers are likely to experience unplanned increases in stocks (inventories).

If, on the other hand, planned expenditure exceeds national income in the previous period – as it may if consumers plan to draw on past savings – national income will rise. However, once expenditure reaches the limit set by economic capacity, a further rise in real expenditure can be achieved only by running a deficit on international trade.

The three alternative situations that we have examined here can be summarized by means of a 45° diagram. In Fig. 18.3 the 45° line indicates the points at which planned expenditure in period $t + 1$ and national income in period t are equal, i.e. these are all potential points of equilibrium. The levels of planned expenditure at various levels of income are indicated by the expenditure function E. It can be seen that the only level of income at which planned expenditure ($t + 1$) and

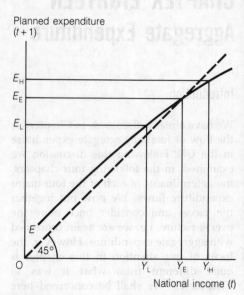

Fig. 18.3
Equilibrium and disequilibrium levels of national income

income (t) are equal is Y_E, i.e. this denotes the equilibrium level of income. If planned expenditure is above national income, e.g. at income Y_L, income will rise. If planned expenditure is below national income, e.g. at Y_H, national income will fall.

The shape of the expenditure function

In order to explain the shape of the expenditure function shown in Fig. 18.3 we can draw upon the analysis presented in Chapters 14–17.

In Chapter 14 we showed that a change in GDP is normally accompanied by a smaller absolute change in consumers' expenditure, and that the consumption function could take the form indicated by line C in Fig. 18.4. In Chapters 15 and 16 we showed that both government consumption and total investment expenditure were likely to increase with GDP. These forms of expenditure are represented in Fig. 18.4 by G and I respectively. For the sake of simplicity we have assumed that both G and I grow at a constant rate as GDP increases.

In order to obtain the aggregate

Planned expenditure

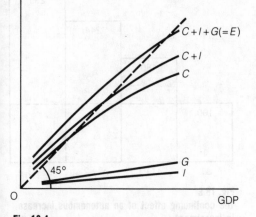

Fig. 18.4
The derivation of the planned expenditure function

expenditure function we simply add the three curves vertically. In Fig. 18.4 we have done this in stages, first adding I to C, and then G to $(C + 1)$. The resulting (planned) expenditure function E corresponds to that in Fig. 18.3.

It will be noticed that we have not included in Fig. 18.4 a schedule relating to expenditure on exports, even though this has been identified as one of the four components of total expenditure. This is because, as we saw in Chapter 13, when GDP is calculated, expenditure on imports

is offset against expenditure on exports, a net figure being included in total expenditure. We cannot say a priori whether this figure is likely to be positive or negative. We have therefore assumed that the net flow is zero (as it would be for the world economy).[3]

If we wished to depict the situation for a particular economy which had a surplus, i.e. whose exports of goods and services exceeded imports, we would include this as a fourth positive expenditure flow. This would cause the total expenditure function to shift upwards. Conversely a deficit, an excess of imports over exports, would shift the function downwards.

Autonomous and induced expenditure

Let us now examine what happens to national income when a change occurs in one of these expenditure flows. For example, assume that the discovery of vast mineral reserves increases the prospective profitability of investment, and thus the volume of investment expenditure. Since the increase in investment is *not* the result of an increase in income we define it as an *autonomous* change in investment.

The initial results of an autonomous increase in investment in period t are

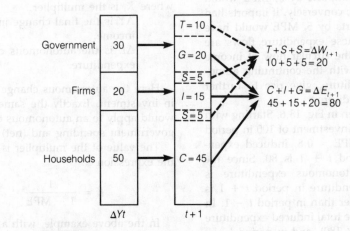

Fig. 18.5
The consequences of an autonomous increase in investment

shown in Fig. 18.5. The additional expenditure increases the incomes of households (in their role as suppliers of labour), firms (who supply other inputs) and the government (in the form of taxation). The additional income obtained by these three groups is shown in the first column. In the second column we show the change in planned expenditure which results from the change in income.

Some of the money accruing to households and firms is saved – this is designated as *S*. The rest is spent; spending by households on consumption goods is designated as *C*, and spending by firms (investment spending) as *I*. Again, of the money received by the government, some is spent (*G*), and the rest (*T*) is retained. The additional spending resulting from the autonomous investment expenditure is known as *induced* expenditure.

The marginal propensity to spend

If we add together the amounts spent, $C + I + G$, and express this as a proportion of the initial increase in GDP we obtain the marginal propensity to spend (MPE). Of the additional 100 units of income received, 80 are spent, i.e. MPE = 0.8. (Note that we have assumed here that the additional spending on exports equals the additional spending on imports. If exports had exceeded imports by 5, MPE would have been 0.85; conversely, if imports had exceeded exports by 5, MPE would have been 0.75.) These expenditure flows are fed back into the circular flow of income and together with the continuing autonomous expenditure, give rise to further induced expenditure.

This is shown in Fig. 18.6. Starting with an increase in investment of 100 in period *t*, and with MPE = 0.8, induced expenditure in period $t + 1$ is 80. Since the continuing autonomous expenditure is 100, total expenditure in period $t + 1$ is 180 units greater than in period $t - 1$. In period $t + 2$ the total induced expenditure is 144 (= 0.8 × 180), and in period $t + 3$ it is 195.2 (= 0.8 × 244).

The series could be continued indefinitely. Fortunately there is an easy

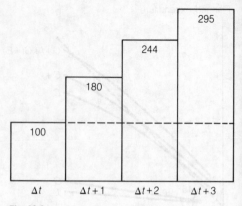

Fig. 18.6
The continuing effect of an autonomous increase in investment

method of calculating what the eventual outcome would be at the end of the process. This involves the concept of the multiplier.

The multiplier

The multiplier is defined as the ratio of the final change in national income (or GDP) resulting from an autonomous change in expenditure, to that autonomous change in expenditure. Using symbols:

$$K = \frac{\Delta Y}{\Delta E}$$

where *K* is the multiplier,
    ΔY is the final change in national income,
    ΔE is the autonomous change in expenditure.

Here the autonomous change occurred in investment. Exactly the same analysis would apply to an autonomous change in government spending and (net) exports.[4]

The value of the multiplier is given by the expression

$$K = \frac{1}{1 - \text{MPE}}$$

In the above example, with a marginal propensity to spend of 0.8, we have:

$$K = \frac{1}{1 - \text{MPE}} = \frac{1}{1 - 0.8} = \frac{1}{0.2} = 5$$

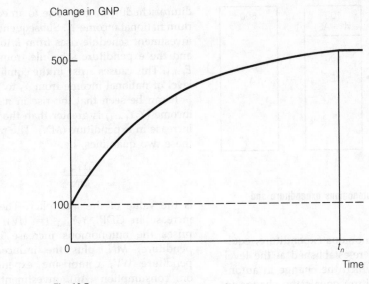

Fig. 18.7
Autonomous and induced expenditure

Applying this value of the multiplier to the autonomous change in expenditure of 100 tells us that the eventual change in national income (and expenditure) would be 500 (= 5 × 100), of which 400 would be induced expenditure. This is illustrated in Fig. 18.7, in which t_n denotes the period in which the multiplier effect would be completed.

An alternative method of calculating the value of the multiplier

An alternative, simpler, method of calculating the value of the multiplier involves the concept of withdrawals. Withdrawals are simply those parts of an increase in GDP that are *not* passed on into the circular flow. Figure 18.5 shows that with an initial increase in income of 100 total withdrawals, comprising saving (S) and taxation (T) equal 20. This means that the marginal propensity to withdraw (MPW) = 0.2 (20/100).[5]

The simpler form of the multiplier is:

$$K = \frac{1}{\text{MPW}} = \frac{1}{0.2} = 5$$

Again, therefore, we arrive at the result that national income (and expenditure)

would eventually rise by 500, comprising the autonomous increase of 100 plus the induced expenditure of 400. At this point the process would cease, i.e. equilibrium would be re-established.

An alternative definition of equilibrium national income

Earlier in this chapter we defined equilibrium national income as the level at which planned expenditure equals income. We are now able to provide an alternative definition. We showed in the above example that equilibrium is re-established when induced expenditure equals 400. When this occurs total withdrawals will equal 100. This is illustrated in Fig. 18.8, in which t_n has the same meaning as in Fig. 18.7, i.e. in period t_n the total additional income (ΔY) is 500. In the following period, with MPE = 0.8, induced expenditure (IE) is 400; consequently withdrawals are 100.

This situation is one of equilibrium because total planned expenditure (and income) in period t_{n+1} is 500. This occurs because withdrawals are exactly balanced by the autonomous expenditure (AE). Consequently we can say that if the equilibrium national income is disturbed by a

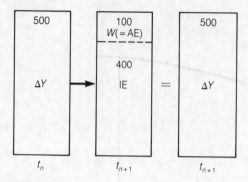

Fig. 18.8
The equality of autonomous expenditure and withdrawals

change in autonomous expenditure, equilibrium will be re-established at the level of income at which the change in autonomous expenditure equals the change in withdrawals.

A diagrammatic representation of the multiplier process
The operation of the multiplier process is illustrated in Fig. 18.9. The initial expenditure schedule E_t gives rise to an equilibrium national income Y_t. Subsequently the investment schedule rises from I_t to I_{t+1}, and the expenditure schedule from E_t to E_{t+1}. This causes a rise in the equilibrium level of national income from Y_t to Y_{t+1}.

It can be seen that the rise in national income $(Y_t Y_{t+1})$ is greater than the initial increase in expenditure (MN). The ratio of these two quantities, i.e.

$$\frac{Y_t Y_{t+1}}{MN}$$

is the value of the multiplier. The final increase in GDP, $Y_t Y_{t+1}$ $(= UV)$, comprises the autonomous increase in expenditure, MN, plus the induced expenditure WV, comprising expenditure on: consumption (AB), investment (PQ) and government current expenditure on goods and services (ST).

The optimum level of expenditure

The desirability of any level of expenditure can be determined only in relation to

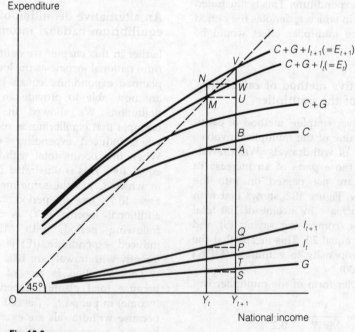

Fig. 18.9
The multiplier

the country's economic capacity; the higher that capacity the higher the optimum level of expenditure. The advantages of a high level of expenditure are, of course, a high level of resource utilization (implying low unemployment) and a high level of consumption. In preceding chapters we have shown how higher levels of expenditure, income, output and employment might be attained.

We now widen our frame of reference in two respects. First, while continuing to recognize resource utilization as important, we examine the implications of changes in expenditure for the behaviour of prices (which in turn has implications for the balance of payments). We do this in the following sections.

Second, we consider a theoretical approach which leads to quite different conclusions, especially for government policy, from those derived from the approach adopted to date. An important assumption of this alternative approach is that the economic system always adjusts so as to maintain full employment. This so-called classical model is examined in Chapter 19.

Expenditure and prices

In order to show the effect of a change in expenditure on prices, we use a 45° diagram, which shows the total *value* of income and expenditure, in conjunction with a second diagram plotting price and output. In Fig. 18.10, with the expenditure function E_1, equilibrium national income is Y_1. Given the aggregate supply curve S, the corresponding level of real output is Q_1. (A certain level of employment, and hence of unemployment, would be associated with this output.) An increase in expenditure, shown by an upward shift of the expenditure function to E_2, would result in an increase in income to Y_2, and in output and employment to Q_2. The additional output is supplied without an increase in price ($P_1 = P_2$).

A further increase in expenditure to E_3 would cause a further increase in income to Y_3, and in output to Q_3. But this further

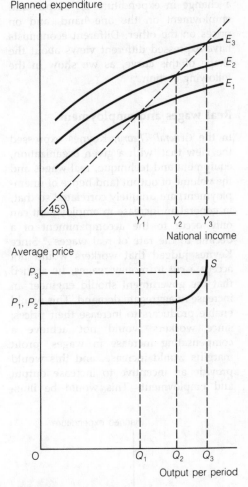

Fig. 18.10
An increase in expenditure, price and output

increase in output is associated with an increase in the average price level from P_2 to P_3. (In other words the increase in the real national income is less than the increase in the money national income Y_2Y_3.)

The aggregate supply curve becomes vertical at Y_3; in other words Y_3 is the full employment level of income. If expenditure were to increase above E_3, the only effect would be to increase prices and money national income. Real output, real national income would not change.

We can see that the shape of the aggregate supply curve determines the effect of a change in expenditure on output and employment on the one hand, and on prices on the other. Different economists have expressed different views about the shape of this curve, as we show in the following section.

Real wages and employment

In the *General Theory*, Keynes expressed the view that 'with a given organization, equipment and technique, real wages and the volume of output (and hence of unemployment) are uniquely correlated so that, in general an increase in employment can only occur to the accompaniment of a decline in the rate of real wages'.[6] Since Keynes judged that workers would not accept a cut in money wages, he argued that the government should engineer an increase in aggregate demand. This would enable producers to increase their prices; since workers would not achieve a compensating increase in wages, profit margins would increase, and this would provide an incentive to increase output and employment. This would be illus-

trated by the upward-sloping segment of the supply curve in Fig. 18.10.

Keynesian economists subsequently argued that producers would increase output to meet an increase in demand even if prices did not increase. The average cost of production is constant and producers would increase output in order to increase total profits. If all producers were in this position, the aggregate supply curve would be horizontal.

An entirely different view is held by the so-called New Classical School of economists. They believe that the number of people willing to take employment, and hence the level of output, can be increased only by an increase in the real wage rate. An increase in expenditure would not increase the real wage rate. (We have seen that Keynes believed that an increase in expenditure would cause real wages to fall.) The only effect would be an increase in prices, i.e. the aggregate supply curve is vertical.

These different views are discussed in more detail in the following chapters. We also show that these different views lead

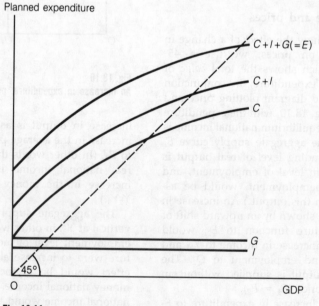

Fig. 18.11
A simplified approach to the determination of national income

to different recommendations for government policy.

Appendix: A simplified approach to the determination of national income

In many textbooks government expenditure (G) and investment (I) are assumed to be independent of the level of national income, i.e. any change in G or I is an autonomous change. This situation is illustrated in Fig. 18.11, which should be compared to Fig. 18.4 above.

Making the assumption that there are no induced changes in G or I has the advantage that the analysis is simplified. For example in Figs. 18.3 and 18.9 we would need to consider the impact of the change in investment on consumption only. Moreover the multiplier can be related to the MPC or the MPS rather than the MPE or the MPW.

However, we have not adopted this simplified approach because its assumptions run counter to the nature of economic systems. As we have shown in earlier chapters, investment and government expenditure have increased as national income has increased. Of course the models adopted in the main body of this chapter also involve simplifying assumptions. For example each diagram includes a single consumption function whereas, as we showed in Chapter 14, the long-run function may differ from the short-run function. This distinction between long-run and short-run functions could also be applied to investment and government expenditure. Indeed we have already shown in Chapter 16 that if firms have excess capacity investment may respond less in the short run than in the long run to an increase in income. It may therefore be difficult to predict the amount of induced investment and government expenditure that will result from a given change in consumption (or more generally GDP), but to assume that induced investment is zero is scarcely consistent with the facts.

Summary

1. National income attains equilibrium when planned expenditure in one period equals national income in the previous period. Provided that the plans of consumers and suppliers are unchanged, national income (the circular flow of income) will remain at that level.
2. If planned expenditure exceeds national income in the previous period, and these plans are fulfilled, national income will rise. Conversely, if planned expenditure is less than national income in the previous period, national income will fall.
3. An autonomous increase in expenditure will give rise to induced expenditure; consequently the final increase in expenditure (and GDP) will exceed the initial, autonomous, increase. The multiplier is defined as the ratio of the final change in GDP to the autonomous change in expenditure.
4. If the equilibrium national income is disturbed by a change in autonomous expenditure, equilibrium will be re-established at the level at which the change in withdrawals equals the change in autonomous expenditure.
5. Some economic models assume that there is a trade-off between a change in output and resource utilization and a change in the price level.

Key terms

Equilibrium national income
Disequilibrium national income

Marginal propensity to spend
Marginal propensity to withdraw

Expenditure function

Multiplier

Autonomous expenditure

Optimum level of expenditure

Induced expenditure

Notes

1. Lipsey R G, *An Introduction to Positive Economics*, 6th edn. Weidenfeld and Nicolson, 1983, p. 518.
2. Lipsey, op. cit., p. 518.
3. An alternative approach would be to interpret C, G and I as referring to expenditure on domestic output only; this would be equivalent to deducting imports from these expenditure flows. Exports could then be added as a fourth flow. However, this approach complicates the diagrammatic presentation of the analysis.
4. The same principle would apply when an upward shift in the consumption function gave rise to induced investment spending. But it is, of course, conventional to deal with this response under the heading of the accelerator, not the multiplier.
5. It must again be remembered that we have assumed the change in exports and imports to be equal. As we noted above, if the change in imports had exceeded exports by 5, MPE would have been reduced to 0.75. The other way of looking at this is that this deficit in foreign trade would represent a third form of withdrawal from the circular flow. Total withdrawals would then be 25, and the MPW 0.25. Incidentally, in practice the multiplier has a much lower value than in this hypothetical example.
6. Keynes J M, *The General Theory of Employment, Interest and Money*. Macmillan, 1936.

Essay questions

1. Define equilibrium national income and discuss the factors which might cause the equilibrium level of national income to change.
2. Explain how equilibrium is re-established when planned expenditure in a given period differs from national income in the previous period.
3. Draw a diagram to show an expenditure function and explain why it assumes that shape.
4. Distinguish between autonomous and induced expenditure and discuss the significance of the distinction.
5. Examine the significance of the multiplier in the determination of national income.
6. Discuss the relationships between consumption and investment.
7. Explain what you understand by the term 'the optimum level of expenditure'.

Exercises

18.1 (i) Calculate on the basis of the data in Table 18.1, the APC when national income is (a) £2,000m., (b) £8,000m.,

(ii) Calculate the MPC when national income is (a) £3,000m., (b) £6,000m.
(iii) What would be the equilibrium level of income in a closed economy with no government sector if investment were (a) zero, (b) £1,000m.?
(iv) Calculate the value of the multiplier.

Table 18.1
A hypothetical schedule of income and consumption

National income (£000m.)	Consumption (£000m.)
0	1.00
1	1.75
2	2.50
3	3.25
4	4.00
5	4.75
6	5.50
7	6.25
8	7.00
9	7.75

18.2 An investment project generates an additional 100 units of gross income, of which 80 per cent comprises income from employment and 20 per cent income from profits.

Tax is levied at the following rates:

On earned income	25%
On profits	50%
On expenditure (except imports)	20%

The MPC is two-thirds of disposable income. One-quarter of expenditure comprises imports (which are not subject to tax).

Companies distribute all their after-tax profits as dividends (not subject to further taxation).

(i) What proportion of the gross income derived from the initial investment is (a) paid as taxation, (b) saved, (c) spent on imports?
(ii) By how much will income eventually rise following the additional investment?
(iii) Describe in a few sentences why the operation of the accelerator might be expected to lead to a rise in income different from that calculated above.

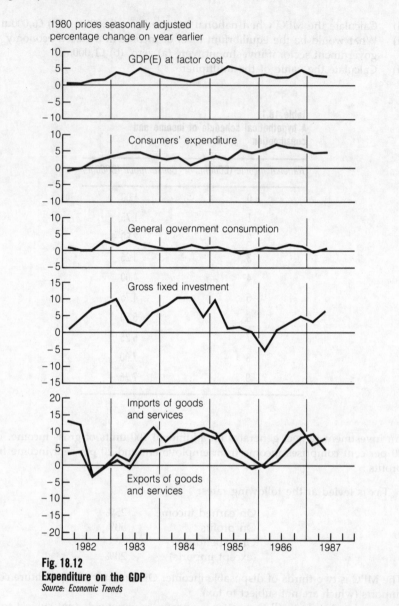

Fig. 18.12
Expenditure on the GDP
Source: *Economic Trends*

18.3 (i)   Explain the arithmetic relationships among the expenditure flows shown in Fig. 18.12.
     (ii) What factors might have caused the changes in these expenditure flows?
     (iii) Discuss the possible implications of these changes.

CHAPTER NINETEEN
Expenditure, Output, Employment and Prices

Introduction

In Chapter 18 we outlined in Keynes's argument that an increase in expenditure would cause an increase in prices and employment (and hence a fall in unemployment). In this chapter we evaluate this argument, and we also consider the counter-argument that an increase in expenditure would cause prices to increase, but would, at least in the long run, have no effect on output and employment.

The relationship between unemployment and inflation

Figure 19.1 shows that the lower the level of unemployment, the higher the rate of increase in prices. This relationship is similar to the one identified by A. W. Phillips in a study of the UK economy in the period 1861–1957.[1] Phillips actually studied the relationship between unem-

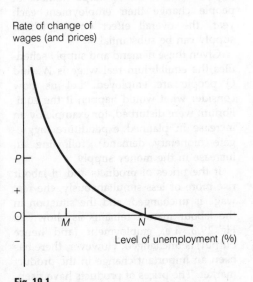

Fig. 19.1
The relationship between unemployment and inflation

ployment and the rate of change in the money wage rate; but it is argued that changes in the price of labour are eventually reflected in product prices.

For the relationship shown in Fig. 19.1 to be compatible with Keynes's analysis, outlined in Chapter 18, it would be necessary to show that an increase in money prices is associated with a fall in real wages (since for Keynes the fall in real wages provided the incentive to increase employment). It is not clear that this is so. Nevertheless, Phillips's findings were seized on by Keynesian economists as support for the view that governments were able to influence the level of unemployment via demand-management policies. Indeed, it used to be argued by some economists that the government could choose the level of unemployment, provided it was willing accept the associated rate of inflation. (Alternatively, it could choose the level of inflation if it accepted the associated level of unemployment.)

However, the idea of a stable and fairly precise relationship or trade-off between inflation and unemployment has gradually fallen into disrepute, for two reasons. Firstly, the empirical evidence has become less convincing. Phillips's results implied that at an unemployment rate of 5.5 per cent wage rates would be stable, whereas when unemployment reached this level during 1976, wage increases well into double figures were being registered. If in Fig. 19.2 we take N as indicating the unemployment rate of 5.5 per cent and P_1 as indicating the double-figure rate of wage increase, we can see that we are not on the curve PC_1, as postulated by Phillips, but on PC_2, i.e. the curve has shifted to the right.

Second, more credence is now given to the theoretical argument that the aggregate supply curve is vertical, at least in the

Rate of change of
wages (and prices)

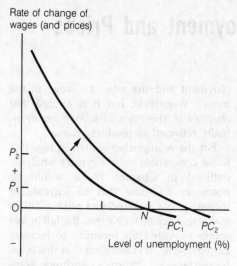

Fig. 19.2
A shifting Phillips curve

long run. (As we have seen, the Phillips
curve implies an upward-sloping supply
curve.)

A vertical supply curve

The explanation of the vertical supply
curve begins with an analysis of the
labour market.[2] In Fig. 19.3 the real wage
is measured on the vertical axis and the

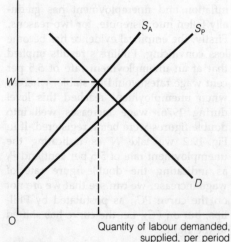

Fig. 19.3
Equilibrium real wage and employment

quantity of labour demanded and supplied
is measured on the horizontal axis. The
real wage reflects the relationship between
the price of labour and the price of goods
and services. A fall in the real wage means
that labour becomes relatively less expensive, either because money wage rates fall
or because the price of goods and services
increases. A fall in the real wage would
cause employers to offer more jobs, as
indicated by the downward-sloping
demand curve D.

In Fig. 19.3 S_A denotes the actual
supply of labour, i.e. the number of
people who, at a given point in time,
would be willing to accept work at a given
real wage; S_P denotes the potential supply
of labour. It can be seen that S_P is greater
than S_A. This is because there are some
people who would not be willing to accept
jobs *at this point in time* because they hope
to receive a better offer in future or
because they wish to extend their job
search before reaching a decision. Also
some people, in the process of changing
their employment, are 'in between' jobs
and so are part of the labour supply at
that particular time. Each person may be
out of the labour supply for only a few
days, but since a very large number of
people change their employment each
year, the overall effect on the labour
supply can be substantial.

Given these demand and supply schedules the equilibrium real wage is W, and
Q people are employed. Let us now
consider what would happen if the equilibrium were disturbed, for example by an
increase in planned expenditure (aggregate monetary demand), following an
increase in the money supply.

If the prices of products and of labour
rise more or less simultaneously, the real
wage is unchanged, and the situation in
the labour market remains as shown in
Fig. 19.3, i.e. employment (and hence
output) is unchanged. However, there has
been an important change in the product
market. The prices of products have risen,
from P_1 to P_2 in Fig. 19.4, even though
output is unchanged.

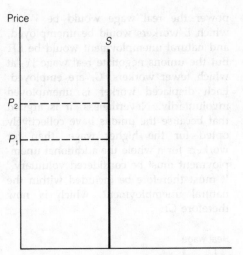

Fig. 19.4
A vertical supply curve

Short-run equilibrium in the labour market

In practice prices (of products and labour) may not react precisely as shown above, especially in the short run. In Fig. 19.5 W_1 is the initial equilibrium money wage rate and Q_E is the equilibrium output. (Associated with this output there would be an equilibrium level of employment, which

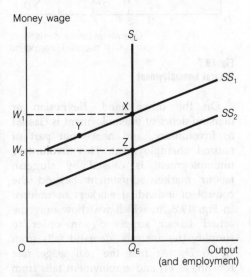

Fig. 19.5
Short-run equilibrium in the labour market

would denote the number of people currently willing to work at that wage rate.) Here S_L is the long-run supply curve and SS_1 is a short-run supply curve, indicating the change in output that would follow from a change in the wage rate.

The increase in output, along SS_1, is obtained by means of an increase in the number of hours worked by the existing labour force. The number of hours can be increased by overtime working, and reduced by short-time working. The basic wage rate is unchanged, but the actual wage rate is modified by the payment of premiums for overtime working, the introduction of bonuses, etc. Varying the number of hours worked by a given labour force is likely to be the preferred reaction on the part of employers and workers to a change in demand whose duration is not known.

Similarly, if demand fell, the initial reaction might be a move along SS_1 from X to Y, e.g. by the introduction of short-time working. However, if the fall in demand proves to be long-lasting employers would wish to make workers redundant (or not replace existing workers who left). Faced with this reduction in demand the money wage rate would eventually fall to W_2 and equilibrium would be re-established at Z on the long-run supply curve S_L. (Any subsequent short-run adjustment following a further change in demand would take place along SS_2.)

At this new equilibrium position, output (and employment) is again Q_E. Note that although the money wage rate has fallen the real wage is unchanged since product prices have fallen.

This change in product prices is shown in Fig. 19.6. With demand D_1 price is P_1 at which Q_1 is sold. When demand falls to D_2 output and price decline as indicated by the short-run supply curve SS_1. A temporary equilibrium is established with price P_2 and output Q_2. However, as demand continues at D_2 price declines further to P_3, at which output returns to Q_1.

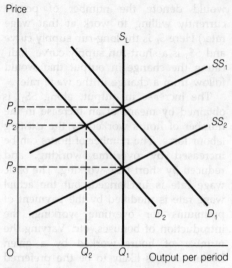

Fig. 19.6
Short-run equilibrium in the product market

The natural rate of unemployment

We have defined the equilibrium real wage as that at which all those people who would be willing to accept jobs at that wage are in employment. We have also shown that equilibrium may be reached when some people remain unemployed. This is known as natural unemployment; similarly the natural rate of unemployment is the rate of unemployment when the labour market is in equilibrium. (Alternative terms include the non-accelerating inflation rate of unemployment and the minimum sustainable rate of unemployment.)

We noted above that this unemployment includes individuals who are holding off in the hope of obtaining a better job offer and individuals who are 'in between' jobs. Such individuals are voluntarily unemployed at that point in time. It has also been argued that natural unemployment includes individuals who would be prepared to accept the additional jobs that employers would offer at a lower real wage but who are prevented from doing so by the action of trade unions.

In Fig. 19.7 S_A and S_P have the same meaning as in Fig. 19.3. Given the labour supply S_A, in the absence of trade union

power the real wage would be W_1 at which E workers would be unemployed, and natural unemployment would be EF. But the unions negotiate real wage W_2 at which fewer workers, G, are employed. Each displaced worker is unemployed involuntarily. Nevertheless, it is argued that because the unions have collectively opted for the higher wage, then for workers for a whole the additional unemployment must be considered voluntary.[3] It must therefore be included within the natural unemployment, which is now therefore GH.

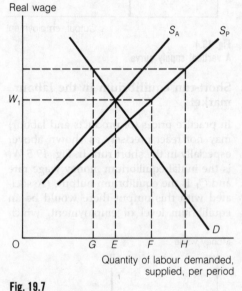

Fig. 19.7
Natural unemployment

On the other hand, Keynesian or demand-deficient unemployment is classed as involuntary, and hence not part of natural unemployment. This involuntary unemployment is caused by sluggish labour market adjustment beyond the control of individual workers or unions. In Fig. 19.8, in which we show only the actual labour supply S_A in order to simplify the analysis, demand falls from D_1 to D_2. At first the real wage rate remains at W_1 and employment falls from Q_1 to Q_3. Subsequently the real wage adjusts to W_2 and employment is partly

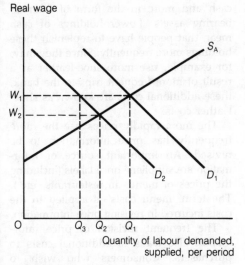

**Fig. 19.8
Involuntary unemployment**

restored to Q_2, Q_3Q_2 is a measure of involuntary or disequilibrium unemployment.

The two approaches compared

We have analysed the consequences of an increase in demand in a Keynesian framework, involving shifting Phillips curves, and a New Classical framework, involving the natural rate of unemployment and a vertical aggregate supply curve.

Neither approach leads to the conclusion, previously held by some economists, that the government can determine the level of unemployment by means of demand-management policies alone. There is general agreement that the power of the government is much more limited in this respect than was once believed.

However, considerable differences remain in the policy recommendations emerging from these two schools of thought. Some Keynesian economists advocate the use of demand-management policies combined with prices and incomes policies (see Ch. 23).

In circumstances in which a prices and incomes policy is judged to be politically unfeasible, many economists (especially of a Keynesian orientation) would advocate

selective reflation as a low-risk method of reducing unemployment. Government expenditure would be increased but the spending would be targeted so as to minimize the inflationary consequences.

Two targets have been proposed most frequently. The first is spending to provide training and at least temporary employment for the long-term unemployed. This spending is justified on the grounds that econometric analysis has not revealed any tendency for a fall in the number of long-term unemployed to be associated with a rise in the rate of wage increase and hence in inflation. (It is also argued that the long-term unemployed may become unemployable unless work is provided for them.)

The second form of selective spending that is often advocated is capital expenditure on the infrastructure – roads, houses, hospitals, etc. The justification for additional spending of this type in the mid 1980s was that spending had been substantially reduced in the first part of the 1980s so that the infrastructure had seriously deteriorated. A further argument was that 'a stitch in time saves nine'. For example minor road repairs undertaken this year might prevent the need for major repairs in the not too distant future. Finally, it was argued that there was substantial excess capacity in the construction industry, the result of the earlier· cutbacks.

New Classical economists, on the other hand, argue that demand-management policies are useful only for controlling inflation. They believe that the best hope for reducing unemployment is in policies designed to make more people willing to accept work at any given real wage, i.e. the aim of policy should be to shift the supply curve to the right. Figure 19.9 shows that if a shift of the supply curve to S_2 was accompanied by a higher level of demand D_2 the result would be a higher output Q_2 (and higher employment) and an unchanged price level P. These 'supply-side' policies are discussed at various points below, and especially in

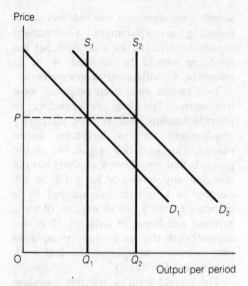

Fig. 19.9
Increased output and stable price

Chapter 24. It is sufficient to mention here that they range from reducing direct tax rates in order to reduce the disincentive to effort, to curbing the power of the trade unions.

The effects of inflation

If expectations of price increases become built into the wage-bargaining process an inflationary spiral may result. Such a situation is obviously very serious. However, even if the rate of inflation does not accelerate in this way, even if prices rise by a constant percentage each year, the consequences both internal and external may be undesirable. We start by examining the consequences internal to an economy.

The internal effects of inflation

The internal effects of inflation depend upon whether the rate of inflation is correctly anticipated. If it is correctly anticipated, three sets of economic effects can be identified.

If, as part of the inflationary process, all prices including the rate of interest rise, people will hold less of their wealth as

cash and more in the form of interest-bearing assets. Lower holdings of cash mean that people have to replenish these holdings more frequently. Since they may, for example, use more shoe-leather as a result of more frequent trips to the bank, these additional costs are known as shoe-leather costs.

The more rapidly prices rise the more frequently has price information to be revised. An important source of information are suppliers' price labels (including the prices of menus in restaurants, etc.). The term 'menu costs' is applied to the costs incurred in revising price information.

The frequent revision of price information also leads to additional costs to purchasers. Consumers who wish to ensure that they buy at the lowest cost can now rely less on their memory of the prices ruling in alternative outlets or sources, since these prices are more likely to have changed. This applies both to the housewife who has a choice of several retail outlets and the industrial purchaser who can choose from among several suppliers of components, raw materials, etc. Both have to incur additional costs in order to achieve a given level of price information. (Incidentally, surveys of attitudes and behaviour reveal that housewives may also incur substantial psychological costs when prices rise rapidly.)

The third set of effects arises because the institutional arrangements are such that not all prices (and incomes) change at the same rate. A failure of institutional arrangements to adapt to correctly anticipated inflation may be due simply to the fact that the adjustment mechanisms are inadequate (as may happen when inflation is at a higher rate than ever experienced previously), or because the arrangements that have been established apply differently to different groups in the community.

For example, inflation may cause some individuals to move into a higher tax bracket so that they pay a higher proportion of their income in tax than was intended by the government. (This process of fiscal drag is discussed in Ch. 20.) Workers in strong unions may be in a better position than other workers to protect their real incomes in times of high inflation. Public sector employees have sometimes found it difficult to protect their real incomes under inflationary conditions because their employer, the government, has the responsibility of trying to control inflation. Finally, the incomes of some groups of non-wage-earners, e.g. pensioners and students, may lag behind prices.

Imperfect adaptation

It is sometimes said that borrowers (debtors) benefit and lenders (creditors) suffer from inflation. The reasoning behind this statement can be easily illustrated by means of a simple example. If a man borrows from his bank £1,000 for a period of a year, and during this year prices rise by 10 per cent, then when the money is repaid it is 'worth' 10 per cent less than when it was borrowed, i.e. it will buy 10 per cent fewer goods.

The lender will, however, have suffered only in so far as he failed to anticipate and adjust to inflation. If he knew that prices were likely to rise by 10 per cent, then he should have charged the borrower a rate of interest, say 15 per cent, that took this into account. (If the borrower realized that the real rate would be reduced considerably by virtue of rising prices, he should be willing to pay a higher nominal rate.)

Of course people's expectations concerning the rate of inflation may prove to be inaccurate. But in principle this is just as likely to benefit lenders as borrowers, since inflation may be higher or lower than anticipated. The fact that lenders tended to suffer from the high rates of inflation in the 1970s was due less to errors in prediction than to a failure of the financial system to adjust to the higher rates. Lenders, and especially individuals with private savings, had to lend at negative real rates of interest because of a lack of better alternatives. The highest yielding savings medium for the private indi-

vidual in the mid 1970s was the index-linked bond (and its equivalents) issued by the government. Since the yield was tied to changes in the index of retail prices the real rate of interest was zero.

Although one can find numerous examples of groups who have suffered as a result of inflation, these internal effects are clearly very dependent upon institutional arrangements, e.g. retirement pensioners in the UK are now better protected than they were previously, by virtue of a government commitment to review pension rates twice a year in the light of changes in prices and earnings. It is possible in principle to evolve a set of arrangements whereby the disadvantageous internal effects of inflation are largely eliminated. However, inflation also has external effects which may be very damaging to a country's economy.

The external effects of inflation

If prices are rising at a higher rate in one country than in other countries the volume of that country's exports is likely to fall, and of its imports to increase. (This assumes that the prices of internationally traded products change in roughly the same way as the prices of all other products and also that these changes are not fully offset by movements in exchange rates.) It is also likely that the *value* of exports will fall in relation to the value of imports, although this will depend upon the elasticities of demand (see Ch. 17). Since trade in goods and services is an important element in our balance of payments, a deficit in this trade will tend to lead to a worsening of our balance of payments position. This tendency will be strengthened in so far as other international financial flows are influenced by the balance of our trade in goods and services. A country whose inflation rate is significantly above those of its main competitors does not find it easy to attract the funds of overseas investors.

Furthermore, even if the effect of inflation on the volume of trade and on the balance of payments was not adverse, the consequences for employment would still be unfavourable. A fall in the volume of exports implies less employment in export industries. Similarly a rise in the volume of imports implies less employment in domestic industries competing with these imports.

This implies that, in evaluating the trade-off between inflation and unemployment, the scales will be balanced more heavily against inflation than they would if only the internal effects were considered. This is not only because inflation may lead to balance of payments problems but also because, even in the absence of such problems, it can lead to a reduction in employment.

Favourable effects of inflation

Are there any considerations that we have not yet taken into account which might tilt the balance more in favour of inflation? It is sometimes claimed that mildly inflationary conditions are desirable since they provide a stimulus to producers to increase their capacity, without giving rise to serious problems of the kind discussed above.

Gently rising prices may indeed be preferable to falling prices accompanied by reductions in output and employment, as has occurred in some periods in the (rather distant) past. But will mild inflation in fact provide a stimulus to producers? It seems that this will occur only if rising prices are not accompanied by costs rising at the same rate. In this situation the stimulus is really a prospective increase in profitability. Moreover the other side of this coin is a prospective fall in the real income of wage-earners. It is therefore doubtful whether we can conclude that, overall, gently rising prices are to be preferred to stable prices.

Employment and unemployment

Table 19.1 shows the relationship between various measures of employment and unemployment, and indicates the trend in each measure. (Another extensively used measure is the civilian labour force, which is the working population minus those employed in HM Forces.)

The number of employees in employment fluctuated between 1965 and 1979, but since then has declined by almost a tenth. The number of self-employed has also fluctuated, but has risen strongly recently and now accounts for around one-tenth of total employment. The number in HM Forces declined until the 1980s when it bottomed out.

In summarizing these changes we can make a distinction between two sub-periods. First, between 1965 and 1979 the employed labour force showed relatively little change. However, because of the rise in the working population, unem-

Table 19.1
Employment and unemployment, Great Britain (000s, March)

	1965	1973	1979	1986
Employees in employment	23,058	22,657	23,045	21,137
Self-employed	1,700	2,023	1,903	2,643
HM Forces	424	367	315	320
Employed labour force	25,182	25,047	25,263	24,100
Unemployed	334	729	1,324	3,016
Working population	25,516	25,776	26,587	27,116

Source: Employment Gazette, Historical Supplement No. 2

ployment increased by around 1 million. Since 1979 the employed labour force has fallen by over 1 million (almost 5 per cent) and unemployment has risen by a further 1.7 million.

Figure 19.10 shows that the civilian labour force (the working population minus HM Forces) has grown steadily apart from a dip in 1981–83. This growth can be seen to be due entirely to a rise in the female labour force, a rise that is projected to continue.

Forty-five per cent of employees are now female. Forty-five per cent of women work part-time, and part-time workers now make up almost a quarter of the total employed labour force. On the other hand more than 750,000 people have two jobs. Of these the majority work less than ten hours a week in their second job, but a tenth work for twenty hours a week or more. Taken together these figures suggest that many of the additional jobs that have

been created in the last two decades may not have been filled by the main breadwinner in a family.

The industrial distribution of employment

Marked changes have occurred in the industrial distribution of employment, as shown by the sample of industries listed in Table 19.2. Job losses have occurred throughout the production and construction industries, the most severe losses

Table 19.2
Employees in employment, by industry

	March 1987 (1971 = 100)
Agriculture, forestry and fishing	72
Metal manufacturing	51
Mechanical engineering	65
Office machinery, electrical engineering, instruments	77
Motor vehicles and parts	49
Food, drink, tobacco	72
Textiles, leather, footwear, clothing	50
Paper products, printing, publishing	82
Construction	82
Wholesale distribution, repairs	125
Retail distribution	110
Hotels and catering	148
Transport	79
Banking, finance, insurance	164
Education	130
Medical and veterinary services	138
All employees	98

Source: Employment Gazette, Historical Supplement No. 2

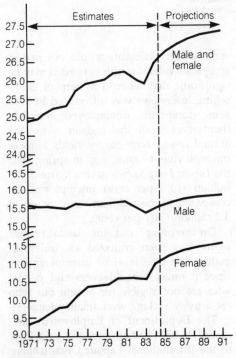

Fig. 19.10
Estimates and projections of the civilian labour force

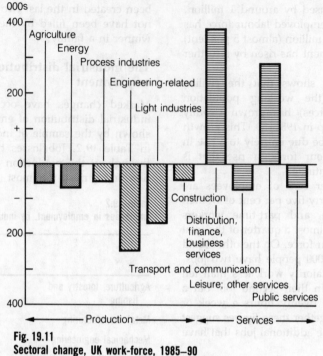

Fig. 19.11
Sectoral change, UK work-force, 1985–90
Source: *Occupation and Employment Trends to 1990* (Institute of
Manpower Studies for the Occupations Study Group, reported in
Financial Times, 13 June 1986).

being in metal manufacturing, motor
vehicles, and textiles, leather, footwear
and clothing. By contrast employment has
risen in the service sector, and especially
in hotels and catering, banking, finance
and insurance, medical and other services.
The result of these changes is that the
service industries now account for around
two-thirds of total employment, and
manufacturing for around a quarter.
Moreover, it seems likely that these trends
will continue (Fig. 19.11).

The measurement of unemployment

The monthly unemployment statistics
published by the Department of Employment comprise people who declare that
they are unemployed and available for
work, and claim (and receive) unemployment benefit. This method of defining or
measuring unemployment has been criticized as yielding too high a figure, since

some of the claimants would not in fact
accept job offers. In this context it may be
significant that when a system of counselling interviews was introduced in 1986
some long-term unemployed removed
themselves from the register. Also the
annual *Labour Force Survey* yields a lower
unemployment figure, e.g. in spring 1986
the *Labour Force Survey* gave a figure of 2.8
million (10.6 per cent) unemployed, as
compared to the claimant count figure of
3.2 million (11.7 per cent).

On the other hand, the claimant count
figure has been criticized as underesti-
mating the true level of unemployment,
since it omits school-leavers and people
who are not eligible for benefit but who
are actively seeking work (mainly females).

The Department of Employment estimated that if it had adopted the guidelines
of the International Labour Organization,
the unemployment figure yielded by its
1985 *Labour Force Survey* would have been
2.97 million instead of 2.82 million, i.e. an

additional 150,000. But even the higher figure would have been below that yielded by the claimant count.

The main forms of unemployment

Having explored some of the complexities of the measurement of unemployment, we now consider the main forms of unemployment. Although in practice there is some overlap, the classification is helpful in suggesting the most appropriate policy response.

Demand-deficient unemployment

This term denotes unemployment which results from a general deficiency in demand affecting virtually all industries. The policy response that would be advocated – at least by Keynesian economists – would be an expansionary fiscal and monetary policy. However, as we noted above, there has been an increasing awareness of the need to supplement such policies by other measures designed to increase employment.

A number of economists have claimed to have found statistical evidence of fairly regular cycles in economic activity. One aspect of this cyclical activity has been fairly regular changes in the level or rate of unemployment. (Some economists have suggested that the high unemployment of the 1980s is part of a fifty-year Kondratieff cycle, previous peaks having occured in the 1880s and the 1930s.) The term 'cyclical unemployment' is sometimes applied to this phenomenon.

Structural unemployment

Structural unemployment arises when there is a long-term decline in the demand for the products of a particular industry, and other industries are unable to absorb the redundant workers. If the declining industry is concentrated geographically, structural unemployment may be associated with regional unemployment.

General demand-management policies are clearly less appropriate here. Greater attention is given to methods of increasing labour mobility – retraining in new skills, providing information about alternative employment opportunities and offering financial assistance to unemployed workers who move to find employment. (Incentives are also offered to firms which set up or expand in regions of high unemployment, as shown in Ch. 12.)

Technological unemployment

Technological unemployment is due to the introduction of new machines or processes which reduce the need for workers of a given type. There is obviously an analogy with structural unemployment – although technological unemployment tends to be concentrated among particular occupations rather than industries – and similar policies are required to counteract the unemployment.

Frictional unemployment

Frictional unemployment arises when a worker leaves one job and finds another, not immediately, but after a short period of time. Although considered less serious than the previous types of unemployment, frictional unemployment may in some years constitute a significant proportion of the total. Consequently governments have tried to reduce frictional unemployment by providing better information concerning vacancies, and by extending worker placement services.

Seasonal unemployment

As the term suggests, seasonal unemployment occurs when the demand for workers is seasonal, as in tourism, catering and parts of agriculture. Governments have not taken any specific measures to deal with seasonal unemployment; nor is it clear that they should do so. Although the establishment of new firms would reduce the seasonal peaks of unemployment, it would, of course, also add to the pressure on the labour market at other times, to the disadvantage of employers in the 'seasonal' industries.

Long-term unemployment

Increasing attention is being given to proposals to provide work for the long-term unemployed (usually defined as those out of work for at least a year). Behind this concern is an increase in the proportion of the long-term unemployed from 25 per cent of the total in 1980 to 40 per cent in 1986. Moreover, it appears that the longer a person has been unemployed the longer he or she can expect to remain unemployed. A study published by the Department of Employment in 1986 found that 80 per cent of those becoming unemployed could expect to leave the jobless count within a year, but for those who had been unemployed for a year only 64 per cent could expect to leave the count within the next year. After two years the expectation fell to 39 per cent.

Unemployment among young people and non-whites

Another area of growing concern is the extremely high unemployment among young people, especially non-whites. In the mid 1980s the unemployment rate for those aged 16–19 was double that for older workers, and the rate for non-whites was double that for whites. An unemployment rate of 40 per cent was recorded for young non-whites.

The cost of unemployment

We discuss in Chapter 20 various policies that might be adopted in order to reduce unemployment. In evaluating these policies their cost should be set against the costs of unemployment. Some of these costs – boredom, a loss of aptitude for work, etc. – are extremely difficult to quantify. It is, however, possible to estimate the financial costs of unemployment to the government, and hence to taxpayers (although there is room for differences of interpretation). The main financial costs are unemployment and other benefits paid to the unemployed, and the loss of tax revenue due to their lower income and spending capacity.

A study by Professor Adrian Sinfield, commissioned by the BBC, concluded that in 1984/85 the cost per unemployed person was £6,300 (or some £20bn. a year in total). Other studies have produced other figures, but none is seriously out of line with Sinfield's estimates.[4]

Summary

1. An increase in expenditure may lead to an increase in the rate of inflation because producers increase their prices, either to earn higher profits or to compensate for increases in wages and other costs.
2. The Phillips curve indicates that the higher the level of unemployment the lower would be the rate of increase of wages (and hence of prices). However, it now appears that the trade-off between unemployment and inflation is much less stable than suggested by Phillips.
3. If, following an increase in expenditure, all prices (including the price of labour) rise to the same extent, the real wage will be unchanged. Consequently the supply of labour, and hence the level of output, will be unchanged. The only effect of the increased expenditure will be an increase in prices, i.e. the aggregate supply curve will be vertical.
4. Some economic models assume that the aggregate supply curve becomes vertical only when economic capacity (including labour) is fully utilized. On the other hand the New Classical model shows that the supply curve may become vertical when some labour remains unemployed.
5. According to the New Classical model the equilibrium real wage is the wage at which all the people who would be willing to accept jobs (at that wage) are

employed. The unemployment that exists at this wage is known as natural unemployment.

6. Keynesian or demand-deficient unemployment is classed as involuntary and hence not part of natural unemployment. This involuntary unemployment is caused by sluggish labour-market adjustment.

7. If inflation is correctly anticipated, people will hold less of their wealth as cash. The more rapid the rate of inflation the greater the need to revise price information. Even if inflation is correctly anticipated, institutional arrangements may not be sufficient to ensure that no one suffers because of the rise in prices.

8. If prices rise more rapidly in one country than in others, that country's volume of exports is likely to fall and of imports to rise, leading to a fall in employment. The balance of payments current account is likely to deteriorate.

9. Several forms of unemployment can be distinguished: demand-deficient, structural, technological, frictional and seasonal.

Key terms

Phillips curve
Vertical supply curve
Equilibrium real wage
Natural (rate of) unemployment
Voluntary unemployment

Demand-deficient unemployment
Involuntary unemployment
Effects of inflation
Imperfect adaptation

Notes

1. Phillips A W, The relation between unemployment and the rate of change of money wage rate in the United Kingdom, *Economica*, 1958.

2. The analysis in this section follows the classical model of the determination of prices (including the price of labour). This model has been refined in recent years by a group of economists known as the New Classical School, whose most prominent member in the UK is Professor A P Minford.

3. Begg D, Fischer S and Dornbusch R, *Economics*. McGraw-Hill, 1984, p. 595.

4. *Financial Times*, 13 June 1986.

Essay questions

1. Examine the possible relationships between the level of expenditure and the rate of inflation.

2. Explain how an increase in expenditure may affect (a) the price level, (b) the level of output.

3. Outline the relationship embodied in the Phillips curve and explain why this relationship appears to have changed in recent years.

4. Discuss the statement that inflation is undesirable only if it runs at a higher rate than in other countries.

5. 'Higher prices mean higher profits which encourage producers to expand. Inflation is, therefore, good for employment.' Discuss.

6. Why might one expect to find a trade-off between employment and inflation? What policies might be adopted in order to try to alter the terms of the trade-off?

7. Discuss the proposition that in the absence of government intervention the economy would be unlikely to reach a full employment equilibrium.
8. Explain what you understand by the term 'the natural rate of unemployment' and suggest what factors may influence its value.
9. Is full employment compatible with stable prices?
10. Explain how knowledge of the numerical values of the accelerator and the multiplier could assist the government in its formulation of economic policy.

Exercises

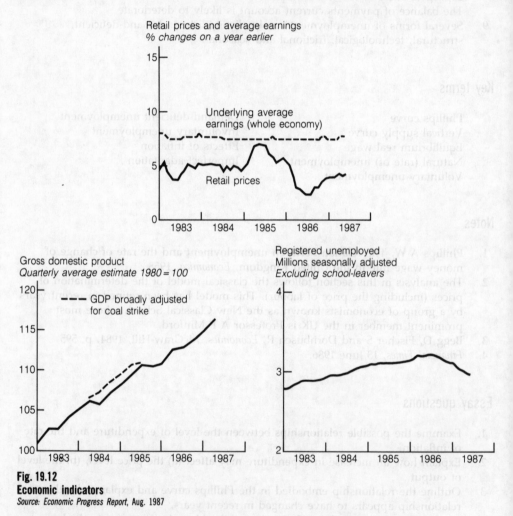

Fig. 19.12
Economic indicators
Source: Economic Progress Report, Aug. 1987

19.1 Discuss the relationships among the four series plotted in Fig. 19.12.
19.2 What factors might have caused the changes in the pattern of employment shown in Table 19.2?
19.3 How would you explain the employment projections shown in Fig. 19.11?
19.4 Table 19.3 originally appeared in *Lloyds Bank Economic Bulletin*.
   (i) Explain the relationships among the various items listed in the table.

Table 19.3
Changes in employment and unemployment 1979–87: Great Britain, seasonally adjusted

	March 1979	March 1983		March 1987		
	Level (000s)	Level (000s)	Change from March 1979 (000s)	Level (000s)	Change from	
					March 1983 (000s)	March 1979 (000s)
1. Manufacturing employees	7,129	5,485	−1,644	5,075	−410	−2,054
2. Other employees	15,413	15,044	−369	16,182	+1,138	+769
3. All employees	22,542	20,529	−2,013	21,257	+728	−1,285
4. Self-employed	1,843	2,147	+304	2,644	+497	+801
5. HM Forces	314	322	+8	320	−2	+6
6. Employed labour force	24,699	22,998	−1,701	24,221	+1,223	−478
7. Unemployed	1,199	2,828	+1,629	3,116	+288	+1,917
8. Working population	25,898	25,826	−72	27,337	+1,511	+1,439
9. Inactive population	6,672	7,474	+802	6,730	−744	+58
10. Working age population	32,570	33,300	+730	34,067	+767	+1,497
Activity rate = 8/10	79.5%	77.5%		80.2%		

1 + 2 = 3   3 + 4 + 5 = 6   6 + 7 = 8   8 + 9 = 10

Source: Employment Gazette, Historical Supplement No. 1, and May 1987, 'Labour force outlook for Great Britain'. Department of Employment press notice 156/87, 16 July, 1987

(ii)   What factors might explain the changes in the numbers of (a) manufacturing employees, (b) other employees, (c) self-employed?

Objective test questions: set 7

1.   An increase in investment expenditure when there is a high level of capacity utilization is most likely to:
 A   increase inflationary pressures in the long term without having any effect in the short term;
 B   increase inflationary pressures in the short term without having any effect in the long term;
 C   increase inflationary pressures in both the short and the long term;
 D   reduce inflationary pressures in the short term but increase them in the long term;
 E   increase inflationary pressures in the short term but reduce them in the long term.

2.   If the MPS is 0.6 the multiplier is:
 A   6;
 B   4;

C   2.5;
D   1.67;
E   none of the above

3. With an equilibrium national income of £10m. an autonomous increase in investment of £1m. occurs. If the new equilibrium national income is £14m., we can conclude that the MPS is:
A   0.25;
B   0.4;
C   0.6;
D   0.75;
E   none of the above.

4.

	Country X		Country Y	
	Food	*Machines*	*Food*	*Machines*
Price per unit	£1	£2	$2	$3

Given the above prices of food and machines in countries X and Y we can conclude that:
A   X will produce food only and Y will produce machines only;
B   X will produce machines only and Y will produce food only;
C   X will produce both food and machines, and Y will produce machines only;
D   both X and Y will produce both food and machines;
E   we can conclude nothing about the pattern of production because we do not know the exchange rate.

5. If the terms of trade change from 105 to 110 we can conclude that:
A   the total value of exports has risen;
B   the total value of imports has risen;
C   the total value of exports has risen more than the total value of imports;
D   the average price of imports has risen relative to the average price of exports;
E   none of the above.

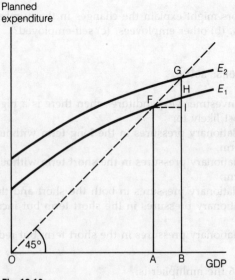

Fig. 19.13

Questions 6 and 7 relate to Fig. 19.13, in which an autonomous change in expenditure causes the expenditure function to shift from E_1 to E_2.

6. The value of the multiplier is:
    A   AB ÷ IG;
    B   AB ÷ HG;
    C   FG ÷ HG;
    D   HG ÷ BH;
    E   IF ÷ BI.

7. The level of induced expenditure is:
    A   FI;
    B   FG;
    C   IH;
    D   IG;
    E   HG.

8. The level of aggregate demand is likely to increase as a result of all of the following factors except:
    A   a reduction in taxation of company profits;
    B   a reduction in personal taxation;
    C   a reduction in tariff barriers;
    D   an increase in unemployment benefit;
    E   an increase in investment.

9.
	Export prices		Import prices	
	Year 1	*Year 2*	*Year 1*	*Year 2*
	100	120	100	80

The terms of trade in year 2 are:
    A   67;
    B   80;
    C   120;
    D   150;
    E   none of the above.

Questions 10 and 11 are based on the following table:

	£m.
Exports of goods	1,500
Imports of goods	2,000
Exports of services	1,000
Imports of services	500
Interest, profits and dividends received from abroad	750
Interest, profits and dividends paid abroad	300

10. The current balance (£m.) was:
    A   zero;
    B   450;
    C   950;
    D   1,450;
    E   2,500.

11. We can deduce from the above table that:
    1   the total currency flow was positive;

2   a surplus was earned on visible trade;
3   a surplus was earned on invisible trade.

12.   The volume of food and machines that could be produced by countries X and Y if all their resources were allocated to either one product or the other are as follows:

	Country X		Country Y	
	Food	or Machines	Food	or Machines
Situation				
1	5,000	8,000	10,000	16,000
2	6,000	6,000	6,000	8,000
3	2,000	4,000	4,000	2,000

In which of the above situations would the principle of comparative advantage suggest that economic welfare would be increased by international specialization and trade?

13.   The Phillips curve would be likely to shift outwards, i.e. away from the point of origin, if:
1   rates of unemployment benefit were reduced;
2   an improved system of notification of job vacancies was introduced;
3   in wage negotiations more weight was given than previously to past price increases.

14.   The opportunity cost ratios, as between food and machines, are as follows

	Country X		Country Y	
	Food	Machines	Food	Machines
	1	4	1	2

At which of the following exchange rates would international trade occur?
1   1 unit of food = 1 machine;
2   2 units of food = 9 machines;
3   3 units of food = 8 machines.

15.   The UK's balance of payments on current account would benefit from
1   an increase in the value of UK sales of cars in the USA;
2   an increase in spending by Japanese tourists in London;
3   the purchase of shares in a UK property company by Kuwait.

16.   The principle of comparative advantage states that a country should specialize in the production of any product which it can make more efficiently than any other country.
    Total production is increased if countries specialize in accordance with the principle of comparative advantage.

17.   The demand for sterling will fall following a rise in the prices of British exports.
    A rise in the price of British exports will cause the volume of exports to fall.

18.   Other things remaining equal the depreciation of a currency will cause a worsening of the terms of trade.
    The terms of trade is an index denoting the ratio of export prices to import prices.

19.   When planned expenditure in one period equals national income in the previous period, the national income is said to have reached the equilibrium level.
    When planned expenditure in one period equals national income in the previous period, there is no tendency for the level of national income to change.

20. The natural or normal rate of unemployment refers to the level of unemployment at which prices would be stable.

    If unemployment is below the natural or normal rate there is a tendency for the rate of inflation to accelerate.

True/false

1. Total production will increase following international specialization and trade provided that the opportunity cost ratios are the same in all countries.
2. The visible balance represents expenditure on the exports of goods minus expenditure on imports of goods.
3. The invisible balance represents expenditure on exports of goods and services minus expenditure on imports of goods and services.
4. Other things remaining equal the depreciation of a currency will cause an improvement in the terms of trade.
5. If in a given period national income equals total expenditure, national income is said to have reached an equilibrium level.
6. If planned expenditure in one period exceeds national income in the previous period the level of national income will tend to rise.
7. An autonomous change in expenditure is one that is caused by a prior change in income.
8. If the equilibrium level of national income is disturbed by an autonomous change in expenditure, equilibrium will be re-established when the change in withdrawals equals the autonomous change in expenditure.
9. The Phillips curve indicates the relationship between the level of unemployment and the change in wage levels.
10. The natural or normal rate of unemployment may be associated with any (constant) rate of change in prices.

CHAPTER TWENTY
Fiscal Policy

Introduction

Fiscal policy encompasses government expenditure on the one hand and taxation on the other. The balance between these two is very important, and is discussed at some length towards the end of the chapter. But first we examine the two elements separately, beginning with government expenditure.

The purposes of government expenditure

The provision of public goods

If we took a very long historical perspective, the provision of public, or collective consumption, goods would probably emerge as the primary function of government expenditure. The reasons for this were explained in Chapter 2.

The provision of other products at a price below the cost of production

This objective might be met by giving subsidies to private producers. But more commonly the products are supplied by public sector producers, e.g. medical services are provided in the UK by the National Health Service.

As noted in Chapter 9, an important purpose of subsidies is to encourage the consumption of products that are felt by the government to be desirable (so-called 'merit goods'). The policy is also likely to bring about a redistribution of real income. Subsidies are mainly financed out of taxation; therefore, given the existence of a system of progressive taxation (discussed below), poorer people will tend to obtain the greatest benefit from subsidies in relation to their share of the cost.

The redistribution of income

A more important method of redistributing income is by the use of transfer payments. Indeed these are called transfer payments because they transfer money from some members of the community, through taxation, to other members in the form of a range of benefits. The benefits include unemployment benefit, sickness benefit, retirement pensions and child benefits. Since they are paid without the recipient providing any service in exchange, they are excluded from the calculation of the national income, and therefore from government expenditure (G) as defined in our earlier analysis of income determination.

The forms of government expenditure

In order to evaluate the contribution of government expenditure to various objectives, including those listed above, it is necessary to examine its composition. Government expenditure can be classified in several alternative ways. We examine first the relative importance of broad categories of spending by general, i.e. central and local, government.

General government expenditure

Table 20.1 shows that over half of government spending comprises *expenditure on goods and services*. Within this category, by far the most important component is current purchases of goods and services, or *consumption*, the form of spending discussed in Chapter 15. The major items of current expenditure by central government are military defence and the National Health Service, while around half of the current spending of the local authorities is accounted for by education.

Table 20.1
UK general government expenditure (1986)

	£m.	%
Current expenditure on goods and services	76,882	47
Gross domestic fixed capital formation	7,296	4
Increase in value of stocks	104	1
Total expenditure on goods and services	84,282	52
Current grants and subsidies	59,245	37
Capital grants	3,117	2
Debt interest	17,022	10
Total transfers	79,384	49
Net lending and other expenditure	−1,475	−1
Total expenditure	162,191	100

Source: United Kingdom National Accounts

Of these three items, which together account for around one-third of total current expenditure, the first is a public good provided at zero price, while the other two comprise facilities and services provided at zero price or at prices below cost.

Spending on housing, transport and communication accounts for almost half of capital expenditure (*gross capital formation*). The rest is spent on education, health and social services, and other services such as swimming-pools, refuse collection, the police and fire services. This category of expenditure was discussed, along with other forms of investment, in Chapter 16.

As noted above, government expenditure on goods and services enters into the expenditure function (being designated G in the 45° diagram). By contrast *transfers* affect the income of recipients and only affect expenditure subsequently as and when they are spent. (If the recipients are households, transfers subsequently affect consumption (C), if producers, transfers affect investment spending (I).

Within total transfers, *grants and subsidies* have become increasingly important in recent years and now account for almost 40 per cent of total government

expenditure. Social security benefits – retirement pensions, unemployment benefits, income support, etc. – account for over two-thirds of total grants, suggesting that this category of expenditure is especially important in relation to the objective of the redistribution of income.

Redistribution of income may also be attained via subsidies. However, these are much smaller in total than grants. Moreover producers receive a much higher proportion of the total expenditure on subsidies than on grants, suggesting that an increase in economic efficiency may be a *relatively* more important objective of subsidies than of grants.

Debt interest, also treated as a transfer payment, accounts for 10 per cent of total government expenditure. This proportion increased in the 1970s and early 1980s, partly because of increases in government borrowing and partly because of the higher rates of interest on this borrowing. The increased interest payments led to concern about the 'growing burden of the national debt'. While higher interest payments obviously do impose a burden currently, the ratio of the national debt to GDP is lower now than it was in the

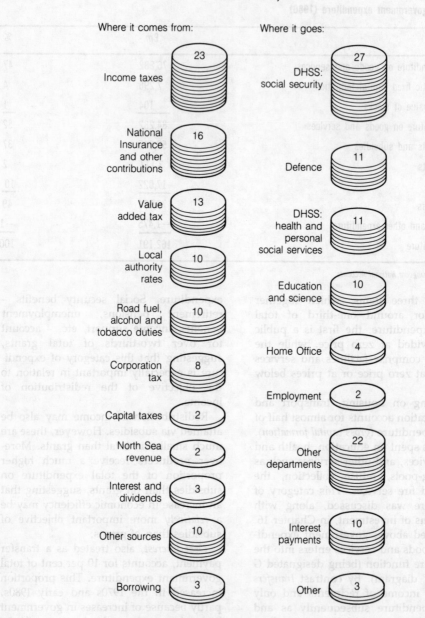

Pence in every £1

Where it comes from:

Income taxes	23
National Insurance and other contributions	16
Value added tax	13
Local authority rates	10
Road fuel, alcohol and tobacco duties	10
Corporation tax	8
Capital taxes	2
North Sea revenue	2
Interest and dividends	3
Other sources	10
Borrowing	3

Where it goes:

DHSS: social security	27
Defence	11
DHSS: health and personal social services	11
Education and science	10
Home Office	4
Employment	2
Other departments	22
Interest payments	10
Other	3

Cash totals of revenue and expenditure £173 bn.

Fig. 20.1
Government revenue and expenditure
Source: *Economic Progress Report Supplement*, March/April 1987

1960s. Indeed the current ratio is one of the lowest seen during the past 100 years. (It should be remembered that if money borrowed by the government is spent in ways that increase economic capacity and thus GDP, the borrowing need not result in a rise in the ratio of national debt to GDP.)

Public expenditure programmes

The final classification of government expenditure that we consider here is expenditure by programme (sometimes known as a functional analysis). Planned expenditure on the main programmes for 1987/88 is shown in Fig. 20.1.

By far the most important programme is social security where, as noted previously, a high proportion of expenditure comprises transfer payments (subsidies, grants and loans). Spending on social security has increased because of an increase in the number of pensioners and unemployed. Next in terms of expenditure come defence, health and personal social services and education. In these programmes, transfers payments are relatively unimportant, most expenditure comprising pay and other purchases of goods and services. As noted above, services under these headings are supplied at zero price or below cost.

Of the remaining programmes law and order has attracted increasing expenditure, but expenditure on others has recently declined. Particularly important here has been the decision of the Conservative government to reduce subsidies to producers and to some households. This has been reflected in a decline in the proportion of spending accounted for by industry, energy, trade and housing.

Government revenue

Figure 20.1 also gives a broad breakdown of the government's planned revenue for 1987/88. We discuss each item in turn, beginning with taxation.

The functions of taxation

To raise revenue

Given the overwhelming importance of taxation within the sum total of government receipts, the primary function of taxation must be to raise revenue. As we shall see below, this function influences both the level and structure of taxation.

Other important functions of taxation may include any of those given under the subheadings below.

To influence the level of total expenditure

The higher the level of taxation the lower the level of real expenditure is likely to be (unless the effects of higher taxation are balanced by higher government expenditure). In the case of direct taxation, i.e. taxes on income and wealth, expenditure is reduced simply because the disposable income of individuals and firms is reduced. When indirect taxes, i.e. taxes on expenditure, are imposed, *money* disposable income is unchanged. However, its real value falls because of the increase in prices, and this fall causes a fall in real expenditure.

To influence the pattern of expenditure

The quantities of various products purchased can be influenced by the imposition of high expenditure taxes on some products and low or zero taxes on others. The pattern of expenditure may also change due to changes in disposable income as a result of direct taxation of income and wealth.

To redistribute income and wealth

A system of differential expenditure taxes can be used – in conjunction with public expenditure – to redistribute real income. Redistribution in favour of poorer members of the community requires that low or zero taxes should be imposed on products that account for a greater proportion of the expenditure of poorer than of richer people. Conversely, higher taxes should be imposed on products that account for a greater proportion of the expenditure of richer than of poorer people.

More important in the UK, however, is redistribution by means of a progressive system of direct taxation. Direct taxation is said to be progressive when the *proportion* of income paid in tax increases as the level of income increases. (The opposite situation is known as a regressive system.) As we show below, direct taxation in the UK is progressive.

Measures which redistribute income will also, in the long term, influence the distribution of wealth. In addition the distribution of wealth may be directly affected by taxes on wealth or capital.

Having identified the main functions of taxation, let us now examine the main features of the structure of taxation in the UK.

The structure of taxation

Table 20.2 gives a breakdown of tax revenue. Social security contributions (for National Insurance, etc.) are included because they function in a very similar way to taxes; they reduce the disposable income of employees and constitute a cost to employers.

A broad distinction can be made between direct taxes (levied on income) and indirect taxes (levied on expenditure). Direct taxes are the most important source of revenue; if employees' National Insurance contributions, which are income-related, are included, direct taxes account for almost half of total tax revenue. Within this category personal income tax is the major item. Since the structure of personal taxation is progressive, as shown below, the tax structure as a whole is mildly progressive.

Indirect taxes account for about one-third of total tax revenue. By far the most important source is value added tax, a general expenditure tax, but substantial

Table 20.2
Government revenue from taxation and social security contributions (1986)

	£m.	%
Taxes on income		
Income tax	37,618	26.2
Petroleum revenue tax	2,703	1.9
Corporation tax	12,046	8.4
Other taxes on income	63	—
Total taxes on income	52,430	36.6
Taxes on capital	2,588	1.8
Taxes on expenditure		
Value added tax	22,724	15.9
Alcoholic drinks	4,240	3.0
Tobacco	4,643	3.2
Hydrocarbon oils	7,151	5.0
Customs/protective duties	1,280	0.9
Other customs and excise revenue	1,964	1.4
Motor vehicle duties	2,518	1.8
Other expenditure taxes	2,646	1.8
Total taxes on expenditure	47,166	32.9
Social security contributions	26,067	18.2
Local authority rates	15,107	10.5
Total	143,358	100

Source: United Kingdom National Accounts

sums are also raised from additional taxes levied on three groups of products, alcoholic drinks, tobacco and oils and petrol.

Of the remaining taxes the most important is local authority rates. However, this source has tended to decline as a proportion of total tax revenue, and of the total receipts of the local authorities (see below).

Having outlined the main features of the tax structure we now examine in greater detail the major forms of taxation, beginning with direct taxation (taxes on income).

Direct taxation

The most important form of direct taxation is personal income taxation. As can be seen from Table 20.2, income tax accounts for more than a quarter of total tax revenue.

Income tax

The current rates of income tax are 25 per cent on the first £19,300 of taxable income (i.e. gross income minus allowances) and 40 per cent on any further taxable income. The higher rate of tax on higher incomes, and allowances which mean that the lowest income group pays no tax, together create a progressive system of income taxation.

With a given scale of allowances and tax rates, an increase in prices can cause an increase in the burden of taxation (a process known as 'fiscal drag'). To take a simple example, consider a situation in which all prices and incomes increase by the same percentage. Real pre-tax incomes are unchanged. However, if the increase in nominal incomes causes the recipients to move to higher tax brackets, i.e. to pay a higher proportion of their income in tax, the real post-tax income falls. (This effect is compounded if, as a result of an increase in nominal income, some recipients cease to qualify for certain benefits, such as free school meals. This is an example of the so-called 'poverty trap'.)

To remedy this consequence of inflation tax allowances would need to be revalued in line with changes in the retail price index. Adjustments are made automatically each year unless overridden by Parliament at the Chancellor's behest. The provision was first overridden in 1981, and it was estimated that pegging the allowances would increase tax payments by £2.5bn. in 1981/82. This can be taken as a measure of fiscal drag in that financial year.

The effect on revenue of a change in personal taxation

In most instances an increase in the rates of personal taxation will lead to an increase in revenue. To understand why on occasions this may *not* be so, we need to realize (a) that for many people, earning a given income is not an end in itself but a means to obtaining a certain standard of living, and (b) that leisure is also an important element in the standard of living.

Each person has some idea of the amount of leisure he is prepared to give up in order to increase his income and hence his consumption. We can represent the preferences of any individual by means of an indifference curve. In Fig. 20.2 we have two curves representing the preference of two different individuals. Each curve indicates combinations of leisure and consumption with which that individual would be equally satisfied (is indifferent between). Line AB indicates the combinations of leisure and consumption that might be available to an individual. The two extremes are indicated by points A and B. If a person were willing to forgo all his leisure, his consumption would be Y. At the other extreme an unemployed man, drawing unemployment benefit, could consume only X.

Let us consider the effect of a change in taxation on an individual who chooses

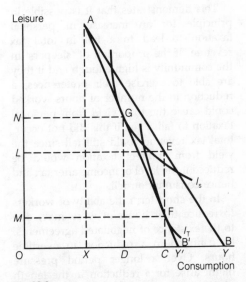

Fig. 20.2
The effect of a change in taxation on the choice between leisure and consumption

point E, representing a combination of *C* consumption and *L* leisure. The imposition of a higher rate of direct taxation means a change in the combination of consumption and leisure available to this individual. For any given level of work (and thus for any given level of leisure), his disposable income, and therefore his consumption, is less than previously. The curves AB pivots to AB', the maximum possible consumption now being Y'.

The effect of this change will depend upon the individual's preferences as between consumption and leisure. Some members of the community may be willing to work longer hours than before in order to maintain their consumption. A typical indifference curve of such a 'thruster' is I_T. This person's new equilibrium position is where I_T is tangential to AB', i.e. at point F, representing an unchanged level of consumption *C*, but a reduction is leisure to *M*.

On the other hand, since the rewards from work have been reduced some people may decide to work less; I_S would be the indifference curve of such a 'sleeper'. At his new equilibrium position G (where I_S is tangential to AB'), his consumption is reduced to *D*, but he enjoys more leisure, *N*.[1]

This demonstrates that it is possible in principle for an increase in personal taxation to lead to a fall in total tax revenue. If the proportion of 'sleepers' in the community is high enough and if they are able to exercise their preferences, a reduction in the number of hours worked could cause the total yield from personal taxation to fall. Even if this did not occur, total tax revenue could still fall since the yield from indirect taxation would be reduced if the level of income after tax and hence consumption fell.

In the short term the ability of workers to reduce their hours of work may, due to the existence of negotiated agreements, be confined to a reduction in overtime hours. Over a longer period pressure might arise for a reduction in the length of the standard working week. In addition

some people might leave the work-force entirely, either by emigrating or by retiring earlier than they would otherwise have done. (On the other hand there might be an increase in the number of housewives seeking work from the households of thrusters.) Finally, as the rewards for working decline, and more specifically as point Y in Fig. 20.2 moves closer to X, there will be less incentive for people drawing unemployment benefit to seek work yielding a (taxable) income.

The Laffer curve

Taking as his starting-point the alleged disincentive effect of high marginal tax rates, Professor A. Laffer suggested that the relationship between the tax rate and tax revenue would be as shown in Fig. 20.3. If we apply this to direct taxes, revenue will obviously be zero at a zero tax rate. Revenue will also be zero at a tax rate of 100 per cent unless work itself has a positive value. (In practice, of course, these two extreme points are not observed.)

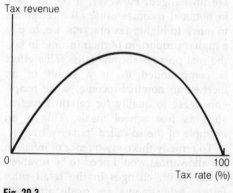

Fig. 20.3
A Laffer curve

Early studies found little evidence that high tax rates have a disincentive effect.[2] However, Professor Lindsey has demonstrated that in the USA, although tax cuts as a whole had resulted in reduced revenues, the cut in the top rate of tax from 70 to 50 per cent in 1982 had caused the revenues from the top tax bracket to increase substantially. Under the previous, higher, rate about $34bn. would have been paid in tax by high-income earners in 1984, whereas in fact $42bn. was paid. About one-third of the increase was estimated to have resulted from additional work (the pure supply-side response, discussed in Ch. 24), the rest from reduced tax avoidance.

In the UK the percentage of tax revenue contributed by the top 1 per cent of taxpayers increased from 11 per cent in 1978/79 to 12 per cent in 1985/86, despite a cut in the maximum tax rate from 83 to 60 per cent. The contribution of the top 10 per cent of taxpayers increased from 34 to 37 per cent.

Other effects of personal taxation

We have explored the effect of an increase in personal taxation on tax revenue in some detail because the analysis also throws light on other possible effects of taxation. In so far as high rates of taxation deter people from working as hard, or cause them to leave the work-force completely, the overall level of economic efficiency is likely to suffer. This is perhaps especially likely to occur if workers have skills that are in demand in other countries which can offer higher real rewards. The emigration of senior managers and of professional people such as doctors would be good examples.

Inheritance tax

The main objective of this tax, which replaced capital transfer tax in 1986, is to redistribute wealth and income by taxing money left by people at death and gifts made up to seven years before death. It has been pointed out that the term 'inheritance tax' is rather misleading. It suggests that tax is levied on the amount inherited by one person, whereas in fact it is levied on the total amount left by the donor. (The difference is, of course, that several people may share in the wealth left by one person.) Previous terms, capital transfer tax or estate duty, would be more meaningful descriptions. A tax of 40 per cent is levied on all transfers above the minimum threshold. This threshold, which is indexable, was set at £110,000 in the 1988 budget.

Corporation tax

Companies pay direct taxes in the form of corporation tax. This is levied on a sliding scale, ranging from 35 per cent on profits above £500,000 to 25 per cent on profits below £100,000. The taxation of company income can again be justified in terms of revenue raising, although the yield is much less than from income tax. There may also be an element of income redistribution if the average shareholder has a higher income than the average non-shareholder. (Such differences in income have to some extent been eroded by the increase in the proportion of shares held by pension and insurance funds, discussed in Ch. 16.)

Another very important factor to be borne in mind when assessing the rate of company taxation is the need of companies to retain sufficient funds, after the payment of taxes, to finance investment. As we showed in Chapter 16 a substantial proportion of companies' capital spending is financed from retained earnings. Consequently a fall in retained earnings – whether due to a fall in pre-tax profits or to an increase in the rate of taxation – may reduce the rate of growth of productive capacity.

Since 1984 the rate of corporation tax has been reduced in stages from 52 to 35 per cent (and the 'small company rate' to 25 per cent). This change obviously increased post-tax profitability. On the other hand there has also been a change from a system of 100 per cent initial allowances, allowing the entire cost of plant and machinery to be offset against tax in its year of purchase, to 25 per cent reducing-balance writing down allowances (4 per cent for industrial buildings). Moreover the previous concession, whereby companies were not taxed on profits arising from stock appreciation, was withdrawn. These changes tended to cancel out the benefit of the lower rate of tax. (The precise balance depends upon the form of investment and the way in which it is financed.[3])

Higher profitability facilitates higher investment. This in turn may lead to faster economic growth, although the link is by no means automatic. If there *is* a link, the fact that rates of return in the UK have been below those in many other industrialized countries for much of the postwar period, may help to explain the UK's relatively low rate of growth. Similarly, the recent improvement in profitability in the UK might have contributed to the increased rate of growth.

Capital gains tax

A capital gain is the difference between the price paid for an asset (e.g. shares) and the price at which that asset is sold. Capital gains are taxed at the individual's marginal rate of income tax, 25 or 40 per cent as appropriate. Since the tax was introduced several steps have been taken to reduce the burden of the tax and hence encourage financial investment.

First, the first £5,000 (indexable) of gains realized in any year are exempt from taxation. Second, tax is paid on the gains expressed in real terms, i.e. after allowing for inflation. Third, capital gains on shares bought through the BES or personal equity plans are, under certain conditions, exempt from tax.

Indirect taxation: taxes on expenditure

The current structure of indirect taxation in the UK, outlined in Table 20.2 and already discussed briefly, is examined in more detail below. But we first discuss three of the functions of taxation listed above which help to explain this structure.

To raise revenue
Since raising revenue is the primary purpose of taxation, one might conclude

that the heaviest taxes should be imposed on the products with the lowest demand elasticities. A low elasticity implies that the quantity demanded would decline only slightly in response to the increase in price that would follow the imposition of an indirect tax. Conversely the lightest taxes should be imposed on products with a high elasticity of demand, since for these products a much greater fall in the quantity demanded would follow a price rise.

This is illustrated in Fig. 20.4, where we assume that producers are willing to supply an unlimited quantity of each of two products A and B at price P. The demand curves for the two products are D_A and D_B respectively. For the sake of simplicity we assume that for each product the initial equilibrium position is X, Q of each product being bought at price P.

The government now imposes an indirect tax of PC per unit on both products. At the higher price, C, the quantity bought of A falls only slightly to R, and the tax revenue is $PCBA$. The demand for B is, however, far more elastic. The quan-

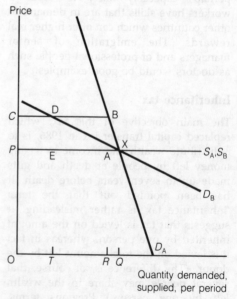

Price

Fig. 20.4
Elasticity of demand and tax revenue

tity bought falls to T and the tax revenue is $PCDE$. This demonstrates the fact that for a given rate of tax, the less elastic the demand the greater will be the tax revenue.

Indeed there may be a point at which an increase in the tax rate on a product with a highly elastic demand would cause a decline in tax revenue. In Fig. 20.5, Q is bought at price P. After the imposition of a tax per unit of PC, R is bought and tax revenue is $PCEF$. However, a further increase in the tax rate to PD would lead to a reduction in the quantity bought to T, and to a fall in the tax revenue ($PDHI < PCEF$).

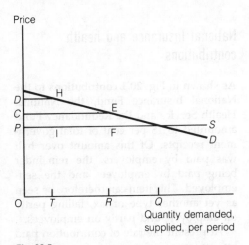

Fig. 20.5
A fall in tax revenue following an increase in the tax rate

To redistribute real income
When one considers the products whose price elasticity of demand is relatively low, one finds that many are so-called necessary goods on which low-income groups spend a higher proportion of their income than high-income groups, e.g. basic foodstuffs, public transport, fuel. Consequently the imposition of high rates of taxation on these products would have a regressive effect. In other words, the objectives of revenue raising and the redistribution of real income are in conflict. (We show

below that the system of indirect taxation in the UK is mildly regressive.)

To influence the pattern of expenditure
Indirect taxation offers considerable scope for influencing the pattern of expenditure, and differential rates of taxation can usually be at least partly explained in these terms. For example, high rates of taxes have been imposed on products considered to be dangerous to health, those having a high import content, etc. However, a proliferation of rates adds to the cost of tax collection, both on the part of the government department collecting the taxes and the firms responsible for making payment. Consequently there has been a tendency in the UK to reduce the number of tax rates.

Having identified the major influences on the structure of indirect taxation, let us now examine that structure in the UK.

The structure of indirect taxation

The main general expenditure tax imposed by the central government is *value added tax* (VAT), which accounts for some 45 per cent of revenue from expenditure taxes. The standard rate of tax is 15 per cent. However, a range of products, including foodstuffs, gas, electricity and public transport services are zero-rated. Petrol is taxed at 25 per cent, and cars bear an additional tax. Overall the structure of VAT appears to be influenced by a desire not to have a regressive effect rather than by an objective of maximizing revenue; at present the structure is slightly progressive.

As shown in Table 20.2 more than a third of the total revenue from expenditure taxes is obtained from duties on three groups of products: alcoholic drinks, tobacco, and hydrocarbon oils (petrol, diesel oil, etc.). The main purpose of these taxes is undoubtedly revenue maximization – experience suggests that their demand elasticities have been fairly low.

There may be a further justification for taxing these products heavily. Their consumption gives rise to social costs –

road accidents, pollution, a need for more hospital beds, etc. If the taxes deter consumption these social costs will thereby be reduced.

Value added tax is an *ad valorem* tax, i.e. for any given rate of tax the amount of tax paid changes in line with the price of the product. Consequently in inflationary conditions the tax yield automatically increases. By contrast most other customs and excise duties are specific, i.e. the tax is levied at a given absolute rate per unit quantity sold, e.g. £1 per gallon of petrol. The yield from specific duties does not increase as a result of inflation. Indeed the real burden of such taxes falls with infla-tion – the tax accounts for a smaller proportion of the selling price. Conse-quently in order to maintain a constant real burden of taxation the rates of specific taxes should be adjusted upwards. This contrasts with the need to reduce nominal rates of direct taxes (assuming direct taxation to be progressive) in order to maintain a constant real burden of taxation.

The final major form of taxation is *local authority rates*, which accounts for 10 per cent of total tax revenue. The rates paid by any household or business depend partly upon the rateable value of the premises and partly upon the rate poun-dage levied in the local authority area in which the premises are situated. Rates can be seen as a tax on assets or wealth (houses, offices, etc.). But they are also similar to an expenditure tax in that there is a rough relationship between the value of the local authority services 'consumed' and the rateable value, and so, for any given area, between 'consumption' and the amount paid in rates.

However, this relationship is so rough that numerous suggestions have been made for alternative methods of financing local authorities. The increasing reliance of local authorities on assistance from the central government has also been ques-tioned. In view of the increasing attention being given to these questions, the expenditure and finance of the local authorities are discussed in a separate section below.

North Sea tax revenues

The revenues arising from the extraction and sale of North Sea oil and gas have received individual treatment in terms of taxation. The basic justification for separate treatment is that oil and gas reserves are natural assets and that part of the revenue accruing from their development should accrue to the nation. Consequently the government obtains revenue from the petroleum revenue tax, levied at a rate of 75 per cent, as well as from corporation tax.

National Insurance and health contributions

As shown in Fig. 20.1 contributions to the National Insurance Fund, the National Health Service and the Redundancy Fund amounted to 18 per cent of total govern-ment receipts. Of this amount over half was paid by employers, the remainder being paid by employees and the self-employed. This item can therefore be seen as yet another type of tax, falling partly on employers and partly on employees.

At present the rate of contribution paid by employees is 5 per cent of weekly earn-ings of £41 rising to 9 per cent of all weekly earnings from £155 to £305, the upper limit for contributions. Employers pay a similar percentage, except that it rises to a maximum of 10.45 per cent.

Taking one year with another these contributions are roughly balanced by National Insurance benefits. However, this does not mean that the overall econ-omic effect is neutral. The contributions increase the costs of labour and so encourage employers to substitute other inputs and especially, perhaps, machinery for labour. On the other side the employee's share of the contribution may have some slight effect on the supply of labour, especially now that the contribution includes an income-related element. This element in effect raises the marginal rates of personal taxation, a process whose dangers were outlined above.

Rent, interest and dividends

This is a miscellaneous group of receipts, emanating from several sources. Most of the 'rent' item refers to the imputed rent income in respect of houses owned by the local authorities. The bulk of the 'interest and dividends' were received by the central government, mainly in respect of loans made to the nationalized industries. Finally a small surplus was earned on the trading activities of the local authorities, e.g. municipal markets.

Borrowing

It was expected that revenue from the above sources in 1987/88 would be 3 per cent less than expenditure and that the shortfall would have to be met by borrowing. (In fact revenue exceeded expenditure by 3 per cent.) The significance of government borrowing is discussed at length in Chapter 21.

The balance between government expenditure and taxation

Having examined government expenditure and taxation separately, we now discuss the significance of the balance between them. We do this first with respect to the overall level of economic activity. It is useful to begin by referring to the 45° diagram introduced during our discussion of total expenditure in Chapter 18. In Fig. 20.6 the expenditure function $C + I$ indicates what planned expenditure would be, at various levels of national income, in the absence of government expenditure and taxation.

Government spending on goods and services (G) shifts the expenditure func-

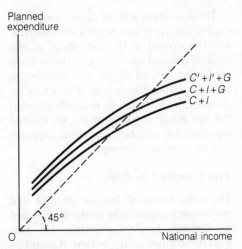

Planned expenditure

$C' + I' + G$
$C + I + G$
$C + I$

45°

O

National income

Fig. 20.6
Government spending and total expenditure

tion upwards to $C + I + G$, having a direct effect on expenditure. Transfer payments, on the other hand, do not have a direct effect on expenditure. However, they do have an indirect effect. They increase the real disposable income of individuals and/or firms, and therefore increase the propensity to spend, i.e. the amount spent from any given level of national income. This is shown in Fig. 20.6 by a further upward shift of the expenditure function to $C' + I' + G$.

The precise effect of a given level of transfer payments depends, of course, upon their composition. Grants to individuals will increase consumption spending and grants to firms investment spending. The effect of a subsidy may be more complicated. If it results in lower prices, real consumption will increase. In addition it may lead to increased company profits and therefore, via the liquidity effect, to higher investment spending.

Taxation has the reverse effects. By reducing the disposable income of individuals and firms, direct taxation (and we can include here National Insurance contributions) reduces consumption and investment. Moreover indirect taxation, although not affecting disposable income, will via higher prices reduce the level of real expenditure.

These changes will, of course, cause the expenditure function to shift downwards. What is crucial is the net effect on the expenditure function of these two conflicting sets of forces, one tending to increase expenditure and the other to decrease it. In order to understand what the net effect is likely to be, let us first examine the situation in which expenditure and taxation are equal.

The balanced budget

The term 'balanced budget' implies that government expenditure is exactly matched by taxation (widely defined), i.e. that government borrowing is zero. It might be felt that a balanced budget would leave total expenditure unchanged, the forces tending to increase expenditure being exactly offset by those tending to decrease it. However, this will be so only if the MPC or the MPE of taxpayers equals the MPE of the government, including the recipients of transfer payments.

This situation is illustrated in Table 20.3, where we assume that government expenditure consists entirely of transfer payments and that the MPE of the recipients is 0.85. Since this equals the MPE of the taxpayers, the net effect on total expenditure is zero.

However, it is extremely unlikely that MPEs will be equal. Since many of the recipients have incomes below average, e.g. the unemployed, retirement pensioners, their MPE is likely to be well above average. So if in the above example the average MPE of recipients were 0.95, the initial impact of the balanced budget

Table 20.3
A balanced budget: equal propensities to spend

	£m.
Amount paid in taxation	100
Reduction in expenditure of taxpayers	85
Government expenditure (transfer payments)	100
Expenditure of recipients of transfer payments	85

would be an increase in total expenditure of £10m. (£95 − 85m.).

Furthermore, we have seen that in practice more than one-half of government expenditure comprises spending on goods and services. This can be seen as analogous to an MPE of 1.0. Consequently the overall 'MPE of the government' is likely to be very high, say 0.98. In the above example this would imply, for a balanced budget of £100m., an initial increase in expenditure of £13m. (£98 − 85m.). Moreover, this would subsequently be extended by the operation of the multiplier and accelerator. Consequently the effect of a balanced budget will almost certainly be expansionary. (As noted in Ch. 19, some economists believe that fiscal policy can induce an expansion of output in the short term only.)

A budget surplus

It is sometimes claimed that a budget surplus, where revenue from taxation exceeds government expenditure, will cause the economy to contract. However, the analysis of the previous section suggests that this need not be so. Since the MPE of the government exceeds that of taxpayers, a modest budget surplus may leave total expenditure unchanged. However, there clearly must come a point at which the surplus is so great as to cause total expenditure to fall, and the economy to contract.

A budget deficit

If a balanced budget is likely to be expansionary, then clearly a budget deficit, where government expenditure exceeds revenue from taxation, is even more likely to be expansionary, at least in the short term.

Government expenditure, taxation and the redistribution of income

Figure 20.7 shows the composition of final income, while the combined effect on the distribution of income of taxation and government expenditure is shown in

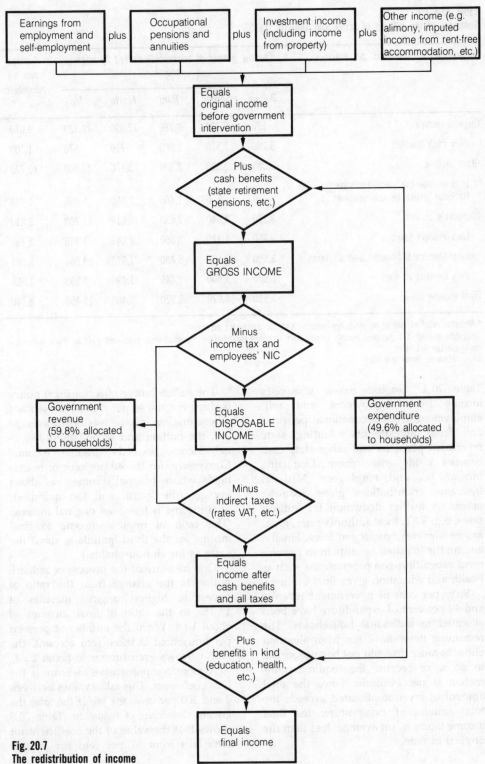

Fig. 20.7
The redistribution of income
Source: Economic Trends, July 1987

Table 20.4
Summary of the effects of taxes and benefits, 1985

Average per household (£ per year)	Quintile groups of households ranked by original income					Average over all households
	Bottom	Second	Third	Fourth	Top	
Original income	120	2,720	7,780	12,390	22,320	9,070
Plus cash benefits	3,260	2,570	1,200	790	670	1,700
Gross income	3,380	5,300	8,980	13,170	23,000	10,770
Less income tax* and employees' National Insurance contributions	−10†	360	1,460	2,560	5,300	1,930
Disposable income	3,390	4,940	7,530	10,610	17,700	8,830
Less indirect taxes	790	1,420	2,050	2,640	3,840	2,150
Income after cash benefits and all taxes	2,590	3,520	5,480	7,970	13,860	6,680
Plus benefits in kind	1,370	1,400	1,440	1,490	1,590	1,460
Final income	3,960	4,920	6,920	9,460	15,450	8,140

* After tax relief at source on mortgage interest and life assurance premiums.
† Negative average tax payment results largely from imputed tax relief on life assurance premiums paid by those with nil or negligible tax liabilities.
Source: Economic Trends, July 1987

Table 20.4. *Original income* comprises income from employment and self-employment, from occupational pensions and from investments. Adding state retirement pensions and other state cash benefits yields *gross income*. Deducting income tax and employees' National Insurance contributions gives *disposable income*. A further deduction for indirect taxes, e.g. VAT, local authority rates, gives *income after cash benefits and taxes*. Finally, adding the imputed benefits from government expenditure on programmes such as health and education gives final income.

Sixty per cent of government revenue and 49 per cent of expenditure have been allocated to individual households. The remaining items have not been allocated either because it would not be appropriate to do so or because the required information is not available. Since the total amount of revenue allocated exceeds the total amount of expenditure, the final income figure is, on average, less than original income.

The redistributive effect of fiscal policy is clear. For the 40 per cent of households whose original income was below average (i.e. the bottom and second quintiles) final income exceeds original income. Conversely, for the 40 per cent of households whose original income was above average (the fourth and top quintiles), final income is less than original income. (The ratio of original income to final income for the third quintile is about the same as for all households.)

One measure of the process of redistribution is the change from the ratio of lowest to highest original incomes of 1 : 186 to the ratio of final incomes of about 1 : 4. When the number of persons per household is taken into account, the ratio narrows even further to about 1 : 2.

A more comprehensive measure is the Gini coefficient. This takes values between 0 and 100 per cent; the *higher the value* the greater the *degree of inequality*. Table 20.5 shows that the value of the coefficient for 1985 falls from 51 per cent for original

Table 20.5
Distribution of household income

	Gini coefficient (%)	
	1975	*1985*
Original income	43	51
Gross income	35	38
Disposable income	32	35
Income after cash benefits and taxes	33	38
Final income	31	34

Source: Economic Trends, July 1987

income to 34 per cent for final income. A comparison of the two columns reveals that the distribution of original and final income became more unequal during the decade.

Table 20.5 also shows that the greatest contribution to the reduction in inequality is made by cash benefits (which convert original income into gross income). Most cash benefits help the aged, the sick and disabled and others on low incomes.

On the other hand the effect of indirect taxes is to increase slightly the degree of inequality. On the whole higher-income households pay a slightly lower proportion of their disposable income in expenditure taxes than lower-income households. In other words the system of indirect taxation is mildly regressive.

Changes in the distribution of income

Changes in taxation and government policy can have a significant effect on the distribution of income, even over a relatively short period of time. We referred above to the reductions in the highest ratio of income tax made by the Conservative government. These changes help to explain the pattern of changes in real after-tax incomes. Taking as an example

a married man with two children under 11 we find the following increases from 1978/89 to 1985/86: those whose earnings were ten times the average enjoyed an increase in real after-tax incomes of 68 per cent; those with five times average earnings 32 per cent; those with half average earnings 16 per cent.

The distribution of wealth

The distribution of wealth may be affected directly by fiscal policy, e.g. by changes in the taxation of money transferred at death. It may also be affected indirectly by those fiscal measures which affect the distribution of income.

The trend towards a more equal distribution of wealth was halted after the Conservatives were returned to power in 1979. Between 1966 and 1979 the share of marketable wealth (excluding pension rights) held by the poorest 75 per cent of the population increased from 13 to 24 per cent. Between 1979 and 1984 this proportion remained roughly constant. The proportion held by the richest 10 per cent, after falling from 69 per cent in 1966 to 51 per cent in 1980, also remained roughly constant in the first half of the 1980s.

While changes in fiscal policy contribute to changes in wealth distribution they are not the only causal factor. The 1980s saw a considerable rise in the value of shares and other marketable securities which constitute a larger proportion of the wealth of the richer than of the poorer members of the community.

Changes in government spending

The long-term trend in the share of aggregate expenditure (GDP) accounted for by government spending is shown in Fig. 20.8. It is clear that the major cause of the increased government's share has been two world wars; although the government's share declined with the return of peace, it remained above the pre-war level on both occasions.

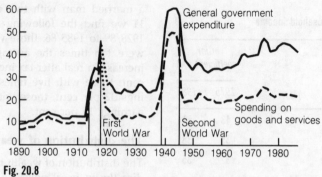

Fig. 20.8
General government expenditure as percentage of GDP
Source: Economic Trends, Oct. 1987

However, significant changes have occurred in other periods. The decline in the government's share that began after the end of the Second World War continued until the late 1950s; a sharp upturn then occurred. This upturn was due more to a rise in government spending than to a decline in the rate of growth of aggregate expenditure. Figure 20.9 shows that during the 1970s government spending rose by just under 3 per cent a year during the 1950s, but by 4.5 per cent in the 1960s.

The growth rate in the 1970s was around 3 per cent, and since the economy was growing less rapidly the government's share of spending continued to increase, reaching 43.4 per cent in 1979. A Conservative government, pledged to reverse this increase, was then elected. However, this pledge proved difficult to fulfil in the face of a recession which involved a substantial increase in spending on unemployment benefit and other transfer payments. Despite the fact that since 1980 government spending has

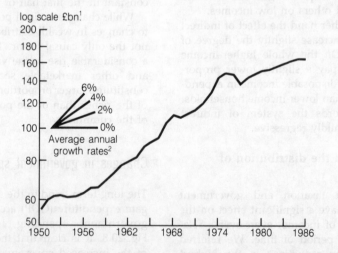

Fig. 20.9
General government expenditure in real terms. *Note*: (1) Real terms figures are the cash figures adjusted to 1986 price levels by excluding the effect of general inflation as measured by the GDP deflator. (2) The different slopes of the lines represent different rates of annual growth. The steeper the gradient the greater the growth rate. By comparing the slopes with particular sections of the graph the reader can determine the appropriate rate of annual growth over the period.
Source: Economic Trends, Oct. 1987

Table 20.6
General government expenditure (% of GDP at market prices)

1979	1980	1981	1982	1983	1984	1985	1986
43.4	45.2	46.0	46.4	45.9	45.5	44.5	42.8

Source: Economic Trends, Oct. 1987

increased by only about 1.25 per cent a year, it was 1983 before the government's share of spending declined (see Table 20.6).

The expenditure and finance of local authorities

In much of the earlier discussion we have included the expenditure and finance of the local authorities (LAs) along with that of the central government. However, the activities of the LAs raise a number of important issues which require separate attention.

Local authority expenditure tended to increase at a rate far in excess of the growth of the economy as a whole, especially in the first part of the 1970s. In fact real expenditure increased by about one-quarter in the first half of the decade. This increase in expenditure no doubt resulted in improvements in some of the services provided by LAs – education, welfare services, recreational facilities, etc. However, it has been suggested that the increase in expenditure was also an indication of a reduction in efficiency in the local authority sector as a whole.

This increased expenditure required increased finance. Rates revenue increased in real terms almost every year, as shown in Fig. 20.10. Between 1963 and 1986 rates revenue doubled in real terms. However, the increase in rates revenue was insufficient to finance all of the increased expenditure, and the LAs came increasingly to rely on central government finance. This trend was strengthened by the fact that the current expenditure of the

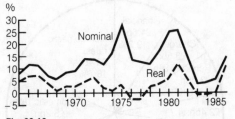

Fig. 20.10
Annual increases in rates
Source: Financial Statistics (published in Lloyds Bank Economic Bulletin, June 1986)

LAs frequently turned out to be greater than indicated when the amount of the annual rate support grant was agreed. Since the amount of rates revenue is fixed at the beginning of the year, an excess of current expenditure over that intended implied that the central government must supplement the rate support grant.

By 1980 central government grants accounted for around two-thirds of the LAs' current expenditure. In the 1980s with a Conservative government committed to a reduction in public spending, this proportion has declined, as shown in Fig. 20.11. Despite this reversal of the previous trend, central government grants remain the major source of finance, as shown in Fig. 20.12.

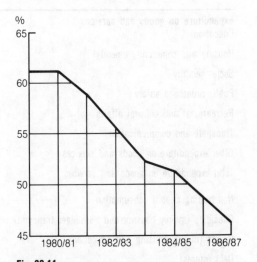
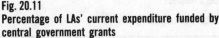

Fig. 20.11
Percentage of LAs' current expenditure funded by central government grants

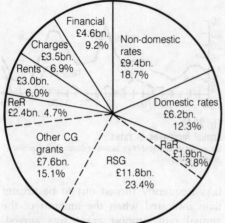

Fig. 20.12
Local government income (1986/87 estimates)
Financial: £2.5bn. borrowing, £1.4bn. capital receipts, £0.7bn. interest. ReR = rent rebate; RaR = rate rebate; RSG = rate support grant; CG = central government
Source: *Lloyds Bank Economic Bulletin*, June 1986

The pattern of local authority spending

The pattern of the LAs' spending is shown in Table 20.7. Almost three-

quarters of the total consists of expenditure on goods and services, by far the most important heading being education.

Although some discretion is exercised at the local level, the broad parameters of spending are established centrally. For example the basic structure of the education service is determined by the Department of Education and Science, and the system for administering law and order by the Home Office. The heavy involvement of the central government, both in the provision of finance and the influencing of the pattern of expenditure, has led to the suggestion that it should take full responsibility for some of the services currently provided by the local authorities. Such a change would also make it easier for central government to control spending on those services and therefore public spending as a whole.

Alternative forms of finance

A Green Paper issued in 1986[4] outlined the major deficiencies of the existing system of rates as a source of finance.

Table 20.7
Local authorities' expenditure (1986)

	£m.	%
Expenditure on goods and services		
Education	15,108	33.7
Housing and community amenity	4,215	9.4
Social security	3,935	8.8
Public order and safety	4,439	9.9
Recreational and cultural affairs	1,683	3.8
Transport and communication	2,333	5.2
Other expenditure on goods and services	1,539	3.4
Total expenditure on goods and services	33,252	74.2
Non-trading capital consumption	1,440	3.2
Subsidies (mainly housing and passenger transport)	1,078	2.4
Grants (mainly housing and education)	4,824	10.8
Debt interest	4,241	9.5
Total expenditure	44,835	100

Source: *United Kingdom National Accounts*

First, it is technically inadequate in that the amount paid by a household does not reflect its use of local services. Second, it is unfair or regressive in that in general those on low incomes pay a higher proportion of their income in rates than higher-income earners.[5] Finally, and perhaps most important, it fails the test of democratic accountability. Rates are paid by householders, not by all voters. Moreover, half of the rates income comes from industry which has no voting rights. Furthermore the existence of rebates and subsidies (including that from central to local government) shields voters, and their elected representatives, from the full impact of their decisions.

The Green Paper contained four main proposals intended to improve the situation. The most important was that domestic rates should be phased out over a period of up to ten years and replaced by a flat rate community charge, or residents' tax, payable by all adults. Second, non-domestic rates should be set by central government, as a uniform rate in the pound. The proceeds would be pooled and redistributed to all local authorities as a common amount per adult. Third, the grants system would be simplified. It would consist of (a) a needs grant, which would compensate for differences in what authorities needed to spend to provide a comparable standard of service, and (b) a standard grant, paid to all authorities as a common amount per adult.

The government subsequently decided that the community charge (popularly termed the poll tax) would operate in Scotland from 1989 and in most of England and Wales from 1990. When the Bill introducing the tax was published in 1987 it was estimated that the tax would be paid by 33 million people in England and Wales, of whom 2.5 million would receive nearly a complete rebate and another 5 million some rebate. (People receiving a rebate include students, resident hospital patients and those living in residential care homes.) By comparison about 19 million people received a bill for domestic rates, of whom between 6 and 7 million received a full rebate. Most of the difference is explained by the fact that rates are paid by households, the community charge by individuals.

The Bill proposed that the community charge should cover about a fifth of local councils' spending. The remaining four-fifths would be provided centrally, partly as a central government grant and partly as a business rate, collected nationally and then redistributed according to each council's population. This would mean that each time a council increased its spending by 1 per cent above government-set targets, it would have to increase the level of the community charge by 4 per cent. Conversely, 1 per cent under-spending would enable the community charge to be reduced by 4 per cent.

Summary

1. The primary function of government expenditure is probably the provision of public, or collective consumption, goods. The essential characteristics of these goods are first, that if the good is provided for one citizen it is provided for all (non-excludability), second, that the consumption of the good by one person does not impede its consumption by others (non-rivalness).
2. Other functions of government expenditure include the provision of merit goods at a price below the cost of production, the redistribution of income and an increase in economic efficiency.
3. Government expenditure on goods and services enters directly into the expenditure function. By contrast transfers increase the income of recipients, and only affect expenditure subsequently if and when they are spent.
4. By far the most important spending programme is social security, followed by defence, health, personal social services and education.

5. The primary function of taxation is to raise the revenue required to finance government expenditure. Other important functions are to influence the level of total expenditure, to influence the pattern of expenditure and to redistribute income and wealth.

6. In the UK most revenue is raised by taxes on income (well over 50 per cent if National Insurance contributions are included). Taxes on expenditure account for about one-third of revenue and rates for one-tenth.

7. Overall the UK tax system is progressive since the effect of a progressive direct tax structure outweighs a mildly regressive indirect tax structure.

8. High rates of taxation may cause workers to substitute leisure for income and may reduce firms' investment spending. This could lead to a fall in total tax revenue.

9. A balanced budget (government spending equals revenue from taxation) will almost certainly have an expansionary effect on aggregate demand, as will a budget deficit. A modest budget surplus may leave total expenditure unchanged, but a large surplus will cause aggregate demand to fall.

10. Government policy often operates to reduce inequalities of wealth. However, in the 1980s inequalities have increased, partly because of changes in government policy and partly because of a rise in the value of shares and other marketable securities which form a larger proportion of the wealth of the richer than of the poorer members of the community.

11. There has been considerable controversy in the 1980s concerning the budgeting of the local authorities. Very rapid growth in expenditure in the 1970s led to attempts by the central government to curb spending in the 1980s. Moreover, as rates revenue has declined as a proportion of the LAs' total revenue, frequent proposals have been made for modifying the structure of financing. The latest of these proposals, soon to come into effect, is to replace rates by a flat rate community charge or residents' tax.

Key terms

Public goods	Poverty trap
Non-excludability	Diminishing rate of substitution
Non-rivalness	Laffer curve
Free-rider problem	Balanced budget
Merit goods	Budget surplus
Transfer payments	Budget deficit
Structure of taxation	Redistribution of income and wealth
Fiscal drag	

Notes

1. Note that although the two individuals react in different ways they must both be worse off than previously. In order to simplify the diagram we have not drawn the original indifference curves passing through E. However, it is clear that each individual must move to a lower curve. (Another simplification is that unemployment benefit is not taxed.)

2. This evidence is reviewed in Griffiths A and Wall S, *Applied Economics*, Longman, 1984, Ch. 14.

3. Sargent J R and Scott M F G, Investment and the tax system in the UK, *Midland Bank Review*, Spring 1986.

4. *Paying for Local Government.* HMSO, 1986.

5. *Lloyds Bank Economic Bulletin*, June 1986, estimated that rates take up 4 per cent of the net income of households earning £100–200 a week, but only 2 per cent of the incomes of those on the highest incomes.

Essay questions

1. Discuss the major characteristics of public goods and explain why such goods are normally supplied by the government.
2. Assess the role of fiscal policy in relation to any three economic objectives.
3. Discuss the major functions of taxation and show how these functions have influenced the structure of taxation in the UK.
4. Discuss the major functions of government expenditure and show how these functions have influenced the pattern of UK government expenditure.
5. Discuss the possible effects on total tax revenue of a reduction in the rates of personal taxation.
6. Discuss the possible effects on the supply of labour of changes in (a) direct, (b) indirect taxation.
7. Analyse the possible effects of a reduction in the rates of corporation tax combined with an increase in the rates of inheritance tax. (Assume that the effect on total tax revenue is neutral.)
8. Analyse the possible effects of an increase in the rates of direct taxation combined with a reduction in the rates of indirect taxation. (Assume that the effect on total tax revenue is neutral.)
9. Analyse the possible effects on total expenditure of a balanced budget.
10. 'A budget surplus will cause a reduction in the level of economic activity.' Discuss.
11. Explain what you understand by the term 'the burden of the national debt'. Under what circumstances, if any, might an increase in the burden of the debt be justified?

Exercises

20.1 The passage below was taken from an article by Anthony Crosland, then Minister of the Environment, and published in *The Guardian* (24 March 1976).

Public spending roughly divides into four broad categories:
First, there is the direct expenditure of resources on services, many of which contain a large social service element – the NHS, the personal social services, housing investment, and the rest.
Secondly, there are transfers. Transfers redistribute money from original income recipients to pensioners and social security beneficiaries, to consumers of subsidized services such as public transport, and to holders of Government debt.
Thirdly, there is public spending designed to increase productive capacity, whether in the form of investment in the nationalized industries, or in the form of grants to private industry.
Fourthly, there is public spending on the acquisition of assets, for example the extension of public ownership in industry, or the municipalization of privately rented housing.
Spending between these categories differs fundamentally in its economic and social effect.

Comment on the conclusion that 'Spending between these categories differs fundamentally in its economic and social effect', discussing especially the implications of each type of spending for (a) economic growth, (b) inflation, (c) the reduction of inequality.

20.2 Table 20.8 shows the expected effect on government revenue of measures introduced in the 1987 budget.

Table 20.8
Expected effects on government revenue 1987/88 (£m.)

Yield (+)/cost (−)	Changes from a non-indexed base	Changes from an indexed base
Income tax		
2p off basic rate	−2,200	−2,200
Increase in allowances	−705	−10
Changes in higher rate thresholds	−65	+40
Excise duties		
Petrol/derv	—	−240
Vehicle excise duty	+5	−90
Tobacco	—	105
Alcohol	—	−105
On-course betting duty	−20	−20
Gaming machine licence duty	+20	+20
VAT		
Small business measures	−115	−115
Tighter rules for certain traders	+300	+300
Inheritance tax: increase in thresholds, etc.	−90	−75
Other changes	−25	−25
Total	**−2,895**	**−2,625**

Source: Economic Progress Report, Supplement March–April 1987

  (i) Why do you think these measures were introduced?
  (ii) Explain why for some items the effect on revenue differs as between an indexed and a non-indexed base?
  (iii) What factors might cause the actual effects of the measures to differ from the expected effects?

20.3 What factors might explain the changes in government spending shown in Fig. 20.13?

20.4 Table 20.9, taken from *Economic Trends*, July 1987, shows indirect taxes as a percentage of disposable income of non-retired households. (Intermediate taxes are costs such as employers' National Insurance contributions and non-domestic rates, part of which are passed on by employers in the form of higher prices.)
  (i) What factors might account for the differences in the relative burden of indirect taxes among different income groups?
  (ii) Examine the case for a change in the rates of indirect taxes.

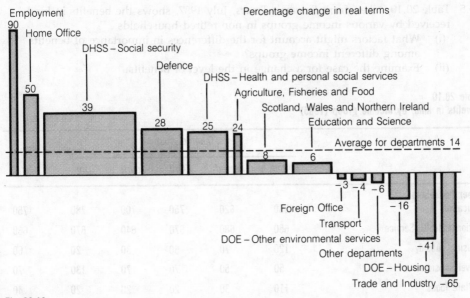

Fig. 20.13
Changes in government spending between 1978/79 and 1986/87
Source: *Public Expenditure White Paper*, reprinted in *Financial Times*, 15 Jan. 1987

Table 20.9
Indirect taxes as percentage of disposable income (1985)

	Quintile group					
	Bottom	*Second*	*Third*	*Fourth*	*Top*	*Total*
Domestic rates	3.9	4.8	4.1	3.7	2.8	3.6
VAT	7.7	8.0	7.8	7.7	7.3	7.6
Duty on beer	1.2	1.3	1.1	1.1	0.9	1.1
Duty on wines and spirits	0.8	0.9	0.9	1.0	1.1	1.0
Duty on tobacco	5.3	3.3	2.5	1.8	1.2	2.2
Duty on hydrocarbon oils	1.2	1.6	1.7	1.7	1.5	1.6
Car tax and vehicle excise duty	0.8	1.1	1.1	1.1	1.0	1.0
Other taxes on final goods and services	2.1	1.9	1.6	1.4	1.1	1.5
Intermediate taxes	5.7	5.5	5.1	4.9	4.5	4.9
Total	28.6	28.3	25.9	24.4	21.4	24.5

20.5   Table 20.10, taken from *Economic Trends*, July 1987, shows the benefits in kind received by various income groups in non-retired households.
    (i)   What factors might account for the differences in importance of benefits among different income groups?
    (ii) Examine the case for a change in the level of benefits.

Table 20.10
Benefits in kind, by income group (1985)

	Quintile group					
	Bottom	*Second*	*Third*	*Fourth*	*Top*	*Total*
£ per household						
Education	880	620	750	700	780	750
National Health Service	650	680	670	640	670	660
Housing subsidy	120	70	50	30	20	60
Travel subsidies	50	50	70	70	130	70
Welfare foods	110	30	20	20	20	40
Total	1,800	1,460	1,460	1,460	1,620	1,580
Benefits in kind as a percentage of post-tax income	56	30	23	16	11	20

Note: All figures are approximations and must be rounded in the second digit.

Objective test questions: set 8

1.   Transfer payments include all of the following except:
    A   salaries of schoolteachers;
    B   interest on the national debt;
    C   retirement pensions;
    D   sickness benefit;
    E   child benefit.

2.   The best definition of a progressive tax system is that:
    A   all taxpayers pay the same absolute amount in taxation;
    B   all taxpayers pay the same proportion of their income in taxation;
    C   high-income earners pay more in taxes than low-income earners;
    D   high-income earners pay a higher proportion of their income in taxes than low-income earners;
    E   there is a bigger absolute range in pre-tax than in post-tax incomes.

3.   Assume that in a closed economy government expenditure and taxation are both £100m., 60 per cent of the government expenditure consists of spending on goods and services, and 40 per cent of transfer payments. The MPC of taxpayers is 0.8. Ignoring any multiplier or accelerator effects, the net effect of fiscal policy will be an increase in total expenditure of (£m.):
    A   100;
    B   60;
    C   25;

D 12;

E zero.

4. 'Any excess of government expenditure over revenue must increase the real burden of the national debt.' This statement is incorrect because:

A most of the national debt is held by UK citizens;

B rates of interest may fall;

C government expenditure may cause an increase in GNP;

D the gap between expenditure and revenue can be filled by borrowing abroad;

E an excess of expenditure over revenue redistributes income in favour of the poorer member of the community.

6.

		Income before tax (£)	Income after tax (£)
1	X	10,000	9,000
	Y	5,000	4,000
2	X	10,000	8,000
	Y	5,000	4,000
3	X	10,000	5,000
	Y	5,000	3,000

Which of the above situations indicate(s) the existence of a progressive system of taxation?

7. Under a regressive tax system:

1 there is a bigger absolute range in post-tax than in pre-tax incomes;

2 all taxpayers pay the same absolute amount in taxation;

3 all taxpayers pay the same proportion of their income in tax.

8. Direct taxes include:

1 personal (income) tax;

2 corporation tax;

3 inheritance tax.

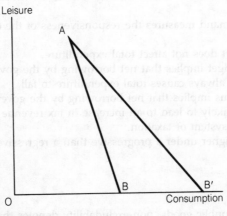

Fig. 20.14

9. In Fig. 20.14 AB indicates all the possible combinations of leisure and consumption available to an individual. The shift of the curve to AB' could be due to a fall in:

1 direct tax rates;

2 indirect tax rates;

3 unemployment benefit.

10. In order to maintain a constant real burden of taxation under inflationary conditions it is usually necessary to increase the rates of:
    1 direct taxes;
    2 *ad valorem* expenditure taxes;
    3 specific expenditure taxes.

11. The effect of a balanced budget on total expenditure is likely to depend upon:
    1 the MPC of taxpayers;
    2 the MPC of the recipients of transfer payments;
    3 the composition of government expenditure.

12. Inheritance tax:
    1 applies to all inherited money;
    2 is a tax on holdings of wealth;
    3 is a progressive tax.

13. Indirect taxes include:
    1 value added tax;
    2 customs and excise duties;
    3 capital gains tax.

14. Personal income tax, as currently levied in the UK, is progressive because:
    1 no tax is payable on incomes below a minimum figure;
    2 on incomes beyond a certain figure the rate of tax increases;
    3 the maximum rate of tax is less than 100 per cent.

15. Transfer payments are not included in the calculation of national income.
    Transfer payments are made without any productive service being provided in exchange.

16. An increase in the rates of direct taxation may cause a fall in total tax revenue.
    The amount of revenue from both direct and indirect taxation may fall following an increase in the rates of direct taxation.

17. The greater the elasticity of demand the greater is the tax revenue for any given rate of tax.
    Elasticity of demand measures the responsiveness of the quantity demanded to a change in price.

18. A balanced budget does not affect total expenditure.
    A balanced budget implies that net borrowing by the government is zero.

19. A budget surplus always causes total expenditure to fall.
    A budget surplus implies that net borrowing by the government is positive.

20. Inflation is more likely to lead to an increase in tax revenue under a progressive than a regressive system of taxation.
    Tax rates are higher under a progressive than a regressive system of taxation.

True/false

1. When applied to public goods, non-excludability denotes that if a good is supplied to one citizen it must be supplied to all.
2. The fee charged by a solicitor for effecting the transfer of ownership of property is an example of a transfer payment.
3. Indirect taxation is most likely to lead to a redistribution of income in favour of poor people if the highest taxes are imposed on those products which account for a greater proportion of the expenditure of rich than of poor people.

4. Under a progressive tax system all taxpayers pay the same proportion of their income in tax.
5. Fiscal drag refers to the fact that with a progressive tax system the proportion of income paid in taxation automatically increases in inflationary conditions.
6. Fiscal policy encompasses both taxation and public expenditure.
7. The 'free-rider problem' refers to the difficulty of preventing someone who has not contributed to the cost of a project, from deriving benefits from the project.
8. Housing is the major item of local authorities' current expenditure.
9. The government provides subsidies and grants both to companies and private individuals.
10. Interest on the national debt is treated in the national accounts as a transfer payment.

CHAPTER TWENTY-ONE
Monetary Policy

Introduction

As we noted at the end of Chapter 20, monetary policy has been used along with fiscal policy in order to influence the level of economic activity. Policy designed to influence the *supply of money* is implemented via a wide range of institutions, both public and private, and we discuss these institutions in some detail.

Monetary policy is also concerned with the *cost of money*, which is influenced not only by supply, but also by demand conditions. Before discussing the supply side, we examine the major determinants of the demand for money.

The demand for money

Keynes specified three types of demand for money: the transactions, precautionary and speculative demand. These three types of demand may be related to three basic reasons why individuals or firms may wish to hold money rather than securities, such as bonds or shares, which would yield a positive return.

The transactions demand

The transactions demand reflects the fact that the pattern of income – of household or firm – seldom coincides with the pattern of expenditure. The worker is paid every week or month, while he (or his wife), makes payments for food, travel, etc. every day. Firms have to pay workers, suppliers of materials, etc. at times different from that at which they receive payment for goods sold. Consequently, both households and firms maintain a stock of money out of which they can make payments at those times when their current income is inadequate.

The most important determinant of the size of the transactions demand is the value of the transactions which the household or firm expects to make in a given period, which itself depends upon the income of the household or firm. If we aggregate these individual demands we can say that the main determinant of the total transactions demand is the level of GDP or national income. Other influences include the flexibility of the financial system – and in particular the ability of an individual or firm to acquire money at short notice when required – and the penalty for non-payment of bills on the due day. The opportunity cost of holding money, i.e. the benefit forgone by not spending money, may also be important.

The precautionary demand

The precautionary demand reflects the fact that uncertainty may exist concerning future financial obligations. The size of the precautionary demand is subject to very similar influences as the transactions demand, and the difference between the two is probably best explained by means of a simple example.

A family setting off for a day's car ride would take a given amount of money to pay for any meals, petrol, etc. that they planned to buy. This would constitute their transactions demand. They would also, if they were sensible, take an additional amount to cover the possibility of a breakdown or accident requiring expenditure on repairs, train fares, etc. This would constitute their precautionary demand.

The speculative demand

In its simplest form, as formulated by Keynes, the speculative demand for money is related to the current rate of interest on fixed interest government stock or bonds. Keynes suggested that the speculative demand would be inversely related to the rate of interest for two reasons. The first reason is that the higher the rate of interest the greater is the opportunity cost of holding money, and consequently the less money will be held.

The second reason is connected with the fact that the rate of interest is inversely related to the price of bonds. For example if a £100 bond bearing a 'coupon' of 5 per cent is issued at par, i.e. at a price of £100, then the actual rate of interest is, of course, 5 per cent. The purchaser of a bond for £100 would receive £5 a year interest. (We ignore taxation.) If the price of that bond were subsequently to fall to £50, a purchaser could now obtain an annual return of £5 for an outlay of £50, i.e. the actual rate of interest to new purchasers would be 10 per cent, double the nominal rate. Conversely, at a price of £125 the actual rate of interest would be 4 per cent (= 5 per cent × 100/125).

Although the price of bonds is influenced by many factors, and although different investors may take different views about the relative importance of these factors, a general feeling is likely to emerge about what the correct or normal rate of interest should be in the prevailing economic circumstances. If the current rate is actually greater than what is adjudged normal, a decline in the rate, i.e. *a rise* in the price of bonds would be expected. Such an expectation would encourage investors to switch from money to bonds. That is to say a high rate of interest tends to give rise to a low speculative demand for money. Conversely, a low rate of interest would induce an expectation of a future fall in bond prices (a rise in the rate of interest) and would therefore encourage a switch from bonds to money, i.e. a low rate of interest tends to give rise to a high speculative demand.

Consequently these two factors, the current return on bonds and expectations about changes in future prices, combine to make the speculative demand sensitive to the rate of interest, i.e. to make demand interest elastic.

The asset demand

It is more usual today to use the term 'asset demand' to describe the third motive for holding money. As mentioned above, Keynes's formulation of the speculative demand related to the choice between holding money or government stock. These are not, of course, the only alternative forms of wealth. Wealth may also be held in the form of debentures issued by companies, shares, property, consumer durable goods, etc. These different forms of assets offer the prospect of different forms of return – interest, dividends, capital gains, etc. (In this context, the expected proportionate change in prices is the yield on consumer durables.) However, as before, the choice is between holding one or more assets which yield a positive return, and holding money which does not.

If money is held in preference to other assets, income (and thus the opportunity for higher consumption in the future) is sacrificed. This sacrifice will be made only if it is felt that the risks incurred in holding these other assets outweigh the benefit of the income earned. (One of the major risks, to which we drew attention above, is that the market price of the asset might fall.) In other words the asset demand for holding money exists because people are risk-averse.

Since the rates of interest on all loans – government stock, debentures, etc. – tend to move together, the analysis of the previous section can be extended to these other forms of loan. It cannot, however, be extended so easily to other assets which yield different forms of return. For example the prices and yields of shares and fixed interest securities frequently move in opposite directions. This limitation of the analysis must be borne in mind. A further limitation is that the assumption that holdings of money attract no return has become increasingly dubious in the light of recent changes in the financial system, and especially the introduction of bank accounts which pay interest and offer depositors the facility of a cheque-book. By the end of 1985 these accounted for 13 per cent of the clearing banks' sterling deposits, as compared to 3 per cent at the end of 1984.

The determinants of the demand for money: summary

Figure 21.1 summarizes the above analysis of the determinants of the demand for money. The transactions and precautionary demands have been combined in curve *L*, which is only slightly sensitive to the rate of interest. The asset or speculative demand, *B*, is much more interest elastic.[1] The total demand function for money, *D*, is obtained by aggregating horizontally the two separate demand functions.

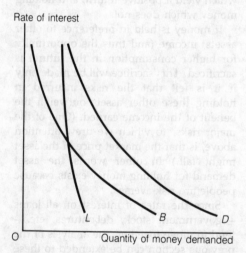

Rate of interest

O — Quantity of money demanded

L   *B*   *D*

Fig. 21.1
A demand function for money

Figure 21.1 represents the situation with a given level of national income. As we noted above, the transactions and precautionary demands and therefore, of course, the total demand for money, will be positively related to the level of national income. This is shown in Fig. 21.2 where the demand function

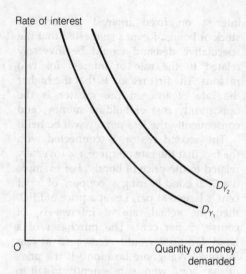

Rate of interest

O — Quantity of money demanded

D_{Y_2}

D_{Y_1}

Fig. 21.2
A change in the demand for money

shifts to the right as the level of national income rises from Y_1 to Y_2.

The supply of money

Before we can examine the factors affecting the supply of money we must briefly discuss the definition of money, since several alternative definitions might be used.

Alternative definitions of the money supply

Money can be defined as anything which is generally acceptable in exchange for goods and services and which acts as a measure and store of value. While this definition has the advantage of being comprehensive, it is not of much help when we are attempting to discover the effect of changes in the supply of money. In order to do this we must be able to measure the money supply, and consequently a more precise definition is required. Several definitions exist in the UK, as shown in Fig. 21.3.

Table 21.1 shows the magnitude of three of the aggregates contained in Fig. 21.3. In all three instances bank

---

Narrow money

M0

Notes and coin in circulation with the public
plus banks' till money
plus banks' operational balances with the Bank of
England

M1

Notes and coin in circulation with the public
plus private sector sterling sight bank deposits

M2

Notes and coin in circulation with the public
plus private sector non-interest-bearing sterling sight
bank deposits
plus private sector interest-bearing sterling bank deposits
plus private sector holdings of retail building society
shares and deposits and National Savings Bank ordinary
accounts

Broad money

M3

M1
plus private sector sterling time bank deposits
plus private sector holdings of sterling bank certificates
of deposit

M3c

M3
plus private sector holdings of foreign currency bank
deposits

M4

M3
plus private sector holdings of building society shares
and deposits and sterling certificates of deposit
minus building society holdings of bank deposits and
bank certificates of deposit, and notes and coin

M5

M4
plus holdings by the private sector (excluding building
societies) of money market instruments (bank bills,
Treasury bills, local authority deposits), certificates of tax
deposit and National Savings instruments (excluding
certificates, save as you earn and other long-term
deposits)

Fig. 21.3
Monetary aggregates: definitions
Source: Economic Progress Report, Aug. 1987

deposits constitute the greater part of the
money supply.[2] It is therefore appropriate
to discuss next the functions of the
banking system.

The functions of a banking system

The basic functions of a banking system
are to accept deposits and to make loans
of one kind or another. Deposits are the
major item on the liabilities side of most
banks' balance sheets, and loans the major
item on the assets side. Liabilities must
always equal assets. Nevertheless banks
are able to extend loans in excess of the
amount of money *initially* deposited with
them.

Credit creation in a single bank system

This can be explained with reference to
Table 21.2 which relates to the simplest
form of banking system with just a single
bank. We start from the point at which,
since beginning operations, the bank has
succeeded in attracting *initial deposits* of
coin to the value of £100,000. At this
stage, designated Stage 1, the coin lies idle
in the bank's vaults. If the bank expects
depositors to withdraw their deposits at
short notice it will be prudent to retain all
the money deposited.

On the other hand, if experience
suggests that depositors will not withdraw
all their deposits at any one time, the bank
will be able to lend the money that is not
required. For example, if it believed that
depositors would not call upon more than
one-tenth of their deposits, it would be
able to lend the remaining nine-tenths.

When people borrow money from a
bank they normally do so because they
wish to buy something. Consequently,
this money (coin) loaned by the bank will
be used for payment for goods and
services. The suppliers of these goods and
services will deposit the money received
with the same bank as made the loans,
since this is the only bank in existence.
This money we call *created deposits.*

The coin that is redeposited with the
bank can be loaned out again and again
provided that the bank continues to hold
coin equal to 10 per cent of its total
deposits or total assets. The limit to this
process of credit creation is represented

Table 21.1
Money stock (end Sept. 1987)

	£m.
Notes and coin in circulation with public	13,206
Private sector sterling sight bank deposits	76,050
M1	89,256
Private sector sterling time deposits	87,343
M3	176,599
Private sector holdings of building society shares, deposits and certificates of deposit	128,107
Building society holdings of M3	− 12,112
M4	292,594

Source: Bank of England Quarterly Bulletin, Nov. 1987

by Stage 2 in Table 21.2. The bank has coin to the value of £100,000 but this now represents only 10 per cent of its assets. The bank has created credit of nine times the level of its initial deposits.

Credit creation in a multi-bank system

Although the arithmetic is slightly different, the principle of credit creation is exactly the same in a multi-bank system. Let us consider the simplest form of multi-bank system, i.e. one comprising two banks. In Table 21.3 we again begin with initial deposits of £100,000, but these are now split equally between the two banks (Stage 1).

If each bank could be sure that for every £100 of loans that it made it would receive a further £100 of (created) deposits, then it could operate on the same cash assets ratio as previously. However, in practice each bank may feel obliged to keep a slightly higher cash ratio in case it loses potential deposits to the other bank. If each bank operates with a 12.5 per cent cash ratio and lends money to this limit, the final position will be as at Stage 2 in Table 21.3. Each bank has created credit of seven times its initial deposits. We have assumed here that neither bank is more successful than the other in attracting deposits. If one bank were more successful, the final distribution of deposits and loans would be different. However, the totals for the system would be the same, provided that both banks continued to work to the same cash ratios.

Table 21.2
Credit creation in a single bank system

Liabilities (£)			Assets (£)	
Stage 1	Initial deposits	100,000	Coin	100,000
Stage 2	Initial deposits	100,000	Coin	100,000
	Created deposits	900,000	Loans	900,000
		1,000,000		1,000,000

Table 21.3
Credit creation in a multi-bank system

	Bank A			
	Liabilities (£)		Assets (£)	
Stage 1	Initial deposits	50,000	Coin	50,000
Stage 2	Initial deposits	50,000	Coin	50,000
	Created deposits	350,000	Loans	350,000
		400,000		400,000

	Bank B			
	Liabilities (£)		Assets (£)	
Stage 1	Initial deposits	50,000	Coin	50,000
Stage 2	Initial deposits	50,000	Coin	50,000
	Created deposits	350,000	Loans	350,000
		400,000		400,000

Credit creation in practice

In the hypothetical banking system described above, the banks attracted deposits on the basis of which they made loans, etc. In practice banks tend to make loans and then find the deposits to match these loans (and other assets). The extreme illustration of this is where banks borrow money overnight in the inter-bank market in order to balance their books. It is scarcely necessary to add that the banks attempt to attract deposits at a lower rate of interest than they earn on their assets.

The value of the credit multiplier (also known as the money or bank multiplier) depends upon which definition of money is adopted. For example Begg, using M1 as his definition of the money stock, derived a multiplier of 3.2, whereas Culyer, using M3, derived a multiplier of 7.5.[3]

The UK banking system

In the UK, as in most industrialized economies, by far the greater part of the

Table 21.4
The sterling assets of UK banks (April 1987)

	£m.	%
Notes and coin	2,155	0.7
Balances with the Bank of England		
Cash ratio deposits	803	0.3
Other	189	0.1
Money at call	7,463	2.4
Other market loans	82,610	26.4
Bills	6,814	2.2
Advances	169,485	54.2
Investments	20,947	6.7
Miscellaneous	22,324	7.1
Total	312,790	100

Source: Financial Statistics

total value of transactions is settled by payment by cheque. Similarly the loans made by the banks mainly comprise accounts against which payment can be made by cheque, rather than coin or notes. However, the principle of credit creation remains the same. The base to which credit creation is related today is discussed further below. But first we discuss the assets of the banking system. The distribution of the sterling assets of the UK banks (in order to simplify the discussion we confine our attention to sterling assets) shown in Table 21.4, reflects a number of influences, in particular the need for profitability, for liquidity and for compliance with government policies. (As we shall see, these last two requirements coincide to some extent.)

Profitability

In order to cover their operating costs, and to earn profits from which to pay dividends to shareholders, the banks must use their deposits in ways which, in total, yield a surplus over the payments made to depositors. The most profitable assets are advances, which account for about half of the total market loans and investments. The rate of interest charged on advances varies with the bank's *base rate*. The margin charged above base rate varies according to the nature and status of the customer but is normally within the range 1–5 per cent. (The rate paid to depositors might be 3–4 per cent below base rate, depending upon the amount deposited and the length of notice of withdrawal required.)

Market loans are made to a variety of institutions at home and overseas including banks, LAs and producers in the public and private sectors. The rate of interest, which is normally fixed (as contrasted with the variable rate on advances), varies with the length of the loan and the status of the borrower. British government stocks are the major item within investments. They usually provide a high yield. However, if the banks wish to sell the stock before the date of maturity, there is the possibility that they will make a capital loss, i.e. obtain a lower price than they paid for the stock. (The longer the period

between the sale and the date of maturity the greater the *possible* capital loss.) In this sense, therefore, investments must be seen as a relatively illiquid type of asset.

Liquidity

In the hypothetical banking systems discussed earlier, the banks' need for liquidity was met by ensuring that reserves of coin were always at least 10 per cent (12.5 per cent in the multi-bank system) of total liabilities or total assets. Precisely the same procedure applies in practice today, in that the banks maintain a certain reserve of notes and coin. The London clearing banks keep relatively higher reserves of notes and coin than do other banks. This reflects the more extensive branch network and the much greater number of depositors of the clearers.

These reserves of notes and coin are intended to meet the day-to-day requirements of the bank's depositors. The fact that the percentage of assets backed by cash is relatively small can be partly explained by the increasing tendency to make payments by cheque. Some of these payments relate to transactions between customers of the same bank. However, many involve customers of different banks, e.g. a firm with an account at Barclays pays a supplier with an account at the Midland; an individual who banks at the Midland makes a cheque out to an account holder at Lloyds; and so on.

These latter (inter-bank) transactions lead to a set of claims and counter-claims among the clearers. Many of these claims simply offset each other. But at the end of the day, when all cheques have been cleared at the clearing house, some banks emerge as net creditors and others as net debtors. These debts are settled by making transfers between the 'other balances' that each bank holds at the Bank of England. These balances are therefore almost as liquid as the reserves of notes and coin.

The next most liquid asset is money loaned 'at call' to the London discount market. If, on a given day, a bank finds that it has more than enough money to meet its immediate requirements, it may lend the surplus to various institutions of which the discount houses are the most important. All of this lending is short term, some of it for as little as twenty-four hours. Money loaned on this basis is known as money at call since the banks can call in these loans, i.e. reconvert them into money, as required. (We show below how the discount houses finance the repayment of the loans that are called in by the banks.)

Bills constitute short-term borrowing by a variety of institutions including the central government. A certain quantity of Treasury bills, normally with a period to maturity of ninety days, is offered each week. (The quantity offered depends upon the government's borrowing requirement.) The banks do not bid for bills when they are offered initially, but subsequently buy them in the market, the bills then having less than the initial ninety days to maturity. The banks normally keep Treasury bills until maturity, and arrange their purchases so that some of their holdings mature each week, i.e. the banks have a regular inflow of money from this source. The same principles apply to their holdings of LA and commercial bills.

Compliance with government policy

For many years the banks have been obliged to keep a certain proportion of their assets in liquid form, as part of government policy designed to control the money supply. The nature of the banks' obligations has been changed on several occasions. (The current regulations are discussed below.)

The Bank of England

The major areas of responsibility of the Bank of England are similar to those of most other central banks. First, the Bank is responsible for the supervision of the activities of the institutions comprising the country's banking and financial system so as to ensure the stability and efficient functioning of the system. Under the Banking Act 1979 the Bank of England was given the right to decide, in the light of guidelines in the Act, which organizations are entitled to designation as 'recognized banks', which to designation as 'licensed deposit-taking institutions' and which are not entitled to either designation. The Act also provided for the establishment of a deposit protection fund with an initial capital of £6m., financed by a levy on all banks and licensed deposit-taking institutions. Depositors with institutions which fail are entitled to compensation of 75 per cent of the funds deposited, up to a limit of £10,000 deposits.

Second, the Bank acts as banker to the government. The Bank must ensure that the government has at all times sufficient money to meet its planned expenditure. Since, as we saw in Chapter 20, public expenditure frequently exceeds revenue from taxation, this implies that the Bank is responsible for managing the government's borrowing programme.

The role of the Bank of England as the government's banker can be explained with reference to the Bank's balance sheet, as shown in Table 21.5.

Looking first at the Issue Department we see that its main liability comprises notes in circulation. These notes are held by persons, firms and other institutions. Its assets are government and other securities. An increase in the note issue generally implies an increase in the department's holding of government securities. Or, putting the matter the other way round, the borrowing requirements of the government can be (partly) met by obtaining notes from the Issue Department in exchange for securities. (These notes are not, of course, held by the government, but are used to finance its expenditure.)[4] Conversely, when the government has excess cash it will, in effect, exchange this for securities. In practice this normally means not issuing new securities to replace those that mature.

Table 21.5
The balance sheet of the Bank of England (Sept. 1987, £m.)

Issue Department			
Liabilities		**Assets**	
Notes issued			
In circulation	13,228	Government securities	8,861
In Banking Department	12	Other securities	4,379

Banking Department			
Liabilities		**Assets**	
Deposits			
Public	97	Government securities	716
Bankers'	934	Advances and other accounts	1,042
Reserves and other accounts	2,040	Premises, equipment and other securities	1,315
		Notes and coin	12

Source: Financial Statistics

Turning to the Banking Department, the liabilities that are of the greatest interest to our present discussion are bankers' deposits. Bankers' deposits belong to the London clearing banks, the Scottish banks, other banks, accepting houses and the discount market. The importance of these deposits to the commercial banks was discussed above.

Like the Issue Department, the Banking Department holds part of its assets in the form of government securities. These include Treasury bills, government stocks and Ways and Means Advances, made overnight to the Exchequer if it finds itself short of funds at the end of the day. The basic effect of purchases by the department of securities from the government is, via government spending, to increase the volume of bankers' deposits. Conversely, sales reduce the volume of these deposits.

Other securities include bills purchased by the bank in order to check on the quality of bills circulating in the London market. The bank will not purchase bills of which it disapproves, and this acts as a deterrent to their issue and circulation.

Notes correspond to the similar item in the Issue Department. Finally, advances and other accounts include discounts and advances to the discount houses.

The discount houses operate at the shorter end of the financial market. Most of their borrowed funds are obtained from the monetary sector, and especially the banks, 90 per cent being borrowed at call or overnight. These funds are invested in assets which are again essentially short term, with a substantial proportion of bills.

We saw above that money loaned to the discount houses is often treated by the banks as a first line of defence, the first asset to be realized if they need to replenish their reserves of money. When the repayment of these loans is demanded, if the discount houses cannot borrow elsewhere, they turn to the Bank of England which makes funds available to them against suitable collateral – which must include a minimum proportion of Treasury bills.

The Bank of England is said here to act as the lender of last resort to the monetary and financial system, via the discount houses, who are the only institutions to have automatic access to the bank in this way.

This privilege is extended to them on the understanding that the discount houses apply each week for the full amount of the Treasury bill issue. (Other institutions also apply, of course, so that the discount houses normally take up only part of each issue.) In this way the government is assured that its short-term borrowing needs will, via the issue of Treasury bills, always be met. The cost of borrowing may, however, vary from week to week in accordance with changes in the balance between the demand for bills and the quantity issued.

Last but by no means least of the Bank of England's areas of responsibility is the implementation, in conjunction with the Treasury, of the government's monetary policy. (The Bank of England and the Treasury are together known as the monetary authorities.) This requires the Bank to operate in the foreign exchange market, the money market and the gilt-edged market. The Bank operates in these markets in order to help achieve the government's objectives with respect to the money supply and the exchange rate. The activities of the monetary authorities are discussed in detail below, but first we present a framework for this discussion.

The framework of monetary policy

The various measures which governments might adopt can be related to Fig. 21.4 (and subsequently to Fig. 21.6). In Fig. 21.4 the initial supply or stock of money is S_1, demand D and the rate of interest R_1. If the authorities wished to dampen spending, they might attempt to reduce supply to S_2. This would cause the equilibrium rate of interest to rise to R_2 and the quantity of money demanded to fall from A to B.

Alternatively the authorities might attempt to directly engineer a rise in

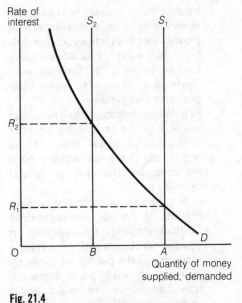

Fig. 21.4
Money supply and demand

interest rates to R_2. The demand for money would again fall from A to B, and since the supply of money responds to changes in demand, supply would fall. (The interdependence between the demand for money and the supply, underlies the process of credit creation discussed earlier and illustrated by Tables 21.3 and 21.4.) In order to re-establish equilibrium supply would, of course, have to fall to S_2.

Whichever approach was adopted the authorities would hope that the higher interest rates and the lower money supply would lead to a reduction in spending on goods and services. (This point is developed at greater length below.)

Having established the broad framework we now consider the alternative forms or mechanisms of control that might be adopted.

Forms of monetary control

1. Regulations and guidance concerning the volume of bank lending. Regulations have been applied to total lending, and also to specific types, e.g. lending to finance consumption. The purpose of restricting bank

lending is, of course, to reduce the money supply, or at least its rate of growth. But in practice such controls have invariably resulted in more lending being made through non-controlled channels, e.g. hire-purchase companies.

2. Regulations relating to balance-sheet ratios, e.g. the cash ratio, liquidity ratio, reserve assets ratio. (These regulations have sometimes been bolstered by the use of special deposits.)

   In principle the existence of these regulations enables the authorities to limit lending. By engaging in open-market operations (selling securities to the public, who pay by drawing on their bank deposits), they can reduce the banks' liquid assets; in order to restore the liquidity ratio to the specified level, the banks have to engineer a multiple contraction of deposits. (This is the converse of the process of credit creation described above.) However, in practice the authorities have usually ensured that lending was not inhibited by these regulations. For example the banks have usually been able to overcome a shortage of liquidity by selling government stock to the authorities at a non-penal price.

3. Measures to limit the growth of deposits and thus the money stock. The supplementary special deposits scheme or 'corset' penalized any banks whose deposits grew at a faster rate than the target specified by the authorities. However, the control was circumvented by the increased use of bankers' accept-ances. Borrowers issue bills which are 'accepted', i.e. countersigned by the bank to make them negotiable, and are then bought by lenders. This process, which constitutes an alternative to that whereby money is deposited with the bank which then lends it, evades the corset.

4. Managing the national debt so as to maximize the proportion held outside the banking system. (Public sector borrowing from the banking system increases the money supply.) In theory it is possible to increase sales of bonds (i.e. increase government borrowing) by reducing their price. However, in general the authorities have been reluctant to lead the market down. This is probably because (a) potential purchasers might see the fall in price as heralding further falls and so hold off from buying, (b) high interest rates (low bond prices) would increase the cost of borrowing by private sector producers, who compete with the government for funds, and so might cause a reduc-tion in investment.

   The inability to sell enough gilts has led to a widening of the range of the government's borrowing instruments which now include National Savings Certificates, Premium Bonds and index-linked bonds.

5. Influencing interest rates. The authorities might change an 'anchor' rate, such as Minimum Lending Rate, or use money-market transac-tions so as to influence short-term interest rates and thus affect the demand for money. Domestic interest rates may also affect external capital flows and hence the exchange rate.

6. Monetary base control. This denotes the situation in which the authori-ties seek to limit the growth of the banks' deposits by controlling the most liquid element in their reserves, their deposits at the central bank (base money). If the money stock started to increase, the banks would bid for funds in the money market in an attempt to secure the extra base money needed to match the growth of their deposits. But as the central bank would not allow the stock of base money to expand

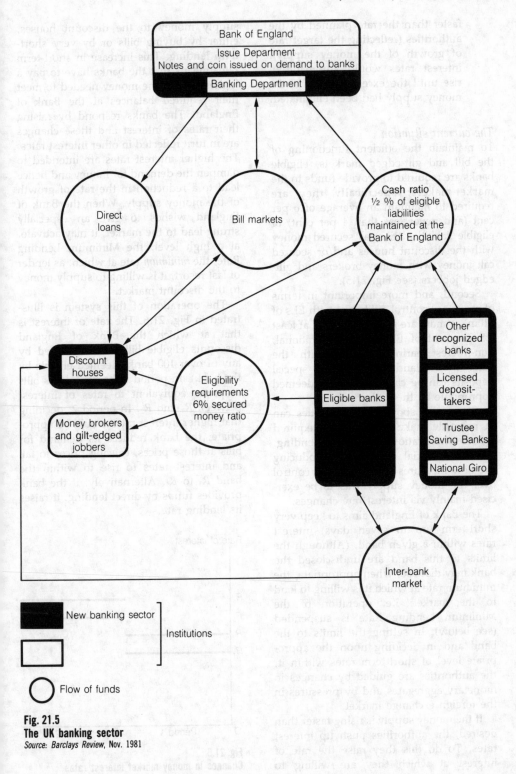

Fig. 21.5
The UK banking sector
Source: Barclays Review, Nov. 1981

faster than the rate planned by the authorities (reflecting the target rate of growth of the money supply), interest rates would automatically rise until the excess growth in the money supply had been eliminated.

The current situation

To maintain the efficient functioning of the bill and gilt-edged markets, eligible banks are required to provide funds to the market-makers; specifically they are required to maintain an average of 6 per cent (and never less than 4 per cent) of eligible liabilities (ELs) as secured money with the discount houses and/or secured call money with money brokers and gilt-edged jobbers (see Fig. 21.5).

Second, and more important in terms of monetary control, all banks with ELs of £10m. or more are required to hold at least 0.5 per cent of ELs as non-operational, non-interest-bearing deposits with the Bank of England. In addition special deposits can be called for when deemed appropriate by the authorities.

As we saw above, the authorities can in principle make use of such required balance-sheet ratios to limit bank lending. However, official statements introducing the new measures suggested that control over the money supply was to be exercised mainly via interest rate changes.

The Bank of England aims to keep very short-term (up to seven days) interest rates within a given band. (Although the limits to this band are undisclosed the bank may disclose, when appropriate, the minimum rate at which it is willing to lend to the market, i.e. operation of the Minimum Lending Rate is suspended (see below). In setting the limits to the band and in deciding upon the appropriate level of short-term rates within it, the authorities are guided by changes in monetary aggregates and by pressures in the foreign exchange market.

If the money supply is rising faster than desired, the authorities push up interest rates. To do this they raise the rate of interest at which they are willing to

supply money to the discount houses, either by buying bills or by very short-term lending. This increase in short-term rates means that the banks have to pay a higher rate on the money needed to meet their required balances at the Bank of England. The banks respond by raising their rates of interest and these changes are in turn reflected in other interest rates. The higher interest rates are intended to dampen the demand for money and hence lead to a reduction in the rate of growth of the money supply. When the Bank of England wishes to give an especially strong lead to the market, it may activate, at a high level, the Minimum Lending Rate, the *minimum* rate at which, as lender of last resort, it is willing to supply money to the discount market.

The operation of this system is illustrated in Fig. 21.6. The rate of interest is that at which the Bank of England discounts eligible bills (bills accepted by any of over 100 banks deemed eligible by the bank). In period 1 the bank buys bills at prices equivalent to rates of interest between R_1 and R_2. In period 2, deciding that higher interest rates would be appropriate, the bank reduces its demand for bills at those prices, causing prices to fall and interest rates to rise to within the band R_3 to R_4. Alternatively, if the bank provides funds by direct lending, it raises its lending rate.

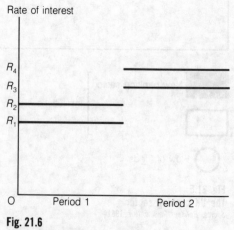

Fig. 21.6
Changes in money market interest rates

In addition, when the increase in the money supply has exceeded the target set by the government, the bank has indulged in overfunding, i.e. it has sold more public sector debt to the non-bank private sector than would be needed in order to finance the public sector borrowing requirement. These open-market sales are intended to reduce bank deposits. But they also inevitably reduce the banks' cash balances, and could cause interest rates to rise.

Interest rates and the exchange rate

We noted above that the Bank of England's reponsibilities include maintaining the exchange rate at the target level set by the government. Under a system of managed floating, such as we have at present, the government seeks to keep the exchange rate within a given band. To achieve the target the bank may intervene directly in the foreign exchange market. It may also seek to influence international capital flows, and hence the exchange rate, via changes in domestic interest rates.

The effect of changes in the supply of money

Having discussed the various measures by means of which the authorities might seek to influence the supply of money, we now examine the possible consequences of changes in the money supply.

The quantity theory of money

One approach to the effects of a change in the supply of money is via the quantity theory of money. In its simplest version this theory can be expressed as follows:

$$MV = PT$$

where M is the supply or stock of money,
V is the velocity of circulation of money,
P is the price level,
T is the volume of transactions.

The equation states that an increase in the supply of money will, unless balanced by a fall in the velocity of circulation, cause an increase in the price level and/or the volume of transactions. (The velocity of circulation can be measured in various ways, depending upon the definitions of expenditure and money supply adopted. But all the measures suggest that velocity increased in the UK in the post-war period until 1980, thereby reversing the previous trend, since when it has again fallen.)

The quantity theory does not allow us to say whether the impact of a change in the money supply will be on the price level, on the volume of transactions or on both. However, where there is a substantial reserve of unemployed resources, part of the initial impact is likely to take the form of an increase in transactions, i.e. in the level of economic activity.

Note that the equation given above does not embody any functional relationship. It is in fact a tautology. The two sides of the equation simply represent different ways of measuring total expenditure. Following on from this it is argued that although the theory may describe what is likely to happen following a change in the money supply, it does not provide an *explanation* of such consequences. In the next section, therefore, we extend the analysis and consider two possible explanations.

The supply of money and aggregate demand

Monetary policy has been given greater emphasis in the 1980s as part of the government's attempts to reduce the level of aggregate monetary demand and rate of inflation. We begin, therefore, by considering the possible effects of a reduction in the money stock or supply. (In practice a restrictionist monetary policy has aimed to reduce the rate of growth of the nominal money stock. This has sometimes caused a reduction in the real money stock. In other instances it has caused the real money stock to grow less than it would otherwise have done.)

A reduction in the money stock

Money is one of a range of assets held by the private sector (individuals and firms). The decision of each individual (or firm) as to how to allocate his resources among these assets depends upon the structure of prices and the expected return from each asset. (This is the basis of the analysis presented at the beginning of the chapter and underlies Fig. 21.1.)

If, given existing preferences, the authorities reduce the money stock, the private sector will attempt to restore the balance, i.e. to exchange other assets, such as gilt-edged securities, for money. However, these attempts will be frustrated if the money stock is maintained at the lower level, i.e. if the system of monetary control functions with perfect efficiency. In these circumstances the balance will be restored when the price of bonds falls, i.e. the rate of interest rises, to the extent required to eliminate the excess supply of bonds.

This is illustrated in Fig. 21.7 where the initial preferences of the private sector, as between money and bonds, are represented by curve D_1. As the money stock falls

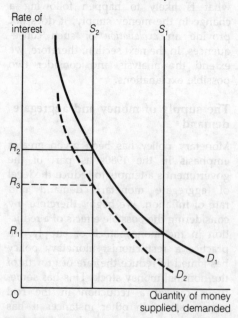

Fig. 21.7
Changes in the rate of interest

from S_1 to S_2 the rate of interest rises from R_1 to R_2.

The interaction between monetary and real variables

As noted earlier the higher interest rate is likely to cause changes in spending. A higher real interest rate makes saving more attractive and hence tends to reduce consumers' expenditure, as shown in Chapter 14. Furthermore, as we showed in Chapter 16, investment may be reduced as the cost of finance rises relative to the prospective return on that investment. The prospective return may itself be reduced because of lower economic activity following a rise in the interest rate. Moreover the ability to finance investment out of retained profits may decline. Finally, a rise in interest rates reflects a reduction in the value of government debt held by the private sector; this 'real wealth' effect may also lead to a fall in expenditure.

In Fig. 21.7 the initial demand for money D_1 reflects the initial level of national income. As national income falls following the increase in the rate of interest, the demand for money shifts to D_2. This causes the increase in the rate of interest to be moderated (R_3) as shown in Fig. 21.7.

An increase in the money stock

On the basis of the above analysis it might be concluded that an increase or expansion of the money stock would result in an increase in expenditure. However, in so far as this is presumed to occur via the mechanism of lower interest rates, the conclusion would be challenged by many Keynesian economists.

Keynes argued that an increase in money supply might not lead to an increase in investment, and hence in national income, for two reasons. First, once the rate of interest has fallen to a certain level the demand for money may become perfectly interest elastic. In Fig. 21.8, with the rate of interest at R_1,

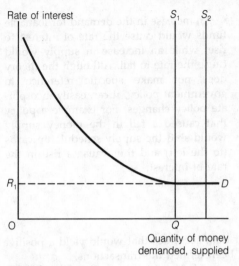

Fig. 21.8
The liquidity trap

people are willing to hold any addition to the money supply. Consequently any increase in the money supply beyond Q, such as from S_1 to S_2, would leave the rate of interest unchanged. This phenomenon has been named the liquidity trap. (In fact there is virtually no evidence that a liquidity trap has existed, at least since the 1950s.)

Second, even if the demand for money is not perfectly interest elastic, i.e. even if an increase in the money supply causes the rate of interest to fall, investment may not respond. The cost of finance is only one of numerous factors which influence investment spending, and these other factors may operate so as to make investment unresponsive to changes in interest rates. For example, if companies are very pessimistic concerning future economic prospects, their investment expenditure may not increase at all in response to a fall in interest rates, i.e. investment may be perfectly interest inelastic.

The implication of a possible failure of investment to respond to an increase in the money supply is that national income may also be unchanged. It was this possibility that led Keynes to advocate an increase in government expenditure as the surest way of increasing national income

and reducing the level of unemployment. He argued that even if there was a tendency for the system to move towards full employment via an increase in investment (or in consumption or exports) the process would proceed at a far slower rate than was required in view of the massive unemployment experienced by the UK and many other countries in the inter-war period.

The controversy concerning the relative effectiveness of monetary and fiscal policy is considered in more detail in Chapter 22. To conclude the present chapter we outline an alternative explanation of interest rate determination.

Appendix: An alternative explanation of interest rate determination

The *loanable funds theory* explains the rate of interest in terms of the demand for and supply of loanable funds. The demand for loanable funds comes from firms wishing to invest. As we showed in Chapter 16, the lower the rate of interest the larger the number of projects that would be profitable, i.e. the greater the demand for loanable funds (*D*, Fig. 21.9).

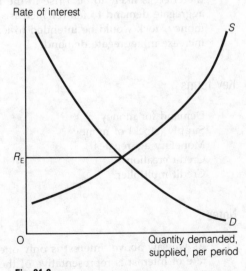

Fig. 21.9
The market for loanable funds

As we showed in Chapters 14 and 16, the supply of funds comes from savings, usually via financial intermediaries. Most people save, i.e. refrain from consumption, only if they are offered sufficient compensation in the form of interest (or some other type of financial return). The higher the interest offered the greater the amount saved (S, Fig. 21.9). The equilibrium rate of interest, R_E, is that which equates demand and supply.

An increase in the demand for loanable funds would cause the rate of interest to rise, while an increase in supply would cause the rate to fall. Although the theory does not make specific reference to government policy, it can easily incorporate policy changes. For example a policy that caused a fall in the money supply would shift the supply schedule upwards (to the left) and thus cause a rise in the rate of interest.

Summary

1. Three motives for holding money rather than securities that would yield a positive return can be distinguished; these have been termed the transactions, precautionary, and asset or speculative demand. The total demand for money varies positively with the level of national income and inversely to the rate of interest.
2. The supply of money (of which there are numerous definitions) is heavily influenced by the credit-creation activities of the banking system.
3. The structure of the banks' assets is influenced by the banks' desire for profitability and liquidity and for the need to comply with government policy. This policy is implemented by the Bank of England and the Treasury (the monetary authorities).
4. Monetary policy may include regulations concerning the volume of bank lending and balance-sheet ratios, measures to limit the growth of deposits and measures to influence interest rates. The Bank of England's responsibilities also include maintaining the exchange rate at the target level set by the government.
5. When the monetary authorities engineer a reduction in the money supply or stock the effect is likely to be a rise in the rate of interest. This it is hoped will cause aggregate demand to fall (or increase less quickly). Conversely, an increase in the money stock would be intended to lead to a fall in the rate of interest and an increase in aggregate demand.

Key terms

Demand for money	Bank of England
Supply (stock) of money	Discount houses
Monetary aggregates	Monetary control
Credit creation	Quantity theory
Credit multiplier	Liquidity

Notes

1. As we saw above, interest is only one of several types of return on assets. The rate of interest is representative of the various rates of return.
2. Bank deposits are not, of course, included within M0.
3. Begg D, Fischer S and Dornbusch R, *Economics*. McGraw-Hill, 1984, p. 515; Culyer A J, *Economics*. Blackwell, 1985, p. 615.

4. The quantity of notes issued also changes in accordance with the public's requirements. For example the public demands more notes to help finance the usual pre-Christmas shopping spree.

Essay questions

1. Discuss the factors which might cause a change in the demand for money and examine the possible implications of such a change.
2. Discuss the factors which might cause a change in the supply of money and examine the possible consequences of such a change.
3. Explain how banks can create credit and discuss the factors which limit their ability to do so.
4. 'The pattern of bank assets reflects the need for profitability, liquidity and for compliance with government policy.' Discuss.
5. Explain why the authorities might wish to restrict the supply of money and discuss the measures which they might adopt in order to do so.
6. Discuss the role within the financial system of (a) of the Bank of England, (b) the London clearing banks, (c) the discount houses.
7. Explain what you understand by the term 'the rate of interest' and show what factors might cause the rate to change.
8. 'The current system of monetary control is designed primarily to influence the demand for money.' Discuss.
9. 'Monetary policy is more useful when the authorities wish to expand the level of economic activity than when they wish to restrict it.' Discuss.
10. Explain, using a numerical example, the multiple expansion of deposits, and discuss its significance.

Exercises

21.1 What factors might account for the spread of interest rates shown in Table 21.6?

Table 21.6
Interest rates: what you should get for your money

	Post-tax return for standard rate taxpayers (%)	Minimum amount invested (£)	Withdrawals (days)
Clearing bank deposit account	5.12	—	7
High interest cheque account	7.82	2,500	0
Building society: ordinary share	6.09	—	0
High interest access	8.50	10,000	0
Premium	8.69	10,000	90
National Savings investment a/c	8.17	5	30
10% Treasury stock 1990	5.96	—	30
Index-linked stock 1990	6.95	—	—

Source: Financial Times, 10 May 1986

21.2 How would you explain the pattern of interest rates shown in Table 21.7?

Table 21.7
Rates of interest (Aug. 1987)

	%
Treasury bills – yield	10.11
Retail banks: call money	9.00
deposit accounts (7 days' notice)	4.95
National Savings Bank investment account	10.00
Building societies: mortgages	11.27
shares	7.39
Deposits with local authorities: 7 days' notice	9.50
3 months' notice	10.38
Long-dated British government securities – redemption yield	10.19

Source: Financial Statistics

21.3 The passage below appeared in the *Financial Times*, 11 April 1986.

The Bank of England acted yesterday to calm UK money markets and head off expectations that Tuesday's cut in bank base rates might be followed by another reduction. In its operations yesterday the bank refused to buy bills from the discount houses, and instead lent money to them for one week at a penal rate of interest (11¾ per cent).

Interest rates for three-month money had earlier moved below 104 per cent, three-quarters of a percentage point below the current level of bank base rates, before firming after the Bank stepped in. The Bank moved in the wake of the failure of disappointing figures for the growth of UK money supply in March, announced the previous day, to dampen the markets; Barclays Bank had followed its base rate cut earlier in the week by announcing a reduction in its mortgage rate by half a percentage point to 11¾ per cent from May 1.

(i)   How does a change in the banks' base rate affect interest rates?
(ii) In what sense do you think the March money supply figures were considered disappointing?
(iii) Why did the authorities hope that these figures would have dampened the markets?
(iv) What would be the likely effects of the Bank of England's actions?

Table 21.8
The PSBR as percentage of GDP

1974–79 (av.)	6.8
1979–80	4.8
1980–81	5.5
1981–82	3.3
1982–83	3.3
1983–84	3.3
1984–85	3.0
1985–86	1.6
1986–87	1.1
1987–88	1.0
1988–89	1
1989–90	1
1990–91	1

Source: Financial Statement and Budget Report 1987–88
Note: Figures for 1986–87 are Treasury estimates and for later
years are Treasury forecasts.

21.4 Discuss (i) the possible causes, (ii) the likely consequences, of the changes in the
public sector borrowing requirement shown in Table 21.8.

CHAPTER TWENTY-TWO
An Evaluation of Demand – management Policies

Introduction

In previous chapters we have examined the relationship between aggregate demand on the one hand and output and employment on the other. We have seen that different economic models lead to different conclusions about this relationship. We have also discussed the various policies that governments might adopt in order to try to influence the level of demand.

Most of this chapter is devoted to what is in effect a large case-study of the UK economy. There are two purposes in presenting this case-study. First, we examine the empirical evidence to see what light, if any, it might shed on the effectiveness of demand-management policies. The period studied was one in which what was claimed to be the most marked shift in policy for many years occurred, with more emphasis being given to monetary policy, and less to fiscal policy.

It is impossible to establish laboratory conditions in which to study economic behaviour, as noted in Chapter 1. Nevertheless, this marked shift in policy appeared to provide a good opportunity to test the effectiveness of alternative policies. However, the second purpose of the case-study is to show how difficult it is in practice to draw hard-and-fast conclusions about the effect of policy changes. This lesson is true for all time, even though the period studied ended a few years ago.

There are several factors that make it difficult to draw hard-and-fast conclusions. First, although we have discussed fiscal and monetary policy separately, in practice they interact, a point discussed in the next section. Second, the shift in policy was by no means the only important economic change in the period studied, as shown below. Finally, severe technical problems arise in the interpretation and implementation of both fiscal and monetary policy. These problems are discussed in the appendix to this chapter.

The interaction between fiscal and monetary policy

We saw in Chapter 20 that in most years government expenditure has exceeded revenue from taxation. Consequently we shall concentrate on the implications of a budget deficit. We examine two alternative sets of implications. First we consider the possibility that the budget deficit may lead to an increase in the money supply, giving a further stimulus to aggregate demand. We then consider the possibility that increased public spending may lead to a reduction in private spending (the 'crowding-out' hypothesis).

The monetary implications of the public sector borrowing requirement

The public sector borrowing requirement (PSBR) is related to, but is not precisely the same as, the budget deficit. It is the net difference between the expenditure and income of the public sector as a whole or, to use the term used in Fig. 22.1, expenditure minus tax revenue.

This excess of expenditure over revenue from taxation results in the net outflow of money designated A. This outflow has two effects. First, if some of the expenditure is on imports, this causes a worsening of the balance of payments current account – flow B. Second, expenditure on domestic output tends to increase commercial bank deposits (flow C) and cash reserves. However, this effect will be neutralized if the government can borrow an equivalent amount from the non-bank private sector (flow 1). This borrowing

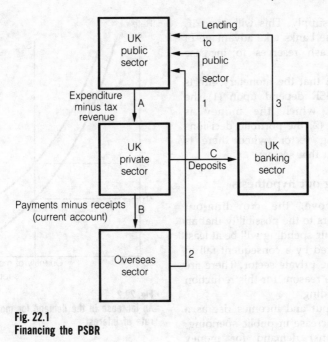

Fig. 22.1
Financing the PSBR

may take place via the issue of government bonds, National Savings Certificates, etc.

The government can also borrow funds from the overseas sector in two ways. First, if the sector wishes to hold its current account surplus in sterling it may buy UK government stock. Alternatively, if it wishes to obtain foreign currencies these will be supplied by the Exchange Equalization Account (EEA). Subsequently the sterling received in exchange will be invested by the EEA in government securities. These two flows are designated 2 in Fig. 22.1.

If the government's borrowing needs are not met from these sources it is said to have a residual financial deficit, and this must cause an increase in the money supply.

It can be seen from Fig. 22.1 that the residual deficit is financed by borrowing from the banking or monetary sector. This borrowing takes two forms. The first, borrowing from the Bank of England via Ways and Means Advances, is strictly temporary. Far more important is the second form, the issue of Treasury bills.

Treasury bills are purchased initially by the discount houses, but with funds provided by the commercial banks. The banks are able to provide these funds since, as shown above, their cash reserves have increased because of the deficit spending. If the discount houses are unable to cover the Treasury bill tender with funds raised from the banks and elsewhere, the Bank of England will meet the shortfall either by making loans to, or purchasing existing bills from, the discount houses.

The banks may choose to increase the proportion of the assets they hold directly or indirectly in the form of Treasury bills, and use their additional cash entirely to make loans to the discount houses or purchase bills from them. In these circumstances the Treasury bill issue can be regarded as having completely mopped up the additional cash injected into the banking system. The money supply increases simply by the amount of the residual deficit.

However, in a fractional banking system such as that in the UK, it is likely that there will be a secondary expansion of the money supply. This will occur if, for example, the banks take advantage of their higher cash reserves to increase advances.[1]

We see then that the monetary effects of a given PBSR depend upon (1) the sources from which the money is borrowed, and (2) the portfolio decisions of the banking sector (when there is borrowing from that sector).

The crowding-out hypothesis

As noted above, the crowding-out hypothesis refers to the possibility that an increase in public spending will be at least partially balanced by a consequent fall in spending by the private sector. There are several possible reasons for this reduction in private spending.

First, as output and incomes rise as a result of the increase in public spending, the (transactions) demand for money rises. Unless this is balanced by an increase in the supply of money, the rate of interest will rise. (We saw above that the authorities often try to finance the PSBR in such a way as to minimize the expansionary effect on the money supply.) In Fig. 22.2 the increase in the demand for money from D_1 to D_2 causes the rate of interest to rise from R_1 to R_2. This rise in the rate of interest is likely to cause private sector spending (especially investment) to fall, as shown in Chapter 16.

Second, consumption may fall because of the wealth effect. If the increase in public expenditure leads to a rise in prices, the real value of consumers' liquid assets will fall. In order to restore the value of these assets consumers may increase saving (i.e. reduce consumption).

Third, the value of assets (and especially of fixed-interest assets) may fall if increased sales of government stocks (to fund the PSBR) cause a fall in the prices of stocks. Again the response may be an increase in saving and a fall in consumption.

We saw in Chapter 16 that the volume of investment spending depends upon the expected yield of that investment. If a budget deficit is seen by businessmen as

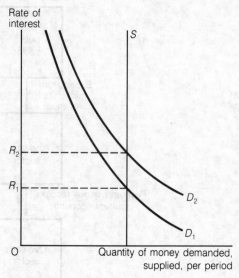

Fig. 22.2
An increase in the demand for money and the rate of interest

an indication of lax economic management, their confidence may fall and they may be more reluctant to invest. (Formally this would be illustrated by a downward shift of the marginal efficiency of capital schedule.)

Real resource crowding out

We noted in Chapter 11 the possibility that the public sector might become so large that private sector producers are unable to obtain all the resources they would require to meet consumers' demand. The possibility of real resource crowding out was explored at length by Bacon and Eltis.[2] They demonstrated that there had been a substantial increase in the proportion of people employed in the non-market sector, i.e. in industries whose output is not sold in the market. They suggested that this could undermine the rate of growth of the economy and the balance of payments, since the market sector provides the bulk of the nation's productive investment and exports.

Empirical evidence on crowding out

After reviewing a range of studies, Robins concluded that 'Despite the impressive array of possible theoretical mechanisms by which crowding-out might undermine the effectiveness of fiscal policy, empirical evidence of the significance and importance of its effect is far from unanimous and is, indeed, often conflicting.'[3]

The fiscal implications of monetary policy

Monetary policy has implications for the PSBR, and for tax revenue.

The public sector borrowing requirement

If a government uses monetary policy to control the economy, fiscal policy should be consistent with the chosen monetary stance. This point was clearly made in the Chancellor of the Exchequer's 1986 budget speech:

At the heart of the Medium Term Financial Strategy lies the objective of steadily reducing the growth of total spending power in the economy, as measured by GDP in cash terms, at a pace that will gradually squeeze inflation out of the system. . . . Over the past six years the rate of growth of money GDP has been halved, and a further significant reduction is envisaged for 1986–87. . . . We shall continue to maintain steady downward pressure on inflation. That means, above all, controlling the growth of money in the economy . . . monetary policy must always be supported by an appropriate fiscal policy. That means, in plain English, keeping borrowing low. . . . The public sector borrowing requirement for 1984–85 was just over 3 per cent of GDP. In my budget last year I planned to reduce it substantially to 2 per cent of GDP . . . for 1986–87 . . . I have decided to . . . provide for a PSBR of . . . 1¾ per cent of GDP.

Tax revenue

Tax revenue is affected whenever the level of economic activity changes as a result of monetary policy. If, for example, interest rates rise, causing expenditure to fall, tax revenue will be reduced. (This in turn will lead to a rise in PSBR unless government

expenditure is reduced.) Moreover, if the higher interest rates cause an increase in the cost of servicing the public debt, as is highly likely, this will require higher taxation or increased borrowing to meet the higher interest payments.

An evaluation of demand-management policies

In the following sections we examine the performance of the UK economy, to see what light this might throw on (a) the relative effectiveness of fiscal policy *vis-à-vis* monetary policy, and (b) the effectiveness of demand-management policies overall.

The historical record

We examine recent UK experience below, but first it is useful to adopt a longer perspective. Figure 22.3 presents estimates of the price level over almost 900 years. Reviewing the evidence on price changes Professor Pearce noted that before 1914 there were only two periods of inflation – both extremely mild in terms of recent experience – in 1520–1620 and 1750–1820. Pearce concluded that: 'The historical norm is obviously stable prices.'[4]

In the light of the historical record it is obviously important to attempt to discover the causes of the faster rates of inflation experienced more recently. As we saw in

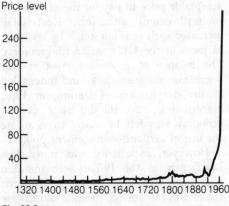

Fig. 22.3
Annual average level of prices 1300–1982

Table 22.1
The UK economy 1961–78

	Unemployment (%)		Inflation (%)		GDP: average annual change (%)
	Range	Average	Range	Average	
1961–64	1.6–2.6	2.0	2.0–4.3	3.3	2.0
1965–68	1.5–2.5	2.0	2.8–4.8	3.7	2.9
1969–73	2.4–3.8	3.0	3.6–10.7	7.8	3.3
1974–78	2.6–6.1	4.9	8.3–27.7	15.9	1.1

Source: United Kingdom National Accounts

Chapter 19 some economists see as the main culprit misguided attempts by governments to prevent increases in unemployment by means of demand-management (and especially fiscal) policies. Let us therefore examine the behaviour of the economy during a period when governments pursued an active demand-management policy, with a heavy reliance on fiscal policy.

Demand management in the 1960s and 1970s

Table 22.1 summarizes experience in terms of three major objectives: inflation, unemployment and growth of GDP. It can be seen that in the 1960s unemployment was low. The rate of inflation was high by historical standards but appeared to be under control (although a slight acceleration can be observed). Inflation at this rate was seen by most people as an acceptable price to pay for the satisfactory unemployment situation. Real GDP increased each year (although by less than in most of the UK's major competitors). The balance of payments position was sometimes unsatisfactory, and indeed led to the devaluation of sterling in 1967. Nevertheless, overall the state of the economy was felt by many to vindicate the use of demand-management policies.

However, experience was much less satisfactory in the 1970s. Both inflation and unemployment increased and, towards the end of the period, the rate of increase in GDP declined. The economy performed particularly badly in the second part of the 1970s, partly as a consequence of increased oil prices, and this period is considered in greater detail below. But it is important to recognize that the deterioration had begun before the first OPEC-inspired oil price increase. Over the period 1969–73 the average inflation rate was double that in the previous period, and the average unemployment rate 50 per cent higher. (These percentage increases were in fact repeated in the next period.)

This deterioration is at least consistent with the view that in the long term demand-management policies can do little to improve economic performance. But this could in principle be due to the fact that the best mix of policies was not chosen. We therefore compare economic performance in the 1970s and the 1980s, a period which saw a significant shift in government policy.

Demand management 1973–85

Table 22.2 compares the behaviour of the economy in the period 1973–79, during which fiscal policy was still the main form of demand management, with 1979–85 when greater reliance was placed on monetary policy (1979 is in fact a transitional year since it saw the change from a Labour to a Conservative government and from reliance on fiscal to reliance on monetary policy). We have not in this chapter presented information relating to later years, because after 1985 rather less emphasis was given to monetary policy.

Table 22.2
The UK economy 1973–85

	1973–79				1979–85		
	Inflation (%)	Unemployment (%)	Change in GDP (%)		Inflation (%)	Unemployment (%)	Change in GDP (%)
1973	8.4	2.7	7.4	1979	13.5	5.1	2.4
1974	16.9	2.6	−1.6	1980	16.4	6.4	−2.3
1975	23.9	3.9	−1.2	1981	11.5	9.9	−1.4
1976	15.7	5.3	2.7	1982	8.6	11.5	2.0
1977	14.9	5.6	2.5	1983	5.4	12.4	3.0
1978	8.9	5.5	3.1	1984	5.0	12.6	2.7
1979	13.5	5.1	2.4	1985	6.1	13.1	3.6

Source: United Kingdom National Accounts

The two periods covered by Table 22.2 were similar in two respects. First, both were affected by steep increases in oil prices. The direct impact on costs of the doubling of oil prices in 1979–80 was probably similar to that of the quadrupling of oil prices in 1973–74, since the later increase started from a higher base. (Because of the development of North Sea oil, the UK's balance of payments was, of course, affected more by the first than the second price increase.)

The second similarity is that both periods began with large public sector pay awards. However, in addition the second period opened with substantial increases in VAT as the government modified the pattern of taxation, from direct to indirect taxes. Despite this fact the rate of inflation was halved during the second period, whereas inflation was higher at the end than at beginning of the first period.

To some extent this improvement reflects the fall in world inflation, but the UK's relative situation also shows a vast improvement. The average annual compound rate of price increase was 15.6 per cent in the UK compared to 9.6 per cent in all OECD countries during 1973–79, whereas the comparable figures during 1979–85 were 8.7 and 8.0 per

cent.[5] Does this indicate that the war against inflation is better waged by monetary than by fiscal policy? Before we can reach this conclusion we must examine other possible contributory factors.

Reasons for the reduction in inflation

In economic matters the process of cause and effect is often complex and difficult to identify. Any of several combinations of factors could in principle have brought about the fall in the rate of inflation. In Fig. 22.4 we set out five alternative routes to lower inflation. We begin, as part of route 1, by considering the relationship between the exchange rate and the rate of inflation.

A change in the exchange rate

We explained in Chapter 17 why a fall in the exchange rate causes import prices to rise and so adds to inflation, and conversely why a rise in the exchange rate causes import prices to fall and so moderates inflation. Figure 22.5 shows that after 1973 the exchange rate fell for four years and was 22 per cent lower at the end than at the beginning of the period. On the other hand, after 1979 the exchange rate

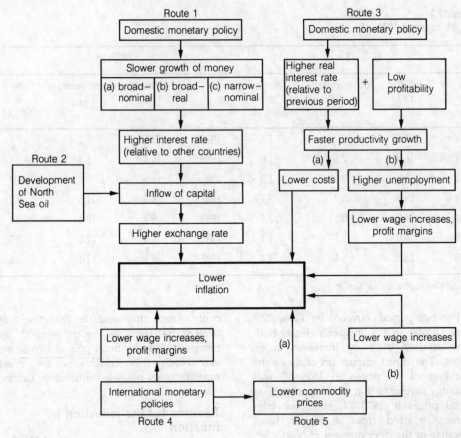

Fig. 22.4
Possible routes to lower inflation

rose, and although it subsequently declined its overall fall was only 10 per cent, less than half that in the previous period.

Commenting on this change, Professor Rose concluded that 'this difference in the behaviour of sterling probably explains the major part of the relative improvement in Britain's inflation record *vis-à-vis* the rest of the world over the past six years'.[6] (Note that in Fig. 22.4 'higher exchange rate' refers to this slower rate of depreciation of sterling.)

But what caused the more favourable behaviour of sterling, government policy or other factors? In seeking to answer this question we cannot look to exchange-rate policy itself, since sterling was allowed to float throughout the period covered by Fig. 22.5. The only policy change under this heading that might in principle have

had an effect was the relaxation of controls on UK overseas investment that occurred in 1979. But this was followed by a rise in sterling, not a fall as might have been expected.

Monetary policy and the exchange rate
What about the effect of monetary policy on the exchange rate (route 1, Fig. 22.4)?

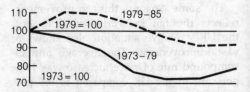

Fig. 22.5
Sterling exchange rate index
Source: *Barclays Review*, Aug. 1985

We saw in Chapter 21 that, with a given demand for money, the slower the growth in the money supply the higher the rate of interest is likely to be. Higher interest rates attract an inflow of capital, which causes the exchange rate to rise.

If, following route 1(a), we take a broad aggregate, sterling M3 (now redefined as M3), we find that the increase was actually greater in the second period (13 per cent a year compound) than in the first (11.4 per cent). See the top chart in Fig. 22.6.

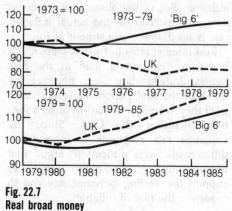

Fig. 22.7
Real broad money
Source: Barclays Review, Aug. 1985

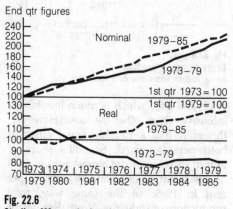

End qtr figures

Fig. 22.6
Sterling M3: nominal and real values
Source: Barclays Review, Aug. 1985

On the evidence that we have considered so far, it does not appear that the slower rate of depreciation of sterling in the second period can be explained by a tighter monetary stance. But let us take the investigation a stage further. It can be argued that the monetary stance is better measured by changes in the real than in the nominal money supply (route 1(b)). In fact when we examine the real money supply we again fail to find any evidence of a tightening of the monetary stance. Indeed, the bottom chart in Fig. 22.6 shows that the real money supply fell in the first period, but rose in the second. Morever, real sterling M3 rose faster than broad aggregates in other countries in 1979–85, in contrast to the earlier period (Fig. 22.7).

It is clear then that we cannot explain the more favourable behaviour of sterling

in the second period by a tightening of the monetary stance as measured by a broad monetary aggregate. However, as we saw in Chapter 21, there are several alternative measures of money, and in fact a different picture emerges when we examine the behaviour of narrow money (route 1(c)). On the IMF's definition of narrow money, the average annual growth in the UK slowed from 14 per cent in the first period to 11 per cent in the second, a little more than in the other major countries (9.5 to 7.5 per cent). A fervent believer in the effectiveness of monetary policy might wish to present this as evidence that policy did affect the exchange rate (and hence inflation). A more balanced view would be that when we consider the behaviour of all the aggregates we find little evidence that changes in the exchange rate can be explained by changes in the money supply.

However, it is still possible that interest-rate changes caused the change in the behaviour of sterling. (We showed in Ch. 21 that the authorities sometimes attempt to influence interest rates directly, not via changes in the money supply.) Therefore we need to examine the behaviour of interest rates.

Interest rates
Borrowers and lenders are influenced by the real rate of interest. Ideally this would be measured by the nominal rate of interest adjusted for the *expected* rate of

inflation. But in the absence of adequate data on expectations, the actual inflation rate is used as the adjustment factor.

Real interest rates in the UK were much higher in the second than in the first period. Indeed they were negative for much of the first period. However, until 1985 they were lower than in other countries including the USA. Since the exchange rate responds to interest-rate differentials, it is difficult to argue that monetary (interest-rate) policy operated to support the sterling exchange rate and so moderate the rate of inflation.

The development of North Sea oil

When we look for other possible reasons for the fact that sterling depreciated less in the second than in the first period, the development of North Sea oil (route 2, Fig. 22.4) is an obvious candidate. The UK's move from being an importer of oil to a net exporter led to increase in the demand for sterling and a fall in the supply.

Unemployment and production

The improved UK performance in terms of inflation has been accompanied by a severe deterioration in unemployment, as shown in Table 22.2. In absolute terms unemployment increased by about 2 million between 1979 and 1985 as compared to an increase of 640,000 between 1973 and 1979.

This difference occurred despite the fact that GDP rose almost identical amounts in the two periods. This is brought out clearly in Fig. 22.8 in which the actual growth in GDP is compared with the trend line for the period 1973–79. It can be seen that in 1985 GDP was at the level that would have been predicted on the basis of the earlier trend.

How do we explain these differences in the behaviour of unemployment and GDP between the two periods? Several factors merit attention.

First, there was an increase in the share of output accounted for by the production

Real UK GDP

—— Gross domestic product in the UK
- - - Trend based, 1973–79

Fig. 22.8
Gross domestic product
Source: National Westminster Bank Review, Aug. 1985

of oil and gas, which is much less labour intensive than other sectors. However, this shift had a roughly equal effect in both periods. North Sea oil's share of output increased from almost zero in 1973 to 3 per cent in 1979, and to nearly 6 per cent in 1985. In the same way, total production outside the North Sea sector rose by about 4 per cent in each period. Therefore we must dismiss this possible explanation.

Another possible explanation is the change in the numbers seeking work. The population of working age increased by 1.1 million in the second period. But there was also a considerable increase of around 900,000 in the first period. Allowing for the fact that some of the additional people would not seek work, we arrive at a difference between the two periods of 150,000. But, this difference is small when set against the additional rise in unemployment, i.e. in the second period as compared to the first, of around 1.3 million.

Finally we come to by far the most important factor, the faster rate of growth of labour productivity (route 3(b), Fig. 22.4). Gross domestic product per person grew by 2 per cent per annum in the second period as compared to 1.1 per cent in the first. (The comparable figures for non-oil productivity were 1.7 per cent and 0.4 per cent.) Rose expresses the significance of this change as follows: 'If since 1979 output per person had grown at the lower rate of the earlier period, *but without pulling down the growth of output itself,* employment would have been about 1½ million higher than it is today and recorded unemployment about 1¼ million lower.'[7]

Does the fact that the higher unemployment was due largely to a faster rate of productivity growth, mean that government policy was in no way responsible for the higher unemployment? In order to answer this question we need to examine the possible causes of the faster rate of productivity growth.

The causes of changes in productivity

One possible cause of an increase in productivity is the substitution of capital for labour. But in fact the country's capital stock grew relatively slowly in the second period. Rose also asserts that the advent of new technologies does not supply an adequate answer.

A far more plausible reason, he suggests, is

the development of high real interest rates in a situation in which the real rate of return on capital employed, which was already poor by international standards in 1979, particularly in manufacturing, fell to an intolerably low level in 1980. The rate of return in manufacturing was not appreciably less in 1980–81 than the very low figure recorded for 1975–76; but this earlier experience had already weakened many firms, and real interest rate had risen substantially in the interval.[8] (See Fig. 22.9.) In order to counteract this squeeze on profitability, firms made substantial reductions in their labour force, and increased labour productivity.

The increase in productivity would, via lower costs, contribute to lower inflation (route 3(a)). In addition the higher unemployment might lead to lower inflation because workers accept lower wage increases and/or because firms accept lower profit margins (route 3(b)).

Even though profitability revived subsequently, the improvement was patchy, and real interest rates remained at a high level. If it was felt that government policy contributed to the high interest

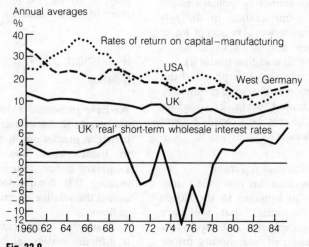

Annual averages %

Rates of return on capital–manufacturing

USA

West Germany

UK

UK 'real' short-term wholesale interest rates

1960 62 64 66 68 70 72 74 76 78 80 82 84

Fig. 22.9
Return on capital interest rates
Source: Department of Trade and Industry (published in *Barclays Review,* Aug. 1985)

rates, it could be concluded that government policy contributed to the growth in labour productivity and in unemployment.

International economic conditions

In the three routes, the three sets of factors, that we have examined so far, domestic policies and developments have been most prominent. We now consider what happened during this period in the international economy.

International inflation

In the previous section we explored possible explanations of the improvement in the UK inflation rate relative to that of other countries since 1979. We concluded that there is little evidence to suggest that the monetary stance had been tighter in the UK than in other countries. However, this leaves open the possibility that the fall in inflation world-wide was due, at least partly, to a *general* tightening of monetary conditions. This explanation would be given by many economists. For example Rose asserts that 'the world inflation rate has been brought down to a lower level than six years ago mainly because tighter monetary policies have been followed in the leading countries'.[9]

These tighter monetary policies might again lead to a moderation in the rate of inflation because workers accept lower wage increases and/or because firms accept lower profit margins (route 4).

Other economists have emphasized the impact on inflation of changing commodity prices. (As indicated in Fig. 22.4, tighter monetary policies may be a cause of lower commodity prices.)

Commodity prices and inflation

Professor Beckerman has concluded that the slowdown in inflation in the dozen industrialized countries that we have studied can be explained entirely by the sharp deceleration of 'commodity prices' i.e. the prices of primary products. . . . Between 1978 and 1980 the prices of goods imported into the advanced market economies from the outside world, or of the major commodities entering into international trade, rose by about 30 to 40 per cent (depending on which price index and which basket of goods one selects) and between 1980 and 1982 they fell by about 15 to 20 per cent. Thus, the total 'swing', or turn-around, in these prices was between 45 and 60 per cent.[10]

This swing was reflected in a swing in the prices of *all* imports into the average OECD country of 22 per cent. Given the proportion of expenditure accounted for by imports 'one would expect a deceleration of the final prices in the typical advanced OECD country of about 5 per cent. And this is almost precisely what took place.'[11] This conclusion could, of course, be applied to the UK (route 5(a)).

This relationship could be purely statistical or arithmetical. But Beckerman took the analysis a stage further. He used econometric techniques to test whether changes in import prices were reflected in changes in wage rates. He found that 'a 10 per cent change in the price of imports into the OECD as a whole would result in roughly a 2.5 per cent change in the wages in the representative OECD country'.[12] A moderation of the rate of wage increase may, of course, be reflected in a moderation of the inflation rate (route 5(b)).

Government policy, unemployment and inflation

We have presented a detailed comparison of changes in the economy in two periods in which greater emphasis was given first to fiscal policy and subsequently to monetary policy. One of the reasons for making this comparison was to try to assess the relative effectiveness of the two policies.

Evaluation of economic policy is always a difficult matter, since it requires decisions as to (a) which facts are most relevant, (b) precisely how these facts should be interpreted, and (c) in some instances, value-judgements. Consequently it is not surprising that our examination of this period of recent economic history allows differing conclusions to be drawn about the effectiveness of monetary policy *vis-à-vis* fiscal policy.

A critical view

Critics of the conduct of monetary policy in the 1980s might concede that the monetary stance did not become tighter in this period, but would nevertheless assert that it was too tight given the circumstances. Moreover the accompanying fiscal stance would also be considered to have been too tight. (The measurement of the fiscal stance is discussed in the Appendix.) An easier or looser stance would have prevented the rise in real interest rates that contributed to the rise in unemployment.

An expansionary policy would have caused only a modest increase in domestic prices, given the existence of a large amount of excess capacity as illustrated by the high level of unemployment. Indeed a higher level of output might have been achieved without any increase in costs (and hence prices) because fixed costs would have been spread over the larger output (see Ch. 5).

A higher level of expenditure would have led to an increase in imports, but the balance of payments was healthy because of the development of North Sea oil, and could have taken the strain.

An alternative view

An alternative answer to the question would emphasize the fact that the UK had lagged behind other countries in the growth of productivity, that the steep rise in productivity in the 1980s helped to correct this imbalance – or at least prevent it from getting worse – and that it left the UK better able to compete in international markets. Being competitive internationally is the best guarantee of a high level of employment in the long term. (The implication of this view is that

greater emphasis should be given to supply-side policies, such as those discussed in Ch. 24.)

Moreover, although the real interest rate was high in the UK it was, until 1985, even higher in other countries. This was a situation which threatened to put pressure on the exchange rate. Indeed sterling depreciated rapidly in 1984, especially in relation to the dollar. A more expansionary government policy would have added to the pressure on sterling. Thus the advantage of a high exchange rate – low import prices and therefore a lower rate of inflation – could have been lost.

Finally, the high level of unemployment is not necessarily an indication of massive excess capacity that is 'economic' or useful. Rapid changes in products and processes can render existing capacity obsolete.

Summary: the relative effectiveness of monetary and fiscal policy

We have made a detailed comparison between two periods, the first characterized by greater reliance on fiscal policy, the second by greater reliance on monetary policy. Unfortunately this comparison has not thrown much light on the relative effectiveness of these policies, for two reasons. First, although the performance of the economy improved considerably with respect to the rate of inflation, it deteriorated with respect to unemployment. Consequently as economists we cannot say that overall performance has improved or deteriorated (although we may, of course, hold private opinions on this matter). Second, there is considerable evidence that at least part, and perhaps, most of the change in performance could be explained by factors other than the change in policy.

On the other hand, confidence in the effectiveness of demand-management policies remains low. This is partly because of the experience of the 1970s and partly because of problems in policy implementation. (Also, as we have seen, some economists have advanced theoretical arguments which lead to the conclusion that demand-management policies, however skilfully implemented, are doomed to fail.) In the following sections we examine some of the problems that arise in implementing policy, beginning with fiscal policy.

Appendix: Problems in the interpretation and implementation of policy

Measuring the fiscal stance

The best measure of the overall impact of fiscal policy is the size of the PSBR. In trying to forecast the PSBR the government has a fairly good idea of its expenditure (although problems may arise in controlling the expenditure of the individual departments of central governments, and especially of the LAs). It has less certainty about revenue from taxation.

Which public sector borrowing requirement?

A problem of a more conceptual nature is to identify the definition of PSBR that would be most appropriate, given the government's aims and the economic circumstances. In presenting their policies governments use the actual (forecast) PSBR. But alternative definitions or measures have been proposed.

The alternative that has probably received most support is the cyclically adjusted PSBR. Even if rates of tax, social security benefits and expenditure programmes were held constant, fluctuations in economic activity would lead to movements in the PSBR. For instance the PSBR tends to increase in a recession, as tax revenue falls and social security payments rise. The cyclically adjusted PSBR attempts to remove the impact of cyclical variations in economic activity from the actual PSBR. It is a measure of

what the PSBR would be, at given tax rates, etc. if economic activity were in some sense 'on trend' or at a 'normal' level.

It is obviously difficult to decide what on trend or normal mean in this context. Nevertheless it is important that the government should be aware of these cyclical influences. If it were not, it might react to an unplanned increase in the PSBR during a recession by reducing its expenditure and/or increasing taxation, policies that would tend to exacerbate the recession.

Two other measures can be discussed briefly. The demand-weighted PSBR takes account of the fact that different forms of government expenditure have different multiplier effects (see Table 20.4). Changes in the relative shares of these various forms of expenditure will cause a change in the overall value of the multiplier, and hence in the size of the PSBR required to achieve a given objective.

Finally the real or inflation-adjusted PSBR would require that the actual PSBR be adjusted by an amount equal to the erosion by inflation of the real value of the stock of public sector debt. This is, perhaps, a rather more esoteric principle, and there is no evidence that it has influenced government policy.

Table 22.3 gives details of these alternative measures of the fiscal stance in the period in which monetary policy was the main weapon of demand management. Column 1 gives that actual PSBR; this is adjusted in column 2 for the first factor mentioned above, in column 3 for the first and second factors and in column 4 for all three factors. It can be seen that all the adjusted measures indicate a far tighter fiscal stance than the unadjusted measure. These adjusted measures are quoted by those economists who, as noted above, claimed that government policy in this period was too restrictive.

The multiplier

As noted above, a budget deficit will have a secondary effect on demand via the

Table 22.3
The PSBR (as % of GDP)

Year	Unadjusted	Cyclically adjusted	Cyclically adjusted and demand-weighted	Fully adjusted
1979	4.40	−0.73	−1.82	−3.59
1980	4.83	−2.07	−2.06	−3.25
1981	3.58	−4.79	−3.50	−4.47
1982	2.82	−5.37	−3.77	−3.11
1983	3.60	−4.34	−3.18	−3.62
1984	4.04	−3.99	−3.64	−4.07

Source: Mark J, Fiscal policy 1979–85: measurement of fiscal stance, *The Economic Review*, May 1986; adapted from table in Bisaras R, John C and Savage D. The measurement of fiscal stances, *National Institute Economic Review* August 1985.

multiplier mechanism. It has always been difficult to obtain precise estimates of the value of the multiplier. But it is argued that the move to a system of floating exchange rates has (a) made the process of estimation more difficult, and (b) made it more likely that the multiplier will have a low value. This would reduce the effectiveness of a given PSBR in raising aggregate demand.

The multiplier is most likely to assume a low value when a budget deficit is not accompanied by an increase in the money supply. In this situation borrowing by the government will cause interest rates to rise. If this increases the attractiveness of the UK as a location for financial investment, funds will flow in from other countries, causing the exchange rate to rise. This rise in the exchange rate will reduce overseas purchases of (dearer) UK exports, and increase UK spending on (cheaper) imports. In other words aggregate demand will fall.

In principle the fall in (net) exports may entirely offset the initial increase in demand, giving a multiplier value of one, i.e. the secondary effects are zero. A series of estimates of the multiplier value are reported by Driffill. He notes that 'all the multipliers are small (between zero and one, roughly speaking) regardless of model, and all indicate that under present con-

ditions fiscal policy is not a powerful tool for changing output and employment'.[13]

Technical problems in the implementation of monetary policy

The first problem, already mentioned above, is that it is not clear which of the various monetary aggregates should be targeted by the authorities. Second, experience has shown that the authorities frequently fail to hit whatever target is chosen. Both of these points are illustrated in Table 22.4.

We noted above that all governments have both a fiscal and a monetary policy, but until the mid 1970s only the fiscal policy objectives were published. An explicit monetary target was first published in connection with the UK's application for a large loan from the IMF. The target was in terms of Domestic Credit Expansion, the aggregate favoured by the IMF. As the balance of payments current account moved into surplus, attention shifted towards the broad aggregate M3.

In the 1980s, M3 continued to be targeted, but attention has also been given to other aggregates, both broader and narrower than M3. In 1988 it was announced that in future, in monitoring changes in broad money, most attention would be given to M4. This change can be

Table 22.4
Monetary targets

Period	Aggregate	Target*	Out-turn*
April 1976–April 1977	DCE	9	4.9
	£M3	9–13	7.7
April 1977–April 1978	£M3	9–13	16.0
April 1978–April 1979	£M3	8–12	10.9
Oct. 1978–Oct. 1979	£M3	8–12	13.3
June 1979–April 1980	£M3	7–11	10.3
June 1979–Oct 1980	£M3	7–11	17.8
Feb. 1980–April 1981	£M3	7–11	22.2
Feb. 1981–April 1982	£M3	6–10	13.5
Feb. 1982–April 1983	M1	8–12	12.1
	£M3	8–12	10.9
	PSL2	8–12	10.8
Feb. 1983–April 1984	M1	7–11	13.5
	£M3	7–11	9.5
	PSL2	7–11	13.2
Feb. 1984–April 1985	M0	4–8	6.6
	£M3	6–10	11.9
April 1985–April 1986	M0	3–7	3.5
	£M3	5–9	14.8

* Percentage growth at an annual rate.
Source: Savage D, Monetary targets – a short history, *The Economic Review*, Sept. 1984, updated

interpreted in different ways. A charitable interpretation would be that the authorities have shown flexibility as they learned from experience and as circumstances changed.

Changes in the financial system
The 1980s have seen very great changes in the financial system. Especially important in the present context has been the increasing level of competition among the financial institutions: banks, building societies, etc. This competition has led to the payment of interest on some current accounts, as noted above, and the abolition of bank charges on current accounts maintained in credit. These changes, it is argued, have caused people to hold a

higher proportion of their assets as deposits in banks, building societies, etc. and less as notes and coin. The spread of credit cards has also been important in this respect. One measure of this change is that the ratio of M3 to M0, after fluctuating between 4 and 5 between 1870 and 1970, doubled in the 1980s. This instability in the ratio is one reason why it became necessary to monitor more than a single aggregate.

A more cynical explanation of the loss of status of £M3 is that the authorities realized that they were unable to control its growth. It can be seen from Table 22.4 that its growth was constantly above the upper end of the target range. Moreover there is little evidence that the authorities are likely to be more successful in hitting other targets.

It is not that the authorities are incompetent; rather that they have an impossible task. Professor Goodhart, now at the London School of Economics but formerly chief economic adviser at the Bank of England, has said that to assume that the monetary authorities can and do control the stock of money appears 'other worldly and academic to a central banker'. He continues: 'Instead we see ourselves as operating within an uncertain market context, fitfully illuminated by unreliable forecasts of other influences on monetary growth.'[14]

The adoption of M0 as a monetary target has been criticized by many commentators. For example Andrew Bain, the Midland Bank's chief economic adviser, commented that as a target M0 'rightly carries little conviction in the financial markets. Quite apart from the indisputable fact that the spread of cash machines has reduced the amount of currency that people hold, and so gives a downward bias to its growth, M0 has virtually none of the characteristics sought in a useful monetary target.'[15]

Samuel Brittan noted that M0 had been chosen

simply because of a supposed statistical relationship between it and national income in the past, without a proper theory or explanation of the connection. Black box regularities are sometimes better than nothing. . . . But the equations behind the Treasury's monetary targets are based on a pitiful few years out of the millennia of human history and cannot be accepted without reasoning to back them.[16]

Brittan's preferred alternative, which he has advocated over a number of years, is to target the change in aggregate monetary demand, or monetary or nominal GDP.

A steady growth in aggregate monetary demand

In this approach, the precise definition of money would become a secondary issue, and the authorities would monitor and control whatever measure or measures (of money, credit or liquidity) experience showed to have the greatest impact on aggregate money demand (AMD).

The relationship between this approach and others is shown in Fig. 22.10. It can be seen that both fiscal and monetary targets are intermediate, the final objective being to control money GDP or AMD.

This approach is claimed to have several advantages. First, the announcement of a target in terms of aggregate

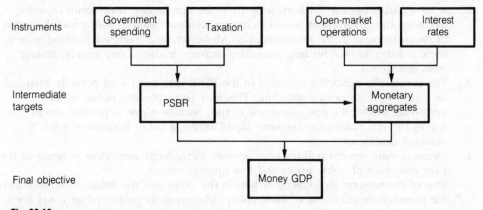

Fig. 22.10
The components of demand-management policies
Source: Brittan S, *How to End the 'Monetarist' Controversy*, 1st edn. Institute of Economic Affairs, p. 66

demand, rather than of an intermediate variable such as M4, makes the implication of a given increase in wages more obvious. If (productivity being unchanged) wages rise by 10 per cent but spending on goods and services is allowed to rise by only 8 per cent, there will be a fall of 2 per cent in output and employment.

Second, the danger is avoided that the government might continue to rely on its control of one monetary variable when this has been rendered less appropriate by a change in some other monetary variable, or by a substantial change in the velocity of circulation.

In principle a target growth of AMD could be implemented as rigidly as a target growth of the money supply. But one of its leading advocates, Samuel Brittan, has suggested that some flexibility in the response to shocks would be in order. If an increase in the price of one product, e.g. oil, were balanced by a fall in the prices of other products, the overall price level could remain unchanged. But

in practice prices tend to be sticky downward and the likelihood is that the overall price level would rise. If the government refuses to accommodate this increase by allowing an increase in AMD, a fall in output and employment will follow. Therefore Brittan suggests that AMD should be allowed to expand to at least partially accommodate a rise in the price of imports, but not to accommodate increased wage claims made to compensate for the price rise. For domestic shock of a wage-push kind, the general rule should be 'no accommodation'.[17]

It has been pointed out that AMD or nominal GDP has disadvantages as a target. It cannot be a *leading* indicator of policy goals since it measures what has already occurred. It cannot be measured accurately, especially in the short term, and the figures are subject to substantial revision. Finally the different ways of measuring GDP, described in Chapter 13, often give differing indications, in the short term, of the state of the economy.

Summary

1. An excess of public expenditure over revenue from taxation may cause a worsening of the balance of payments current account. It also tends to increase commercial bank deposits and cash reserves. However, this effect will be neutralized if the government borrows an equivalent amount from the non-bank private sector.

2. If the PSBR is not met by borrowing from the non-bank private sector or from overseas, the government is said to have a residual financial deficit and this must cause an increase in the money supply. Moreover, in a fractional banking system there is likely to be a further, secondary increase in the money supply, arising from this deficit.

3. The potentially expansionary effect of the PSBR may be at least partially balanced by a fall in private sector spending. This may occur because public sector borrowing causes the rate of interest to rise, because a rise in product prices causes the real value of consumers' liquid assets to fall or because of a fall in business confidence.

4. Demand-management policies have become increasingly ineffective in terms of the twin objectives of stable prices and low unemployment.

5. One of the reasons for higher inflation in the 1970s was the failure to understand the monetary implications of fiscal policy. Moreover, as greater reliance has been placed on monetary policy in the 1980s, the rate of inflation has declined. On the other hand the level of unemployment has risen dramatically.

6. Evaluation of economic policy is difficult because it requires decisions as to which facts are most relevant, and the exercise of judgement in the interpretation of these facts. Moreover value-judgements are sometimes involved. A detailed examination of the recent behaviour of the economy allows opposing conclusions to be drawn about the role and effects of government policy.

7. Technical problems in the interpretation and implementation of policy include difficulties in measuring the fiscal stance, in estimating the multiplier, and in choosing the monetary aggregate(s) to target.

Key terms

Public sector borrowing requirement
Crowding out
Inflation
Unemployment
Monetary implications of fiscal policy

Fiscal implications of monetary policy
Monetary targets
Exchange rate and inflation
Productivity
Commodity price changes

Notes

1. Numerical examples of both situations are given in Gilbody S H, The public sector borrowing requirement and the money supply: a simple descriptive account of the United Kingdom institutional mechanisms, *Economics*, Autumn 1985.
2. Bacon R W and Eltis W A, *Britain's Economic Problem: Too Few Producers*, 2nd edn. Macmillan, 1978.
3. Robins P, Keynesian economic policy and the 'crowding-out' hypothesis, *Economics*, Autumn 1984.
4. Pearce I F, What is wrong with inflation, *The Economic Review*, Sept. 1983.
5. Rose H, A tale of two periods: 1973–79 and 1979–85, *Barclays Review*, Aug. 1985, p. 51. This section draws heavily on Rose's article.
6. Rose, op. cit., p. 51.
7. Rose, op. cit., p. 54.
8. Rose, op. cit., p. 54.
9. Rose, op. cit., p. 51.
10. Beckerman W, How the battle against inflation was really won, *Lloyds Bank Review*, Jan. 1985, p. 5.
11. Beckerman, op. cit., p. 6.
12. Beckerman, op. cit., p. 8.
13. Driffill J, Why increasing government expenditure may have little effect on unemployment, *The Economic Review*, Nov. 1985.
14. Goodhart C A E, The operational role of the Bank of England, *The Economic Review*, May 1985. It appears that the French authorities have been more successful than the British in hitting monetary targets – see Cobham D and Serre J M, Monetary targeting: a comparison of French and UK experience, *The Royal Bank of Scotland Review*, March 1986.
15. *Midland Bank Review*, Spring 1986.
16. Brittan S, Time to relegate M0 target, *Financial Times*, 16 Sept. 1985.
17. Brittan S, *How to End the 'Monetarist' Controversy*, 1st edn. Institute of Economic Affairs, 1981, p. 26.

Essay questions

1. 'The debate between Keynesians and monetarists is a debate about the use rather than the choice of policy.' Discuss.
2. Explain why it is important to distinguish between the direct (physical) and indirect (monetary) effects of a budget deficit.
3. 'The precise effect of a given public sector borrowing requirement depends mainly upon the way it is financed.' Discuss.
4. Analyse the possible effects of a budget deficit on the level of fixed capital formation.
5. Evaluate a policy designed to permit the money supply to grow at a constant rate.
6. Explain why it is not sensible to think of a government operating only fiscal policy or only monetary policy.
7. Why might a government adopt an exchange rate target?
8. Discuss the relevance of the 'crowding-out' hypothesis to government economic policy.
9. 'Changes in the international economy have a more powerful impact than changes in domestic economic policies.' Discuss.
10. Examine the difficulties that arise in trying to measure (a) the fiscal stance, (b) the monetary stance.

Exercises

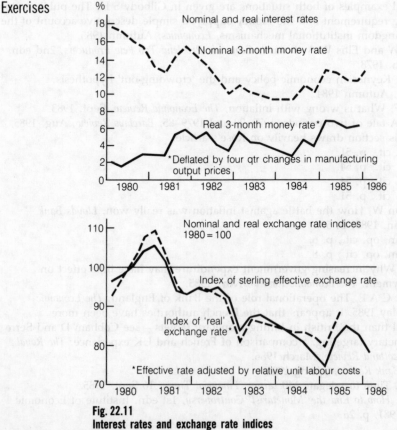

Fig. 22.11
Interest rates and exchange rate indices
Source: Barclays Review, Feb. 1986

22.1 Exercise 22.1 is based on Fig. 22.11.
  (i)   Explain the difference between (a) nominal and real interest rates, (b) nominal and real effective exchange rate indices.
  (ii) What factors might explain the changes in (a) nominal, (b) real interest rates?
  (iii) Discuss the likely consequences of the changes in real interest rates.
  (iv) What factors might explain the changes in (a) nominal, (b) real, exchange rate indices.
  (v)   Discuss the likely consequences of the changes in the real exchange rate.

22.2 The passage below is extracted from an article in *Barclays Review*, February 1986.

The response of government policy to the fall in oil prices has given a new twist to the conflict which had been developing between industry, as represented by the CBI, and the Chancellor. The former had for several months been asking for a reduction in interest rates and, therefore, in the exchange rate, but Mr Lawson had replied by saying in effect that interest rates had to be held until the level of wage increases had subsided.

Early in January money market rates were allowed to rise by 1 per cent in response to money market reactions to the incipient fall in oil prices, even though sterling had not actually weakened. The authorities were apparently anxious to avoid a repetition of events a year ago. Then interest rates had to be raised sharply to reverse a collapse of sterling which had been sparked off by the expectation of a sharp fall in the price of oil (that did not actually materialize) but which gathered momentum because markets interpreted the initial stability of officially influenced money rates as evidence of official indifference to the fate of sterling.

  (i)   Explain why the Confederation of British Industry (CBI) had been asking for a reduction in (a) interest rates, and (b) the exchange rate.
  (ii) Why had the Chancellor refused to lower interest rates in advance of a reduction in the rate of wage increases?
  (iii) Why did money market rates rise following the fall in oil prices?
  (iv) Why might the initial stability of officially influenced money rates have led to a collapse of sterling 'a year ago'?

22.3 The link between the size of the borrowing requirement and the growth in the quantity of money is very erratic. It depends on the size of *the balance-of-payments deficit on current account*, which determines the extent to which foreigners finance the borrowing requirements; it depends on the *private sector's appetite for gilt-edged securities* and on *the policy of the government and the Bank about interest rates*. In any case, with modern methods of control by the Bank of the banking system, the financing of the borrowing requirement by the banks can be largely prevented from enabling the banks to expand credit by more than is regarded as desirable.

  (i)   Explain why the factors given in italics influence the relationship between the PSBR and the growth in the quantity of money.
  (ii) In what ways may the undesirable consequences of financing the borrowing requirement by the banks be prevented?

22.4 Exercise 22.4 refers to the data on the next page, which first appeared in the *Midland Bank Review*, 1985. Figure 22.12 plots annual changes in the money supply and in the RPI. Table 22.5 presents estimates, by Professors M J Artis and M K Lewis, of the contribution of various factors to inflation. The rate of inflation is measured by changes in the consumer price index (CPI), a series that is similar to the RPI.

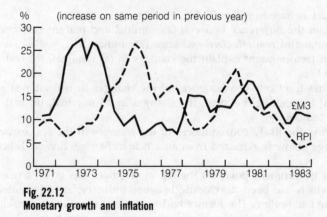

Fig. 22.12
Monetary growth and inflation

Table 22.5
Estimated contributions to inflation

	1971	1972	1973	1974	1975	1976	1977	1978	1979	1980	1981	1982	1983
Increase in CPI*	8.4	6.6	8.6	17.3	23.6	15.7	15.2	8.8	12.8	16.5	10.9	8.5	5.4
Contribution to inflation													
Increase in employment costs	2.5	4.1	2.7	7.2	11.2	3.5	3.2	3.9	5.6	7.6	3.8	1.5	1.2
Increase in non-employment costs	3.2	3.9	2.6	0.8	4.3	5.0	7.4	3.4	2.6	3.0	2.5	2.8	2.7
Increase in import prices	0.8	0.6	5.0	9.0	3.0	4.7	3.0	0.6	1.6	2.0	1.1	1.6	1.7
Increase in indirect taxes	0.2	0.4	−0.1	−0.3	3.8	3.1	4.4	1.6	4.7	3.8	3.1	1.8	0.2
Unidentified	1.7	−2.4	−1.6	0.6	1.3	−0.6	−2.8	−0.7	−1.7	0.1	0.4	0.8	−0.4

* Implicit deflator of the consumers' expenditure series
† Mainly profits.
Source: CSO, *Economic Trends*, annual supplements (various)

With reference to these data assess the role of monetary policy in controlling inflation.

22.5 Table 22.6 gives details of the economic performance of the UK and of other countries. (The figures in brackets are the UK's ranking out of twelve countries: Belgium, Canada, Denmark, France, West Germany, Ireland, Italy, Japan, Netherlands, Switzerland, UK, USA.)

What light does the data throw on the effectiveness of the UK government's economic policy since 1979?

Table 22.6
Real GDP growth 1960–86 (% per year)

	1960–69	*1970–79*	*1980–86*	*1982–86*	*1960–86*
UK	3.1 (12)	2.4 (11)	1.4 (8 =)	2.6 (3)	2.4 (12)
USA	3.9 (11)	2.7 (9)	2.1 (3)	2.5 (4)	3.0 (10)
Japan	10.1 (1)	5.1 (1)	3.8 (1)	3.6 (1)	6.6 (1)
European Community	—	3.3	1.4	1.8	—
OECD	—	3.3	2.1	2.4	—

Output per person employed 1970–86
Whole economy

	1971–74	*1975–79*	*1980–86*	*1982–86*
UK	2.5 (8)	1.8 (6 =)	1.8 (3 =)	2.4 (2)
USA	1.0 (12)	0.8 (9)	0.7 (10 =)	0.6 (12)
Japan	4.1 (1 =)	3.6 (1)	2.8 (1)	2.7 (1)
European Community	3.5	2.5	1.6	1.9
OECD	2.7	2.0	1.5	1.7

Unemployment 1960–86
Per cent of labour force. ILO common definitions. Averages

	1960–69	*1970–79*	*1980–86*	*1982–86*	*1960–86*
UK	1.9 (4)	4.3 (7)	10.6 (10)	11.7 (10)	5.1 (4)
USA	4.8 (6)	6.1 (9)	7.8 (4)	8.1 (4)	6.1 (6)
Japan	1.3 (3)	1.7 (2)	2.5 (2)	2.6 (2)	1.7 (2)
European Community	—	4.2	9.9	11.0	—
OECD	—	4.2	7.5	8.1	—

Consumer price inflation
(% per year)

	1960–69	*1970–79*	*1980–86*	*1982–86*	*1960–86*
UK	3.6 (6)	12.5 (11)	8.1 (9)	5.5 (6)	8.0 (10)
USA	2.3 (1)	7.1 (3 =)	6.1 (5 =)	3.8 (5)	5.0 (3)
Japan	5.4 (12)	8.9 (7 =)	3.2 (1)	1.9 (1)	6.1 (7)
European Community	3.5	9.3	8.4	6.9	6.8
OECD	2.9	8.3	6.9	5.1	5.9

Source: Lloyds Bank Economic Bulletin, April 1987

CHAPTER TWENTY-THREE
Prices and Incomes Policies

Introduction

As noted in Chapter 19, prices and incomes policies are usually adopted in conjunction with demand-management policies. We have shown that measures to increase demand, in order to try to increase output and employment, can also cause prices to rise. It is claimed that prices and incomes policy can reduce the inflationary impact of higher demand. Incomes policy may also be used in order to counteract cost-push inflation.

A comprehensive policy involves controls on both prices and incomes. However, since the costs of implementing such a policy are high, governments have sometimes preferred to adopt a less comprehensive approach, seeking to control either prices or incomes. In examining the principles on which policies might be formulated it is convenient to start with the less comprehensive approach. We consider first a policy designed to control prices only.

The control of prices

If we were to adopt a very simple definition of inflation, namely an increase in the level of prices, the immediate effect of successfully controlling prices would be to reduce the rate of inflation. However, a wider definition of inflation would take account of the underlying forces which have led, or might lead, to rising prices. According to this view the control of prices moderates inflation only if it moderates these underlying inflationary forces.

This throws us right back to the controversies concerning the operation of the economy that we discussed in earlier chapters. If the crucial factor is the balance between demand and supply of goods and services, price controls will do nothing to moderate inflationary tendencies. They will simply cause open inflation to be replaced by suppressed (or repressed) inflation.

An important aspect of a system of price controls is the proportion of prices to which controls are applied. Clearly the more products covered by the controls the greater will be the cost of administering the system. On the other hand, if only some products are covered the result is likely to be that the price of the remaining products will rise even faster than they would have done in the absence of controls. This is due to the 'real income' effect, i.e. to the fact that since less money is spent on products whose prices are controlled, consumers are left with more money to spend on non-controlled products.

The effect of price controls on aggregate demand

When the control of prices is not accompanied by the control of incomes, important changes in real incomes are likely to occur. The real income of wage- and salary-earners is likely to rise, and the real income of companies – and thus of shareholders – to fall.

This change in the distribution of income is likely to be reflected in the pattern of expenditure – with consumption rising and investment falling. The effect on aggregate expenditure of these changes depends upon the magnitude of the changes and the propensities to spend of the various groups concerned. It is very difficult to predict what the overall effect will be, but the fact that consumption is by far the major form of expenditure suggests that aggregate demand is more likely to increase than to decrease.

A further boost to aggregate demand may also occur if imported goods are exempt from price controls – as is likely. In these circumstances there is likely to be some switching away from (non-controlled) imports to (controlled) domestic products.

The effect of price controls on aggregate supply

Some producers may react to controls on domestic prices by switching supplies to export markets. This would cause the aggregate supply curve to shift to the left. This might also occur if company profits, and therefore investment, were squeezed to the extent that a reduction in economic capacity resulted.

The overall effect of price controls on inflationary pressures

We suggested above that price controls are likely to cause aggregate supply to fall. Since there is unlikely to be a corresponding fall in aggregate demand it appears that price controls, unaccompanied by controls on incomes, are likely to accentuate rather than moderate the underlying inflationary pressures.

The only circumstances in which this conclusion might not apply are if supply conditions are modified as a result of changing expectations about the behaviour of prices. Wage claims may take into account both past changes in prices and expected future changes. If price controls have an appreciable impact on the rate of price increases this may lead to a moderation of wage claims and to wage costs being lower than they would be otherwise. This would cause the supply curve to shift to the right, indicating that producers would be willing to supply more at any given price. This increase in supply would, of course, tend to reduce the underlying inflationary pressures.

If expectations are very important, the reduction in the rate of price increases in one period may lead to a reduction in the pressure for higher wages in succeeding periods, and hence establish a 'virtuous

circle'. Given the disadvantages involved in price controls many economists have concluded that they can be justified only if they operate on expectations in the way outlined here.

The control of incomes

We now consider the likely effects of a policy which controls incomes but which does not *directly* control prices. Such a policy is most likely to be adopted if it is felt that the basic cause of inflation is a rise in factor costs, and in particular in the cost of domestic inputs. (It is extremely difficult to control or combat increases in the prices of imported factors, although a method that may be appropriate in some circumstances is a revaluation of the currency, a policy discussed in Ch. 25.) Inflation which is believed to arise from this cause is sometimes termed cost-push inflation.

It is argued that if the rise in factor costs can be checked or moderated, price increases will also be moderated. This will occur because producers typically set their prices by adding a fixed mark-up to their costs. The implication of this argument is that it is not necessary to control prices, and thus incur additional adminstrative costs.

If this reasoning is valid (and this point is discussed further below), this might appear to be the ideal method of preventing or halting inflation. However, to be successful an incomes policy requires the co-operation of all members of the community and especially, perhaps, of employees. Many employees may not accept the mark-up theory of pricing outlined above. They may not believe that the rate of price increase will respond to the rate of wage increase in the way suggested here. They may feel that prices will rise faster than money wages.

Should this happen, real wages would of course fall. (The only circumstances in which this may not happen are if the rise in domestic prices is balanced by a fall in import prices.) Furthermore, company profits and therefore dividend payments are likely to rise. (Even if dividends are controlled as part of the incomes policy, shareholders are likely to benefit in the long run if higher profits cause share prices to rise.) The belief that the control of incomes may result in a redistribution of income away from employees, suggests that they are unlikely to accept controls on incomes unless accompanied by price controls.

One of the likely consequences of rising incomes and prices is a reduction in employment via a fall in exports and a rise in imports. But even if there is no effect on foreign trade, for example because prices are rising at the same rate in other countries, a fall in employment might result from a rise in real wages. As one commentator has put it, 'The logic of the incomes policy case is: (a) union power has added to the sustainable (natural) rate of unemployment by distorting the market pattern of real wages; and (b) incomes policy can reproduce something more nearly approaching market wages.'[1]

Expressing the matter in this way highlights the fact that an incomes policy may well involve modifying the pattern of relative earnings of different groups of workers, and this could provide a further source of conflict.

The control of prices and incomes

We have suggested that it may be especially difficult to implement a policy that aims to control only prices or incomes (earnings), because the group affected – firms or workers – might believe that the other group would benefit at their expense. A policy to control both prices and incomes will not arouse the same degree of suspicion and may find a greater degree of public acceptance in principle. However, problems are still likely to arise because of a lack of agreement as to what would constitute an appropriate division of the national income as between income from employment on the one hand, and

from profits, etc. on the other. In addition the conflicts within a group, e.g. concerning the size of differentials between skilled and unskilled workers, would remain.

In the next section we consider some of the evidence relating to the effects of prices and incomes policies. But first we briefly consider some of the questions and problems that have arisen in the implementation of policy.

1. Should a figure be stated as a guideline or norm or as a maximum? The advantage of a norm is that it allows some flexibility, e.g. for pay increases above the norm where a particular type of labour is scarce. The disadvantage is that in practice the norm tends to become the minimum.

2. Should the target be expressed in absolute or percentage terms? A percentage target avoids the problem of erosion of differentials, and has been a feature of most policies. But it has not always been acceptable and has frequently been modified.

3. If departures from the target are to be allowed, what criteria or conditions should be met: a shortage of a particular type of labour or product, the working of unsocial hours, the introduction of a productivity agreement, upgrading, promotion or some other change in the nature of the job? All of these, and other, criteria have been adopted. Introducing flexibility in this way is desirable in principle. But in practice difficulties of definition and measurement have made it impossible to ensure that increases in excess of the target have been within the spirit of the legislation.

4. Should price controls be exercised in isolation, as when a price freeze is imposed, or should they be based on the relationship between the price of a product and its cost? The former is less costly to administer and in principle should be more effective in the short term. However, it has usually been found necessary

to allow some exemptions, e.g. fresh foodstuffs.

5. If controls are to be related to the relationship between the price of a product and its cost, should the price be allowed to reflect all increases in cost or should the firm be expected to absorb part of those increases? If firms have to absorb cost increases they must increase their efficiency to protect their profits. On the other hand, if firms are required to maintain the same percentage profit rate as before they will be discouraged from trying to reduce their costs, since this would result in a reduction in the absolute profit allowed.

6. What prices should firms be allowed to charge for new products? It might seem appropriate to allow a profit rate similar to that on other products. But this may not be very meaningful given the many alternative ways of allocating costs between products.

The effects of prices and incomes policies

Since prices and incomes policies have become less used recently, we have to go back a number of years in order to find evidence about their effects.

It is difficult to determine the effects of any economic policy since this requires knowledge of what would have happened in the absence of the policy. However, it appears that countries that have operated prices and incomes policies have suffered higher inflation rates than countries which placed more reliance on demand-management policies. In the period 1953–72, before the first of the OPEC-induced oil price rises, the UK, the Netherlands and Sweden, in the first group, had inflation rates about twice those of West Germany, Switzerland, Belgium and the USA, in the second group.

Moreover, detailed studies of UK ex-perience show that the long-term benefit of prices and incomes policies is negligible. Considering the period 1952–66 *The Economist* (5 April 1975) concluded that during periods in which an incomes policy was 'full on', wages were lower than would have been expected. This was seen as 'prima facie evidence that a short-lived freeze works'. However, in subsequent periods when policy was only 'half on' or had been completely abandoned, 'wages soon catch up again – prima facie evidence that the ground gained in the freeze is subsequently lost'.

The authors of a later study reached similar conclusions:

Our results indicate that, whilst some incomes policies have reduced the rate of wage inflation during the period in which they operated, this reduction has only been temporary. Wage increases in the period immediately following the ending of the policies were higher than they would otherwise have been, and these increases match losses incurred during the operation of the incomes policy.[2]

The strongest case for an incomes policy is probably that it can be used to break an inflationary cycle as, for example, when the inflation rate declined from an annual rate of 26 per cent in June 1975 to 15 per cent in 1976. However, even this rate was substantially in excess of the rates experienced by many of the UK's major competitors, including those without an incomes policy. Moreover it is possible that the inflation rate would have fallen in the absence of an incomes policy in the UK. The prices of some imported commodities fell in 1976. Furthermore, monetarist economists had predicted that the inflation rate would decline following a decline in the real money supply in 1975 and 1976.

Incomes policy via taxation

The disadvantages of conventional incomes policies and the apparent failure of demand-management policies have led to proposals for a different form of incomes policy, in which taxation would be used.

to influence changes in earnings. Under a scheme proposed by Professor Layard there would be a pay norm. Any employer paying above the norm would be liable to a tax equal to the tax rate times that part of his wage bill representing the excess growth of pay. There could also be a provision whereby firms awarding increases lower than the norm might pay a negative tax. In this way employers would have an additional incentive to negotiate lower wage increases.[3]

Summary

1. Prices and incomes policies are usually adopted to reduce the potentially inflationary impact of government policies intended to increase aggregate demand.
2. Policy may be designed to control either prices or incomes or both.
3. If the prices of only some products are controlled the real income effect may cause an increase in demand for other products, and therefore a faster rate of increase in their prices.
4. Price controls unaccompanied by controls on incomes are likely to accentuate underlying inflationary pressures.
5. An incomes policy may be introduced to counteract cost-push inflation.
6. In the absence of price controls, the control of incomes may lead to a redistribution of income.
7. Alternative criteria exist for allowable increases in prices and incomes.
8. Evidence suggests that the long-term benefit of prices and incomes policies is negligible.

Key terms

Price controls
Suppressed (repressed) inflation
Real income effect
Control of incomes
Cost-push inflation

Redistribution of income
Mark-up theory of pricing
Norms
Criteria
Incomes policy via taxation

Notes

1. Brittan S, *How to End the 'Monetarist' Controversy*. Institute of Economic Affairs, 1981, p. 113.
2. Henry S G B and Ormerod P A, Incomes policy and wage inflation: empirical evidence for the UK, 1961–1977, *National Institute Economic Review*, Aug. 1978.
3. Shaw R, Price controls and inflation, *Economics*, Winter 1980.

Essay questions

1. 'In situations where incomes policies are effective they are not required whereas in situations where they are required they are not effective.' Discuss.
2. Explain the statement that the basic rationale of an incomes policy is that by reducing inflationary tendencies or pressures it permits a higher degree of resource utilization than would otherwise be possible.

3. 'Although producers may suffer as a result of price controls, consumers must benefit.' Discuss.

4. Explain why it is sometimes claimed that prices and incomes policies are successful only in so far as they influence expectations.

5. Under what circumstances are prices and incomes policies most likely to contribute usefully to the management of the economy?

6. 'It is easier to identify the benefits than the costs of incomes policies.' Discuss.

Exercises

The following is taken from A A Walters, *Money and Inflation*. Aims of Industry, 1974, p. 11.

23.1 The reaction of a businessman to an increase in the demand for his product is well known. He will not immediately increase the price. First he will wish to make sure that the increase in demand is permanent and not a flash in the pan. Thus the first reaction is to produce more from existing resources. Any slack is taken up, stocks are run down, short-time working is eliminated, and the quantity of output of the firm is increased and sold readily at the existing prices. Thus it seems that there is an increase in the rate of growth without any increase in the price level. It seems, therefore, that one can have unusually high growth without inflation. And it is tempting to end the story at this point; but we must face the consequences and go on.

The businessmen who have run down their stocks and eliminated part-time working will be induced to attempt to hire more labour and to buy more stocks of raw materials to keep the higher rate of production going. But, of course, all businessmen will be there trying to buy labour and commodities. The price of such raw materials would be increased, and one would find that the wage rates of labour, particularly those of skilled workers in short supply, would rise quickly. The businessman will then say that 'costs have risen', and so he must put up his prices; he will agree that it was not the rise in demand that gave rise to his need to increase prices; on the contrary the higher demand kept down costs because of the greater throughput. It was the cost-push that caused it all. The corollary is that if we could only keep down the prices of raw materials and commodities and the wages of labour, then we would beat inflation.

Comment on the conclusion presented in the final sentence of this passage.

23.2 The passage below is from the *Midland Bank Review*, 1981, p. 1.

When the difficulties of operating an incomes policy and the lack of clear evidence that it can be more than temporarily effective are added to the natural reluctance of trade unions to see their role diminished by it, there seems a case for consigning it to the limbo of policies tried and found wanting. The present Government eschews it in the belief that monetary policy backed by fiscal restraint is sufficient to bring down the rate of inflation; and so it probably is, for that purpose alone. But an incomes policy may still be required in order to minimize the cost of monetary and fiscal restraints in terms of lower real output and employment.

Critically examine the above passage.

CHAPTER TWENTY-FOUR
Supply-side Policies

Introduction

In Chapter 23 we examined prices and incomes policies, favoured by Keynesian economists as a supplement to demand-management policies. We now consider policies intended to influence the supply side of the economy, i.e. to shift the aggregate supply curve to the right, by increasing the flexibility of labour and capital markets. Most of the measures that we discuss were introduced by the Conservative government first elected in 1979, and may reflect both political and economic considerations. However, we concentrate on the alleged economic merits of these measures.

The labour market

The government has attempted to increase the flexibility of the labour market by fiscal policy, by measures to increase training, and by legislation relating to the activities of trade unions.

Fiscal policy

A number of fiscal measures have been introduced with a view to increasing the incentive to work (and to take more highly paid but demanding work). The basic rate of income tax has been reduced in stages from 33 to 25 per cent, and the maximum rate from 83 to 40 per cent. Moreover the various tax thresholds have been increased since 1978/79 by over 20 per cent more than would have been required to keep them in line with inflation. (For workers on average incomes much of the reduction in the tax burden has, however, been balanced by increases in National Insurance contributions.)

The balance of rewards between work and leisure has also been altered by changes in the treatment of unemployment benefit. The earnings-related supplement to unemployment benefit has been abolished, and the benefit itself is now taxed. These changes should have the effect of increasing the number of people willing to work (or more generally the total amount of effort supplied) at a given wage rate.

Small businesses

There were an estimated 750,000 (40 per cent) more self-employed in 1987 than in 1979. Many of these have used the Enterprise Allowance Scheme under which the government can pay a formerly unemployed person a weekly allowance for a year to help set up his or her own business. The small companies' rate of corporation tax has been reduced from 42 to 25 per cent; and assistance to small businesses has been extended in various other ways, as shown in Chapter 16.

Obstacles to mobility

The efficient operation of the labour market requires that workers should change jobs in response to changes in the demand for labour. Mobility of labour has been impeded by a number of factors. People who change jobs have usually ended up with lower occupational pensions than those who stay with one employer. Legislation has been introduced to remove this anomaly. In order to reduce the difficulty and cost involved in moving house, the stamp duty paid on house purchase has been reduced and solicitors' monopoly on conveyancing has been ended. Finally, many council house tenants have been enabled to buy their houses at concessionary rates.

Profit-related pay

In a move to encourage wage flexibility the government introduced in 1987 a scheme whereby the pay of employees linked to their firm's profits could qualify for income tax relief. It was estimated that this relief would be worth up to 4p off the basic rate of income tax to a worker on average earnings.

When pay is related to profits, shareholders and workers benefit (or suffer) together from changes in profitability, a factor which the government hoped would help to reduce the 'them and us' feeling in industry. A more particular advantage would occur in periods of falling profits. In these circumstances the wages bill would automatically decline, i.e. the cost of labour would fall. The firm would therefore be able to retain some workers who might otherwise have been made redundant.

Measures to increase training

In the 1960s and 1970s the training of workers was encouraged in two main ways. First, under the 1964 Industrial Training Act a levy and grant system penalized employers whose training was considered to be inadequate (in terms of quantity or quality) and rewarded employers whose training was considered to be satisfactory. The government monitored the scheme and made a contribution towards its costs. Second, training was offered under the Training Opportunities Scheme at government training centres (subsequently renamed skillcentres), colleges of further education, etc.

The scope of the 1964 Act was reduced by further legislation in 1973 and 1981, and this no doubt contributed to the fall in privately funded training; between 1972 and 1984 the number of apprentices in manufacturing fell from 225,000 to 122,000, and the number of students on day and block release from 289,000 to 168,000. (The decline in apprenticeships also reflects the decline in total employment in manufacturing, and a move away from time-serving to the acquisition of standards of skill as the criteria for qualifications.) The proportion of all manufacturing employees receiving training is estimated to have fallen from 5.5 per cent in 1967 to just over 2 per cent in 1985.

Government-sponsored training scheme

As privately funded training declined, public spending on training increased. In cash terms expenditure by the Manpower Services Commission (MSC), the main spending agency, increased by over three-quarters between 1982/83 and 1985/86.

The number of people benefiting from special employment and training schemes in the financial year 1987/88 are shown in Table 24.1, and a wide range of training opportunities is now sponsored by the government.

Table 24.1
Numbers benefiting from special employment and training schemes (000s)

Community Programme	300
Youth Training Scheme	373
Job Release Scheme	25
Enterprise Allowance Scheme	103
New Workers Scheme	25
Jobstart Allowance Scheme	40

Source: National Institute Economic Review, Nov. 1987

The *Youth Training Scheme* provides a two-year training programme for 16-year-old school-leavers and a one-year programme for 17-year-old leavers. The two-year programme involves at least twenty weeks off-the-job training, e.g. at the local technical college, in addition to on-the-job training and planned work experience. The second year provides specific skill training leading, wherever possible, to vocational qualifications.

Sixteen-year-old entrants receive a tax-free allowance, currently £27.30 a week in the first year and £35 in the second. Up to half a million trainees a year are expected, and the government's total contribution for 1987/88 was estimated at £1.1bn.

The *Job Training Scheme* provides a wide choice of training for unemployed people over the age of 18 who have been out of full-time education for at least two years. Special emphasis has been given to opportunities in the technician and new technology fields, in skills which are in relatively short supply.

The acquisition of new skills is also emphasized in the *Wider Opportunities Training Programme*, open to all unemployed people and those taking part in the Community Programme (see below). These skills may be in areas of new technology, in management, in work-related language training, etc.

The *Training for Enterprise* programme provides training for the owners or managers of new or existing businesses and for those considering starting up a business.

Grants are also available to employers for retraining existing employees or training new recruits for hard-to-fill vacancies, and to employ consultants to analyse their training needs.

The government has introduced a number of other measures intended to improve the quality of the labour force. It has encouraged the introduction of more flexible patterns of apprenticeship, and has modified the school curriculum, e.g. through the Technical and Vocational Education Initiative (TVEI).

Measures to provide a temporary stimulus to employment

The measures discussed in this section may also cause the aggregate supply curve to shift (to the right). But their main purpose is to provide a temporary stimulus to employment.

The most important of these measures is the *Community Programme*, which gives the long-term unemployed the chance to work either full- or part-time for up to a year. Although the degree of training may be limited, the work experience itself, and the chance to make contacts, increases the worker's chance of finding future employment.

The projects, which all benefit the local community, include clearing derelict land, the creation of adventure playgrounds, gardening and decorating for elderly and disabled people, and adapting buildings for community use.

Participants are paid the local rate for the job, and project sponsors are paid an allowance for operating costs. A project may be sponsored by any organization or group, e.g. companies, LAs, charities. In the first three years of its existence the Community Programme dealt with about 300,000 workers, and was targeted to expand to 230,000 places by the summer of 1986.

It is recognized that the productivity of young workers is often less than that of more experienced workers, and that employers may be reluctant to recruit the less experienced except at a considerably lower wage. In order to encourage the creation of such jobs the government provides assistance to employers under the *New Workers Scheme*. A subsidy of £15 a week is given for up to a year for every new job provided for people under 21 at rates of pay which reflect their age and relative inexperience.

With the same objective in mind, financial assistance is provided to workers under the *Jobstart Allowance Scheme*. People aged 18 and over who have been out of work for more than twelve months and who then take a full-time job with gross earnings of less than £80 a week are eligible for an allowance of £20 a week for six months.

At the other end of the career path, the *Job Release Scheme* allows workers to retire a year before the normal retirement age with an allowance, currently up to £74 a week. Their employer must agree to their retirement and replace them with an unemployed person.

Another measure intended to spread job opportunities more widely is the *Job Splitting Scheme*. Employers receive £840 towards the cost of administration and training if they create new part-time jobs by splitting an existing full-time job, by combining regular overtime hours into a new part-time job or by recruiting part-time workers from, for example, the Community Programme or the Job Training Scheme.

A number of measures have been introduced to increase people's chances of finding and filling vacancies. Vacancies are notified at *Jobcentres*. In addition the staff run *Jobclubs*, at which coaching sessions are given to restore self-confidence and motivate job-hunters. Members are provided (free of charge) with a telephone, typewriters, stationery, directories, etc. and are given advice on job-hunting techniques. Under the *Restart Programme* all long-term unemployed are invited to counselling interviews at which they are given information about vacancies and the various forms of assistance that are available.

The effectiveness of policy

In order to evaluate the effectiveness of policy, information is required on the number of jobs created and the cost of provision. Hard information is, in fact, available only on a piecemeal basis (and there is virtually no evidence on improvements in the quality of the labour force, an important policy objective).

The current budget of the MSC, which operates most of the schemes discussed above, is about £3bn. Around a third of this budget is devoted to the Community Programme. Research by the MSC revealed that 25 per cent of the long-term unemployed went into jobs immediately after leaving the programme. Eight months after leaving, 31 per cent were in employment, 3 per cent on training courses, 3 per cent on another Community Programme and 55 per cent were unemployed.[1] While it is disappointing that over half were unemployed, the MSC concluded that entering the programme roughly doubles the chances of long-term unemployed people finding conventional work.

A breakdown of the destinations of people leaving the Youth Training Scheme was published by the MSC in 1985. It found that only 56 per cent of former trainees were in full-time jobs. However, a subsequent study by the Department of Applied Economics at Cambridge University found that 95 per cent of former trainees were in employment, two-thirds with their placement firms and the rest with other firms.[2]

The Department of Employment issued a report on the operation of the Young Workers Scheme (YWS) between its inception in 1982 and 1986 when it was replaced by the New Workers Scheme.[3] Assistance was provided under the YWS to employers of 440,000 young people. At least 90 per cent of these workers had continued (or were expected to continue) in their current jobs beyond the period of their eligibility for YWS support. The net cost per person employed was found to have fallen from £5,000 in 1982/83 to £1,400 in 1985/86.

Estimates of the costs of job creation by means of manpower and other policies were given in a paper prepared for stockbrokers Simon and Coates by Gavyn Davies and Professor David Metcalf. They estimated the annual cost per job created by special employment measures to be £2,050 (in 1984/85 prices). This compares extremely favourably with the cost of job creation by other policies, which were estimated as follows: increasing current public expenditure £15,300; increasing public infrastructure investment £26,200; tax cuts £47,000–£59,200.[4] It also compares favourably with the estimated cost to the government of £6,300 per person unemployed (see Ch. 19).

Legislation relating to trade unions

We explained in Chapter 8 how trade unions might influence the supply of labour, and in Chapter 19 we showed that some workers who would be prepared to take jobs at wage rates below the existing level might be prevented by unions from doing so. Legislation has been passed making unions more democratic and so more responsive to their members.

It has strengthened the rights of employees losing their jobs because of not joining a union; provided for financing of union ballots; removed legal immunities for some types of picketing and for secondary strikes; introduced measures controlling setting up of closed shops; and provided for ballots before strike action. The 1988 Employment Act carried this process further. It provided for a special commissioner to help individual members to enforce their fundamental rights; protection for individual union members from disciplinary action if they refuse to join a strike they disagree with; removal of legal immunity from strikes called to establish or enforce a closed shop; legal protection for the closed shop to be completely removed; mandatory secret postal ballots for union executive elections. In 1988 the government asked the Monopolies and Mergers Commission to investigate the activities of the trade unions in the television industry, the first reference of its kind to be made under the Fair Trading Act.

Flexibility of wages might also be inhibited by government policy, and steps have recently been taken to lessen this possibility. The 1946 Fair Wages Resolution which enabled some workers to obtain wage increases on the ground of comparability, and so prevented employers from offering jobs which would have been viable only at lower rates of pay, has been rescinded. Wages Councils set minimum wages in certain industries; the scope of these councils has been reduced in that workers under 21 are no longer covered, while for others a minimum and an overtime rate are the only ones fixed. This should make it easier for employers to take on young and unskilled workers at wages they are prepared to accept.

The capital market

In order to increase the flexibility of the capital market, various controls have been abolished and wider share ownership has been encouraged.

The abolition of controls

Many controls on financial markets have been abolished. Foreign exchange controls were abolished in 1979, and companies are now free to follow whatever dividend policy they wish. Direct controls on bank lending were last used in 1980, and hire-purchase controls in 1982. These measures allow savings to go to where there is the best combination of risk and return, i.e. where the most efficient use is made of capital.

Amendments to its legal status has put the Trustee Savings Bank on a par with other clearing banks in terms of financial structure and freedom in competing for, and the use of, funds. Legislation has been introduced to enable building societies to compete more freely with banks and other financial institutions.

Wider share ownership

It is felt that if workers derive some of their income from company profits, they may be more inclined to co-operate with innovations designed to increase efficiency, and less inclined to press for wage increases that would depress profits.

The number of shareholders was estimated to have increased threefold to around nine million between 1979 and 1988. This increase was largely the result of employee share schemes and privatization. (The BT share flotation in November 1984 attracted over 2 million investors, of whom about half had not previously bought any shares; BT still had around 1.7 million shareholders a year later, and more than 1.5 million in May 1986.)

Until recently the long-term trend had been for the private shareholder to become less important, as shown in Chapter 16, and the government has taken a number of steps to encourage wider share ownership. These include a reduction in the stamp duty on Stock Exchange transactions, abolition of the investment income surcharge and tax incentives for profit-sharing and share option schemes.

Markets for goods and services

All the measures discussed above relate to factor (labour and capital) markets. Aggregate supply is also affected by changes in the efficiency with which goods and services are produced. Increased efficiency is one of the aims of the micro-economic policies discussed in earlier chapters, and especially of competition policy (Ch. 10) and of privatization (Ch. 11).

An evaluation of supply-side policies

As we saw in Chapter 22, different economists have arrived at varying conclusions about the effectiveness of economic policies, partly because of different interpretations of the 'evidence'. There may be even more scope for different views when the policies are relatively new and the evidence scarce, as tends to be the case with supply-side policies. For example, estimates derived from simulations of the increase in employment that would follow from the abolition of Wages Councils range from 300,000 by Patrick Minford, an enthusiastic supply-sider, through 70,000 by David Metcalf, to 8,000 by Henry Neuberger, an advocate of demand-management policies.

These estimates are reported in a survey by Shackleton of recent studies of the labour market. Shackleton reaches the conclusion that

although there are real rigidities in the U.K. economy, the labour market is perhaps not as inflexible as is sometimes supposed. . . . This must cast doubt on the view that this country's exceptional vulnerability to unemployment in the 1980s can be put down essentially to supply-side rigidities. . . . At the very least, it does not seem obvious that the particular causes of inflexibility singled out recently by the Government – minimum wage and other regulations, trade unions and the tax-benefit system – can fully account for such rigidities as exist.[5]

Professor Nicholl, who has himself conducted a great deal of research in this area, reaches a similar conclusion:

The important policies are those dealing with trade unions, Wages Councils, employment protection, labour monopolies, taxes on labour, and the public sector. In our analysis of these policies we conclude that their overall contribution to reducing wage pressure has not been and is not likely to be, very great.[6]

One of the main reasons leading to this conclusion is that while many of these policies are particularly concerned with wage pressure generated in the lower half of the pay distribution, the main source of wage pressure in recent years appears to have come from the upper half.[7]

This last point is illustrated in Table 24.2 which shows a significant increase since 1979 in the dispersion of earnings.[8]

A Treasury Green Paper issued in 1985[9] was concerned with the effects, not of supply-side policies as such, but of a moderation of the rate of increase in real wage rates (which might, of course, result from an increase in aggregate supply). It

Table 24.2
Dispersion of gross weekly earnings – full-time adult workers as percentage of the corresponding median

	Lowest decile	Lowest quartile	Upper quartile	Highest decile
Men				
1975	67.0	81.0	125.3	157.6
1979	66.0	80.3	125.1	156.9
1984	61.6	77.2	130.5	171.5
Women				
1975	67.4	81.5	125.2	164.5
1979	69.4	82.1	124.7	158.6
1984	66.2	79.2	130.2	166.4

Source: Department of Employment Gazette, 1981, 1984

noted a number of reasons for expecting a moderation of the rate of wage increases to be followed by a faster growth of employment. First, the less the rise in real wages the lower the incentive to substitute capital for labour. Second, lower costs would increase the profitability of production, increase the UK's international competitiveness and enable the public sector to buy more goods and services for a given level of cash expenditure.

The Green Paper then considered the argument that if people had lower pay rises they would have less money to spend so that demand would fall, leaving employment unchanged. The Treasury believes that this outcome would be unlikely. The tendency towards lower spending due to lower wages would be balanced by higher spending by firms out of higher dividends. When account is also taken of the higher incomes of the newly employed workers, 'the empirical evidence suggests that the net effect would be to increase demand'.[10]

Economists of different 'schools' disagree as to whether a reduction in the real wage is required in order to increase the number of workers willing to take jobs. There is also disagreement, as noted above, about the effectiveness of supply-side policies in isolation. On the other hand, as shown in Chapter 19, there is a growing consensus that government attempts to increase employment via an increase in demand will be more successful if supplemented by measures to increase the flexibility of markets for labour, capital and goods and services.

Summary

1. A number of measures have been introduced with the aim of making the labour market more flexible. These include reductions in income tax, the taxation of unemployment benefit, financial assistance to the self-employed, increased government expenditure on training, reductions in the scope of Wages Councils and the weakening of employment protection legislation.
2. Measures have also been introduced to increase the flexibility of the capital market, including the abolition of foreign exchange controls, dividend controls and direct controls on bank lending, and a number of measures to encourage wider share ownership.
3. Although it is difficult to measure the effects of any government policies, supply-side policies do not in themselves appear to have had a great impact on the economy to date.
4. There is a growing consensus that government attempts to increase employment by means of demand-side policies will be more successful if supplemented by measures to increase the flexibility of markets.

Key terms

Aggregate supply
Flexible labour markets
Obstacles to mobility
Training
Flexible capital markets
Wider share ownership
Real wages

Notes

1. Reported in the *Financial Times*, 11 March 1986. In 1988 the name of the MSC was changed to the Training Commission and the Community Programme was merged in the new Employment Training Programme.
2. Department of Employment, *Employment News*, Sept. 1987.
3. Bushell R, Evaluation of the Young Workers Scheme, *Employment Gazette*, May 1986.
4. Davies G and Metcalf D, *Generating Jobs*. Simon and Coates, 1985.
5. Shackleton J R, Is the UK labour market inflexible? *The Royal Bank of Scotland Review*, Sept. 1985.
6. Nicholl S J, The government's policy for jobs: an analysis, *Oxford Review of Economic Policy*, **1** (1985), 114.
7. Nicholl, op. cit., p. 114.
8. This table appears in Metcalf D and Nicholl S J, Jobs and pay, *Midland Bank Review*, 1985.
9. *The Relationship between Employment and Wages: Empirical Evidence for the UK*. HMSO, 1985.
10. *Economic Progress Report*, Jan. 1985.

Essay questions

1. Outline the measures taken by the government to increase the flexibility of the labour market. Why is increased flexibility thought to be desirable?
2. Outline the measures taken by the government to increase the flexibility of the capital market. Why is increased flexibility thought to be desirable?
3. Distinguish between supply-side and demand-side policies. Discuss the circumstances in which each set of policies is likely to be most appropriate.
4. 'A government which operates only demand-side or supply-side policies is like a boxer fighting with one hand tied behind his back.' Discuss.
5. Examine the view that the government's best chance of reducing unemployment is to reduce the level of real wages.

Exercises

24.1 The passage below appeared in *Economic Progress Report*, Oct. 1987.
   (i) What is the link between increases in oil prices and the subsequent world recessions?
   (ii) Explain why it is believed that job prospects are harmed by (a) increased tax burdens, (b) higher replacement ratios and (c) rising trade union power.
   (iii) What restructuring in the UK was required (a) in response to North Sea oil, (b) following the breakdown of incomes policy?
   (iv) Comment on the proposition that real wages in the UK have risen too fast.

   The rest of Europe has therefore shared the UK's unfavourable experience of unemployment in the 1970s and 1980s. Much of the initial impetus to the rise in unemployment stemmed from large adverse shocks, in particular from the increases in oil prices in 1973 and 1979 and the subsequent world recessions. These took place against the background of trends on both the demand and supply sides, in many economies, that harmed job prospects – for example, increased tax burdens, higher replacement ratios (the ratio of unemployment benefits to earnings), and rising trade union power. Real growth in gross domestic product (GDP) in the major seven OECD economies fell from an average of 4.5 per cent a year in the years 1968–73 to 2.7 per cent in the 1973–79 period and to only 2.3 per cent between 1979 and 1985. At the same time employment in these major economies grew more slowly, especially in the 1980s. In the case of the UK, other special factors were also at work – the need to restructure in response to North Sea oil and a sharp rise in wages following the breakdown of incomes policy in 1979.

The persistence of high European unemployment reflects the slow adjustment of labour markets to the disequilibrium produced by these shocks. Moreover, the British labour market appears to have adjusted more slowly than that in other countries, including many European countries. If the labour market is functioning properly, high levels of unemployment, indicating that labour is in excess supply, should reduce the growth in real wages in order to bring supply and demand back into balance. But real wages in the UK have not been sufficiently responsive to labour market conditions, and have risen too fast.

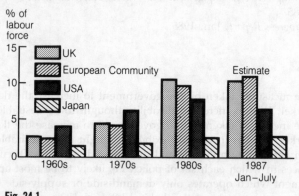

Fig. 24.1
Unemployment in the industrialized countries
Source: Economic Progress Report, Oct. 1987

24.2 (i) Discuss, with reference to Fig. 24.1, the effectiveness of the supply-side policies adopted in the UK.

(ii) What additional information would have helped you to give a better answer to (i)?

24.3 The passage below was adapted from an article in *Lloyds Bank Economic Bulletin*, Dec. 1985. Discuss the likely consequences of the trends described in the passage, with reference to the likely behaviour of (a) prices, (b) profits, (c) investment, (d) unemployment, (e) the distribution of income, (f) the balance of payments.

The increase in average earnings in the whole economy has been a remarkably constant $7\frac{1}{2}$–8 per cent a year for the last two and a half years. Manufacturing earnings have been about one per cent higher than the average, and public sector pay about one per cent lower. The government has forecast a growth in real earnings of 3–4 per cent in 1986–87.

Pay has been rising over 3 per cent faster than in competing countries, and productivity has increased rather less than in these countries.

CHAPTER TWENTY-FIVE
International Economic Policies and Institutions

Introduction

In Chapter 17 we discussed international economic transactions as they might influence, and be influenced by, the economy of the UK. We made no reference to specific government policies. Indeed we assumed that the government allowed international trade to be determined by the free interplay of economic forces.

We now examine government policies which influence international economic transactions and relationships. Policies in this sphere can be broadly divided into those relating to the exchange rate, those which involve the imposition, or the removal, of barriers to trade, and those relating to membership of international economic organizations. As far as possible we shall discuss each of these three sets of policies separately, although, as we shall see, there is a considerable degree of overlap.

Policies relating to the rate of exchange

The first distinction to be made here is between a policy of allowing exchange rates to float, i.e. to move to a level determined by the free interplay of market forces, and a policy of fixed exchange rates – or more precisely the stabilization of the exchange rate for long periods of time. It is convenient to discuss floating rates first, since this provides a useful frame of reference within which we can subsequently evaluate government intervention designed to stabilize the exchange rate.

Floating exchange rates: the effects of depreciation

In Chapter 17 we discussed the factors that influence the rate of exchange in the absence of government intervention. We now consider the effects of a change in the exchange rate. The exchange rate may, of course, float either up or down. However, since 1972, when sterling was allowed to float, its value in relation to most other currencies has declined, i.e. sterling has depreciated. Consequently we concentrate on the effect of the depreciation of a currency. We discuss the effects on resource utilization, the rate of inflation and the balance of payments.

Depreciation and resource utilization

Depreciation implies a fall in the price of exports and hence an increase in their volume, and a rise in the price of imports and hence a fall in their volume. Consequently depreciation increases the level of utilization of domestic resources, at least in the short term. (The reverse applies when the currency appreciates, i.e. the exchange rate moves upwards. The appreciation of sterling in 1980 contributed to the steep rise in unemployment in the UK, as shown in Ch. 22.)

Depreciation and the rate of inflation

As we have shown in earlier chapters, an increase in resource utilization may give rise to inflationary pressures. For this reason alone depreciation tends to be inflationary. In addition the fall in the exchange rate affects the level of prices. We have already seen that imports become dearer. The prices charged by domestic producers are also likely to rise for three reasons. First, those producers who use materials and components bought from abroad suffer increased costs. Second, suppliers whose products are in competition with imported goods may take advantage of the increase in the prices of these competitive goods to raise their own prices. Finally, since prices in the UK have risen, workers may press for and achieve wage increases, thus putting up the costs of all domestic producers.

There is a danger that, due to these various factors, the costs and prices of domestic producers may rise so much that the initial price effect of the fall in the exchange rate is cancelled out. A simulation using the Treasury macro-economic model yielded a prediction that a year after a 5 per cent depreciation of sterling, the sterling price of imports would have risen by 4.4 per cent, and that of exports by 3.3 per cent, even on the assumption that earnings did not change. When account is taken of the possibility of higher wage claims, following the rise in import prices, a vicious circle of increasing costs and prices may arise. This could cause resource utilization to be *lower* than it would have been had the currency not depreciated.

Depreciation and the balance of payments
The effect of depreciation on the balance of payments depends upon the price elasticities of demand for exports and imports. The balance of payments, or more strictly the balance in relation to trade in goods and services, will improve following the depreciation of a currency if the sum of the demand elasticities is greater than unity. (It is conventional to ignore the negative signs.) For example the balance of payments will improve if the elasticity of demand for imports is (negative) 0.4 and the elasticity of demand for exports is (negative) 0.7. (This assumes that sufficient spare capacity exists to meet the additional demand.) The balance will worsen if the sum of the demand elasticities is less than unity.

In most instances one would expect the sum of the demand elasticities to exceed unity, and hence a depreciation to lead to an improved balance of payments, at least in the long term. However, the short-term effect may be less favourable. The shorter the time period, the more difficult it is for purchasers to modify their purchasing patterns. In particular, manufacturers may find it difficult to change their sources of supply for materials and components because of technical specifications and requirements. This means that demand may be highly inelastic in the short term, i.e. a currency depreciation may worsen the balance of payments in relation to trade in goods and services.

The effect on the balance of payments as a whole will depend also upon the behaviour of the remaining currency flows, discussed in Chapter 17. There is a danger that international investors, observing the initial weakening of the balance of payments, may lose confidence in the currency. For example if sterling begins to weaken, investors may sell pounds and buy safer currencies such as German marks. Similarly, UK importers, observing the weakening of sterling, may anticipate a further fall in the exchange rate. This will be an incentive to pay for their imports as quickly as possible, before the value of their sterling falls further. Conversely, purchasers of UK exports may delay payment in the hope of eventually being able to obtain a larger number of pounds for their own currency. (These actions by importers and exporters are known as 'leads and lags'.) Finally the pressure on the exchange rate may be increased by the speculative selling of sterling. (On the other hand, if depreciation results in a strengthening of the current account, this may give investors confidence in that country's currency and lead to capital inflows.)

It is difficult to identify the precise effect of these various sets of factors. Nevertheless British experience suggests that the initial effect of a fall in the exchange rate on the current account (and therefore on the balance of payments) may well be adverse. This effect and the subsequent improvement in the current balance are illustrated in Fig. 25.1. In this figure the plus and minus signs on the vertical axis indicate an improvement or a worsening of the current balance in relation to its level before the currency depreciated. If, for the sake of simplicity, we assume that the current balance was

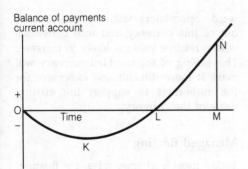

Fig. 25.1
Depreciation and the current account

initially zero, a plus indicates a current account surplus, and a minus indicates a deficit.

A most important consideration is obviously the length of time that elapses before the current account moves back into surplus, i.e. period OL, and also the period at which the accumulated surpluses equal the accumulated deficits, i.e. period OM (areas LMN = OLK). Following the devaluation (i.e. depreciation by government action) of sterling in November 1967, more than a year elapsed before a current account surplus was achieved, and considerably longer before the accumulated deficits were eliminated.

Fixed exchange rates

Although many currencies have been allowed to float since the early 1970s, this was a reversal of the previous situation. For most of the post-war period the major international trading nations had operated a system of fixed exchange rates. We now examine the major implications of such a system, beginning again with resource utilization.

The implications of fixed exchange rates for resource utilization

We showed above that a fall in the exchange rate leads, via a change in the relative prices of products, to an increase in the volume of exports and a decline in the volume of imports, both of which imply an increase in the level of resource utilization. If follows, therefore, that when the authorities intervene to support a currency at a level above that which would be established in a free market, the result is likely to be a lower level of resource utilization. In addition, if the market forces which are causing the pressure on the currency are strong, the government may take positive steps (via fiscal and/or monetary policy) to reduce the level of aggregate expenditure. United Kingdom governments have frequently felt obliged to adopt such policies when in balance of payments difficulties. Such action will, of course, lead to a further fall in resource utilization.

On the other hand, if the authorities intervene to prevent a currency rising to the free market level it will thereby increase, or at least prevent a fall in, the level of utilization of domestic resources.

Fixed exchange rates and the rate of inflation

We can again refer to our earlier discussion, where we showed that a depreciation of the currency tends, for several reasons, to be inflationary. It follows that intervention to prevent a fall in the exchange rate will result in prices increasing less than they would otherwise have done. Conversely, preventing an upward movement in the exchange rate will lead to a relatively higher rate of domestic price increase.

Fixed exchange rates and the balance of payments

We showed above that the depreciation of a currency would lead to an improvement in the current balance, and hence probably in the overall balance of payments, provided that the sum of the elasticities of demand for imports and exports exceeded unity. Conversely, an (upward) appreciation of the currency would lead to an improvement in the balance of payments provided that the sum of the demand elasticities is less than unity. It follows that the effect on the balance of payments of intervention to prevent a change in the exchange rate will depend on the values of the demand elasticities.

Devaluation and revaluation

When a country feels unable to sustain the existing parity of its currency because there is a fundamental persistent disequilibrium in its international trading position, it will devalue. The extent of the devaluation will depend mainly upon how serious the disequilibrium is felt to be, and in particular how much the prices of its products which are traded internationally are out of line with competitive products. In practice devaluations tend to be substantial. For example sterling was devalued against the dollar by 14 per cent in 1967.

The effects of a devaluation are similar to those of a currency depreciation, discussed above. However, since the international value of the currency is changed by a substantial amount literally overnight, the impact is more dramatic.

The effects of a revaluation (or upvaluation) are similar to the appreciation of a currency. A currency is most likely to be revalued when the country has a persistent balance of payment surplus, especially if this is accompanied by significant inflationary pressures. Since a revaluation has a potentially adverse effect on resource utilization, revaluations tend to be more modest than devaluations. For example the Deutschmark has been revalued several times by around 5 per cent.

Fixed exchange rates and speculation

There has been considerable controversy concerning the role of speculation – the buying and selling of currencies in the hope of profit rather than for use in settling trading transactions. It is especially difficult to identify the effect of speculation when currencies are floating. However, when currencies are fixed speculation is almost certain to add to whatever pressures on a currency may already exist. For example if a country is suffering balance of payments difficulties then any change in the value of its currency will be downward. Speculators will, therefore, move out of this currency and into currencies whose relative value is likely to increase. This selling of the troubled currency will make it more difficult and expensive for the authorities to support the existing value of the currency.

Managed floating

Today most exchange rates are floating. However, they are all subject, to some degree, to government intervention designed to steady the rate or slow the pace at which it changes. Thus although the rates are allowed to respond to market forces, governments reserve the right to intervene. For instance a government might intervene to counteract a movement which it feels is due purely to speculative activity, or which is inconsistent with its economic strategy, e.g. a rapid depreciation of the currency which would be reflected in a rapid rise in import prices and hence in domestic costs and prices. Governments may also have in mind, when acting to steady the exchange rate, that rapid fluctuations create added uncertainties for traders – although these uncertainties can, at a cost, be overcome by buying or selling currencies in forward markets.

The European Monetary System

In 1978 all the existing members of the European Community (EC) with the exception of the UK agreed to establish a European Monetary System (EMS), a 'scheme for the creation of closer monetary co-operation leading to a zone of monetary stability in Europe'. The EMS, which came into operation in March 1979, is a system of fixed but adjustable currency parities. The three main components of the EMS are:

(a) a European Currency Unit (ECU);
(b) an exchange rate mechanism;
(c) a system of credit arrangements through the European Monetary Fund (EMF).

The European Currency Unit

The ECU is the common denominator used in fixing parities. It is a 'basket' of ten currencies mixed in proportion to the relative size of each country's economy. For example the Deutschmark currently has a weight of 32 (in 100), and the £ sterling a weight of 15.

The rules allow the composition of the basket to be reviewed every five years, or on request if the weight of any currency changes by more than 25 per cent. Revisions are made in such a way as to hold the value of the ECU constant at the moment of change.

The values of the individual currencies, in terms of the ECU, are determined as a result of negotiations among all the governments concerned. So for example in April 1986 the newly elected French government wished to devalue the franc against the mark by 8 per cent. West Germany and other countries were unwilling to agree to so large a devaluation and eventually a compromise devaluation of 6 per cent was agreed, giving a new central rate of 1 ECU = 6.96 francs. (Other central rates were ECU = 63p sterling and 2.14 Deutschmarks.)

The exchange rate mechanism

This mechanism currently applies to all the ECU currencies except the £ sterling and the drachma. The central rates are used to establish a set of bilateral exchange rates. Margins of fluctuation are set at 2.5 per cent of these exchange rates (although Italy has opted to utilize the provision of a 6 per cent margin). Each currency also has a limit for its divergence from the central rate against the ECU. When fluctuations reach 75 per cent of this limit – the 'divergence threshold' – the country concerned is expected to take corrective measures, such as buying or selling the currency by the country's central banks or a change in fiscal or monetary policy. If such measures are not sufficient to correct the divergence, a change in the central rate may be negotiated.

The credit mechanism

To facilitate the functioning of the exchange mechanism, credit facilities are made available through the EMF. The countries whose currencies comprise the ECU have agreed to deposit 20 per cent of their gold and dollar reserves with the EMF and in exchange receive an equal amount of unconditional drawing rights denominated in ECUs.

Since the ECU is the 'currency' in which debts and credits in the EMS are denominated, this system of credit leads to a sharing of risk. For example assume that the Netherlands is running a current account deficit with West Germany, to meet which the Central Bank of the Netherlands swaps guilders with the Bundesbank. Normally the Netherlands must repay its debts in Deutschmarks, and if the guilder depreciates, the Netherlands incurs a loss because it will cost more to obtain the required marks. Under the EMS system the debt is expressed in ECUs, and the loss of the Netherlands will equal the guilder–ECU depreciation, which will be less than the guilder–mark depreciation. In effect West Germany shares the risk of depreciation.

The United Kingdom and the European Monetary System

Although the UK did not join the EMS at its inception, it has co-operated on a narrower front, as noted above, and full membership continues to be a matter of debate. The existing members have benefited from much greater stability in exchange rates. The 1986 realignment was the first for more than three years, whereas during the same period sterling underwent marked fluctuations. It may also be that the greater stability of exchange rates has reduced the need to raise interest rates to protect currencies. It is also argued that an exchange rate that is virtually fixed – at least in the short run – exerts discipline on producers and workers, since it is no longer possible to compensate for a rise in relative prices by a depreciation of the currency.

However, although the EMS has successfully created a zone of monetary stability, its record in terms of the ultimate objectives, inflation, employment and growth, is less clear-cut. All EMS countries have experienced rising unemployment, and their economic growth has lagged behind that of Japan and the USA. There may be many reasons for this, but it appears that the EMS has had a generally deflationary bias. As usual with fixed exchange rate arrangements, it has been difficult to persuade the members with the strongest currencies, in this case West Germany and the Netherlands, to adopt more expansionary policies.

Additional reasons have been advanced for continuing to defer UK membership. Sterling, like the D-mark but unlike the other EMS currencies, is one of the main international investment currencies. Consequently a substantial shift out of, say, the dollar, could lead to a swing in the sterling/D-mark exchange rate, depending upon how international investors redistributed their portfolios between the two currencies. Moreover, despite the fall in the UK inflation rate, it remains above that of West Germany, a situation which might necessitate high interest rates in the UK to defend a fixed exchange rate. (A desire to reduce interest rates was one of the justifications for the devaluation of the franc, discussed above.)

Barriers to trade

We said above that a country can attempt to overcome its balance of payments difficulties either by changing its exchange rate or by reducing the level of domestic expenditure. A third alternative is to erect barriers designed to reduce imports. Erecting import barriers invites retaliation and opens up the possibility that international trade will decline, and that some of the advantages of specialization will thereby be lost. Moreover, even if trade barriers lead to an improvement in a country's balance of payments, the overall

level of economic welfare in that country may fall. This point is developed below as we consider the various types of trade barriers that might be erected.

Tariffs

Tariffs are taxes imposed on imports. They may be levied on an *ad valorem* basis, i.e. as a certain percentage of the price (value), or on a specific basis, i.e. as a given amount per unit. The effects of a tariff are illustrated in Fig. 25.2 which is assumed to relate to the market for shoes. The demand curve is D, while S_H indicates the amount that would be supplied at various prices by domestic producers. The price at which foreign producers would supply the domestic market, in the absence of a tariff, is £25. The supply curve S_W is horizontal at this price because the UK is only a small part of the world market. (With a horizontal supply curve the impact of an *ad valorem* and a specific tariff is identical.)

Given free trade, OM pairs of shoes would be sold at a price of £25. Of this output, OQ would be supplied by domestic producers and QM by foreign producers. Assume that a 20 per cent tariff is now imposed. The price charged by overseas producers rises to £30 (the new

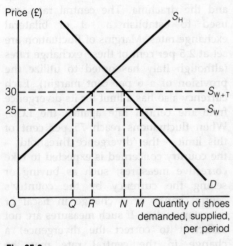

Fig. 25.2
The imposition of a tariff

supply curve S_{W+T} is horizontal at this price). The quantity demanded falls to *ON*; of this output *OR* is supplied by domestic producers and *RN* by overseas producers. If the overseas countries do not retaliate by imposing tariffs on UK exports, the UK balance of payments will improve, because of the fall in the volume of imports from *QM* to *RN*.

Tariffs and economic welfare

In order to calculate the overall change in UK economic welfare it is necessary to consider the impact on the various groups affected by the tariff. We do this with the help of Fig. 25.3, which reproduces and builds on Fig. 25.2.

The additional cost to consumers of the shoes that they now buy is *PLJT*. Much of this additional cost is transferred (as a benefit) to domestic producers and the government. Let us consider these two sets of transfers in turn, beginning with transfers to producers.

Here S_H indicates the quantities that domestic producers would supply at various prices. They would have been willing to increase output by *QR* for additional revenue *WKV*. But in fact their revenue has increased by *PLKV*. The revenue in excess of that required to

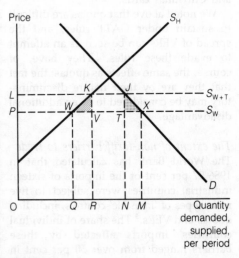

Fig. 25.3
The welfare effects of a tariff

increase output, *PLKW*, is known as economic rent. In company accounts it would be represented by additional profits.

The second transfer is the tariff paid on the imported shoes, *VKJT*. Although the tariff is paid by producers, it is recovered from consumers and in effect is a transfer from consumers to the government.

When we take into account the two sets of transfers that we have identified, we are left with the shaded area *WKV*. If we make certain assumptions, this area would constitute part of the welfare loss arising from the imposition of the tariff. The first assumption is that the community attaches the same weight or value to changes in welfare experienced by different groups. So, for example, the gain to producers from a given transfer would exactly balance the loss to consumers. (Not everyone might be happy with this assumption if, for example, it was found that the income of shareholders was well above the average for all consumers.)

The second assumption relates to the area *WKV*. This indicates the additional cost of supplying *QR* shoes by domestic rather than by foreign producers. It is assumed that these domestic resources would have been better employed in the production of other goods, allowing the demand for shoes to be met by more efficient foreign manufacturers. (In other words the principle of comparative advantage would be allowed to operate.) But it is, of course, only an assumption that if resources were released from the shoe industry they would be absorbed in other industries. In times of heavy unemployment this might not be true, implying that the welfare loss of the tariff might be less than indicated above.

The second element of the welfare loss identified in Fig. 25.3 is the shaded area *JXT*. The demand curve *D* denotes the value that consumers place on shoes. Their valuation of an increase in consumption *NM* is the area under the demand curve *NJXM*. But the removal of the tariff would enable them to increase their consumption of shoes at a cost of only *NTXM*. The difference, *JXT*, is known as consumer surplus. The imposition of the tariff causes the loss of this surplus.

Quotas

Quotas are quantitative restrictions on imports. A quota may relate to the total quantity or value of a commodity that can be imported in a given period, or to the quantity or value that can be imported from a particular source, e.g. a certain country or group of countries.

Quantitative restrictions are less efficient than tariffs, for reasons explained below. Moreover their economic effects are less easily identified. Consequently the use of quotas is proscribed under the Charter of the General Agreement on Tariffs and Trade (GATT, see below), except under specified circumstances such as a balance of payments crisis.

The effects of a quota

In order to compare the effects of a tariff and a quota we can refer again to Fig. 25.3. If the government wished to reduce imports to the level that they would be with a tariff, the quota would, of course, be *RN*. Total consumption would again be *ON* at price *L*, and many of the previous arguments apply. There is, however, one important difference. The revenue *VKJT*, which previously accrued to the government, now goes to the foreign producers who are lucky enough to obtain a share of the quota. Clearly, therefore, the domestic country's loss of economic welfare is greater with a quota than with a tariff.

Other barriers to trade

The post-war period has seen a substantial reduction in the overall level of tariffs. On the other hand there has been an increase in the extent of other barriers to trade. These include a number of administrative procedures – technical standards, marks of origin, environmental controls, customs valuation procedures, etc. –

which put foreign suppliers at a disadvantage. Government procurement policies often favour domestic producers, sometimes to the complete exclusion of foreign competitors. United Kingdom governments have usually 'bought British' in the field of armaments, computers, etc. Aid may be given to overseas countries on condition that some or all of it is spent on imports from the donor country; this obviously puts other countries' producers at a disadvantage. Exchange controls, most commonly imposed by less developed countries, often operate to restrict imports.

Voluntary export restraints

A voluntary export restraint (VER) is 'an arrangement between two parties, which may be governments or industries, whereby one party "voluntarily" agrees to restrict the volume of its exports to the other country to a specified amount, over a given period of time'.[1]

A well-known example is the agreement that imports of Japanese cars should not exceed a certain proportion of the UK market (11 per cent in 1985). Other agreements negotiated by the UK involved limitations on exports of footwear, pottery, colour televisions, cutlery, music centres and Christmas cards.

We noted above that quotas are difficult to sustain under GATT rules, and the spread of VERs can be seen as an attempt to evade these rules.[2] They have, of course, the same effects as quotas; the fact that they are by their nature discriminatory may be considered to be an additional disadvantage.

The extent of non-tariff barriers to trade

The World Bank has calculated that in 1986 27 per cent of the imports of sixteen industrial countries were subject to five main types of 'invisible' controls, including quotas and VERs.[3] The share of individual countries' imports affected by these barriers ranged from over 50 per cent in France and over 40 per cent in the USA to 10–20 per cent in Italy, Norway and Austria.

The goods most affected are food, textiles, minerals, fuel and iron and steel. The proportion of agricultural imports estimated to be covered by non-tariff barriers was 36 per cent in the EC, 24 per cent in the USA, 43 per cent in Japan and as high as 73 per cent in Switzerland. The Multifibre Arrangement (MFA) is even more restrictive, covering an estimated 80 per cent of world trade in textiles and clothing. (The MFA is discussed below.)

Countertrade

The term 'countertrade' covers several mechanisms, including:

Barter: the exchange of an exporter's goods and services for goods and services provided by the importer.

Counterpurchase: this requires an exporter to accept part payment for his shipment in goods. Cash is usually the main ingredient, but the exchange of goods is crucial to the completion of the deal.

Buy-back: regularly used in trade with centralized economies, it often applies to projects whose output is used to finance the deal.

Offset: this is frequently used in large transactions, especially relating to defence or aerospace equipment, and requires the exporter to make investments in the client country in terms of plant or components, to 'offset' the cost of the goods sold.

In a report issued in 1985 the OECD estimated that countertrade accounts for 5 per cent of total world trade, while other estimates have suggested a higher figure. Recently concluded deals include the exchange of 100,000 tonnes of New Zealand lamb for 6 million barrels of Iranian oil, valued at $160m., and the sale by General Dynamics of the USA, of $4.2bn. of aircraft to Turkey, of which $2bn. is likely to be offset by trade.

Partly because of its bilateral nature, the growth of countertrade has caused concern in a number of international agencies. To quote from a recent GATT report: 'Substituting discriminatory, bureaucratic decision-making for the impersonal workings of market forces may buy some peace in the short run, but only at a heavy cost in terms of its impact on the medium-term prospects for friendly commercial and political relations.'[4]

The costs of protection

A number of recent reports have emphasized the costs of protection and have thrown doubts on the alleged benefits often used to justify protection. An OECD report concluded, on the basis of a wide range of studies, that:

Trade restrictions have not only diverted imports but have also reduced them in total.

Quantitative restrictions have put up prices in the protected markets; even in the short term, protection has only a limited impact on employment in the protected sectors, typically of the order of 2 or 3 per cent; in the longer term, the impact may be even more limited, as capital is substituted for labour.

The employment gain to protected sectors may be offset by jobs lost in other industries, as the exchange rate appreciates or higher inflation leaves less room for real growth.

Although some industries have used the breathing-space afforded by protection to achieve structural adjustments, most have not.

Protection by the developed world harms developing countries; it worsens their debt problems by restricting their access to export markets, and it distorts their investment plans by creating uncertainty about future markets.

Import controls are fairly ineffective at transferring resources to the protected sector, and often the jobs saved do not go to the groups or regions it is intended to help.[5]

In a report published in 1986 the Trade Policy Research Centre estimated that the annual cost to the UK of VERs in four industries, cars, videos, clothing and footwear, probably approaches £1bn.

Moreover the cost per job saved was extremely high, ranging from £7,500 a year in footwear to £80,000 a year for videos.

Professor Silberston studied the effects on the UK economy of trade policies for textiles and clothing, with particular reference to the MFA[6]: the MFA, which was established in 1973, and is excluded from the normal GATT rules, comprises a set of bilateral agreements between importing and exporting countries.

Silberston *estimated* that if the MFA were abandoned, then in the UK textile and clothing markets after five years:

Landed import prices would be 5–10 per cent lower.

UK producer prices and retail prices would be 5 per cent lower.

UK employment would be 10,000–50,000 lower.

The benefit to consumers would be £500m.; this means that the annual cost per job saved in these industries by the MFA is from £10,000 to £50,000.

Moreover, although employment in textiles and clothing would fall, unemployment in the economy as a whole would be reduced by 37,000. This would happen partly because consumers, given their higher real incomes, would increase their consumption of other products, and partly because the increase in textile imports would cause the exchange rate to depreciate, which would lead to an increase in the exports of other UK products. These estimates are subject to a wide margin of error. Nevertheless they indicate that it is by no means certain that a country will benefit by imposing import controls.

Conditions favouring trade barriers

Trade barriers are least likely to invite retaliation if certain conditions are fulfilled. A developed country should seek to indicate that the restriction is intended to be temporary and that other steps are also being taken to solve the problem that made the restriction necessary. For example

the UK would be in a better position to justify the protection of the textile industry if it could show that, during the period of protection, it had planned an orderly run-down of the industry, including an accelerated programme of retraining employees for work in other industries.

There tends to be greater tolerance of restrictions imposed by less developed countries because of their lower living standards. However, even here temporary restrictions are likely to be viewed most favourably. An argument frequently advanced by these countries is that an industry that is just developing in that country may be inherently as efficient there as in any other country, but that it requires protection in order to allow it to gain the advantages that come only with experience and large-scale production. This so-called infant industry argument is particularly appealing since it implies that once the industry has matured, and the restrictions on competition from imports are removed, specialization and trade will take place in accordance with the principle of comparative advantage. However, it should be pointed out that protection from competition can breed inefficiency, and that many infant industries take much longer to grow up than one might expect!

Finally, retaliation is less likely for the less 'visible' forms of protection, such as technical specifications, than for quotas and tariffs. This no doubt helps to explain the growth in the importance of such forms in recent years.

International economic institutions

The General Agreement on Tariffs and Trade

The advantages to be derived from international specialization and trade were the main reason for the establishment in 1947 of the GATT, an international organization based on Geneva. The members of GATT are pledged to the expansion of multilateral trade, and to the removal or at least a reduction of measures which distort the pattern of trade, such as import restrictions and export incentives.

Since its foundation GATT has sponsored seven rounds of negotiations which have resulted in the average import tariffs of the industralized nations being reduced from about 40 per cent to 4–8 per cent. This has, of course, aided trade among the industrialized nations, and has helped to widen the markets for the products of the developing countries. These countries also enjoy considerable dispensation from the GATT rules, including duty-free exports under the generalized system of preferences, and the right to control imports when they get into balance of payments difficulties. These departures from the usual GATT principle of non-discrimination in trade policy were justified by the need to aid the development, and raise the living standards, of the less developed nations. Unfortunately the reduction in tariffs has been followed by an increase in other barriers to trade, as we showed above.

Regional trade groupings

Membership of GATT implies some limitation of the freedom of members to adopt policies which they consider to be in their own interest. This restriction is also inherent in membership of a regional trade grouping, the most important forms of which are the free trade area and the customs union.

Free trade areas
In a free trade area all restrictions on trade between members are removed. But each member remains free to decide upon its policy in relation to non-members. Examples of this type of grouping include the European Free Trade Association, of which the UK was formerly a member, and the Latin American Free Trade Area, which currently comprises ten South American countries.

Customs unions
As in a free trade area, all restrictions on trade between members are abolished.

However, a member of a customs union also gives up the right to decide upon its policy towards non-members. Instead a common external tariff, observed by all members, is established. A customs union may also oblige its members to adopt common policies in other spheres. This is certainly so for members of the EEC (the Common Market).

The European Community

The European Community comprises three bodies, the EEC, the European Coal and Steel Community (ECSC) and the European Atomic Energy Community (Euratom). We shall be mainly concerned with the policies and institutions of the EEC, and we begin by considering its budgetary policy.

The budgetary policy of the EEC

The Community's revenue
The Community's revenue, or 'own resources' consist of: (i) duties levied on imports entering the Community from third countries under the common external tariff; (ii) levies charged on agricultural products from outside the Community to bring their prices up to the levels prevailing under the CAP price support regime; and (iii) the yield of a national VAT rate applied to spending on a common basket of goods and services.

Originally the ceiling rate of the VAT was 1 per cent, but this was increased in 1986 to 1.4 per cent, and there have been suggestions that it might be increased further. Even before the increase VAT provided over half of the Community's own resources, with about a quarter coming from the common external tariff and one-tenth from agricultural levies.

The UK government has argued that the application of these procedures would result in the UK making a net contribution to the Community greater than what would be justified in the light of the UK national income. An agreement reached whereby the UK receives an abatement to its VAT contribution equivalent to two-thirds of its VAT expenditure gap – broadly the difference between what it would pay to the budget if there were no levies and duties and it paid only VAT – and its receipts from the budget. This rebate brought the UK's net contribution in 1988 down from almost £3bn. to around £1bn. But even this contribution exceeded those of some richer members of the Community. Indeed some richer members such as Denmark and Luxembourg, received more than they paid. This was due to the pattern of the Community's expenditure, discussed below.

The Community's expenditure

The increase in the Community's resources, via the higher VAT rate, was required to meet the increase in its commitments. Spending more than doubled between 1980 and 1986, and outstanding commitments increased at an even faster rate.

Expenditure on agriculture
Almost two-thirds of spending is accounted for by farm price support under the CAP. (In addition the agricultural industry benefits from spending under the structural policies head.) Since the CAP was discussed in Chapter 9, we concentrate here on other Community expenditure. It is sufficient to note here that the CAP has put an increasing strain on the Community's finances. To take a small example by way of illustration, the cost in 1986 of disposing of stocks of old beef and butter was estimated at 1.155bn. ECUs (£750m.).

Other Community expenditure
Although agriculture accounts for the bulk of the Community's expenditure, sums of considerable significance are spent by several other Community institutions.

The principal role of the *European Investment Bank* (EIB) is to make loans for projects that:
(a) benefit less developed regions, or

(b) are concerned with developments of such a size or nature that they cannot be entirely financed by the means available in individual member countries, or
(c) are of common interest to several member countries, e.g. improving cross-border communications.

Since its establishment, about two-thirds of EIB lending has gone towards meeting the first objective, making the EIB the main Community source of funds for furthering regional development.

In 1985 the EIB's lending reached nearly 7.2bn. ECUs (nearly £5bn). Over 90 per cent was spent on capital investments within the Community (including investments in Spain and Portugal in preparation for their accession to the Community in 1986), the UK's share being 17 per cent. Most of the rest was spent in African, Caribbean and Pacific countries under the terms of the Second Lomé Convention (see below).

The EIB normally finances up to 50 per cent of the cost of a project, loans being made for up to twenty years. Interest rates follow movements in the capital markets; the EIB is able to borrow at very 'fine' terms and passes this benefit on to its borrowers.

The *European Regional Development Fund* which accounts for about 8 per cent of the Community budget, was established in 1975 to help to correct regional economic imbalance in member countries.

Since 1975 the UK has received almost £2bn. from the ERDF, mostly to support projects in the assisted areas (see Ch. 12). Roughly three-quarters has been used to support infrastructure projects in transport and communications, energy, etc. and a quarter to support industrial investment projects. It was estimated that by 1984 this spending had created or saved about 180,000 jobs.

The *European Social Fund*, which now accounts for some 6 per cent of the Community budget, was established in 1957 to improve the employment opportunities for workers in the Common

Market. The main types of scheme assisted are:

(a) training and retraining schemes;
(b) the resettlement of workers and their families who have to move home to gain or retain employment;
(c) schemes to improve access to employment for disabled workers and workers over the age of 50;
(d) vocational preparation and job creation schemes for unemployed young people;
(e) some schemes for allowances for newly engaged workers.

One example was the assistance offered by the fund to meet the cost of retraining workers whose jobs in the newspaper industry were threatened by technological change.

Not all Community institutions are concerned primarily with the interests of their own members. The *European Development Fund* was established in 1971 to provide loans and non-repayable credits for specific projects in the developing countries, such as the building of roads and bridges and radio and telecommunications networks.

The impact on the pattern of trade

The establishment of the Common Market has led to a substantial increase in the relative importance of intra-Community trade. For the nine countries who were members in 1980, intra-Community exports accounted for over a half of all exports, compared to a third in 1958.

In the UK there has been a steady upward trend in the percentage of manufactured imports and exports accounted for by the EEC. In 1973 the EEC took 31 per cent of the UK's total exports of manufactures and provided 39 per cent of imports. By 1984 this had increased to 39 per cent of exports and 50 per cent of imports.

Since the UK joined the Common Market the rate of increase in the value of imports from the Community has consistently exceeded the rate of growth of exports and the UK's trade deficit increased from £2.2bn. in 1976 to £8.4bn. in 1986. The trend in the *volume* of trade is even more unfavourable; between 1973 and 1984 manufactured exports rose by 66 per cent, while manufactured imports rose by 300 per cent.[7] It cannot be assumed that these trends are entirely the result of EEC membership. As we saw in Chapter 17 there has been a general deterioration in the UK balance of trade in manufactures. However, the deterioration has been more marked in trade with the EEC than with other OECD countries, and with the world as a whole.

The single most important explanation of the widening deficit in manufactured trade with the EEC is trade in road vehicles. The deficit on this trade increased from £93m. in 1973 to £3,200m. in 1982, when it accounted for 44 per cent of the total deficit.

The economic effects of regional groupings

Regional groupings can be evaluated in terms of their effects on the total welfare of all countries, the welfare of their members as a whole and the welfare of individual members. It might be thought that total welfare would be increased by the formation of a regional grouping since the abolition of barriers to trade among members encourages, within that grouping, specialization and trade in accordance with the principle of comparative advantage. However on a wider international scale, regional groupings – and especially customs unions – may be inconsistent with that principle. One member of the grouping may have a comparative advantage in a particular product when compared to other members, but not when compared to non-members. To put the matter slightly differently, a low-cost producer may be excluded from a market, leaving it to be supplied by a relatively high-cost producer.

The total welfare of all the nations in the world may not, therefore, increase as a result of the formation of a regional grouping. Moreover, even when we confine our attention to the members of the grouping it is not inevitable that total welfare should increase. The high-cost producer will benefit by being sheltered from the competition of low-cost non-members, but this is at the expense of consumers, who have to pay higher prices.

Finally the producers of some member countries may benefit at the expense of producers in other member countries. As noted above, there is some evidence to suggest that on the whole UK industry has lost rather than gained sales as a result of our entry into the EEC.

Other international economic institutions

The main objectives of the international institutions that we consider below are twofold. The first is to facilitate the expansion of international trade. The policies required in order to meet this objective are (a) reductions in barriers to trade (discussed above), (b) an increase in world liquidity, (c) the provision of assistance to countries facing balance of payments difficulties.

The second objective is to aid the economic development of the less developed countries. The provision of longer-term finance has been seen as one of the best ways of meeting this objective.

The International Monetary Fund

The IMF was established in 1945 and now has 146 members. The IMF's resources are provided by members according to a system of quotas related to the size of their economies – 75 per cent of the quota is paid in the member's own currency and 25 per cent in reserve assets.

In addition the Group of 10 (the major European countries, USA, Canada and Japan) provide further resources under the General Arrangements to Borrow. The IMF has also from time to time provided a widely distributed increase in world liquidity through the issue of Special Drawing Rights (SDRs). These are in effect entries in members' bank balances with the IMF, and are available for settlements between central banks and with the IMF.

The main use of IMF funds has been to help countries to deal with temporary balance of payments difficulties without resorting to excessive deflation, protectionism or competitive devaluations. It provides short-term financial assistance to such countries, usually on condition that the country adopts policies (including demand-management policies) designed to restore equilibrium.

However, this type of assistance has become less important as countries have increasingly met their need for temporary finance by borrowing from commercial banks without submitting to the policy conditions imposed by the IMF. The IMF has responded by offering assistance on longer maturities and with less strict conditions. Thus in 1974 the Extended Fund Facility was established to help member countries deal with more persistent balance of payments problems such as those arising from structural defects in production and trade, especially where an active development policy was being inhibited by slow growth and an inherent balance of payments weakness.

More recently the IMF has acted as mediator in negotiations between less developed countries which have difficulty in meeting their international obligations and the banks from which they have previously borrowed. The arrangements have had three essential ingredients:

1. The commercial banks agree to reschedule their outstanding debt and to make a modest contribution to new net lending.
2. This lending is supplemented by finance from the IMF.
3. The IMF's contribution is conditional on the borrower implementing an austerity programme.

In 1987 repayments to the IMF exceeded new lending, leading to renewed criticisms of the IMF's operations by some Third World countries. These countries have argued for an increase in the total amount of assistance. They have also demanded that the system of quotas should be changed so as to increase the share of Third World countries, and that there should be an increased allocation of SDRs, made according to need rather than quota, thus using the SDR as a form of aid. Finally they want a lengthening of maturities, an easing of conditions and subsidies to reduce the interest cost for poor countries borrowing from the IMF.

The International Bank for Reconstruction and Development

The International Bank for Reconstruction and Development (IBRD) was established at the same time as the IMF and has virtually the same membership. It is popularly known as the *World Bank*, and this title is used by the IBRD itself to describe collectively the IBRD and the International Development Association (see below).

Capital subscriptions to the IBRD are related to the wealth of the member states, but the major source of funds for its lending is borrowing on world markets. Interest charged on its loans is therefore market-related.

Loans are made either to governments or under government guarantee for a wide range of development and welfare purposes, almost entirely to less developed countries. The IBRD also provides various kinds of technical assistance.

In recent years the IBRD's lending policies have evolved in a way which has brought them closer to those of the IMF, especially the latter's Extended Fund Facility. Although project lending comprises nine-tenths of the IBRD's total lending, it has introduced programme lending, not tied to specific projects, for the support of development programmes in countries with short-term foreign exchange problems.

The net lending of the IBRD has risen rapidly in the 1980s (by a quarter between 1983 and 1985), partly because it has introduced new forms of lending, and partly

because it has begun to participate in joint operations with the commercial banks. The aim of this co-operation is to provide longer maturities to less developed countries than would normally be available directly from private sector sources and, by strengthening investors' confidence, to promote an increase in capital flows. There is an obvious parallel here with the benefits flowing from co-operation between the IMF and the commercial banks.

The *International Finance Corporation* (IFC), an affiliate of the IBRD, was established mainly to stimulate the provision of aid from private sources to the less developed countries. In addition to providing loans, the IFC can hold shares in companies. Also affiliated to the IBRD, the *International Development Association* provides loans at little or no interest for projects in developing countries that would not be feasible if finance had to be obtained at normal commercial rates. These projects often have a long life and are capital intensive, e.g. roads, power supplies, etc.

The main purpose of the *Bank for International Settlements* is to promote central bank co-operation, including the provision of short-term liquidity to central banks in need. In recent years it has played an important role in providing bridging finance to countries with liquidity problems. For example it made bridging loans of $925m. to Mexico, and $1.45bn. to Brazil while these countries were negotiating credits from the IMF. (However, it subsequently decided not to make further loans of this type.)

The contribution of international economic institutions

Despite the increase in the financial and non-financial assistance provided by these institutions, grave problems remain. This could be seen as a failure by these institutions to discharge their responsibilities. (We have already noted criticisms of the IMF.) But a more realistic interpretation is that the contribution of these institutions is bound to be limited, given the nature of international economic forces. This point will become clear as we examine, first world liquidity, and second the problems of the less developed countries.

World liquidity

Despite numerous increases since its establishment, IMF credits and SDRs account for less than a tenth of *world official reserves*. The bulk of the reserves comprise foreign currencies (the most important being the dollar), and gold. Moreover, these reserves themselves are only a part of total world liquidity, since they exclude various important practices such as the General Arrangements to Borrow, Eurocurrency swaps, etc.

Underdevelopment and development

There is considerable controversy about what are the characteristics of underdevelopment and development, and about which countries should be given particular labels such as less developed countries. However, there is no doubting the fact of substantial international inequalities. The World Bank has estimated that 5 per cent of the world's output is shared by the 47 per cent of the population who live in low-income countries such as Bangladesh, China, India, Pakistan and the majority of countries in sub-Saharan Africa. National income (GDP) per head (US dollars) varies from 17,010 in Switzerland to 80 in Chad.[8]

We saw in Chapter 13 that differences in national income are only an approximate indicator of differences in welfare,

but many other measures also point to substantial inequality. Infant mortality rates (per 1,000 births) range from 7 in Japan to 133 in Bangladesh, the male life expectancy at birth is 74 in Japan and 51 in Pakistan, the percentage of adult illiteracy is less than 1 per cent in the USA and 96 per cent in Ethiopia.[9]

The percentage rate of growth of national income (GDP) has on the whole been higher in the poorer than in the richer countries in recent years. However, the absolute increase has been greater in richer countries. Moreover, when account is taken of population growth, even the percentage growth rate (GDP per head) has been lower in the poorer countries for much of the post-war period (Table 25.1). In sub-Saharan Africa the population growth has outstripped the increase in GDP, and in the period 1980–86 GDP per head has fallen by about 0.4 per cent a year.

The bases of growth

In the next three sections we consider the role in the process of economic growth and development of agriculture, industrialization (manufacturing) and foreign economic assistance.[10]

The role of agriculture in economic development

The expansion of agriculture helps to feed the increasing domestic population. It can also aid economic development via higher export earnings with which to purchase capital equipment, components, etc.

Table 25.1
Gross domestic product per head

	GDP per head ($) 1986	Growth of GDP per head (annual % changes)		
		1965–73	1973–79	1980–85*
Low-income developing countries	380	2.9	2.5	5.4
Industrial countries	11,920	3.7	2.1	1.6

* Estimate.
Source: World Bank, *World Development Report*, 1987

The less developed countries have been successful in increasing the output of many crops by means of the increased use of fertilizers, improved irrigation and drainage and better seeds. Unfortunately, it has been possible to sell this increased output only at substantially lower real prices. The World Bank has estimated that the real prices of agricultural products in the 1970s was almost a quarter lower than the average level in the 1950s.

The problem of a downward trend in real prices has been accompanied by substantial fluctuations in price. (The pricing of primary products was discussed at length in Ch. 7.) The combination of these factors has led to more attention being given to industrialization.

Development through industrialization

The proportion of the labour force in industry in the low-income economies has slowly increased. The benefits that industrialization can in principle yield include the creation of extensive employment opportunities, an increase in output per head and in living standards, an improvement in the balance of payments and the diffusion of advanced technologies.

A broad distinction can be made between import-substituting industrialization (ISI) and export-led industrialization. (Some countries may, of course, adopt a mixture of the two strategies.) Nixson notes that the ISI strategy has been widely adopted by the majority of LDCs, and that this has usually involved 'the establishment of large scale, capital-intensive, urban-based industries, protected by high tariff and other barriers, catering to the demands of middle and upper-income groups in the LDCs'.[11]

This strategy has been extensively criticized on two grounds. First, the high level of protection countervenes the principle of comparative advantage, leading to a misallocation of resources and the development of an inefficient industrial sector.

Second, it creates a reliance on an inappropriate type of technology. Much of the plant required for mass production has to be purchased from, and often serviced by, the rich industrialized nations. Moreover the number of jobs created is less than would occur if a simpler, 'intermediate'· technology were used. An example of the use of intermediate technology is the development by the Intermediate Technology Group of a machine costing £30,000 that can make 8,000–12,000 glass bottles a day for medical, cosmetic and other consumer products. Automatic machines used in developed countries cost $500,000 and can produce up to several hundred thousand containers a day, far more than required by most developing countries. Moreover the machines are extremely complex and need highly skilled personnel.

The critics of ISI advocate the alternative strategy, export-led industrialization, pointing to the very high growth rates of the newly industrializing countries (NICs) that have adoped this strategy. For example South Korea and Hong Kong, whose exports of manufactures account for around 90 per cent of their total exports, achieved a growth in real GDP of around 10 per cent a year in the 1970s.

The contribution of foreign assistance to economic development

It is easy to demonstrate how in principle foreign assistance can contribute to economic development. As we showed in Chapter 2, a country that wishes to increase the resources devoted to the production of capital goods may have to reduce its output of consumption goods. This reduction in output may cause severe hardship, and even loss of life, if consumption is already close to the subsistence level. Foreign assistance can help to avoid this dilemma by making funds available for the import of capital equipment. (The purchase of consumption goods is less important in the context of economic development but may, of course, contribute greatly to current welfare.)

Sources of assistance

In the 1980s assistance provided at non-concessional (commercial) rates increased in relative importance and now accounts for some 60 per cent of the total, considerably in excess of Official Development Assistance (ODA) and voluntary assistance which together constitute economic aid as usually understood. Bilateral ODA accounts for around 30 per cent of the total, and multilateral agencies (World Bank, etc.) for under 10 per cent. Voluntary agencies contribute around 2 per cent of total assistance.

The volume of assistance

The volume of assistance has fallen in the 1980s. A report by the OECD indicated that the total flow of economic resources into developing countries declined in 1985 for the fourth year running.[12] The flow of resources from OECD countries, OPEC and the Eastern bloc fell to $80bn., about 40 per cent below the 1981 peak of $139bn.

The OEDC countries' official development assistance was almost $30bn., an increase of almost 2 per cent in real terms on the previous year. Bilateral aid, paid directly to Third World countries, increased by 12 per cent to $22bn., reflecting the response of OEDC governments to the famine in sub-Saharan Africa.

However, these increases were outweighed by a decline in banking flows and export credits from OEDC countries, and in assistance from OPEC countries (from $3.7bn. to $2.3bn.). Eastern bloc aid was unchanged at around $3bn.

Figure 25.4 shows the contributions of various OECD countries in 1985. It can be seen that some countries exceeded the United Nations target of 0.7 per cent of GNP in official development assistance, while others fell short of this target. The UK contribution fell from 0.43 per cent in 1981 to 0.34 per cent in 1985, and is now less than half the target figure.

International debt

As we noted above, foreign assistance can be used to purchase plant and equipment in order to build up a country's economic capacity. If the assistance takes the form of a loan rather than a grant, it involves interest payments which appear as a

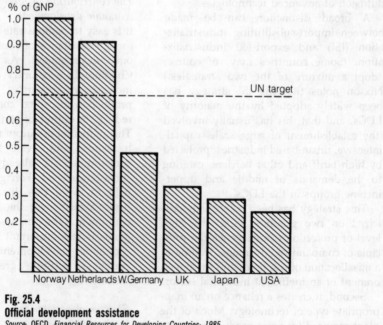

Fig. 25.4
Official development assistance
Source: OECD, *Financial Resources for Developing Countries: 1985* and *Recent Trends*. 1986

negative item on the balance of payments current account. (Subsequently the repayment of the loan gives rise to an outflow on the capital account.)

During the 1970s the current account deficits of the non-oil developing countries increased rapidly, mainly because of the increase in the price of oil. To meet these increased deficits bank borrowing was stepped up, and debt service payments (interest payments and repayments of principal) as a percentage of exports rose from 15.5 per cent in 1973 to 18 per cent in 1979.

This increased reliance on bank borrowing left some countries very vulnerable to further shocks, such as the further increase in oil prices in 1979. The initial response was to increase bank borrowing even further (as after the previous oil price rise, much of the borrowing was financed by recycled OPEC funds). In 1981 private borrowing by the non-oil developing countries (most of it from banks) peaked at almost £80bn.

Further details of the position of these countries is given in Table 25.2. It shows that the current deficit, external debt and debt service ratio all rose after 1980. The rise in the external debt and debt service ratio was, of course, due partly to the increased borrowing, but other factors were also responsible. The dollar exchange rate rose. Since four-fifths of the debt of the developing countries is denominated in dollars, this rise caused an increase in

the share of export revenues needed to service their debts. Interest rates also rose, causing a further increase in the debt burden. (More recently the fall in the dollar has eased the situation somewhat.)

A rise in the debt service ratio implies a greater danger of default by the borrower, which can discourage new lending. This was precisely what happened. Between 1981 and 1985 private borrowing fell from £80bn. to £10bn. This swing would probably have been even greater if the banks had not been 'locked in' and effectively forced to reschedule loans.

We have shown that the difficulties faced by these countries stemmed partly from the rise in the price of oil. Ironically the subsequent fall in the oil price caused immense difficulties for countries such as Mexico, Venezuela and Nigeria which had embarked on highly ambitious development programmes, to be financed from oil revenues. Indeed the high point of the debt crisis came when Mexico declared a moratorium on repayments, threatening the stability of Western banks which had made extensive loans to Mexico and other Latin-American countries. As we saw above, this crisis was resolved mainly through the efforts of the IMF.

Economic aid

Economic aid includes grants, loans at subsidized rates, technical assistance, gifts

Table 25.2
Non-oil developing countries: selected indicators

	1979	1980	1981	1982	1983	1984	1985
Current account ($bn.)	−61	−87	−108	−86	−54	−39	−44
External debt							
As % of GDP	25	25	29	33	36	36	37
As % of exports	122	115	128	150	154	152	158
Debt service ratio (%)	19	18	21	25	22	23	25

Source: IMF, *World Economic Outlook*, 1984, 1985

of food and equipment, etc. We have already noted that official aid provided by the UK is well below the United Nations target, a situation for which governments have been regularly criticized.

The case for aid is often argued purely in terms of the benefits to the recipients. But it is sometimes claimed that aid also benefits the donors. One benefit is greater political stability. There may also be economic benefits arising from the fact that poorer nations are assumed to have a higher propensity to spend than rich nations. Transferring purchasing power from rich to poor will lead to a higher level of aggregate demand and thus to a higher level of resource utilization. This case was argued strongly in the Brandt Report. However, the logic of Brandt's case has been challenged by a number of development economists.[13]

The more general case for economic aid has also been challenged. For example Professor Lord Bauer has asserted that economic aid is often used inefficiently, in projects that contribute more to the prestige than the development of the country, or even, in some instances, to help undemocratic governments to retain power. It is also argued that foreign funds are often substituted for domestic funds. Moreover the receipt of aid may sap local initiative, making the recipients even more dependent on the donors. (This last point is made by both right- and left-wing critics.)[14]

Aid versus trade

Whether the present scale of aid is too little, too great or just about right, will continue to be a matter for debate. Moreover, views will no doubt change with circumstances. Whatever the circumstances, however, it is generally accepted that the LDCs would benefit if they were allowed greater freedom in their international trading relationships.

One method of increasing freedom is to reduce the proportion of aid that is tied, i.e. where the recipient is required to spend a certain percentage (which may be 100 in extreme instances) of the aid in the purchase of products from the donor country. It is estimated that about three-quarters of UK bilateral trade is tied in this way.

Another method is, of course, to reduce the various barriers that might be raised against products exported from the less developed countries. In 1970, following negotiations conducted under the auspices of GATT, an agreement was reached whereby the developed nations of EFTA, the EEC and the USA give preferential treatment in specific manufactured goods to the developing countries.

Multinational enterprises

A multinational enterprise (MNE) is an enterprise which owns production or service facilities in two or more countries.[15] The United Nations estimated that in the late 1970s there were 10,000–11,000 firms with at least one foreign affiliate, of which just over 2,000 had affiliates in six or more countries.[16] The biggest MNEs are based in the USA, and three of these, Exxon, Ford and General Motors, each had a turnover in 1983 that was larger than the GNPs of all but fourteen countries.[17] Well-known European MNEs are Royal Dutch Shell, Unilever and ICI.

Griffiths and Wall estimate that the output of existing MNEs is growing at an annual rate of 10–17 per cent, more than twice as fast as world output and faster than world trade. In some instances direct foreign investment (DFI) is undertaken to gain improved access to markets where imports are restricted. Nissan's UK factory is a case in point. In other instances DFI is intended to take advantage of specific locational advantages, e.g. sources of cheap labour or raw materials. Another reason is a desire to meet the specific needs of the local market, including the provision of after-sales service.

It is estimated that between one-quarter and one-third of the DFI of the multinationals is located in the less developed countries. However, this share has tended to fall, and the investment is heavily concentrated in a relatively few countries, including Hong Kong, Singapore, South Korea, Mexico and Brazil.

The effects of multinational investment in the UK

It is important to try to evaluate the effects of the activities of MNEs since governments may wish to influence (encourage or curb) these activities. A useful summary of these effects is provided by Griffiths and Wall[18]:

Employment: employment in manufacturing has held up better in foreign-owned than British-owned companies.

Balance of payments: industries in which foreign participation in the UK is high tend to have a relatively favourable balance of trade.

Technology: the welfare effects of technology transfer were found to be 'ambiguous'.

International competitiveness: the inflow of manufacturing investment into the UK has been biased towards the more technology-intensive sector. However, it appears that the effect of the inflow has been to exploit the UK market rather than to reinforce the UK's export capability. If this is so the effect may be to perpetuate the technological gap that is one of the reasons for the decline in UK international competitiveness.

Summary

1. Under a system of floating exchange rates currency parities may change frequently, in line with changes in market forces. Under a system of fixed rates, parities change infrequently, and then by government action.

2. The depreciation or devaluation of a currency implies a fall in the price of that country's exports and a rise in the price of its imports. As the volume of exports increases and the volume of imports falls, resource utilization increases. However the rate of inflation tends to rise, which cancels out some of the initial effects of the depreciation.

3. The balance on trade in goods and services will improve following depreciation if the sum of the PED for imports and exports exceeds one.

4. The EMS has three components: an ECU, an exchange rate mechanism and a system of credit arrangements. The exchange rate mechanism is based on a system of fixed but adjustable currency parities.

5. A country may attempt to overcome balance of payments difficulties by a change in its exchange rate, by reducing the level of domestic expenditure, by imposing barriers to trade or by stimulating exports.

6. A common barrier to trade is the tariff, a tax on imports. Tariffs benefit the producers of the goods on which the tariff is imposed. They also increase government revenue. But these benefits are obtained at the expense of domestic consumers (who have to pay higher prices) and overseas producers (whose markets are restricted). The loss of economic welfare to the country imposing the restriction is even greater with a quota (a quantitative restriction) than a tariff.

7. In recent years there has been an increase in VERs. These have the same effects as quotas but their discriminatory nature is an additional disadvantage. The growth of VERs has been criticized by many observers, including GATT.

8. The two main forms of regional economic groupings are the free trade area and the customs union, the best-known example of which is the EEC. Both are characterized by an absence, at least in principle, of barriers to trade among

members. A feature of a customs union, but not of a free trade area, is a common external tariff. The existence of this tariff means that the total welfare may not increase following the formation of a customs union.

9. A number of international economic institutions have been established in order to facilitate the expansion of international trade. This objective has required policies to reduce barriers to trade, increase world liquidity and provide assistance to countries facing balance of payments difficulties. Especially important in this context are GATT and the IMF. The main objective of the World Bank is to aid the economic development of the less developed countries.

10. There are few signs that overall the distribution of the world's output is becoming less unequal. Some poorer countries have expanded the output of the agricultural sector as the main way of trying to improve living standards, while others have emphasized industrialization (the expansion of manufacturing).

11. Foreign assistance is often used to purchase plant and equipment in order to expand economic capacity. If the assistance is in the form of a loan the yield of the additional capacity should be sufficient to service the interest on, and the eventual repayment of, the loan. If this does not happen the country's indebtedness will increase. In the 1980s a number of developing countries were unable to repay the debts that they had incurred. The IMF played a major part in resolving these difficulties.

12. Economists disagree about the role of aid in economic development. But there is general agreement that the less developed countries would benefit by a reduction in barriers against their imports.

Key terms

Depreciation
Appreciation
Devaluation
Revaluation
Floating exchange rates
Fixed exchange rates
European Monetary System
Tariffs
Quotas
Voluntary export restraints
Costs of protection

Free trade area
Customs union
European Economic Community
International Monetary Fund
General Agreement on Tariffs and Trade
World Bank
Bases for economic growth
International debt
Economic aid
Multinational enterprises

Notes

1. Greenaway D, New ways of restricting imports, *Economic Review*, Nov. 1985.
2. Greenaway D, Multilateral trade policy, *Lloyds Bank Review*, Jan. 1984.
3. World Bank, *Staff Paper 1986*, reported in *Financial Times* 23 June 1986.
4. *Financial Times*, 11 Jan. 1986.
5. OECD, *Costs and Benefits of Protection*, summarized in *Economic Progress Report*, May 1985.
6. Silberston Z A, *The Multi-fibre Arrangement and the UK Economy*. HMSO, 1985, summarized in *Economic Progress Report*, May 1985.
7. Dearden S, EEC membership and the United Kingdom's trade in manufactured goods, *National Westminster Bank Quarterly Review*, Feb. 1986, p. 16.
8. World Bank, *World Development Report 1984*. Oxford Univ. Press, 1985.

9. These and other useful statistics are contained in Donaldson P, *Worlds Apart*, 2nd edn. Penguin, 1986.
10. This approach follows that adopted by Begg D, Fisher S and Dornbusch R, *Economics*. McGraw-Hill, 1984, Ch. 33.
11. Nixson F, Development economics. In Atkinson G B J, *Developments in Economics*, vol. 1, Causeway Press, 1985, p. 167.
12. OECD, *Financial Resources for Developing Countries: 1985* and *Recent Trends*, 1986.
13. Bird G, The Brandt Report and economic theory, *Economics*, Winter 1980; Kirkpatrick C H and Nixson F I, The North–South debate: reflections on the Brandt Commission Report, *The Three Banks' Review*, Sept. 1981.
14. Bauer P, *Reality and Rhetoric*. Weidenfeld and Nicolson, 1984; Hayter T, *Aid as Imperialism*. Penguin, 1971.
15. The term 'transnational corporation' is favoured by the United Nations, but multinational enterprise is used more frequently.
16. Nixson, op. cit., p. 171.
17. Griffiths A and Wall S, *Applied Economics*. Longman, 1984, Ch. 7.
18. Griffiths and Wall, op. cit., pp. 123ff.

Essay questions

1. Discuss the relative advantages and disadvantages of fixed and floating exchange rates.
2. Analyse the possible effects of the appreciation of a currency's external value.
3. 'Devaluation is more likely to have a favourable effect on resource utilization than on the balance of payments.' Discuss.
4. 'As a result of inflation Belgradia's currency depreciated.' 'The depreciation of Belgradia's currency increased the inflationary pressures.' Comment.
5. Analyse the circumstances under which devaluation is likely to result in an improvement in the balance of payments.
6. 'A deficit on the balance of payments current account has favourable short-run, but unfavourable long-run consequences.' Discuss.
7. Analyse the relationship between a fixed exchange rate and the rate of inflation.
8. Discuss the proposition that the move towards floating exchange rates in the post-war period indicates that they are to be preferred to fixed rates.
9. Explain the meaning of the term 'dirty floating' and why it occurs.
10. 'Since barriers to trade inhibit international specialization in accordance with the principle of comparative advantage they must reduce the overall level of economic welfare.' Discuss.
11. Compare and contrast the characteristics and objectives of customs unions and free trade areas.
12. 'Although a customs union increases the economic welfare of each of its members, this is at the expense of non-members.' Discuss.
13. Describe the major objectives of the following: the IMF, the World Bank, the EIB.
14. 'Trade is always to be preferred to aid.' Discuss.

Exercises

25.1 The passage on the following page is extracted from the *Financial Times*, 3 April 1986.
   (i) Why was the exchange rate expected to fall following the fall in the price of oil?

(ii)   What might explain the fact that the actual fall was less than expected?
(iii) Explain why the effect of lower oil prices might be broadly neutral with respect to output and inflation.

The effect of lower oil prices on both output and inflation in the UK should be 'broadly neutral – if anything slightly beneficial', says the Treasury. Lower oil costs should be offset by the exchange rate, which would be expected to fall in response to the probable drop in the UK's trade surplus. A fall of about £1.5bn. from the Treasury's projected oil trade surplus of £5bn. in 1986 would be likely if oil prices remained at $10.

The exchange rate, however, has remained high. As measured by the Bank of England's trade-weighted index the pound has been trading around 76, scarcely $2\frac{1}{2}$ per cent lower than when the oil price stood at $26 a barrel.

25.2   Under a fixed exchange rate a persistent deficit on current account implies a tendency for the money stock of the country to decline unless this effect is deliberately neutralized by the actions of the central bank. The loss of reserves implies an excess demand for foreign exchange, matched by an excess supply of the domestic currency absorbed by the central bank as a result of its intervention in the foreign exchange market.

(i)   Why does a persistent deficit on current account imply a tendency for the money stock of the country to decline?
(ii)   How might the central bank neutralize this tendency?
(iii) Would this process of neutralization be likely to contribute to or impede a solution of the current account deficit?

25.3   A realignment of EMS currencies in April 1986 had the effect of devaluing the French franc by 6 per cent. The following statistics indicate the background to the devaluation: prices had risen by only 0.6 per cent during the previous six months; however, since the previous realignment, prices in France had risen by 12 per cent more than prices in West Germany; in the previous year the volume of manufactured exports had risen by 2 per cent in France as compared to 9 per cent in West Germany and 10 per cent in the UK. In 1985 France's deficit in manufactured goods trade with West Germany reached more than 40bn. francs. The Bank of France's intervention rate – the leading money market rate – was 8.25 per cent, very high historically.

(i)   Explain why the state of the economy might have persuaded the French government to seek a devaluation of the franc.
(ii)   Assess the probable consequences of devaluation with respect to (a) the rate of inflation, (b) output, (c) interest rates, (d) share prices.

25.4   The passage below is based on an article in *Economic Progress Report*, July 1973.

International competitiveness depends in part on the factors reflected in the relative-price or cost-based measures of competitiveness, but it also depends on a host of less tangible factors.

The most widely used of the various price- and cost-based measures of competitiveness are the indices of relative unit labour costs, adjusted for exchange rates, compiled by the IMF.

A change in cost competitiveness can come through a change in the exchange rate, a change in the growth of earnings relative to that abroad or a change in the growth of productivity relative to that abroad. The different routes have implications for other aspects of the economy especially for inflation and real incomes.

(i) Explain why indices of relative unit labour costs, adjusted for exchange rates, can be used as a measure of international cost competitiveness.

(ii) Why might these indices be an imperfect measure of cost competitiveness?

(iii) What 'less tangible factors' affect international competitiveness?

(iv) Explain the final sentence in the passage.

Objective test questions: set 9

Questions 1–3 are based on the following table:

Amounts outstanding, 31 Aug. 1987	*£bn.*
Notes and coin in circulation	13,747
Private sector sterling sight bank deposits (non-interest bearing)	30,550
Private sector sterling sight bank deposits (interest bearing)	43,441
Private sector sterling interest bearing retail deposits	135,889
Private sector sterling time deposits	87,185
Private sector deposits in other currencies	30,634

1. M3 (£bn.) is:
   A   44,297;
   B   57,188;
   C   87,185;
   D   174,923;
   E   205,557.

2. M1 (£bn.) is:
   A   44,297;
   B   73,991;
   C   87,738;
   D   118,372;
   E   131,634.

3. M3c (£bn.) is:
   A   57,188;
   B   87,738;
   C   118,372;
   D   174,557;
   E   205,557.

4. If VAT is imposed on a product for which demand elasticity is zero, price will rise by the full extent of the tax if:
   A   the supply curve slopes up to the right;
   B   the supply curve is horizontal;
   C   the supply curve slopes down to the right;
   D   the supply curve has any of these shapes;
   E   none of these will apply (i.e. the price could not rise by the full extent of the tax).

5. Assume a banking system with ten banks each having total assets of £10m., of which £1m. comprises cash. If each bank now obtained an additional £1m. of cash

and wished to continue operating with a cash/assets ratio of 10 per cent, the total amount of *additional* assets that the system could support would be (£m.):

A   9;
B   10;
C   90;
D 100;
E 110.

6. In which of the following situations will the appreciation of the currency cause an improvement in the balance of payments?

	Elasticity of demand for exports	Elasticity of demand for imports
A	0.5	0.5
B	0.2	0.8
C	0.6	0.8
D	0.0	1.1
E	None of the above.	

7. The formation of a customs union must lead to an increase in:
   A the welfare of every country in the world;
   B the total welfare of all countries in the world;
   C the welfare of each member of the union;
   D the total welfare of all members of the union;
   E none of the above.

8. The main difference between a customs union and a free trade area is that in a customs union, but not a free trade area:
   A floating exchange rates are allowed;
   B specialization and trade take place in accordance with the principle of comparative advantage;
   C a common external tariff must be observed by all members;
   D tariffs on trade between members are permitted;
   E quotas on trade between members are permitted.

9. Special Drawing Rights are assets of the members of the:
   A International Bank for Reconstruction and Development;
   B European Investment Bank;
   C International Monetary Fund;
   D European Social Fund;
   E International Finance Corporation.

10. Which of the following is/are included within the M1 definition of the money supply?
   1 Notes and coin in circulation.
   2 Private sector sterling sight bank deposits.
   3 Private sector sterling time bank deposits.

11. According to the quantity theory of money an increase in the price level may be caused by an increase in:
   1 the supply of money;
   2 the velocity of circulation of money;
   3 the volume of transactions.

12. The national income may fail to rise following an increase in the money supply if:
   1 the demand for money is perfectly interest elastic;

    2   investment expenditure is perfectly interest elastic;
    3   all economic resources are fully utilized.

13.   In which of the following situations would the depreciation of a currency be likely to result in an improvement in the balance of payments in relation to trade in goods and services?

	Elasticity of demand for imports	Elasticity of demand for exports
1	0.4	0.6
2	0.0	1.2
3	0.2	0.9

14.   For which of the following reasons would the depreciation of a currency be likely to a result in an increase in the domestic price level?
    1   The prices of imports would rise.
    2   The costs of domestic producers would rise.
    3   Domestic producers would meet less competition from overseas producers.

15.   Which of the following constitute quantitative controls on imports?
    1   Quotas.
    2   Tariffs.
    3   Import deposit schemes.

16.   Membership of GATT involves a commitment to:
    1   a reduction in import restrictions;
    2   a reduction in export incentives;
    3   an expansion of multilateral trade.

17.   Keynes suggested that the speculative demand for money is inversely related to the price of bonds.
    If the price of bonds falls below the issue price the rate of interest also falls.

18.   If government controls prevent the prices of some products from increasing, this may lead to greater increases in the prices of other products.
    Price controls may result in the real incomes of consumers being higher than they would otherwise have been.

19.   The balance of payments will improve following the depreciation of the currency provided that the elasticity of demand for exports is greater than that for imports.
    If the elasticity of demand for exports exceeds unity the value of exports will increase following a fall in their price.

20.   Devaluation is likely to lead to an increase in domestic resource utilization.
    Devaluation will cause the value of exports to rise and the value of imports to fall.

True/false

1.   If a bond with a nominal value of £100 and a nominal rate of interest of 6 per cent can be bought for £50, the actual rate of interest is 12 per cent.
2.   A fall in the exchange rate usually leads to a fall in domestic interest rates.
3.   The quantity theory of money states that an increase in the quantity of money will always lead to an increase in the price level.
4.   The term 'suppressed inflation' indicates that the government has eliminated all inflationary pressures in the economy.
5.   The minimum lending rate was abolished in August 1981.

6. Devaluation of the currency will always lead to an improvement in the balance of payments in the long term.
7. If the foreign exchange value of a currency is tending to fall, this tendency will be counterbalanced by the operation of leads and lags in international payments.
8. If the authorities intervene to prevent a currency from rising to its free market level, this would have a favourable effect on the level of domestic resource utilization.
9. If the authorities intervene to prevent a currency from rising to its free market level this will moderate the rate of inflation.
10. The 'infant industry' argument provides justification for granting an industry permanent protection from foreign competition.

Index